Handbook of Research on Learning and Instruction

During the past twenty years researchers have made exciting progress in the science of learning (i.e., how people learn) and the science of instruction (i.e., how to help people learn). This handbook examines learning and instruction in a variety of classroom and non-classroom environments and with a variety of learners, both K-16 students and adult learners. The chapters are written by leading researchers from around the world, all of whom are highly regarded experts on their particular topics.

The book is divided into two sections: learning and instruction. The learning section consists of chapters on how people learn in reading, writing, mathematics, science, history, second languages, and physical education, as well as learning to think critically, learning to self-monitor, and learning with motivation. The instruction section consists of chapters on effective instructional methods—feedback, examples, self-explanation, peer interaction, cooperative learning, inquiry, discussion, tutoring, visualizations, and computer simulations. Each chapter reviews empirical research in a specific domain and is structured as follows:

- **Introduction**—Defines key constructs and provides illustrative examples or cases.
- **Historical Overview**—Summarizes the historical context for the topic or domain.
- **Theoretical Framework**—Summarizes major models or theories related to the topic or domain.
- **Current Trends and Issues**—Synthesizes the research literature and highlights key findings or conclusions.
- **Practical Implications**—Suggests relevance of the research for educational practice.
- **Future Directions**—Considers next steps or stages needed for future research.

Richard E. Mayer is Professor of Psychology at the University of California, Santa Barbara.

Dr. Patricia A. Alexander is the Jean Mullan Professor of Literacy and Distinguished Scholar-Teacher in the Department of Human Development at the University of Maryland.

Educational Psychology Handbook series

Handbook of Research on Learning and Instruction

Edited by
Richard E. Mayer
University of California, Santa Barbara
and
Patricia A. Alexander
University of Maryland

Routledge
Taylor & Francis Group

NEW YORK AND LONDON

First published 2011
by Routledge
270 Madison Avenue, New York, NY 10016

Simultaneously published in the UK
by Routledge
2 Park Square, Milton Park, Abingdon, Oxon OX14 4RN

Routledge is an imprint of the Taylor & Francis Group, an informa business

© 2011 Taylor & Francis

The right of the editors to be identified as the authors of the editorial material, and of the authors for their individual chapters, has been asserted in accordance with sections 77 and 78 of the Copyright, Designs and Patents Act 1988.

Typeset in Minion by Swales & Willis Ltd, Exeter, Devon
Printed and bound in the United States of America on acid-free paper by Edwards Brothers, Inc.

Library of Congress Cataloging-in-Publication Data
Handbook of research on learning and instruction / edited by Richard E. Mayer and Patricia A. Alexander.
    p. cm
    Includes bibliographical references and index.
    1. Learning—Handbooks, manuals, etc. 2. Teaching—Methodology—Handbooks, manuals, etc.
    3. Education—Research—Handbooks, manuals, etc. I. Mayer, Richard E., 1947–
    II. Alexander, Patricia A.
    LB1060.H34575 2011
    370.15'23—dc22
    2010020096

ISBN13: 978–0–415–80460–8 (hbk)
ISBN13: 978–0–415–80461–5 (pbk)
ISBN13: 978–0–203–83908–9 (ebk)

CONTENTS

PREFACE

How do people learn in subject areas, such as reading, writing, mathematics, science, and history, and how can we help people learn, using instructional methods such as feedback, examples, self-explanation, tutoring, and visualizations? These questions about how learning works and how instruction works are central to both educational practice and learning theory. These are the questions that motivate this handbook. If you are interested in what research has to say about learning and instruction in academic subject areas, then this handbook is for you.

GOAL AND RATIONALE

The goal of the *Handbook of Research on Learning and Instruction* is to provide a focused, organized, and evidence-based review of what research has to say about how people learn and how to help people learn. The *Handbook* seeks to examine learning and instruction in a variety of learning environments including in classrooms and out of classrooms, and with a variety of learners including K-16 students and adult learners. The *Handbook* is written at a level that is appropriate for graduate students, researchers, and practitioners interested in an evidence-based approach to learning and instruction.

Decisions about educational practice are often based on opinions, advice, or common practice. In contrast, the contributors to the *Handbook of Research on Learning and Instruction* were asked to demonstrate how educational practice can be guided by research evidence concerning what works in instruction (i.e., the science of instruction) and why it works (i.e., the science of learning).

During the past 20 years, researchers have made exciting progress in the science of learning (i.e., how people learn) and the science of instruction (i.e., how to help people learn). This *Handbook* is intended to provide an overview of these research advances. The chapters are written by leading researchers from around the world who are highly regarded experts on their particular topics and active contributors to the field.

DESCRIPTION

The book is divided into two sections—learning and instruction. The learning section consists of chapters on how people learn in subject matter areas—reading, writing, mathematics, science, history, second language, and physical education—as well as how people acquire the knowledge and processes required for critical thinking, self-regulation, and motivation. The instruction section consists of chapters on effective instructional methods—feedback, examples, self-explanation, peer interaction, cooperative learning, inquiry, discussion, tutoring, visualizations, and simulations.

To maintain focus and organization, each chapter has a similar structure:

- *Introduction* in which key constructs are defined with illustrative examples,
- *Historical overview* that summarizes the historical context for the chapter topic or domain,
- *Theoretical framework* in which authors summarize predominant models or theories pertinent to the topic or domain,
- *Current trends and issues* where authors synthesize the relevant literature and summarize key findings or conclusions,
- *Practical implications*, in which authors suggest the relevance of the research for educational practice, and
- *Future directions* in which authors consider the next steps or stages required to inform research and practice in the years ahead.

The central feature of each chapter is a review of empirical research in a specific domain. Each chapter underwent an intensive review process.

FOCUS

As editors, we seek to produce a handbook that showcases the best research work being done in our field, so readers can appreciate the advances being made in research on learning and instruction. We value empirical evidence so the heart of each chapter is a review of empirical research central to the domain. The chapter is not a narrow review of any author's research program but rather explores the most important advances in the domain. We value theoretical grounding so each chapter includes a description of a testable model or theory related to the learning or instructional topic under consideration. We value educational relevance, so the chapters address issues that have practical implications for education, are based on a research evidence base, and are grounded in a theory of how people learn. We value readability so each chapter is written with an eye for clarity, conciseness, and organization. Rather than provide an encyclopedia, each chapter focuses on a few major advances that represent progress in the field. We value timeliness, so each chapter provides up-to-date coverage, while putting the topic or domain into its historical context so you can see the roots of that topic or domain. We value comprehensiveness so the chapters of the book represent a broad array of academic domains, learning constructs, and instructional methods.

ACKNOWLEDGMENTS

We wish to thank the chapter authors who have shared their expertise by contributing excellent chapters, revised them based on our feedback, and worked hard to craft chapters that meet the *Handbook*'s standards. We gratefully acknowledge our colleagues who have produced the high quality research and theory that make up the content of this *Handbook*. We appreciate the work of the Taylor and Francis staff, and we are particularly grateful to Lane Akers for his continued support and encouragement of this project.

Patricia A. Alexander   Richard E. Mayer
College Park, Maryland   Santa Barbara, California

ABOUT THE EDITORS

Patricia Alexander is the Jean Mullan Professor of Literacy and Distinguished Scholar-Teacher in the Department of Human Development at the University of Maryland. She has served as President of Division 15 (Educational Psychology) of the American Psychological Association, and as Vice-President of Division C (Learning and Instruction) of the American Educational Research Association. A former middle-school teacher, Dr. Alexander received her reading specialist degree from James Madison University (1979) and her Ph.D. in reading from the University of Maryland (1981). Since receiving her Ph.D., Dr. Alexander has published over 250 articles, books, or chapters in the area of learning and instruction. She has also presented over 250 papers or invited addresses at national and international conferences. Currently, she serves as the editor of *Contemporary Educational Psychology*, Associate Editor of *American Educational Research Journal-Teaching, Learning, and Human Development*, and on 12 editorial boards including those for *Reading Research Quarterly, Journal of Literacy Research, Educational Psychologist*, and the *Journal of Educational Psychology*. Among her many honors and awards, Dr. Alexander is a Fellow of the American Psychological Association, and was a Spencer Fellow of the National Academy of Education. She was recently named the second most productive scholar in Educational Psychology, and was the 2001 recipient of the Oscar S. Causey Award for outstanding contributions to literacy research from the National Reading Conference. She is also the 2006 recipient of the E. L. Thorndike Award for Career Achievement in Educational Psychology from APA Division 15 and the 2007 recipient of the Sylvia Scribner Award from AERA Division C. In addition, she has received various national, university, and college awards for teaching.

Richard E. Mayer is Professor of Psychology at the University of California, Santa Barbara (UCSB) where he has served since 1975. He received a Ph.D. in Psychology from the University of Michigan in 1973, and served as a Visiting Assistant Professor of Psychology at Indiana University from 1973 to 1975. His research interests are in educational and cognitive psychology. His current research involves the intersection of cognition, instruction, and technology with a special focus on multimedia learning and computer-supported learning in science and mathematics. He is past-President of the Division of Educational Psychology of the American Psychological Association, former editor of the *Educational Psychologist*, former co-editor of *Instructional Science*, former Chair of the UCSB Department of Psychology, and the year 2000 recipient of the E. L. Thorndike Award for career achievement in educational psychology. He is the winner of 2008 Distinguished Contribution of Applications of Psychology to Education and Training Award from the American Psychological Association. He was ranked #1 as the most productive educational psychologist in *Contemporary Educational Psychology*. Currently he is Vice President for Division C (Learning and Instruction) of the American Educational Research Association. He is on the editorial boards of 14 journals mainly in educational psychology. He has served as a local school board in Goleta, California since 1981. He is the author of more than 400 publications including 25 books, such as *Applying the Science of Learning* (2011), *Multimedia Learning* (2009), *Learning and Instruction* (2008), *E-Learning and the Science of Instruction* (with R. Clark, 2008), and the *Cambridge Handbook of Multimedia Learning* (editor, 2005).

CONTRIBUTORS

EDITORS

Patricia A. Alexander
University of Maryland (USA)

Richard E. Mayer
University of California, Santa Barbara (USA)

CHAPTER AUTHORS

Eric M. Anderman
Ohio State University (USA)

Christina Rhee Bonney
Tufts University (USA)

Whitney Cade
University of Memphis (USA)

Ang Chen
University of North Carolina, Greensboro (USA)

Michelene T. H. Chi
Arizona State University (USA)

Heather Dawson
Ohio State University (USA)

Ton de Jong
University of Twente (The Netherlands)

Susan De La Paz
University of Maryland (USA)

Sidney D'Mello
University of Memphis (USA)

Richard Duschl
Pennsylvania State University (USA)

Ann R. Edwards
University of Maryland (USA)

Catherine D. Ennis
University of North Carolina, Greensboro (USA)

Indigo Esmonde
University of Toronto (Canada)

Brenda A. Fonseca
Arizona State University (USA)

Emily Fox
University of Maryland (USA)

Mark Gan
University of Auckland (New Zealand)

Arthur C. Graesser
University of Memphis (USA)

Richard Hamilton
University of Auckland (New Zealand)

John Hattie
University of Auckland (New Zealand)

Linda S. Levstik
University of Kentucky (USA)

Sofie M. M. Loyens
Erasmus University Rotterdam (The Netherlands)

Deborah McCutchen
University of Washington (USA)

P. Karen Murphy
Pennsylvania State University (USA)

Alexander Renkl
University of Freiburg (Germany)

Remy M. J. P. Rikers
Erasmus University Rotterdam (The Netherlands)

Robert E. Slavin
Johns Hopkins University (USA)

Anna O. Soter
Ohio State University (USA)

Robert J. Sternberg
Oklahoma State University (USA)

Marcel V. J. Veenman
Leiden University (The Netherlands)

Joseph F. Wagner
Xavier University (USA)

Min Wang
University of Maryland (USA)

Deborah E. Watkins
York College of Pennsylvania (USA)

Kathryn R. Wentzel
University of Maryland (USA)

Ian A. G. Wilkinson
Ohio State University (USA)

Part I
Research on Learning

1

INTRODUCTION TO RESEARCH ON LEARNING
Richard E. Mayer and Patricia A. Alexander

The psychology of subject matter is the scientific study of how people learn school subjects such as reading (Huey, 1908/1968), writing (Gregg & Steinberg, 1980; Kellogg, 1994), and mathematics (Resnick & Ford, 1981; Thorndike, 1922). Although research on learning in academic content areas has a long history dating back to classic research by Huey (1908/1968) and Thorndike (1922), much progress has been made, particularly in the past 20 years. For this reason, the development of the psychology of subject matter has been recognized as one of the major accomplishments of educational psychology (Alexander, Murphy, & Greene, in press; Mayer, 1999, 2004, 2008; Shulman & Quinlan, 1996). This first section of the *Handbook* provides a research-based overview of the exciting progress being made in our understanding of learning in subject areas. In addition to chapters on reading, writing, and mathematics, we have expanded Part I to include the subject areas of science, history, second language learning, and physical education, as well as the hidden curriculum areas of critical thinking, metacognition, and motivation.

In "Learning to Read" (Chapter 2), Emily Fox and Patricia Alexander provide a lifespan approach to what is widely recognized as the most central of all academic skills, reading, which they define as "the complex communicative behavior of deriving meaning from presented text." Building on foundational scholarship by Gray (1951), the authors describe six important themes in research on learning to read: (1) recognizing the changed role of reading; (2) developing a broad concept of reading; (3) accepting the idea that growth in reading is a continuous process; (4) broadening the reading program in harmony with expanding interests and needs of pupils; (5) recognizing that guidance in reading is essential in each curriculum field; and (6) adjusting reading programs to the unique characteristics and needs of pupils. They call for more longitudinal research that provides a broader picture of the developmental dynamics of learning to read.

In "Learning to Write" (Chapter 3), Susan De La Paz and Deborah McCutchen focus on three cognitive processes in writing as first articulated by Hayes and Flower (1980; Flower & Hayes, 1980): planning, translating (or text production), and reviewing.

Importantly, the authors review intervention programs that have been successful in promoting each of these processes in writing, and thereby improving students' written products. The authors recommend that future research examine writing specific to each discipline, rather than writing in general.

In "Learning Mathematics" (Chapter 4), Ann Edwards, Indigo Esmonde, and Joseph Wagner begin with a case study of a sixth-grade student's mathematical thinking, and seek to show the value of studying mathematical activity *in situ*. The authors describe how the field has been influenced by behaviorist, cognitive, and situated theoretical frameworks. They review current research on the structures and processes of mathematical cognition, the role of discourse and language on mathematics learning, identity in mathematics learning, and the cognitive neuroscience of mathematics learning. Challenges in future research include taking into account the complexity of the context of mathematical thinking, creating effective multidisciplinary collaborations, and bridging across different theoretical approaches.

In "Learning Science" (Chapter 5), Richard Duschl and Richard Hamilton provide a vision of the progress that has been made in the field of science education over the past 20 years. Building on dozens of recent reports on science learning, they show how the field has been enriched by learning theory in cognitive science and the naturalistic turn in the philosophy of science. Some important current issues involve theory of mind, learning progressions, and the domain specificity/generality of learning. The authors conclude that future research is needed that focuses on science learning in context.

In "Learning History" (Chapter 6), Linda Levstik notes that empirical research on how students learn history is a relatively new field, which started to take hold in the 1980s. She describes a theoretical shift from reflective inquiry—understanding history in terms of current problems—to sociocultural theories—in which people's understanding of history is influenced by the social and cultural context and available sociocultural tools. The chapter reviews research on early learning in history, learning official and vernacular histories, the role of gender in historical narratives, learning to recognize others' perspectives, learning to use historical sources, the role of technology in history learning, the role of motivation in history learning, and learning of world history. The author calls for future research on emergent historical thinking, sense-making in the context of world history, and transfer.

In "Learning a Second Language" (Chapter 7), Min Wang makes an excellent case for the importance of second language learning in schools to prepare students for the global economy and to address the needs of immigrants. She describes three major constituents in second language learning: (1) phonology, the sounds of the language; (2) orthography, the writing system for putting words into print; and (2) morphology, meaningful word parts (e.g., suffixes, prefixes, a change to plural or past tense, or compound words). She outlines major theories of cross-language transfer concerning how knowledge about phonology, orthography, and morphology in one language affects learning a second language. The chapter closes with a call for more focused research on the causal mechanisms underlying cross-language transfer in learning a second language.

In "Learning Motor Skill in Physical Education" (Chapter 8), Catherine Ennis and Ang Chen examine how to help people improve their motor skills in physical education. The authors show how research on motor skill learning began in the 1930s, and since the 1970s has been influenced by information-processing theories, expert–novice comparison theories, and dynamical systems theories. The authors show the benefits of taking an evidence-based approach to promoting skill learning in physical education, and point to the need for future research on motor skill learning in complex sports environments.

In "Learning to Think Critically" (Chapter 9), Christina Rhee Bonney and Robert Sternberg examine the important, but sometimes unstated, curricular objective of helping students become critical thinkers. The authors summarize core concepts concerning developmental considerations, motivational considerations, the role of the student, the role of the teacher, and the role of context. The authors summarize foundational research on teaching and learning of critical thinking skills, including Lipman's (2003) Philosophy for Children, Feuerstein et al.'s (1980) Instrumental Enrichment, Bransford et al.'s (1988) anchored instruction, and Sternberg's (2008) successful intelligence. The authors call for future research on the role of a collection of thinking skills including critical, analytic, practical, creative, and wisdom skills.

In "Learning to Self-Monitor and Self-Regulate" (Chapter 10), Marcel Veenman focuses on the student's learning of metacognitive knowledge for academic learning, that is, knowledge about how to learn. Veenman provides an historical overview of research on key concepts including metacognitive knowledge, metacognitive skills, and development of metacognitive skills. Some current research topics include assessment of metacognitive skills and instruction of metacognitive skills. The author calls for research that goes beyond narrow, short-term studies of metacognitive instruction, and suggests that cognitive neuroscience research is also a valuable methodology for understanding metacognitive processing during learning.

In "Learning with Motivation" (Chapter 11), Eric Anderman and Heather Dawson show how motivation is a pervasive and fundamental issue in academic learning that has blossomed as a research area in the past 30 years. The chapter begins with Pintrich and Schunk's (2002, p. 5) classic definition of motivation as "the process by which goal-directed activity is instigated and sustained." The study of motivation has shifted from behavioral theories based on drive reduction, which were popular prior to the 1970s, to social cognitive theories, which have generated a substantial research base relevant to academic motivation since the 1970s. The chapter reviews some of the most influential theories of academic motivation: achievement goal theory, which focuses on the learner's academic goals; social cognitive theory, such as motivation based on self-efficacy; self-determination theory, which includes the distinction between intrinsic and extrinsic motivation; and expectancy-value theory, which considers how the learner values various academic experiences. Some of current research issues reviewed in the chapter include the debate about whether extrinsic rewards harm intrinsic motivation; and the debate about the consequence of having performance goals, in which the learner seeks to demonstrate high test performance, for example. The authors establish how research on motivation has implications for student testing and grouping of students for instruction. Concerning future directions for motivation research, they point to the need for research on motivation-based interventions as well as developmental and qualitative studies of motivation.

Overall, Part I of the Handbook helps you understand the advances being made in the scientific study of learning in subject areas. Whether dealing with traditional academic domains (e.g., reading or history) or with dimensions of the hidden curriculum (e.g., critical thinking), the contributing authors have effectively followed in the footsteps of such forbears as Huey and Thorndike—further endowing the discipline of educational psychology and supporting those who benefit for the knowledge educational psychology affords.

REFERENCES

Alexander, P. A., Murphy, P. K., & Greene, J. A. (in press). Projecting educational psychology's future from its past and present: A trend analysis. In K. A. Harris, & S. Graham (Eds.), *Handbook of educational psychology*. Washington, DC: American Psychological Association.

Bransford, J., Hasselbring, T., Barron, B., Kulewicz, S., Littlefield, J., & Goin, L. (1988). Uses of macro-contexts to facilitate mathematical thinking. In R. Charles, & E. A. Silver (Eds.), *The teaching and assessment of mathematical problem solving* (pp. 125–147). Hillsdale, NJ: Lawrence Erlbaum.

Feuerstein, R., Rand, Y., Hoffman, M., & Miller, R. (1980). *Instrumental enrichment: An intervention program for cognitive modifiability*. Baltimore, MD: University Park Press.

Flower, L., & Hayes, J. R. (1980). The dynamics of composing: Making plans and juggling constraints. In L. W. Gregg, & E. R. Steinberg (Eds.), *Cognitive processes in writing* (pp. 31–50). Hillsdale, NJ: Erlbaum.

Gray, W. S. (1951). Foundation stones in the road to better reading. *The Elementary School Journal, 51*, 427–435.

Gregg, L. W., & Steinberg, E. R. (Eds.). (1980). *Cognitive processes in writing*. Hillsdale, NJ: Erlbaum.

Hayes, J. R., & Flower, L. S. (1980). Identifying the organization of writing processes. In L. W. Gregg, & E. R. Steinberg (Eds.), *Cognitive processes in writing* (pp. 3–30). Hillsdale, NJ: Erlbaum.

Huey, E. B. (1968). *The psychology and pedagogy of reading*. New York: Macmillan. (Original published in 1908.)

Kellogg, R. T. (1994). *The psychology of writing*. New York: Oxford University Press.

Lipman, M. (2003). *Thinking in education* (2nd ed.). Cambridge: Cambridge University Press.

Mayer, R. E. (1999). *The promise of educational psychology: Learning in the content areas*. Upper Saddle River, NJ: Merrill Prentice Hall.

Mayer, R. E. (2004). Teaching of subject matter. In S. T. Fiske, D. L. Schacter, & C. Zahn-Waxler (Eds.), *Annual review of psychology* (vol. 55, pp. 715–744). Palo Alto, CA: Annual Reviews.

Mayer, R. E. (2008). *Learning and instruction* (2nd ed.). Upper Saddle River, NJ: Pearson Merrill Prentice Hall.

Pintrich, P.R., & Schunk, D.H. (2002). *Motivation in education: Theory, research, and applications* (2nd ed.). Upper Saddle River, NJ: Merrill/Prentice Hall.

Resnick, L. B., & Ford, W. W. (1981). *The psychology of mathematics for instruction*. Hillsdale, NJ: Erlbaum.

Shulman, L. S., & Quinlan, K. M. (1996). The comparative psychology of school subjects. In D. C. Berliner, & R. Calfee (Eds.), *Handbook of educational psychology*. New York: Macmillan.

Sternberg, R. J. (2008). Schools should nurture wisdom. In B. Z. Presseisen (Ed.), *Teaching for intelligence* (2nd ed.). Thousand Oaks, CA: Corwin Press.

Thorndike, E. L. (1922). *The psychology of arithmetic*. New York: Macmillan.

2

LEARNING TO READ
Emily Fox and Patricia A. Alexander

Our view of learning to read aligns with that articulated by Strang, McCullough, and Traxler more than fifty years ago: "Learning to read is a lifetime process" (1955, p. 82). Understanding learning to read as a lifelong process has strong entailments in terms of what reading is taken to be. In particular, it means that the nature of reading changes as the reader develops. As Strang and her colleagues put it:

> From birth to old age, each period of life makes its contribution to the development of reading abilities, interests, and attitudes. Reading ability, as part of the individual's total development, increases with [his] growth in interests and general ability and with the challenges of increasingly complex and difficult reading tasks at each successive educational level.
>
> (1955, p. 90)

Further, the view of reading across an entire lifespan necessarily incorporates context. Reading becomes viewed as essentially embedded in the context of the reader's life and as oriented toward contextually meaningful purposes. When thus contextualized, reading is positioned as a behavior (Russell, 1961) rather than as a skill set or ensemble of processes.

The adoption of such a developmental view of reading taken as a behavior makes complex how we, as researchers and educators, approach the enterprise of understanding what learning to read involves. To begin with, it means that any definition of reading that we offer must be broad enough to encompass developmental changes and a variety of modes of contextualized reading behaviors, while still remaining identifiably reading. The broad definition we use is this: *Reading is the complex communicative behavior of deriving meaning from presented text.* The corresponding definition of learning to read takes this form: *Learning to read is becoming able to participate in the behavior of reading in ways that support one's purposes and satisfy one's needs.* As the reader's contextualized purposes and needs change with development, so will the texts encountered, the meanings derived, and the appropriate modes of reading behavior.

Our definitions of reading and of learning to read are intentionally broad, to accommodate a wide range of reading behaviors and purposes. For the beginning reader, reading may involve using rhyme to sound out words in a Dr. Seuss book, or narrating the sequence of events in a wordless picture book about the cycle of the seasons. For a middle-school student, reading may involve searching the social studies textbook to find the answers to the homework questions on the age of exploration, or reading the schedule and the map of the school building successfully in tandem to ensure arrival at the right classroom at the right time. For a high-school student, reading may involve eliminating obvious wrong answers in multiple-choice questions on the SAT, or finding out that you are nothing like Holden Caulfield, or getting the cheat codes for a video game from an online magazine.

For a college student, reading may involve identifying the important details in a lengthy chapter in your organic chemistry textbook, or locating a downloadable article in a peer-reviewed journal that you can use for your research methods assignment. For an adult, reading may include deciphering a text message from your teenager saying that he forgot his lunch, figuring out whether you can take a tax deduction or a tax credit for the college tuition you paid, or reading through the materials from the League of Women Voters to decide which political candidate to support. And at any age, reading may involve reading engaged in for its own sake, for self-directed learning and pleasure. Learning to read is both specific to particular developmental moments and also encompasses the entire varied spectrum of contextualized purposes, encountered texts, and requisite reading abilities.

By characterizing reading as complex, we signal our commitment to a view of reading as inherently interactive, dynamic, and layered. This means that explanations of reading, in our view, include acknowledgment of: the layering of multiple systems (themselves also complex and layered), such as perception, cognition, and motivation; the interactions of multiple factors, such as those arising from text, context, and individual; and the continuous adjustments and adaptations within and among these systems and factors. By characterizing it as communicative, we link reading to its predominantly language-based social role in the exchange of ideas and information. And by characterizing reading as a behavior, we signal a perspective on reading in which it is viewed as something readers do as part of their lives. We acknowledge that there are many separate aspects of reading upon which an investigative lens can focus and toward which instructional practices can be geared, and there is often good reason to adopt a narrower focus or orientation. However, the foundation and reference point for our investigations of reading must be how it operates within readers' lived experiences. The explanations and interpretations that arise from more narrow conceptualizations benefit from being grounded in an understanding of reading as a behavior that develops across the lifespan. When investigating, theorizing, or making claims about reading, it is critical to consider how the path back out to reading in this largest sense would be specified (Fox & Alexander, 2009).

This is the heart of our enterprise in this chapter, which we undertake by considering recent research on learning to read as organized around six broad principles for the improvement of reading that are drawn from such a lifespan developmental perspective (Gray, 1951). These principles address: (1) recognition of the changing role of reading as communication practices evolve; (2) broadening of the concept of reading beyond word recognition; (3) acknowledgment that growth in reading continues throughout the lifespan; (4) consideration of students' developing interests and needs; (5) instruction in domain-specific reading practices; and (6) attention to readers' individual differences. The review of recent research is preceded by a brief overview of key events and theories shaping the current landscape in research on learning to read, and a discussion of the theoretical framework behind our view of reading.

HISTORICAL OVERVIEW

The lifespan developmental view of reading had its heyday beginning in the 1930s and extending into the early 1960s. Topics of interest to researchers and educators included such areas as Americans' reading habits (Waples & Tyler, 1931), the nature of mature reading (Gray & Rogers, 1956), the social effects of reading (Waples, Berelson, & Bradshaw, 1940), the importance of developing interest in reading and lifelong reading habits (Russell, 1961), and the relation of how reading was taught in school to how it would be used in life (Gray, 1949). There was widespread interest in improving reading, particularly adult reading, with emphasis both on reading rapidly to get through the increasing volume of printed material adults were expected to encounter in the workplace and in their personal lives (Judson, 1954) and on the ability to read to satisfy one's purposes in gaining knowledge (Adler, 1940). The development of reading into adulthood was seen as important for citizenship and for personal fulfillment (Powell, 1949).

A confluence of social, political, and theoretical forces (more fully discussed in Alexander & Fox, 2004) in the late 1950s and early 1960s turned the attention of the field to beginning reading and the processes involved in the successful identification of words. This truncated the trajectory of reading development, so that the main task of learning to read became getting access to print. The cognitive emphasis fueled by the emergence of the information-processing perspective in psychology had a role as well in shifting the types of questions asked and explanations sought. Reading processes became compartmentalized into separate strands of research on perception, cognition, motivation, and sociocultural context. This fragmentation of the reader, on the one hand, and emphasis on word reading, on the other, meant that the lifespan developmental framework moved offstage, with an appearance in Chall's model of stages of reading development (1983) but otherwise not much of a role in the work being done in reading.

An influential contribution to the thinking on what was involved in learning to read was the introduction in 1986 by Gough and Tunmer of their simple model of reading. The simple model identifies reading as the product of decoding (measured as ability to pronounce pseudowords) and linguistic comprehension (measured as listening comprehension). In this view, once the reader can decode the individual words, linguistic comprehension enables their assembly into meaningful text. The simple model was intended both to support the preeminent role of decoding in learning to read and to provide an explanation for failure to understand what is read; the reader could fall short in decoding ability, in language comprehension, or in both. There are many problems with this view of reading, with a primary concern being its inadequacy in explaining what goes on in learning to read. The appeal to listening comprehension to explain reading comprehension merely pushes our questions about the origins of comprehension back another level. Further, the difference between what is involved in understanding speech and what is involved in understanding written text is not just decoding. The explicit consideration of how listening and reading are different would be a valuable addition to most interpretations and explanations of reading processes.

For one thing, comprehension of oral language benefits from the speaker's understanding of what is being uttered, which enables the shaping of the speech with expressiveness, intonation, and pauses. Any access to this prosody when reading written text must come from what the reader is able to supply in the way of meaning-based interpretation and use of the conventions of text that signal appropriate pauses and expression. How this is accomplished is an important and difficult question. If the simple model were accurate, a reader with perfect decoding ability should be able to derive the identical level of comprehension from perusing a written text as from hearing it presented orally as an uninflected stream of words, with each word articulated at a uniform rate and with a uniform tone, as by a machine.

A further issue for the simple model of reading is the role of reading-related experience in the development of listening comprehension; it is difficult to imagine how to measure pure oral language comprehension that has in it no contribution from exposure to written text. In our literate society, the influence of written text on our language activities is ubiquitous and inescapable (Ong, 1982). Despite these and other difficulties with the simple model, it has remained a potent force in the research on learning to read, spawning studies aiming to test the model, supplement the model, and predict individual differences in reading development using the model. Its decomposition of reading into decoding and oral language capabilities and its identification of learning to decode words as the essence of learning to read have had a lasting impact.

The emphasis on learning to read as a childhood task was reinforced strongly in more recent years by the National Reading Panel (NRP) Report (2000) on teaching children to read. The NRP Report emphasized the importance of scientific, evidence-based research on how best to teach children to read. It highlighted the key areas of alphabetics (phonemic awareness and phonics), fluency, and comprehension (vocabulary and text comprehension). Phonemic awareness concerns discrimination of basic sound units (phonemes) in speech, while phonics links these sound units to the letters of the alphabet. In the NRP Report, fluency is defined as speed, accuracy, and proper expression in oral reading, vocabulary is word knowledge, and comprehension involves development of an understanding of what is read.

The appearance of the NRP Report marked something of a watershed in research on reading and learning to read, in its singling out of experimental research as providing the highest quality of evidence, its selection of the key components of reading, and its synthesis of *best evidence* research and identification of research gaps. In this chapter, we will consider research on learning to read and reading development that has appeared since 2000, under the assumption that the NRP Report represented a boundary event likely to have shaped the direction taken by the field.

Although the NRP Report identified the five pillars of reading instruction as phonemic awareness, phonics, fluency, vocabulary, and comprehension, how these five pillars might come together during reading development remained unclear, as did what might be involved in reading beyond high school (Pressley, Duke, & Boling, 2004). In addition, the incorporation of motivational, contextual, or sociocultural factors remained problematic, as noted in Yatvin's Minority View appended to the report (NRP, 2000). The RAND Reading Study Group offered a more complex and nuanced view of the specific area of comprehension in their 2002 report outlining directions for future research on improving reading comprehension. Their conceptualization of reading comprehension included explicit acknowledgment of the interaction of person-level, text-level, and activity-level factors, embedded the reader in a sociocultural context, and positioned motivation alongside cognition as shaping the course of a given reading experience. They suggested that learning to read well is "a long-term developmental process" (p. 9) in which the meaning of reading well changes at different developmental points, and identified the adult reader and adult purposes for reading as the goals of reading comprehension development. Their approach to reading provided a counterbalance to the emphasis on word reading and access to print, but limited its developmental range by its strong demarcation of the separate areas of beginning reading (up through Grade 3) and reading for understanding and to learn (after Grade 3).

Another important recent influence in the field of reading has been the accountability movement spearheaded by the passage of the No Child Left Behind Act of 2001 (2002). This nationally-mandated program of assessment, with its requirement of universal grade-level proficiency in reading by 2014, has put the articulation of the markers of appropriate development in reading in the hands of each state's test developers. For teachers and students across the country, learning to read has become learning to do what will be asked for on the test (Alexander & Riconscente, 2005). The understandable desire to avoid the penalties associated with failure to make adequate yearly progress toward universal proficiency has led to a focus in schools on intensive remediation for those students at risk of falling just short. Learning to read in the accountability framework becomes not a matter of reaching one's potential but of avoiding failure. The mandatory achievement of a minimum level of competence according to grade-level reading standards regardless of initial level of motivation or ability is the very antithesis of a developmental approach to reading, which advocates consideration of what the individual brings to the situation in the way of capabilities, needs, and goals.

THEORETICAL FRAMEWORK

Our lifespan developmental view portrays reading as a complex communicative behavior that involves deriving meaning from presented text, as changing over the course of development, and as oriented toward the reader's contextualized purposes. The theoretical framework associated with this view is Alexander's Model of Domain Learning (MDL), fitted to the domain of reading (Alexander, 2003, 2006). The MDL postulates three stages of development in academic domains: (1) the entry-level stage of acclimation; (2) the mid-level and often terminal stage of competence; and (3) the more rarely achieved highest stage of proficiency or expertise. Each stage manifests its own typical range of patterns in the learner's possession of and reliance on situational and individual interest, domain and topic knowledge, and surface-level and deep strategic processing. Although the MDL is a model of learning in academic domains, the learner is not viewed as isolated in an academic setting. Learners' interests, knowledge, goals, and choices are held to be informed by their activities and identities both inside and outside the classroom.

As outlined by Alexander in her discussions of reading development per the MDL (2003, 2006), readers in the stage of acclimation do not yet have much breadth or depth of knowledge. When they read, their strategic processing tends to be superficial, aiming more at word-level processing or local coherence than at integration of the text with their own understanding. They may respond to surface features of the reading situation or text with interest, but this may or may not result in more effective processing and greater comprehension. Over time and with practice, their interest in reading can increase, their knowledge increases, and their ability to engage in deeper processing also increases, leading to a transition to the stage of competence.

The competent reader has a relatively broad store of knowledge about reading (domain knowledge), as well as a certain depth of knowledge of relevant topics that may be addressed or invoked during typical reading tasks (topic knowledge). In addition, this knowledge is structured and interconnected to a degree, making recall and application of it more fluent. Correspondingly, the competent reader has achieved a level of automaticity in carrying out routine procedures (surface-level processing); this skillful navigation of the reading terrain enables the reader's attention to be possibly turned to deeper meaning-building, reflective, evaluative, and even transformational strategic behaviors (deep-level processing).

Finally, as the motive force behind the operation of all this reading machinery, competent readers have a certain level of interest in reading and in learning from text (individual interest); they do not necessarily require the attention-grabbing devices of a controversial or personally-relevant topic or a colorful spread of pictures (situational interest) to lure them into interaction with a text. Should the reader be strongly enough interested to pursue learning from and about reading further, the progression to proficiency can occur. Proficient readers are likely to be those who have made the study of it their profession. Their identity is bound up with the study of the domain and their interest is clearly enduring and internal. Their body of principled knowledge has grown and will continue to grow, and their strategic processing is deep, efficient, and engaged.

Unlike in Chall's (1983) stage model of reading development, there are no particular ages or levels of school experience associated with developmental status in the MDL. Quite young readers can be well into competence, and quite mature readers can be at its very beginnings. While Chall draws a clear boundary between learning to read (Stages 1–2, Grades 1–3) and reading to learn (Stages 3–5, Grades 4 and up), in the MDL, our view is that reading is at every point about both learning to read and reading to learn. This point is nicely addressed by Strang and her colleagues:

> There was a time when we thought that children in the first three grades were to learn to read, in the middle grades were to read to learn, and were to begin to evaluate what they read after they had arrived at the high school or college level . . . Now we are realizing that there is no skill or aspect of reading for which some preparation is not made in the kindergarten, no process in reading on the college level that does not have its counterpart on every one of the earlier levels.
>
> (1955, p. 90)

There are particular aspects of the MDL framework for reading development that are most salient for our discussion of the empirical research. The MDL gives an important role to the reader's knowledge, which includes both knowledge about reading and knowledge relating to what is read. The MDL includes explicit consideration of the reader's motivation to read and learn from text, and of the way that motivation and knowledge can interact in the formulation of reading goals and the implementation of reading strategies. How the reader employs both skillful and strategic processing and the role of practice and automaticity are also addressed by the MDL. And finally, the MDL considers how the reader's development is part of an overall lifespan developmental trajectory reflecting participation in a variety of discourse communities and pursuit of individual purposes and interests.

CURRENT TRENDS AND ISSUES

Our approach to the identification and synthesis of relevant current literature on learning to read is structured around six foundational principles for improving reading identified by Gray in 1951. His principles are admirably suited for our enterprise of situating the current research base on learning to read within the particular lifespan developmental perspective afforded by the MDL. These principles are not independent, but relate to a coherent view of reading development, and studies often could legitimately fall under more than one. The articles selected appeared in peer-reviewed journals from 2000 to 2009. Articles about specific interventions or instructional practices were not included; our focus was research on learning to read that would illuminate the status of the field for each of Gray's six foundation stones.

Recognizing the Changed Role of Reading

Gray (1951) began by addressing the need for explicit consideration of changes in the role of reading following upon the emergence of new forms of mass communication and entertainment such as radio, movies, and television. He emphasized the continued importance of reading as a source of information, for the reflective and critical study of personal and social problems, and as a form of vicarious exposure to experience.

In our own era, electronic media and communications are the latest source of change. We wonder, as did Gray, what the role of reading becomes as the social and economic landscape shifts yet again with the introduction and infiltration into our daily lives of new forms of communication, information storage, and entertainment. For example, the expanded view of what counts as text, partially driven by the introduction of new media, has prompted a call to reconsider how the field conceptualizes reading comprehension (Fox & Alexander, 2009). Gray's urging to consider the changed role of reading has been echoed recently by Hassett (2006), who raised a particular concern that elementary education and reading instruction remain centered around a vision of traditional print literacy that no longer aligns well with the literacies and texts students will encounter in the world. Studies under this heading addressed the role of reading in the daily lives of adults, investigated children's management of complex reading tasks, and considered possible consequences for young adult readers of using new modes of communication and entertainment.

Adult Reading

Among the issues associated with an explicit consideration of the role of reading is the important question of how adults use reading in their daily lives and whether these uses are supported by the reading instruction presented in schools. In their daily lives, adults are likely to encounter a variety of types of texts and documents and to use a variety of information sources, both printed and electronic. An ethnographic study by Taylor (2006) of the informal literacy activities of adults with low reading skills found that these adults needed to be able to read printed instructional materials and to use computers to meet information needs related to both work and home life. How well adults can cope with the demands of document use may relate to their familiarity with the documents.

Using a constructed index of typical familiarity, level of use, and frequency of encountering a range of document types, Cohen and Snowden (2008) found that adults' performance in document-related reading tasks on national assessments of adult literacy tended to be higher for document types more likely to be familiar, used regularly, and encountered frequently. However, many reading situations require engagement with unfamiliar text content or formats, at which point ability as a reader would be an asset and lack of ability could prove a liability. In her correlational investigation of reading skills and exam performance in Danish adults taking adult education courses, Arnbak (2004) found that poor decoding and comprehension could be a real handicap, particularly in courses with heavy reading loads.

Managing Complex Reading Tasks

The need for the school curriculum to address the document skills required for successful performance in the modern workplace was noted by Conley (2008) in his discussion of cognitive strategy instruction for adolescents. Some document-related skills have broad utility across educational, personal, and workplace settings, such as the location and identification of information to answer questions. Studies of children performing search tasks in complex print (Rouet & Coutelet, 2008) and online (Coiro & Dobler, 2007) environments suggest that document search behaviors represent an additional skill beyond reading comprehension as typically framed. For print text, this involves maintenance of focus on the question, suppression of irrelevant information, and targeting of relevant information using top-down search strategies (Rouet & Coutelet, 2008). Older students were more successful and faster at print text search tasks in Rouet and Coutelet's cross-sectional comparison of third, fifth, and seventh graders, suggesting that search behaviors are complex higher-level skills not available to younger students.

Coiro and Dobler explored the internet search strategies of 11 sixth-grade skilled readers in a qualitative think-aloud study, concluding that the additional complexity of searching across the multiple information sources available online required their participants to call upon strategic search and comprehension processes specific to the demands of locating information in an online environment. Such processes included use of knowledge about typical structures of informational websites and rapid cycling through prediction, search, location, and evaluation in managing navigational decisions. The requirement for flexibility and management of reading across and within multiple texts was also highlighted by Lewis and Fabos (2005) in their case study of the uses of instant messaging (IM) by seven teenagers selected as being frequent and relatively expert users of IM.

New Media Use and Consequences

Another issue associated with consideration of the role of reading involves the use by young adults of particular forms of new electronic media and modes of communication and possible associated changes in reading habits, patterns, or abilities (e.g., text speak). Change can often be perceived as threatening, as Carrington (2005) noted in her discussion of negative perceptions of students' uses of text messaging. Two recent studies addressed possible negative consequences of participation in the use of new media for college students' reading, but found no apparent ill effects. In a cross-sectional comparison of 34 college student users and 46 non-users of text messaging abbreviations, Drouin and David (2009) found that non-users of text speak tended to be older, but that there were no observable differences between the two groups on measures of spelling, word recognition, or reading fluency. However, they found that about half of their participants reported believing that use of text speak could negatively affect memory for and use of standard English. The displacement of recreational or academic reading time by time spent online or watching television was investigated in a time-diary survey of college students (Mokhtari, Reichard, & Gardner, 2009), in which time spent on the internet did not appear to be displacing time spent on reading, possibly as a consequence of activity overlap in multitasking.

Developing a Broad Concept of Reading

Here Gray (1951) addressed what he saw as the critical need to broaden the understanding of what reading means and what reading development should entail beyond successful word recognition and fluent oral reading. Although he held these to be important elements in reading development, he also stressed that our understanding of reading should include much more, such as reflection, critical evaluation, identification of patterns and relations, accommodation of new ideas, and application.

We embrace Gray's delineation of a broader concept of reading and his inclusion of higher-order goals and activities, and would add in also engagement in intertextual reading, and social engagement around text. Along with consideration of how readers develop toward successful participation in these various levels of reading activities, such acknowledgment of multiple levels of reading includes the need to consider the reader's goals and intentions in a given reading situation (Fox, Maggioni, Dinsmore, & Alexander, 2008; Linderholm, 2006). It becomes important to take into account what the reader thinks reading is, and what behaviors and activities the reader views as appropriate to reading in a particular context and toward a particular purpose (Gee, 2001). Studies under this heading addressed broader aspects of reading including texts as presenting argument and requiring evaluation, interaction with multiple texts, metacognition and monitoring, and peer discussions.

Argument and Evaluation

Evaluation of text is one of the higher-order aspects of reading identified by Gray. In order to evaluate an argument presented by a text, the reader must be aware of the argument as such. Chambliss and Murphy (2002) investigated the performance of fourth and fifth graders in detecting and representing argument structure in their recall of argumentative texts. Observed responses included the accurate or inferred approximate representation of the text's hierarchical argument structure, a topic-details organization scheme, and lists. Grade-level comparisons using chi-square analysis indicated that older children were more likely to see the text as following an argument pattern, but the low performance overall together with the use by some children of the topic-details arrangement familiar from textbooks suggested to the authors the need for more reading of argumentative texts in elementary classrooms.

Beyond the ability to identify the text's argument structure, the reader also brings to the evaluation of an argumentative text certain relevant beliefs. The role of undergraduates' epistemological and topic-specific beliefs in how they read and what they recalled was studied by Kardash and Howell (2000), in a think-aloud study using a dual-positional argumentative text on a controversial topic. Of particular note was their finding that readers engaged in more evaluative processing of text that conflicted with their current beliefs on the topic, while they tended to check their understanding for the consistent text. This suggests that readers may make different use of texts depending on how well the texts align with their already formed opinions and beliefs. More overt decisions about how to make use of texts include readers' evaluations of trustworthiness when trying to construct an understanding of a complex topic using multiple and possibly conflicting texts (Bråten, Strømsø, & Britt, 2009). In their study of the relation of Norwegian under-graduates' ratings of trustworthiness to their performance in building comprehension of an issue across multiple texts, Bråten and his colleagues found that trusting reliable sources was associated with better comprehension, with additional variance accounted for by the use of appropriate criteria for trustworthiness.

Multiple Texts

Multiple text situations call particularly for management of content, both in piecing together what is derived from the various texts and in deciding what to access when. McEneaney, Li, Allen, and Guzniczek (2009) found that reader stance toward an exposi-tory hypertext was related to both navigation and learning. Those undergraduate and graduate students prompted to consider their own response to the hypertext format (an aesthetic stance) tended to use a more built-in path through the hypertext and also achieved higher ratings for understanding in post-test comparisons than those prompted to direct their attention to the information being presented (an efferent stance). Over-all, how readers moved through the environment changed over the course of the task, with faster reading rates and simpler paths seen as readers became more familiar with the content and its arrangement. A change over time was also observed by Strømsø, Bråten, and Samuelstuen (2003) in their think-aloud study of the reading behaviors of seven Norwegian pre-law students reading self-selected course-related texts. Their participants' strategic processing came to focus more on text-external sources over the course of a semester and involved more monitoring and elaboration, particularly for better-performing students. The authors saw this shift as suggesting a modification in the participants' goals and perception of the task as they drew nearer to the final exam.

Metacognition and Monitoring

The broadening of reading into multiple levels with multiple associated goals means that the monitoring supporting successful attainment of these goals and the forms of metatextual or metalinguistic knowledge guiding the monitoring also expand. Children's metacognition and monitoring in reading were considered in three studies in the recent literature. Eme, Puustinen, and Coutelet (2006) compared third and fifth graders on their knowledge of reading skills, tasks, and goals and on their ability to assess the likely correctness of their responses to reading comprehension questions. They found low accuracy in self-evaluation at both grades, and relatively little in the way of verbalizable knowledge about reading, with a slight trend for fifth graders to know more. Although self-evaluation and comprehension appeared to be independent, better comprehenders tended to have greater metatextual knowledge related to reading.

Another angle on metacognition was addressed by Zipke (2007), who used riddle and ambiguity resolution tasks to assess metalinguistic awareness in sixth and seventh graders. Performance on these tasks was correlated to reading comprehension and vocabulary scores; riddle solving, in particular, explained additional variance in reading comprehension over and above vocabulary scores. Bornholt (2002) looked at the test-taking strategies of 9- and 10-year-olds for a cloze test of reading comprehension and found large individual differences in strategies, which related to performance differences. Children with effective strategies were able to give explicit explanations for their choices in a group discussion after the test, which appeared to assist the initially poorer performers during a retest. That test-wiseness may be related to metacognitive knowledge about reading and that both may be related to performance on reading assessments raise interesting questions regarding what is being assessed in tests of reading comprehension and why good readers might do better on them.

Peer Discussions

What readers know and can communicate about reading can emerge directly or indirectly in their discussions about text with other readers. Two recent studies focused specifically on reading comprehension strategy use during group discussions by ninth graders (Berne & Clark, 2006) and 5th graders (Clark, 2009). Ninth graders most often used comprehension strategies related to interpretation or questioning, but generally appeared to lack a planful approach to developing understanding of the text together (Berne & Clark, 2006). Common strategies used by fifth graders also included questioning and interpreting (Clark, 2009). Clark found that students of different reading abilities did not differ in patterns of strategy use; however, the quality of strategy use did vary, and post-discussion comprehension tended to reflect more the contributions of the better readers.

Accepting the Idea That Growth in Reading Is a Continuous Process

In discussing the continuous nature of growth in and through reading, Gray (1951) highlighted both the changes in what is demanded in the way of reading competence as readers progress into higher levels of schooling and readers' continued growth into adulthood in underlying aspects of reading such as vocabulary and comprehension of meaning, those labeled by Paris (2005) as unconstrained skills. Gray strongly emphasized the need for systematic instructional support for reading into the higher grades and on into college. Mastery of earlier stages of reading does not guarantee competent reading when pursuing new interests, addressing new problems, and facing new demands for interpretive depth, reflective and critical response, and technical reading.

We stand with Gray in viewing growth in reading as a continuous process, with the theoretical framework of the MDL providing a broad characterization of the patterns of changes in knowledge, interest, and strategy use as readers advance (Alexander, Jetton, & Kulikowich, 1995). Readers' knowledge of reading and of what they read about becomes richer, deeper, and more principled; their strategy use shifts to match their increasingly higher-level goals and their development of automaticity at lower-level processes; and their interest becomes more focused and self-sustaining, directing cognitive, attentional, and motivational resources toward understanding reading and toward reading for understanding. We add to Gray's emphases the challenges now presented by the expectation that most students will finish high school and attend college.

Little attention has been given recently to growth in reading into and beyond high school, with little work done on reading tasks and goals beyond a grasp of literal or inferential meaning and on the reader capabilities that might support pursuit of them, such as author awareness, openness to the unfamiliar, and acknowledgment of conflict (Scholes, 2002). This dearth of attention (to levels beyond early reading) may be due to the lack of a well-specified model of reading development beyond early reading to support assessments beyond those addressing basic comprehension (Fox & Alexander, 2009; Johnston, Barnes, & Desrochers, 2008). On the other hand, there has been extensive research in recent years on early reading development and on the early determinants of subsequent reading performance. Of particular interest have been the predictors of and connections between word reading (discussed in Nation, 2008) and comprehension of connected text (for reviews, see Johnston et al., 2008; Nation & Angell, 2006). Studies under this heading looked at growth in reading using cross-sectional or longitudinal designs, and focused on word reading, reading comprehension, or both.

Growth in Word Reading

In studies addressing factors related to growth in the ability to read words, development in word reading was found to be related to: home literacy environment (Burgess, Hecht, & Lonigan, 2002); concept of a word in print (Flanigan, 2007; Morris, Bloodgood, Lomax, & Perney, 2003); rhythm (David, Wade-Woolley, Kirby, & Smithrim, 2007); letter knowledge, phonemic manipulation, and Rapid Automatized Naming (RAN) (Lervåg, Bråten, & Hulme, 2009); and phonological awareness, orthographic knowledge, and morphological awareness (Roman, Kirby, Parrila, Wade-Woolley, & Deacon, 2009). While greater separability of the different constructs composing word reading speed was observed for older children (Lervåg et al., 2009), the contributions of orthographic knowledge, morphological and phonological awareness to word reading appeared to be stable across the three ages measured by Roman et al. (2009), with orthography most important for real word reading and phonological awareness for pseudowords.

Growth in Reading Comprehension

There appeared to be relatively strong stability in individual differences in reading comprehension development. In a large-scale longitudinal study of Dutch schoolchildren from first through sixth grade, Verhoeven and van Leeuwe (2008) found that children's initial scores for listening comprehension and vocabulary strongly predicted their later development in reading comprehension, with individual differences remaining stable throughout the course of the study. In a longitudinal twin study, stability in reading achievement scores appeared to relate substantially to genetic influences (Harlaar, Dale, & Plomin, 2007), with new age-specific genetic influences appearing at each age studied, possibly related to the differences in what was expected in the way of reading. A longitudinal study of college undergraduates (Bray, Pascarella, & Pierson, 2004) found that students' initial levels of reading comprehension and reading attitude were the strongest predictors of later reading comprehension and reading attitude. Although other factors associated with aspects of college experience were found to be related to growth in reading comprehension, these relations were moderated by reader characteristics such as gender, ethnicity, and initial reading ability.

The importance of the development of automaticity for growth in reading comprehension was investigated in a cross-sectional study of third, fifth, and seventh graders (Walczyk et al., 2007), in which older students tended to compensate more efficiently to prevent and resolve confusions when reading, while level of efficiency enabled students to cope more effectively with restrictive reading situations, such as the time pressure often involved in reading assessments. Speed, accuracy, and automaticity of oral word reading were found to predict reading comprehension for first, second, and third graders, but had diminishing influence with age (Schwanenflugel et al., 2006), while smoother and more adult-like intonations when reading aloud in first grade predicted better reading comprehension in third grade (Miller & Schwanenflugel, 2008).

Meaning-based factors in reading comprehension growth were explored in two cross-sectional studies of children's comprehension of narratives, where it was found that choice of appropriate superordinate goals and outcomes as titles for narrative texts increased with age (van den Broek, Lynch, Naslund, Ievers-Landis, & Verduin, 2003), as did sensitivity to underlying narrative structure (Lynch et al., 2008) although even the youngest participants in both studies showed awareness of narrative structure. Children's knowledge of story structure was among the component skills of comprehension assessed in a longitudinal study (Cain, Oakhill, & Bryant, 2004); after controlling for word reading, vocabulary, and verbal ability, both working memory and component skills contributed to the prediction of reading comprehension. In a three-year longitudinal study, working memory capacity was found to become more important as a predictor of reading comprehension over the early years of reading development, while growth in vocabulary and in reading comprehension appeared to be reciprocally related during this period (Seigneuric & Ehrlich, 2005).

With regard to learning from expository text, possible developmental differences were found in a study comparing older adults (mean age 67) and younger adults (mean age 21; Noh et al., 2007). Older adults tended to work more toward incorporating prior knowledge and experience in building an elaborated situation model, while younger readers focused more on the content presented in the textbase and had better recall of textbase details.

Distinguishing and Relating Word Reading and Comprehension

Recent studies exploring the determinants of growth in word reading and reading comprehension were generally consistent in finding that different sets of factors predicted growth in these two aspects of reading. Typical findings included the role of phonological skills in word reading and the importance of some form of language ability in the development of reading comprehension (e.g., de Jong & van der Leij, 2002). Aspects of language-related ability found to be independent predictors of growth in reading comprehension included: vocabulary and grammatical skills at school entry (Muter, Hulme, Snowling, & Stevenson, 2004); oral language ability in preschool (Storch & Whitehurst, 2002) and at age 8 (Nation & Snowling, 2004); semantic skills at age 3 (Frost, Madsbjerg, Niedersøe, Olofsson, & Sørensen, 2005), in kindergarten (Roth, Speece, & Cooper, 2002), and in Grades 2–3 (Vellutino, Tunmer, Jaccard, & Chen, 2007); vocabulary and listening comprehension in Grade 1 (de Jong & van der Leij, 2002); and text integration and metacognitive monitoring (Oakhill, Cain, & Bryant, 2003).

Word reading and reading comprehension appear to follow different developmental trajectories within overall reading development (Frost et al., 2005; Roth et al., 2002;

Storch & Whitehurst, 2002; Vellutino et al., 2007). A two-year twin study of early reading found considerable overlap in the genetic influences on decoding and comprehension; however, these data were from quite young readers at a point when word reading capability typically constrains comprehension (Petrill et al., 2007). Overall, these findings suggest the complex, dynamic, and interactive nature of relations among word reading, language ability, reading comprehension, and other knowledge-related, cognitive, attentional, and motivational factors in reading development.

Broadening the Reading Program in Harmony with Expanding Interests and Needs of Pupils

Gray (1951) also outlined developmental changes in students' interests and in their purposes for reading as they mature, viewing these changes in interests and needs as occurring in tandem with changes in requisite aspects of reading competence. He recommended that reading materials and instruction be aligned with students' interests and be supportive of their purposes, with a central goal being the development of the habit of independent reading both for enjoyment and as an essential tool for adult life.

Interest has a key role in the understanding of reading development in the MDL (Fox & Alexander, 2004), where the developmental trajectories of situational and individual interest are constitutive elements of readers' growth profiles. Along with Gray's emphasis on developmental changes in students' reading interests and purposes, we see other associated topics of current relevance as including readers' motivational responses to new forms of text, the role of out-of-school reading, and social interactions around text, including collaboration and discussion. Studies under this heading fell into two groups, one considering mechanisms related to the action or development of interest, and the other considering reading interest, reading behaviors, and reading attitudes in and out of school.

Mechanisms of Interest

Interest helps determine the course of an individual reading experience as well as shaping the choices and decisions associated with longer-term progress. The role of interest in motivating the choice to continue reading a passage was investigated by Ainley, Corrigan, and Richardson (2005), who had young adolescents read expository texts addressing topics similar to those appearing in popular magazines. Students' levels of domain interest related to the subject of the text influenced their initial topic interest when presented with the passage titles; unless the text content was able to sustain that topic interest, students stopped reading. Beyond interest's role in sustaining attention, more interesting stories were found to require fewer attentional resources for comprehension than less interesting stories in a study reporting on a pair of experiments in which undergraduates were presented with stories differing in rated interest (McDaniel, Waddill, Finstad, & Bourg, 2000); however, overall recall did not differ depending on rated story interest.

The possible development of long-term intrinsic motivation for reading from accumulation of satisfying experiences with individual books was explored in a study looking at changes in reading motivation for third grade students from September to December (Guthrie, Hoa, Wigfield, Tonks, & Perencevich, 2006). Changes in students' situated motivation for individual books predicted changes in general intrinsic and extrinsic reading motivation over this period. Guthrie and his colleagues also found that fourth graders' reading motivation predicted reading comprehension growth from September to December, while initial level of reading comprehension did not predict growth in interest (Guthrie et al., 2007). Together these findings suggest not only that positive reading experiences should be encouraged, but also that negative reading experiences may have longer-term harmful consequences, a concern raised by Lenters in her discussion of adolescent resistant readers (2006).

Reading In and Out of School

A theme in the research related to reading behaviors, reading attitudes, and reading interest in and out of school was the need for sensitivity to the multiple sources of potentially important variability, as Moje, Dillon, and O'Brien emphasized in their discussion of secondary literacy (2000). Studies discussed here documented variability related to culture, gender, and interest in collaboration and social engagement. For instance, in her case study of African American middle-school students' classroom discussions of children's books presenting African American culture, Brooks (2006) found that although African American culture as presented in these books provided a valuable connection to the students' interests and shared relevant background knowledge, there was considerable variability and complexity in how students responded to the elements of shared culture presented, such as dealing with racism or use of vernacular language. The author suggested that similarity in interpretations and uses of culture should not be taken as a given even for those with a shared cultural background. Gender was found to be a source of differences in reading interest and behavior in a survey of students at a large urban middle school (Hughes-Hassell & Rodge, 2007), with females more likely to report enjoying reading and reading for pleasure. Varying attitudes toward collaboration and social engagement around reading were expressed by fourth grade students (Guthrie et al., 2007), with some young readers reporting enjoyment of reading with others, discussing books with others, and having others choose books for them, while among the most highly motivated and competent readers, some valued instead autonomy, independence, and personal choice.

Autonomy and pursuit of personal interests and goals are an important part of the distinction seen by adolescents between reading in school and out of school (Alexander & Fox, in press). A large-scale survey of sixth graders (Ivey & Broaddus, 2001) found a clear difference between students' reported reading activities and purposes in school and out of school. When reading on their own, students had individual and varied reasons for reading, including following up on topics of personal interest to learn more. Independent reading to pursue personally-valued knowledge, one of Gray's key goals in reading development, was mentioned in association with out-of-school reading by adolescent participants in two other recent studies as well (Hughes-Hassell & Rodge, 2007; Smith & Wilhelm, 2004). In Smith and Wilhelm's interview-based study of a diverse group of 49 adolescent boys, participants reported finding school texts difficult and distant from their experiences and uses for texts, while they felt competent and validated when engaging in out-of-school reading to support their own inquiries and purposes.

Guidance in Reading Essential in Each Curriculum Field

In terms of instructional guidance for reading, Gray (1951) focused on the connection between reading purposes and appropriate reading behaviors. He considered that reading activities in the different content areas are associated with different purposes and therefore call for different attitudes and skills. According to Gray, the more differentiated and specialized the content areas become, the more critical it is that students understand clearly the purposes for which they are reading in each content area, understand which reading behaviors are called for, and can carry out those reading behaviors effectively.

The linking of reading behaviors to reader purposes within the context of a given content area is fundamental to the understanding of reading development within the MDL (Fox et al., 2008). Along with the purpose-related and domain-specific reader attitudes and skills noted by Gray, we would also include a strong role for knowledge both of reading and of the domain and of its discourse practices. Studies pertinent to this section fell into two groups, one addressing what goes into successful reading of domain-related texts and the other considering issues arising in the context of content-area reading instruction.

Reading of Domain-Specific Texts

Gray's suggestion that there are different reading requirements for different content areas was addressed by Behrman and Street (2005) and by Best, Floyd, and McNamara (2008). In an investigation of possible different competencies supporting the reading of expository and narrative texts, Best et al. (2008) found that world knowledge predicted third graders' recall of an expository passage on plants, while their recall of a narrative passage of comparable difficulty was better predicted by decoding ability. For community college students in an anatomy course, neither prior content knowledge nor general reading ability predicted their final grade as strongly as did their scores on an initial measure of content-specific reading ability based on the course textbook (Behrman & Street, 2005).

Readers' understanding of, memory for, and learning from domain-specific text depend in multiple ways on their relevant knowledge (Fox, 2009). Tenth grade students' prior knowledge about the topic of a sociology text was found to contribute most strongly to the prediction of their recall and comprehension, with lesser contributions from decoding skill and reported use of organization and monitoring strategies (Samuelstuen & Bråten, 2005). Kendeou and van den Broek (2005) found that undergraduates engaged in similar patterns of processing and of knowledge use as they read a passage on how flashlights work, regardless of the correctness or incorrectness of their prior knowledge; this resulted in the generation of invalid inferences and corruption of recall for those with misconceptions. Compartmentalization of their knowledge appeared to prevent readers from realizing the conflict between their misconceptions and the text content. A different aspect of students' failure to incorporate relevant information from text was noted by Britt and Aglinskas (2002) in their investigation of undergraduates' and high school students' spontaneous and prompted use of appropriate sourcing heuristics for a set of texts related to a historical event. Use of source information was low overall, even when prompted, and students did not look to corroborate information across multiple sources.

Other forms of discipline-specific reading behaviors addressed in the recent literature include the reasoning supporting literary interpretations (Graves, 2001) and the specific competencies associated with the reading of graphs (Friel, Curcio, & Bright, 2001; Roth & Bowen, 2003). Graves (2001) found that her six literary expert participants used analogical reasoning to support the generation and elaboration of global themes and management of an array of interpretive possibilities when reading the opening passage of a novel, *The English Patient*. This analogical reasoning built upon connections to each expert's interests, general knowledge of literature, and particular area of expertise, resulting in interpretations linked to a variety of initial associations, including Shakespeare, Milton, and Emily Dickinson. The bulk of the experts' statements were at the local or factual levels, however, with global or integrative statements making up only one-tenth of their comments.

Movement between a local and global focus of attention and the role of both individually specialized and more general discipline-related knowledge also emerged as a critical element in conceptualizations of expertise in the reading of graphs. Competence in the reading of statistical graphs was described by Friel, Curcio, and Bright (2001) in their review of literature as having three progressive levels involving information identification, manipulation, and application, calling for different forms of supporting knowledge and a shift of attention from local to more global features. Information identification, that is, the determination of what data are being presented in the graph, requires an understanding of the conventions of graph design. Information manipulation involves drawing relationships among the data presented, while application moves beyond the immediate data and relationships to consider their meaning in the larger context. Comparison of expert scientists' readings of graphs from their own work and less familiar graphs found that the scientists moved directly to application with the familiar graphs, while the unfamiliar graphs required effortful identification of information and determination of appropriate manipulations to uncover relations in the data (Roth & Bowen, 2003).

Issues in Content-Area Reading Instruction

When older students are reading to learn in a particular content area, they typically encounter some form of informational text, such as a textbook. In her content analysis of informational books for young children, Pappas (2006) argued that even young children need exposure to informational texts that follow the conventions of typical scientific discourse in order to learn science content and to develop an awareness of the way scientists organize and communicate knowledge. She found that informational books available for primary grade students included hybrid texts mingling informational content with conventions appropriate for other genres, such as personal or episodic narrative structures. Socialization of students into the communicative practices and knowledge structures used in the disciplines is critical to reading and learning in secondary education (Moje, 2008), with a key element being what students think counts as learning in a given area of knowledge, which shapes their purposes and behaviors when reading domain-specific texts.

Several tensions were observable in the recent literature related to content-area reading and instruction. One was that content-area teachers may not be explicitly aware of the contextualized reading practices associated with their discipline and of the need to make students explicitly aware of these as well (Fisher & Frey, 2008). Another was that teachers may feel that the content-area reading strategies they are being told to instruct lack utility or relevance for the actual reading practices associated with their content area (Siebert & Draper, 2008). A third was the push to acknowledge, value, and connect to the personal interests, competencies, and knowledge that students bring with them to school, while still moving them into participation in disciplinary discourse in science (Moje et al., 2004), mathematics (Siebert & Draper, 2008), and architecture (Smagorinsky, Cook, & Reed, 2005).

Adjusting Reading Programs to Unique Characteristics and Needs of Pupils

Gray's final principle (1951) concerns the acknowledgment and accommodation of learners' individual differences in capabilities, interests, and needs, which he considered to be at the heart of any program for improving reading. For Gray, it was evident that learners differ widely and that support for learning to read requires recognition of the full range and implications of individual differences. He noted that "growth in reading is influenced by the total development of the child and by all the factors that promote it" (p. 434), and identified the factors involved as: "the reader's background; his capacity to learn; his physical, mental, and emotional status; his interests, motives, and drives; his immediate and oncoming developmental needs; his biases, prejudices, and preconceptions; and his home and community environment" (p. 434). He felt that there was a shift underway in education at that time toward greater attention to individual variability and away from an expectation of lock-step progression at a uniform rate through a program of universally desirable and attainable reading benchmarks.

We are in complete agreement with Gray in positioning this principle as central to the understanding of reading development. In the MDL framework for reading development (Alexander, 2003), there are no expectations for rate of progress and no ages assigned to different stages. The course of development is complexly determined both by what learners bring with them and the dynamic interactions of their capabilities, interests, and goals with instruction, tasks, and other environmental influences impinging upon them, both in and out of school. In contrast to the shift Gray identified away from pressure for uniformity of instruction and reading achievement, we see rather the presence in the current educational milieu of exactly such pressure. Studies included here addressed cognitive and attitudinal factors related to individual differences in reading or learning to read, considered readers' compensatory behaviors to overcome difficulties associated with such differences, and evaluated the long-term effects of early individual differences in success at learning to read.

Factors Relating to Individual Differences

A number of cognitive factors contributing to individual differences in reading capability or reading development were investigated in the recent literature. Among the aspects of reading capability considered, individual differences in reading comprehension, in particular, were found to be significantly related to: measures of intelligence, particularly non-verbal intelligence (Ferrer et al., 2007); simultaneous use of phonological and semantic categories in a classification task by elementary students (Cartwright, 2002) and college students (Cartwright, 2007); text search efficiency and memory for word order (Cataldo & Oakhill, 2000); oral vocabulary (Ricketts, Nation, & Bishop, 2007); word-to-text integration processes (Perfetti, Yang, & Schmalhofer, 2008); and phrase-level prosody (Whalley & Hansen, 2006).

Besides cognitive factors, there was also some recent attention to attitudinal factors. For early adolescents, attitude toward reading made an additional contribution to the prediction of reading comprehension beyond what was explained by orthographic processing, nonverbal ability, and word identification; perceived reading competence was also a significant independent predictor of reading outcomes (Conlon, Zimmer-Gembeck, Creed, & Tucker, 2006). Chapman and Tunmer (2003) argued that children who have difficulty with word-level reading processes at the initial stages of learning to read are likely to develop low reading self-efficacy that could prove to be a lasting handicap.

Compensation for Deficits

In their investigation of word reading fluency and comprehension, Walczyk and Griffith-Ross (2007) found that less fluent readers can compensate and arrive at the same level of comprehension as more fluent readers, particularly in less restrictive reading situations and when they are highly motivated. Undergraduate readers' compensation for low memory span was investigated by Burton and Daneman (2007), who found that their low memory span participants who scored higher on a measure of epistemic sophistication were more likely to look back in the text at content that was unfamiliar or relevant to the task, and also recalled more of the targeted information. Jackson and Doellinger (2002) found that their undergraduate participants who were poor at pseudoword reading but good at comprehending did not differ in their reading performance or in their strategic behaviors from participants who were strong at both pseudoword reading and comprehending, suggesting that their compensation was occurring at a level not apparent in this situation.

Long-Term Effects of Early Individual Differences

Studies considering the long-term effects of early reading differences addressed whether the Matthew effects in reading hypothesized by Stanovich (1986) were seen to occur in various populations. Empirical findings tended to suggest that, by and large, they did not. For example, a cross-language comparison of English and Finnish children found that although individual differences in reading capabilities were stable, they tended to decrease rather than increase over time (Parrila, Aunola, Leskinen, Nurmi, & Kirby, 2005). Similarly, a three-cohort longitudinal study of students up through Grade 6 found that readers who started out with poorer reading comprehension, vocabulary, and spelling tended to catch up to those who started off stronger (Aarnoutse & van Leeuwe, 2000), which the authors saw as a possible effect of instruction.

Another possible effect of instruction was observed by Stainthorp and Hughes (2004), who followed for six years a group of 14 British children who had been identified as self-taught precocious readers at age 5. These students tended to progress at the same rate as the average reader comparison group on all measures of reading development except receptive vocabulary, where the reading done by the precocious readers appeared to support greater vocabulary growth. The authors suggested that the observed lack of specific instructional support for these strong readers may have inhibited their reading development.

FUTURE DIRECTIONS

Our overview of the recent research on learning to read considered this research in light of Gray's (1951) six foundational principles for improving reading and with reference to a lifespan developmental view on reading development structured around the MDL

(Alexander, 2003, 2006). From that perspective, understudied areas in reading development include: the transition from high school to college and from college to adult roles and responsibilities; motivation in older readers; reading of different types of texts as associated with different purposes and behaviors; readers' perspectives on what reading is and on their own goals in reading; the inherently social nature of all reading, particularly its aspect as communication with an author; and the intimate connection between the competencies and perspectives involved in reading and in writing. There is need for more longitudinal research that would allow the developmental dynamics of reading to be better understood; even the extensive research on early reading, much of it longitudinal, falls short of giving a complete picture of how children move into and onward in reading. A more broadly framed consideration of what children are learning about reading as they learn to read might provide a clearer understanding of their progress through the developmental tasks encountered in elementary school and beyond.

Areas that appear poised for extensive research activity include the question of how readers get from reading words to an understanding of an entire text. Although this is an important issue, it appears to be situated more properly in the sphere of overall language comprehension rather than in reading development per se, as does the related issue of vocabulary and its role in word reading and text comprehension. To the extent that readers' text-related understandings, knowledge, and strategic behaviors are implicated in the building of a connected representation of a text from the word level, however, such investigations would be revelatory regarding reading development.

A specific methodological issue that emerged in trying to gain a coherent picture of what the recent research has to say about reading development and learning to read was the variety of conceptualizations and operationalizations of the various forms of reading capabilities and outcomes assessed. With regard to reading comprehension, the frequently observed use of some form of commercially-produced standardized assessment was understandable, but made claims regarding growth in reading difficult to evaluate and limited in developmental scope. These commonly used measures of reading comprehension have been criticized as insensitive to the developmental complexities of reading comprehension growth (RAND Reading Study Group, 2002). Aspects of reading performance beyond comprehension were rarely addressed.

The value and importance of framing our understanding of learning to read within a lifespan developmental perspective are in this perspective's insistence that it matters who the learner is, it matters what they choose to read and what we give them to read, it matters what they think reading is, it matters what they know about reading and about texts, it matters why they think they are reading, it matters what they are interested in, know about, and want to know about, and it matters how they make reading a part of their life. Although reading is a complex and fascinating psychological phenomenon in itself, in our psychologizing about reading and its myriad processes, we cannot lose sight of its tremendous potentiality and power as a behavior, and why, after all, we think learning to read is important. We close with this reminder of the transformative power of reading and encountering the unknown, from the autobiography of Richard Wright:

> And it was out of these novels and stories and articles, out of the emotional impact of imaginative constructions of heroic or tragic deeds, that I felt touching my face a tinge of warmth from an unseen light; and in my leaving I was groping toward that invisible

light, always trying to keep my face so set and turned that I would not lose the hope of its faint promise, using it as my justification for action.

(Wright, 1937/1966, p. 283)

REFERENCES

Aarnoutse, C., & van Leeuwe, J. (2000). Development of poor and better readers during the elementary school. *Educational Research and Evaluation, 6,* 251–278.

Adler, M. J. (1940). *How to read a book: The art of getting a liberal education.* New York: Simon & Schuster.

Ainley, M., Corrigan, M., & Richardson, N. (2005). Students, tasks, and emotions: Identifying the contribution of emotions to students' reading of popular culture and popular science texts. *Learning & Instruction, 15,* 433–447.

Alexander, P. A. (2003). Profiling the developing reader: The interplay of knowledge, interest, and strategic processing. In C. M. Fairbanks, J. Worthy, B. Maloch, J. V. Hoffman, & D. L. Schallert (Eds.), *The Fifty-first Yearbook of the National Reading Conference* (pp. 47–65). Oak Creek, WI: National Reading Conference.

Alexander, P. A. (2006). The path to competence: A lifespan developmental perspective on reading. *Journal of Literacy Research, 37,* 413–436.

Alexander, P. A., & Fox, E. (2004). A historical perspective on reading research and practice. In R. B. Ruddell, & N. J. Unrau (Eds.), *Theoretical models and processes of reading* (5th ed., pp. 33–68). Newark, DE: International Reading Association.

Alexander, P. A., & Fox, E. (in press). Adolescents as readers. In M. L. Kamil, P. D. Pearson, E. B. Moje, & P. Afflerbach (Eds.), *Handbook of reading research,* Vol. IV. New York: Routledge.

Alexander, P. A., Jetton, T. L., & Kulikowich, J. M. (1995). Interrelationship of knowledge, interest, and recall: Assessing a model of domain learning. *Journal of Educational Psychology, 87,* 559–575.

Alexander, P. A., & Riconscente, M. M. (2005) A matter of proof: Why achievement ≠ learning. In J. S. Carlson, & J. R. Levin (Eds.), *The* No Child Left Behind *legislation: Educational research and federal funding* (pp. 27–36). Greenwich, CT: Information Age Publishers.

Arnbak, E. (2004). When are poor reading skills a threat to educational achievement? *Reading and Writing: An Interdisciplinary Journal, 17,* 459–482.

Behrman, E. H., & Street, C. (2005). The validity of using a content-specific reading comprehension test for college placement. *Journal of College Reading and Learning, 35,* 5–20.

Berne, J. I., & Clark, K. F. (2006). Comprehension strategy use during peer-led discussions of text: Ninth graders tackle "The Lottery." *Journal of Adolescent & Adult Literacy, 49,* 674–686.

Best, R. M., Floyd, R. G., & McNamara, D. S. (2008). Differential competencies contributing to children's comprehension of narrative and expository texts. *Reading Psychology, 29,* 137–164.

Bornholt, L. J. (2002). An analysis of children's task strategies for a test of reading comprehension. *Contemporary Educational Psychology, 27,* 80–98.

Bråten, I., Strømsø, H., & Britt, M. A. (2009). Trust matters: Examining the role of source evaluation in students' construction of meaning within and across multiple texts. *Reading Research Quarterly, 44,* 6–28.

Bray, G. B., Pascarella, E. T., & Pierson, C. T. (2004). Postsecondary education and some dimensions of literacy development: An exploration of longitudinal evidence. *Reading Research Quarterly, 39,* 306–330.

Britt, M. A., & Aglinskas, C. (2002). Improving students' ability to identify and use source information. *Cognition and Instruction, 20,* 485–522.

Brooks, W. (2006). Reading representations of themselves: Urban youth use culture and African American textual features to develop literary understandings. *Reading Research Quarterly, 41,* 372–392.

Burgess, S. R., Hecht, S. A., & Lonigan, C. J. (2002). Relations of the home literacy environment (HLE) to the development of reading-related abilities: A one-year longitudinal study. *Reading Research Quarterly, 37,* 408–426.

Burton, C., & Daneman, M. (2007). Compensating for limited working memory capacity during reading: Evidence from eye movements. *Reading Psychology, 28,* 163–186.

Cain, K., Oakhill, J., & Bryant, P. (2004). Children's reading comprehension ability: Concurrent prediction by working memory, verbal ability, and component skills. *Journal of Educational Psychology, 96,* 31–42.

Carrington, V. (2005). Txting: The end of civilization (again)? *Cambridge Journal of Education, 35,* 161–175.

Cartwright, K. B. (2002). Cognitive development and reading: The relation of reading-specific multiple classification skill to reading comprehension in elementary school children. *Journal of Educational Psychology, 94,* 56–63.

Cartwright, K. B. (2007). The contribution of graphophonological-semantic flexibility to reading comprehension in college students: Implications for a less simple view of reading. *Journal of Literacy Research, 39,* 173–193.

Cataldo, M. G., & Oakhill, J. (2000). Why are poor comprehenders inefficient searchers? An investigation into the effects of text representation and spatial memory on the ability to locate information in text. *Journal of Educational Psychology, 92,* 791–799.

Chall, J. S. (1983). *Stages of reading development.* New York: McGraw-Hill.

Chambliss, M. J., & Murphy, P. K. (2002). Fourth and fifth graders representing the argument structure in written texts. *Discourse Processes, 34,* 91–115.

Chapman, J. W., & Tunmer, W. E. (2003). Reading difficulties, reading-related self-perceptions, and strategies for overcoming negative self-beliefs. *Reading & Writing Quarterly, 19,* 5–24.

Clark, K. F. (2009). The nature and influence of comprehension strategy use during peer-led literature discussions: An analysis of intermediate grade students' practice. *Literacy Research & Instruction, 48,* 95–119.

Cohen, D. J., & Snowden, J. L. (2008). The relations between document familiarity, frequency, and prevalence and document literacy performance among adult readers. *Reading Research Quarterly, 43,* 9–26.

Coiro, J., & Dobler, E. (2007). Exploring the online reading comprehension strategies used by sixth-grade skilled readers to search for and locate information on the Internet. *Reading Research Quarterly, 42,* 214–257.

Conley, M. W. (2008). Cognitive strategy instruction for adolescents: What we know about the promise, what we don't know about the potential. *Harvard Educational Review, 78,* 84–106.

Conlon, E. G., Zimmer-Gembeck, M. J., Creed, P. A., & Tucker, M. (2006). Family history, self-perceptions, attitudes and cognitive abilities are associated with early adolescent reading skills. *Journal of Research in Reading, 29,* 11–32.

David, D., Wade-Woolley, L., Kirby, J. R., & Smithrim, K. (2007). Rhythm and reading in school-age children: A longitudinal study. *Journal of Research in Reading, 30,* 169–183.

de Jong, P. F., & van der Leij, A. (2002). Effects of phonological abilities and linguistic comprehension on the development of reading. *Scientific Studies of Reading, 6,* 51–77.

Drouin, M., & Davis, C. (2009). R u txting? Is the use of text speak hurting your literacy? *Journal of Literacy Research, 41,* 46–67.

Eme, E., Puustinen, M., & Coutelet, B. (2006). Individual and developmental differences in reading monitoring: When and how do children evaluate their comprehension? *European Journal of Psychology of Education, 21,* 91–115.

Ferrer, E., McArdle, J. J., Shaywitz, B. A., Holahan, J. M., Marchione, K., & Shaywitz, S. E. (2007). Longitudinal models of developmental dynamics between reading and cognition from childhood to adolescence. *Developmental Psychology, 43,* 1460–1473.

Fisher, D., & Frey, N. (2008). Student and teacher perspectives on the usefulness of content literacy strategies. *Literacy Research & Instruction, 47,* 246–263.

Flanigan, K. (2007). A concept of word in text: A pivotal event in early reading acquisition. *Journal of Literacy Research, 39,* 37–70.

Fox, E. (2009). The role of reader characteristics in processing and learning from informational text. *Review of Educational Research, 79,* 197–261.

Fox, E., & Alexander, P. A. (2004). Reading, interest, and domain learning. In C. Kardash (Chair). The role of affect in text processing/comprehension: Theoretical and practical implications. Symposium conducted at the annual meeting of the American Educational Research Association, San Diego, April.

Fox, E., & Alexander, P. A. (2009). Text comprehension: A retrospective, perspective, and prospective. In S. E. Israel, & G. G. Duffy (Eds.), *Handbook of research on reading comprehension* (pp. 227–239). New York: Routledge.

Fox, E., Maggioni, L., Dinsmore, D., & Alexander, P. A. (2008). The multi-layered reading goals of expert readers: Bridging between knowledge, interest, and strategy use. Paper presented at the annual meeting of the American Educational Research Association, New York, March.

Friel, S. N., Curcio, F. R., & Bright, G. W. (2001). Making sense of graphs: Critical factors influencing comprehension and instructional implications. *Journal for Research in Mathematics Education, 32,* 124–158.

Frost, J., Madsbjerg, S., Niedersøe, J., Olofsson, Å., & Sørensen, P. M. (2005). Semantic and phonological skills in predicting reading development: From 3–16 years of age. *Dyslexia, 11,* 79–92.

Gee, J. P. (2001). Reading as situated language: A sociocognitive perspective. *Journal of Adolescent & Adult Literacy, 44,* 714–725.

Gough, P. B., & Tunmer, W. E. (1986). Decoding, reading, and reading disability. *Remedial and Special Education, 7,* 6–10.

Graves, B. (2001). Literary expertise and analogical reasoning: Building global themes. *Empirical Studies of the Arts, 19,* 47–63.

Gray, W. S. (Ed.) (1949). *Reading in an age of mass communication.* New York: The National Council of Teachers of English.

Gray, W. S. (1951). Foundation stones in the road to better reading. *The Elementary School Journal, 51,* 427–435.

Gray, W. S., & Rogers, B. (1956). *Maturity in reading, its nature and appraisal.* Chicago: The University of Chicago Press.

Guthrie, J. T., Hoa, A. L. W., Wigfield, A., Tonks, S. M., Humenick, N. M., & Littles, E. (2007). Reading motivation and reading comprehension growth in the later elementary years. *Contemporary Educational Psychology, 32,* 282–313.

Guthrie, J. T., Hoa, L. W., Wigfield, A., Tonks, S. M., & Perencevich, K. C. (2006). From spark to fire: Can situational reading interest lead to long-term reading motivation? *Reading Research & Instruction, 45,* 91–117.

Harlaar, N., Dale, P. S., & Plomin, R. (2007). From learning to read to reading to learn: Substantial and stable genetic influence. *Child Development, 78,* 116–131.

Hassett, D. D. (2006). Technological difficulties: A theoretical frame for understanding the non-relativistic permanence of traditional print literacy in elementary education. *Journal of Curriculum Studies, 38,* 135–159.

Hughes-Hassell, S., & Rodge, P. (2007). The leisure reading habits of urban adolescents. *Journal of Adolescent & Adult Literacy, 51,* 22–33.

Ivey, G., & Broaddus, K. (2001). "Just plain reading": A survey of what makes students want to read in middle school classrooms. *Reading Research Quarterly, 36,* 350–377.

Jackson, N. E., & Doellinger, H. L. (2002). Resilient readers? University students who are poor recoders but sometimes good text comprehenders. *Journal of Educational Psychology, 94,* 64–78.

Johnston, A. M., Barnes, M. A., & Desrochers, A. (2008). Reading comprehension: Developmental processes, individual differences, and interventions. *Canadian Psychology, 49,* 125–132.

Judson, H. (1954). *The techniques of reading: An integrated program for improved comprehension and speed.* New York: Harcourt Brace & Company.

Kardash, C. M., & Howell, K. L. (2000). Effects of epistemological beliefs and topic-specific beliefs on undergraduates' cognitive and strategic processing of dual-positional text. *Journal of Educational Psychology, 92,* 524–535.

Kendeou, P., & van den Broek, P. (2005. The effects of readers' misconceptions on comprehension of scientific texts. *Journal of Educational Psychology, 97,* 235–245.

Lenters, K. (2006). Resistance, struggle, and the adolescent reader. *Journal of Adolescent & Adult Literacy, 50,* 136–146.

Lervåg, A., Bråten, I., & Hulme, C. (2009). The cognitive and linguistic foundations of early reading development: A Norwegian latent variable longitudinal study. *Developmental Psychology, 45,* 764–781.

Lewis, C., & Fabos, B. (2005). Instant messaging, literacies, and social identities. *Reading Research Quarterly, 40,* 470–501.

Linderholm, T. (2006). Reading with purpose. *Journal of College Reading and Learning, 36,* 70–80.

Lynch, J. S., van den Broek, P., Kremer, K. E., Kendeou, P., White, M. J., & Lorch, E. P. (2008). The development of narrative comprehension and its relation to other early reading skills. *Reading Psychology, 29,* 327–365.

McDaniel, M. A., Waddill, P. J., Finstad, K., & Bourg, T. (2000). The effects of text-based interest on attention and recall. *Journal of Educational Psychology, 92,* 492–502.

McEneaney, J. E., Li, L., Allen, K., & Guzniczak, L. (2009). Stance, navigation, and reader response in expository hypertext. *Journal of Literacy Research, 41,* 1–45.

Miller, J., & Schwanenflugel, P. J. (2008). A longitudinal study of the development of reading prosody as a dimension of oral reading fluency in early elementary school children. *Reading Research Quarterly, 43,* 336–354.

Moje, E. B. (2008). Foregrounding the disciplines in secondary literacy teaching and learning: A call for change. *Journal of Adolescent & Adult Literacy, 52,* 96–107.

Moje, E. B., Ciechanowski, K. M., Kramer, K., Ellis, L., Carrillo, R., & Collazo, T. (2004). Working toward third space in content area literacy: An examination of everyday funds of knowledge and discourse. *Reading Research Quarterly, 39,* 38–70.

Moje, E. B., Dillon, D. R., & O'Brien, D. (2000). Reexamining roles of learner, text, and context in secondary literacy. *Journal of Educational Research, 93,* 165–180.

Mokhtari, K., Reichard, C. A., & Gardner, A. (2009). The impact of internet and television use on the reading habits and practices of college students. *Journal of Adolescent & Adult Literacy, 52,* 609–619.

Morris, D., Bloodgood, J. W., Lomax, R. G., & Perney, J. (2003). Developmental steps in learning to read: A longitudinal study in kindergarten and first grade. *Reading Research Quarterly, 38,* 302–328.

Muter, V., Hulme, C., Snowling, M. J., & Stevenson, J. (2004). Phonemes, rimes, vocabulary, and grammatical skills as foundations of early reading development: Evidence from a longitudinal study. *Developmental Psychology, 40,* 665–681.

Nation, K. (2008). Learning to read words. *The Quarterly Journal of Experimental Psychology, 61,* 1121–1133.

Nation, K., & Angell, P. (2006). Learning to read and learning to comprehend. *London Review of Education, 4,* 77–87.

Nation, K., & Snowling, M. J. (2004). Beyond phonological skills: Broader language skills contribute to the development of reading. *Journal of Research in Reading, 27*, 342–356.

National Reading Panel (2000). *Report of the National Reading Panel.* Washington, DC: National Institute of Child Health and Human Development.

Noh, S. R., Shake, M. C., Parisi, J. M., Joncich, A. D., Morrow, D. G., & Stine-Morrow, E. A. L. (2007). Age differences in learning from text: The effects of content preexposure on reading. *International Journal of Behavioral Development, 31*, 133–148.

Oakhill, J. V., Cain, K., & Bryant, P. E. (2003). The dissociation of word reading and text comprehension: Evidence from component skills. *Language and Cognitive Processes, 18*, 443–468.

Ong, W. J. (1982). *Orality and literacy: The technologizing of the word.* London: Routledge.

Pappas, C. C. (2006). The information book genre: Its role in integrated science literacy research and practice. *Reading Research Quarterly, 41*, 226–250.

Paris, S. G. (2005). Reinterpreting the development of reading skills. *Reading Research Quarterly, 40*, 184–202.

Parrila, R., Aunola, K., Leskinen, E., Nurmi, J., & Kirby, J. R. (2005). The development of individual differences in reading: Results from longitudinal studies in English and Finnish. *Journal of Educational Psychology, 97*, 299–319.

Perfetti, C., Yang, C., & Schmalhofer, F. (2008). Comprehension skill and word-to-text integration processes. *Applied Cognitive Psychology, 22*, 303–318.

Petrill, S. A., Deater-Deckard, K., Thompson, L. A., Schatschneider, C., Dethorne, L. S., & Vandenberg, D. J. (2007). Longitudinal genetic analysis of early reading: The Western Reserve Reading Project. *Reading & Writing, 20*, 127–146.

Powell, J. W. (1949). *Education for maturity.* New York: Hermitage House, Inc.

Pressley, M., Duke, N., & Boling, E. (2004). The educational science and scientifically based instruction we need: Lessons from reading research and policymaking. *Harvard Educational Review, 74*, 30–61.

RAND Reading Study Group (2002). *Reading for understanding: Toward an R&D program in reading comprehension.* Santa Monica, CA: RAND.

Ricketts, J., Nation, K., & Bishop, D. V. M. (2007). Vocabulary is important for some, but not all reading skills. *Scientific Studies of Reading, 11*, 235–257.

Roman, A. A., Kirby, J. R., Parrila, R. K., Wade-Woolley, L., & Deacon, S. H. (2009). Toward a comprehensive view of the skills involved in word reading in grades 4, 6, and 8. *Journal of Experimental Child Psychology, 102*, 96–113.

Roth, F. P., Speece, D. L., & Cooper, D. H. (2002). A longitudinal analysis of the connection between oral language and early reading. *Journal of Educational Research, 95*, 259–272.

Roth, W., & Bowen, G. M. (2003). When are graphs worth ten thousand words? An expert-expert study. *Cognition and Instruction, 21*, 429–473.

Rouet, J., & Coutelet, B. (2008). The acquisition of document search strategies in grade school students. *Applied Cognitive Psychology, 22*, 389–406.

Russell, D. H. (1961). *Children learn to read* (2nd ed.). New York: Ginn and Company.

Samuelstuen, M. S., & Bråten, I. (2005). Decoding, knowledge, and strategies in comprehension of expository text. *Scandinavian Journal of Psychology, 46*, 107–117.

Scholes, R. (2002). The transition to college reading. *Pedagogy, 2*, 165–172.

Schwanenflugel, P. J., Meisinger, E. B., Wisenbaker, J. M., Kuhn, M. R., Strauss, G. P., & Morris, R. D. (2006). Becoming a fluent and automatic reader in the early elementary school years. *Reading Research Quarterly, 41*, 496–522.

Seigneuric, A., & Ehrlich, M. (2005). Contribution of working memory capacity to children's reading comprehension: A longitudinal investigation. *Reading & Writing, 18*, 617–656.

Siebert, D., & Draper, R. (2008). Why content-area literacy messages do not speak to mathematics teachers: A critical content analysis. *Literacy Research & Instruction, 47*, 229–245.

Smagorinsky, P., Cook, L. S., & Reed, P. M. (2005). The construction of meaning and identity in the composition and reading of an architectural text. *Reading Research Quarterly, 40*, 70–88.

Smith, M., & Wilhelm, J. D. (2004). "I just like being good at it": The importance of competence in the literate lives of young men. *Journal of Adolescent & Adult Literacy, 47*, 454–461.

Stainthorp, R., & Hughes, D. (2004). What happens to precocious readers' performance by the age of eleven? *Journal of Research in Reading, 27*, 357–372.

Stanovich, K. E. (1986). Matthew effects in reading: Some consequences of individual differences in the acquisition of literacy. *Reading Research Quarterly, 21*, 340–406.

Storch, S. A., & Whitehurst, G. J. (2002). Oral language and code-related precursors to reading: Evidence from a longitudinal structural model. *Developmental Psychology, 36*, 934–947.

Strang, R., McCullough, C. M., & Traxler, A. E. (1955). *Problems in the improvement of reading* (2nd ed.). New York: McGraw-Hill.

Strømsø, H. I., Bråten, I., & Samuelstuen, M. S. (2003). Students' strategic use of multiple sources during expository text reading: A longitudinal think-aloud study. *Cognition and Instruction, 21,* 113–147.

Taylor, M. C. (2006). Informal adult learning and everyday literacy practices. *Journal of Adolescent & Adult Literacy, 49,* 500–509.

van den Broek, P., Lynch, J. S., Naslund, J., Ievers-Landis, C. E., & Verduin, K. (2003). The development of comprehension of main ideas in narratives: Evidence from the selection of titles. *Journal of Educational Psychology, 95,* 707–718.

Vellutino, F. R., Tunmer, W. E., Jaccard, J. J., & Chen, R. (2007). Components of reading ability: Multivariate evidence for a convergent skills model of reading development. *Scientific Studies of Reading, 11,* 3–32.

Verhoeven, L., & van Leeuwe, J. (2008). Prediction of the development of reading comprehension: A longitudinal study. *Applied Cognitive Psychology, 22,* 407–423.

Walczyk, J. J., & Griffith-Ross, D. A. (2007). How important is reading skill fluency for comprehension? *The Reading Teacher, 60,* 560–569.

Walczyk, J. J., Wei, M., Griffith-Ross, D. A., Goubert, S. E., Cooper, A. L., & Zha, P. (2007). Development of the interplay between automatic processes and cognitive resources in reading. *Journal of Educational Psychology, 99,* 867–887.

Waples, D., Berelson, B., & Bradshaw, F. R. (1940). *What reading does to people.* Chicago: University of Chicago Press.

Waples, D., & Tyler, R. W. (1931). *What people want to read about: A study of group interests and a survey of problems in adult reading.* Chicago: American Library Association and University of Chicago Press.

Whalley, K., & Hansen, J. (2006). The role of prosodic sensitivity in children's reading development. *Journal of Research in Reading, 29,* 288–303.

Wright, R. (1937/1966). *Black boy.* New York: Perennial Library.

Zipke, M. (2007). The role of metalinguistic awareness in the reading comprehension of sixth and seventh graders. *Reading Psychology, 28,* 375–396.

3

LEARNING TO WRITE

Susan De La Paz and Deborah McCutchen[1]

Writing can be defined in a variety of ways. In this examination of learning to write, we view writing as a complex cognitive process and examine instruction that is designed to enable writers to communicate their ideas effectively and perform well in academic settings, on standardized assessments such as the Nation's Report Card (Salahu-Din, Persky, & Miller, 2008), and in the modern workplace (e.g., Brandt, 2005). We do not discuss literary writing as done by writers such as Toni Morrison, Ian McEwan, and others whose interviews appear in *The Paris Review;* nor do we examine the relation between writing and other modes of communicative expression (i.e., other aspects of the traditional language arts or combinations of text, visuals, and sound as discussed in the emerging field of New Literacies Studies). In this review, we examine what is known about writing development from empirical research with children and youth, and we summarize 30 years of writing intervention research that addresses one or more cognitive process deemed central in theoretical accounts of the writing process.

A BRIEF HISTORY: SHIFTING THEORETICAL LANDSCAPE

In the teaching and learning of writing, focus on the writing process, as opposed to only the written product, is so widely accepted today that it may be difficult to imagine alternative instructional approaches. In classrooms from elementary schools to universities, it is now common to see students taking part in writers' workshops and explicitly discussing their planning, drafting and revising strategies. Such a process-focused approach contrasts sharply with product-focused instructional models, prevalent even in the 1970s. These product-focused models engaged students in detailed analyses of sample texts in books with chapters entitled "Writing a cause-and-effect paper" and "Writing a definition paper" (e.g., Skwire, Chitwood, Ackley, & Fredman, 1975) and then sent students off (typically alone) to mimic the genre.

Janet Emig's (1971) publication of *The Composing Processes of Twelfth Graders* is often cited as the beginning of the empirical study of the writing process, at least in North America. As Nystrand (2006) reported in a recent review, empirical studies of writing had appeared previously, but such work was largely isolated, without identifiable professional organizations and publication outlets. The field of composition and rhetoric emerged as a legitimate academic specialization in the 1980s, as doctoral programs began to train writing researchers (Nystrand, 2006).

The Zeitgeist of the 1970s no doubt helped fuel an interest in writing among cognitive psychologists. Cognitive psychology had replaced behaviorism as the dominant paradigm in the United States, and after abandoning studies of complex human thinking for much of the middle part of the twentieth century (e.g., Huey, [1908] 1968), psychologists renewed their interest in human activities such as reading (e.g., LaBerge & Samuels, 1974) and complex problem solving (e.g., Hayes, 1981; Hayes-Roth & Hayes-Roth, 1979; Larkin, McDermott, Simon, & Simon, 1980; Newell & Simon, 1972). In the 1970s, on the campus of Pittsburgh's Carnegie Mellon University, the fields of process-oriented composition studies and cognitive psychology converged in the collaboration between Linda Flower and John R. Hayes, which provided a theoretical frame (Flower & Hayes, 1977, 1980; Hayes & Flower, 1980) that has influenced writing research for over thirty years.

Like other contemporaneous studies of human problem-solving in complex domains (e.g., Hayes, 1981; Newell & Simon, 1972), Hayes and Flower's approach to writing followed the example of models developed within computer science, emphasizing constraint identification and problem decomposition. They described three primary processes—planning, translating (i.e., the production of text), and reviewing—that operated under the executive control of a monitor, all within the constraints of the external task environment and the writer's long-term memory (Hayes & Flower, 1980). The model has been revisited and revised over the years (see Hayes, 1996; Hayes 2006). Yet it has retained its cognitive character, as well as its influence on the field.

Writing instruction also evolved from multiple traditions, each with a different approach to the writing process. Writers and teachers such as Donald Graves, Nancy Atwell, Lucy Calkins, and James Gray, from the National Writing Project, helped make what has come to be known as the *process approach* to writing instruction accessible to thousands of teachers (Atwell, 1987; Calkins, 1986; Graves, 1983; Gray, 2000). The process approach is typically characterized by an emphasis on personally-meaningful writing contexts and development of students' identities as writers. Other educational researchers, influenced more by theorists such as Vygotsky (1978), Meichenbaum (1977), Brown (Brown, Campione, & Day, 1981), and Hillocks (1982), developed various forms of expert–novice apprenticeship models. Because the writing process is complex, requiring the coordination of multiple and simultaneously occurring cognitive elements, such apprenticeship models are forms of instruction that allow teachers to scaffold discrete thinking processes for students, and give students progressively more responsibility for decision-making over a series of lessons. Other forms of writing instruction (e.g., direct instruction and procedural facilitation; Bereiter & Scardamalia, 1987) are less widely practiced, but have also figured prominently in empirical intervention research in writing.

THE EMPIRICAL RESEARCH: CURRENT TRENDS AND ISSUES

Although writing warrants study from a range of theoretical perspectives (see Bazerman, 2008), the seminal cognitive model outlined by Hayes and Flower (1980) has generated a substantial body of empirical research on writing processes and writing instruction, which is the primary focus of the present chapter. We use the three major processes proposed by Hayes and Flower (i.e., planning, translating and reviewing), as well as an examination of more current influences on writing (e.g., knowledge of genre and text structure), to organize our review. For each of these key processes, we overview the empirical research pertaining to that process and its development, and then specifically consider findings from the instructional research that show promise for improving classroom practice. We end with calls for researchers to parse effects of individual components within complex interventions, and to attend to disciplinary writing purposes.

Planning What to Write

Processes and General Development

Planning received considerable emphasis in early versions of the Hayes and Flower model (1980; Flower & Hayes, 1984), as it did in many problem-solving models of the time (e.g., Hayes-Roth & Hayes-Roth, 1979), and planning was held almost as the *sine qua non* of writing expertise. According to Hayes and Flower (1980), planning entails setting goals, generating content, and organizing that content in terms of the developing text. Plans can be general or local, and they can be made in advance or evolve during writing (Galbraith, 1996). The importance of planning as the hallmark of writing expertise has been downplayed considerably in Hayes' later refinements of the model (Hayes, 1996, 2006), and currently planning is considered one thing, among many, that expert writers do more than novices, and especially more than children.

In addition to differences in the quantity of planning, the qualitative nature of the planning tends to differ strikingly between experts and children, in the absence of instruction. Even without prompting, expert writers can be quite articulate about the conceptual aspects of their planning. They formulate goals for their texts (e.g., to reach a given audience, to present a particular persona) and then develop plans to achieve those goals. Consider, for example, the protocol of a particular professional sports writer as he prepared his responses to readers' letters for his weekly newspaper column:

> I try to read them [the readers' letters] and react to them in a way that is entertaining. And I will not be deadly serious about it unless I feel that it is demanded by the subject matter . . . And I try to avoid being jargonistic or requiring expertise for a reader to understand the answers, because I believe that this is a pretty good way to bring a lot of nontraditional sports readers into the section. So I don't want to alienate them by, by writing in a way, which requires them to know—presupposes that they know a lot of things.
>
> (McCutchen, 1988, p. 309)

Most writers, including young children, engage in some form of planning. Children may use drawings to generate ideas and "plan" their stories (Dyson, 2008; Teale & Sulzby, 1986). Young children's protocols, however, typically reveal little explicit conceptual planning, especially in advance of writing. Analyses of prewriting pauses reveal that children often begin writing within a minute of receiving a writing task, and they are often incredulous when told that some writers spend 15 minutes or more before they write (Bereiter & Scardamalia, 1987). The protocols produced by children in the early elementary grades frequently consist of the words being written, rather than interplay among planning, text production and reviewing processes (Bereiter & Scardamalia, 1987). The protocol of one second-grade writer is illustrative. The child said, "My dad can swim better than us all" and immediately wrote *My dad is the swimmer;* she said, "Then sometimes my brother dunks me" and wrote *Sometimes my brother dunk's [sic] me;* she said, "My mom makes me swim back and forth ten times" and wrote *My mother make's [sic] makes me swim back and forth over and over* (McCutchen, 1988, p. 314).

It is not the case, however, that children are unable to plan. When the contexts are meaningful, even children as young as kindergarten show signs of implicit planning for a specific audience. Children can adapt the texts they produce (sometimes orally) for audiences who vary in age or setting (Lee, Karmiloff-Smith, Cameron, & Dodsworth, 1998) or who are physically present or absent (Littleton, 1998), although they are not often explicit about their reasons for doing so.

Still, *content* planning, in contrast to conceptual planning or audience considerations, dominates children's planning through much of the school years. Bereiter and Scardamalia (1987) analyzed protocols from children at age 10, 12, 16, and 18, and they reported that approximately 90% of the statements produced by the two youngest groups involved either (a) generation of content or (b) explicit dictation or rereading. Content generation remained the predominant form of planning across all the age groups (see also Langer, 1986).

Still, amid the content generation, it is possible to see glimpses of emerging on-line attention to audience and the developing text, as in the following excerpt from the protocol of a 10-year-old writing about roller-skating:

> Hold it, no, "the wheels." I'm going to put *"the* wheels," not just "wheels" 'cause they won't know where the wheels—well, *"the* wheels."
>
> (McCutchen, 1988, p. 315)

Although not a fully articulated conceptual plan for audience, this young writer was clearly thinking about her audience, wondering whether "they," her readers, would know which wheels she was describing. Granted, this young writer's plans for audience were not separate goals that she set in advance, but issues of audience surfaced momentarily.

When explicitly asked to plan in advance, children in the later elementary and middle school grades show signs of beginning to recognize planning as a process separate from other aspects of writing. Cameron and Moshenko (1996) reported that, on average, sixth-grade students that they observed spent slightly over two minutes planning before beginning to write. Similarly, the 12- and 14-year-olds described by Bereiter and Scardamalia (1987) produced notes that they later expanded into text, whereas 10-year-olds typically wrote what amounted to a first draft of the composition itself. Further, children of middle-school age begin to distinguish among various types of planning. When shown a videotape of an adult planning a text, 12- and 14-year-olds correctly identified far more of the planning activities than did 10-year-olds (Bereiter & Scardamalia, 1987).

High-school students seem more likely than younger children to intentionally plan their texts and reference those intentions when asked (Bereiter, Burtis, & Scardamalia, 1988), although Paxton (2002) found that the context of the writing task influenced high school students' planning and attention to audience. Students who read a text written with a strong personal voice wrote essays that contained more overt references to their readers than did essays written by students who read more typical textbook excerpts, and more often mentioned conceptual plans in their protocols. For example, one student in the strong-voice condition stated:

> I'm just sort of thinking of my English class, and how you're supposed to write a paper, and it seems kinds of—um. Now, I'm thinking what quote I'm going to use to get this thing going.

(Paxton, 2002, p. 229)

Although the student was searching for a quote (i.e., content), she clearly had in mind rhetorical goals as well as content goals.

Thus, by approximately age 12, children may begin to distinguish between plans and text; however, their plans are dominated by content generation. Conceptual planning remains relatively rare well into adolescence, in the absence of instruction.

Instruction: A Focus on Planning

Efforts to teach children to plan before composing have varied across instructional traditions. These traditions include process approaches, expert-novice apprenticeship models, direct instruction, and procedural facilitation. Studies involving instruction in planning within a process model are relatively rare, however Pritchard and Honeycutt (2006) compare studies within the process approach to writing instruction, and report that in contrast to earlier years, teachers using the process approach now explicitly address prewriting, with the goal to create structure and organization, not only to generate content. Troia and Graham (2002) compared planning instruction within a process writing approach with direct instruction in three planning strategies with elementary students who experienced learning and writing problems. The process approach was based on the work of Calkins (1986) and Graves (1983) and emphasized purposeful writing, mini-conferences, sharing and publishing written work. The contrasting condition included direct instruction in three planning strategies: goal setting, brainstorming, and organizing. Students learned to write narrative compositions; at post-test and maintenance, children who learned via direct instruction wrote qualitatively better narratives and they also wrote longer stories at maintenance. Troia and Graham (2002) concluded the explicit instruction benefited children with writing difficulties more than the incidental learning environment under comparison.

Bereiter and Scardamalia (1987) proposed that students could be scaffolded to execute more complex composing processes through *procedural facilitation*—the provisions of cues, prompts, routines or other forms of support that allow children to make better use of the knowledge and skills they already possess, or to recruit higher order strategies (Baker, Gersten, & Scanlon, 2002; Englert, Mariage, & Dunsmore, 2006). In a landmark study involving several procedural facilitators as well as an apprenticeship model, Englert and her colleagues (Englert, Raphael, Anderson, Anthony, & Stevens, 1991) demonstrated the benefit of using mnemonics, text frames, or "think sheets" and graphic organizers, combined with teacher and peer interaction, to teach students more sophisticated approaches to planning. With such instructional support, children across a broad range of ability showed increased metacognitive knowledge of the planning process and greater improvement in their expository texts, compared to children in a control group.

However, as Troia and Graham (2002) demonstrated, some students need more explicit forms of planning instruction than are typical in process approaches or procedural facilitation. These children, often identified as having learning disabilities (LD), are typically limited in their awareness of the differences between their writing skills and grade-level expectations in text generation, content elaboration, organization, adherence to theme, and audience awareness (Englert & Raphael, 1988). They are also less able to coordinate the separate processes involved in writing. Both Thomas, Englert, and Gregg (1987) and Graham (1990) reported that students with LD typically approached writing by converting the assigned writing task into a question-answering task, telling whatever came to mind and then ending their responses.

To illustrate, consider an essay composed by Aaron, an African American seventh-grader with learning and writing disabilities. When responding to the prompt, "Do you think children should be required to clean their rooms?" and asked to "Remember to plan your essay before you begin writing," Aaron immediately wrote the following text.

> I think children should be required to clean their room because if they derdy their room then they should clean it up. In my house you clean up if you derdy up
>
> (De La Paz, 2001, p. 234)

In this essay, Aaron stated his position (i.e., a premise), and then continued with a single supporting reason and one personal example (elaborating the reason), ending abruptly without a conclusion.

For students such as Aaron, explicit instruction may be required. In response to the instructional needs of students with LD, researchers from several universities have developed various forms of apprenticeship models to teach planning strategies and self-regulation procedures, so students may develop more sophisticated approaches to writing and improve the quality of their compositions. When first conceived by Deshler and colleagues for application with adolescents with LD, planning strategies were thought to specify not only the sequence of actions to complete a task, but also provide guidelines and rules that help students make decisions during a problem-solving process (Deshler & Schumaker, 1986). Deshler and Schumaker and their colleagues (Schmidt, Deshler, Schumaker, & Alley, 1988; Schumaker & Deschler, 1992) developed a curriculum of strategies (strategic instruction model, SIM) to teach adolescents with LD how to generate different types of sentences, paragraphs, and five paragraph themes. Developers of the SIM model focused more on disseminating their work over the past 25 years than providing research evidence that their strategies are effective. However, several studies employing single subject design reveal effective to highly effective results when the percentage of non-overlapping data (PND) is considered for important dependent variables, such as number of complete sentences written (Mason & Graham, 2008).

As described previously, Englert and her colleagues designed a cognitive strategy instruction program that emphasized the development of students' metacognitive knowledge about writing, including planning (Cognitive Strategy Instruction in Writing, CSIW, Englert et al., 1991). Through modeling, scaffolding, procedural facilitation, and peer conferencing, teachers emphasized the role of dialogue and the use of text structure as prompts to generate text, and the transformation of writing from a solitary to a collaborative activity, and improvements in expository writing were documented even for students with learning disabilities (Englert et al., 1991). In more recent studies, Englert and her colleagues have added scaffolds to the writing environment via Web-based technology (see Englert, Zhao, Dunsmore, Collins, & Wolbers, 2007; Englert, Wu, & Zhao, 2005). Efficacy data regarding CSIW dates back to Englert's original research studies (summarized in Englert, 2009); additional support for the teaching of text structure, one of the underlying tenets of CSIW, comes from Graham and Perin's (2007) meta-analysis of instructional research on writing.

Another apprenticeship model was developed by Wong and her associates (Wong, 1997; Wong, Butler, Ficzere, & Kuperis, 1997; Wong, Hoskyn, Jai, Ellis, & Watson, 2008). Wong's work emphasizes the transfer of interactive dialogue between teacher and students, as well as the use of dialogue between peers, teaching students to use language to regulate their writing behaviors (planning behaviors as well as revising). Through dialogue, teachers involve students in the writing process, encouraging writing partners to request clarifications and elaborations of one another and thereby identify ambiguities in their writing (Wong, Butler, Ficzere, & Kuperis, 1996). In work focused more explicitly on planning, Wong and her colleagues taught poor writers a variety of planning strategies for writing compare-and-contrast and persuasive essays (Wong et al., 1997; Wong et al., 2008). The strongest empirical evidence for the effectiveness of this instruction comes from Wong et al.'s most recent (2008) study in which a multilevel modeling procedure was used with three assessment waves for each dependent variable (clarity, organization, and cogency). Results revealed that planning instruction helped students learn to write stories that were more clearly developed and well organized than those written in the control condition; moreover, children in the intervention condition learned at a faster rate. Despite some variation in rate and level of individual learning, the apprenticeship model plus teacher conferencing promoted positive changes in students' writing.

In addition, Graham and Harris and their colleagues (Graham et al., 1991; Harris & Graham, 1996) developed an approach referred to as the Self-Regulated Strategy Development model (SRSD) for teaching writing. This approach is similar in many ways to the above teaching approaches in that students learn specific strategies for accomplishing writing tasks. In contrast to other approaches, however, SRSD places a strong emphasis on self-regulation. Teachers give explicit definitions and examples of self-regulatory procedures and demonstrate their use. Such procedures typically include goal setting, self-instructions (e.g., defining what to do to execute a strategy), and self-monitoring. Thus, teachers typically model and help students identify verbal statements and physical actions to promote student mastery of the targeted writing process. Use of self-regulation can be differentiated for students in general education classrooms, and as students mature (De La Paz, 2005; De La Paz & Felton, 2010).

Using the SRSD model, students with LD have been taught various planning strategies, such as semantic webbing (MacArthur, Schwartz, Graham, Molloy, & Harris, 1996), brainstorming (Harris & Graham, 1985), using text structure to generate writing content (Danoff, Harris, & Graham, 1993), and setting process and product goals (Graham, MacArthur, Schwartz & Page-Voth, 1992). In addition, in their more recent work, Harris and Graham and their colleagues have extended the use of SRSD planning instruction to younger children in settings in which students worked with partners as they planned and composed (Graham, Harris, & Mason, 2005). Moreover, other researchers have independently used the SRSD model to teach planning strategies to students with and without learning problems in middle school (De La Paz, 1999, 2005), to gifted and normally-achieving elementary students (Albertson & Billingsley, 2001; Glaser & Brunstein, 2007), and to students with attention deficit disorder (Reid & Lienemann, 2006).

Instruction in SRSD strategies has demonstrated results in teaching students to self-regulate their performance, with improvements in the quantity and quality of writing, and those results are maintained over time. In addition, SRSD procedures have been successfully integrated in classrooms using a process approach to writing (e.g., Danoff et al., 1993; MacArthur et al., 1996). A recent meta-analysis of studies involving group designs by Graham and Perin (2007) found that strategy instruction is a highly effective approach for students from the fourth through the tenth grade (weighted effect size = .62). Importantly, the effect size was even greater when strategy instruction included self-regulation (ES = 1.14). Students who struggle with writing and who are emerging writers benefit from learning approaches that employ these apprenticeship models.

Translating Ideas into Text: Transcription and Text Generation

Processes and General Development

To provide a better account of children's writing processes, Berninger and Swanson (1994) refined Hayes and Flower's (1980) original conceptualization of translating by distinguishing two distinct components: transcription and text generation. Text generation shares many components with oral language generation, such as content refinement, lexical retrieval, and syntactic formulation. Transcription, in contrast, entails the cognitive and physical acts of forming written (as opposed to spoken) text.

Transcription

In many cognitive models of writing, spelling is not distinguished from other aspects of translating; but for young children, spelling represents a considerable challenge (Berninger et al., 1998). Many researchers have observed patterns in the growth of children's spelling (e.g., Chomsky, 1970; Henderson & Beers, 1980; Treiman, 1993; Varnhagen, 1995), leading to various stage models of the development of spelling.

Gentry's (1982) well-known model of children's spelling of English is typical, entailing five stages extending through the early elementary years. The initial *precommunicative stage* involves the child's emerging use of symbols to represent language. Children are not yet mapping individual letters to sounds, and they may confuse letters and numbers or the number of letters in a word with quantifiable aspects of the referent such as size or number, writing longer letter strings to represent larger objects (Ferreiro & Teberosky, 1982; Share & Levin, 1999).

Phonological strategies begin to emerge in the *semiphonetic stage*, as the child begins to use letters to represent some, but not necessarily all, sounds within words. During the semiphonetic stage, children may use the names of letters to represent entire words, as in the example from Bissex (1980), RUDF (i.e., "Are you deaf?"). Children's spelling captures more complete representations of the phonological structure of words during the *phonetic stage*, but often with unconventional orthography (e.g., EGL for eagle). As children move into the *transitional stage*, and then to *conventional* spelling, they show a growing awareness of orthography (Varnhagen, 1995) and how it reflects word meaning (morphology) as well as sound (Ehri, 1992; Carlisle, 1988).

Like spelling skill, handwriting skill develops with age and experience. Clearly, the motor and cognitive aspects of writing words on a page require effort on the part of young children, and one issue examined by writing researchers is the extent to which other aspects of writing are compromised by the effort required by transcription. Using a correlational approach, Berninger and Swanson (1994) documented that transcription-related measures were stronger predictors of writing quality for children in their primary grade sample than in their intermediate or junior high sample.

Resource demands imposed by transcription were also examined in a series of experiments by Bourdin and Fayol (1994), who varied response modality (written versus spoken) in a recall task. Bourdin and Fayol found that serial recall was significantly poorer in the written condition for second- and fourth-grade children but not for college students. Bourdin and Fayol argued that handwriting processes of children were still relatively inefficient and drew on working memory resources, whereas the college students' handwriting processes were more automatic. In similar studies involving text recall (Bourdin, Fayol, & Darciaux, 1996) and text generation (Olive & Kellogg, 2002), handwriting was again found to impose higher resource costs for children than for adults. Interestingly, when adults' fluent transcription processes were interrupted by novel response requirements (e.g., writing only in cursive uppercase), they too demonstrated interference during writing (Bourdin & Fayol, 1994; Olive & Kellogg, 2002).

Text Generation

According to Berninger and Swanson (1994; see also Chenoweth & Hayes, 2001; Hayes & Chenoweth, 2007), text generation involves the mental production of a linguistic message, distinct from transcription of that message into written text. Like speech, text generation involves turning ideas into words, sentences, and larger units of discourse within working memory. Pauses in the stream of language generated during writing are influenced by syntactic junctures such as paragraph, sentence and clause boundaries (Chanquoy, Foulin, & Fayol, 1996), text genre (Matsuhashi, 1981), knowledge of the language (Chenoweth & Hayes, 2001) and working memory demands (Hayes & Chenoweth, 2007).

There is evidence that the fluency of children's text generation processes develop with age and increasing writing experience. McCutchen et al. (1994) observed that older children (seventh and eighth grades) generated sentences more fluently than did younger children (third and fourth grades), but at all grades, skilled writers were more fluent than less skilled writers. The ability to generate language efficiently remains a potent predictor of writing quality even for high-school students (Dellerman, Coirier, & Marchand, 1996). Unlike transcription, text generation may never approach automaticity; text generation continues to require working memory resources even among college students (Hayes & Chenoweth, 2007; Kellogg, 2001).

Instruction: A Focus on Spelling, Handwriting, and Transcription

Early work in spelling instruction by Berninger and colleagues (1998) showed promise in teaching second graders to generalize alphabetic principles and write longer compositions. However, Graham (2000) found it was common in the 1980s and 1990s for systematic teaching of spelling to be renounced in favor of incidental teaching, such as when teachers provide rules to small groups of students during teachable moments, even in the absence of empirical support for such an approach. In contrast, Graham, Harris, and Fink-Chorzempa (2002) demonstrated the efficacy of a direct instruction approach in teaching second graders sound–letter combinations, spelling patterns involving long and short vowels, and common words that fit those patterns. Outcomes included improved spelling as well as better decoding and sentence writing skills. Berninger, Winn, Stock, Abbott, Eschen, Lin, et al. (2007) randomly assigned children with dyslexia (Grades 4–6 and 7–9) to an intervention focused on orthography (in which students tried to recall visual images of written words, with particular attention to the order of letters) or morphology (focused on base words, affixes, and morphological spelling rules applied to word parts) in addition to phonology. Although the reported results go beyond those mentioned here, it is relevant to note that the orthographic treatment helped students spell novel real words and the morphological treatment helped children spell pseudowords—confirming that complex interventions are needed for students who struggle to make significant progress in spelling.

Literature on handwriting instruction includes a trivial (but longstanding) controversy over the initial use of manuscript alphabet that is later replaced by cursive script, versus calls for an italic or slanted version of print that is designed to ease students' transition (Schlagal, 2007). However, a national survey of primary teachers suggests that teachers have moved past that controversy, and most (60%) report using effective practices when teaching students to write letters (Graham et al., 2008). Graham, Harris, and Fink (2000) describe one such program, using direct instruction to teach children to write lowercase manuscript letters accurately and fluently. Results indicate improved handwriting and writing skills more generally. Direct instruction in writing letters using visual cues appears an effective way to help children develop their ability to write letters automatically (Berninger et al., 2005), which is related to length and quality of composing throughout elementary schools (Graham, Berninger, Abbott, Abbott, & Whitaker, 1997).

Speech recognition software, according to proponents (see MacArthur, 2006, for a recent review) provides the means to bypass the mechanical demands involved in transcription (handwriting and spelling) and in turn gives writers a more fluent means of composing. Students who are especially weak writers seem to benefit from opportunities to compose orally, especially if this is combined with planning instruction (De La Paz & Graham, 1997). MacArthur and Cavalier (2004) found that high-school students with LD derive specific benefit from composing to an adult scribe or when using speech recognition software (when they could see their text as they composed), in comparison to writing by hand (see also Quinlan, 2004). In comparison, students without special needs were not affected by different writing conditions.

Instruction: A Focus on Text Generation

Some students will benefit from direct instruction that focuses on a different aspect of mechanics (i.e., grammar) during elementary or secondary school. Unfortunately, common exercises (diagramming sentences, daily oral language exercises) do not have evidence demonstrating their effectiveness, most likely because most students do not apply what they learn from these activities to their own writing (Andrews et al., 2006); thus, we next discuss a more promising approach for teaching sentence construction skills.

Sentence combining appears to be an effective approach for teaching sentence construction skills when the goal is to increase a student's syntactic complexity, regardless of the student's age (ranging from 5 to 16), writing genre (persuasive, narrative, or expository) or presence of a learning disability (as demonstrated with fourth grade students; Saddler & Graham, 2005). Briefly, sentence combining refers to explicitly teaching students how to restructure sentences, for example, revising two simple sentences (referred to as "kernel sentences") to form a more interesting complex sentence (often by modifying nouns, or by creating complex sentences with coordinate or subordinate phrases). Students then use standards such as clarity and directness of meaning, to judge the adequacy of their new sentence combinations. In their evaluation of the effectiveness of this approach, Saddler and Graham (2005) randomly assigned 44 average and struggling fourth-grade writers to receive 30 sentence-combining or grammar lessons across 10 weeks. Students in the sentence-combining group learned to use connectors "and," "but," and "because" and how to embed an adjective or adverb from one sentence into another (e.g., "They passed the ball before shooting" and "They passed quickly" combined to "They quickly passed the ball before shooting.") Subsequent objectives included learning to embed two syntactic forms into one new sentence. Students in the comparison grammar condition learned parts of speech. The focus of instruction was to generate better target sentence parts for a sentence completion task. Students also wrote and revised short stories using target parts of speech. Outcomes from this and other sentence combining studies are robust; an overall effect size of .50 was reported by Graham and Perin (2007).

Reviewing and Revision

Processes and General Development

Hayes (1996, 2004) elaborated the original description of the revision process (Hayes & Flower, 1980) to include critical reading, text evaluation, and rewriting. Thus, skilled revision involves critically reading the actual text and comparing it to a representation of the intended or ideal text, noting discrepancies and initiating changes to bring the actual text more in line with the ideal text (Bereiter & Scardamalia, 1987; Flower, Hayes, Carey, Shriver, & Stratman, 1986).

Several processes in this sequence can be problematic for children, the first being the representation of the intended text. Because young children are less likely to engage in much conceptual planning, they have fewer specified intentions, and their memory representations of the intended text are often vague (Bereiter et al., 1988). Second, children may have difficulty with reading critically and then differentiating their interpretations from the actual text. Young children are less able than older children to distinguish inferred from explicit text information (Beal, 1990, 1996) and less likely to add information to support necessary inferences (although difficulties assessing readers' knowledge and inference abilities are not unique to children; see Hayes & Bajzek, 2008). Third, children may have difficulty generating alternative language, even if they identify problematic text. Beal (1990) reported that younger children had more difficulty than older children in diagnosing and correcting text problems, even when the problems were pointed out to them.

Most students (from grade school to college) focus most of their revision efforts on changing surface features of the text (e.g., spelling, punctuation word choice), rather than attending to text meaning (e.g., Chanquoy, 2001; Faigley & Witte, 1981; Fitzgerald, 1987). There is considerable evidence that critical reading is crucial for meaning-focused revision. McCutchen, Francis, and Kerr (1997) listened as middle-school students collaboratively revised, and observed that skilled and less skilled writers employed markedly different reading strategies. Skilled revisers developed a macrostructure of the text they were revising (see Kintsch, 1998) and considered large sections of text as they worked, whereas less skilled revisers edited sentence by sentence. Thus, sophisticated revision may depend, in part, on sophisticated reading strategies (see also Beal, 1996) that go beyond reading for surface understanding. Such reading strategies can, however, present challenges even for college students (Piolat, Roussey, Olive, & Amada, 2004).

Part of the focus on surface revision may however, be the result of the task schema that writers bring to the revision task. With very brief instruction, Wallace and Hayes (1991; Wallace et al., 1996) were able to reorient college writers to revise for meaning. The instruction was so brief (eight minutes) that Wallace and colleagues argued they could not have taught students revision processes per se; rather, they argued they simply altered the students' revision schema by directing students' attention to meaning over mechanical features of texts (see also Graham, MacArthur, & Schwartz, 1995). Such brief instruction, however, was not effective for struggling college writers (Wallace et al., 1996).

Instruction: A Focus on Revising

Direct instruction, procedural facilitation, and apprenticeship models have been used to improve the revision skills of students at different ages and varying levels of writing competence. Direct instruction attempts to describe, and explicitly model, what revision is about and how to revise. Research on direct instruction in revision appears limited, but at least one study revealed beneficial effects of teaching in this way to sixth-graders. In Fitzgerald and Markham's (1987) study, students learned four types of revisions (how to add, delete, rewrite, and move text) in a series of three-day lesson cycles. When compared to a control group, direct instruction in the revision process improved students' knowledge of revision, their efforts to make revisions, and the quality of their stories across drafts. A recent example of direct instruction involving a contrast between collaborative and individual revision on fourth-, sixth-, and eighth-grade students' abilities to anticipate lack of clarity in narratives (Boscolo & Ascorti, 2004) revealed clear advantages for having students work together to identify and resolve ambiguities in text.

Procedural Facilitation

Scardamalia and Bereiter (1983, 1985) developed procedural routines for students in a series of studies to reduce the executive burden involved in revising, by signaling movement from one element of revising to the next and by limiting the number of evaluative and tactical decisions to be made. Their *compare, diagnose, and operate* (CDO) routines helped students identify problem areas, evaluate and explain the problems, select a revising tactic if needed, and carry it out. These routines generally elicited more revisions in students' writing, and enabled students to focus on higher-level features of text than typically reported for similar students. Because students with disabilities are more likely to have problems with executive control, Graham (1997) taught fifth- and sixth-graders with LD how to use a modified version of the routine used by Scardamalia and Bereiter (1983). Revising one sentence at a time, the student selected one of seven possible evaluations (e.g., "This doesn't sound right") for each sentence (compare), explained orally how the evaluation applied (diagnose), and selected one of five directives (e.g., "Say more") to execute (operate). Unfortunately, despite increases in the number of nonsurface (e.g., meaning-changing) revisions, which improved local aspects of text, gains in overall quality were not evident because the global structures of the texts were largely unchanged.

De La Paz, Swanson, and Graham (1998) replicated and extended Graham's (1997) study. They used a CDO procedure to teach a revising strategy to twelve eighth-grade students with LD. A primary difference in the more recent study was the inclusion of additional steps to engage students in applying the directives twice, first at a global level and then at a local level. Results indicated that when revising with the CDO procedure, students were more likely to improve the quality of their essays than under normal conditions. Meaning-preserving revisions tended to improve quality under the CDO procedure; in contrast, meaning-changing revisions appeared to lower quality. Thus, while students made more changes affecting the meaning of their text, some changes resulted in lower quality ratings, because these students with LD were limited in their ability to carry out evaluative and tactical decisions.

Recent evidence from a study by Midgette, Haria, and MacArthur (2008) demonstrates that setting content and audience awareness goals can function as procedural facilitators for students during revising. In their study, fifth- and eighth-grade students wrote persuasive essays and then revised them under one of three goal setting conditions: a condition that prompted students to make changes in general, a content condition that encouraged students to include reasons and a conclusion, and an audience awareness plus content condition that suggested students consider a reader's position, especially one who might have another point of view. Older students were more successful than younger students in responding to the content plus audience awareness goals; however, all students in this condition outperformed other students in addressing and rebutting reasons in their essays. Moreover, the two content goal conditions appeared equivalent in terms of effects on overall quality.

Apprenticeship Models

The strategic instruction model (SIM), described previously in the context of instruction to support students' planning, has also been used to support revising strategies in several studies on editing and proofreading (McNaughton, Hughes, & Ofiesh, 1997; Schumaker et al., 1982). Other researchers using the SRSD model, which combines strategy instruction with self-regulation support, have focused on changes in meaning (e.g., revising; Graham & MacArthur; 1988; Stoddard & MacArthur, 1993), or on both revising and editing, with word processors and peer review to facilitate the revising process (e.g., MacArthur, Graham, Schwartz, & Schafer, 1995). The study by MacArthur and colleagues (1995) was longitudinal and embedded instruction within a writer's workshop model, making it more similar to the type of apprenticeship model developed by both Englert and Wong and their colleagues. In general, positive effects on the type of changes and quality of the revised texts have been found as a result of these interventions, which often include peer revising as a component of instruction.

It is important to note that some investigators have developed holistic writing programs that focus on both planning and revising instruction (Bui, Schumaker, & Deshler, 2006; De La Paz & Graham, 2002; Englert et al., 1991; Wong et al., 1996). In addition, recent studies have attempted to determine the effects of direct instruction in both planning and revising (Fidalgo, Torrance, & Garcia, 2007) and the benefits of planning versus revising strategy instruction, relative to a student's initial writing profile (Kieft, Rijlaarsdam, Galbraith, & van den Bergh, 2007). Thus, our characterization of multi-pronged studies such as these as either planning or revising was done partly for convenience.

KNOWLEDGE OF GENRE

General Development

All writers rely on knowledge of shared rhetorical conventions, such as genre. By the term *genre*, we refer to more than the structural features of text and include the illocutionary purposes that texts serve within the contexts of specific disciplines and discourse communities. However, genre knowledge develops, in part, from experience with text structures. As a consequence of their broad early experience with narratives (Duke, 2000; Teale & Sulzby, 1986), even young children show signs of emergent narrative schemata (Stein & Glenn, 1979). Young children's exposure to informational texts, even in school, is more limited than their exposure to narratives (Duke, 2000), and it is therefore not surprising that children's knowledge of expository genres generally develops later than knowledge of narrative (Englert, Stewart, & Hiebert, 1988; Langer, 1986). Comparisons typically reveal that children's written narratives are superior to their expositions (e.g., Cox, Shanahan, & Tinzmann, 1991; see Langer, 1986, and McCutchen, 1987, for qualifications). Crammond (1998) documented that students' control over the argumentative text structure continues to develop throughout high school and beyond. However, use of non-traditional text structures may sometimes reflect purposeful genre selections that have more to do with expressions of personal identity than with lack of knowledge, especially for adolescents (Ball, 1992).

Instruction: A Focus on Genre and Text Structure

A survey of empirical intervention research revealed more published work on text structure than on genre; one reason for this finding might be the predominant use of qualitative or descriptive approaches by researchers who study the writing process more broadly (including genre), rather than the experimental designs that typify intervention research (Pritchard & Honeycutt, 2006). Ironically, however, a review of writing standards published on websites for state Departments of Education show a plethora of genres expected for students across K-12 (e.g., writing letters and journalistic feature writing). Moreover, popular books on the writing process for teachers often focus on genre and writing purposes more generally (e.g., Calkins, 1986). Thus, expectations around students' genre knowledge are increasing despite a lack of empirical research on how to develop that knowledge.

With respect to research on text structure, writing intervention researchers have focused on teaching students basic elements of narrative, persuasive, or compare–contrast texts (e.g., Fitzgerald & Teasley, 1986; Gordon & Braun, 1986; Kirkpatrick & Klein, 2009; Scardamalia & Bereiter, 1985), but typically with more emphasis on the writing process than was common in product-focused instruction (e.g., Skwire et al., 1975). More generally, it is important to note that researchers who employ expert–novice apprenticeship models typically embed instruction in text structure as a means to communicate information about the genre under consideration to students. Many writing intervention studies involving planning include a focus on text structure (e.g., Bui et al., 2006; Danoff et al., 1993; De La Paz, 1999; Wong et al., 2008). To illustrate, teaching students to understand text structures and to use them as ways to organize their writing has featured prominently in Englert's research, from her early research on generic writing strategies (Englert et al., 1991) to her most recent work on content area writing (Englert, Okolo, & Mariage, 2009).

Briefly, Englert and her colleagues describe ACCelerating Expository Literacy (ACCEL) as a program designed to integrate reading and writing strategies in learning about science and social studies from expository texts. The ACCEL instruction includes Plan-It, Highlight-It, Read-It, Mark-It, Note-It, Map-It, Respond-to-It, and Write-It. Each strategy becomes a tool to be used in conjunction with knowledge about common text structures in expository text: cause/effect, problem/solution, compare/contrast, time (sequential order), classification, and explanation. Together, both strategies and text structure form the basis of the overall curriculum. In sum, the overall effort was to help students develop writing-to-learn strategies that would help them in the expository curriculum (Englert, 2009). In their most recent program evaluation, organizing information was difficult for students with and without learning difficulties to master. However, students with LD made relatively larger gains than students without learning problems, based on an improved ability to selectively identify main ideas and details in printed texts, take well-organized notes, and generate written retellings that contained related details and ideas.

Finally, we were able to locate one intervention study that involved a comparison of text structure and an expert–novice apprenticeship model (Reynolds & Perin, 2009). In this study, middle school students learned to summarize sources using text structure or a modified self-regulatory planning strategy. Students in the text structure condition received explicit instruction in composing from textbook sources, relying on the use of summarization rules and text structure (e.g., main idea, details, topic sentences). Students in the self-regulatory strategy condition followed mnemonics in addition, and engaged in personal goal setting. Results, while indicating nearly comparable performance, should be viewed as tentative, because essential elements in most expert-novice apprenticeship models were omitted (e.g., teacher modeling self-regulatory statements, collaborative practice among students, and criterion-based instruction). Moreover, independent practice was limited to completing assignments that teachers began for students (either in class or as homework) as opposed to independent execution of the planning and composing process, as is typical in true expert–novice apprenticeship models. What is most appealing about this study, however, is the authors' attempt to separate the effects of text structure from its usual role as an embedded element within most expert–novice apprenticeship models. More work on the differential effects of components in multi-pronged intervention research is needed, both to be parsimonious and to understand which elements contribute most to the effects produced by complex interventions.

PRACTICAL IMPLICATIONS AND FUTURE DIRECTIONS

The model of writing proposed by Hayes and Flower in 1980 was intended to be general, not specific to a discipline. However, as writing research has matured, the importance of disciplinary perspectives, including genre, has become apparent. There is increasing interest in knowledge of genre and writers' broader knowledge of the disciplinary community *for* whom (or perhaps more appropriately *with* whom) they write. For example, writers generally learn the discourse forms and honor the rhetorical values of their respective discourse communities, defined in terms of social and/or disciplinary affiliations (MacDonald, 1992; Myers, 1985; essentially *Discourse*, as discussed by Gee, 1996). Skilled writers seem to have ready access to, if not explicit awareness of, such Discourse and rhetorical knowledge (Langer, 1992; Stockton, 1995). Genre and stylistic knowledge seem to influence many aspects of the writing process, including even lexical and syntactic choices (Barton, 1995; Bazerman, 1984; MacDonald, 1992; Vande Kopple, 1998).

Argumentation: A Crucial Genre for Academic Discourse

One genre of central importance in written communication is argumentation. Students' argumentation skills have been studied as milestones of conceptual development (e.g., Kuhn, 2005), as rhetorical conventions (e.g., Toulmin's 1958 model and Fulkerson's 1996 explication of classical claims to teachers), and as grade-related benchmarks. For instance, in the Nation's Report Card, Salahu-Din et al. (2008, p. 37) indicated that only 24% of twelfth-graders were able to compose texts that "persuade[d] the reader" at levels judged as "sufficient" or better. Although the scoring criteria used in the Nation's Report Card 2007 were not published, most standards for evaluating arguments suggest that good arguments are organized, elaborated, and supported by evidence (Perloff, 2003). In addition, Rieke and Sillars (2001) describe argument structure as presenting a clear position, supporting claims with relevant justification and elaborations, considering counterarguments, and finding ways of refuting those counterarguments.

However, Ferretti, Andrews-Weckerly, and Lewis (2007) contend that argumentative strategies are more complex, as they are influenced by the nature of the writing task, the degree to which writers hold shared knowledge about a topic, and the writing purpose. Moreover, Stevens, Wineburg, Herrenkohl, and Bell (2005) argued that the nature of effective argumentation differs across disciplines because the epistemological criteria for causal explanations differ. Thus, argument is a common text structure employed in many disciplines as a means for persuading or convincing others, but the nuances of the argumentation genre can vary across disciplines.

Disciplinary Perspectives

Students then must understand how arguments vary across disciplines. In recent years, advocates for disciplinary literacy articulate differences in the ways teachers should guide adolescents to approach reading and writing tasks in secondary content classes based on inherent differences in the ways that experts think in the sciences (e.g., biology; Carter, Ferzli, & Wiebe, 2007), mathematics (Brown, 2007), and history (Shanahan & Shanahan, 2008; National Research Council, 2000). It follows that in secondary social studies classes, students must learn to use historical evidence to write compelling arguments whether taking the role of novice historian (Wineburg, 2001) or democratic citizen (Barton, 2005). In science classrooms, students identify claims and evidence when constructing and defending scientific explanations (Berland & Reiser, 2009). Recent evidence from McNeil (2009) indicates that dialogue is a critical vehicle for helping students learn to justify claims as they write scientific arguments. Thus, more research is needed to explore how expert teachers help students learn to develop interpretations that are supported with evidence (see Monte-Sano, 2008), as well as research on interventions aimed at improving disciplinary argumentation (e.g., De La Paz & Felton, 2010).

CONCLUSION

We have presented an overview of empirical research on how writing develops and how researchers and teachers have endeavored to scaffold students' learning using theoretical perspectives common to cognitive and process approaches. Although experienced writers describe overlapping and recursive processes during writing (such as revising the beginning of a sentence before returning to generate content that concludes the sentence), the ability to capture the development of such phenomenon in writing research, as well as our strategies for systematically teaching youngsters how to think about writing in such sophisticated ways, remain limited.

Interestingly, much of what we know about effective practices in the teaching of writing comes from the study of children and youth who struggle with this form of communication (Graham & Perin, 2007). Researchers who employ an empirical tradition have found benefit in direct instruction, procedural facilitation, and expert–novice apprenticeship models for teaching planning, translating, and reviewing. Knowledge of genre and text structure have an effect on the writer and writing task and as such may be viewed as influences from the task environment (Hayes, 1996); however, writing that is purposeful also has disciplinary meanings, and we note that recent activity, such as research on argumentation, has considered such contexts. We join others in a call for continued exploration of writing development and interventions that have disciplinary connections, especially for adolescents who are expected to connect writing to content area learning. This is an exciting time to engage in writing research, as the examination of writing within disciplines such as history and science provides opportunities for researchers and teachers to explore new avenues to support student writing and thinking.

NOTE

1 Both authors contributed equally to this chapter, the order of mention is alphabetical.

REFERENCES

Albertson, L. R., & Billingsley, F. F. (2001). Using strategy instruction and self-regulation to improve gifted students' creative writing. *Journal of Secondary Gifted Education, 12*, 90–101.

Andrews, R., Torgerson, C., Beverton, S., Freeman, A., Locke, T., Low, G., Robinson, A., & Zhu, D. (2006). The effect of grammar teaching on writing development. *British Educational Research Journal, 32*, 39–55.

Atwell, N. (1987). *In the middle: Writing, reading, and learning with adolescents*. Portsmouth, NH: Heinemann.

Baker, S., Gersten, R., & Scanlon, D. (2002). Procedural facilitators and cognitive strategies: Tool for unraveling the mysteries of comprehension and the writing process, and for providing meaningful access to the general curriculum. *Learning Disabilities: Research and Practice, 17*, 65–77.

Ball, A. F. (1992). Cultural preference and the expository writing of African-American adolescents. *Written Communication, 9*, 501–532.

Barton, E. L. (1995). Contrastive and non-contrastive connectives: Metadiscourse functions in argumentation. *Written Communication, 12*, 219–239.

Barton, K. C. (2005). Primary sources in history: Breaking through the myths. *Phi Delta Kappan, 86*, 745–753.

Bazerman, C. (1984). Modern evolution of the experimental report in physics: Spectroscopic articles in *Physical Review*, 1893–1980. *Social Studies of Science, 14*, 163–196.

Bazerman, C. (Ed.) (2008). *Handbook of research on writing*. Mahwah, NJ: Erlbaum.

Beal, C. R. (1990). Development of text evaluation and revision skills. *Child Development, 61*, 1011–1023.

Beal, C. R. (1996). The role of comprehension monitoring in children's revision. *Educational Psychology Review, 8*, 219–238.

Bereiter, C., Burtis, P. J., & Scardamalia, M. (1988). Cognitive operations in constructing main points in written composition. *Journal of Memory and Language, 27*, 261–278.

Bereiter, C., & Scardamalia, M. (1987). *The psychology of written composition*. Hillsdale, NJ: Erlbaum.

Berland, L.K., & Reiser, B. J. (2009). Making sense of argumentation and explanation. *Science Education, 93*, 26–55.

Berninger, V. W., Rutberg, J. E., Abbott, R. D., Garcia, N., Anderson-Youngstrom, Brooks, A., & Fulton, C. (2005). Tier 1 and Tier 2 early intervention for handwriting and composing. *Journal of School Psychology, 44*, 3–30.

Berninger, V. W., & Swanson, H. L. (1994). Modifying Hayes and Flower's model of skilled writing to explain beginning and developing writing. In Jerry S. Carlson (Series Ed.), & Earl C. Butterfield (Vol. Ed.), *Advances in cognition and educational practice, Vol. 2: Children's writing: Toward a process theory of the development of skilled writing* (pp. 57–81). Greenwich, CT: JAI Press.

Berninger, V. W., Vaughn, K., Abbott, R. D., Brooks, A., Abbott, S. P., Rogan, L., Reed, E., & Graham, S. (1998). Early intervention for spelling problems: Teaching functional spelling units of varying size with a multiple-connections framework. *Journal of Educational Psychology, 90*, 587–605.

Berninger, V. W., Winn, W. D., Stock, P., Abbott, R. D., Eschen, K., Lin, S.J., et al. (2007). Tier 3 specialized writing instruction for students with dyslexia. *Reading and Writing, 21*, 95–129.

Bissex, G. L. (1980). *GNYS AT WRK: A child learns to read and write.* Cambridge, MA: Harvard University Press.

Boscolo, P., & Ascorti, K. (2004). Effects of collaborative revision on children's ability to write understandable narrative texts. In L. Allal, L. Chanquoy, & P. Largy (Eds.), *Revision: Cognitive and Instructional Processes* (pp. 157–187). Norwell, MA: Kluwer Academic Publishers.

Bourdin, B., & Fayol, M. (1994). Is written language production more difficult than oral language production? A working memory approach. *International Journal of Psychology, 29*, 591–620.

Bourdin, B., Fayol, M., & Darciaux, S. (1996). The comparison of oral and written modes on adults' and children's narrative recall. In G. Rijlaarsdam, H. van den Bergh, & M. Couzijn (Eds.), *Studies in writing, Vol. 1: Theories, models, and methodology in writing research* (pp. 159–169). Amsterdam: Amsterdam University Press.

Brandt, D. (2005). Writing for a living: Literacy and the knowledge economy. *Written Communication, 22*, 166–197.

Brown, R. (2007). Exploring the social positions that students construct within a community of practice. *International Journal of Educational Research, 46*, 116–118.

Brown, A. L., Campione, J. C., & Day, J. D. (1981). Learning to learn: On training students to learn from texts. *Educational Researcher, 10*(2), 14–21.

Bui, Y.N., Schumaker, J.B., & Deshler, D. D. (2006). The effects of a strategic writing program for students with and without learning disabilities in inclusive fifth-grade classes. *Learning Disabilities Research & Practice, 21*, 244–260.

Calkins, L. M. (1986). *The art of teaching writing.* Portsmouth, NH: Heinemann.

Cameron, C. A., & Moshenko, B. (1996). Elicitation of knowledge transformational reports while children write narratives. *Canadian Journal of Behavioural Science, 28*, 271–280.

Carlisle, J. F. (1988). Knowledge of derivational morphology and spelling ability in fourth, sixth, and eighth graders. *Applied Psycholinguistics, 9*, 247–266.

Carter, M., Ferzli, M., & Wiebe, E. N. (2007). Writing to learn by learning to write in the disciplines. *Journal of Business and Technical Communication, 21*, 278–302.

Chanquoy, L. (2001). How to make it easier for children to revise their writing: A study of text revision from 3rd to 5th grades. *British Journal of Educational Psychology, 71*, 15–41.

Chanquoy, L., Foulin, J. N., & Fayol, M. (1996). Writing in adults: A real-time approach. In G. Rijlaarsdam, H. van den Bergh, & M. Couzijn (Eds.). *Theories, models, and methodology in writing research* (pp. 36–43). Amsterdam: Amsterdam University Press.

Chenoweth, N. A., & Hayes, J. R. (2001). Fluency in writing: Generating text in L1 and L2. *Written Communication, 18*, 80–98.

Chomsky, C. (1970). Reading, writing, and phonology. *Harvard Educational Review, 40*, 287–309.

Cox, B. E., Shanahan, T., & Tinzmann, M. B. (1991). Children's knowledge of organization, cohesion, and voice in written exposition. *Research in the Teaching of English, 25*, 179–218.

Crammond, J. G. (1998). The uses and complexity of argument structures in expert and student persuasive writing. *Written Communication, 15*, 230–268.

Danoff, B., Harris, K. R., & Graham, S. (1993). Incorporating strategy instruction within the writing process in the regular classroom: Effects on the writing of students with and without learning disabilities. *Journal of Reading Behavior, 25*(3), 295–322.

De La Paz, S. (1999). Self-regulated strategy instruction in regular education settings: Improving outcomes for students with and without learning disabilities. *Learning Disabilities Research & Practice, 14*, 92–106.

De La Paz, S. (2001) Stop and dare: A persuasive writing strategy. *Intervention in School and Clinic, 36*, 234–243.

De La Paz, S. (2005). Effects of historical reasoning instruction and writing strategy mastery in culturally and academically diverse middle school classrooms. *Journal of Educational Psychology, 97*, 137–156.

De La Paz, S., & Felton, M. K. (2010). Reading and writing from multiple source documents in history: Effects of strategy instruction with low to average high school writers. *Journal of Contemporary Educational Psychology, 35*, 174–192.

De La Paz, S., & Graham, S. (1997). The effects of dictation and advanced planning instruction on the composing of students with writing and learning problems. *Journal of Educational Psychology, 89*, 203–222.

De La Paz, S., & Graham, S. (2002). Explicitly teaching strategies, skills and knowledge: Writing instruction in middle school classrooms. *Journal of Educational Psychology, 94*, 687–698.

De La Paz, S., Swanson, P. N., & Graham, S. (1998). The contribution of executive control to the revising of students with writing and learning difficulties, *Journal of Educational Psychology, 90*, 448–460.

Dellerman, P., Coirier, P., & Marchand, E. (1996). Planning and expertise in argumentative composition. In G. Rijlaarsdam, H. van den Bergh, & M. Couzijn (Eds.), *Theories, models, and methodology in writing research* (pp. 182–195). Amsterdam: Amsterdam University Press.

Deshler, D. D., & Schumaker, J. B. (1986). Learning strategies: An instructional alternative for low-achieving adolescents. *Exceptional Children, 52*, 583–590.

Duke, N. K. (2000). 3.6 minutes per day: The scarcity of informational texts in first grade. *Reading Research Quarterly, 35*(2), 202–224.

Dyson, A. H. (2008). Staying in the (curricular) lines: Practice constraints and possibilities in childhood writing. *Written Communication, 25*, 119–159.

Ehri, L. C. (1992). Review and commentary: Stages of spelling development. In S. Templeton, & D. R. Bear (Eds.), *Development of orthographic knowledge and the foundations of literacy: A memorial festschrift to Edmund H. Henderson* (pp. 307–332). Hillsdale, NJ: Erlbaum.

Emig, J. (1971). *The composing processes of twelfth graders.* Urbana, IL: National Council of Teachers of English.

Englert, C. S. (2009). Connecting the dots in a research program to develop, implement, and evaluate strategic literacy interventions for struggling readers and writers. *Learning Disabilities Research & Practice, 24*, 104–120.

Englert, C. S., Mariage, T. V., & Dunsmore, K. (2006). Tenets of sociocultural theory in writing instruction research. In C. A. MacArthur, S. Graham, & J. Fitzgerald (Eds.), *Handbook of writing research* (pp. 208–221). New York: Guilford Press.

Englert, C. S., Okolo, C. M., & Mariage, T. V. (2009). Informational writing across the curriculum. In G. Troia (Ed.), *Instruction and assessment for struggling writers: Evidenced-based practices* (pp. 132–161). New York: Guilford Press.

Englert, C. S., & Raphael, T. E. (1988). Constructing well-formed prose: Process, structure, and metacognitive knowledge. *Exceptional Children, 54*, 513–520.

Englert, C. S., Raphael, T. E., Anderson, L. M., Anthony, H. M., & Stevens, D. D. (1991). Making strategies and self-talk visible: Writing instruction in regular and special education classrooms. *American Educational Research Journal, 28*, 337–372.

Englert, C. S., Stewart, S. R., & Hiebert, E. H. (1988). Young writers' use of text structure in expository text generation. *Journal of Educational Psychology, 80*, 143–151.

Englert, C. S., Wu, X., & Zhao, Y. (2005). Cognitive tools for writing: Scaffolding the performance of students through technology. *Learning Disabilities Research and Practice, 20*, 184–198.

Englert, C. S., Zhao, Y., Dunsmore, K., Collins, N., & Wolbers, K. (2007). Scaffolding the writing of students with disabilities through procedural facilitation: Using an internet-based technology to improve performance. *Learning Disability Quarterly, 30*, 9–29.

Faigley, L., & Witte, S. (1981). Analyzing revision. *College Composition and Communication, 32*, 400–414.

Ferreiro, E., & Teberosky, A. (1982). *Literacy before schooling.* Exeter, NH: Heinemann International.

Ferretti, R., Andrews-Weckerly, S., & Lewis, W. (2007). Improving the argumentative writing of students with learning disabilities: Descriptive and normative considerations. *Reading & Writing Quarterly, 23*, 267–285.

Fidalgo, R., Torrance, M., & Garcia, J-N. (2007). The long-term effects of strategy-focused writing instruction for grade six students. *Contemporary Educational Psychology, 33*, 672–693.

Fitzgerald, J. (1987). Research on revision in writing. *Review of Educational Research, 57*, 481–506.

Fitzgerald, J., & Markham, L. R. (1987). Teaching children about revision in writing. *Cognition and Instruction, 4*, 3–24.

Fitzgerald, J., & Teasley, A. B. (1986). Effects of instruction in narrative structure on children's writing. *Journal of Educational Psychology, 78*, 424–432.

Flower, L., & Hayes, J. R. (1977). Problem-solving strategies and the writing process. *College English, 39*, 449–461.

Flower, L., & Hayes, J. R. (1980). The dynamics of composing: Making plans and juggling constraints. In L. W. Gregg, & E. R. Steinberg (Eds.), *Cognitive processes in writing* (pp. 31–50). Hillsdale, NJ: Erlbaum.

Flower, L., & Hayes, J. R. (1984). Images, plans, and prose: The representation of meaning in writing. *Written Communication, 1*, 120–160.

Flower, L., Hayes, J. R., Carey, L. L., Shriver, K., & Stratman, J. (1986). Detection, diagnosis, and the strategies of revision. *College Composition and Communication, 37,* 16–55.

Fulkerson, R. (1996). *Teaching the argument in writing.* Urbana, IL: National Council of Teachers of English.

Galbraith, D. (1996). Self-monitoring, discovery through writing and individual differences in drafting strategy. In G. Rijlaarsdam, H. van den Bergh, & M. Couzijn (Eds.). *Theories, models, and methodology in writing research* (pp. 121–141). Amsterdam: Amsterdam University Press.

Gee, J. P. (1996). *Social linguistics and literacies: Ideology in discourse* (2nd ed.). London: Taylor & Francis.

Gentry, J. R. (1982). An analysis of developmental spelling in GNYS at WRK. *Reading Teacher, 36,* 192–200.

Glaser, C., & Brunstein, J. (2007). Improving fourth-grade students' composition skills: Effects of strategy instruction and self-regulation procedures. *Journal of Educational Psychology, 99,* 297–310.

Gordon, C. J., & Braun, C. (1986). Mental processes in reading and writing: A critical look at self-reports as supportive data. *Journal of Educational Research, 79*(5), 292–301.

Graham, S. (1990a). Should the natural learning approach replace spelling instruction? *Journal of Educational Psychology, 92,* 235–247.

Graham, S. (1990b). The role of production factors in learning disabled students' compositions. *Journal of Educational Psychology, 82,* 781–791.

Graham, S. (1997). Executive control in the revising of students with learning and writing difficulties. *Journal of Educational Psychology, 89,* 223–234.

Graham, S., Berninger, V. W., Abbott, R. D., Abbott, S., & Whitaker, D. (1997). The role of mechanics in composing of elementary school students: A new methodological approach. *Journal of Educational Psychology, 89,* 170–182.

Graham, S., Harris, K. R., & Fink, B. (2000). Is handwriting causally related to learning to write? Treatment of handwriting problems in beginning writers. *Journal of Educational Psychology, 92,* 620–633.

Graham, S., Harris, K. R., & Fink Chorzempa, B. (2002). Contribution of spelling instruction to the spelling, writing, and reading of poor spellers. *Journal of Educational Psychology, 94,* 669–686.

Graham, S., Harris, K., MacArthur, C., & Schwartz, S. (1991). Writing and writing instruction with students with learning disabilities: A review of a program of research. *Learning Disability Quarterly, 14,* 89–114.

Graham, S., Harris, K. R., & Mason, L. (2005). Improving the writing performance, knowledge, and self-efficacy of struggling young writers: The effects of self-regulated strategy development. *Contemporary Educational Psychology, 30,* 207–241.

Graham, S., Harris, K. R., Mason, L., Fink-Chorzempa, B., Moran, S., & Saddler, B. (2008). How do primary grade teachers teach handwriting? A national survey. *Reading and Writing, 21,* 49–69.

Graham, S., & MacArthur, C. A. (1988). Improving learning disabled students' skills at revising essays produced on a word processor: Self-instructional strategy training. *Journal of Special Education, 22,* 133–152.

Graham, S., MacArthur, C., & Schwartz, S. (1995). Effects of goal setting and procedural facilitation on the revising behavior and writing performance of students with writing and learning problems. *Journal of Educational Psychology, 87,* 230–240.

Graham, S., MacArthur, C., Schwartz, S., & Page-Voth, T. (1992). Improving the compositions of students with learning disabilities using a strategy involving product and process goal setting. *Exceptional Children, 58,* 322–334.

Graham, S., & Perin, D. (2007). A meta-analysis of writing instruction for adolescent students. *Journal of Educational Psychology, 99,* 445–476.

Graves, D. H. (1983). *Writing: Teachers and children at work.* Exeter, NH: Heinemann.

Gray, J. (2000). *Teachers at the center: A memoir of the early years of the National Writing Project.* Berkeley, CA: National Writing Project.

Harris, K.R., & Graham, S. (1996). *Making the writing process work: Strategies for composition and self-regulation.* Cambridge, MA: Brookline.

Hayes, J. R. (1981). *The complete problem solver.* Philadelphia, PA: Franklin Press Institute.

Hayes, J. R. (1996). A new framework for understanding cognition and affect in writing. In C. M. Levy, & S. Ransdell (Eds.). *The science of writing* (pp. 1–27). Mahwah, NJ: Erlbaum.

Hayes, J. R. (2004). What triggers revision? In L. Allal, L. Chanquoy, & P. Largy (Eds.), *Studies in writing, Vol. 13: Revision: Cognitive and instructional processes* (pp. 9–20). Boston: Kluwer.

Hayes, J. R. (2006). New directions in writing theory. In C. A. MacArthur, S. Graham, & J. Fitzgerald (Eds.), *Handbook of writing research* (pp. 28–40). New York: Guilford Press.

Hayes, J. R., & Bajzek, D. (2008). Understanding and reducing the knowledge effect: Implications for writers. *Written Communication, 25,* 104–118.

Hayes, J. R., & Chenoweth, N. A. (2007). Working memory in an editing task. *Written Communication, 24,* 283–294.

Hayes, J. R., & Flower, L. S. (1980). Identifying the organization of writing processes. In L. W. Gregg, & E. R. Steinberg (Eds.), *Cognitive processes in writing* (pp. 3–30). Hillsdale, NJ: Erlbaum.

Hayes-Roth, B., & Hayes-Roth, F. (1979). A cognitive model of planning. *Cognitive Science, 3*, 275–310.

Henderson, E. H., & Beers, J. W. (Eds.) (1980). *Developmental and cognitive aspects of learning to spell: A reflection of word knowledge.* Newark, DE: International Reading Association.

Hillocks, G. (1982). Inquiry and the composing process: Theory and research. *College English, 44*, 659–673.

Huey, E. B. (1908/1968). *The psychology and pedagogy of reading.* Cambridge, MA: MIT Press.

Kellogg, R. T. (2001). Long-term working memory in text production. *Memory & Cognition, 29*, 43–52.

Kieft, M., Rijlaarsdam, G., Galbraith, D., & van den Bergh, H. (2007). The effects of adapting a writing course to students' writing strategies. *British Journal of Educational Psychology, 77*, 565–578.

Kintsch, W. (1998). *Comprehension: A paradigm for cognition.* New York: Cambridge.

Kirkpatrick, L.C., & Klein, P.D. (2009). Planning text structure as a way to improve students' writing from sources in the compare-contrast genre. *Learning and Instruction, 19*, 309–321.

Kuhn, D. (2005). *Education for thinking.* Cambridge, MA: Harvard University Press.

LaBerge, D., & Samuels, S. J. (1974). Toward a theory of automatic information processing in reading. *Cognitive Psychology, 6*, 293–323.

Langer, J. A. (1986). *Children reading and writing: Structures and strategies.* Norwood, NJ: Ablex.

Langer, J. (1992). Speaking and knowing: Conceptions of understanding in academic disciplines. In A. Herrington, & C. Moran (Eds.), *Writing, teaching, and learning in the disciplines* (pp. 68–85). New York: Modern Language Association.

Larkin, J. H., McDermott, J., Simon, D. P., & Simon, H. A. (1980). Models of competence in solving physics problems. *Cognitive Science, 4*, 317–345.

Lee, K., Karmiloff-Smith, A., Cameron, C. A., & Dodsworth, P. (1998). Notational adaptation in children. *Canadian Journal of Behavioural Science, 30*, 159–171.

Littleton, E. B. (1998). Emerging cognitive skills for writing: Sensitivity to audience presence in five- through nine-year-olds' speech. *Cognition and Instruction, 16*, 399–430.

MacArthur, C. A. (2006). The effects of new technologies on writing and writing processes. In C. A. MacArthur, S. Graham, & J. Fitzgerald (Eds.), *Handbook of writing research* (pp. 248–262). New York: Guilford Press.

MacArthur, C. A., & Cavalier, A.R. (2004). Dictation and speech recognition technology as test accommodations. *Exceptional Children, 71*, 43–58.

MacArthur, C.A., Graham, S., Schwartz, S., & Shafer, W. (1995). Evaluation of a writing instruction model that integrated a process approach, strategy instruction, and word processing. *Learning Disability Quarterly, 18*, 278–291.

MacArthur, C., Schwartz, S., Graham, S., Molloy, D., & Harris, K. (1996). Integration of strategy instruction into a whole language classroom: A case study. *Learning Disabilities Research and Practice, 11*, 168–176.

MacDonald, S. P. (1992) A method for analyzing sentence-level differences in disciplinary knowledge making. *Written Communication, 9*, 533–569.

Mason, L., & Graham, S. (2008). Writing instruction for adolescents with learning disabilities: Programs of intervention research. *Learning Disabilities Research & Practice, 23*, 103–112.

Matsuhashi, A. (1981). Pausing and planning: the tempo of written discourse production. *Research in the Teaching of English, 15*, 113–134.

McCutchen, D. (1987). Children's discourse skill: Form and modality requirements of schooled writing. *Discourse Processes, 10*, 267–286.

McCutchen, D. (1988). "Functional automaticity" in children's writing: A problem of metacognitive control. *Written Communication, 5*, 306–324.

McCutchen, D., Covill, A., Hoyne, S. H., & Mildes, K. (1994). Individual differences in writing: Implications of translating fluency. *Journal of Educational Psychology, 86*, 256–266.

McCutchen, D., Francis, M., & Kerr, S. (1997). Revising for meaning: Effects of knowledge and strategy. *Journal of Educational Psychology, 89*, 667–676.

McNaughton, D., Hughes, C. A., & Ofiesh, N. (1997). Proofreading for students with learning disabilities: Integrating computer and strategy use. *Learning Disabilities Research and Practice, 12*, 16–28.

McNeil, K. (2009). Teachers' use of curriculum to support students in writing scientific arguments to explain phenomena. *Science Education, 93*, 233–268.

Meichenbaum, D. (1977). Cognitive behavior modification: An integrative approach. New York: Plenum Press.

Midgette, E., Haria, P., & MacArthur, C. (2008). The effects of content and audience goals for revision on the persuasive essays of fifth- and eighth-grade students. *Reading and Writing, 21*, 131–151.

Monte-Sano, C. (2008). Qualities of historical writing instruction: A comparative case study of two teachers' practices. *American Educational Research Journal, 45*, 1045–1079.

Myers, G. (1985). Text as knowledge claims: The social construction of two biologists' proposals. *Written Communication, 2,* 219–245.

National Research Council (2000) *How people learn: Brain, mind, experience, and school.* John D. Bransford et al. (Eds; Committee on Developments in the Science of Learning). Washington, DC: National Academy Press. Available online at: http://www.nap.edu.

Newell, A., & Simon, H. (1972). *Human problem solving.* Englewood Cliffs, NJ: Prentice Hall.

Nystrand, M. (2006). The social and historical context for writing research. In C. A. MacArthur, S. Graham, & J. Fitzgerald (Eds.), *Handbook of writing research* (pp. 11–27). New York: Guilford Press.

Olive, T., & Kellogg, R. T. (2002). Concurrent activation of high- and low-level production processing in written composition. *Memory & Cognition, 30,* 594–600.

Paxton, R. J. (2002). The influence of author visibility on high school students solving a history problem. *Cognition and Instruction, 20*(2), 197–248.

Perloff, R. M. (2003). *The dynamics of persuasion* (2nd ed.). Mahwah, NJ: Erlbaum.

Piolat, A., Roussey, J.-Y., Olive, T., & Amada, M. (2004). Processing time and cognitive effort in revision: Effects of error type and of working memory capacity. In L. Allal, L. Chanquoy, & P. Largy (Eds.), *Studies in writing, Vol. 13: Revision: Cognitive and instructional processes* (pp. 21–38). Norwell, MA: Kluwer Academic Press.

Pritchard, R. J., & Honeycutt, J. (2006). Process writing. In C. MacArthur, S. Graham, & J. Fitzgerald (Eds.), *Handbook of writing research* (pp. 275–290). New York: Guilford.

Quinlan, T. (2004). Speech recognition technology and students with writing difficulties: Improving fluency. *Journal of Educational Psychology, 96,* 337–346.

Reid, R., & Lienemann, T. O. (2006). Self-regulated strategy development for written expression with students with attention deficit hyperactivity disorder. *Exceptional Children, 73,* 53–67.

Reynolds, G.A., & Perin, D. (2009). A comparison of text structure and self-regulated writing strategies for composing from sources by middle school students. *Reading Psychology, 30,* 265–300.

Rieke, R. D., & Sillars, M. O. (2001). *Argumentation and critical decision making* (5th ed.). New York: Longman.

Saddler, B., & Graham, S. (2005). The effects of peer-assisted sentence-combining instruction on the writing performance of more and less skilled young writers. *Journal of Educational Psychology, 97,* 43–54.

Salahu-Din, D., Persky, H., & Miller, J. (2008). *The Nation's Report Card: Writing 2007* (NCES 2008–468). Washington, DC: National Center for Education Statistics, Institute of Education Sciences, U.S. Department of Education.

Scardamalia, M., & Bereiter, C. (1983). The development of evaluative, diagnostic, and remedial capabilities in children's composing. In M. Martlew (Ed.), *The psychology of written language: Development and educational perspectives* (pp. 67–95). New York: Wiley.

Scardamalia, M., & Bereiter, C. (1985). Development of dialectical processes in composition. In D. R. Olson, N. Torrance, & A. Hildyard (Eds.), *Literacy, language, and learning: The nature and consequences of reading and writing* (pp. 307–329). Cambridge: Cambridge University Press.

Schlagal, B. (2007). Best practices in spelling and handwriting. In S. Graham, C.A. MacArthur, & J. Fitzgerald (Eds.), *Best practices in writing instruction* (pp. 179–201). New York: Guilford Press.

Schmidt, J. L., Deshler, D. D., Schumaker, J. B., & Alley, G. R. (1988). Effects of generalization instruction on the written language performance of adolescents with learning disabilities in the mainstream classroom. *Reading, Writing, and Learning Disabilities, 4,* 291–309.

Schumaker J. B., & Deshler, D. D. (1992). Validation of learning strategy interventions for students with LD: Results of a programmatic research effort. In B. Y. L. Wong (Ed.), *Contemporary intervention research in learning disabilities: An international perspective* (pp. 22–46). New York: Springer-Verlag.

Schumaker, J. B., Deshler, D. D., Alley, G. R., Warner, M. M., Clark, F. L., & Nolan, S. (1982). Error monitoring: A learning strategy for improving adolescent academic performance. In W. M. Cruikshank, & J. W. Lerner (Eds.), *Coming of age, Vol. 3: The best of ACLD* (pp. 170–183). Syracuse, NY: Syracuse University Press.

Shanahan, T., & Shanahan, C. (2008). Teaching disciplinary literacy to adolescents: Rethinking content-area literacy. *Harvard Educational Review, 78*(1), 40–59.

Share, D., & Levin, I. (1999). Learning to read and write in Hebrew. In M. Harris, & G. Hatano (Eds.), *Learning to read and write: A cross-linguistic perspective* (pp. 89–111). New York: Cambridge University Press.

Skwire, D., Chitwood, F., Ackley, R., & Fredman, R. (1975). *Students book college English.* Beverly Hills, CA: Glencoe Press.

Stein, N. L., & Glenn, C. G. (1979). An analysis of story comprehension in elementary school children. In R. O. Freedle (Ed.), *Advances in discourse processing, Vol. 2: New directions in discourse processing* (pp. 53–120). Norwood, NJ: Ablex.

Stevens, R., Wineburg, S., Herrenkohl, L. R., & Bell, P. (2005). Comparative understanding of school subjects: Past, present, and future. *Review of Educational Research, 75,* 125–157.

Stockton, S. (1995). Writing in history: Narrating the subject of time. *Written Communication, 12*, 47–73.

Stoddard, B., & MacArthur, C.A. (1993). A peer editor strategy: Guiding learning-disabled students in response and revision. *Research in the Teaching of English, 27*, 76–103.

Teale, W., & Sulzby, E. (1986). *Emergent literacy: Writing and reading.* Norwood, NJ: Ablex.

Thomas, C., Englert, C., & Gregg, S. (1987). An analysis of errors and strategies in the expository writing of learning disabled students. *Remedial and Special Education, 8*, 21–30.

Toulmin, S. E. (1958). *The uses of argument.* Cambridge: Cambridge University Press.

Treiman, R. (1993). *Beginning to spell.* New York: Oxford University Press.

Troia, G. A., & Graham, S. (2002). The effectiveness of a highly explicit, teacher-directed strategy instruction routine: Changing the writing performance of students with learning disabilities. *Journal of Learning Disabilities, 35*, 290–305.

Vande Kopple, W. J. (1998). Relative clauses in spectroscopic articles in the *Physical Review,* Beginnings and 1980: Some changes in patterns of modification and a connection to possible shifts in style. *Written Communication, 15*, 170–202.

Varnhagen, C. K. (1995). Children's spelling strategies. In V. W. Berninger (Ed.), *The varieties of orthographic knowledge II: Relations to phonology, reading, and writing* (pp. 251–290). Dordrecht: Kluwer Academic Press.

Vygotsky, L. (1978) *Mind in society: The development of higher psychological processes.* (M. Cole, V. John-Steiner, S. Scribner, & E. Souberman, Trans.). Cambridge, MA: Harvard University Press.

Wallace, D. L., & Hayes, J. R. (1991). Redefining revision for freshmen. *Research in the Teaching of English, 25*, 54–66.

Wallace, D. L., Hayes, J. R., Hatch, J. A., Miller, W., Moser, G., & Silk, C. M. (1996). Better revision in 8 minutes? Prompting first-year college writers to revise more globally. *Journal of Educational Psychology, 85*, 682–688.

Wineburg, S. (2001). *Historical thinking and other unnatural acts: Charting the future of teaching the past.* Philadelphia, PA: Temple University Press.

Wong, B. Y. L. (1997). Research on genre-specific strategies in enhancing writing in adolescents with learning disabilities. *Learning Disability Quarterly, 20*, 140–159.

Wong, B. Y. L., Butler, D. L., Ficzere, S. A., & Kuperis, S. (1996). Teaching low achievers and students with learning disabilities to plan, write, and revise opinion essays. *Journal of Learning Disabilities, 29*, 197–212.

Wong, B. Y. L., Butler, D. L., Ficzere, S. A., & Kuperis, S. (1997). Teaching adolescents with learning disabilities and low achievers to plan, write, and revise compare and contrast essays. *Learning Disabilities Research & Practice, 12*, 2–15.

Wong, B. Y. L., Hoskyn, M., Jai, D., Ellis, P., & Watson, K. (2008). The comparative efficacy of two approaches to teaching sixth graders opinion essay writing. *Contemporary Educational Psychology, 33*, 757–784.

4

LEARNING MATHEMATICS

Ann R. Edwards, Indigo Esmonde, and Joseph F. Wagner

INTRODUCTION

In 1973, Stephen Erlwanger published a groundbreaking article in the *Journal of Children's Mathematical Behavior* reporting on a case study of one sixth grade student's mathematical thinking. "Benny's conceptions of rules and answers in IPI [Individually Prescribed Instruction] Mathematics," or "Benny" as it came to be called, employed protocol analysis of clinical interviews to reveal the "rules" Benny had developed to operate on fractions and decimals. Benny was a successful student in IPI, a curriculum in which students individually progress through sequentially ordered behavioral objectives via continuous cycles of assessment and feedback. Erlwanger showed that while Benny demonstrated mastery on the IPI assessments using his rules, he had little conceptual understanding of fractions and decimals. Perhaps more importantly, he also argued that Benny's "rules" could be seen as a sensible effort on the part of the learner to construct meaning out of instructional experiences that made little mathematical sense.

This work was important in several ways. It catalyzed the articulation and development of the constructivist perspective in mathematics education research. "Benny" was both a rebuke of prevailing behaviorist conceptualizations of and methodological approaches to mathematics learning and an existence proof that alternative paradigms for mathematics education research, grounded in theoretical and methodological advances in cognitive science and developmental psychology, could reveal how students actually think mathematically. But in a broader sense, it raised questions that are still fundamental to inquiry into mathematics learning: What constitutes mathematical knowledge or knowing? What is mathematical learning? How is mathematics learned? And, therefore, how should mathematical knowing and learning be studied?

Since "Benny," the field has revisited and re-contested these questions many times. For example, radical constructivists called into question the most basic ontological and epistemological assumptions of mathematical thinking and learning—that mathematics exists outside of the learner's active construction of it and that learning mathematics is the acquisition of an objective representation of that external reality. Cognitive science has focused the field's attention on the nature, construction, and use of mentally repre-sented mathematical knowledge, and is increasingly studying these processes of learning *in situ*, in addition to its historical focus in the laboratory. Work in anthropology, soci-ology, and cultural psychology broadened the field's notions of who does mathematics, where and how, thereby opening up avenues of inquiry into mathematical activity as situated and into mathematical learning as participation in cultural practices. Increasing recognition of the diversity of students learning mathematics in schools today has begun to draw our attention to issues of identity in mathematics learning, particularly as relates to gender, race, culture, and language. The resultant theoretical, methodological and moral considerations are profoundly reshaping our understandings of what constitutes mathematics, mathematics thinking and mathematics learning.

Mathematics education research today is diverse in its foci of inquiry, methodological approaches, and epistemological commitments. This diversity reflects the complexity of the phenomena constituting mathematical doing and knowing and their relation to stu-dents' mathematical learning. It also reflects the field's willingness to draw upon theoretical and methodological resources from other fields and disciplines within and outside of edu-cational research. Each of the aforementioned examples, grounded in different theoretical perspectives, can be seen as a thread in the fabric of research on mathematics learning. Tensions and even contradictions exist within this fabric, yet each line of research seeks to shed light on the same questions that Erlwanger's (1973) work raised, questions that reflect the most fundamental theoretical issues in research on mathematics learning.

In this chapter, we highlight several current threads in research on mathematics learn-ing that take up timely yet enduringly important questions for mathematics education. In our choices, we forefront the theoretical paradigms that inform the threads, repre-senting some of the diversity of epistemological commitments underpinning current research on mathematical knowing and learning. In the next section, we briefly discuss the intellectual grounds of research in mathematics learning during the last several decades, describing the predominant theoretical perspectives that have shaped and con-tinue to shape research on mathematics learning. That is followed by syntheses of four current threads of research on mathematics learning: (1) research on the structures and processes of mathematical cognition; (2) research on the role of discourse and language on mathematics learning; (3) research addressing identity and mathematics learning; and (4) research in neuroscience relevant to mathematics learning. We conclude with thoughts on future directions for research.

THEORETICAL FRAMEWORK

The nature of an inquiry into mathematical thinking and learning (i.e., the phenom-ena examined, questions posed, modes of inquiry employed, etc.) is grounded in the researchers' understandings of the nature of mathematics, what constitutes mathemati-cal knowledge or knowing, and how that knowledge is learned. Reflective of the broader intellectual history of inquiry into thinking and learning, the field of mathematics edu-cation research over its history has been predominantly influenced by three theoretical perspectives that take contrasting, perhaps divergent, views on these issues: the behav-iorist perspective, the cognitive/constructivist perspective and the situative/sociocul-tural perspective. Of course, any categorization of a landscape as complex as theories of cognition and learning is necessarily simplistic and limited. We offer this formulation to reflect current discourse about the dominant theoretical traditions in mathematics education (Gutierrez & Boero, 2006; Lerman, 2000) as well as for reasons of brevity.

In mathematics education, behaviorism dominated research on learning through the first half the 20th century. Research in the behaviorist tradition, particularly that of Skinner (1953), conceptualized mathematical behavior in terms of observable skills characterized as responses to stimuli and mathematical learning as the formation and strengthening of those stimulus–response associations. Although strictly behaviorist accounts of mathematical learning all but disappeared in the later 20th century (though neo-behaviorist psychological theory continues to contribute to understandings of conditions for learning and, increasingly, biological bases of learning (Mowrer & Klein, 2001)), a continued legacy of this line of work has been the analysis of mathematical tasks into component subskills. The hierarchical organization of the components constitutes the sequence of skills to be learned in order to achieve mastery of the task (Gagné, 1965). Researchers adopting methods from cognitive science later reconceptualized this analysis of mathematical tasks through cognitive task analysis, and component cognitive processes underlying the completion of mathematical tasks became the focus of investigation.

Beginning in the 1960s, due to the influences of developmental psychology and insights from the emerging fields of information processing and cognitive psychology that highlighted the limitations of the behaviorist theoretical and methodological paradigm, research on mathematics learning shifted toward inquiry into the mental bases of mathematical thinking and learning. Cognitive research on mathematics learning has proved highly productive and valuable to the field's understandings of the organization of the knower's knowledge of specific mathematical content, problem-solving and metacognitive processes, the role of internal and external representations in mathematical sense-making and learning, and the reorganization of knowledge structures in conceptual growth, among other crucially important aspects of mathematical cognition. A key cognitive paradigm in mathematics education research is constructivism, particularly as it emerged from the learning and developmental theories of Piaget. The impact of constructivist perspectives has been to place active exploration, inquiry, and modeling activities at the heart of mathematical learning, in contrast to the previous and sometimes exclusive emphasis on the acquisition of computational and algebraic rules and skills.

As cognitive/constructivist research on mathematical thinking and learning has established itself as the dominant paradigm in mathematics education in recent decades, it has been critiqued from alternative epistemological perspectives, particularly sociocultural perspectives including situated learning and situated cognition. In this view, mathematical knowledge is situated—located in particular forms of experience—and involves "competence in life settings" rather than or in addition to mathematically specific psychological or mental structures (Lerman, 2000, p. 26). Research on mathematics learning in the situated/sociocultural tradition spans research on out-of-school mathematical practices (e.g., Saxe, 1991) to interactional accounts of the accomplishment of mathematical activity as coordinated productions of talk, gesture and inscription (e.g., Hall & Stevens, 1995) to analyses of the practices of mathematics classrooms (e.g., Cobb, Stephan, McLain, & Gravemeijer, 2001). Generally, the impact of this body of work has been to remove the individual as the sole focus of theory and research on mathematics learning and locate individuals in relation to others, objects, activities, settings and histories in conceptualizations of learning.

Much of the current research on mathematics learning reflects influences from these major perspectives, particularly the cognitive/constructivist and the situated/sociocultural. The first three research threads presented in this chapter are situated within these broader traditions, grounded in their fundamental epistemological commitments, but taking on focused issues of import to theory and practice in mathematics education today. The first section focuses on current directions in research on mathematics thinking and learning in the cognitivist tradition. The second addresses several important conceptualizations of the role of discourse and language in mathematics learning. The third section takes up the construct of identity and synthesizes literature concerned with the nature and role of identity in mathematics learning. The final research thread presents a relatively new yet important field of inquiry, research in neuroscience relevant for mathematics learning.

These threads do not, of course, provide a comprehensive survey of current research on mathematics learning—that is beyond the scope of this chapter (see handbooks on mathematics education research for more comprehensive treatments: e.g., Bishop, Clements, Keitel, Kilpatrick, & Leung, 2003; Lester, 2007). Even so, there are many viable ways to structure such a chapter: historically, by mathematical domains (e.g., arithmetic, geometry), by processes (e.g., abstraction, representation, problem-solving), or by age or grade level. Our choice to foreground theoretical paradigms is grounded in our conviction that advances in the field's understandings of how people learn mathematics depend on explicit and robust theoretical formulations of the phenomena of mathematical knowing and learning. Additionally, we believe that the diversity of the theoretical perspectives represented in research on mathematics learning is a strength of the field, despite or perhaps due to the tensions that this diversity naturally raises. We hope that our choices capture that diversity.

CURRENT TRENDS AND ISSUES IN RESEARCH IN MATHEMATICS LEARNING

Research on the Organization and Processes of Mathematical Cognition

Historically, research in the nature of mathematical knowledge and learning has been dominated by a variety of cognitive epistemologies, reflecting mathematics education's strong historical roots in educational and cognitive psychology, and later developments of cognitive modeling with the rise of computational metaphors of cognitive processes. Throughout its history, mathematics education research has attended both to the acquisition of mathematical rules and procedures as well as the development of mathematical meaning and sense-making. A thorough historical consideration would include the early and mid-20th-century work of Judd (1908), Wertheimer (1945), and Brownell (1948), for example, each of whom highlighted the importance of meaningful mathematics learning, in contrast to the then dominant connectionist and behaviorist approaches of Thorndike (1913) and Skinner (1953) that focused on the acquisition of computational skills. More recently, mathematics education researchers have been greatly influenced by Piagetian and subsequent constructivist theories in educational and developmental psychology, which have shown promise in informing the development of both skills and sense-making in mathematics education.

Cognitive researchers have traditionally focused on identifying and typifying knowledge and mental functions such as memory, declarative and procedural knowledge, frames, schemata, routines, heuristics, and the nature of mental (internal) representations. The unit of analysis is the thinking individual, or more specifically, the individual's mental constructs and processes. Such approaches have been used to study and model arithmetic procedures, mental arithmetic, algebraic skills, and the solutions of word problems throughout the mathematics curriculum.

One reason for the close relation between cognitive research and mathematics has been the perception that the logical and structural constraints of mathematical activity make it perhaps more readily modeled than other cognitive processes. As research has advanced, however, particularly to better accommodate higher levels of mathematical thinking, complex problem solving, conceptual understanding, and sense-making, the cognitive study of mathematical learning has expanded. Schoenfeld (2006) identified a consensus among cognitive researchers that a thorough analysis of an individual's mathematical performance requires attention to that individual's knowledge base, available problem-solving strategies or heuristics, metacognitive processes (particularly self-regulation and monitoring), beliefs and affective variables, and acquired practices typical of the classroom or mathematical community.

Research attention to conceptual understanding and sense-making has examined students' abilities to invent or discover their own strategies and solutions to mathematical problems when given sufficient opportunities and support. Such research has suggested new learning trajectories and instructional approaches that support mathematical sense-making. The Cognitively Guided Instruction program (CGI: Fennema et al., 1996; Fennema, Franke, Carpenter, & Carey, 1993) remains a preeminent example of how mathematics teaching and learning in the early grades benefit when teachers are made aware of and attend to students' ways of thinking about mathematics problems. Fennema et al. (1996) demonstrated that teachers' learning about students' mathematical thinking is related to changes in the teachers' instructional practices and subsequent student achievement. Students showed higher achievement in concepts and problem solving without diminishing computational performance. Cognitive research on student thinking has further inspired, at least in part, the development and dissemination of mathematics reform curricula for middle- and high-school mathematics (Martin et al., 2001), calculus (Darken, Wynegar, & Kuhn, 2000), and differential equations (Rasmussen, 2002).

Among cognitive researchers behind mathematics education reform efforts, constructivism has played a dominant role since the late 1980s. Rooted in the research and developmental theories of Piaget (1954, 1970), constructivism posits that individuals generate knowledge and understanding through their experiences and reflection. Thus, knowledge arises from the active mental processes of the learner as new experiences are interpreted through existing knowledge structures. Prior knowledge may be called upon to assimilate experience as familiar, or restructured to accommodate new experience.

Sociocultural critiques challenged cognitive researchers to attend more directly to the role of the sociocultural context of the learner in mathematical thinking. Lave (1988), in particular, argued the inadequacy of then dominant cognitive approaches to address mathematical learning and transfer. Lave's critique emerged, in part, from research using interviews and pencil-and-paper arithmetic tasks, alongside *in situ* observations of adults performing price-comparisons while grocery shopping. Despite successfully navigating price comparisons, the same shoppers were much less successful at what Lave argued to be equivalent arithmetic tasks presented on paper in standard arithmetic notation. Lave asserted that such evidence revealed the dynamic relation between learner, activity and context, and that mathematics learned in the classroom was not transferred to other contexts as cognitive researchers expected. If so, the interpretation of cognitive studies of individuals working within controlled laboratory conditions must be carefully nuanced.

Advances in cognitive research methods have subsequently prompted some cognitive researchers to expand the types of mathematical knowledge and activity studied. Laboratory studies of cognition have no access to the role of social interaction and collaboration in classroom mathematical learning; or mathematical conjecturing, argumentation, and debate. As a result, some researchers have made strides toward moving cognitive studies into classrooms. Jaworski (1994) examined the tensions inherent in studying students as individual, cognizing subjects in the social context of the classroom. Cobb and Yackel (1996) have pursued an approach to classroom research that coordinates individual psychological analysis with interactionist analyses of classroom activity and discourse.

Cognitive research has supported the study of mathematics learning through a variety of approaches, from information processing models (e.g., Singley & Anderson, 1989) to Piagetian constructivism (Simon, Tzur, Heinz, & Kinzel, 2004). It has been highly successful in modeling differences between novices and experts, mapping the complexities of learning transfer, and revealing learning and developmental trajectories of children in mathematics and in other domains (see, for example, Bransford, Brown, & Cocking, 1999). A number of mathematics curricula, informed largely (though not exclusively) by cognitive research, have recently been implemented on a large scale and have shown signs of success in improving students' conceptual learning without diminishing computational skills (Schoenfeld, 2002).

Despite much success, cognitive research in mathematics learning has considerable room for growth. We identify two specific tasks for cognitive researchers in mathematical thinking and learning that have begun to receive more attention yet remain essential challenges for future research. First, cognitive researchers must take on the challenge of studying mathematical thinking and learning in natural settings, especially in the classroom. Above all, this challenge entails the development of new research methods that enable the study of individual cognition within a social collective (e.g., Cobb & Yackel, 1996). Additionally, careful study of students in classroom settings, particularly as students are actively engaged in mathematical activities involving collaboration in problem solving, debates of mathematical ideas, or verbal communication of mathematical thinking, can open windows into aspects of mathematical knowledge and learning not observable through laboratory settings or clinical interviews.

A recent example of primarily cognitive research that has moved into actual classrooms has been that of Rasmussen and colleagues. Rasmussen (2001) began with clinical interviews of undergraduate students studying differential equations, and he outlined a framework for understanding significant conceptual difficulties that students face when learning the subject. Using his own and others' research on student learning, Rasmussen (2002) developed the *Inquiry Oriented Differential Equations Curriculum* (IO-DE). The one-semester set of curricular materials guides students through problem-solving activities, enacted through small group work and whole class discussion, to discover the methods and concepts of a first course in differential equations. Experimental studies suggest that the curriculum supports students' increased development and retention of conceptual understanding of differential equations, while matching the procedural competence of traditionally taught comparison groups (Kwon, Allen, & Rasmussen, 2005; Rasmussen, Kwon, Allen, Marrongelle, & Burch, 2006). Rasmussen and others supplemented clinical interview research with real-time classroom research to reveal students' own patterns and progression of thinking that led to their discoveries of various mathematical concepts (Rasmussen & Blumenfeld, 2007; Rasmussen, Zandieh, King, & Teppo, 2005). Taken as a whole, the still-growing body of research around Rasmussen's IO-DE work has entailed both cognitive and sociocultural research methods, using clinical interviews and real-world classroom settings, to reveal aspects of individual and cooperative learning that have direct implications for classroom instruction.

A second essential task of contemporary cognitive researchers must be to continue probing more deeply the nature of mathematical knowledge itself. This includes identifying new forms of knowledge as well as examining existing theoretical constructs such as Piaget's (1954) notions of assimilation and accommodation at a fine-grained level to account for how such processes take place in real time and over time. A major issue for cognitive researchers remains the problem of transfer and the role of context in mathematical thinking and learning. One emerging epistemological approach in mathematics education research, arising from cognitive research in physics education, is diSessa's (1993) *knowledge in pieces* perspective. Developed to examine how intuitive or naïve knowledge progresses toward expertise, a knowledge-in-pieces epistemology posits that some forms of conceptual knowledge are best modeled as complex systems of knowledge consisting of many more fundamental knowledge elements, often sensitive to context, in that different knowledge elements may be called upon in different contextual circumstances (diSessa, 1993; Wagner, 2006). This approach has shown promise for hypothesizing specific types of knowledge constructs (e.g., phenomenological primitives (diSessa, 1993), coordination classes (diSessa & Sherin, 1998), concept projections (diSessa & Wagner, 2005), meta-representational knowledge (diSessa, Hammer, Sherin, & Kolpakowski, 1991)), and it uses the context-sensitivity of such knowledge elements (rather than their abstractness) to model knowledge transfer.

A key tenet of a knowledge-in-pieces perspective is that new knowledge often entails the systematization and (re)organization of a variety of already existing knowledge elements. In this way, new concepts, for example, do not necessarily replace old or insufficient ideas, but they emerge as existing knowledge elements are refined, put to new uses (perhaps in new contexts), and coordinated with previously unassociated knowledge. One potentially promising line of research that has emerged from a knowledge-in-pieces approach concerns the role of meta-representational knowledge (diSessa et al., 1991). Meta-representational knowledge refers to knowledge by which individuals create or evaluate the suitability of representations within problem-solving contexts. Izsák (2003) first introduced the notion of meta-representational knowledge to mathematics education research in a clinical interview study of pairs of eighth grade students learning to model the behavior of a physical device with algebra. Knowledge-in-pieces analysis requires very fine-grained analysis of students' extended problem-solving sessions, with careful attention to verbal responses and engagement with external tools and representations. Using such methods, Izsák revealed how students coordinated meta-representational knowledge with elements of algebraic knowledge as their abilities to algebraically model the given situation grew and changed. In follow-up work, Izsák (2005) extended the study of meta-representational knowledge to younger (fifth grade) students learning array and area models of multiplication. Most recently, Izsák, Caglayan, and Olive (in press) focused the same analytic lens on both the students and the teacher of an eighth grade algebra classroom, demonstrating that attention to meta-representational knowledge could reveal different perspectives on the part of the teacher and the students that impeded learning and instruction. In this way, Izsák's work suggests that a knowledge-in-pieces epistemology can reveal aspects of knowledge not evident through other analytical lenses, yet demonstrate very practical consequences in a typical mathematics classroom. The extent to which such work can inform instructional practice remains a significant question for further research.

Research on the Role of Discourse and Language in Mathematics Learning

Reflecting the "turn to discourse" in the social sciences in recent decades, research in mathematics education is undergoing its own "linguistic turn" (Lerman, 2004), with increasing attention to the role that language plays in mathematical activity and learning. Much has been made in discussions about reform in mathematics education regarding mathematical discourse not only as an object of study (i.e., what is the nature of the discourse of the mathematical community? What are the structural and semantic characteristics of language use in mathematical activity?), but also as a desired outcome of students' mathematical learning and a key component of a classroom environment that promotes mathematical learning. The ubiquity of the idea of mathematical discourse (sometimes at the expense of clarity) points to the growing recognition of the stance that language and learning are inextricably intertwined, and that understanding mathematical learning, assessing students' mathematical learning, and designing mathematical learning environments require examining the role of language in mathematical activity. Research in mathematics education that focuses on language or discourse varies widely in terms of foci and methods of analysis (as does the work in linguistics, discourse and conversation analysis, ethnomethodology, and other related fields from which mathematics education researchers draw), and this diversity is both a source of fresh insights and also a potential barrier to coherence and depth. Since representing the diversity of this work in its entirety is beyond the scope of this section, we have chosen to highlight four areas—two relatively mature and two emerging lines of work—that represent distinctly different points in the landscape. The section ends with comments on strengths and weaknesses of this thread of research as a whole and suggestions for future research.

The first area of research relevant to the role of discourse and mathematics learning focuses on the characteristics of mathematics as a discursive and textual disciplinary practice. A key starting point for this work is the notion that mathematics is a language—a semiotic system with particular syntactic and semantic entailments that differ from those of "everyday" language. Halliday (1978) described this "mathematics register" as "a set of meanings that is appropriate to a particular function of language, together with the words and structures which express these meanings" (p. 195). Following Halliday, researchers in systemic functional linguistics have characterized the linguistic features of the mathematics register. The mathematics register is highly technical, including particular uses of everyday words (e.g., *set, order*), specialist vocabulary that is specifically mathematical (e.g., *sine, equation*), composite words and expressions with mathematical meanings distinct from everyday usage (e.g., *square root, differential operator*), precise and specific meanings of linguistic features (e.g., conjunctions such as *if, therefore*; directives such as *assume*; modifiers such as *clearly, obvious*), highly dense nominal structures (e.g., *the sum of the squares of two sides of a right triangle*), and grammatical constructions that imply logical relationships (e.g., *if . . . then . . .*) (Lemke, 1990; O'Halloran, 2000; Pimm, 1987).

From this perspective, mathematical discourse is seen as an idealized semiotic system and mathematical learning involves the appropriation of the vocabulary as well as the "styles of meanings and models of argument" (Halliday, 1978, p. 195) that characterize this system. Developing mathematical fluency therefore requires recognizing and shifting between everyday and mathematical registers. Word meaning and grammatical structures are key concerns here, in particular when the same words or structures exist in both mathematical and everyday registers and students must learn to negotiate their multiple, situationally dependent meanings and uses. Research on students' appropriation or learning of the mathematics register has included attention to what Pimm has called "semantic contamination" (1987, p. 88) by which word meanings in the everyday register are used in attempts to make sense of new mathematical language. For example, Cornu's (1981) interview study comparing high school and university mathematics students' notions of limit revealed that students' difficulties with limit in the mathematically technical sense were, in part, due to the "spontaneous models" they used to describe limiting behavior, particularly their use of the expression *tends to*. Similarly, MacGregor's (2002) linguistic analysis of students solving word problems showed not only that students' construction of mathematical ideas using informal yet common language structures can be technically incorrect, but furthermore that "students who described a relation between numbers in an informal, unclear or immature way were unable to relate it to a mathematical operation" (p. 1).

While this area of research has provided insights into students' difficulties appropriating the mathematics register, some have noted that its focus on characterizing an idealized form of "mathematics as language" is limiting and have suggested an alternate conceptualization of mathematical discourse that forefronts the notion of mathematics as social practice (e.g., Moschkovich, 2002). Research in this area, informed by sociocultural theories of cognition and learning, assumes that mathematics is constituted by complex social practices (which are crucially discursive but not limited to specific categories of vocabulary and grammatical structure), and defines mathematical learning as the socialization into the practices of the mathematics community—including, conjecturing, explaining, justifying, representing, and evaluating mathematical ideas, claims and solutions (e.g., Forman, Larreamendy-Joerns, Stein, & Brown, 1998; Moschkovich, 2003; O'Connor, 1998).

Drawing upon theoretical work in sociolinguistics on language socialization (e.g., Schieffelin & Ochs, 1986) and sociocultural participationist theories of cognition (Sfard, 1998), one productive line of inquiry within this area examines how teacher-mediated classroom participation structures create opportunities for student participation, and therefore learning, in school-based mathematical practices. For example, several researchers have examined how the discursive move of revoicing—the repetition, restatement or reformulation of a student's utterance by another classroom participant (usually the teacher)—facilitates student engagement and appropriation of mathematical discourse practices (Enyedy et al., 2008; Forman et al., 1998; O'Connor & Michaels,

1993). In one influential study, Forman et al. (1998) drew upon analytical tools in socio-linguistics and rhetoric to investigate the discursive structure and propositional content of mathematical argumentation in one lesson in an urban middle school classroom. The study showed how teachers' revoicing moves orchestrate classroom discussion in ways that recruit and ratify students' contributions, position students as authors and legiti-mizers of knowledge, align students and their contributions with one another and with the mathematical content, expand and refine students' contributions into more conven-tional forms of mathematical discourse, and socialize them into mathematical discourse practices such as conjecturing, justifying, argumentation, and evaluating ideas. Despite the focus on teaching, this study and other studies in this area have contributed to the field's understandings of student learning by demonstrating how particular structures of participation and discursive moves in classroom interactions support students' appro-priation of mathematical processes.

A third area of research relevant to the role of discourse in mathematics learning focuses on how ordinary language resources—features or structures of ordinary talk as identified in linguistics, sociolinguistics, pragmatics, ethnomethodology and con-versation analysis among others—are employed by interactants in mathematical activ-ity. Researchers in this area view mathematical activity as discursive and interactional accomplishments and take the perspective that doers and learners of mathematics rou-tinely and systematically deploy features of talk-in-interaction to accomplish math-ematical work (Stevens & Hall, 1998). While the range of this body of work is broad, we highlight one line of inquiry focused on pronoun use in mathematical talk. In an early example, Rowland (1992) demonstrated how the pronoun "it" functions as a *con-ceptual deictic*—a linguistic pointer to (mathematical) concepts or ideas which are as yet unnamed in the course of the interaction and whose meanings are to be inferred by the context of the utterance. For example, he shows how one child, while working on a multiplication task, uses the pronoun "it" to name the notion of commutativ-ity—a concept that is useful for making sense of the task but that she has not formally encountered. Her use of this deictic pointer allows her to "share and discuss a concept which [she] possesses as a meaningful abstraction, yet is unable to name" (p. 47), in this way serving as a resource for mathematical sense-making. While his study was per-haps limited by the focus on a single, somewhat unique case, Rowland's use of linguis-tic methods of analysis to illuminate mathematical functions of language elements in micro-interaction suggests that close examination of structures of talk can reveal how more complex mathematical processes are accomplished in interaction. For example, Rowland's later work (1999, 2000) and more recent analyses of students' mathematical talk in problem-solving or sense-making activities (Edwards, Farlow, Liang, & Hall, 2009; Jurow, 2004) show how pronouns and other structures of talk (such as shifts in verb tense) and coordination with gesture are employed by speakers when engaged in processes of generalizing, proving, and abstraction.

Finally, studies of discourse and language have illuminated dynamics of power and ideology manifest through language in mathematics learning and teaching contexts. These studies have shown how the discourse of mathematics classrooms (including "reform" mathematics classrooms) are often reflective of the practices of dominant groups. These classroom discourse practices can alienate or exclude some students, in particular those from cultural groups or with class backgrounds whose discourse practices differ from the discourses in schools (e.g., Zevenbergen, 2000). For example,

Lubienski (2000a, 2000b) examined the influence of class on students' experiences in a middle grades reform-based mathematics classroom. Drawing upon multiple sources of qualitative data, including surveys, interviews, observations, and student written work, she found that lower SES and higher SES students responded differently to and had different understandings and opinions about several reform-oriented instructional practices, including the use of open-ended problems and discussion-intensive classroom pedagogy. In particular, the discursive practices of the reform classroom seemed more closely aligned with middle-class students' ways of learning and knowing than those of lower- and working-class students, which raised important questions about whether and how reforms intended to serve all students can support powerful mathematical learning for students with different class backgrounds. Like Walkerdine and Lucey's seminal work on early childhood mathematical development (Walkerdine, 1988; Walkerdine & Lucey, 1989), this work points to the power of language to exclude and oppress—a power that is often invisible to those exercising it—and the particular power that mathematics as a discourse holds as a form of cultural or linguistic capital (Bourdieu & Wacquant, 1992).

Some researchers seeking to reveal and interrogate the dynamics of power in mathematical classrooms have employed analytical tools from critical discourse analysis (CDA), a tradition that focuses on how discourse manifests, reproduces and can resist social and political domination (Fairclough, 1989). In one recent example, Wagner and Herbel-Eisenmann (2008) used CDA to analyze a large corpus of classroom transcripts to examine how a specific discursive move—the use of the word "just," common in mathematics classroom talk—invited or suppressed student dialogue. Their analysis of occurrences of "just" across the data corpus shows how teachers' use of the term positioned students in relation to mathematics, often shutting down dialogue, and, in particular, how it seemed to shape students' perceptions of their authority and legitimacy to take mathematical initiative.

The diverse body of work pertaining to the role of discourse in mathematics learning has provided insight into the processes that constitute the doing and learning of mathematics as participatory and interactional activities. In addition, the focus on discursive practices has provided needed analytical meat to the application of situated and sociocultural theories of cognition to mathematics learning. However, the relationships between mathematics as language, mathematical talk and interaction, and learning mathematics are complex; the field has only begun to identify and unpack key constructs and relations through which they can be understood. Consequently, such studies are often very specific and focused on single cases of a particular phenomenon, and, as such, findings can be limited in scope.

In addition, across this field of work, there is often a lack of clarity in how key ideas are conceptualized, resulting in lack of theoretical coherence. This is problematic not only for researchers seeking to respond to and build upon one another's work and, thus, for developing theory and building new knowledge, but also for those seeking to translate insights about the role of discourse in mathematics learning into meaningful contributions to practice. In a related note, this body of work draws from diverse traditions with varied commitments and intellectual histories; while appropriating theoretical and methodological resources from other disciplines has provided valuable insights and resources to our inquiries into mathematics learning, this can also result in a hodge-podge of constructs and methods with little coherence or resonance.

Research Addressing Identity and Mathematics Learning

As sociocultural theories of learning have gained in prominence within the field of mathematics education, the concept of identity has received increased attention from the field, both theoretically and empirically. An ERIC search with keywords *mathematics* and *identity* from 1990 to 2009 netted a total of 86 relevant papers; of these, 73 were published between 2000 and 2009. In this body of work, a variety of different definitions and methods were used to study identity, with the only broad area of agreement being that identity should not be conceived as purely individual, nor purely social. The different definitions currently in use have important empirical and theoretical implications, and open up different kinds of possibilities for research. Although there are many approaches we could discuss here (e.g., Castanheira, Green, Dixon, & Yeager, 2007; Sfard & Prusak, 2005; Solomon, 2007; Walshaw, 2005), we limit ourselves to three definitions and analytic strategies for studying identity as it relates to mathematics learning. For each approach, we present the definition and describe a representative study. We close this section by discussing the strengths and weaknesses of these various approaches to the study of mathematics learning.

Nasir and Hand (2008) use the term *practice-linked identities* to describe "identities that people come to take on, construct, and embrace that are linked to participation in particular social and cultural practices" (p. 147). Practice-linked identities are simultaneously social (reflecting the practice) and individual (integrated into an individual sense of self). In their analysis, they consider both the moment-to-moment shifting of identity (sometimes called *positioning;* Davies & Harré, 1990; Holland, Lachiotte, Skinner, & Cain, 2001) and longer-term trajectories of identity as a relatively stable sense of self (Erikson, 1968). Nasir and Hand conducted ethnographic studies of two different practices—a high school basketball team, and a high school mathematics classroom—drawing on participant observation, ethnographic fieldnotes, and structured interviews with young African American men who participated in both of the practices. Their analysis considered how each of these practices afforded opportunities for participants to develop practice-linked identities. They found that the school and the team differed in the ways participants were offered: (a) access to the domain itself (basketball or mathematics); (b) integral roles in the practice; and (c) opportunities for self-expression. The structure of the basketball team's practice afforded deeper engagement (in all aspects of the sport, including mathematical aspects) than the mathematics classroom.

A second strand of research in this area has coalesced around the concept of a *mathematics identity* (Martin, 2000, 2006, 2007). Martin (2007) examined the interplay between a *mathematics identity* and a *racial identity,* specifically for African American learners. A mathematics identity refers to "the dispositions and deeply held beliefs that individuals develop about their ability to participate and perform effectively in mathematical contexts and to use mathematics to change the conditions of their lives" (p. 150). These identities are shaped by one's experiences, how one perceives oneself, and also how one is seen by others. One's racial identity, presumably, is one's sense of self as a racialized being—once again, partially reflecting one's own self-perceptions, as well as the perceptions of others. This concept of identity differs from the notion of practice-linked identities in that while practice-linked identities are conceived as being primarily local, the mathematics and racial identities are conceived as going beyond local contexts or practices to develop in a relatively enduring fashion over the life-span.

For his analysis of these forms of identity, Martin (2007) drew on lengthy interviews with adults and adolescents in which he asked participants to describe their life experiences with mathematics in and outside of school and to articulate their attitudes and beliefs about mathematics. These interviews were then analyzed thematically. Based on analysis of these interviews, Martin argued that although mathematical and racial identities are often considered to be separate, in fact they reflect two "intersecting realms of experience" (p. 146). Interview narratives showed that for the interview participants, all of whom are African American adults who grew up in the U.S., racial identities have influenced mathematics identities, and vice versa. When faced with struggles to understand and learn mathematics, interview subjects appealed to their ongoing struggles for racial justice to help overcome the educational barriers they faced. Conversely, interview subjects argued that mathematics itself was often presented as a domain that is unwelcoming of or unimportant to African American people, and they spoke of the ways achievement in mathematics affected their racial identities as well. Through these interview studies, Martin found that successful African American students of mathematics (middle school students and adult learners alike) drew on their African American identities as sources of strength to support their learning.

A recent paper by Cobb, Gresalfi, and Hodge (2009) built on the body of Martin's work to operationalize definitions of identity that can be applied to analysis of local classroom interaction (although, notably, the racial specificity of Martin's work does not translate into this operationalization). Their definitions are related to both local, practice-linked identities, and more global, domain-specific identities (such as mathematics or racial identities). Cobb et al. referred to the "*normative identity* as a doer of mathematics that is established in the classroom and the *personal identities* that individual students develop as they participate in classroom activities" (p. 43). Normative identities encompass the range of attitudes, values, ways of speaking about mathematics, and so on, with which students would have to affiliate in order to be positioned as a good student in a particular classroom. Personal identities involve the extent to which individuals affiliate or resist the normative identities. They claim that there is one normative identity in any particular classroom context, whereas each individual develops their own personal identity.

Cobb et al. (2009) provided an illustrative case in which they use this analytic framework to compare the normative and personal identities in two different middle school mathematics classes. These classes were taught by different teachers and addressed different mathematical content areas (data analysis, algebra) but had many of the same students. To discern classroom normative identities, they used ethnographic methods to collect fieldnotes and video of classroom events and analyzed the general and specifically mathematical obligations that were imposed on students. Cobb et al. used in-depth interviews with students to examine student understandings and values about classroom obligations as well as the students' sense of their own and other students' mathematical competence. This analytic framework highlights general and specifically mathematical aspects of classroom life that influence the normative and personal identities that develop. In the case study, students developed personal identities that were strongly aligned with the normative identities in the classroom in which students and teachers shared authority and agency about mathematical methods and solutions. In the classroom where authority rested almost solely with the teacher, students developed more resistant personal identities, or complied with classroom normative identities without strong affiliation.

The three distinct, yet related, ways of conceptualizing identity presented here have strengths and weaknesses for the study of mathematics learning. These conceptualizations elucidate the relationship between participation in collective practices and individual development. All three of these frameworks attempt to elaborate on how broad social structures shape opportunities for participation, making space for particular kinds of individual and practice-linked identities. These identities are both constantly in flux and relatively enduring.

A general weakness of research in this area is that, perhaps as a result of the proliferation of definitions and stances towards the concept of identity, it is difficult to compare results across studies to develop a coherent body of knowledge on this topic. Some of the key assumptions of this research appear to be untested (such as Cobb et al.'s (2009) claim that each classroom will have a single normative identity). Further, although the metaphor of learning as participation has provided traction in investigating how and why mathematics learning happens, studies have rarely addressed the learning of specific mathematical topics or processes.

Research in Cognitive Neuroscience Relevant to Mathematics Learning

Neuroscience is a field currently generating much interest among mathematics education researchers and the general public, although the field is still in its infancy and there are few substantive results illustrating the process of *learning*. In this brief review, we will focus on the way learning has been conceptualized in neuroscientific research, then discuss some underlying assumptions and theoretical framings, and close by highlighting some examples of research in this area to consider what this field has contributed to our understanding of mathematics learning.

It should be noted at the outset that much of neuroscientific research is not concerned with learning; instead, neuroscience research excels at studying cognition, or more properly, brain function. However, much of this research is based on an implicit definition of learning as a change in either the quantity or speed of brain function (i.e., reduced or increased activation in a particular part of the brain) or a shift in the network of brain areas that work to perform a particular task (i.e., a qualitative change in terms of which areas of the brain are active during the task). In practice, mathematics learning is also measured outside of the brain in a fairly traditional manner, usually using experimental tasks, from the simple (number recognition) to the complex (geometric proof).

Learning has often been studied by proxy, for example, by comparing the brain function of younger vs. older people (Rivera, Reiss, Eckert, & Menon, 2005) or comparing people researchers call "prodigies" vs. people they consider "normal"[1] (Pesenti et al., 2001). In both of the studies cited here, researchers found that increasing expertise in particular mathematical tasks was associated with a shift in brain function; when comparing the brain function of the two groups, different areas of the brain were activated, or similar areas were activated but to greater or lesser degrees. Another approach to investigating learning has been to train participants in particular tasks, and then compare brain function on the trained vs. untrained tasks. For example, in one study, participants memorized a set of multiplication facts, and subsequent fMRI scans demonstrated that different areas of the brain were activated for facts that were recalled versus facts that were untrained and were, therefore, presumably computed on the spot (Ischebeck et al., 2009). This study went on to examine what brain function looked like when these memorized facts were leveraged to solve related division problems.

In contrast, Anderson, Betts, Ferris and Fincham (2009) recently investigated whether neuroscientific research could study the process of learning itself. The research design they used is markedly different from the type of study described above; in this design, they constructed a computer model of the learning process, and used the model to predict how long various tasks should take and which parts of the brain would be activated at a given time. They compared the results from their computer model with the brain scans of human participants doing the same set of tasks and used the differences between the results to refine their model. They found their model to be fairly accurate, but had underestimated the activation of areas of the brain associated with visualization and with motor functions. They argue that this provides evidence of the importance of visualization in mathematical (especially geometric) problem-solving.

The two research designs we have described here—one to identify which brain *areas* are associated with which cognitive functions, and the other to identify how different regions of the brain coordinate (in *networks*) to accomplish complex tasks—highlight two major competing approaches to the study of the brain: what Varma and Schwartz (2008) call the "area" focus and the "network" focus. Whichever approach one takes, it is commonly accepted that neuroscientific research can tell us little, as yet, about the processes of teaching or schooling (Bruer, 1997). The tasks that have been studied are usually broken down into basic components and simplified such that participants can expect to solve each in a few seconds. The selection of tasks is further limited because head movements (e.g., moving the lips for speech) can interfere with imaging techniques. A typical experiment involves asking a participant to perform the same (usually quite basic) task dozens, sometimes hundreds, of times, while their brain function is being scanned. These experimental trials are usually preceded by dozens of trials in which the scanner is not used; this is to habituate the participant to the task so the images of brain function capture only (or mostly) the functions relevant to the task itself (e.g., adding one-digit numbers) rather than functions related to figuring out the technology or the context (e.g., which button to push). As the technology for this research advances, perhaps more complex tasks and tasks requiring social interaction or a longer time span can be studied.

We report key findings from neuroscientific research on mathematics learning in three areas: seemingly universal aspects of mathematical cognition, individual differences in brain function that might help to explain achievement differences, and cultural differences in brain function.

Universals in Brain Function

One of the most robust findings in mathematical neuroscience is the existence of the *numerical distance effect* (also well known in cognitive psychology). In brief, this finding states that if people are asked to decide which is the larger of two numbers, the decision time gets longer the closer the two numbers are (Dehaene, Dehaene-Lambertz, & Cohen, 1998; Goobel & Rushworth, 2004; Halberda, Mazzocco, & Feigenson, 2008; Holloway & Ansari, 2009; Zhou et al., 2006). Brain mapping has shown that parts of the brain that are associated with visual processing are active during such tasks, suggesting that humans represent numbers as a mental number line and use this number line representation to make comparisons.

The fact that there are certain regions of the brain that are associated with visual processing, others with speech, and others with motion, is also taken as evidence for some universal neurological human capacities. Further, primate brains are often roughly similar to the organization of human brains, indicating that primates are evolutionarily endowed with particular capacities (e.g., number, language).

Individual Differences and Mathematics Achievement

Although all humans display the numerical distance effect, there are differences in terms of the size of this effect for different people. In one recent study of schoolchildren, the size of the numerical distance effect (for symbolic numbers only) was found to correlate positively to mathematics achievement scores in school, and not to reading achievement (Holloway & Ansari, 2009). Thus, these individual differences in the speed of brain functioning for this task appear to be related to mathematics learning in school, although from this study design it is not possible to determine whether one causes the other, or both are related to some third factor.

Another area of study for mathematical neuroscience has been dyscalculia or mathematical learning disabilities. In these studies, dyscalculia is defined simply as a deficit in mathematics learning that does not affect other areas. Scientists study brain function to determine whether and how individuals diagnosed with dyscalculia have systematically different brain function from their "normal" peers. As one example, it has been shown that individuals differ in their ability to estimate number from a visual or auditory array. These differences correlate with school achievement from the very beginning of schooling (Halberda, Mazzocco, & Feigenson, 2008). Again, it is unknown whether this estimation ability influences math achievement, math achievement influences estimation ability, or some other factors influence both, but in children diagnosed with dyscalculia, the part of the brain that is believed to play a key role in number representation was not activated in the same way as it was for typically developing children (Price, Holloway, Räsänen, Vesterinen, & Ansari, 2007). This suggests that the functioning of this area of the brain (the right intraparietal sulcus) may be a root cause of this type of learning disability.

Cultural Differences

Although neuroscience does at times focus on universals, we know that the human brain goes through enormous changes from the moment of birth and remains plastic throughout the life span. The brain changes because of human experience in cultural communities; the development of the brain is therefore "biologically cultural" (Rogoff, 2003, p. 63). As Rogoff points out, some universals are also profoundly cultural, for example, the use of language may be universal across human cultural groups, but the ways in which language is used are undoubtedly cultural.

Differences in language can also influence the nature of brain function for particular mathematical tasks. In one study comparing the ways in which Chinese speakers and English speakers represented numbers, it was found that different parts of the brain were used by the different groups (Tang et al., 2006). The results indicated that

> [T]he different biological encoding of numbers may be shaped by visual reading experience during language acquisition and other cultural factors such as mathematics learning strategies and education systems, which cannot be explained completely by the differences in languages per se.
>
> (p. 10775)

That is, the verbal language, reading practices, and schooling experiences all influenced the way information was encoded in and retrieved from the brain. These and similar findings highlight the importance of considering the ways in which everyday human activity influences learning. In other words, it is critical for neuroscientific research to focus further on processes of learning, and not just cognition, in order to understand how the brain functions.

Strengths and Weaknesses

There are strengths and weaknesses to taking this approach to understanding learning. First, cognitive neuroscience has supported the diagnosis and understanding of learning disabilities such as dyscalculia. Understanding which components of particular tasks might cause difficulty for people diagnosed with specific learning disabilities allows educators to focus on training or developing that specific brain area, in the hope that overall mathematical achievement will improve.

However, there is a danger in assuming that learning is only, or even primarily, about brain function. While neuroscience is appealing precisely because it can be so concrete— it does not depend on nebulous ideas like identity or discourse—there is little evidence that for most children learning difficulties are primarily about brain function so much as they are about opportunities to engage in rich mathematical tasks in culturally responsive contexts. It is unclear at this point whether it is possible for neuroscientific research to capture these phenomena.

Another danger of brain-based learning science is in the way the technology, coupled with a research base still in its early stages, has a hand in deciding which topics will be studied. Because we know little about basic building blocks for mathematical tasks and because the scanners are extremely limited in the contexts in which they can work, tasks are selected that can be performed in the scanner and that are of a repetitive and very discrete character. In addition, the use of the machines is very expensive, and cost prohibits experimental studies in which participants solve a small number of unfamiliar tasks slowly. Experimental designs require a large number of participants and a large number of trials; results of scans are averaged, and too much idiosyncrasy (e.g., participants solving problems in radically different ways) would make the data difficult to interpret. When the technology supports a broader range of studies, we look forward to neuroscientific studies of more complex mathematical content and of mathematical processes such as problem-solving, reasoning and proof.

FUTURE DIRECTIONS FOR RESEARCH ON MATHEMATICS LEARNING

The aim of this chapter has been to highlight threads of research that have broadened and deepened our understandings of mathematics learning. These threads reflect some of the theoretical and methodological diversity of the current state of the field, a diversity that enriches the development of knowledge about mathematics learning but that also creates certain challenges for the field of research in mathematics education. We briefly discuss three of these challenges and propose avenues of inquiry that may address them.

The Challenge of Addressing the Complexity of Context

The role of context in mathematical cognition and learning has been an enduring challenge and source of debate within the field of research in mathematics education. In part, the challenge arises from the accountability of the field to understanding not only how people learn mathematics in a universal sense, but also how students, with histories and identities, learn mathematics in their school and classroom contexts. Furthermore, the very notion of context is perhaps too broad and encompasses issues too complex to expect research to embrace a single, coherent conceptualization of the role of context in mathematics learning. However, the relationship between contextual factors or forces and mathematics learning is critical for understanding how students learn mathematics and how we can support that learning. Consequently, research in both the cognitive/constructivist and situated/sociocultural traditions has sought to understand aspects of context in mathematics learning, for example, the situational sensitivity of knowledge in studies of transfer or the role of culture and race in students' mathematical engagement and learning. Indeed, much of the current research on mathematics learning attends to some aspect of context. Through our review of the current research, we have identified a few directions for future research that seem productive for furthering the field's theoretical understandings of mathematics learning and context, particularly those that may be important for addressing the current challenges facing mathematics learning and teaching.

First, in our discussions of research on discourse, identity, and neuroscience, we outlined some research findings that focus on single social categories, like race or ethnicity. Greater attention should be paid to issues of intersectionality, in particular, how the interplay of race, gender, socioeconomic status, language proficiencies, and so on, affects mathematics learning and how students experience mathematics in particular contexts of learning. Mathematics education research might be well served to consider theoretical frameworks outside of mathematics education, for example, current formulations of Critical Race Theory, that draw upon theoretical paradigms of intersectionality in the recognition that the dynamics of race manifest in and through gender, sexuality, class, ethnicity, and culture (e.g., Crenshaw, 1991).

Second, research on mathematics learning needs to better address how the sociopolitical contexts of schooling interact with how students experience and learn mathematics. For example, while studies have long included school and community categories such as urban, rural, and so on in their research design, little progress has been made in understanding how urban or rural contexts shape students' mathematical experiences and, thus, their learning. Indeed, there is little consensus about what constitutes an urban school or district (and even less attention paid to rural communities). Furthermore, the significant body of research that has been conducted on urban schooling and urban students' learning has not, by and large, examined the particular dynamics of how mathematics is experienced and learned in urban settings. For example, how does the "high stakes" status of mathematical performance—for students as well as teachers and schools—shape the perceptions of mathematics and mathematics identities of students in large urban schools serving high minority and high poverty populations? How do urban youth experience school mathematics as relevant in their futures and how does this shape their mathematical participation and learning? Broadly speaking, this work necessitates understanding how mathematical performance and expertise are constructed in the social, economic and political discourses that frame current debates in educational policy and then how policies emerging from those debates effect how school mathematics is structured, taught and learned in specific settings.

The Challenge of Disciplinary Diversity
As illustrated by the studies reviewed in this chapter, the field of research on mathematics learning is truly multi-disciplinary. The broad range and complexity of the phenomena

relevant to mathematics learning necessitate a diversity of theoretical and methodological tools. Sometimes driven by challenges of understanding contextual forces (e.g., how race and culture shape mathematical learning) or by advances in other disciplines (e.g., neurological imaging technologies), researchers of mathematics learning often draw upon resources outside of the traditional boundaries of mathematics education research grounded in psychology and cognitive science. However, as has been said of educational research more generally, researchers in mathematics education have not always had an adequate understanding of the intellectual histories and disciplinary groundings of theories and methods of analysis borrowed from other fields. As a result, methods such as "discourse analysis" are sometimes cited or employed inappropriately and theoretical notions such as "community of practice" get taken up in so many different ways that their original purpose, context and characterization are muddied. In such cases, what is lost is the methodological rigor and theoretical robustness that allow for the reliability and comparability of findings. That is not to suggest that tools should not be repurposed; rather, that tools are created for particular purposes and within particular intellectual contexts, and so using them to build knowledge within mathematics education and across disciplinary boundaries requires that we educate ourselves about those intellectual traditions.

The Challenge of Theoretical Bridging Given the Limits of Commensurability

Much has been written about the need and potential for bridging the seemingly divergent theoretical perspectives that inform current research on learning (e.g., Greeno, Collins, & Resnick, 1996; Sfard, 1998)—particularly those theoretical perspectives that center on individuals' cognition and learning versus those that focus on the social or the situated nature of cognitive activity. A decade or so ago, it seemed desirable and plausible to conceptualize how these perspectives could be unified or made commensurable—Greeno, Collins and Resnick (1996), for example, suggested that cognitive, behaviorist, and situative views could be seen as analyzing learning at different levels of "aggregation" (p. 40, i.e., individual cognitive structures and processes, individuals' behaviors, and activity systems within which individuals participate and interact with others and material resources); thus, theoretical coherence might be accomplished through further theoretical developments that showed the nested relations between those levels. In current research, researchers are pushing on the boundaries of their theoretical frameworks in order to examine phenomena in different contexts or at different units of analysis. Cognitive researchers are seeking to understand students' learning by taking into account the social processes that structure individuals' cognitive activity; some research in the situative/sociocultural tradition has sought to characterize individual students' trajectories of learning within communities of practice and arising from interaction. However, it remains to be determined whether and how a kind of "grand unified theory" of learning can be developed, or is even desirable, given the apparent incommensurability of some fundamental assumptions and commitments. We do not necessarily believe that overarching theoretical unity is necessary or achievable within a field so diverse and multidisciplinary; however, in order for the field to progress and for new knowledge to relate to and build upon existing work, researchers need to be explicit about their theoretical and analytical assumptions and provide explicit and robust formulations of theoretical constructs. In this way, greater coherence may be achieved as points of resonance and contrast are more clearly visible.

Finally, progress toward greater clarity and coherence is critical if the field is to be relevant to practitioners and policymakers. Too often, research on mathematics learning is seen as irrelevant to or difficult to realize within today's classrooms and schools; even more so when district, state and federal organizations are seeking interventions that are effective at large scales and for diverse populations of students. In order to better communicate what has been learned about mathematics learning and how to support it, and to translate these findings into tools, practices and policies that are meaningful for students, practitioners and policymakers, we must understand and build upon connections across theoretical perspectives, levels of aggregation, and methodological approaches.

ACKNOWLEDGMENTS

We are grateful to Sashank Varma for suggestions, comments, and feedback on the section on neuroscientific research. In addition, the chapter benefited from constructive feedback from Patricia Alexander and Richard Mayer.

NOTE

1 Comparing different groups of people is central to some areas of research in cognitive neuroscience. In such comparisons, researchers frequently compare one group that they describe as "normal" to another group that is in some way deemed "abnormal" (e.g., individuals with learning disabilities, individuals deemed to be prodigies, etc.). Throughout this review, we adopt the language used by the researchers.

REFERENCES

Anderson, J. R., Betts, S., Ferris, J. L., & Fincham, J. M. (2009). Can neural imaging investigate learning in an educational task? Unpublished manuscript.

Bishop, A. J., Clements, K., Keitel, C., Kilpatrick, J., & Leung F. (Eds.). (2003). *Second international handbook of mathematics education*. Dordrecht: Kluwer Academic.

Bourdieu, P., & Wacquant, L. (1992). *An invitation to reflexive sociology*. Cambridge: Polity Press.

Bransford, J., Brown, A. L., & Cocking, R. R. (Eds.). (1999). *How people learn: Brain, mind, experience, and school*. Washington, DC: National Academy Press.

Brownell, W. A. (1948). Learning theory and educational practice. *Journal of Educational Research, 41*, 481–497.

Bruer, J. T. (1997). Education and the brain: A bridge too far. *Educational Researcher, 26*(8), 4–16.

Castanheira, M. L., Green, J., Dixon, C., & Yeagerb, B. (2007). (Re)formulating identities in the face of fluid modernity: An interactional ethnographic approach. *International Journal of Educational Research, 46*(3–4), 172–189.

Cobb, P., Gresalfi, M., & Hodge, L. L. (2009). An interpretive scheme for analyzing the identities that students develop in mathematics classrooms. *Journal for Research in Mathematics Education, 40*(1), 40–68.

Cobb, P., Stephan, M., McLain, K., & Gravemeijer, K. (2001). Participating in classroom mathematical practices. *The Journal of the Learning Sciences, 10*(1&2), 113–163.

Cobb, P., & Yackel, E. (1996). Constructivist, emergent, and sociocultural perspectives in the context of developmental research. *Educational Psychologist, 31*(3&4), 175–190.

Cornu, B. (1981). Limits. *Advanced Mathematical Thinking, 11*, 153–166.

Crenshaw, K. (1991). Mapping the margins: Intersectionality, identity politics, and violence against women of color. *Stanford Law Review, 43*(6), 1241–1299.

Darken, B., Wynegar, R., & Kuhn, S. (2000). Evaluating calculus reform: A review and a longitudinal study. In E. Dubinsky, A. H. Schoenfeld, & J. Kaput (Eds.), *Research in collegiate mathematics education IV* (pp. 16–41). Providence, RI: American Mathematical Society.

Davies, B., & Harré, R. (1990). Positioning: The discursive production of selves. *Journal for the Theory of Social Behavior, 20*, 43–63.

Dehaene, S., Dehaene-Lambertz, G., & Cohen, L. (1998). Abstract representations of numbers in the animal and human brain. *Trends in Neurosciences, 21*(8), 355–560.

diSessa, A. A. (1993). Toward an epistemology of physics. *Cognition & Instruction, 10*(2–3), 105–225.

diSessa, A. A., Hammer, D. M., Sherin, B., & Kolpakowski, T. (1991). Inventing graphing: Children's representational expertise. *The Journal of Mathematical Behavior, 10*, 117–160.

diSessa, A. A., & Sherin, B. L. (1998). What changes in conceptual change? *International Journal of Science Education, 20*(10), 1155–1191.

diSessa, A. A., & Wagner, J. F. (2005). What coordination has to say about transfer. In J. P. Mestre (Ed.), *Transfer of learning from a modern multidisciplinary perspective*. Greenwich, CT: Information Age Publishing.

Edwards, A. R., Farlow, K., Liang, S., & Hall, R. (2009). Witness to a demonstration: Recipient design of mathematical argument among undergraduate calculus students. Paper presented at the annual meeting of the American Educational Research Association, San Diego, CA, April.

Enyedy, N., Rubel, L., Castellon, V., Mukhopadhyay, S., Esmonde, I., & Secada, W. (2008). Revoicing in a multilingual classroom. *Mathematical Thinking and Learning, 10*(2), 134–162.

Erikson, E. H. (1968). *Youth and crisis*. New York: Norton.

Erlwanger, S. H. (1973). Benny's conception of rules and answers in IPI Mathematics. *Journal of Children's Mathematical Behavior, 1(2)*, 7–26.

Fairclough, N. (1989). *Language and power*. London: Longman.

Fennema, E., Carpenter, T. P., Franke, M., Levi, L., Jacobs, V. R., & Empson, S. B. (1996). A longitudinal study of learning to use children's thinking in mathematics instruction. *Journal for Research in Mathematics Education, 27*(4), 403–434.

Fennema, E., Franke, M., & Carpenter, T., & Carey, D. (1993). Using children's mathematical knowledge in instruction. *American Educational Research Journal, 30*(3), 555–583.

Forman, E. A., Larreamendy-Joerns, J., Stein, M. K., & Brown, C. A. (1998). "You're going to want to find out which and prove it": Collective argumentation in a mathematics classroom. *Learning and Instruction, 8(6)*, 527–548.

Gagné, R. M. (1965). *The conditions of learning*. New York: Holt, Rinehart and Winston.

Goobel, S. M., & Rushworth, M. F. S. (2004). Cognitive neuroscience: Acting on numbers. *Current Biology, 14*(13), R517–R519.

Greeno, J. G., Collins, A. M., & Resnick, L. (1996). Cognition and learning. In D. C. Berliner, & R. C. Calfee (Eds.) *Handbook of educational psychology* (pp. 15–46). New York: Macmillan.

Gutierrez, A., & Boero, P. (2006). *Handbook of research on the psychology of mathematics education*. Rotterdam: Sense Publishers.

Halberda, J., Mazzocco, M. M. M., & Feigenson, L. (2008). Individual differences in non-verbal number acuity correlate with maths achievement. *Nature, 455*(7213), 665–668.

Hall, R., & Stevens, R. (1995). Making space: A comparison of mathematical work in school and professional design practices. In S. L. Star (Ed.), *The cultures of computing* (pp. 118–145). London: Basil Blackwell.

Halliday, M. (1978). *Language as social semiotic: The social interpretation of language and meaning*, Baltimore, MD: University Park Press.

Holland, D., Lachiotte Jr., W., Skinner, D., & Cain, C. (2001). *Identity and agency in cultural worlds*. Cambridge, MA: Harvard University Press.

Holloway, I. D., & Ansari, D. (2009). Mapping numerical magnitudes onto symbols: The numerical distance effect and individual differences in children's mathematics achievement. *Journal of Experimental Child Psychology, 103*(1), 17–29.

Ischebeck, A., Zamarian, L., Schocke, M., & Delazer, M. (2009). Flexible transfer of knowledge in mental arithmetic – an fMRI study. *NeuroImage, 44*(3), 1103–1112.

Izsák, A. (2003). "We want a statement that is always true": Criteria for good algebraic representations and the development of modeling knowledge. *Journal for Research in Mathematics Education, 34*(3), 191–227.

Izsák, A. (2005). "You have to count the squares": Applying knowledge in pieces to learning rectangular area. *The Journal of the Learning Sciences, 14*(3), 361–403.

Izsák, A., Caglayan, G., & Olive, J. (2009). Meta-representation in an algebra classroom. *The Journal of the Learning Sciences, 18*(4), 549–587.

Jaworski, B. (1994). *Investigating mathematics teaching: A constructivist enquiry*. London: Falmer Press.

Judd, C. M. (1908). The relation of special training to general intelligence. *Educational Review, 36*, 28–42.

Jurow, S. (2004). Generalizing in interaction: Middle school mathematics students making mathematical generalizations in a population-modeling project. *Mind, Culture and Activity, 11(4)*, 279–300.

Kwon, O. N., Allen, K., & Rasmussen, C. (2005). Students' retention of mathematical knowledge and skills in differential equations. *School Science and Mathematics, 105*(5), 227–239.

Lave, J. (1988). *Cognition in practice*. New York: Cambridge University Press.

Lemke, J. (1990). *Talking science: Language, learning and values*. Norwood, NJ: Ablex Publishing.

Lerman, S. (2000). The social turn in mathematics education research. In J. Boaler, *Multiple perspectives on mathematics teaching and learning* (pp. 19–44). Westport, CT: Ablex.

Lerman, S. (2004). Challenging research reading (Commentary 3). In A. Chronaki, & I.M. Christiansen (Eds.), *Challenging perspectives on mathematics classroom communication* (pp. 349–358). Charlotte, NC: Information Age Publishing.

Lester, F. K. (2007). *Second handbook of research on mathematics teaching and learning.* Charlotte, NC: Information Age Publishing.

Lubienski, S. (2000a). A clash of social class cultures? Students' experiences in a discussion-intensive seventh-grade mathematics classroom. *The Elementary School Journal, 100*(4), 377.

Lubienski, S. (2000b). Problem solving as a means toward mathematics for all: An exploratory look through a class lens. *Journal for Research in Mathematics Education, 31*(4), 454–4892.

MacGregor, M. (2002). Using words to explain mathematical ideas. *Australian Journal of Language and Literacy, 25*(1), 78–89.

Martin, D. B. (2000). *Mathematics success and failure among African-American youth: The roles of sociohistorical context, community forces, school influence, and individual agency.* Mahwah, NJ: Lawrence Erlbaum.

Martin, D. B. (2006). Mathematics learning and participation as racialized forms of experience: African American parents speak on the struggle for mathematics literacy. *Mathematical Thinking and Learning, 8*(3), 197–229.

Martin, D. B. (2007). Mathematics learning and participation in African American context: The co-construction of identity in two intersecting realms of experience. In N. S. Nasir, & P. Cobb (Eds.), *Improving access to mathematics: Diversity and equity in the classroom* (pp. 146–158). New York: Teachers College Press.

Martin, T. S., Hunt, C. A., Lannin, J., Leonard, W., Jr., Marshall, G. L., & Wares, A. (2001). How reform secondary mathematics textbooks stack up against NCTM's Principles and Standards. *Mathematics Teacher, 94*(7), 540–545, 589.

Moschkovich, J. (2002). A situated and sociocultural perspective on bilingual mathematics learners. *Mathematical Thinking and Learning, 4*(2 & 3), 189–212.

Moschkovich, J. (2003). Examining mathematical discourse practices. *For the Learning of Mathematics, 27*(1), 24–30.

Mowrer, R. R., & Klein, S. B. (2001). *Handbook of contemporary learning theories.* Mahwah, NJ: Lawrence Erlbaum Associates.

Nasir, N. S., & Hand, V. (2008). From the court to the classroom: Opportunities for engagement, learning, and identity in basketball and classroom mathematics. *Journal of the Learning Sciences, 17*(2), 143–179.

O'Connor, M.C. (1998). Language socialization in the mathematics classroom: Discourse practices and mathematical thinking. In M. Lampert, & M. L. Blunk (Eds.), *Talking mathematics in school: Studies of teaching and learning. Learning in doing* (pp. 15–55). Cambridge: Cambridge University Press.

O'Connor, M. C., & Michaels, S. (1993). Aligning academic task and participation status through revoicing: Analysis of a classroom discourse strategy. *Anthropology and Education Quarterly, 24*(4), 318–335.

O'Halloran, K. L. (2000). Classroom discourse in mathematics: A multisemiotic analysis. *Linguistics and Education, 10*(3), 359–388.

Pesenti, M., Zago, L., Crivello, F., Mellet, E., Samson, D., Duroux, B., et al. (2001). Mental calculation in a prodigy is sustained by right prefrontal and medial temporal areas. *Nature Neuroscience, 4*(1), 103–107.

Piaget, J. (1937/1954). *The construction of reality in the child* (M. Cook, Trans.). New York: Basic Books.

Piaget, J. (1970). *Genetic epistemology* (E. Duckworth, Trans.). New York: Columbia University Press.

Pimm, D. (1987). *Speaking mathematically: Communication in mathematics classrooms.* London: Routledge.

Price, G. R., Holloway, I., Räsänen, P., Vesterinen, M., & Ansari, D. (2007). Impaired parietal magnitude processing in developmental dyscalculia. *Current Biology, 17*(24), 1042–1043.

Rasmussen, C. (2001). New directions in differential equations: A framework for interpreting students' understandings and difficulties. *Journal of Mathematical Behavior, 20*, 55–87.

Rasmussen, C. (2002). Instructional materials for a first course in differential equations. Unpublished document, Purdue Calumet University.

Rasmussen, C., & Blumenfeld, H. (2007). Reinventing solutions to systems of linear differential equations: A case of emergent models involving analytic expressions. *The Journal of Mathematical Behavior, 26*(3), 195–210.

Rasmussen, C., Kwon, O. K., Allen, K., Marrongelle, K., & Burtch, M. (2006). Capitalizing on advances in mathematics and K-12 mathematics education in undergraduate mathematics: An inquiry oriented approach to differential equations. *Asia Pacific Education Review, 7*(1), 85–93.

Rasmussen, C., Zandieh, M., King, K., & Teppo, A. (2005). Advancing mathematical activity: A practice-oriented view of advanced mathematical thinking. *Mathematical Thinking and Learning, 7*(1), 51–73.

Rivera, S. M., Reiss, A. L., Eckert, M. A., & Menon, V. (2005). Developmental changes in mental arithmetic: Evidence for increased functional specialization in the left inferior parietal cortex. *Cerebral Cortex, 15*(11), 1779–1790.

Rogoff, B. (2003). *The cultural nature of human development.* New York: Oxford University Press.

Rowland, T. (1992). Pointing with pronouns. *For the Learning of Mathematics, 12*(2), 44–48.

Rowland, T. (1999). Pronouns in mathematical talk: Power, vagueness and generalisation. *For the Learning of Mathematics, 19*(2), 19–26.

Rowland, T. (2000). *The pragmatics of mathematics education: Vagueness in mathematical discourse.* London: Falmer Press.

Saxe, G. B. (1991). *Culture and cognitive development: Studies in mathematical understanding.* Hillsdale, NJ: Lawrence Erlbaum Associates, Inc.

Schieffelin, B. B., & Ochs, E. (1986). *Language socialization across cultures.* Cambridge: Cambridge University Press.

Schoenfeld, A. H. (2002). Making mathematics work for all children: Issues of standards, testing, and equity. *Educational Researcher, 31*(1), 13–25.

Schoenfeld, A. H. (2006). Mathematics teaching and learning. In P. A. Alexander, & P. H. Winne (Eds.), *Handbook of educational psychology* (2nd ed.) (pp. 479–510). Mahwah, NJ: Erlbaum.

Sfard, A. (1998). On two metaphors for learning and the dangers of choosing just one. *Educational Researcher, 27*(2), 4–13.

Sfard, A., & Prusak, A. (2005). Telling identities: In search of an analytic tool for investigating learning as a culturally shaped activity. *Educational Researcher, 34*(4), 14–22.

Simon, M. A., Tzur, R., Heinz, K., & Kinzel, M. (2004). Explicating a mechanism for conceptual learning: Elaborating the construct of reflective abstraction. *Journal for Research in Mathematics Education, 35*(5), 305–329.

Singley, M. K., & Anderson, J. R. (1989). *The transfer of cognitive skill.* Cambridge, MA: Harvard University Press.

Skinner, B.F. (1953). *Science and human behavior.* New York: The Free Press.

Solomon, Y. (2007). Experiencing mathematics classes: Ability grouping, gender and the selective development of participative identities. *International Journal of Educational Research, 46*, 8–19.

Stevens, R., & Hall, R. (1998). Disciplined perception: Learning to see in technoscience. In M. Lampert, & M. Blunk (Eds.), *Talking mathematics in school: Studies of teaching and learning* (pp. 107–150). Cambridge: Cambridge University Press.

Tang, Y., Zhang, W., Chen, K., Feng, S., Ji, Y., Shen, J., et al. (2006). Arithmetic processing in the brain shaped by cultures. *Proceedings of the National Academy of Sciences, USA, 103*(28), 10775–10780.

Thorndike, E. L. (1913). *Educational psychology, Vol. II: The psychology of learning.* New York: Teachers College.

Varma, S., & Schwartz, D. L. (2008). How should educational neuroscience conceptualise the relation between cognition and brain function? Mathematical reasoning as a network process. *Educational Research, 50*(2), 149–161.

Wagner, D., & Herbel-Eisenmann, B. (2008). "Just don't": The suppression and invitation of dialogue in the mathematics classroom. *Educational Studies in Mathematics, 67*(2), 143–157.

Wagner, J. F. (2006). Transfer in pieces. *Cognition and Instruction, 24*(1), 1–71.

Walkerdine, V. (1988). *The mastery of reason: Cognitive development and the production of rationality.* London: Routledge.

Walkerdine, V., & Lucey, H. (1989). *Democracy in the kitchen: Regulating mothers and socialising daughters.* London: Virago.

Walshaw, M. (2005). Getting political and unraveling layers of gendered mathematical identifications. *Cambridge Journal of Education, 35*(1), 19–34.

Wertheimer, M. (1945). *Productive thinking.* New York: Harper.

Zevenbergen, R. (2000). "Cracking the code" of mathematics classrooms: School success as a function of linguistic, social, and cultural background. In J. Boaler (Ed.), *Multiple perspectives on mathematics teaching and learning* (pp. 201–223). Stamford, CT: Ablex.

Zhou, X., Chen, C., Dong, Q., Zhang, H., Chen, C., Qiao, S., et al. (2006). Numerical distance effect in the N240 component in a number-matching task. *Neuroreport, 17*(10), 991–994.

5

LEARNING SCIENCE
Richard Duschl and Richard Hamilton

INTRODUCTION

We arrive at the beginning of the 21st century with new agendas, challenges, insights and issues facing the science of learning and science education. The research on learning and reasoning over the past 20 years has ushered in new and important ideas about the science of learning (NRC, 1999) and the important role of assessment in learning (NRC, 2001). Other developments influencing science learning include the new NAEP 2009 Science Framework (NAGB, 2008). The NAEP Framework emphasizes the assessment of outcomes that include both the target content and the context of its use (i.e., learning performances). In doing so, the assessment of science learning is taken beyond questions of what we know toward the inclusion of questions and tasks addressing how we know and why we believe what we know. New computer tools and technologies both in the classrooms and in support of classrooms and schools are making possible new forms of information on learning that can: (a) guide teachers in assessment for learning as well as assessment of learning; and (b) bring databases to classrooms for further inquiry and engagement in complex scientific/mathematical reasoning (NRC, 2006).

Science education has been in flux for a half century. First there was the launch of Sputnik and the race to space Cold War politics that stimulated the curriculum reforms in the 1960s (Duschl, 1990; Rudolph, 2002). Second, there was the 1980s economic crisis that stimulated the Standards movement and then a decade later the national assessments of annual cumulative progress. Finally, there is the current OECD countries' clarion warning calls of a waning STEM (science, technology, engineering and math) workforce that seeks to recruit students and teachers into STEM disciplines and to develop 21st-century skills for new and yet unknown products and services (NCEE, 2007; NRC, 2005).

Alongside the various agendas for national and global economic health and well-being there has been 50 plus years of basic and applied research on bringing psychology to bear on learning, learning environments and assessments. During this same 50-year period there has been a rethinking by philosophers of science about the nature of scientific inquiry (i.e., the practices and process of the growth of scientific knowledge).

In this chapter, we take up a review of the literature on science learning and teaching that is guided by the concomitant and ongoing developments in cognitive sciences and science studies begun during the second half of the 20th century. We have chosen to focus our review on a few salient topics that capture the vibrant debates and current challenges among researchers that have emerged when the study of science learning, science discourse and scientific inquiry is examined in contexts (e.g., conceptual, epistemological, and social), at different ages (e.g., pre-school, K-8, secondary, adult) and in various learning environments (e.g., formal and informal). Our choice of topics was guided by a set of recent policy reports and research synthesis reports on science learning and on STEM workforce initiatives:

- Australian Department of Education, Employment and Workplace Relations (2008). *Opening up pathways: Engagement in STEM across the primary-secondary school transition.*
- Carnegie Corporation of New York (2009). *The opportunity equation: transforming mathematics and science education for citizenship and the global economy.*
- Corcoran, Mosher, & Rogat (2009). *Learning progressions in science: An evidence-based approach to reform.* (Consortium for Policy Research in Education-CPRE).
- European Commission (2004). *Europe needs more scientists: report by the high level group on increasing human resources for science and technology.*
- European Commission (2007). *Science education now: A renewed pedagogy for the future of Europe.*
- National Center on Education and the Economy (2007). *Tough choices, tough times.*
- National Research Council (1999). *How people learn.*
- National Research Council (2001). *Knowing what students know: The science and design of educational assessment.*
- National Research Council (2005). *Systems for state science assessment.*
- National Research Council (2006). *Rising above the gathering storm.*
- National Research Council (2007). *Taking science to school: Learning and teaching science in grades K-8.*
- National Research Council (2009). *Learning science in informal environments: People, places, and pursuits.*
- Nuffield Foundation (2008). *Science education in Europe: critical reflections.*

The first topic we examine is the research on the knowledge and skills that young children bring to school, the results of which are shaping how we think about the learning and teaching of science and the design of learning environments. The second topic looks at research on the role of adaptive instruction and instruction-assisted development that argues for an alignment of curriculum, instruction and assessment to foster learning progressions. The third and final topic discussed is the domain-general vs. domain-specific perspectives debate of science learning and constructivism as a pedagogical framework. The review of research in these three topic domains is preceded by brief historical overviews of: (a) learning theory in science education; and (b) naturalized philosophical views about the nature of science, views that embrace cognitive and social exchange practices as key components of scientific inquiry.

HISTORICAL AND THEORETICAL OVERVIEW
Learning Theory in Science Education

There is a long and storied history of learning theory perspectives in science education. The most recent developments are presented in the Linn and Eylon (2006) science education chapter in the second edition of the *Handbook of Educational Psychology*. In developing an adequate picture of learning within a science education context, Linn and Eylon identify the contributions of developmental, socio-cultural, cognitive and constructivist theory and research. The picture that emerges is one in which there is not one best way to engage students in the learning of science but a need for a variety of principles which will engage all students in important aspects of knowledge integration. Linn and Eylon identify four interrelated processes of knowledge integration that need to be addressed in science learning context: (a) eliciting existing student ideas; (b) introduction of new normative ideas; (c) develop criteria to evaluate the scientific ideas students encounter; and (d) sort out new and current ideas using appropriate criteria. Linn and Eylon suggest that most approaches to knowledge integration within science education contexts have focused on the initial two processes and ignored the final two. They propose a set of design patterns that focus on specific instructional sequences (e.g., construct and argument, collaborate) that, when implemented, are aimed at ensuring that all-important aspects of knowledge integration are addressed during science instruction. Linn and Eylon indicate that future research needs to explore how these design patterns impact learning within domain specific science education contexts and to assess their value in ensuring knowledge integration.

Twenty years earlier, the White and Tisher (1986) science education chapter in the *Handbook of Teacher Education Research* had as its principal focus conceptual change learning environments and the competing perspectives between two science education research programs: (a) Piagetian domain-general stages view of cognitive development with an emphasis on concrete–abstract stages of reasoning; and (b) the information-processing/metacognitive view of cognitive development with an emphasis on prior knowledge and memory capacity. In the NSTA-sponsored *Handbook of Research on Science Teaching and Learning* (Gabel, 1994), the summary research reported on cognition and learning was parceled out into two sections: one on *Learning* and one on *Problem Solving*. The topics and paradigms within the chapters demonstrate the progress and the tensions operating then, and to some extent now as well, in research on science learning.

For example, the chapter by Lawson (1994) examined and used Piaget's process of equilibration to examine knowledge acquisition and to consider neurological mechanisms involved in learning and knowing. The focus for Lawson was strongly on the domain-general logical-mathematical reasoning constructs that guide deduction, induction, inference and analogy. In contrast, the second *Learning* chapter by Wandersee, Mintzes, and Novak (1994) examined the research on alternative conceptions in science with a strong focus on domain-specific characteristics of emergent knowledge claims. Here the review of research is grounded in Ausubel's (1963) meaningful learning theory and the bulk of the chapter examines the methodological practices for conducting research on children's science. The consideration of domain-general thinking about children's learning in science is the framework for the third *Learning* chapter that addressed the affective dimension of science (Simpson, Koballa, Oliver, & Crawley, 1994).

The *Problem Solving* chapters take up domain-specific research summaries in six contexts: elementary school (Barr, 1994), middle school (Helgeson, 1994), Earth science (Ault, 1994), genetics (Stewart & Hafner, 1994), chemistry (Gabel & Bunce, 1994), and physics (Maloney, 1994). Here we see a decisive turn, particularly in the Stewart and Hafner genetics chapter, toward domain-specific research in science education.

The trend toward domain-specific research in science education is further evidenced in the *International Handbook of Science Education* (Fraser & Tobin, 1998) section on *Learning*. The lead chapter by Duit and Treagust (1998) "Learning in Science—From Behaviourism Towards Social Constructivism and Beyond" provides a concise overview of 20th-century developments on views of learning in science education. The remaining seven chapters take up the role of language in science (Sutton, 1998), cultural aspects (Cobern & Aikenhead, 1998), models and modeling (Gilbert & Boulter, 1998), teaching that attends to students' informal conceptions (Scott & Driver, 1998), young children's inquiry reasoning (Metz, 1998), theories of knowledge acquisition (Chinn & Brewer, 1998) and students' epistemologies (Désautels & Larochelle, 1998).

Returning to the Linn and Eylon (2006) chapter, we find that many of the 1998 *International Handbook* topics persist, however, a wider variety of influential learning contexts have been identified and research has begun to assess their influence. Research on science learning appears to be moving away from a focus on general principles of learning science to a focus on the psychological, social, and cultural factors that influence the development of domain specific science knowledge. New images of science coupled with new images of learning have in rapid succession decade after decade led to a plethora of perspectives on precisely what the foundations of science education might be. Is it the epistemological framework of the scientific discipline? Is it the sociological contexts of the investigative communities? Is it the psychological mechanisms that govern thinking and reasoning? Or, is it the cultural contexts that shape what it is that is important to know and to do? Such epistemic, social, psychological, and cultural perspectives have spawned a wide array of frameworks, and debates, for conceptualizing science learning and teaching over the years. In parallel with the development of new frameworks and debates comes the development of research agendas and programs that are aimed at evaluating the contrasting frameworks and address the ensuing debates about the nature of effective science learning and related teaching (Tobias & Duffy, 2009).

Consider, for example, the recent discussions and debates in *Educational Psychologist* around minimally guided instruction being less effective than direct-guided instruction for science learning. On one side of the debate are theorists and researchers who indicate that the nature of our cognitive architecture (i.e., our need to search through and retrieve an incredibly large number of schema in long-term memory paired with a limited capacity working memory) support the need to retrieve knowledge efficiently and to develop usable knowledge through a directive and guided approach to science instruction. The thesis is that cognitive architecture and working memory theory dictate that instruction should be direct and explicit (Kirschner, Sweller, & Clark, 2006; Sweller, Kirschner, & Clark, 2007). In contrast, the other side of the debate focuses on the need for authenticity of the learning context and the need to situate the development of relevant science knowledge and skills within social and collaborative context which parallel the contexts within which scientific knowledge is developed and modified (Hmelo-Silver, Chinn, & Duncan, 2007, Kuhn, 2007; Schmidt, Lyens, van Gog, & Paas, 2007).

Next, consider, also from *Educational Psychologist*, the wide-ranging discussions in response to Geary's (2008) article on applying evolutionary psychology to education theory and practice. Geary's article makes an important distinction between primary "core" knowledge that we have evolved to acquire and secondary knowledge that is culturally sanctioned, taught in schools but which we have not evolved to acquire. An example of primary "core" knowledge is the biological causal device of vitalism (i.e., bodily processes are meant to sustain life by taking in and exchanging vital force, such as a substance, energy or information; Inagaki & Hatano, 2006). An example of a secondary knowledge is the Arabic numeral system (Spelke, 2000). Geary (2008) suggests that although there has been much research on documenting the primary knowledge of young children (see later discussion), there is a need to identify how these primary core understandings influence the development of related secondary knowledge.

Relevant to but not directly related to this issue is the emerging perspective on learning progressions research (Corcoran, Mosher, & Rogat, 2009; Duncan & Hmelo-Silver, 2009). Learning progressions, discussed more thoroughly in a separate section, are strategically developed cycles of activities that aim to engage learners in successively more sophisticated ways of thinking about an idea that build on one another as the students move through an area or domain (Smith, Wiser, Anderson, & Krajcik, 2006). As an example, with respect to the concept of "natural selection," the progression would begin by focusing on activities aimed at developing students' ability to identify and represent mathematically "variation," then present activities that will help students develop the capability to generate hypotheses aimed at identifying the function of traits and link this to explanations of variation, and then engage them in activities aimed at supporting the development skills and knowledge underlying the ability to generate predictions of how variation of a particular trait will support the survival of individuals (Reiser, Krajcik, Moje, & Marx, 2003).

Finally, consider the current conversations in educational psychology for consilience around competing learning theories (e.g., Alexander, Schallert, & Reynolds, 2009). Here the proposal is to frame learning around a set of nine domain-general content independent principles:

- Principle 1 Learning is change.
- Principle 2 Learning is inevitable, essential, and ubiquitous.
- Principle 3 Learning can be resisted.
- Principle 4 Learning may be disadvantageous.
- Principle 5 Learning can be tacit and incidental as well as conscious and intentional.
- Principle 6 Learning is framed by our humanness.
- Principle 7 Learning refers to both a process and a product.
- Principle 8 Learning is different at different points in time.
- Principle 9 Learning is interactional.

These principles attempt to identify the essence of learning at a level that gives it the power to take an inclusive view of learning theories and related research in order to contribute to our broader knowledge of learning and the implications for practice. The focus on change, whether a change in behavior, attitudes, beliefs, knowledge, and whether one is intentionally trying to change, changing unconsciously or resisting change allows for discussion of a wide range of types and kinds of learning. Learning is also identified as inevitable and essential in that all humans learn and that they are required to learn if they are to survive. However, it is also noted that the outcome of learning may not always be appropriate or positive either for the individual or for those surrounding the individual. The "humanness" of learning highlights that what we learn and how we learn are influenced by evolution in the same way as other aspects of our biological selves. The last three principles focus on the dynamic aspects of learning in that, given that learning is a change, it has a time course and a trajectory that require that we consider both the route and nature of change (process) as well as the end product of the change in any explanation of learning. In addition, the factors that influence the route and nature of change will be different depending on the developmental and experiential level of the learning, as well as the products of ongoing and previous learning. That learning is interactional underscores the dynamic quality of learning in which the characteristics of the learner (who), the learning environment (where), the timing and the nature of learning (when) come together to influence what is learned.

The synthesis research report on science learning *Taking Science to School* (TSTS; NRC, 2007) takes a very different tack from domain-general principles by recommending that science learning be organized around select conceptual knowledge frameworks and practices that, in turn, are coordinated around core content and learning progressions. What the current research in cognitive development and philosophy of mind suggests is that very young children have a surprising capacity for reasoning and prior knowledge in select domains (Keil, 1989; Subrhmanyam, Gelman, & Lafosse, 2002). The current research on cognitive development and reasoning in science also demonstrates that context matters both in terms of content, learning environment, and learning goals (Atran, 2002; Koslowski, & Thompson, 2002; Siegal, 2002). That is, learning is linked to the domain within which learning is taking place and dependent on the acquisition of select practices and ways of representing and communicating science ideas and critiques. Consequently, *core knowledge* learning and *learning progressions* designs for the alignment of curriculum, instruction and assessment are seen as robust areas for future science learning research.

Embedding research on science learning within specific contexts has produced valuable insights into pathways or trajectories of learning in the disciplines (Catley, Lehrer, & Reiser, 2005; Smith et al., 2006). The research on learning in contexts challenges many of the *received views* of child and adolescent science learning, views that assume that development involves broad mental structures that facilitate mastery of a variety of tasks. These domain-general learning mechanisms are seen to support concept acquisition across a variety of domains (Gelman & Brenneman, 2004).

THE NATURALISTIC TURN IN PHILOSOPHY OF SCIENCE

Educational, cognitive and developmental psychology are not the only domains where cognitive and social dynamics of learning are taking hold. Ideas from interdisciplinary research communities labeled *learning sciences* and *science studies* are extending our understandings of science learning, science practices, scientific knowledge, and scientific discourse (Duschl, 2008; Duschl & Grandy, 2008). New views in philosophy of science and more broadly in the set of disciplines that comprise science studies have adopted cognitive and social frameworks to understand the growth of knowledge.

Consider the following core questions posed by Carruthers, Stich, and Siegal (2002) from an edited volume examining *The cognitive basis of science*: "[W]hat makes science possible? Specifically, what features of the human mind, of human cognitive development and of human social arrangements permit and facilitate the conduct of science?" (p. 1) The editors go on to state that such questions are interdisciplinary in nature thus "requiring co-operation between philosophers, psychologists, and others in the social and cognitive sciences [and] as much about the psychological underpinnings of science as they are about science itself" (p. 1).

Cognitive, historical, sociological, and anthropological studies of individuals working in knowledge-building contexts reveal the importance of practices to the professional activities in these knowledge-growth communities. With respect to the scientific disciplines, cognitive models of science (Giere, 1988; Goldman, 1986; Kitcher, 1993; Thagard, 1992) coupled with sociocultural models of science (Knorr-Cetina, 1999; Kuhn, 1996; Longino, 1990, 2002) have established the importance that models and modeling, visual representations, knowledge exchange mechanisms and peer interactions have in the advancement and refinement of knowledge and in the growth of scientific knowledge. In brief, doing science takes place in complex settings of cognitive, epistemic and social practices.

Science learning when viewed generally as the growth of knowledge has many parallels with scientific inquiry among scientists as a set of knowledge building and refining activities and practices. These activities and practices progress from experiments on to models and then to explanatory theories. Models are seen as cognitive tools that sit between experiments and theory (Giere, 1988, 2002; Nersessian, 2002, 2008). What has come to gain traction is the view of science and science learning as fundamentally a model building and refining enterprise. The synthesis research report *Taking Science to School* (NRC, 2007) takes the position that the teaching and learning of science should be based on an image of science that sees the growth of knowledge as involving the following epistemic and social practices:

1. building theories and models;
2. constructing arguments;
3. using specialized ways of talking, writing and representing phenomena.

This tripartite perspective on school science reflects a synthesis of ideas about the growth of knowledge and the nature of scientific reasoning taken from the learning sciences community and from the science studies community. While it is well beyond the scope of this chapter to delve into a thorough accounting of developments in philosophy of science, philosophy of mind, and developmental psychology, a brief overview is needed to understand the emergent view of science learning/reasoning and recommendations for research on science learning/reasoning found in *Taking Science to School*. For a concise and yet thorough introduction, from which this overview draws, interested readers should refer to Chapter 1 of *The Cognitive Basis of Science* (Carruthers et al., 2002). Godfrey-Smith (2003) also provides an effective introduction to the naturalized view of the philosophy of science. A good overview source for the learning sciences is the Introduction chapter to *The Cambridge Handbook of the Learning Sciences* (Sawyer, 2006).

The learning sciences emerged from the earlier constructivist theories of learning and from the pioneering research in the cognitive sciences. Our deeper understanding of how children's thinking is fundamentally different from that of adults coupled with richer understandings of expertise, representation, reflection, problem solving and thinking provided a foundation for a major tenet of the learning sciences; "students learn deeper knowledge when they engage in activities that are similar to the everyday activities of professionals who work in a discipline" (Sawyer, 2006, p. 4). This perspective on the importance of activities is also found in the critiques of logical positivism:

> [P]hilosophy of science had been conducted in a relatively *a priori* fashion . . . with philosophers of science just thinking about what scientists *ought* to do, rather than about what they actually *do* do. This all began to change in the 1960s and 1970s, when philosophy of science took is so-called "historical turn."
>
> (Carruthers et al., 2002, p. 3; emphasis in the original)

During the *historical turn* of philosophy of science that began with the work of Kuhn (1996), Feyerabend (1970), and Lakatos (1970), a concurrent development in philosophy—epistemology, philosophy of mind, philosophy of science—was the *naturalistic turn*. Here, philosophers started to realize that any attempts to account for the growth of scientific knowledge or theory change needed to view science inquiry through the natural human mental processes and human modes of acquiring knowledge. This philosophical perspective aligns somewhat with research on informal learning that reveals the importance of participation structures and the development of practices in culturally valued activities (Cole, 1996; NRC, 2009). Focusing on scaffolding, apprenticeship, legitimate peripheral participation and guided participation, informal learning researchers provided "broader units of analysis . . . these views move beyond the study of individuals alone to consider how learning occurs within enduring social groups such as families and communities" (Bransford et al., 2006, p. 24).

A strong tradition in psychological research on science learning is to frame learning in terms of knowledge as distinct from beliefs with beliefs here to imply values. Another tradition in psychology is to separate the learning of content (e.g., conceptual knowledge) from the learning of skills, practices, and processes. The philosophical tradition for the growth of scientific knowledge, on the other hand, does not separate knowledge and belief (Duschl, Hamilton, & Grandy, 1993), beliefs are explanatory claims about nature. Contemporary philosophical accounts of the growth of scientific knowledge (e.g., Knorr-Cetina's (1999) epistemic cultures) have adopted naturalistic accounts to explain the emergence of new conceptual (what we know), methodological (how we know), and epistemological (why we believe) criteria or standards for the growth of scientific knowledge and the mechanisms of scientific reasoning.

> It became important, then, to see science, too, as a natural phenomenon, somehow recruiting a variety of natural processes and mechanisms–both cognitive and social–to achieve its results. Philosophers of science began to look, not just to history, but also to cognitive psychology in their search for an understanding of scientific activity.
>
> (Carruthers et al., 2002, p. 4)

Grounded strongly in perspectives from philosophy of science, philosophy of mind, and developmental psychology, the interdisciplinary approach to understanding science learning, knowing, and doing has established in no uncertain terms that learning, cognition and reasoning are contingent on context and content. Twentieth-century interdisciplinary efforts in understanding science and science learning contributed to developments in both our understandings of science learning and our understandings of doing science.

In summary, having students' image of science as a learning goal is not about establishing a process of science as seeking justified true beliefs but rather it requires pursuing rational beliefs and explanatory coherence that are influenced and shaped by new tools, instruments, theories, and methods. The strong recommendation from *Taking Science to School* is the teaching of conceptual knowledge should not be independent of learning science practices. In short, our understandings of the growth of scientific knowledge and scientific reasoning are grounded both philosophically and psychologically (Carruthers et al., 2002). Each domain has contributed to our understandings about *learning how to learn*; a phrase, interestingly, used both about the nature and growth of science knowledge (Shapere, 1982) and about the nature and development of science learning (Novak, 1977). The emerging consensus is that science learning and teaching ought to be grounded in and informed by conceptual, epistemological, and social structures and practices. Within science education, changes in our understandings of what is science—the nature of science—have influenced our understandings of what's involved in learning and doing science. Conversely, our understandings of what's involved in learning and doing science have influenced our understandings about the nature of science.

CURRENT ISSUES AND TRENDS

The following sections discuss three current issues or trends in theory and research on science learning in which there is much potential for identifying factors that impact the learning of science as well as identifying gaps and possible future directions for expanding our knowledge of both learning and the learning of science. These three issues/trends are theory and research on core knowledge and theory of mind, learning progressions, and domain-specific and domain-general learning frameworks.

Following the tenet of current cognitive psychological theory—that it is easier to learn more about what one already knows—documenting what children come to school with is critically important. There is much research that has focused on describing the knowledge and skills of pre-school children, particularly within the areas of simple mechanics of solid bounded objects, behaviors of psychological agents, actions and organization of living things, and makeup and substance of materials. Charting the course of development of children's conceptions and skills within these areas is critically important to better understanding the nature of learning within science as well as the influence of specific contexts on their development.

As indicated earlier and developed below, learning progressions are strategically developed cycles of instructional activities which aim to engage learners in successively more sophisticated ways of knowing and thinking about an idea that build on one another as the students moves through an area or domain (Smith et al., 2006). The application of learning progressions within the area of science learning is a natural outgrowth of current views of learning that focus on the importance of epistemic and social influences on learning and development. Learning progressions represents a shift in emphasis from teaching that focuses on what we know (e.g., facts and skills) to teaching that focuses on how did we come to know and develop scientific knowledge and on why we believe what we know over alternatives. This in turn balances the thrust and focus of research on science learning to include not only the acquisition of science content but also to focus on the practices of science. Hence an important expansion of the focus of theory and research on science learning needs to be an understanding of how students learn the practice of science (e.g., building and refining theories and models, formulating and refining useful scientific questions, evaluating competing claims, generating and evaluating relevant evidence). Relevant to this issue are the tensions that are created by different learning goals and outcomes and the best approach (i.e., a domain-general approach versus a domain-specific approach) by which to advance the specific learning goals and outcomes.

Core Knowledge—What Children Bring to School

The *TSTS* report (NRC, 2007) includes a research review on infant and young children's cognitive capacities to address the guiding question: What do children bring to school? As documented in recent reviews of research on the capabilities of elementary school children, many of these children are able to think in abstract terms, make sense of their world through creating intuitive models or theories, and can engage in experimentation to develop their ideas (Metz, 1995).

As part of a research program aimed at documenting pre-school biological conceptions, Godfried and Gelman (2005) performed two studies to investigate children's knowledge of internal parts within living and non-living things and their potential involvement in immanent causes for their behaviors. An example of an immanent cause is vital energy that is somehow generated by and emanates from a living thing. Previous research has suggested that pre-school children endorse abstract immanent causes such as the living thing moved by itself, however, there has not been much research to link conceptions of vital energy to causing movement and/or growth in pre-school children. In Study 1, participants included pre-school children in three separate age groups, 3-, 4-, and 5-year-olds. Each participant was asked questions about what was inside objects presented in photos and were also asked to match photos of possible internal structures of either animals, plants, or machines. The experimental materials consisted of 12 target photos of four animals (eland, tapir, pacarana, cavy), four plants (fern, moss, water lily, liverwort), and four machines (espresso maker, intercom, mini-TV, electric razor). The match-to-sample items included four-color photographs of animal insides (i.e., brain, bones, muscles, heart), four of plant insides (i.e., cross-section of banana plant, cellular structure of blade of grass, cross-section of wood, plant cells), and four of machine insides (i.e., circuit board, batteries, wires, gears). The results showed that domain-specific knowledge of internal parts develops between ages 3 and 4.

In Study 2, using similar materials as employed in Study 1, participants (4-year-olds, 8-year-olds, and adults) were asked yes or no questions about the relation between the specific internal parts, their insides, or energy to either move, sit, or grow. Participants were also asked to justify their answers. Results showed that pre-schoolers did not endorse internal parts as causally responsible for familiar biological events (e.g., movement, growth). Pre-schoolers, however, were able to attribute an abstract cause (vital energy) for the movement of animals but not for machines. These latter results mirrored the results found for adults and older children. In summary, the results suggest that children recognize domain-specific internal parts as early as age 4 but that their causal attributions are not yet linked to a detailed biological system.

When development or learning is stalled because of cognitive complexity or the need for abstract reasoning, thoughtful and informed curriculum designs and effective mediation on the part of teachers and peers can move learners forward. Research on instruction-assisted development (e.g., Lehrer, Schauble, & Lucas, 2008; Metz, 2008) is discussed in learning progression and design of learning environments sections. In addition, researchers are learning that young children are capable of complex reasoning when children are provided with multiple opportunities that sustain their engagement with select scientific practices over time such as predicting, observing, testing, measuring, counting, recording, collaborating, and communicating (Carey, 2004; Gelman & Brenneman, 2004; Gopnik et al., 2004; Hapgood, Magnusson, & Palincsar, 2004; Metz, 2004; Spelke, 2000). Hapgood et al. (2004) documented how a targeted curriculum and pedagogy were used to create a learning community in which second grade children were engaged in investigations of scientific relations such as mass and speed. Within this learning community, the children were supported and held responsible for generating and testing their knowledge claims.

In the course of instruction, the children and the teacher participated in two forms of investigation in which children were: (a) directly exploring the physical world by manipulating variables in phenomena, making observations and measurements, and drawing conclusions about how the target variables are related (e.g., mass and momentum); and (b) asking other children about their investigations and using text-based resources to compare their own and other children's interpretations of the target relations.

In order to document teacher and student classroom behaviors: (a) all whole-class instruction and most small-group and individual writing activity were videotaped; and (b) student-generated texts in response to classroom activities and tasks were collected. These texts included students' assertions about the nature of "motion" as they engaged in both types of classroom investigations, data tables and records, records of children's predictions for various situations, publicly displayed records of children's ideas about the investigations, and children's' responses to five writing prompts (given to them by their teacher) in their journals. Finally, paper and pencil pre- and post-tests were administered that focused on the children's knowledge of those factors that influenced the motion of balls down inclined planes. All videotapes were analyzed to create a detailed account of the activities in which the class was engaged. Student texts were entered into a database and organized so that one could look at changes within individual children's entries as well as across all students' entries for a specific date and within set time periods.

Hapgood et al. (2004) used videotapes and student texts to document that the children in the class were able to use data as evidence to support their claims regarding the target relations regarding "motion," evaluate approaches to assessing knowledge claims (e.g., experiments, discussion with other students, seek out relevant text), and use and understand multiple forms of representing data and claims (e.g., tables, diagrams, text). These practices required that the children engage in complex reasoning which are integral to scientific inquiry.

By the time young children enter school, they already possess a surprising amount of capability to reason about the natural and social world. For example, they appear to be sensitive to a variety of high-level causal and relational patterns that are particularly useful for reasoning about living things (Inagaki & Hatano, 2006). Inagaki and Hatono (2002) in their experiments with 5-year-olds have found that children of this age, when instructed to compare animals and plants by analogy, were able to recognize similarities between animals and plants in terms of their reliance on food and water, respectively. That is, by using their rich knowledge of humans, they could make human-based inferences when asked about other living things.

This knowledge is more robust for some areas than others, such as naïve biology (e.g., Inagaki & Hatano, 2006; Keil, 2003), naïve psychology (e.g., Wimmer & Perner, 1983), and naïve physics (e.g., Baillargeon, 2004). Underpinning these nascent understandings are several core knowledge systems that serve as the foundations upon which novel knowledge, skills, and beliefs are built (Spelke & Kinzler, 2007). These core knowledge systems appear to be innate and common to both human infants and some other primate animals, and have been shown to represent mechanical interactions between inanimate objects, goal-directed actions of animate objects, numerical relationships and ordering, and geometric relations and spatial layout (Spelke, 2000). An additional system for representing social relationships has recently been proposed as well (Spelke & Kinzler, 2007).

Several studies suggest that even preverbal infants have a sense of mechanism and causality. In some of these studies (Baillargeon, 2004), infants were shown a toy resting at the bottom of a ramp. A cylinder is then rolled down the ramp hitting the toy at the bottom. Using eye-tracking and eye-gazing methods researchers have shown that infants as young as 8 months old correctly understand that a larger cylinder will move the toy farther away from the ramp. These infants can also understand that a barrier between the toy and the ramp would block the rolling cylinder and that the toy would not move. Thus, awareness of cause and effect, including the relation between magnitude of action and magnitude of effect, emerges very early on.

This early sense of cause and effect develops further during the pre-school years. In several studies, Gopnick and colleagues (Gopnik & Sobel, 2000; Gopnik, Sobel, Schulz, & Glymour, 2001) showed young children a setup of multiple toy blocks, some of which were categorized as being "blickets," and a contraption that can detect blickets ("blicket detector"). The young subjects were asked to identify the blicket blocks either by allowing them to experiment themselves or by having them observe a researcher place blocks (one or more at a time) on the blicket detector (without being told which are blickets). Gopnik and her colleagues found that even 2-year-olds could draw appropriate conclusions about causality and covariation by observing contingency patterns as blocks were placed on the detector by the researcher. Pre-schoolers in these studies were able to infer causality in complex situations involving multiple causes and probabilistic causality (Gopnick et al., 2001). Reasoning about causal mechanisms is a core aspect of scientific practice and scientific explanations as exemplified by the second proficiency advocated by the *TSTS* report (generate and evaluate scientific evidence and explanations). Thus, young children can reason about causal mechanisms even before formal schooling begins. Carefully planned and mediated instruction at the kindergarten and early grades can capitalize on these abilities and continue to develop them further (Gelman & Brenneman, 2004).

The Preschool Pathways to Science (PrePS©), a science and mathematics program for pre-K children developed by Rochel Gelman and her colleagues (Gelman & Brenneman, 2004), is an example of a theory-based curriculum that builds on young learners emerging scientific understanding. In this program the teachers introduce the language and ideas of *observe*, *predict*, and *check*, early on in the year (during separate circle time sessions). Children then use their five senses to observe phenomena and objects such as an apple while the teacher records these observations on a publicly displayed chart. Using prior knowledge children then predict what they cannot observe—what is inside the apple—and their ideas are recorded using drawings and labels. By cutting the apple, and examining the inside, children can then check their recorded predictions against the available data. The practices of observe, predict, and check are repeatedly used throughout the year and serve as a framework for thinking and talking about the natural world in scientific ways. Social learning and language play an important role in supporting the development of these ideas and their meaning in context. Tools, such as magnifying glasses, are made available through the day for children to practice their scientific skills of observing, predicting and recording.

The interplay between engaging in science practice and developing understandings of science content allows the learning to spiral as skills and practices are applied to familiar content supporting the development of new knowledge. The PrePS© curriculum takes place over multiple months and is centered on core concepts, or big ideas, in domains that young children already have some substantive experience with and thus already possess some relevant knowledge about (such as insides and outsides of objects, form and function, systems and interactions). Over an extended period, young children engage with different experiences, encompassing different topics that are related to the core concepts. This instructional structure provides multiple entry points for learners and strengthens connections between prior knowledge and new knowledge thus aiding in the development of more robust understandings of the central ideas (Gelman & Lucariello, 2002). Similar understandings are not present when curricula cover multiple disconnected topics over short amounts of time (Winnett, Rockwell, Sherwood, & Williams, 1996). Thus, the PrePS© focus is on deepening students' understanding of a few core ideas over time. In this way the curriculum covers dramatically fewer concepts but covers those in much more depth thereby contributing to the *TSTS* 4th scientific proficiency—using specialized ways to talk, write, and represent phenomena.

A key finding from Gelman's work within this setting is that children may be capable of scientific thinking far more complex than most casual observers might expect, and that scholars such as Piaget had considered possible (e.g., successfully distinguish between the real and non-real animals and between those that could or could not move on their own power). Although the anecdotal evidence suggests that the PrePS© curriculum is having a positive impact on pre-school children's development of science knowledge, no independent assessments have been performed to assess the value and impact of the curriculum.

Along with an emergent understanding of physical mechanism and causal interactions, infants and young children have knowledge of social interactions (Spelke & Kinzler, 2007) that develops into a theory of mind later in childhood (Perner, Leekam, & Wimmer, 1987; Wellman, 1990). Infants are very much aware of differences between animate and inanimate objects. They assume different qualities and attribute different interpretations to the actions of people and other organisms as opposed to inanimate objects (Spelke, Phillips, & Woodward, 1995). Infants interpret human actions as goal-directed, reciprocal, and contingent (Spelke & Kinzler, 2007). For example, 12-month-old infants will follow the "gaze" of an object, if the object had earlier responded to the vocalizations of the infant and thus is assumed to be animate (Johnson, Slaughter, & Carey, 1998). While surprised if shown two cylinders acting on each other at a distance, infants are not surprised to see people acting on each other at a distance (Spelke et al.,

1995). At infancy, the stage is set for the development of a more sophisticated theory of mind during the pre-school years.

Before the age of 3, most pre-schoolers assume that others have the same thoughts and knowledge as they do. At this stage they are unaware that other individuals possess minds that are different than their own. A theory of mind, the idea that others may think and believe differently, emerges around the age of 3 and at this point pre-schoolers are able to understand that others may have false beliefs, that is believe something that is at odds with reality (or at least the child's perception of reality). The notion of false belief is tested through the Sally-Anne task (Wimmer & Perner, 1983) in which a child is shown a doll, Sally, placing an object in a certain place (marble in basket); the doll is then removed and another doll, Anne, moves the object to a new location. The child is asked where the marble is, and to predict where Sally will look for the marble. Children who possess a notion of false belief will correctly predict that Sally will search in the old location even though the child knows the sought-after object is not there. By the age of 5, most pre-schoolers are aware that others may have different beliefs and ideas and that these can be at odds with reality (Wimmer & Perner, 1983).

An individual's theory of mind is a critical precursor to several aspects of their scientific reasoning. A theory of mind affords the understanding that knowledge can be subjective and people may have different interpretations of natural phenomena. This is relevant in grasping the revisionary nature of scientific knowledge and the existence of alternative models for explaining a phenomenon. It follows that in order to engage in scientific argumentation (a core practice we would like students to master), children need to have a theory of mind and notion of false belief that allows them to assume that explanations vary and that explanations may be more or less accurate depictions of a the phenomenon in question. There is clear need to investigate the link between the development of children's theory of mind and their ability to act on and benefit from engaging in modeling phenomena and arguing about alternative models and theories (NRC, 2007). It also follows that if learning environments do not present science as a theory-building or model-building enterprise with a specialized way of talking, writing, and representing ideas, then these innate abilities may fade away (Gopnik, 1996).

Let us now turn to children's capacities for representation and the ways in which this practice can also serve as a foundation for model building in science. In many respects, children's engagements in pretend play, in which one object stands in for another (a spoon for a rocket), is a beginning notion of symbolism—one thing can represent another. Early understandings of words as representing objects or actions are also indicative of emerging symbolic capacities. Engagement with measurement and data representation can be introduced early on as the PrePS© curriculum (Gelman & Brenneman, 2004) demonstrates. Pre-school children can sort objects based on size, color, shape, or other features and then be guided to display this information in the form of lists, tables and simple graphs. Children can compare measurements, for example, shoe size and height of children in different classes (and ages), as well as chart growth in these quantities over time (Gelman & Brenneman, 2004). Understandings about counting, measuring, and illustrating patterns provide a necessary foundation for developing more sophisticated notions of descriptive statistics and data modeling that can be introduced in formal schooling.

Research on elementary students' ability to measure and represent data suggests that young children can engage in productive discussions about aspects of an object to measure (e.g., how would one measure plant growth?) and how these data should be graphically represented (Lehrer, Jaslow, & Curtis, 2003; Lehrer & Schauble, 2000a, 2000b, 2002). Lehrer and Schauble (2004) employed a design study approach to investigating the development of student understanding of natural variation through learning and reasoning about the statistical concept of distribution in a data-modeling context. The focus of the research was to document the learning of students' understanding of variation when the students are exposed to good but not extraordinary instructional experiences. In order to facilitate fifth grade students' understanding of variation, students engaged in a series of activities focused on taking responsibility for the growing of batches of native plants and attempting to find out how the plants would change over time and be influenced by different growth conditions. Over a two-month period, students' reasoning related to and understanding of the concept of "distribution" and "natural variation" significantly improved through their experiences in generating, evaluating, and revising models of data recorded on the growth of these native plants. The students' invented and teacher-guided representations of data served as a focus for discussions about simple statistical qualities of data, as well as the values of different forms of representations for illustrating different features of data patterns (Lehrer & Schauble, 2004).

The extensive research on infants' and young children's cognitive development underscores the multitude of knowledge resources and reasoning capabilities children bring to formal schooling. Young learners are anything but empty minds. They are, within effective instructional conditions (Lehrer & Schauble, 2002), capable of noticing patterns and attributes in the natural world, linking the patterns and attributes to science concepts, developing explanations of natural phenomena, and reasoning about abstract ideas in meaningful and productive ways.

Whether or not we choose to capitalize on children's emerging scientific reasoning abilities and further develop them depends on how we construe the goals of science learning and how such learning outcomes can be achieved. A focus on understanding the doing of science and how scientific knowledge is developed and evaluated will entail building on students' emerging capacities for representation, model-building, casual reasoning, and the like. If the focus of science education is on the accumulation of scientific facts, then it is not clear how one might capitalize on the emerging understandings we describe in this section. We, of course, argue for a science education focus on the practices and discourse of scientific theory-building; and with such a perspective it is clear that students bring significant conceptual resources that can, and should be, used as a leverage for developing more sophisticated understandings of the scientific enterprise throughout schooling.

Learning Progressions and Pathways

In the introduction to a *Journal of Research in Science Teaching* special issue on Learning Progressions, Duncan and Hmelo-Silver (2009) correctly remind readers that Learning Progressions, henceforth LPs, by their very nature are hypothetical; they are conjectural models of learning over time that need to be empirically validated. There is some consensus (Corcoran, Mosher, & Rogat, 2009) that four features characterize LPs:

1. Targeting core and generative disciplinary understandings and practices that merges science content with science practices.

2. Lower and upper boundaries that describe entry assumptions and exiting expectations for knowing and doing.
3. Descriptions of LPs that inform progress levels or steps of achievement.
4. Purposeful curriculum and instruction that mediate targeted student outcomes.

The recommendation for LPs represents a shift in emphasis from teaching that focuses on what we know (e.g., facts and skills) to teaching that focuses on how did we come to know and develop scientific knowledge and on why we believe what we know over alternatives. The emphasis on how and why reflects the *Taking Science to School* (NRC, 2007) recommendation that science learning needs to be strongly grounded in the use and consideration of evidence. This, in turn, leads to the recommendation that science learning be connected through longer sequences of instruction (e.g., immersion units; LPs) that function vertically across and horizontally within months and years of instruction. The rationale is to facilitate the learning of core science knowledge and practices that are critical for development of scientific knowledge and of the reasoning inherent in the four strands of proficiency. Developing rich, conceptual knowledge takes time and requires instructional support via sound assessment practices. The content of the LPs is the core conceptual knowledge as well as the epistemic practices (e.g., science talk and argumentation) and social practices (e.g., critique, communication, and representation) that characterize a domain of scientific inquiry:

> The core concepts used in this practice [learning progressions] would be dramatically fewer in number than those currently focused on or included in standards and curriculum documents . . . a grade-level teacher would need to be concerned not only with the relevant "slice" of a given core idea in her particular grade, but also with the longer continuum of learning that K-8 students experience. Thus, teachers and science teacher educators . . . would need to build structures and social processes to support the exchange of knowledge and information related to core concepts across grade levels.
>
> (NRC, 2007, p. 61)

The LPs approach to the design and alignment of curriculum, instruction, and assessment is grounded in domain-specific or core knowledge theories of cognitive development and learning as documented in recent National Research Council reports (NRC 1999, 2001, 2007). The emerging notion is for LPs at the K-8 grades to be built around the most generative and core ideas that are central to the discipline of science and that support students' science learning. Additionally, the core ideas should be accessible to students in kindergarten and have the potential for sustained exploration across K-8 (NRC, 2007).

An examination of school curriculum, as stated above, reveals disconnected and isolated units of instruction to be the norm in K-8 science education (NRC, 2007). An examination of the growth of scientific knowledge as provided by longitudinal studies around LPs (Corcoran et al., 2009) and by science studies scholars (Nersessian, 2008) can provide some helpful insights on how to proceed with the redesign agenda.

Corcoran and Silander (2009) conducted a review that examined the effects on high school student learning of instructional strategies. The strategies included interdisciplinary teaching, cooperative learning, problem-based learning, adaptive instruction, inquiry and dialogic teaching. The results found that well-designed student grouping strategies, allowing students to express their ideas and questions, and offering students challenging tasks were powerful strategies for advancing student learning. In addition, adaptive instruction in which teachers monitor how students vary in what they are learning and adapt their instruction in response to students' progress and needs was found to be a strong factor that supports student learning.

> We believe that a research and development program that emphasizes adaptive instruction is essential as it has the greatest potential for improving the efficacy of instruction in today's standards-based policy environment. New applications of technology are making adaptive instruction feasible even in situations where teachers have to deal with large numbers of students, and applications of cognitive science to the development of online learning opportunities . . . may redefine and enhance the power of adaptive instruction. Admittedly, the evidence supporting the effectiveness of adaptive instruction is weak at this point, but the theoretical argument is persuasive, and we believe adaptive instruction can be combined with student teaming, discussion methods, and even project-based learning to create more powerful pedagogies.
>
> (p. 177)

One promising context for adaptive instruction is LPs. The Corcoran et al. (2009) synthesis report is of several workshops that included a group of experts exploring LPs and looking at two questions: "What promise might LPs have for improving instruction in schools?" and "What further might be required to make the promise real?" LPs are seen as empirically grounded and testable hypotheses about how students' understandings of and abilities to use core ideas grow and become more sophisticated over time. A key component of LPs is the notion of instruction-assisted development that, like adaptive instruction, is grounded in robust learning performances (Wilson, 2009) that serve as "assessments for learning" (Black & Wiliam, 1998). The hypotheses represent pathways of learning that are based on research of students' progress, like the well-researched learning pathway on matter and the atomic molecular theory (Smith, Carey, & Wiser, 1985; Smith et al., 2006). The extant alternative is the selection of topics and sequences based on a logical analysis of content domains and personal experiences with teaching (e.g., the American Association for the Advancement of Science (2001) *Atlas of Science Literacy* and the scope and sequence curriculum frameworks common in national, state, and local school districts).

The report by Corcoran et al. (2009) states "progressions can play a central role in supporting the needed shift toward adaptive instruction" (p. 9) and that the following are seen as possible learning outcome benefits of establishing LPs:

- providing a basis for setting standards that are tighter and more clearly tied to instruction;
- providing reference points for assessment to report on levels of progress and thereby facilitate teacher interventions and instruction-assisted development;
- informing the design of curricula that are aligned with progressing students (e.g., assessments for learning).

However, they also caution that while some promising efforts exist in select science domains and practices, the work is just beginning to produce valid and reliable evidence on the usefulness of progressions. A larger issue concerns whether progressions around core ideas and scientific practices are a potential alternative to standards. As we contemplate LPs as an approach to the organization and alignment of science learning, Schauble (2008) cautions that while we certainly want to answer the question "Where does reasoning and learning come from?", we must also ask "Where is reasoning going" and, "What conditions support productive change?"

> Answers to the first question help us better understand the foundation on which further development can build. Answers to the second provide a sense of developmental trajectory, or more likely, trajectories. What characteristic changes are coming up? What pathways of change are usually observed? And answers to the third question focus on how those changes can get supported in a productive way.

> (p. 51)

Two LPs research projects, one by Kathleen Metz and one by Richard Lehrer and Leona Schabule, provide insights on how instruction-assisted development can inform adaptive instruction strategies. Metz (2008) reports on two curriculum-based studies with first graders, one in botany research on plant growth and one in animal behavior on crickets. The first grade students' engagements in knowledge-building practices are based on curricula scaffolded around seven interrelated features that support engagement in science practices:

1. immersion in strategically selected scientific domains;
2. centrality of big ideas in the practices;
3. entwining of content and process;
4. centrality of curiosity as a drive for doing science;
5. discovery and explanation as top level goals;
6. challenge of making sense of the ill-structured; and
7. the social nature of scientific knowledge-building practices.

The initial versions of the curricula that demonstrated that children can design investigations around researchable questions and cope with uncertainty were designed and used successfully across several elementary grade levels (Metz, 2004). The first grade vignettes draw from beginning, mid-point, and end of curriculum reports on the ways the deepening of knowledge supports thinking and contributes to increased accountability.

Another example of a study of instruction-assisted development is that by Lehrer et al. (2008). They engaged 6th grade students in school year-long pond studies. A part of the instruction had students design and build models of ponds in gallon jars. This provided a basis for studying questions the students had about the ponds. Lehrer et al. report that unintended outcomes like algae blooms and bacteria colonies afforded opportunities to examine how ecosystems function. Subsequent efforts to model the pond ecologies were supported by weekly research meetings. Here students would exchange ideas and discuss relations between evidence and explanations. The struggles students had with the material design of the jar-ponds were found by the researchers to foster pedagogy of inquiry.

End-of-year interviews with students were conducted to assess understandings about ecology and research design and beliefs about epistemology of inquiry. To get at views about the nature of inquiry, interviewers asked students to contrast the extended inquiry on ponds with kit-based science. The researchers found that the weekly research meetings were a major influence on students' views about the nature of inquiry. Also, students reported that the repeated efforts and struggles to make the jar-ponds work was preferred over the clearer outcomes found in kits. Such a finding has important implications for research on motivating students to engage in science and build identities in science (Blumenfeld et al., 2006). Another finding from the pond study—students developing model-based views of inquiry "in which collective practice and authority are intertwined with individual agency" (p. 17)—challenges current research findings on teaching and learning about the nature of science and on epistemic cognition. Namely, the absolutist views (Driver, Leach, Millar, & Scott, 1996; Lederman, 1992) students and teachers have about the nature of science and the absence of model-based views of science among learners are not present when instruction-assisted inquiry is sustained. With the right context, students can develop sophisticated views about the nature of science.

The content of LPs—core ideas and practices—can also be informed by science studies research. Consider as an example the work of Nersessian (2008) that is extending her research program studying the cognitive basis of model-based reasoning in science (Nersessian, 2002). In her most recent research she is studying the cognitive practices of biomolecular scientists and biomedical engineers working together on interdisciplinary problems concerning cultivating/engineering tissues. The work is guided by the premise that "studying inquiry practices in research laboratories could lead to development of effective pedagogical strategies for improving the instructional laboratory" (2008, p. 72). In the context of cutting edge science, she maintains, everyone is a learner—undergraduates, Ph.D. candidates, post-doctoral researchers and lab directors. Nersessian refers to such contexts as "agentive learning environments" and found several significant features:

- With conceptual and methodological knowledge and skills distributed, everyone, even undergraduate students, makes contributions.
- The organization is non-hierarchical—no one person is the expert, neophyte members can contribute and achieve legitimacy and identity.
- Interactional structures allow for membership routes into the laboratory that motivate learning.
- Multiple social support systems bolster resiliency in a research context that has frequent failures.

Commenting on the potential bridges from science labs to science classrooms and recognizing the differences, she writes,

[These contexts have] their own unique constraints and affordances that need to be figured into the development of strategies for learning and using model-based reasoning . . . the point is that the *kinds of reasoning processes* should aim to approximate those of a scientist. A good example here is Marianne Wiser's (1995) "dots-in-a-box" visual analogical models for teaching thermodynamic concepts.

(1995, p. 78)

Lehrer and Schauble (2006) report that getting students to engage in resemblance representation tasks is an entrée to modeling. Lehrer and Schauble (2006, 2004) maintain that with instruction-assisted inquiry, modeling and reasoning as scientific practices can support: (a) sustained engagement with epistemic and social practices; and (b) the construction of mathematical representational forms that afford quantification and investigation of relations among quantities. Lehrer and Schauble (2002) provide additional teaching examples and student artifacts of engagements in representation tasks that model data from investigations carried out by students in grades Kindergarten to Grade 5. These instruction-assisted-development teaching sequences have students using and learning from data modeling, bridging mathematics and science, engaging in inquiry studies and using emergent representational forms.

The Lehrer et al. (2008), Metz (2008), and Nersessian (2008) results, along with research results from Carey and Smith (1993), Smith, Machlin, Houghton, and Hennessey (2000), Sandoval (2005) and Ford (2008), show that sustained engagements in instruction-assisted inquiry does indeed effect views about the nature of science. Thus, this research challenges recommendations that (a) the nature of science should be explicitly taught during lab lessons (Akerson, Abd-El-Khalick, & Lederman, 2000); and (b) that such teaching should focus on a common agreed upon set of features about the nature of science (McComus & Olson, 1998). Finally, the research on extended instruction-assisted inquiry challenges the 'justified true belief' image of science knowledge held by researchers studying epistemic cognition (Greene, Azevedo, & Torney-Purta, 2008; Murphy, Alexander, Greene, & Edwards, 2007). Here though the research targets conceptual learning only as the goal, not epistemic practices and images of the nature of science as a learning goal.

Domain-General/Specific Learning Frameworks

The recent debate over constructivist instruction (Tobias & Duffy, 2008) has at its core a debate between domain-general and domain-specific frameworks or processes for guiding the teaching and learning of science. The domain-general view adopts a traditional information-processing model (Anderson, 1983: Atchinson & Shiffrin, 1968) that attributes the outcomes of learning to the interaction between working memory processes and the content and organization of long-term memory. Current views and research on the nature of working memory processes have been concerned with how the nature of instruction and instructional materials, and learners' prior knowledge interact to impact the outcomes of learning (Mayer, 1989; Mayer & Moreno, 2003; Van Merriënboer & Sweller, 2005). Here the focus is on the individual learner and the domain-general nature and characteristics of their processing capabilities. However, the specific nature of the learner's existing knowledge in long-term memory as well as the specific nature of the knowledge to be learned are also considered and deemed influential to the amount and nature of learning that can occur within educational contexts. In essence, the influence of these domain-general aspects of the model (i.e., nature and interaction between working memory and long-term memory) are weighed equally with the domain-specific nature of the target knowledge and context when looking for explanations of learning and resulting prescriptions for practice.

In contrast, the domain-specific view of learning draws heavily from situated-cognition theory in that the two approaches share a focus on the importance of contextual factors on learning and the importance of scaffolding for complex reasoning and meaning making (Hmelo-Silver, Chinn, & Duncan, 2007; Kuhn, 2007). Both the domain-specific and domain-general views support the importance of scaffolding, however, in latter case the scaffolding consists primarily of cognitive supports, while in the former, the scaffolding consists primarily of social and collaborative forms of supports.

Three critical aspects of the nature of contexts and situations that are embedded in most views and research on learning within domain specific contexts are issues of authenticity, collaboration and inquiry (Blumenfeld et al., 2006). Authenticity, within the context of science learning, focuses on embedding the learning within the learners' everyday world and the practice of the discipline. Collaboration, within the context of science learning, encourages the sharing and contrasting of ideas within other individuals within a community who are engaged in similar tasks and who have similar aims. Finally, inquiry, that plays a foundational role within science, requires the students to engage in problem-stating and problem-solving activities which require planning, synthesis and evaluation skills, as well as, relevant domain-specific content knowledge. Lehrer and Schauble (2004) bring these three aspects together in their research on developing students' conceptions of "natural variation" and "distribution" by embedding the focus activities within the natural and native ecology (i.e., growing of local plants). In addition, students engaged in inquiry through such processes as question posing, hypothesis generation and design, collection and synthesis of data, and the development and testing of models.

What one finds when looking at the two sides of the debate is a clear difference with respect to learning goals. The views differ as to the primary focus or intent of the instruction (e.g., to develop increased knowledge of science content and skill or to develop increased generic scientific process and method skills). Hence, it is not surprising that there is evidence on both sides that support the value of both a minimally guided approach as well as directive approach to the teaching of science knowledge and skills (Blumenfeld et al., 2006; Tobias & Duffy, 2009). Future research should be focused on identifying under what conditions each approach works best (i.e., what contexts and contents are well suited for a minimally guided approach and which are well suited for a directive approach).

PRACTICAL IMPLICATIONS FOR THE DESIGN OF LEARNING ENVIRONMENTS—PRACTICES, REASONING, AND DISCOURSE

The emergent tradition for teaching and learning science is to frame learning in contexts that merge content knowledge with skills, practices, and processes. The naturalistic turn in philosophy of science with its focus on activities and practices that are cognitive, epistemic and social has implications for science learning and the framing of research on science learning and reasoning. An undeniable trend in STEM (Science Technology Engineering Mathematics) education is that more and more contemporary science is being done at the boundaries of disciplines (e.g., Earth systems science, biophysics, geochemistry, bioengineering, among others). Thus, we recognize now a connectedness in the practices of science that are not typically found in school classrooms environments or the design of science curricula.

Many of the extant K-8 science curriculum programs have been found wanting in terms of the lean reasoning demands required of students (Ford, 2005; Hapgood et al., 2004; Metz, 1995; NRC, 2007). What the research shows is that curricula addressing domain-general reasoning skills and surface level knowledge dominate over curricula addressing core knowledge and domain-specific reasoning opportunities that meaningfully integrate knowledge. This situation, they claim, is partially due to a lack of consensus in curricula about what is most worth learning, and to K-8 teachers' weak knowledge of science. The reasoning-lean curriculum approaches (a) tend to separate reasoning and learning into discrete lessons, thus blurring and glossing over the salient themes and big ideas of science, thereby making American curricula "a mile wide and an inch deep" (Schmidt, McKnight, & Raizen, 1997); and (b) in the case of middle school textbooks, tend to present science topics as unrelated items with little or no regard to relations among them (Kesidou & Roseman, 2002).

Metz (2008) also finds that "science curricula have frequently been critiqued as reflecting an impoverished model of the practices of scientific knowledge construction." (p. 139). First, there is her critique that the reasoning capacities of children have been underestimated because when tested and found to be weak reasoning strategies, this can be due to weak domain knowledge. Brown (1990) found differences in knowledge as the basis for apparent superiority in the reasoning of pre-schoolers. A second reason given for underestimating children's capabilities is that cognitive development research has not paid attention to the important role of instruction (Metz, 2008).

Ohlsson (1992) recognized some years ago that the focus on teaching scientific theories did not include using the theories; missing were cognitive processes involved with theory articulation and refinement. Ford (2005) in a study examining third grade students' engagement with a kit-based unit on Rocks and Minerals found that the principal learning goals for the set of lessons was classification reasoning. Descriptive observational features of rocks and minerals were used to assign rocks to types (e.g., sedimentary, igneous, metamorphic) and to kinds (e.g., sandstone, siltstone, shale, limestone). Missing from the curriculum learning goals Ford laments was any expectation for using information from rocks (e.g., larger grain size in sedimentary rocks implies higher energy water environments) and minerals (e.g., larger grain size in rocks implies a slower cooling) to tell a story about the rocks. Ford concludes that the lessons in the kit were impoverished and underestimated the known capabilities of children to engage in science.

Research on young children's learning (as described in previous sections) demonstrates that children entering school are well equipped cognitively and socially to engage in theory and model building. The role of modeling natural phenomenon and then reasoning from those models has led Ford (2008), Herrenkohl and Guerra (1998), Lehrer and Schauble (2004, 2006), Smith (2007), among others, to investigate ways to design classroom learning environments that promote students' theory and model-building reasoning.

Lehrer and Schauble (2006) report on a 10-year program of longitudinal research that examines planned instructional sequences across grades K-5. The focus is model-based reasoning and instruction in science and mathematics. Critical to the design of these learning environments is engagement in analogical mapping of students' representational systems and emergent models to the natural world. Important instructional supports are coordinated around three forms of collective activity: (a) finding ways to help students understand and appropriate the process of scientific inquiry; (b) emphasizing the development and use of varying forms of representations and inscriptions; and (c) capitalizing on the cyclical nature of modeling (p. 381).

Sandoval (2003) has explored how high school students' epistemological ideas interact with conceptual understandings. Written explanations in the domain of natural selection were used as the dependent measure. Analyses showed students did seek causal accounts of data and were sensitive to causal coherence but they failed to support key claims with explicit evidence critical to an explanation. Sandoval posits that while students have productive epistemic resources to bring to inquiry, there is a need to deepen the epistemic discourse around student-generated artifacts. The recommendation is to hold more frequent public classroom discourse focused on students' explanations. "Epistemically, such a discourse would focus on the coherence of groups' claims, and how any particular claim can be judged as warranted" (p. 46).

Sandoval (2005) argues that having a better understanding of how scientific knowledge is constructed makes one better at doing and learning science. The goal is to engage students in a set of practices that build models from patterns of evidence and that examine how what comes to count as evidence depends on careful observations and building arguments. Schauble, Glaser, Duschl, Schultz, and Johns (1995) found that students' participating in sequenced inquiry lessons with explicit epistemic goals (e.g., evaluating causal explanations for the carrying capacity performance of designed boats) showed improved learning over students who simply enacted the investigations. They found that students' understanding the purposes of experimentation made a difference. Other reports of research that have found positive learning effects of students working with and from evidence and seeing discourse and argumentation as a key feature of doing science include Kelly and Crawford (1997), Sandoval and Reiser (2004), Songer and Linn (1991), and Toth, Suthers, and Lesgold (2002).

Additional insights for the design of reflective classroom discourse environments comes from research by Rosebery, Warren, and Conant (1992), Smith, Maclin, Houghton, and Hennessey (2000), van Zee and Minstrell (1997), and Herrenkohl and Guerra (1998). Rosebery et al.'s (1992) study spanned an entire school year while that of Smith et al. (2000) followed a cohort of students for several years with the same teacher. Both studies used classroom practices that place a heavy emphasis on (a) requiring evidence for claims, (b) evaluating the fit of new ideas to data, (c) justifications for specific claims, and (d) examining methods for generating data. Engle and Conant (2002) refer to such classroom discourse as "productive disciplinary engagement" when it is grounded in the disciplinary norms for both social and cognitive activity.

The research by van Zee and Minstrell (1997) shows the positive gains in learning that come about when the authority for classroom conversation shifts from the teacher to the students. Employing a technique they call the *reflective toss*, van Zee and Minstrell found that students become more active in the classroom discourse with the positive consequence of making student thinking more visible to both the teacher and the students themselves. Herrenkohl and Guerra (1998) examined the effect on student engagement of guidelines for students who constituted the audience, that is, the scaffolding was on listening to others. The intellectual goals for students were predicting and theorizing, summarizing results and relating predictions, theories, and results. The audience role assignments were designed to correspond with the intellectual roles and required students to check and critique classmates' work. Students were directed to develop a *question chart* that would support them in their intellectual roles (e.g., What questions could we ask when it is our job to check summaries of results?) Examples of students' questions are, *What helped you find your results? How did you get that? What were your results? What made that happen? Did your group agree on the results? Did you like what happen?* Following the framework developed by Hatano and Inagaki (1991), Herrenhkohl and Guerra used the audience role procedures to engage students in (a) asking clarification questions; (b) challenging others' claims; and (c) coordinating bits of knowledge. The focus on listening skills and audience roles helps to foster productive community discourse around students *thinking in science.*

CONCLUSION AND FUTURE DIRECTIONS

In conclusion, researchers studying science learning are learning that with proper supports (e.g., instruction-assisted development, assessment for learning) and sequencing (e.g., immersion units and learning progressions) young children and adolescents are capable of complex reasoning and engaging in sophisticated scientific critique and communication practices. The research reported here demonstrates that theory-building, modeling, and other forms of scientific reasoning are possible when children are provided with multiple opportunities that sustain their engagement with select scientific practices over time (e.g., predicting, observing, testing, measuring, counting, recording, collaborating, and communicating). When sustained engagement and assisted development occurs the research shows that learners develop images of the nature of science and of scientific inquiry as an enterprise that is fundamentally a theory/modeling building and refining process. Viewing classrooms and other formal and informal learning environments as a scientific community in which learners participate in scientific practices and discourse processes akin to communities in professional sciences is advantageous but under studied. The growth of knowledge (among scientists and among learners) advances through interactions within communities. Studies of scientific communities can inform our understandings of the cognitive, epistemic and social practices to bring to children's learning of science.

Posing and refining questions, posing and refining hypotheses, posing and refining designs of investigations, developing shared representations and models, considering alternatives, providing feedback are but some of the interactive scientific practices that advance understandings. This view is reflected in a recent NRC report: "[P]articipation in scientific practices in the classroom helps students advance their understanding of scientific argumentation and explanation, engage in the construction of scientific evidence, representations, and models; and reflect on how scientific knowledge is constructed" (NRC, 2007, p. 40).

The future research on science learning and teaching needs to focus more on learning in context. Research is needed on developmental trajectories/progressions that examine learning and reasoning. Such research while informed by lab studies must be grounded in the study of learning environments where student learning is examined in instruction-assisted contexts with mediation by teachers, educators, parents, or peers. The emerging consensus position is to organize and align curriculum, instruction, and assessment and to do so around core knowledge, enduring understandings and learning progressions. The research agenda is complex given the new images we have of science through naturalized philosophy of science, of capable young learners, of scientific participatory practices being more than doing investigations and conducting inquiry and of the importance of context when constructing and evaluating scientific knowledge. Here, then, some of the critical areas for research and development identified in *Taking Science to School* (NRC, 2007, pp. 351–355):

- Students' understanding of how scientific knowledge is constructed and how they come to understand and negotiate different knowledge communities.
- More research is needed to further elaborate the interplay between domain-specific and domain-general knowledge over the course of development and to better understand how to leverage these interconnections to inform instructional models.
- Extensive research and development efforts are needed before learning progressions are well established and tested. Longitudinal studies over multiple ages are particularly important to get better understandings of continuities and discontinuities in students' understanding across grades.
- Research is needed to develop a better understanding of whether and how instruction should change with children's development. Research on curriculum materials is a critical area.
- Research on supporting science learning from culturally, linguistically, and socio-economically diverse students is an area of critical need.

REFERENCES

Akerson, V. L., Abd-El-Khalick, F., & Lederman, N. G. (2000). Influence of a reflective explicit activity-based approach on elementary teachers' conceptions of nature of science. *Journal of Research in Science Teaching, 37*(4), 295–317.

Alexander, P., Schallert, D. L., & Reynolds, R. E. (2009). What is learning anyway? A topographical perspective considered. *Educational Psychologist, 44*(3), 176–192.

American Association for the Advancement of Science (2001). *Atlas of science literacy: Mapping K-12 learning and goals.* Washington, DC: AAAS.

Anderson, J. R. (1983). *The architecture of cognition.* Cambridge, MA: Harvard University Press.

Atchinson, R.C., & Shiffrin, R.M. (1968). Human memory: A proposed system and its control processes. In K. W. Spence, & J. T. Spence, *The psychology of learning and motivation* (Vol. 2, pp. 89–195). New York: Academic Press.

Atran, S. (2002). Modular and cultural factors in biological understanding: An experimental approach to the cognitive basis of science. In P. Carruthers, S. Stich, & M. Siegal (Eds.), *The cognitive basis of science* (pp. 41–72). Cambridge: Cambridge University Press.

Ault, C. (1994). Research on problem solving: Earth science. In D. Gabel (Ed.), *Handbook of research on science teaching and learning* (pp. 269–283), New York: Macmillan Publishing Company.

Australian Department of Education, Employment and Workplace Relations (2008). *Opening up pathways: Engagement in STEM across the primary-secondary school transition.* Canberra: Government Printer.

Ausubel, D. (1963). *The psychology of meaningful verbal learning.* New York: Grune & Stratton.

Baillargeon, R. (2004). Infants' physical world. *Current Directions in Psychological Science, 13*(3), 89–94.

Barr, B. (1994). Research on problem solving: Elementary school. In D. Gabel (Ed.), *Handbook of research on science teaching and learning* (pp. 248–268). New York: Macmillan Publishing Company.

Black, P., & Wiliam, D. (1998). Assessment and classroom learning. *Assessment in Education, 5*(1), 7–74.

Blumenfeld, P. C., Kempler, T. M., & Krajcik, J. S. (2006). Motivation and cognitive engagement in learning environments. In R. K. Sawyer (Ed.), *The Cambridge handbook of the learning sciences.* New York: Cambridge University Press.

Bransford, J., Barron, B., Pea, R., Meltzoff, A., Kuhl, P., Bell, P., Stevens, R., Schwartz, D., Vye, N., Reeves, B., Roschelle, J., & Sabelli, N. (2006). Foundations and opportunities for an interdisciplinary science of learning. In R. K. Sawyer (Ed.), *The Cambridge handbook of the learning sciences.* (pp. 19–34) New York: Cambridge University Press.

Brown, A. L. (1990). Domain-specific principles affect learning and transfer in children. *Cognitive Science, 14*, 107–133.

Carey, S. (2004). Bootstrapping and the origin of concepts. *Daedalus, Winter*, 59–68.

Carey, S., & Smith, C. (1993). On understanding the nature of scientific knowledge. *Educational Psychologist, 28*(3), 235–252.

Carruthers, P., Stich, S., & Siegal, M. (Eds.) (2002). *The cognitive basis of science.* Cambridge: Cambridge University Press.

Carnegie Corporation of New York (2009) *The opportunity equation: Transforming mathematics and science education for citizenship and the global economy.* Available at: www.opportunityequation.org.

Catley, K., Lehrer, R., & Reiser, B. (2005). Tracing a prospective learning progression for developing understanding of evolution. Paper Commissioned by the National Research Council Board of Testing and Assessment, Committee on Test Design for K-12 Science Achievement. Washington, DC: National Research Council.

Coburn, W. W., & Aikenhead, G. S. (1998). Cultural Aspects of Learning Science. In Fraser, B.J., & Tobin, K.G. (Eds.) *International handbook of science education* (pp. 39–52.) Dordrecht: Kluwer.

Cole, M. (1996). *Cultural psychology: A once and future discipline.* Cambridge, MA: Belknap Press.

Corcoran, T., Mosher, R., & Rogat, A. (2009). *Learning progressions in science: An evidence-based approach to reform.* CPRE Research Report #RR-63. Philadelphia, PA: Consortium for Policy Research in Education.

Corcoran, T., & Silander, M. (2009). Instruction in high schools: The evidence and the challenge. *The future of children: America's high schools,* 19(1), 157–183. Available at: www.futureofchildren.org.

Désautels, J., & Larochelle, M. (1998). The epistemology of students: the "thingified" nature of scientific knowledge. In B. J. Fraser, & K. G. Tobin (Eds.), *International handbook of science education* (pp. 115–126). Dordrecht: Kluwer.

Driver, R., Leach, J., Millar, R., & Scott, P. (1996). *Young people's images of science.* Philadelphia, PA: Open University Press.

Duit, R., & Treagust, D.F. (1998). Learning in science: From behaviourism towards social constructivism and beyond. In B. J. Fraser, & K. G. Tobin (Eds.), *International handbook of science education* (pp. 3–25). Dordrecht: Kluwer.

Duncan, R., & Hmelo-Silver, C. (2009). Learning progressions: Aligning curriculum, instruction, and assessment. *Journal of Research in Science Teaching, 46*(6), 606–609.

Duschl, R. (1990). *Restructuring science education: The importance of theories and their development.* New York: Teachers' College Press.

Duschl, R. (2008). Science education in 3 part harmony: Balancing conceptual, epistemic and social learning goals. In J. Green, A. Luke, & G. Kelly (Eds.), Review *of research in education, V32* (pp. 268–291). Washington, DC: AERA.

Duschl, R., & Grandy, R. (Eds.) (2008). *Teaching scientific inquiry: Recommendations for research and implementation.* Rotterdam: Sense Publishers.

Duschl, R., Hamilton, R., & Grandy, R. (1993). Tension and issues between epistemological and psychology frameworks in science education. In R. Duschl, & R. Hamilton (Eds.), *Philosophy of science, cognitive psychology, and educational theory and practice.* Albany, NY: SUNY Press.

Engle, R. A., & Conant, F. C. (2002). Guiding principles for fostering productive disciplinary engagement: Explaining an emergent argument in a community of learners' classroom. *Cognition and Instruction, 20*(4), 399–483.

European Commission (2004). *Europe needs more scientists: Report by the high level group on increasing human resources for science and technology.* Brussels: European Commission.

European Commission (2007). *Science education now: A renewed pedagogy for the future of Europe.* Brussels: European Commission.

Feyerabend, P. (1970). Against method: Outline of an anarchistic theory of knowledge. In M. Radner, & S. Winokur (Eds.), *Minnesota studies in the philosophy of science* (Vol. IV, pp. 170–230). Minneapolis, MN: University of Minnesota Press.

Ford, D. (2005). The challenges of observing geologically: Third grades descriptions of rock and mineral properties. *Science Education, 89,* 276–295.

Ford, M. (2008). "Grasp of practice" as a reasoning resource for inquiry and nature of science understanding. *Science & Education, 17,* 147–177.

Fraser, B., & Tobin, K. (Eds.). (1998). *International handbook of research in science education.* Dordrecht: Kluwer.

Gabel, D. (Ed.). (1994). *Handbook of research on science teaching and learning.* New York: Macmillan Publishing Company.

Gabel, D., & Bunce, D. (1994). Research on problem solving: Chemistry. In D. Gabel (Ed.), *Handbook of research on science teaching and learning.* (pp. 301–326). New York: Macmillan Publishing Company.

Geary, D. (2008). An evolutionarily informed education science, *Educational Psychologist, 43*(4), 179–195.

Gelman, R., & Brenneman, K. (2004). Science pathways for young children. *Early Childhood Research Quarterly, 19*(1), 150–158.

Gelman, R., & Lucariello, J. (2002). Learning in cognitive development. In H. Pashler, & C. R. Gallistel (Eds.), *Stevens' handbook of experimental psychology* (3rd ed., Vol. 3, pp. 395–443). New York: John Wiley & Sons, Ltd.

Gier, R. (1988). *Explaining science: A cognitive approach.* Chicago: University of Chicago Press.

Giere, R. (2002). Scientific cognition as distributed cognition. In P. Carruthers, S. Stich, & M. Siegal (Eds.), *The cognitive basis of science* (pp. 285–299). Cambridge: Cambridge University Press.

Gilbert, J. K., & Boulter, C. J. (1998). Learning science through models and modeling. In B. J. Fraser, & K. G. Tobin (Eds.), *International handbook of science education* (pp. 53–66). Dordrecht: Kluwer.

Godfrey-Smith, P. (2003). *Theory and reality: An introduction to the philosophy of science.* Chicago: The University of Chicago Press.

Godfried, G., & Gelman, R. (2005). Developing domain-specific causal-explanatory frameworks: The role of insides and immanence. *Cognitive Development, 20,* 137–158.

Goldman, A. (1986). *Epistemology and cognition.* Cambridge, MA: Harvard University Press.

Gopnik, A. (1996). The scientist as child. *Philosophy of Science, 63*(4), 485–514.

Gopnik, A., Glymour, C., Sobel, D., Schulz, L., Kushnir, T., & Danks, D. (2004). A theory of causal learning in children: Causal maps and Bayes nets. *Psychological Review, 111*(1), 1–31.

Gopnik, A., & Sobel, D. M. (2000). Detecting blickets: How young children use information about causal properties in categorization and induction. *Child Development, 71,* 1205–1222.

Gopnik, A., Sobel, D. M., Schulz, L., & Glymour, C. (2001). Causal learning mechanisms in very young children: Two, three, and four-year-olds infer causal relations from patterns of variation and co-variation. *Developmental Psychology, 37,* 620–629.

Greene, J., Azevedo, R., & Torney-Purta, J. (2008). Modeling epistemic and ontological cognition: Philosophical perspectives and methodological directions. *Educational Psychologist, 43*(3), 142–160.

Hapgood, S., Magnusson, S., & Palincsar, A.S. (2004). Teacher, text, and experience: a case of young children's scientific inquiry. *The Journal of the Learning Sciences, 13*(4), 455–505.

Hatano, G., & Inagaki, K. (1991). Sharing cognition through collective comprehension activity. In L. B. Resnick, J. M. Levine, & S. D. Teasley (Eds.), *Perspectives on socially shared cognition* (pp. 331–348). Washington, DC: American Psychological Association.

Helgeson, S. (1994). Research on problem solving: Middle school. In D. Gabel (Ed.), *Handbook of research on science teaching and learning* (pp. 248–268). New York: Macmillan Publishing Company.

Herrenkohl, L., & Guerra, M. (1998). Participant structures, scientific discourse, and student engagement in fourth grade. *Cognition and Instruction, 16*(4), 431–473.

Hmelo-Silver, C., Chinn, C., & Duncan, R. (2007). Scaffolding and achievement in problem-based and inquiry learning: A response to Kirschner, Sweller, and Clark (2006). *Educational Psychologist, 42,* 99–108.

Inagaki, K., & Hatano, G. (2002). *Young children's thinking about the biological world.* New York: Psychology Press.

Inagaki, K., & Hatano, G. (2006). Young children's conception of the biological world, *Current Directions in Psychological Science, 15*(4), 177–184.

Johnson, S., Slaughter, V., & Carey, S (1998). Whose gaze would infants follow? The elicitation of gaze following in 12-month-olds. *Developmental Science, 1,* 233–238.

Keil, F. (1989). *Concepts, kinds and cognitive development.* Cambridge, MA: MIT Press.

Keil. F. (2003). That's life: Coming to understand biology. *Journal of Human Development, 46,* 369–377.

Kesidou, S., & Roseman, J. (2002). How well do middle school science programs measure up? Findings from Project 2061's curriculum review. *Journal of Research in Science Teaching, 39*(6), 522–549.

Kelly, G. J., & Crawford, T. (1997). An ethnographic investigation of the discourse processes of school science. *Science Education, 81*(5), 533–560.

Kirschner, P., Sweller, J., & Clark, R. E. (2006). Why minimal guidance during instruction does not work: An analysis of the failure of constructivist, discovery, problem-based, experiential and inquiry-based teaching. *Educational Psychologist, 41,* 75–86.

Kitcher, P. (1993). *The advancement of science: Science without legend, objectivity without illusions.* New York: Oxford University Press.

Koslowski, B., & Thompson, S. (2002). Theorizing is important, and collateral information constrains how well it is done. In P. Carruthers, S. Stich, & M. Siegal (Eds.), *The cognitive basis of science* (pp. 171–192). Cambridge: Cambridge University Press.

Knorr-Cetina, K. (1999). *Epistemic cultures: How science makes knowledge.* Cambridge, MA: Harvard University Press.

Kuhn, D. (2007). Is direct instruction an answer to the right question? *Educational Psychologist, 42,* 109–114.

Kuhn, T. (1996). *The structure of scientific revolutions* (4th ed.). Chicago: University of Chicago Press.

Lakatos, I. (1970) Falsification and the methodology of scientific research programmes. In I. Lakatos, & A. Musgrave (Eds.), *Criticism and the growth of knowledge*. Cambridge: Cambridge University Press.

Lawson, A. (1994). Research on the acquisitions of science knowledge; epistemological foundations of cognition. In D. Gabel (Ed.), *Handbook of research on science teaching and learning* (pp. 131–176). New York: Macmillan Publishing Company.

Lederman, N. G. (1992). Students' and teachers' conceptions of the nature of science: A review of the research. *Journal of Research in Science Teaching, 29*(4), 331–359.

Lederman, N. G. (1999). Teachers' understanding of the nature of science and classroom practice: Factors that facilitate or impede the relationship. *Journal of Research in Science Teaching, 36*, 916–929.

Lehrer, R., Jaslow, L., & Curtis, C. (2003). Developing understanding of measurement in the elementary grades. In D. H. Clements, & G. Bright (Eds.), *Learning and teaching measurement: 2003 yearbook* (pp. 100–121). Reston, VA: National Council of Teachers of Mathematics.

Lehrer, R., & Schauble, L. (2000a). Inventing data structures for representational purposes: Elementary grade students' classification models. *Mathematical Thinking and Learning, 2*, 49–72.

Lehrer, R., & Schauble, L. (2000b). The development of model-based reasoning. *Journal of Applied Developmental Psychology, 21*(1), 39–48.

Lehrer, R., & Schauble, L. (Eds.) (2002). *Investigating real data in the classroom: Expanding children's understanding of math and science*. New York: Teachers College Press.

Lehrer, R., & Schauble, L. (2004). Modeling natural variation through distribution, *American Educational Research Journal, 41*(3), 635–679.

Lehrer, R., & Schauble, L. (2006). Cultivating model-based reasoning in science education. In K. Sawyer (Ed.), *The Cambridge handbook of the learning sciences*. New York: Cambridge University Press.

Lehrer, R., Schauble, L., & Lucas, D. (2008). Supporting development of the epistemology of inquiry. *Cognitive Development, 23*, 512–529.

Linn, M., & Eylon, B. (2006). Science education: integrating views of learning instruction. In P. Alexander, & P. Winne (Eds.), *Handbook of educational psychology* (2nd ed., pp. 511–544). Mahwah, NJ: Lawrence Erlbaum.

Longino, H. (1990). *Science as social knowledge*. Princeton, NJ: Princeton University Press.

Longino, H. (2002). *The fate of knowledge*. Princeton, NJ: Princeton University Press

Maloney, D. (1994). Research on problem solving: Physics. In D. Gabel (Ed.), *Handbook of research on science teaching and learning* (pp. 327–354). New York: Macmillan Publishing Company.

Mayer, R. (1989). Models for understanding. *Review of Educational Research, 59*, 43–64.

Mayer, R., & Moreno, R. (2003). Nine ways to reduce cognitive load in multimedial learning. *Educational Psychologist, 38*, 43–52.

McComas, W. F., & Olson, J. K. (1998). The nature of science in international science education standards documents. In W. F. McComas (Ed.), *The nature of science in science education: Rationales and strategies* (pp. 41–52). Dordrecht: Kluwer.

Metz, K. (1995). Reassessment of developmental constraints on children's science instruction. *Review of Educational Research, 65*, 93–127.

Metz, K. (1998). Scientific inquiry within reach of young children. In B. J. Fraser & K. G. Tobin (Eds.), *International handbook of science education* (pp. 81–96). Dordrecht: Kluwer.

Metz, K. (2004). Children's understanding of scientific inquiry: Their conceptualization of uncertainty in investigations of their own design. *Cognition and Instruction, 22*, 219–290.

Metz, K. (2008). Narrowing the gulf between the practices of science and the elementary school classroom. *Elementary School Journal, 109*(2), 138–161.

Murphy, P. K., Alexander, P. A., Greene, J. A., & Edwards, M. N. (2007). Epistemological threads in the fabric of conceptual change. In S. Vosniadou, A. Baltas, & X. Vamvakoussi (Eds.), *Re-framing the conceptual change approach in learning and instruction* (pp. 105–122). Dordrecht: Elsevier.

National Assessment Governing Board (2008). NAEP 2009 science framework development: issues and recommendations. Available at: http://www.nagb.org.

National Center on Education and the Economy (2007). *Tough choices or tough time: The report of the New Commission on the Skills of the American Workforce*. San Francisco: Jossey-Bass. Available at: http://www.ncee.org.

National Research Council (1999). *How people learn*. Washington, DC: National Academy Press. Available at: http://www.nap.edu.

National Research Council (2001). *Knowing what students know: The science and design of educational assessment*. Washington, DC: National Academy Press. Available at: http://www.nap.edu.

National Research Council (2005) *Systems for state science assessment*. Washington, DC: National Academy Press. Available at: http://www.nap.edu.

National Research Council (2006). *Rising above the gathering storm*. Washington, DC: National Academy Press. Available at: http://www.nap.edu.

National Research Council (2007). *Taking science to school: learning and teaching science kindergarten to eighth grade*. Washington, DC: National Academy Press. Available at: http://www.nap.edu.

National Research Council (2009). *Learning science in informal environments: People, places, and pursuits*. Washington, DC: National Academy Press. Available at: http://www.nap.edu.

Nersessian, N. (2002). The cognitive basis of model-based reasoning in science. In P. Carruthers, S. Stich, & M. Siegal (Eds.), *The cognitive basis of science* (pp. 133–153). Cambridge: Cambridge University Press.

Nersessian, N. (2008). Inquiry: How science works: Model-based reasoning in scientific practice. In R. Duschl, & R. Grandy (Eds.), *Teaching scientific inquiry: Recommendations for research and implementation* (pp. 57–79). Rotterdam: Sense Publishers.

Novak, J. (1977). *A theory of education*. Ithaca, NY: Cornell University Press.

Nuffield Foundation (2008). *Science education in Europe: Critical reflections*. London: Author.

Ohlsson, S. (1992). The cognitive skill of theory articulation: A neglected aspect of science education. *Science & Education, 1*(2), 181–192.

Perner, J., Leekam, S. R., & Wimmer, H. (1987). Three-year-olds' difficulty with false belief: The case for a conceptual deficit. *British Journal of Developmental Psychology, 5*, 125–137.

Reiser, B.J., Krajcik, J., Moje, E., & Marx, R. (2003). Design strategies for developing science instructional materials. Paper presented at the National Association for Research in Science Teaching Annual Meeting, Philadelphia, PA, March.

Rosebery, A. S., Warren, B., & Conant, F. (1992). Appropriating scientific discourse: Findings from language minority classrooms. *Journal of the Learning Sciences, 2*(1), 61–94.

Rudolph, J. (2002). *Scientists in the classroom: The cold war reconstruction of American science education*. New York: Palgrave Macmillan.

Sandoval, W. A. (2003). Conceptual and epistemic aspects of students' scientific explanations. *The Journal of the Learning Sciences, 12*(1), 5–51.

Sandoval, W. A. (2005) Understanding students' practical epistemologies and their influence on learning through inquiry. *Science Education, 89*(4): 345–372.

Sandoval, W. A., & Reiser, B. J. (2004). Explanation-driven inquiry: Integrating conceptual and epistemic scaffolds for scientific inquiry. *Science Education, 88*, 345–372.

Sawyer, R. K. (Ed.). (2006). *The Cambridge handbook of the learning sciences*. New York: Cambridge University Press.

Schauble, L. (2008). Commentary: Three questions about development. In R. Duschl, & R. Grandy (Eds.), *Teaching scientific inquiry: Recommendations for research and implementation* (pp. 50–56). Rotterdam: Sense Publishers.

Schauble, L., Glaser, R., Duschl, R., Schultz, S., & John, J. (1995). Students' understanding of the objectives and procedures of experimentation in the science classroom. *The Journal of the Learning Sciences, 4*(2) 131–166.

Schmidt, H. G., Lyens, S. M. M., van Gog, T., & Paas, F. (2007). Problem-based learning is compatible with human cognition architecture: Commentary on Kirschner, Sweller and Clark (2006). *Educational Psychologist, 42*, 91–98.

Schmidt, W., McKnight, C., & Raizen, S. A. (1997). *A splintered vision: An investigation of US science and mathematics education*. Boston: Kluwer Academic Publishers.

Scott, P. H., & Driver, R. H. (1998). Learning about science teaching: Perspective from an action research project. In B. J. Fraser, & K. G. Tobin (Eds.), *International handbook of science education* (pp. 67–80). Dordrecht: Kluwer.

Shapere, D. (1982). The concept of observation in science and philosophy. *Philosophy of Science, 59*, 485–525.

Siegal, M. (2002). The science of childhood. In P. Carruthers, S. Stich, & M. Siegal (Eds.), *The cognitive basis of science* (pp. 300–315). Cambridge: Cambridge University Press.

Simpson, R., Koballa, T., Oliver, S., & Crawley, F. (1994). Research on the affective dimension of science learning. In D. Gabel (Ed.), *Handbook of research on science teaching and learning* (pp. 211–234). New York: Macmillan Publishing Company.

Smith, C. (2007). Bootstrapping processes in the development of students' possessive common sense matter theories: Using analogical mappings, thought experiments, and learning to promote conceptual restructuring, *Cognition and Instruction, 25*(4), 337–398.

Smith, C., Carey, S., & Wiser, M. (1985). On differentiation: a case study of the development of size, weight, and density. *Cognition, 21*(3), 177–237.

Smith, C., Maclin, D., Houghton, C., & Hennessey, M. G. (2000). Sixth-grade students' epistemologies of science:

The impact of school science experience on epistemological development. *Cognition and Instruction, 18*(3), 285–316.

Smith, C., Wiser, M., Anderson, C., & Krajcik, J. (2006). Implications of research on children's learning for assessment: Matter and atomic molecular theory. *Measurement: Interdisciplinary Research and Perspectives, 4,* 11–98.

Songer, N., & Linn, M. (1991). How do students' views of the scientific enterprise influence knowledge integration? *Journal of Research in Science Teaching, 28*(9), 761–784.

Spelke, E. (2000). Core knowledge, *American Psychologists, 55,* 1233–1243.

Spelke, E., & Kinzler, K. (2007). Core knowledge. *Developmental Science, 10,* 89–96.

Spelke, E. S., Phillips, A. T., & Woodward, A. L. (1995). Infants' knowledge of object motion and human action. In D. Sperber, D. Premack, & A. Premack (Eds.), *Causal cognition: A multidisciplinary debate.* Oxford: Oxford University Press.

Stewart, J., & Hafner, R. (1994). Research on problem solving: Genetics. In D. Gabel (Ed.), *Handbook of research on science teaching and learning* (pp. 284–300). New York: Macmillan Publishing Company.

Subrahmanyam, K., Gelman, R., & Lafosse, A. (2002). Animates and other separable moveable objects. In E. Fordes, & G. Humphreys (Eds.), *Category specificity in brain and mind* (pp. 341–373). London: Psychology Press.

Sutton, C. (1998). New perspectives on languages in science. In B. J. Fraser, & K. G. Tobin (Eds.), *International handbook of science education* (pp. 27–38). Dordrecht: Kluwer.

Sweller, J., Kirschner, P. A., & Clark, R. E. (2007). Why minimally guided teaching techniques do not work: A reply to commentaries. *Educational Psychologist, 42*(2), 115–121.

Thagard, P. (1992). *Conceptual revolutions.* Princeton, NJ: Princeton University Press.

Tobias, S., & Duffy, T. (Eds.) (2009). *Constructivist instruction: Success or failure?* New York: Routledge.

Toth, E., Suthers, D., & Lesgold, A. (2002). "Mapping to know": The effects of representational guidance and reflective assessment on scientific inquiry. *Science Education, 86*(2), 265–286.

Van Merriënboer, J. J. G., & Sweller, J. (2005). Cognitive load theory and complex learning: Recent developments and future directions. *Educational Psychology Review, 17*(2), 147–177.

Van Zee, E., & Minstrell, J. (1997). Using questioning to guide student thinking. *The Journal of the Learning Sciences, 6,* 227–269.

Wandersee, J., Mintzes, J., & Novak, J. (1994). Research on alternative conceptions in science. In D. Gabel (Ed.), *Handbook of research on science teaching and learning* (pp. 177–210). New York: Macmillan Publishing Company.

Wellman, H. (1990). *The child's theory of mind.* Cambridge, MA: MIT Press.

White, R., & Tisher, R. (1986). Research on natural sciences. In M. Wittrock (Ed.), *Handbook of research on teaching* (3rd ed., pp. 874–905). New York: Macmillan.

Wilson, M. (2009). Measuring progressions: Assessment structures underlying a learning progression. *Journal of Research in Science Teaching, 46*(6), 716–730.

Wimmer, H., & Perner, J. (1983). Beliefs about beliefs: Representation and constraining function of wrong beliefs in young children's understanding of deception. *Cognition, 13,* 41–68.

Winnett, D. A., Rockwell, R. E., Sherwood, E. A., & Williams, R. A. (1996). *Explorations for the early years: Grade pre-kindergarten.* Menlo Park, CA: Addison-Wesley.

Wiser, M. (1995). Use of history of science to understand and remedy students' misconception about time and temperature. In D. Perkins (Ed.), *Software goes to school.* New York: Oxford University Press.

6

LEARNING HISTORY
Linda S. Levstik

INTRODUCTION AND HISTORICAL OVERVIEW

Interest in history education is rooted in fundamental questions about what students can and should learn about how the world came to be the way it is, about how power and exclusion operate in the world, and about how an understanding of the past might influence the present and the future. Because history is never a neutral force or a complete worldview, arguments persist about *whose* history appears in (or disappears from) the curriculum, *how* history is taught and learned, and *for what purposes* (Barton & Levstik, 2004; Berkin, Crocco, & Winslow, 2009; Epstein, 2008; Seixas, 2004; Thornton, 2004, 2008; Wineburg, 2001). These arguments have buffeted history education in the U.S. for over a hundred years and show little sign of disappearing any time soon (Nash, Crabtree, & Dunn, 2000; National Governing Board [NGB], 2000; Levstik, 1996; Lybarger, 1991; Snedden, 1924; Thornton, 2004).

None of this should be surprising given disciplinary history's shifts and upheavals in the 20th century. In the United States, the dominant narrative of national history with which the century began fractured into multiple and often-contending narratives. As challenges to traditional ideas about objectivity became more widespread and historians examined the impact of changing sociocultural and political contexts on historical scholarship, they also considered the role historical narratives played in preserving and challenging power relations (Appleby, Hunt, & Jacob, 1994; Novick, 1988; Seixas, 2004; Willinsky, 2000). In a period of multiple historical narratives, too, it became clear that public and private uses of history varied considerably (Blight, 2002; Bodnar, 1993; Lowenthal, 1998; Nora, 1989; Novick, 1988; Smith, 2003).

Interestingly, although scholars invoked various educational theories to explain learning in history, relatively little empirical work focused on how students made sense of the past until well into the 1980s (Downey & Levstik, 1991). From the 1980s on, however, newer theories on human cognition exerted considerable if not always explicit influence on researchers' ways of examining student learning in history. The following discussion focuses first on theoretical shifts and their impact on investigating student learning in history, then on current research directions, and finally on implications for practice and future research.

EXAMINING STUDENT LEARNING IN HISTORY: THEORETICAL SHIFTS

Reflective Inquiry

History educators have long argued that some form of what Alan Griffin ([1942] 1992) described as *independent reflection* provides a coherent and disciplinarily appropriate theoretical base for learning history. From Griffin's perspective, the independence to thoughtfully examine the past developed as students engaged in inquiry into historical problems with current resonance. Later, when Bruner (1962) called for attention to disciplinary forms of inquiry, he struck a note that resonated among history educators already inclined to an inquiry-based approach to history. Despite the persistence of arguments for inquiry-based teaching and learning and the popularity of related materials and programs with some history educators, however, classrooms only rarely reflected an inquiry perspective. Indeed, critics doubted that students could reasonably be expected to learn much history from inquiry-based instruction. In particular, scholars influenced by Piagetian theory suggested that the cognitive foundation for historical inquiry appeared too late in students' development to be of much use either as an instructional tool or as a theoretical model for developing historical thinking (Hallam, 1972).

In challenging this view, others argued that Piagetian theory offered too narrow an understanding of historical thinking as well as of secondary students' intellectual capacities (Booth, 1984; Dickinson, Lee, & Rogers, 1984; Shemilt, 1980). In one of the earliest studies to investigate the impact of inquiry on students' learning in history, Shemilt (1980) reported that students described historical inquiry as more challenging, worthwhile, and interesting than their previous work in history. Further, content analysis of students' written work suggested a more sophisticated use of evidence than Piagetian formulations would have predicted.

Encouraged by these results, and drawing on emerging theories regarding pedagogical content knowledge (Shulman, 1987; Wilson & Wineburg, 1988) and domain-specific cognition (Alexander & Judy, 1988), researchers on both sides of the Atlantic became increasingly interested in investigating the nature of expert historical practice and novice-to-expert shifts in the context of historical inquiry. In the UK, researchers involved with the CHATA (Concepts of History and Teaching Approaches, 7–14) project investigated second-order concepts (use of evidence, causation, perspective) related to historical inquiry (see, for instance, Lee, Ashby, & Dickinson, 1996). Using a combination of video observation, student interviews and analysis of students' written responses to historical stimuli, investigators postulated levels (or progression) in students' evaluation of historical evidence.

This approach—examining problem-solving in the context of a historical task—is indicative of a broader movement among researchers examining thought in-process rather than extrapolating thinking based on recall of historical information. As researchers attended more to learning contexts they began drawing more heavily on sociocultural theory. This emphasis on culturally and historically situated practices rather than single, immutable domains proved a useful framework for making sense of students' differing historical conceptions and misconceptions.

SOCIOCULTURAL CONSTRUCTIONS OF HISTORICAL THINKING AND LEARNING

James Wertsch's (1998) conception of *mediated action* has been particularly influential among researchers interested in applying sociocultural theories to historical thinking. Wertsch describes thinking not only as socially, culturally, and historically situated, but also as mediated by an array of cultural tools for a variety of purposes. Using his own work in Estonia as an example, he demonstrates how students come to resist "official" histories and rely on alternative narratives. In similar fashion, other researchers drew on sociocultural theory in explaining some African American students' resistance to school histories (Epstein, 2008) as well as students' ascriptions of historical significance to people, events, and ideas in different cultural contexts (Barton & McCully, 2005; Levstik, 2001; Seixas, 1993). By shifting attention from individual cognition to learning in community, sociocultural theory called attention to history as a cultural tool used for often-competing purposes.

From its introduction as a school subject, history has served a variety of aims and purposes, including acquiring disciplinary "ways of knowing," preparing well-informed, rational citizens, and developing democratic humanism (Barton & Levstik, 2004; Rüsen, 2004; Simon, 2004). Back in 1898, when Lucy Salmon bemoaned the sad state of history education, she laid much of the blame on "a patriotism that would seek to present distorted ideas of the past with the idea of glorifying one country at the possible expense of truth" (1898, p. 1). But there are other cultural uses for history. Barton and Levstik (2004) described four cultural practices or stances common to school history in the United States: Identifying with people or events in the past, analyzing causal linkages in history, responding morally, and displaying information about the past. Salmon's (1898, p. 1) "spurious patriotism . . . at the expense of truth" represents one form of identification, but it is not the only possibility. As Epstein's (2008) research suggests, an identification stance can also help students historically situate overlapping identities and encourage rich and interesting dialogue about contending and coalescing interests in a pluralist democracy. Different stances may also overlap in the classroom: In the same unit of study, students may be called upon to analyze sources, identify with historical actors, respond morally to historical dilemmas and display the results of their inquiries to peers or interested others.

Among the varying purposes claimed for learning history, citizenship goals have lately garnered attention (Aitken & Sinnema, 2008; Barton & Levstik, 2004; Hughes, 2004; Lee, 2004; Parker, 2002; Simon, 2004). Jörg Rüsen's (2004) conception of *historical consciousness*, for instance, makes a civic case for history as "rendering present actuality intelligible" (p. 67). He argues that by locating students in a *temporal whole* larger than an individual life, historical study prepares them for present and future problem-solving. Rüsen as well as other scholars also suggest some caution in this regard. Not only do narrow conceptions of the past handicap civic action, they argue, but there is little evidence that students easily transfer what they learn in history to the larger civic arena (Aitkin & Sinnema, 2008; Arthur, Davies, Kerr, & Wrenn, 2001; Clark, 2004; Nash et al., 2001).

As the remainder of this chapter suggests, despite disparate purposes claimed for history, and the subtle and not-so-subtle differences attached to terms characterizing learning in history—*historical thinking, historical understanding* and *historical consciousness*, among them—sociocultural theories undergird a reasonably robust set of research findings that offer considerable insight into students' ideas about the past and suggest ways in which classroom practice might better support learning for transfer.

CURRENT TRENDS AND ISSUES: STUDENTS' IDEAS ABOUT HISTORY AND THE PAST

Early Learning in History

In the past few decades, researchers have primarily relied on naturalistic inquiry to trace the development of students' historical thinking. Based on this research we know that children begin developing ideas about the past at an early age. They enter school able to identify ways in which life changes over time and their ideas tend to become more sophisticated as they advance in school (Lee & Ashby, 2000, 2001; Barton, 2002; Cooper & Chapman, 2009; Downey, 1996; Harnett, 1993; Levstik & Barton, 2008; Lynn, 1993; Seixas, 1997; Vella, 2001). Even in the earliest school years, students can sequence broad historical eras with reasonable accuracy by drawing on changes in material and popular culture (Barton & Levstik, 1996; Foster, Hoge, & Rosch, 1999; Harnett, 1993; Hoodless, 2002). Over time, they are more likely to identify long-term social and political patterns related to national development and to have reference to alternative histories that may challenge the national history presented in school (Apostolidou, 2008; Barton & Levstik, 1998; Epstein, 2008, Epstein & Shiller, 2009; Körber, 1997; Yeager, Foster, & Greer, 2002; Seixas, 2006; Yeager & Terzian, 2007).

History and Literacy Studies

Despite knowing considerably more about early learning in history now than in the past, this remains one of the least researched areas in the field. In part, this is a legacy of Piagetian developmental theory; in part, a reflection of the lack of emphasis on history in early schooling. Perhaps not surprisingly, then, when researchers turned their attention to younger children's historical thinking they drew on theories and methods common in a field notable for attention to young learners—literacy studies.

One line of research drew on reader response theory to investigate how narrative influences children's historical thinking. Levstik and Pappas (1987), for instance, investigated how children's retellings of a tradebook historical narrative varied relative to Piagetian stage expectations and how historical elements featured in retellings. Isabel Beck and Margaret McKeown (1988) also drew on research in literacy to investigate student comprehension, but they focused on textbooks rather than tradebooks. In an analysis of fifth-grade textbook accounts of the American Revolution, Beck and McKeown described texts that lacked clarity in the relation between the content presented and instructional goals, appeared to operate out of erroneous assumptions regarding students' background knowledge, and provided inadequate explanations of relations among events and outcomes.

Based on this analysis, Beck and her colleagues revised text passages to better support reader comprehension. Beck, McKeown, and Sinatra (1991) and Beck, McKeown, and

Worthy (1995) then revised the text passages and tested the effects of these more coherent and "voiced" texts on students' comprehension. Quantitative analyses indicated that students who read the revised text passages and those who received background instruction before reading text passages scored significantly higher on comprehension tests than did students who read the original unrevised text passages. Qualitative analysis of student interviews further suggested that students better recalled passages exhibiting a strong sense of voice.

A second area of literacy-related research focuses on student-constructed narratives. In these studies, students are asked to use various sources to construct an explanatory narrative in response to a historical question. Researchers generally combine textual analysis, observation and interview protocols in these studies. Overall results indicate that students tend to recount the central features of historical events but simplify, conflate, reorganize, or invent historical details to maintain narrative cohesion. Without instructional intervention, they tend to flatten perspectives, emphasizing the actions of dominant groups and individuals and ignoring marginalized or minority perspectives. With instructional intervention, however, even younger students better recognize and account for historical within and across-group differences as well as differences between the past and present (Afflerbach & VanSledright, 2001; Barton & Levstik, 2004; VanSledright, 2002).

A third set of studies focus less on reading comprehension and more on how students explain, rework or resist elements of national history. Because these studies are not confined to early learning, but include adolescent learners, they are treated separately, below.

National Stories: Learning Official and Vernacular Histories

Studies investigating students' national narratives generally ask participants to identify significant elements of national history. Students may create a timeline of significant people, events and ideas (Barton & McCully, 2005; Epstein, 2008; Foster, Hoge, & Rosch, 1999; Levstik, 2001), respond to a particular construction of the past (Grant, 2003; VanSledright & Frankes, 2000; Wertsch, 1998), or interpret historical evidence (Ashby, 2004; Boix-Mansilla, 2005; Lee & Guy, 2003, VanSledright, 1995). Results of these and similar studies suggest that students' ideas about national development vary considerably across countries.

In the United States, for instance, students often know elements of a quest-for-freedom narrative and a related story of national progress (Barton & Levstik, 2004; Wertsch, 1998). But not all national narratives are quite so upbeat. In Northern Ireland and Germany, students offer evidence of national decline as well as progress (Barton, 2002, 2005; King, 2009; Kölbl & Straub, 2001). French Quebecois often describe a history of conquest and subjugation, while Ghanaian students emphasize self-rule achieved through ancestral sacrifice (Levstik & Groth, 2005; Seixas, 2006). Students in New Zealand may imagine themselves distant from centers of power yet able to offer problem-solving skills to the rest of the world (Levstik, 2001), and Greek students recall a story of an ancient people whose distinctive Hellenistic characteristics carry into the present (Apostolidou, 2008).

Students' national narratives also demonstrate marked similarity in several important respects. First, barring a significant disjunction between students' home and school identities, they tend not to seek alternatives to prevailing narratives. Second, in recounting national narratives, they tend also to ignore significant differences in perspective among people living in the past as well as between past and present. As a result, they may ignore the impact of differential agency on human behavior, reducing some people to historical shadows and exaggerating the agency of others (Epstein & Shiller, 2009; Levstik & Groth, 2002).

Although many students may accept these simplified national narratives, others turn to alternative or vernacular histories that represent groups with whom they identify (Epstein, 2008; Epstein & Shiller, 2009; Raupach, 2008). Histories constructed in home and community serve as filters through which students view the texts, tasks, and historical interpretations introduced in school (Epstein & Schiller, 2009). Although impact varies within and between groups, researchers note differences in how children and adults from different racial and ethnic backgrounds ascribe significance to historical events, people, and ideas (Epstein, 2008; Seixas, 1997). In analyzing data collected in a national telephone survey, Rosenzweig and Thelan (2000) found that African American and Sioux study participants thought it more important to situate their families' experiences in the broader history of their racial group than did European Americans or Mexican Americans. Overall, Sioux and African Americans emphasized group rather than individual agency more often than did other respondents. Misco (2008) and Wertsch (1998) describe a more profound disconnect between official and vernacular histories in former Soviet bloc countries where continuing silences regarding aspects of the past perpetuate distrust of historical narratives.

Finally, popular culture also intervenes in students' engagement with history. Whether students draw on *Forrest Gump* or *Amistad*, the combination of sound, image and story offered by film provides a more powerful version of the past than most textbooks manage (Marcus, Metzger, & Stoddard, 2010; Wineburg et al., 2009). Similarly, toys, fiction, non-fiction, and television mediate students' experiences with the past. While researchers report that vernacular histories and popular culture influence students' developing ideas about the past, they also argue that ignoring alternate histories can generate resistance that stymies any substantive engagement with the past. In culturally diverse and divided societies, too, research suggests that vernacular histories sometimes frustrate the achievement of civic goals, especially in pluralist societies (Apostolidou, 2008; Barton & McCully, 2006; Ben-David Kolikant & Pollack, 2008; Porat, 2004).

Gender(ed) Narratives

Amid current attention to alternatives to some aspects of history, it is interesting to note the dearth of research regarding alternatives to traditional masculinist history or, more broadly, to the influence of gender in learning history (Berkin, Crocco, & Winslow, 2009). Although some studies include gender in their analyses, few note significant differences in male and female performance. On the other hand, the few studies that focus primarily on gender, usually in the context of women's history, note differences in how students respond to explicit attention to gender.

In one case, researchers combined assessment data and interviews to investigate the impact of a required women's history course in the Netherlands, noting that while female students tended to do better on assessments in women's history, they also expressed concern about the perceived emphasis on women as historical victims (ten Dam & Rijkschroeff, 1996). Similarly, in a study in the U.S. that combined observation, interviews and analysis of student work, eighth graders worried that investigating women's experiences and perspectives was not *real history* and risked leaving men out

(Levstik & Groth, 2002). As some history educators have noted, women may, indeed, be hard to find or marginalized in the history curriculum while men are everywhere but not understood as gendered (Berkin et al., 2009). As is the case in so much of the research on learning history, however, when instruction explicitly attends to gender in conjunction with attention to perspective recognition and agency, so do students (Levstik & Groth, 2002).

Perspective Recognition

Because perspective recognition or empathetic understanding is fundamental to making sense of the past, researchers have investigated this area in some depth (Davis, Foster, & Yeager, 2001; Epstein, 1998; Barton, & Levstik, 2004; Shemilt, 1980). In an early such study, Peter Knight (1990) suggested a less linear progression than that posited later by Lee and Ashby (2002). Knight described differential development of various subcompetencies influencing students' ability to recognize historical perspectives. Lee and Ashby (2001), on the other hand, identified five levels of empathetic understanding, beginning with seeing the past as largely unintelligible and, finally, placing human actions within a broader socio-cultural context of differences in beliefs, values, and material conditions within a given time and society. They based their model of progression on written responses to three perspective recognition tasks from 320 students, aged 7–14 and follow-up studies with a subset of 92 students. While these tasks were not part of regular classroom instruction, they were structured to approximate "natural" classroom activity.

Levstik (2001) also employed a naturalistic strategy, first observing New Zealand students as they engaged in identifying significant people, events, and ideas and then interviewing them about how different perspectives might influence ascriptions of historical significance. She found that students engaged more easily with more distant perspectives, becoming less sure about and more dismissive of perspectives closer to them in time and place. Interestingly, VanSledright (2001) noted similarities between adolescent and adult student approaches to perspective. Adult learners, for instance, tended to presentize past perspectives—imagining that people in the past shared the same world view as their own—a pattern common among younger students.

Several studies in the U.S. also took an ethnographic approach to investigating perspective or empathy. Barton's (1996) report of narrative simplifications in elementary children's historical thinking took note of the difficulties students had in imagining past perspectives as more than evidence of ignorance or inferior intellect. Levstik and Groth's (2002) ethnographic investigation of an eighth grade study of antebellum American history found that although students could identify different perspectives within and between groups, sustaining perspective recognition required considerable teacher mediation. In reviewing this and related literature, Barton and Levstik (2004) suggest five competencies related to perspective recognition: a sense of "otherness," shared "normalcy," historical contextualization, differentiation of perspectives, and contextualization of the present. Although they do not suggest a hierarchy, they do note that the most challenging competency appears to be contextualizing the present. Students may contextualize actions distant in time and place, but when asked to consider alternative perspectives on "closer-to-home" issues, they are more likely to discount them as ill-informed or simply in error (Apostolidou, 2008; Levstik, 2001). Based on their study of Israeli and Palestinian students, Ben-David Kolikant and Pollack (in press) note, however, that these initial responses can be ameliorated with sensitive instruction.

Overall, the research on students' ability to recognize different historical perspectives suggests that this is a long-term development, amenable to instruction but often fragile, especially in the face of personal loyalties and identities (Barton & McCully, 2006; Davis et al., 2001; Levstik & Groth, 2002; Porat, 2004). Further, an instructional emphasis on perspective primarily in relation to historical causation can lead to further misunderstandings of individual, collective, and institutional agency. Indeed, without substantive attention to the sometimes devastating consequences of differing perspectives, students struggle to make connections between past ideas and events and current circumstances (Barton & Levstik, 2004; Rüsen, 2004; Simon, 2006; Seixas, 2006).

Back to Historical Inquiry

Following in the tradition of earlier history educators, current research continues to focus on learning to use the cultural tools related to historical inquiry. Researchers examine how students acquire and use these tools, especially in regard to making sense of historical evidence and building evidence-based historical interpretations. Overall, research on students' acquisition of historical tools suggests that *how* students learn influences *what* they learn. Without specific instruction in school, students rarely understand how the history they encounter came to be known (Barton, 2001; Brophy & VanSledright, 1997; Cooper, 1992; Fasulo, Girardet, & Pontecorvo, 1998; Shemilt, 1980; VanSledright & Afflerbach, 2005). Even with specific instruction, historical inquiry challenges students at all ages. Unfortunately for our understanding of student inquiry, research has tended to focus on some aspects of inquiry more than on others, and often in isolation rather than in the context of actual student inquiry.

Students' understanding of source materials remains the most investigated aspect of historical inquiry. As a result, more is known regarding the challenges students encounter in accessing and evaluating source material than is the case with other aspects of inquiry such as question-setting. Overall, researchers note a number of problems experienced by students as they work with historical sources. Students tend not to recognize the need to interpret sources nor the possibility that similar sources might lead to quite disparate interpretations (Ashby, 2004; Ferretti, MacArthur, & Okolo, 2001; Lee & Ashby, 2000). Rather than consider authors' intentions or the contexts within which sources originally appeared, they account for differences in terms of bias or incomplete information (Afflerbach & VanSledright, 2001; Britt & Aglinskas, 2002; Foster et al., 1999; Kohlmeier, 2005; VanSledright, 2002; von Borries, 1997; Wineburg, 2001). Further, students may assess reliability based on the quantity or specificity of information obtained from a source (Ashby, 2004; Barca, 2005; Boix Mansilla, 2005; Gago, 2005; VanSledright & Afflerbach, 2005; VanSledright & Frankes, 2000).

These challenges are not insurmountable. Relatively minor interventions lead students to be more critical of sources (Ashby, 2004; Barton, 2001; Britt & Aglinskas, 2002; Hoodless, 2004; Kohlmeier, 2005; Levstik & Groth, 2002; VanSledright, 2002). It is unclear, however, if such gains hold up over time. And, even when students do take a more critical stance towards sources, they tend to be less critical when those sources conform to their own social and political commitments (Epstein, 2008; Seixas, 1996; VanSledright, 2002).

As a number of studies demonstrate, students tend also to struggle with the evidentiary uses of historical sources (Ashby, 2004; Ferretti et al., 2001; Kohlmeier, 2005). They sometimes describe interpretation as a matter of balancing sources. In other cases students explain the process as fitting pieces together in a historical jigsaw puzzle, or of forensic-like reconstructions—all with the aim of creating a single correct picture of the past (Levstik, Henderson, & Schlarb, 2005; Medina, Pollard, Schneider, & Leonhard, 2000; VanSledright, 2002). Once again, given opportunities to engage in historical inquiry, students better explain how the same evidence can support multiple possible interpretations and are more likely to write connected historical arguments and to support those arguments with evidence (Ashby, 2004; Kohlmeier, 2005; Levstik & Groth, 2002; Voss & Wiley, 1997; Wiley & Voss, 1999; Yeager, Foster, Maley, Anderson, & Morris, 1998). Other researchers note, however, that even as students improve, the tendency to abandon evidence in favor of narrative remains strong among students of all ages (Levstik & Smith, 1996; Stahl et al., 1996; Young & Leinhardt, 1998).

One of the least investigated aspects of historical inquiry involves question-setting. Perhaps because the task can be time-consuming and challenging, studies of historical inquiry tend to avoid student-initiated questions altogether. In the few studies where this issue is addressed, well-developed questions appear to generate interest in historical inquiry, to encourage better use of sources and to lead to more evidence-based interpretations (Hicks & Doolittle, 2008; Levstik & Smith, 1997; Saye & Brush, 2002; VanSledright, 2002). This is particularly interesting in light of students' more general difficulty in understanding the development of historical accounts and use of evidence (Ashby, 2004; Barton, 2001; Cooper, 1992; Fasulo et al., 1998; Saye & Brush, 2002, 2005). Knowing why someone might investigate one idea or event rather than another and where questions come from, for instance, might help students better evaluate the evidentiary use of historical documents and artifacts, and understand the development of historical accounts that otherwise presents such problems.

Developing questions that address significant historical issues, are open to multiple evidence-based interpretations, and can be investigated using available resources takes considerable time and requires careful scaffolding and relatively few researchers investigate student inquiry from question-setting through interpretation. Overall, those who do investigate student performance in inquiry-based instruction find high levels of student engagement with and interest in history combined with a more analytical stance towards evidence and interpretation (Barton & McCully, 2005; Brophy & VanSledright, 1997; Brush & Saye, 2001; Dimitriadis, 2000; Hicks & Doolittle, 2008; Levstik & Groth, 2005; VanSledright, 2002; Wineburg, 2000; Yeager & Terzian, 2007). At the same time, when students face complex reading tasks, have difficulties in accessing and synthesizing information from multiple sources, and suffer from lack of experience producing different history genres, they benefit from careful instructional scaffolding (Brush & Saye, 2001; Levstik & Groth, 2002; Milson, 2002; Saye & Brush, 2002, van Boxtel & van Drie, 2004; van Drie & van Boxtel, 2003; VanSledright & Frankes, 2000; VanSledright & Kelly, 1998).

This appears to be especially the case when students attempt to explain social, cultural, political and economic forces that influence people's actions. Students tend to ascribe social and cultural patterns to personal preferences and prejudices and change to alterations in individual attitudes, rather than to larger forces (Beck et al., 1995; Brophy & VanSledright, 1997; Carretero, Jacott, Limón, López-Manjón, & León, 1994; Halldén, 1997, 1998; P. Lee & Ashby, 2001; Riviere, Núnez, & Fontela, 1998; Rose, 2000; Wills, 2005). Although this tendency lessens somewhat with age, it requires sustained instructional attention to institutional agency to lead students to take such factors into account on any consistent basis (Barton, 2001; Bermudez & Jaramillo, 2001; Carretero, López-Manjón, & Jacott, 1997; Jacott, López-Manjón, & Carretero, 1998; Levstik & Groth, 2002; Mosberg, 2002). Increasingly, researchers have turned to technological supports in investigating this kind of student learning.

Technological Supports for Student Learning

A number of researchers investigating the impact of technological scaffolding for inquiry note some familiar response patterns. Some students follow the path of least resistance, uncritically downloading data and recording factual information with little or no attempt at synthesis. Some struggle in crafting evidence-based interpretations in newer history genres just as they did in traditional narratives, and some reduce their interpretations to the equivalent of text messages—sound bites rather than substantive historical arguments (Saye et al., 2009; Swan & Hofer, 2008). New problems also arise as students encounter difficulties in selecting and analyzing on-line sources, following through on web-based instructions, or navigating unfamiliar interfaces (Hicks & Doolittle, 2008; Saye & Brush, 2005). On the other hand, careful investigations of on-line problem-based inquiries with point-of-need assistance describe students more likely to draw on historical information, include multiple perspectives, and account for counterarguments in their historical presentations than did students in a traditionally instructed comparison group (Brush & Saye, 2001; Saye & Brush, 2005).

The findings related to digital moviemaking are a bit more complicated. In some cases the constraints of the medium—the need for concision, the opportunity to triangulate visual, textual, and aural sources—encourage attention to interpretation and discourage the information dump common in traditional essays. With point-of-need assistance, students more often produce interesting and evidence-based historical analyses. At the same time, without considerable assistance, they tend to such concision that they fail to connect question to evidence or evidence to interpretation or get lost in the complications of synchronizing all the elements on a screen (Hofer & Swan, 2006). As Swan and Hofer (2008) noted in reviewing this research, while newer technologies require considerable soft scaffolding—the kind of in-the-moment assistance provided by teachers or other experts—they also offer considerable motivational impact.

MOTIVATING STUDENTS' HISTORICAL INTERESTS

Very few researchers specifically examine student motivation in history. Studies of students' historical interests and conceptions of the purposes of school history, however, are suggestive in this regard. Students often say they enjoy learning about history from sources outside the school and express interest in ordinary people and the impact of extraordinary historical events on individual lives, especially those related to human rights violations (Barton & McCully, 2005; Dimitriadis, 2000; Grant, 2001; Kohlmeier, 2005; Kölbl & Straub, 2001; Levesque, 2003; Levstik & Groth, 2002; Schweber, 2009; Wills, 2005; Wineburg, 2000; Yeager & Terzian, 2007). This preference may relate to one of the purposes students often perceive for history—avoiding the mistakes of the past—and to the appeal of historical tradebooks (Biddulph & Adey, 2004; VanSledright, 1997).

As noted, studies suggest that reading clearly voiced trade book-like depictions of the past improves student comprehension (Beck et al., 1995; Paxton, 1997; VanSledright

& Kelly, 1998). At least one recent study (Smith & Niemi, 2001) also associates such texts with higher scores on achievement tests in U.S. history. Students may prefer trade books to textbooks, but they also express interest in non-text sources—visual images and artifacts. In an investigation of the impact of archaeological study on fifth graders' historical thinking, students described their work with artifacts as motivating not only because they excavated historical artifacts, but because the experience was investigative and interpretive. They described previous work with history textbooks as learning a "finished story" rather than investigating an open question (Levstik, Henderson, & Schlarb, 2005).

In Europe, Prangsma, Van Boxtel, and Kanselaar (2008) focused on other aspects of visualizing the past, finding positive correlations between the use of visual organizers (e.g., charts, graphs) and students' comprehension of more abstract aspects of history. In particular, they found a positive impact on comprehension when combining visualizations and text with opportunities for student dialogue—another instance where a relatively minor instructional intervention produced positive effects on student learning.

HISTORY BEYOND THE NATION-STATE

Considering the amount of academic attention to new ways of conceptualizing world history, it is surprising that almost no research in history education focuses on this area. Ross Dunn (2009) describes academic world history as a wide umbrella encompassing explorations of patterns, connections and comparisons within limited frames of time and space as well as studies that consider the "history of our species within large scales of change" (p. 184). Little of this work, he contends, ends up in schools. Even less often is it the subject of research in history education (Zevin & Gerwin, 2005).

Archaeology educators echo Dunn's concern for an analytical emphasis on the deep past and on collective behavior. Archaeologists tend to view behavior as mediated by tools and marked by patterns that connect people and places over long periods of time (LaMotta & Schiffer, 2001). Studies of the impact of archaeological experience suggest, however, that while motivating, experiences with archaeological processes do not necessarily lead to attention to pattern or connection—understandings advocated by archaeologists and world historians (Davis, 2005; Levstik et al., 2005).

Although there is very little research on world history per se, some scholarship in global education relates to world history. There is evidence, for instance, that teachers with international experience are more inclined to include studies of world cultures in their curriculum and that students respond positively to internationally experienced teachers (Zong, Quashigah, & Wilson, 2008). Gaudelli's (2002) description of global education also has much in common with Dunn's description of the new world history—a search for pattern, connection, and a long view across cultures and time. Gaudelli notes, however, that there are some tensions between advocates of infusing global education in all aspects of the curriculum and world history advocates who worry that disciplinary history will lose out to what they perceive as a more amorphous global education.

Some on-line simulations attempt to call attention to world history, too. In a study of the impact of an on-line game that simulates world history crises, Squires (2004) found that students rarely focused on the historical parallels built into the game. In the context of the simulation, some students discussed the circumstances under which a pan-African civilization might thrive or considered how history might have been reversed, but they tended not to see this as related to "what actually happened" in world history. Squire concluded that the game allowed students to challenge historical power structures without developing the kinds of historical understandings claimed by the games' advocates.

Beyond these few studies, we know very little about how (or if) students make sense of world history. Dunn's (2009) *World History for Us All* program reflects current historical scholarship and offers teachers a much-needed theoretical and practical base for developing world history lessons and curriculum, but to date the field lacks systematic investigation of student learning in the context of world history.

CONCLUSION AND IMPLICATIONS

History educators face an interesting set of challenges: contested purposes, a broad purview (all of time and every place), challenging sources (the fragmentary remains of the past), complex cultural tools and difficulties in helping students transfer what they've learned to venues outside the classroom. In regard to purpose, students are fairly consistent in their expectations. They expect to learn how the world got to be the way it is and they expect to use this knowledge to make more informed decisions in the present and future (VanSledright, 1997). They share this expectation with a number of historians and history educators who argue that understanding how societies evolve over time broadens the basis for individual and collective decision-making (Levstik & Barton, 2008; Rüsen, 2004; Seixas, 2004).

Unfortunately, traditional chronological history curricula may limit students' opportunities to achieve these goals. Dunn's (2009) *World History for Us All* program offers a promising if empirically untested alternative, a "unified chronology" that emphasizes global change and "patterns of historical meaning and significance" (p. 1). Other alternatives such as problem-based instruction have been empirically tested with good results, suggesting that explicit attention to links between past and present and to the varying perspectives that influence people's actions can offer support for at least some civic and humanistic goals claimed for history education (Saye & Brush, 2005). In fact, there is considerable evidence that, although student misperceptions about human behavior are fairly predictable, they are also amenable to instruction, especially in the context of historical inquiry. Although inquiry skills are sometimes fragile, with sustained classroom practice, elementary as well as secondary students can locate, evaluate and synthesize evidence, contextualize historical perspectives, and differentiate among the types of agency available to historical actors. The fragility of these skills argues for consistent reinforcement, sensitivity to students' social identifications, and attention to the challenges of analyzing issues with strong contemporary relevance (Bransford, Brown, & Cocking, 1999; Epstein, 2008; McCully, Pilgrim, Sutherland, & McMinn, 2002).

Wade (2007) developed a nationwide program, *CiviConnections*, to address this issue. Teachers learned to help students conduct historical inquiries into local issues and to take ameliorative action. Students not only analyze historical values, beliefs, and attitudes, but consider the intersections between past and present perspectives and how that might inform current decision-making on locally sensitive issues. With specific training in democratic decision-making and discussion of controversial issues, students develop skills important in other contexts as well, yet we know very little about when and if students transfer these skills from historical inquiry to civic discourse (Hess, 2009; Parker, 2002; Wade, 2007). Given the claims made for history education—almost all of them dependent on students' willingness and ability to transfer knowledge and skills from the classroom to public arenas—it is surprising how little research investigates transfer.

Considerable scholarly attention focuses on students' narrative recreations of the past and their ability to understand how others' historical narratives come to be. In fact, no other historical tool receives quite so much attention and is so regularly and uncritically suggested for instructional use as narrative. This is likely due to a human tendency to internalize story structures and rely on them as one important way to organize experience. By suggesting an underlying logic to events and a "moral to the story," narratives have been shown to help students remember and make sense of some features of the past, but they also pose difficulties that are too rarely noted. The emphasis on individual agency in fiction, biography, and autobiography, for instance, may exaggerate individual efficacy and ignore or underestimate the power of collective or institutional agency.

Similarly, students may recognize perspectives other than those of the protagonists in narratives, but nonetheless dismiss them as undesirable. Careful use of contrasting narratives from textbooks, monographs, interactive media and student-created narratives can work against this tendency by calling attention to how narratives are structured or how evidence supports or fails to support alternate interpretations, as well as to call attention to narratives as artifacts of time and place, but again, there is little evidence that these practices are common in schools (Barton & Levstik, 2004; Rüsen, 2004).

Overall, students benefit from reading, watching, and listening to multiple genres of historical narratives, as well as from writing or producing their own evidence-based narratives. Ultimately, however, history education researchers suggest that narrative is not enough and argue for the importance of bringing the past to bear in democratic negotiation (Arthur, Davies, Kerr, & Wrenn, et al., 2001). At present, however, the field lacks a strong research base regarding how (or if) students make this transfer.

FUTURE DIRECTIONS

Three aspects of learning history remain under-researched: (1) emergent historical thinking; (2) sense-making in the context of world history; and (3) transfer. Some recent work has focused on elementary teachers' ideas about the purposes of history and the social studies (James, 2008) and the loss of instructional time at the elementary level (Rock, Hefner, O'Conner, et al., 2004). These are important and interesting investigations, but history education would also benefit from investigating the historical aspects of the cultural universals so prevalent in primary classrooms (Brophy & Alleman, 2005). In regard to world history, researchers might attend to how a world perspective alters (or fails to alter) students' ideas about the normalcy of other ways of living, about the impact of long-term global patterns or about historical connections across cultures (Dunn, 2009; Stearns, 2001). Finally, the lack of research on transfer, especially in regard to the citizenship and humanistic or historical consciousness goals of history education undermines the achievement of these goals. Under what instructional conditions do students transfer historical information or ideas to other arenas, both in and out of school? What issues generate interest in historical antecedents? How can students learn to use historical information or ideas in democratic discourse when they feel personal commitments regarding controversial ideas? Given its relation to some of the primary goals claimed for history education, transfer certainly merits research attention.

REFERENCES

Afflerbach, P., & VanSledright, B. A. (2001). Hath! Doth! What? Middle graders reading innovative history texts. *Journal of Adolescent and Adult Literacy, 44*, 696–707.

Aitken, G., & Sinnema, C. (2008). *Effective pedagogy in social sciences/Tikanga a Iwi: Best evidence synthesis iteration.* Wellington, New Zealand: New Zealand Ministry of Education.

Alexander, P. A., & Judy, J. E. (1988). The interaction of domain-specific and strategic knowledge in academic performance. *Review of Educational Research, 58*(4), 375–404.

Apostolidou, E. (2008). Greek students' official narrative and its role in learning history. Paper presented at the Annual Meeting of the American Educational Research Association, New York.

Appleby, J., Hunt, L., & Jacob, M. (1994). *Telling the truth about history.* New York: W. W. Norton.

Arthur, J., Davies, I., Kerr, D., & Wrenn, A. (2001). *Citizenship through secondary history.* New York: Routledge.

Ashby, R. (2004). Developing a concept of historical evidence: Students' ideas about testing singular factual claims. *International Journal of Historical Learning, Teaching and Research, 4*(2), 44–55.

Barca, I. (2005). "Till new facts are discovered": Students' ideas about objectivity in history. In R. Ashby, P. Gordon, & P. Lee (Eds.), *International review of history education, Vol. 4: Understanding history: Recent research in history education* (pp. 68–82). New York: Routledge.

Barton, K. C. (1996). Narrative simplifications in elementary children's historical understanding. In J. Brophy (Ed.), *Advances in Research on Teaching, 4*, 51–83.

Barton, K. C. (2001). A sociocultural perspective on children's understanding of historical change: Comparative findings from Northern Ireland and the United States. *American Educational Research Journal, 38*, 881–913.

Barton, K. C. (2002). "Oh, that's a tricky piece!": Children, mediated action, and the tools of historical time. *Elementary School Journal, 103*, 161–185.

Barton, K. C. (2005). "Best not to forget them": Secondary students' judgments of historical significance in Northern Ireland. *Theory and Research in Social Education, 33*(1), 9–44.

Barton, K. C. (2008). Research on students' ideas about history. In L. S. Levstik, & C. Tyson (Eds.), *Handbook of research in social studies education* (pp. 239–251). New York: Routledge.

Barton, K. C., & Levstik, L. S. (1996). "Back when God was around and everything": The development of children's understanding of historical time. *American Educational Research Journal, 33*, 419–454.

Barton, K. C., & Levstik, L. S. (1998). "It wasn't a good part of history": Ambiguity and identity in middle grade students' judgments of historical significance. *Teachers College Record, 99*, 478–513.

Barton, K. C., & Levstik, L. S. (2004). *Teaching history for the common good.* Mahwah, NJ: Erlbaum.

Barton, K. C., & McCully, A. W. (2005). History, identity, and the school curriculum in Northern Ireland: An empirical study of secondary students' ideas and perspectives. *Journal of Curriculum Studies, 37*, 85–116.

Barton, K. C., & McCully, A. W. (2006). Secondary students' perspectives on school and community history in Northern Ireland. Paper presented at the European Social Science History Conference, Amsterdam.

Beck, I., & McKeown, M. G. (1988). Towards meaningful accounts in history texts for young learners. *Educational Researcher, 17*(6), 31–39.

Beck, I. L., McKeown, M. G., Sinatra, J. A. (1991). Revising social studies texts from a text-processing perspective: Evidence of improved comprehensibility. *Reading Research Quarterly, 26*(3), 251–276.

Beck, I., McKeown, M. G., & Worthy, J. (1995). Giving a text voice can improve students' understanding. *Reading Research Quarterly, 30*, 220–238.

Ben-David Kolikant, Y., & Pollack, S. (2008). The asymmetrical influence of identity: A triad encounter of Israeli Jews, Arabs, and historical text. *Journal of Curriculum Studies.*

Berkin, C., Crocco, M., & Winslow, B. (2009). *Clio in the classroom: A guide to teaching U.S. women's history.* New York: Oxford University Press.

Bermudez, A., & Jaramillo, R. (2001). Development of historical explanation in children, adolescents and adults. In A. Dickinson, P. Gordon, & P. Lee (Eds.), *International review of history education* (Vol. 3, pp. 146–167). Portland, OR: Woburn Press.

Biddulph, M., & Adey, K. (2004). Pupil perceptions of effective teaching and subject relevance in history and geography at Key Stage 3. *Research in Education, 71*(1), 1–8.

Blight, D. (2002). *Race and reunion: The Civil War in American memory.* Cambridge, MA: Harvard University Press.

Bodnar, J. (1993). *Remaking America: Public memory, commemoration, and patriotism in the twentieth century.* Princeton, NJ: Princeton University Press.

Boix-Mansilla, V. (2005). Between reproducing and organizing the past: Students' beliefs about the standards and acceptability of historical knowledge. In R. Ashby, P. Gordon, & P. Lee (Eds.), *International review of history education* (Vol. 4, pp. 98–115). New York: RoutledgeFalmer.

Booth, M. (1984). Skills, concepts and attitudes: The development of adolescent children's historical thinking. In

History and Theory: Studies in the Philosophy of History (pp. 101–117). Hanover, NH: Wesleyan University Press.

Bransford, J. D., Brown, A. L., & Cocking, R. R. (Eds.) (1999). *How people learn: Brain, mind, experience, and school.* Washington, DC: National Academy Press.

Britt, M. A., & Aglinskas, C. (2002). Improving students' ability to identify and use source information. *Cognition and Instruction, 20,* 485–522.

Brophy, J., & Alleman, J. (2005). *Children's thinking about cultural universals.* Mahwah, NJ: Erlbaum.

Brophy, J., & VanSledright, B. A. (1997). *Teaching and learning history in elementary schools.* New York: Teachers College Press.

Bruner, J.S. (1962). *On knowing: Essays for the left hand.* Cambridge, MA: Harvard University Press.

Brush T., & Saye, J. (2001). The use of embedded scaffolds with hypermedia-supported student-centered learning. *Journal of Educational Multimedia and Hypermedia, 10,* 333–356.

Carretero, M., Jacott, L., Limón, M., López-Manjón, A., & León, A. (1994). Historical knowledge: Cognitive and instructional implications. In M. Carretero, & J. F. Voss (Eds.), *Cognitive and instructional processes in history and the social sciences* (pp. 357–376). Hillsdale, NJ: Erlbaum.

Carretero, M., López-Manjón, A., & Jacott, L. (1997). Explaining historical events. *International Journal of Educational Research, 27*(3), 245–254.

Clark, A. (2004). History teaching, historiography, and the politics of pedagogy in Australia. *Theory and Research in Social Education, 32*(3), 379–396.

Cooper, H. (1992). *The teaching of history.* London: David Fulton.

Cooper, H., & Chapman, A. (2009). *Constructing history 11–19.* London: Sage.

Davis, E. (2005). *How students understand the past: From theory to practice.* Walnut Grove, CA: Altamira Press.

Davis, O. L., Foster, S. J., & Yeager, E. (2001). *Historical empathy and perspective taking in the social studies.* Lanham, MD: Rowman & Littlefield.

Dickinson, A. K., Lee, P., & Rogers, P. J. (Eds.). *Learning history.* New Hampshire: Heinemann.

Dimitriadis, G. (2000). "Making history go" at a local community center: Popular media and the construction of historical knowledge among African American youth. *Theory and Research in Social Education, 28,* 40–64.

Downey, M. (1996). *Writing to learn history in the intermediate grades: Final report.* Berkeley, CA: National Center for the Study of Writing and Literacy, School of Education, University of California. ERIC Document Reproduction Service No. ED 397 422.

Downey, M., & Levstik, L.S. (1991). Teaching and learning history: The research base. In J. Shaver (Ed.), *Handbook of research in social studies* (pp. 400–410). New York: Macmillan.

Dunn, R. (2009). World history for us all. Available at: http://worldhistoryforusall.sdsu.edu

Epstein, T. (1998). *Interpreting national history: Race, identity, and pedagogy in classrooms and community.* New York: Routledge.

Epstein, T., & Shiller, J. (2009). Race, gender, and the teaching and learning of national history. In W. Parker (Ed.), *Social studies today: Research and practice* (pp. 95–104). New York: Routledge.

Fasulo, A., Girardet, H., & Pontecorvo, C. (1998). Seeing the past: Learning history through group discussion and iconographic sources. In J. F. Voss, & M. Carretero (Eds.), *Learning and reasoning in history: International review of history education* (Vol. 2, pp. 132–153). London: Woburn Press.

Ferretti, R. P., MacArthur, C. D., & Okolo, C. M. (2001). Teaching for historical understanding in inclusive classrooms. *Learning Disability Quarterly, 24,* 59–71.

Foster, S. J., Hoge, J. D., & Rosch, R. H. (1999). Thinking aloud about history: Children's and adolescents' responses to historical photographs. *Theory and Research in Social Education, 27,* 179–214.

Gago, M. (2005). Children's understanding of historical narrative in Portugal. In R. Ashby, P. Gordon, & P. Lee (Eds.), *International Review of history education* (Vol. 4, pp. 83–97). New York: Routledge.

Gaudelli, W. (2002). *World class: Teaching and learning in global times.* New York: Routledge.

Grant, S. G. (2001). It's just the facts, or is it? Teachers' practices and students' understandings of history. *Theory and Research in Social Education, 29*(1), 65–108.

Grant, S. G. (2003). *History lessons: Teaching learning and testing in U.S. high school classrooms.* New York: Routledge.

Griffin, A. F. (1942/1992). *A philosophical approach to the preparation of teachers of history.* Washington, DC: NCSS.

Hallam, R. (1972). Thinking and learning in history. *Teaching History, 2,* 337–346.

Halldén, O. (1997). Conceptual change and the learning of history. *International Journal of Educational Research, 27,* 201–210.

Halldén, O. (1998). On reasoning in history. In J. F. Voss, & M. Carretero (Eds.) *Learning and reasoning in history: International review of history education* (Vol. 2; pp. 272–278). London: Woburn Press.

Harnett, P. (1993). Identifying progression in children's understanding: The use of visual materials to assess primary school children's learning in history. *Cambridge Journal of Education, 23*, 137–154.

Hess, D. (2009). *Controversy in the classroom: The democratic power of discussion.* New York: Routledge.

Hicks, D., & Doolittle, P.E. (2008). Fostering analysis in historical inquiry through multimedia embedded scaffolding. *Theory and Research in Social Education, 36*(3), 206–232.

Hofer, M., & Swan, K.O. (2006). Standards, firewall and general classroom mayhem: Implementing student centered research projects in a social studies classroom. *Social Studies Research and Practice, 1*(1). Available at: http//www.socstrp.org/issues/viewarticle.cfm?vol11)=1&IssueID=1&ArticleID=3 (accessed November 9, 2009).

Hoodless, P. A. (2002). An investigation into children's developing awareness of time and chronology in story. *Journal of Curriculum Studies, 34*, 173–200.

Hughes, R. T. (2004). *Myths America lives by.* Urbana: University of Illinois Press.

Jacott, L., López-Manjón, A., & Carretero, M. (1998). Generating explanations in history. In J. F. Voss, & M. Carretero (Eds.), *Learning and reasoning in history. International review of history education* (Vol. 2; pp. 294–306). London: Woburn Press.

James, J. (2008). Teachers as protectors: Making sense of preservice teachers' resistant to interpretation elementary history teaching. *Theory and Research in Social Education, 36*(3), 172–205.

King, J. T. (2009). Teaching and learning about controversial issues: Lessons from Northern Ireland. *Theory and Research in Social Education, 37*(2), 215–246.

Knight, P. (1990). A study of children's understanding of people in the past. *Research in Education, 44*, 39–53.

Kohlmeier, J. (2005). The impact of having ninth-graders "do history." *The History Teacher, 38*, 499–524.

Kölbl, C., & Straub, J. (2001). Historical consciousness in youth: Theoretical and exemplary empirical analysis. *Forum: Qualitative Social Research, 2*(3), unpaginated. Retrieved from http://www.qualitative-research.net/fqs-texte/2003-2001/2003-2001koelblstraub-e.htm

Körber, A. (1997). Chronological knowledge, historical association and historico-political concepts. In M. Angvik, & B. von Borries (Eds.), *Youth and history* (Vol. A: *Description*; pp. 106–152). Hamburg: Körber-Stiftung.

La Motta, V. M., & M. B. Schiffer (2001). Behavioral archaeology: Toward a new synthesis. In I. Hodder (Ed.), *Archaeological theory today* (pp. 14–64). Malden, MA: Polity Press.

Lee, J. K., & Guy, C.W. (2003). High school social studies students' uses of online historical documents related to the Cuban Missile Crisis. *The Journal of Interactive Online Learning, 2*, 1–15.

Lee, P. (2004). "Walking backwards into tomorrow": Historical consciousness and understanding of history. *International Journal of Historical Learning, Teaching and Research, 4(1)*, 1–45. Retrieved from http://www.cshc.ubc.ca>.

Lee, P., & Ashby, R. (2000). Progression in historical understanding among students age 7–14. In P. N. Stearns, P. Seixas, & S. Wineburg (Eds.), *Knowing, teaching, and learning history: National and international perspectives* (pp. 199–222). New York: New York University Press.

Lee, P., & Ashby, R. (2001). Empathy, perspective taking, and rational understanding. In O. L. Davis, E. A. Yeager, & S. J. Foster, *Historical empathy and perspective taking in the social studies* (pp. 21–50). New York: Rowman & Littlefield.

Lee, P., Ashby, R., & Dickinson, A. (1996). Progression in children's ideas about history. In M. Hughes (Ed.), *Progression in Learning.* London: Cromwell Press.

Levesque, S. (2003). "Bin Laden is responsible; it was shown on tape": Canadian high school students' historical understanding of terrorism. *Theory and Research in Social Education, 31*(2), 174–202.

Levstik, L. S. (1996). NCSS and the teaching of history. In O. L. Davis (Ed.), *NCSS in retrospect.* Bulletin 92. Washington, DC: NCSS.

Levstik, L. S. (2001). Crossing the empty spaces: New Zealand adolescents' understanding of perspective-taking and historical significance. In O.L. Davis, E. A. Yeager, & S. J. Foster, *Historical empathy and perspective taking in the social studies* (pp. 69–96). New York: Rowman & Littlefield.

Levstik, L. S. (2008). What happens in social studies classrooms? Research on K-12 social studies practice. In L. S. Levstik, & C. Tyson (Eds.), *Handbook of research in social studies.* New York: Routledge.

Levstik, L. S., & Barton, K.C. (2008). *Researching history education.* New York: Routledge.

Levstik, L. S., & Groth, J. (2002). Scary thing, being an eighth grader: Exploring gender and sexuality in a middle school U.S. history unit. *Theory and Research in Social Education, 30*(2), 233–254.

Levstik, L. S., & Groth, J. (2005). "Ruled by our own people": Ghanaian adolescents' conceptions of citizenship. *Teachers College Record, 107*(4), 563–586.

Levstik, L. S., Henderson, A. G., & Schlarb, J. (2005). Digging for clues: An archaeological exploration of historical cognition. In P. Lee (Ed.), *The international review of history education*, Vol. 4. London: Taylor and Francis.

Levstik, L. S., & Pappas (1987). Exploring the development of historical understanding. *Journal of Research and Development in Education, 21*(1), 1–15.

Levstik, L. S., & Smith, D. B. (1997). "I've never done this before": Building a community of inquiry in a third grade classroom. In J. Brophy (Ed.), *Advances in research on teaching: Case studies of teaching and learning in elementary history*, Vol. 5. Greenwich, CT: JAI.

Lowenthal, D. (1998). *The heritage crusade and the spoils of history*. Cambridge: Cambridge University Press

Lybarger, M. B. (1991). The historiography of social studies: Retrospect, circumspect, and prospect. In J. Shaver (Ed.), *Handbook of research on social studies teaching and learning* (pp. 3–26). New York: Macmillan.

Lynn, S. (1993). Children reading pictures: History visuals at Key Stages 1 and 2. *Education 3–13, 21*(3), 23–29.

Marcus, A., Metzger, S. A., & Stoddard, J. (2010). *Teaching history with film: Strategies for secondary social studies.* New York: Routledge.

McCully, A., Pilgrim, N., Sutherland, A., & McMinn, T. (2002). "Don't worry, Mr. Trimble, we can handle it": Balancing the rational and emotional in the teaching of contentious topics. *Teaching History, 106*, 6–12.

Medina, K., Pollard, J., Schneider, D., & Leonhardt, C. (2000). How do students understand the discipline of history as an outcome of teachers' professional development? ERIC Document Reproduction Service No. ED 466 465.

Milson, A. (2002). The internet and inquiry learning: Integrating medium and method in a sixth grade social studies classroom. *Theory and Research in Social Education, 30*, 330–353.

Misco, T. (2008). "We did also save people": A study of Holocaust education in Romania after decades of historical silence. *Theory and Research in Social Education, 36*(2), 61–94.

Mosberg, S. (2002). Speaking of history: How adolescents use their knowledge of history in reading the daily news. *Cognition and Instruction, 20*(3), 323–358.

Nash, G., Crabtree, C., & Dunn, R. (2001). *History on trial: Culture wars and the teaching of the past*. New York: Knopf.

National Governing Board of the National Assessment of Educational Progress (2000). *U.S. history framework*. Washington, DC: National Governing Board.

Nora, P. (1989). *Between memory and history: Les lieux de Mémoire, Representations 26* (special issue: Memory and Counter-Memory), 7–25.

Novick, P. (1988). *That noble dream: The "objectivity question" and the American historical profession*. Cambridge: Cambridge University Press.

Parker, W. (2002). *Unity and diversity in public life*. New York: Teachers College Press.

Paxton, R. J. (1997). "Someone with like a life wrote it": The effects of a visible author on high school history students. *Journal of Educational Psychology, 89*, 235–358.

Porat, D. A. (2004). It's not written here, but this is what happened: Students' cultural comprehension of textbook narratives on Israeli-Arab conflict. *American Educational Research Journal, 42*(4), 963–996.

Prangsma, M. E., Van Boxtel, C. A. M., & Kanselaar, G. (2008). Developing a "big picture": Effects of collaborative construction of multimodal representations in history. *Instructional Science, 36*, 117–136.

Raupach, M. P. (2008). "From then and now": Secondary students' historical understanding of race. Paper presented at the Annual Meeting of the American Educational Research Association, New York.

Riviere, A., Núnez, B. B., & Fontela, F. (1998). Influence of intentional and personal factors in recalling historical texts: A developmental perspective. In J. F. Voss, & M. Carretero (Eds.), *International Review of History Education*, (Vol. 2; pp. 214–226). Portland, OR: Woburn Press.

Rock, T., Hefner, T., O'Connor, K., Passe, J., Oldendorf, S., Good, A., et al. (2004). One state closer to a national crisis: A report on elementary social studies education in North Carolina schools. *Theory and Research in Social Education 34*(4), 455–483.

Rose, S. L. (2000). Fourth graders theorize prejudice in American history. *International Journal of Historical Learning, Teaching and Research*, 1(1), unpaginated. Retrieved from http://www.ex.ac.uk/historyresoruce/journal2001/roseed-kw.doc.

Rosenzweig, R., & Thelan, D. (2000). *The presence of the past*. New York: Columbia University Press.

Rüsen, J. (2004). Historical consciousness: Narrative structure, moral function and ontogenetic development. In P. Seixas (Ed.), *Theorizing historical consciousness* (pp. 63–86). Toronto: University of Toronto Press.

Salmon, L. (1898). Appendix II: Study of history below the secondary grades. AHA Committee of Seven. Retrieved from http://www.historians.org/pubs/archives/committeeof Seven/index.cfm.

Saye, J., & Brush, T. (2002). Scaffolding critical reasoning about history and social issues in multimedia-supported learning environments. *Educational Technology Research & Development, 50*(3), 6–30.

Saye, J., & Brush, T. (2005). The persistent issues in history network: Using technology to support historical inquiry and civic reasoning. *Social Education, 69*(4), 168–171.

Saye, J., & Brush, T. (2006). Comparing teachers' strategies for supporting student inquiry in a problem-based multimedia-enhanced history unit. *Theory and Research in Social Education, 34*(2), 183–212.

Saye, J., Kohlmeier, J., Brush, T., Mitchell, L., & Farmer, C. (2009). Using mentoring to develop professional teaching knowledge for problem-based historical inquiry. *Theory and Research in Social Education, 37(1)*, 6–41.

Schweber, S. (2009). Holocaust fatigue in teaching today. In W. Parker, *Social studies today: Research and practice* (pp. 151–164). New York: Routledge.

Seixas, P. (1993). The community of inquiry as a basis for knowledge and learning: The case of history. *American Educational Research Journal, 30,* 313–345.

Seixas, P. (1994). Students' understanding of historical significance. *Theory and Research in Social Education, 22,* 281–304.

Seixas, P. (1997). Mapping the terrain of historical significance. *Social Education, 61*(1), 22–27.

Seixas, P. (2004). *Theorizing historical consciousness.* Toronto: University of Toronto Press.

Shemilt, D. (1980). *Evaluation study: Schools Council History 13–16 Project.* Edinburgh: Holmes McDougall.

Shulman, L. L. (1987). Knowledge and teaching. *Harvard Educational Review, 57*(1), 1–22.

Simon, R. (2004). The pedagogical insistence of public memory. In P. Seixas (Ed.), *Theorizing historical consciousness* (pp. 183–201). Toronto: University of Toronto Press.

Smith, J..& Niemi, R. G. (2001). Learning history in school: The impact of course work and instructional practices on achievement. *Theory and Research in Social Education, 29*(1), 18–42.

Smith, R. (2003). *Stories of peoplehood: The politics and morals of political membership.* Cambridge: Cambridge University Press.

Snedden, D. (1924). History studies in schools: For what purposes? *Teachers College Record, 25,* 7–9.

Squires, K. (2004). Replaying history: Learning world history through playing Civilization III. Unpublished dissertation, Indiana University.

Stahl, S. A., Britton, B. K., Hynd, C., McNish, M., & Bosquet, D. (1996). What happens when students read multiple source documents in history? *Reading Research Quarterly, 31,* 430–456.

Stearns, P. N. (2001). *Consumerism in world history: The global transformation of desire.* New York: Routledge.

Swan, K. O., & Hofer, M. (2008). Technology and social studies. In L.S. Levstik, & C. Tyson (Eds.). *Handbook of research in social studies education* (pp. 307–327). New York: Routledge.

ten Dam, G., & Rijkschroeff, R. (1996). Teaching women's history in secondary education: Constructing gender identity. *Theory and Research in Social Education 24,* 71–88.

Thornton, S. J. (2001). Subject specific teaching methods: History. In J. Brophy (Ed.), *Subject specific instructional methods and activities, Vol.8, advances in research on teaching* (pp. 295–309) New York: Elsevier Science.

Thornton, S. J. (2004). *Teaching social studies that matters: Curriculum for active learning.* New York: Teachers College Press.

Thornton, S. J. (2008). Continuity and change in social studies curriculum. In L. S. Levstik, & C. Tyson (Eds.), *Handbook of research in social studies* (pp. 15–32). New York: Routledge.

van Boxtel, C., & van Drie, J. (2004). Historical reasoning: A comparison of how experts and novices contextualise historical sources. *International Journal of Historical Learning, Teaching and Research, 4*(2), 89–97. (Retrieved from http://www.ex.ac.uk/historyresource/journalstart.htm.)

van Drie, J., & van Boxtel, C. (2003). Developing conceptual understanding through talk and mapping. *Teaching History, 110,* 27–32.

VanSledright, B. (1995). "I don't remember—the ideas are all jumbled in my head": 8th graders' reconstructions of colonial American history. *Journal of Curriculum and Supervision, 10,* 317–345.

VanSledright, B. (1997). And Santayana lives on: Students' views on the purposes for studying American history. *Journal of Curriculum Studies, 29*(5), 529–557.

VanSledright, B. (2001). From empathetic regard to self-understanding: Im/positionality, empathy, and historical contextualization. In O. L. Davis, E. A. Yeager, & S. J. Foster, *Historical empathy and perspective taking in the social studies* (pp. 51–68). Lanham, MD: Rowman & Littlefield.

VanSledright, B. (2002). *In search of America's past: Learning to read history in elementary school.* New York: Teachers College Press.

VanSledright, B. (2009). What does it mean to think historically: and how do you teach it? In W. Parker, *Social studies today: Research and practice* (pp. 113–120). New York: Routledge.

VanSledright, B., & Afflerbach, P. (2005). Assessing the status of historical sources: An exploratory study of eight U.S. elementary students reading documents. In R. Ashby, P. Gordon, & P. Lee (Eds.), *International review of history education, Vol. 4: Understanding history: Recent research in history education* (pp. 1–20). New York: Routledge.

VanSledright, B., & Frankes, L. (2000). Concept-and strategic-knowledge development in historical study: A comparative exploration in two fourth-grade classrooms. *Cognition and Instruction, 18,* 239–283.

VanSledright, B., & Kelly, C. (1998). Reading American history: The influence of multiple sources on six fifth graders. *Elementary School Journal, 98,* 239–265.

Vella, Y. (2001). Extending primary children's thinking through the use of artifacts. *International Journal of Historical Learning, Teaching and Research, 1, 2.* Retrieved from http://www.ex.ac.uk/historyresource/journal2002/VELLA.doc .

von Borries, B. (1997). Exploring the construction of historical meaning: Cross-cultural studies of historical consciousness among adolescents. In W. Bos, & R. H. Lehmann (Eds.), *Reflections on educational achievement: Papers in honour of T. Neville Postlethwaite to mark the occasion of his retirement from his chair in comparative education at the University of Hamburg* (pp. 25–59). New York: Waxman Münster.

Voss J. F., & Wiley, L. (1997). Developing understanding while writing essays in history. *International Journal of Educational Research, 27,* 255–265.

Wade, R. (2007). *Community action rooted in history: The CiviConnections model of service learning,* Bulletin 106. Washington DC: NCSS.

Wertsch, J. (1998). *Mind as action.* New York: Oxford University Press.

Wiley J., & Voss, J. F. (1999). Constructing arguments from multiple sources: Tasks that promote understanding and not just memory for text. *Journal of Educational Psychology, 92,* 301–311.

Willinsky, J. (2000). *Learning to divide the world: Education at empire's end.* Minneapolis: University of Minnesota University Press.

Wills, J. A. (2005). Who needs multicultural education? White students, U.S. history and the construction of a usable past. *Anthropology and Education Quarterly, 27*(3), 365–389.

Wilson, S., & Wineburg, S. (1988). Peering at history through different lenses: The role of disciplinary perspectives in teaching history. *Teachers College Record, 89*(4), 525–539.

Wineburg, S. (2000). Making historical sense. In P. Stearns, P. Seixas, & S. Wineburg (Eds.), *Knowing, teaching, and learning history: National and international perspectives* (pp. 331–352). New York: New York University Press.

Wineburg, S. (2001). *Historical thinking and other unnatural acts: Charting the future of teaching the past.* Philadelphia, PA: Temple University Press.

Wineburg, S., Mosborg, S., & Porat, D. (2009). What can *Forrest Gump* tell us about students' historical understanding? In W. Parker, *Social studies today: Research and practice* (pp. 105–112). New York: Routledge.

Yeager, E. A., Foster, S., & Greer, J. (2002). How eighth graders in England and the United States view historical significance. *Elementary School Journal, 103,* 199–210.

Yeager, E. A., Foster, S., Maley, S.D., Anderson, T., & Morris, J. W. I. (1998). Why people in the past acted as they did: An exploratory study in historical empathy. *International Journal of Social Education, 13,* 8–24.

Yeager, E. A., & Terzian, S. (2007). "That's when we became a nation": Urban Latino adolescents and the designation of historical significance. *Urban Education, 42*(1), 52–81.

Young, K. M., & Leinhardt, G. (1998). Writing from primary documents: A way of knowing history. *Written Communication, 15,* 25–68.

Zevin, J., & Gerwin, D. (2005). *Teaching in history: World history.* Mahwah, NJ: Erlbaum.

Zong, G., Quashigah, A. Y., & Wilson, A. (2008). Global education. In L. S. Levstik, & C. Tyson (Eds.), *Handbook of research in social studies education* (pp. 197–218). New York: Routledge.

7

LEARNING A SECOND LANGUAGE

Min Wang

In this age of globalization, the need for communication in a second or foreign language has dramatically increased (Committee for Economic Development, 2006). In the United States, a large proportion of linguistically diverse students are learning to read English as a Second Language (ESL). Camarota (2007) estimated that there were 10.8 million school-aged children of immigrants in the US in 2007, accounting for 20.2% of the total school-aged population. Many ESL children have difficulty acquiring even the most basic English literacy skills and are therefore at risk for reading difficulties and school drop-out (Fleischman & Hopstock, 1993; Gottardo, 2002). Second language learning has become one of the most important components of our educational system. Understanding the important theoretical issues and empirical evidence in research on second language learning is critical for improvement of second language education in both home and school settings.

Learning a language entails learning to comprehend and produce different levels of linguistic information including word, phrase, sentence and text level information. Word learning is an important first step in learning a language. Learning to read and write at the text level, on the other hand, requires not only word level knowledge but also sentence level knowledge as well as experience and knowledge of the world. This chapter focuses on word level learning among second language learners, both adults and children. The three major constituents in learning a word are: orthographic, phonological and meaning-related processes (e.g., Plaut, McClelland, Seidenberg, & Patterson, 1996; Seidenberg & McClelland, 1989). The key development in word learning is the improvement of the qualities of orthographic, phonological and meaning representations of a given word. In other words, learners develop fully specified and precise phonological, orthographic and semantic knowledge about the word (Perfetti, 1991, 1992). In this chapter, the nature and importance of each of the three constituents—phonology, orthography and meaning—in learning a second language are examined. Meaning here is considered in terms of morphological awareness. Indeed, morphological information is critical in processing meaning information in complex words (e.g., Shu, McBride-Chang, Wu, & Liu, 2006).

Phonological awareness generally refers to the ability to perceive and manipulate sound units of spoken language (Goswami & Bryant, 1990). According to Treiman and her colleagues' linguistic structure hypothesis (e.g., Bruck, Treiman, & Caravolas, 1995; Treiman, 1995; Treiman, Mullennix, Bijeljac-Babic, & Richmond-Welty, 1995), the syllable is at the top of the hierarchical structure; it is the largest and most accessible unit. The phoneme is at the bottom of the hierarchical structure; it is the smallest unit and is a later-developing one for children. Between syllables and phonemes lie intermediate onset and rime units. Studies demonstrate the importance of processing both large and small phonological units for reading skills. For example, processing of relatively large phonological units in tasks such as rhyme and alliteration has been shown to be important for promoting young children's learning to read (e.g., Bradley & Bryant, 1983; Bryant, MacLean, Bradley, & Crossland, 1990; Goswami & Bryant, 1990; see Bryant, 2002, for a review). Other studies have suggested that children's skills at processing the smallest phonological units (i.e., phonemes) are powerful predictors of individual differences in learning to read and that training children in phonemic-level skills can benefit their later reading progress (e.g., Byrne & Fielding-Barnsley, 1995; Hulme et al., 2002; Lundburg, Frost, & Petersen, 1988; Muter, Hulme, Snowling, & Taylor, 1998). The role of phonological awareness in learning to read has received the most attention in the past two decades. Relatively less research has been devoted to studying the roles of orthographic awareness and morphological awareness.

Orthographic knowledge generally refers to "children's understanding of the conventions used in the writing system of their language" (Treiman & Cassar, 1997, p. 631). One important orthographic processing skill is children's ability to detect acceptable and unacceptable letter sequences and their relation to letter positions in words (Cassar & Treiman, 1997; Treiman, 1993). For example, Cassar and Treiman (1997) found that by late kindergarten, children have acquired some knowledge of the acceptable form and position of consonant doublets. These young children preferred spellings with final doublets (e.g., *baff*) to those with beginning doublets (e.g., *bbaf*). They also preferred spellings with acceptable doublets (e.g., *yill*) to those with unacceptable ones (e.g., *yihh*). Some researchers have argued that phonological and orthographic knowledge mutually facilitate each other and that grapheme-phoneme knowledge provides young readers with a powerful tool to bind the spelling patterns of individual and multiple letters with their pronunciations in words (e.g., Ehri, 1991, 1998). Recent empirical research suggests that this orthographic knowledge may contribute significantly to word recognition skill in children over and above phonological factors (e.g., Cunningham, Perry, & Stanovich, 2001; Cunningham & Stanovich, 1990, 1993).

Morphological knowledge refers to children's understanding of the "morphemic structure of words and their ability to reflect on and manipulate that structure" (Carlisle, 1995, p. 194). There are three major types of morphological structures in English: compound, inflection, and derivation. Compound morphology is concerned with the formation of new words by combining two or more stem morphemes (e.g., *cupcake*). Inflectional morphology refers to the formation of new words in order to express grammatical features, such as singular/plural form (e.g., *one flower → two flowers*) or past/present tense (e.g., *explain → explained*). Derivational morphology refers to the formation of new words by adding morphemes to change the meaning of a stem morpheme without reference to the specific grammatical role a word might play in a sentence (e.g., the verb *teach* becomes the noun *teacher* by adding a suffix -*er*; however, the adjective *possible* remains an adjective, *impossible*, after adding a prefix *-im*). Children acquire these three types of morphological awareness at different rates. Acquisition of inflectional and compound morphology is completed earlier than derivational morphology and has been related to reading progress during the first and second grades (Berko, 1958). Mastery of derivational morphology emerges later and takes longer, and has been shown to contribute to reading skill in later primary grades (e.g., Nagy, Berninger, Abbott, Vaughan, & Vermeulen, 2003; Nagy, Berninger, & Abbott, 2006).

There is a close relation between morphological and phonological awareness. Researchers such as Carlisle and Nomanbhoy (1993) found that both phonological and morphological awareness contributed significantly to word reading in first graders, but the contribution of phonological awareness was greater. These results suggest that phonological sensitivity may provide a foundation for morphological learning. Since each morpheme is represented by a cluster of sounds, children must learn to segment the speech stream and identify those recurring sound units before they can identify the sound units that bear certain linguistic functions. Since two of the same morphemes can share the same or similar phonology, it is also possible that the observed morphological effect is indeed a sort of phonological effect.

Concerning learning a second language, recent research has focused on the importance of the aforementioned awareness of phonology, orthography and morphology in second language reading. Cross-language transfer, a concept used to refer to general facilitation from one language to the other language in second language learners, is an important theoretical framework in second language research (e.g., Durgunoglu, Nagy, & Hancin-Bhatt, 1993). Recent research has accumulated overwhelming evidence for cross-language facilitation from phonological and morphological awareness in one language to word reading in a second language. More importantly, these studies have shown that morphological awareness is important for reading a second language over and above phonological awareness (e.g., Deacon & Kirby, 2004; Deacon, Wade-Woolley, & Kirby, 2007).

A large volume of literature has documented the effects of differences in orthographic depth on learning to read and spell in different orthographies (e.g., Cossu, Shankweiler, Liberman, Tola, & Katz, 1988; Durgunoglu & Oney, 1999; Frith, Wimmer, & Landerl, 1998; Geva, 1995; Geva & Siegel, 2000; Goswami, Gombert, & de Barrera, 1998; Shimron, 1999; see Ziegler & Goswami, 2005, for a review). For example, readers of a shallow orthography demonstrate an advantage in phonological awareness over readers of a deep orthography (Cossu et al., 1988). Goswami et al. (1998) found that children who learn to read in a less transparent orthography such as English are more likely to benefit from processing large orthographic units such as rimes than children who learn to read in a highly transparent orthography such as German. Native readers of Chinese, a logographic writing system, rely on syllable-level rather than phoneme-level phonological information, and more importantly visual-orthographic information in character recognition (e.g., Chen, Flores d'Arcais, & Cheung, 1995; Perfetti, Liu, & Tan, 2005; Perfetti & Tan, 1998; Zhou & Marslen-Wilson, 1996). This review examines how cross-language differences in terms of orthographic depth have cognitive consequences for learning to read in a second language.

In second language research, cognitive researchers are interested in whether or not the two languages share an integrated lexicon. Models such as the Bilingual Interactive Activation Model (BIA) support an integrated bilingual lexicon in which the lexical access is non-selective (Dijkstra & Van Heuven, 1998). Models such as the Revised Hierarchical Model (RHM) suggest that the two languages may have both shared semantic representation and separated lexical form representation (including phonology and orthography; Kroll & Stewart, 1994). All of these models are based on research on adult second language learners exclusively, and are reviewed briefly in this chapter. These models have great potential to be extended to bilingual children.

In summary, this chapter provides an overview of the nature and importance of the three major constituents—phonology, orthography, and morphology—in learning a second language. Three major theoretical frameworks—cross-language transfer, cognitive consequences of cross-language orthographic depth differences, and bilingual mental lexicon—are introduced and empirical research guided by each of these frameworks is reviewed. Future research directions are discussed.

HISTORICAL OVERVIEW

Cummins's (1979, 1986, 1991) Linguistic Interdependence Hypothesis proposes that once the child develops skills in the first language, he or she is able to transfer those skills to the second language. Although this hypothesis was not detailed enough to allow for empirical testing in its early form, recent second language researchers have refined and modified this hypothesis in the context of learning to read a second language (e.g., Comeau, Cormier, Grandmaison, & Lacroix, 1999; D'Angiulli, Siegel, & Serra, 2001; Geva & Siegel, 2000). The cross-language transfer framework has been greatly used in an emerging line of bilingual reading research to address the relationships among phonological, orthographic and morphological awareness and reading skills across the two languages among various second language or bilingual children. For example, there is a great deal of evidence supporting a strong facilitation from first language phonology to second language reading in research in Canada on English-speaking children learning to read French (e.g., Comeau et al., 1999; Deacon & Kirby, 2004; Deacon, Wade-Woolley, & Kirby, 2007), Italian (e.g., D'Angiulli et al., 2001), and Hebrew (Geva & Siegel, 2000), and in the US on Chinese and Korean children learning to read English (e.g., Wang, Park, & Lee, 2006; Wang, Perfetti, & Liu, 2005).

In this line of research, children's language and reading skills are tested in both first and second languages. Cross-language prediction between first language phonological, orthographic and morphological skills and reading outcome in the second language are the focus of this line of research. The relations between phonological, orthographic and morphological skills and reading outcome within the first and second language are also addressed. For example, a large body of literature has suggested that children's skill at processing the smallest phonological units (i.e., phonemes) is a powerful predictor of individual differences in learning to read and that training children in phonemic-level skills can benefit their later reading progress. Second language researchers have attempted to address whether this is also true in acquiring a second language. However, a more important question in this line of research is whether there is cross-language prediction from phonology, orthography, or morphology in the first language to reading outcomes in the second language.

Although early second language researchers focused on learning a second language from a more universal perspective, in which second language learning follows a similar process for learners with different first language backgrounds, recent researchers have started to acknowledge the need to take into account the role of different first language backgrounds on the way a second language is learned. This line of research is greatly influenced by a theoretical framework called Orthographic Depth Hypothesis (e.g., Katz & Frost, 1992), which originated from monolingual reading research. This hypothesis posits that orthographies differ in terms of their degree of transparency in mapping between graphemes to sounds. A growing number of second language researchers have since given attention to the cross-language differences in terms of orthographic depth between the first and second language in studying second language reading. The cognitive consequences of cross-language orthographic depth differences have been mostly shown among second language learners with a logographic first writing system (e.g., Akamatsu, 1999, Holm & Dodd, 1996; Jackson, Lu, & Ju, 1994; Wang & Geva, 2003; Wang & Koda, 2005; Wang, Koda, & Perfetti, 2003). In this line of research, English as the second language was the language under investigation; second language learners are more typically compared with native English-speaking counterparts. In some studies, second language learners with a nonalphabetic first language versus those with an alphabetic first language background are compared.

Since the 1990s, cognitive scientists who are interested in bilingual language processing have proposed a set of bilingual processing models for understanding the adult bilingual mental lexicon. These models are largely the extensions of monolingual-based interactive models (e.g., McClelland & Rumelhart, 1981). The Bilingual Interactive Activation Model (e.g., Dijkstra & Van Heuven, 1998) is such a model, which claims that the bilingual lexicon is integrated and that lexical access in non-selective. Another set of bilingual lexicon models (e.g., Word Association, Conceptual Mediation, and Revised Hierarchical Model) were proposed, however, to argue for an integrated but simultaneously separated bilingual lexicon, depending on whether it is the representation of lexical form information or semantic/conceptual information (e.g., Kroll & Stewart, 1994; Potter et al., 1984).

THEORETICAL FRAMEWORK

Cross-Language Transfer

Built upon earlier theoretical work by Cummins (1979, 1986, 1991), cross-language transfer is a widely used framework for second language research. In the current literature, the term cross-language transfer has been used in a general way to indicate the tendency of learners to utilize knowledge and experience gained from one language in learning another language (Kuo & Anderson, 2007). Some researchers suggest that cross-language transfer arises from the shared or overlapping features of first and second languages (e.g., grapheme-phoneme correspondences), and such transfer can occur between typologically related languages such as Spanish and English (e.g., Cisero & Royer, 1995).

Other researchers suggest that bilingual facilitation can occur at a more abstract or systemic level. Children are able to apply their metalinguistic skills in one language even to a typologically distant language, as in moving between English and Chinese (e.g., Kuo & Anderson, 2007; Wang et al., 2005). One of the powerful ways to demonstrate cross language transfer in educational psychology research is to reveal the additional variance explained by a target language measure in one language (e.g., score on a phonological task in the first language) to reading outcomes in another language over and above the within-language predictors (e.g., score on a within-language phonological task in the second language).

Cognitive Consequences of Cross-Language Orthographic Depth Differences

Reading in different orthographies entails different phonological and visual-orthographic processes. One major theoretical framework for discussing differences in reading among alphabetic language systems is the Orthographic Depth Hypothesis (see Frost, 1994; Katz & Frost, 1992). According to this hypothesis, there are differences among alphabetic orthographies in terms of how regularly orthography and phonology can be mapped onto each other. In shallow orthographies, such as Spanish, Italian, and Serbo-Croatian, there is a relatively simple one-to-one correspondence between letters and sounds.

Conversely, in deep orthographies, such as English, there is a more complex or opaque relation between letters and sounds. The orthographic depth framework can be extended to nonalphabetic writing systems such as Chinese. Chinese is often referred to as a deep orthography (e.g., Hu & Catts, 1998). It is considered a logographic system, or, more accurately, a morphosyllabic system (DeFrancis, 1989; Mattingly, 1992; Perfetti & Zhang, 1995). Second language researchers have argued that the linguistic and ortho-graphic differences among different language systems affect second language reading acquisition in adults, and that learners apply their strategies from the first language to the second language (Akamatsu, 1999; Haynes & Carr, 1990; Koda, 1994, 1999, 2000; Verhoeven, 1990; Wade-Woolley, 1999). Recent research has also shown some evidence among young ESL children of the effect of cross-language orthographic depth differ-ences (e.g., Sun-Alperin & Wang, 2008; Wang & Geva, 2003).

Bilingual Mental Lexicon Models

Currently, all the Bilingual Mental Lexicon Models are derived for the purpose of explain-ing adult second language learning. In general, the majority of these models agree that the two languages have shared semantic representations but separate lexical form repre-sentations. The main difference among these models is how words in second language are mapped to their respective meanings. The three major models are the Word Associa-tion Model, Concept Mediation Model and Revised Hierarchical Model (see Figure 7.1). According to the word association model (Figure 7.1a), words in the second language are linked to their translation equivalents in the first language, and there are no direct links between the second language words and their meanings. Consequently, the second language words access their meanings via their first language translation equivalents. According to the concept association model (Figure 7.1b), however, the second lan-guage words are directly linked to concepts; there are no direct links between the second language words and their translation equivalents in the first language; and the second language words access their meanings directly, without the activation of their translation equivalents in the first language.

Given the differences between beginning second language learners and proficient bilinguals, Kroll and Stewart (1994) proposed the revised hierarchical model, in which both word and concept associations are allowed (Figure 7.1c). In order to acquire the meaning of a new word in the second language, learners must depend on the translation equivalent of the word in the first language. Thus, there is a strong lexical link mapping second language to first language and a weak link mapping first language to second lan-guage. Initially, there was no link between the second language words and concepts, but

Learning a Second Language • 133

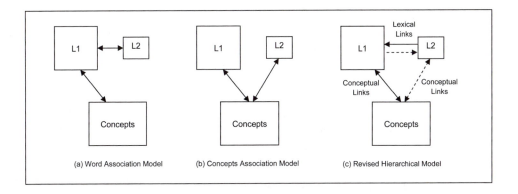

Figure 7.1 Word association model, concept association model, and revised hierarchical model

Source: Adapted from Kroll & Stewart (1994).

the link begins to develop with increasing second language proficiency. The strength of links becomes more balanced when second language proficiency improves.

CURRENT TRENDS AND ISSUES

Cross-Language Phonological and Orthographic Transfer

Cross-language transfer of phonological skills in one language to reading in the other is the most studied topic in the line of research on cross-language transfer among second language or bilingual children. Durgunoglu, Nagy, and Hancin-Bhatt (1993) tested first grade Spanish-speaking children who were enrolled in a transitional bilingual education program in the US on both Spanish and English reading skills. Their results demonstrated that children who could perform well on Spanish phonological awareness tasks were more likely to be able to read English words and pseudowords than were children who performed poorly on these tasks. The phonological awareness tasks included different linguistic units (the onset-rime and the phoneme) in Spanish words. Moreover, phonological awareness was a significant predictor of performance on word recognition tests both within and across languages (see also Cisero & Royer, 1995). Gottardo (2002) also found that Spanish phonological awareness explained the highest proportion of variance in English word reading for English-Spanish bilingual speakers. Several studies examining the effect of Spanish phonological processing on English word reading have echoed these findings (e.g., Lindsey, Manis, & Bailey, 2003; Manis, Lindsey, & Bailey, 2004). Similar findings were also shown in studies of native-English speaking children learning French in their French immersion programs in Canada (e.g., Comeau et al., 1999).

Limited research has been done on cross-language orthographic transfer. Wang, Perfetti, and Liu (2005) investigated cross-language phonological and orthographic transfer simultaneously, in one study among a group of Chinese-English bilingual children in grades 2 and 3 of their English and Chinese classes. Comparable experiments in Chinese and English were designed to focus on phonological and orthographic processing. Onset, rime and phoneme awareness tasks were administered in English, while onset, rime and tone awareness tasks were administered in Chinese. The orthographic task in both English and Chinese was a choice task in which the children were asked to judge which of the two stimuli was more like a real English word or Chinese character. This task tapped into children's sensitivity to various orthographic patterns in English and Chinese. For example, in English, *ff* does not occur at the beginning of a word, so the correct choice for the pair of stimuli *ffeb* and *beff* is *beff*. In Chinese, in the pair 对 and 对, 对 contains a legal radical in an illegal position. Word reading skill in both writing systems was tested.

The critical finding was that Chinese tone skill predicted English pseudoword reading over and above English phonemic processing skill. This finding suggests that even when children learn to read in two different writing systems, there is a level of phonological transfer (see Figure 7.2a). Tone is a suprasegmental feature of Chinese phonology that does not occur in the English phonological system. The four Chinese tones attached to the same syllable segment carry different lexical information. For example, the only difference between the syllable */man3/* and */man4/* is the tone. The first syllable with tone 3 corresponds to 满 which means *full*, and the second syllable with tone 4 corresponds to 慢 which means *slow*. The predictive power of Chinese tone awareness for English pseudoword reading was interpreted as reflecting some shared phonological sensitivity in learning to read Chinese and English. Chinese tone and English pseudoword reading both require children's attention to spoken word forms and their constituents, that is, the phonemes for English and tones for Chinese. The authors also suggested an alternative interpretation that a more general auditory processing skill is an underlying factor.

In a parallel study with Korean-English bilingual children (Wang, Park, & Lee, 2006), Korean phonemic skill was found to contribute to English pseudoword reading after controlling for within-English variables including English phonemic skill (see Figure 7.2b). In both studies, no significant contribution was found from orthographic skill in one language to reading skill in the other. For Chinese-English bilingual children, this suggests that there is a writing system-specific component in biliteracy acquisition in Chinese and English. This result reflects the contrasts in mapping principles and visual forms across the two writing systems. The consequence of these contrasts was difficulty in transfer of orthographic skills from Chinese to English. For Korean-English children, this result reflects the differences in visual forms and possibly in orthographic transparency between the two languages. In summary, findings from the Chinese-English and

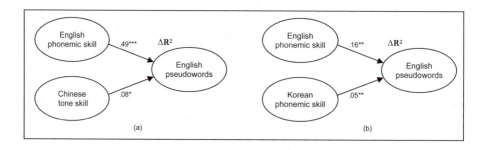

Figure 7.2 Chinese tone skill (a) and Korean phonemic skill (b) predicting English pseudoword reading

Korean-English biliteracy studies suggest that there may be a joint function of shared phonological processes and language-specific orthographic skill. These findings are important in delineating the universal and language-specific processes involved in learning to read two languages simultaneously.

In contrast to the non-significant contribution of Chinese or Korean orthographic awareness to English reading in Chinese and Korean children, Sun-Alperin and Wang (in press) showed that Spanish orthographic awareness predicted English real word and pseudoword reading in Spanish children, after taking English phonological, orthographic awareness and Spanish phonological awareness into consideration. It is possible that the similarities between English and Spanish orthographies facilitated Spanish-speaking children's performance on English real word and pseudoword reading, even though Spanish orthography is more transparent. Indeed, Spanish is more similar to English than is Korean; Spanish and English not only share the alphabetic principle, but are also based on a linear system with the Roman alphabet. The two orthographies share many similar features. For example, several of the shared graphemes between Spanish and English map onto the same phonemes, such as the /s/ as in *sit* (English) and *seis* ("six" in Spanish) or the /m/ as in *man* (English) and *mano* ("hand" in Spanish).

Therefore, it seems that cross-language transfer of phonology to reading is universal across different languages. However, cross-language transfer of orthography to reading is language-specific. It is difficult to transfer orthographic knowledge to reading across different writing systems such as Chinese and English as well as between different alphabetic scripts such as Korean and English. Nonetheless, such transfer is likely to occur across similar scripts within the same alphabetic writing system such as Spanish and English. The findings of cross-language phonological transfer in second language reading obviously have important educational implications. Classroom teachers need to pay attention to second language children's strong first language skills and be aware that these strong first language skills can be transferred to second language learning, in other words, teachers can make full use of the children first language skills as a facilitator or springboard to develop their second language literacy skills (see Durgunoglu, 2002, for discussion).

Cross-Language Morphological Transfer

Very limited research has so far addressed the transfer between morphological awareness in one language and reading in another language. Wang, Cheng, and Chen (2006) examined the contribution of morphological awareness to Chinese and English reading skill after taking into account phonological awareness among Chinese-English bilingual children in grades 2 to 4. Two tasks assessing morphological awareness were used, a compound structure task and a derivational morphology task, in both Chinese and English. In the compound structure task, the child was presented with a riddle followed by two choices. The child's task was to choose the better answer to the riddle. For example, "Which is a better name for a bee that lives in the grass: a *grass bee* or a *bee grass*?" In the derivational awareness task, children were asked to complete a sentence based on a clue word. For example, for the clue word *farm*, the sentence to be completed was, "My uncle is a _____" (farmer). Results showed that English compound awareness contributed to Chinese character reading and reading comprehension after taking into account Chinese-related variables. It seems that bilingual children are able to apply their knowledge about shared morphological structure from one language to reading in another language. In a parallel study on Korean-English bilingual children (Wang, Ko, & Choi, 2009), morphological awareness of derivational structure in one language uniquely predicted a significant amount of variance in reading real words in the other language, suggesting that morphological awareness facilitates word reading across different alphabetic orthographies.

Bindman (2004) studied the cross-language relationship between morphological awareness and reading skill in 6- to 10-year-old native-English speakers learning Hebrew as a second language. Bindman included morphological and syntactic tasks (e.g., word analogy and sentence cloze tasks). After taking into account age and vocabulary, morphological awareness in Hebrew was shown to be significantly related to the consistent representation of roots in the spelling of derived forms in English (e.g., *know-knowledge*). This result supports the cross-linguistic role of morphological awareness in spelling by children learning to write in two different alphabetic orthographies.

Deacon and colleagues (Deacon, Wade-Woolley, & Kirby, 2007) tracked the relations between performance on a past tense analogy task, an index of morphological awareness, and reading of English and French in a group of 58 French immersion children across grades 1 to 3. Early measures of English morphological awareness at grade 1 were significantly related to both English and French reading at grade 2 and grade 3, after controlling for several variables. Later measures of morphological awareness at grade 2 in French were significantly related to English and French reading at grade 3. These relations persisted even after controlling for several variables. Results of this study suggest that morphological awareness can be applied to reading across orthographies. The cross-time contribution of morphological awareness to reading across orthographies points to a potential causal relation between the two.

COGNITIVE CONSEQUENCES OF CROSS-LANGUAGE ORTHOGRAPHIC DEPTH DIFFERENCES

A number of adult-based studies have demonstrated the effects of linguistic and orthographic differences in second language reading for learners with a nonalphabetic first language background (e.g., Akamatsu, 1999; Haynes & Carr, 1990; Holm & Dodd, 1996; Jackson, Lu, & Ju, 1994; Koda, 1999, 2000; Wade-Woolley, 1999; Wang, Koda, & Perfetti, 2003). Results of these studies are consistent with the notion that logographic readers learning to read English tend to rely more on orthographic information and less phonological information for word identification than English readers do.

Holm and Dodd (1996) found that ESL university students from Hong Kong did not differ from the other ESL groups with alphabetic first language backgrounds in reading and spelling real English words. These ESL groups included Chinese Mandarin readers who were taught Chinese characters via Pinyin. Pinyin is an alphabetic transcription used in Mainland China to assist children in learning to read Chinese characters. Hong Kong students learn to read Chinese characters via a whole-word or look-and-say method. Hong Kong ESL students were significantly less competent than all other ESL readers on a set of phonological awareness tasks, as well as in reading and spelling pseudowords. It is apparent that ESL students' first language experience had a significant impact on their ESL reading and spelling. Hong Kong students' whole-word character learning experience did not impede their reading and spelling real English words, however, it negatively affected their reading and spelling English pseudowords where fine-grained skills on grapheme-phoneme correspondence is required.

In Wang et al. (2003), alphabetic and non-alphabetic first language effects in English word identification were systematically investigated via comparison between native Chinese and Korean college students learning to read English as a second language. English proficiency was matched between the two groups. This is an important control which was not given enough attention in previous research. The ESL learners' relative reliance on phonological and orthographic information was examined. Van Orden's (1987) semantic category judgment task was selected to test the involvement of orthography and phonology in reading for meaning. In the semantic category judgment task, the participants were asked to judge whether the target word is a member of a category, for example, whether *rows* is a *flower*, or whether *tow* is *the end of your feet*). By varying the phonological and spelling similarity of the target words to the category exemplars, the use of phonological and visual-orthographic information in second language learners with a nonalphabetic first language background was examined.

The second task was a phoneme deletion task developed by Hart and Perfetti (2000) and shown to correlate with reading skill for adult readers. This task requires phoneme deletion in an English word, followed by a spelling of the new word that results from the deletion. The uniqueness of this task is that the deletion of the required phoneme in the word leads to a new word with a different spelling form from the original one (e.g., removing the /t/ sound from *might* creates a word *my* which has a distinct spelling from *might*). This feature requires the participants not only to manipulate the individual phonemes in the word, but also to accurately access their spelling knowledge of the new word.

In the semantic category judgment task, the Korean ESL learners made more false positive errors in judging stimuli that were homophones to category exemplars than they did in judging spelling controls. However, there were no significant differences in responses to stimuli in these two conditions for Chinese ESL learners. Chinese ESL learners, on the other hand, made more accurate responses to stimuli that were less similar in spelling to category exemplars than those that were more similar. Chinese ESL learners may rely less on phonological information and more on orthographic information in identifying English words than their Korean counterparts.

Further evidence supporting this argument came from the phoneme deletion task, in which Chinese subjects performed more poorly overall than their Korean counterparts and made more errors that were phonologically incorrect but orthographically acceptable. The researchers suggest that cross writing system differences in first languages and first language reading skills influence could be responsible for these ESL performance differences. These findings received support from neuroimaging work by Tan and his colleagues (e.g., Tan et al., 2001; Tan et al., 2003). Their work has shown that reading Chinese resulted in more activation in some brain areas that are responsible for coordinating and integrating visual-spatial analyses of logographic Chinese characters compared with reading English. More importantly, they also showed that when Chinese-English bilingual subjects performed a phonological task on English words, areas that are responsible for spatial information representation, spatial working memory, and coordination of cognitive resources were most active. Areas mediating English monolinguals' fine-grained phonemic analysis were only weakly activated.

Haynes and Carr (1990) compared Chinese ESL and native English-speaking American undergraduates' visual efficiency skills in making visual same–different matching judgments on orthographically irregular (i.e., illegal) four-letter strings, orthographically legal four-letter pseudowords, and real four-letter words. The orthographically illegal letter strings were found to be the most difficult to judge and real words were the easiest for both groups. In order to further examine whether the two groups contrasted in efficiency gains when the stimuli were more familiar, the authors computed "lexicality effect" (word efficiency–pseudoword efficiency) and "orthography effect" (pseudoword efficiency–letter string efficiency). The results revealed that the Chinese ESL readers benefited relatively little from orthography and relatively more from lexicality, compared to their American counterparts. Similar results were obtained by Koda (1989) for Japanese-speaking ESL adults. She found that Japanese ESL readers, literate in Kanji symbols (borrowed from Chinese), performed better in recalling strings of unpronounceable letters than in recalling strings of pronounceable letters. Koda maintained that phonological inaccessibility is less debilitating for logographic readers (e.g., Japanese) than for alphabetic readers.

Wang and Geva (2003) found a similar pattern of performance in a spelling task even among young Chinese ESL readers whose logographic first language experience was very limited. The difference between spelling performance on pronounceable and unpronounceable letter strings, controlling for visual similarity, was significantly smaller for Chinese ESL children than the difference for English-speaking children. These findings together seem to suggest that logographic readers rely less on phonological information from the graphemic form in order to access its lexical representation than do alphabetic readers. On the other hand, for alphabetic readers a direct analysis of phonological information from the graphemic form is necessary for encoding subsequent lexical representation.

Bilingual Lexicon

Potter et al. (1984) reported the earliest study which tested the Word Association Model and Concept Mediation Models by contrasting bilinguals' performance on a translation task from first language to second language and a picture-naming task in their second language. The Word Association Model hypothesizes that translation from the first language to the second language is faster than naming a picture in the second language. Since there is a direct link between first language and second language words, translation from first to second language does not need to activate the shared meanings of those words. By contrast, when naming a picture in the second language, one has to go through the links between concepts and the first language word, and then go through from first language word to the second language word. The Concept Mediation Model hypothesizes that performance of the two tasks is similar, because both the first language and second language words are mediated by the concepts. Participants showed similar performance on a translation task and a picture-naming task, which is consistent with the concept association model. Potter et al. found similar results for both proficient and less proficient second learners, but their results were challenged by other studies. Kroll and Curley (1988), for example, tested beginning learners with very low second language proficiency and found that translation was faster than picture naming for beginning learners.

De Groot and Hoeks (1995) examined Dutch–English–French trilinguals who were more proficient in their second language (English) than in their third language (French).

In a translation task, the participants were to translate first language Dutch words into either second language English or third language French. The critical experimental manipulation was word concreteness. The Concept Mediation Model predicts that concrete words would facilitate translation compared to non-concrete words. The Word Association Model predicts the same performance on the two types of words. Interesting, there was a concreteness effect in first language to second language (Dutch-to-English) translation, thus supporting the Concept Mediation Model. However, the concreteness effect disappeared in first language to third language (Dutch-to-French) translation, thus supporting the Word Association Model. There seems to be a possible developmental shift for adult second language learners: from reliance on word association at an early, less proficient stage to concept mediation at a later, more proficient stage.

Sunderman and Kroll (2006) tested the developmental aspect of the Revised Hierarchical Model regarding accessing the concepts from second language lexical forms. A translation recognition paradigm was used, in which native English speakers with high or low Spanish second language proficiency were asked to judge whether the second word in a pair was the translation equivalent of the first word (e.g., *cara—face*, where *face* is the English translation equivalent for the Spanish word *cara*). The first word in the pair was in the second language. The critical condition involved pairs that were not translation equivalents, but were related to the first word (first language) or the second word (second language) either in lexical form or in meaning (e.g., *cara—card*, *cara—fact*, and *cara—head*). Results showed that all participants experienced interference for lexical form related (e.g., *cara—card*) and meaning related stimuli (e.g., *cara—head*), but only those with low second language proficiency experienced interference for distracters that were related to the lexical form of the translation equivalents (e.g., *cara—fact*). Learners with low second language proficiency needed to access the meaning of second language words through first language translation equivalents, whereas participants with higher second language proficiency did not. Therefore, the mediator role of second language proficiency was supported.

In a very recent study, Chen and Wang (2009) used a lexical decision experiment to investigate cross-language activation in compound processing in a group of Chinese-English bilingual children. The compound words/nonwords in one language contained two free constituent morphemes that mapped onto the desired translations in the other language, such as *tooth (牙) brush (刷)* and *fire (火) mountain (山)*. A significant interaction between the lexicality of the target language, English, and that of the nontarget language, Chinese, was found, but not in the direction of target language being the Chinese. This finding, as the researchers suggested, supports asymmetric cross-language activation between the first and the second language. When the target language is English (the second language), constituents of the compound in English and their translation equivalents in Chinese are activated. Further, the compound of the translated constituents is activated as well. In other words, the translated constituents are recomposed into the corresponding compound word in Chinese. For example, when a child heard a real English compound word *toothbrush*, he/she decomposed the word into *tooth* and *brush*. Then the Chinese translation equivalents of the two constituents—牙 *(tooth)* and 刷 *(brush)* — were activated and recomposed into 牙刷. Since 牙刷 is a real Chinese word, it helped the child to judge *toothbrush* as a real word in English. On the contrary, when a child heard another real English compound word *schoolbook*, the Chinese translation equivalents of the two constituents—校 *(school)* and 书 *(book)* — were activated and

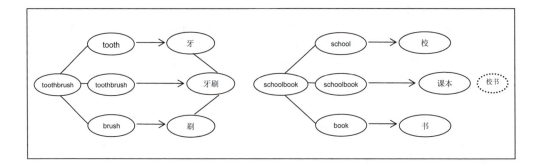

Figure 7.3 Compound processing in Chinese bilinguals

recomposed into a novel compound word 校书 in Chinese. Since 校书 is not a real compound word in Chinese, the contradiction of the lexical status in the two languages was more likely to confuse the child and result in a mistaken judgment (see Figure 7.3).

The bilingual lexicon has frequently been investigated through cross-language priming experiments in adults. In a cross-language priming experiment, the target words in one language are preceded by the translation equivalents or semantically related words in the other language. These translation equivalents or semantically related words are called primes. For example, 牙刷 is the translation equivalent of *toothbrush* in Chinese. When 牙刷 is presented as the prime and *toothbrush* is the target word, we can measure the response time and accuracy of lexical judgment or naming of the target (i.e., the related prime-target pair), and then compare it to the unrelated prime-target pair such as 鞋子 (*shoes*) and *toothbrush*, the cross-language activation can be revealed if there is a significant difference between the two.

Kim, Wang, and Ko (2008) reported findings from Korean-English bilingual adults on their processing of derived words in English. Three experiments, using a priming lexical decision paradigm, were conducted to examine whether cross-language activation occurs via decomposition during the processing of derived words in Korean-English adult bilingual readers. In Experiment 1, when participants were given a real Korean derived word (e.g., 매력적, *attractive*) and an interpretable derived pseudoword (i.e., illegal combination of a stem and a suffix, e.g., 매력화, *attractization*) as a prime, response times for the corresponding English-translated stem (e.g., *attract*) were significantly faster than when they had received an unrelated word (e.g., 공격수, *playground*). These results suggest that cross-language activation of morphologically complex words occurs in bilingual reading and, furthermore, bilingual readers decompose complex words and are sensitive to morphological structure, not lexicality.

In Experiment 2, in order to test the role of morphological structure further, words with non-morphological endings (i.e., an illegal combination of a stem and an orthographic ending, e.g., 매력래, *attract-em*) were included; this did not show a priming effect. Finally, in Experiment 3, semantically related words of the stems in the primes (e.g., *pretty*) were used as the target words. Results showed that morphologically decomposable primes in the first language (Korean) did not prime semantically related target stems in the second language (English). This result provided evidence that cross-language activation only occurs reliably at the lexical form level but not at the semantic

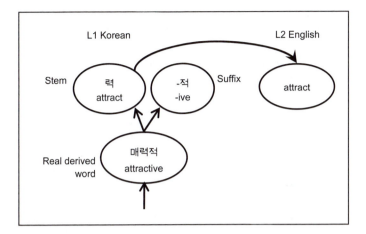

Figure 7.4 Derivational word processing in Korean bilinguals

level. Figure 7.4 illustrates how the priming effect occurs in the real derived word condition in Experiment 1.

The findings of cross-language activation of morphological constituent morphemes have important implications for classroom instruction for second language learners. For example, if second language learners indeed decompose morphological complex words in processing their two languages, teachers need to help the learners understand both the meanings of whole words and the meanings of constituent morphemes. Further, if it is the case that when second language learners process morphological complex words in one language, the translated equivalents in the other language are activated, one pedagogical implication would be the need for teachers to take into account both languages that are spoken by the second language learners.

In summary, the three major lines of research on learning a second language have addressed how the two languages facilitate or interfere with each other. The line of cross-language transfer research has focused on children's learning of the two languages simultaneously. The main research methodology used is correlational. There is a great deal of evidence for the universal cross language transfer of phonological and morphological awareness.

Cross-language orthographic transfer may be language-specific depending on whether the two languages use a similar script. When adults learn to read a second language, obviously there are some cognitive consequences when the languages are across different writing systems. This line of research has used various experimental tasks tapping into phonological and orthographic processing skills in the target language, which is normally English. It appears that when second language learners come from a logographic first language writing system such as Chinese, they tend to rely on less phonemic-based phonological information in processing English words.

The bilingual mental lexicon models have attempted to address the question of how the two languages in mostly adult second language learners are connected to each other. Lexical form level (i.e., phonological and orthographic information) and semantic form level activation across the two languages are the focus of these studies. Clearly, language proficiency in the second language determines which level of mental lexicon information is accessed and retrieved. With low second language proficiency, the two lexicons are linked at the lexical form level. Presumably, most second language learners pass through this level of learning. With high second language proficiency, the activation of semantic information becomes stronger and more immediate.

FUTURE DIRECTIONS

Causal Relation between Phonology, Orthography, Morphology and Second Language Reading

In the line of research addressing the cross-language transfer issue in learning a second language, most current studies have reported correlational data where the language- and reading-related tasks were administered simultaneously (e.g., D'Angiulli, Siegel, & Serra, 2001; Geva & Siegel, 2000; Wang et al., 2005; Wang, Park et al. 2006). Therefore, we cannot make any suggestions concerning the directionality of the relation between phonological, orthographic, or morphological skills and second language literacy acquisition. To better understand this relation, future research needs to address the issue of bidirectional relations, that is, whether the better reading skills are the outcome of the better phonological, orthographic or morphological skills, or the better phonological, orthographic or morphological skills are the outcome of the better reading skills. In line with monolingual research on the reading processes and reading acquisition, future studies should examine the predictive power of phonological, orthographic, and morphological awareness in second language reading acquisition over time. It would be especially interesting to test the relation between phonological, orthographic, or morphological processes in one language at early time points and reading skills in another language at later time points, as well as to explore the reciprocal developmental relation between reading skills and the three related processes (i.e., phonology, orthography, and morphology).

Further, future research also should consider phonological, orthographic, and morphological training studies on bilingual children to see if phonological-, orthographic- or morphological-awareness training in one language would produce substantive gains in students' word reading and reading comprehension in another language. Combining longitudinal studies and training studies will allow researchers to establish the causal relation between reading processes and reading skills in second language reading acquisition.

Control for General Abilities and Language Proficiency

In the line of research addressing the issue of the cognitive consequences of cross-language orthographic depth in learning a second language, it is necessary to control for general cognitive abilities such as intelligence level and overall language proficiency in the second language when comparing second language learners with monolingual English speakers, or comparing second language learners with different first language backgrounds.

Inclusion of Varieties of First Language Backgrounds

Future research is also needed to include second language learners with various first languages. Not only can second language learners with a logographic first language (e.g., Chinese) background be compared with those with an alphabetic first language background, second language learners with alphabetic first languages of varying ortho-graphic depths can also be compared among each other. For example, native French speakers learning to read English as second language can be compared to native Italian speakers learning to read English as second language. French and Italian are different in their transparency in mapping between letters and sounds. The effect of cross-language orthographic depth can thus be tested even within the alphabetic orthographies. Another future research direction is to identify the specific linguistic elements that may lead to different performance between the different first language groups.

Bilingual Lexicon in Children with Varying First and Second Language Proficiency

In the line of research addressing the bilingual mental lexicon, given the fact that the majority of the work is on adult second language learners, it is important to take into consideration the extension of current models to bilingual children. Bilingual children allow us to test the current bilingual lexicon models via varying not only second language proficiency but also first language proficiency, given the fact that bilingual children normally have an unbalanced growth of first and second language proficiency. The asymmetric link between the first and second language lexical forms is expected to become more balanced given children's increasing second language proficiency. It is also possible that if children's second language proficiency becomes higher than their first language proficiency, the direction of the asymmetric lexical link will be changed. The lexical form link from first to second language will become stronger than that from second to first language.

One way to examine the effects of both first and second language proficiency is to manipulate their proficiency levels orthogonally. Four groups can be formed according to their proficiency in the two languages: Low in first (L1) and second language (L2) (LL1-LL2), High in L1 and Low in L2 (HL1-LL2), Low in L1 and High in L2 (LL1-HL2), and high in both languages (HL1-HL2).

Multi-Measure Approach in Language Proficiency Assessment

In order to gain a global picture of children's language proficiency in their two languages, a multiple-measure approach is helpful. First, an oral receptive vocabulary measure can be administered, similar to the Peabody Picture Vocabulary Test-III (PPVT-III; Dunn & Dunn, 1997), which has served as the index of English proficiency in previous research (e.g., Nicoladis, 2003, 2006; Wang, Cheng, & Chen, 2006; Wang, Park, & Lee, 2006; Wang et al., 2008; Wang et al., 2009). An expressive vocabulary measure can be included as a second measure of language proficiency (e.g., the Expressive Vocabulary Test–Second Edition, EVT-2, Williams, 2007). A listening comprehension test can be added as a third measure of proficiency (e.g., the Listening Comprehension Cluster of the Woodcock-Johnson III (WJ III) Tests of Achievement, Woodcock, McGrew, & Mather, 2001). A composite standard score is generated to categorize children's first and second language proficiency levels. Finally, parents and teachers can be asked to fill out a Language Background and Experience Questionnaire to provide subjective ratings of their children's proficiency in the two languages.

In summary, there is a great deal of work needed to advance research on learning a second language in the future. In particular, we need to examine systematically how children develop their language and reading skills in their first and second languages simultaneously, the roles of language exposure at home and at school, and oral language proficiency. Second language learners from varied first language backgrounds need to be included in a more comprehensive research program to form careful comparisons of the similarities and differences across different second language and bilingual populations.

REFERENCES

Akamatsu, N. (1999). The effects of first language orthographic features on word recognition processing in English as a second language. *Reading and Writing, 11,* 381–403.

Berko, J. (1958). The child's learning of English morphology. *Word, 14,* 150–177.

Bindman, M. (2004). Grammatical awareness across languages and the role of social context: Evidence from English and Hebrew. In T. Nunes, & P. Bryant (Eds.), *Handbook of children's literacy* (pp. 691–709). Dordrecht: Kluwer.

Bradley, L., & Bryant, P. E. (1983). Categorizing sounds and learning to read: A causal connection. *Nature, 301,* 419–421.

Bryant, P. E. (2002). It doesn't matter whether onset and rime predicts reading better than phoneme awareness does or vice versa. *Journal of Experimental Child Psychology, 82,* 41–46.

Bryant, P. E., MacLean, M., Bradley, L., & Crossland, J. (1990). Rhyme, alliteration, phoneme detection and learning to read. *Developmental Psychology, 26,* 1–10.

Bruck, M., Treiman, R., & Caravolas, M. (1995). The syllable's role in the processing of spoken English: Evidence from a nonword comparison task. *Journal of Experimental Psychology: Human Perception & Performance, 21,* 469–479.

Byrne, B., & Fielding-Barnsley, R. (1995). Evaluation of a program to teach phonemic awareness to young children: A 2- and 3-year follow-up and a new preschool trial. *Journal of Educational Psychology, 87,* 488–503.

Camarota, S. (2007). *Immigrants in the United States 2007: A profile of America's foreign-born population.* Washington, DC: Center for Immigration Studies. Retrieved from http://www.cis.org/articles/2007/back1007.pdf.

Carlisle, J. (1995). Morphological awareness and early reading achievement. In L. B. Feldman (Ed.), *Morphological aspects of language processing* (pp. 189–209). Hillsdale, NJ: LEA, Inc.

Carlisle, J. F., & Nomanbhoy, D. (1993). Phonological and morphological awareness in first graders. *Applied Psycholinguistics, 14,* 177–195.

Cassar, M., & Treiman, R. (1997). The beginnings of orthographic knowledge: Children's knowledge of double letters in words. *Journal of Educational Psychology, 89,* 631–644.

Chen, H-C., Flores D'Arcais, G. B., & Cheung, S. L. (1995). Orthographic and phonological activation in recognizing Chinese characters. *Psychological Research, 58,* 144–153.

Cheng, C., & Wang, M. (2009). Bilingual compound processing: Decomposition and cross-language activation. Paper presented at the Annual Conference of the Society of Scientific Studies in Reading, Boston, USA, June.

Cisero, C. A., & Royer, J. M. (1995). The development and cross-language transfer of phonological awareness. *Contemporary Educational Psychology, 20,* 275–303.

Comeau. L., Cormier, P., Grandmaison, E., & Lacroix, D. (1999). A longitudinal study of phonological processing skills in children learning to read in a second language. *Journal of Educational Psychology, 91,* 29–43.

Committee for Economic Development (2006). *Education for global leadership: The importance of international studies and foreign language education for U.S. economic and national security.* Washington, DC: Author. Available at: www.ced.org/docs/report/report_foreign languages.pdf.

Cossu, G., Shankweiler, D., Liberman, I. Y., Tola, G., & Katz, L. (1988). Reading and awareness of phonological segments in Italian children. *Applied Psycholinguistics, 9,* 1–16.

Cummins, J. (1979). Linguistic interdependence and the educational development of bilingual children. *Review of Educational Research, 49,* 222–251.

Cummins, J. (1986). Empowering minority students: A framework for intervention. *Harvard Educational Review, 56,* 18–36.

Cummins, J. (1991). Interdependence of first- and second-language proficiency in bilingual children. In E. Bialystok (Ed.), *Language processing in bilingual children* (pp. 70–89). New York: Cambridge University Press.

Cunningham, A. E., Perry, K. E., & Stanovich, K. E. (2001). Converging evidence for the concept of orthographic processing. *Reading and Writing, 14,* 549–568.

Cunningham, A. E., & Stanovich, K. E. (1990). Assessing print exposure and orthographic processing skill in children: A quick measure of reading experience. *Journal of Educational Psychology, 82,* 733–740.

Cunningham, A. E., & Stanovich, K. E. (1993). Children's literacy environments and early word recognition sub-skills. *Reading and Writing, 5,* 193–204.

D'Angiulli, A., Siegel, L. S., & Serra, E. (2001). The development of reading in English and Italian in bilingual children. *Applied Psycholinguistics, 22,* 479–507.

Deacon, S. H., & Kirby, J. R. (2004). Morphological awareness: Just "more phonological"? The roles of morpho-logical and phonological awareness in reading development. *Applied Psycholinguistics, 25,* 223–238.

Deacon, S. H., Wade-Woolley, L., & Kirby, J. (2007). Cross-over: The role of morphological awareness in French immersion children's reading. *Developmental Psychology, 43,* 732–746.

DeFrancis, J. (1989). *Visible speech: The diverse oneness of writing systems.* Honolulu: University of Hawaii Press.

De Groot, A. M. B., & Hoeks, J. C. J. (1995). The development of bilingual memory: Evidence from word transla-tion by trilinguals. *Language Learning, 45,* 683–724.

Dijkstra, A., & Van Heuven, W. J. B. (1998). The BIA model and bilingual word recognition. In J. Grainger, & A. M. Jacobs (Eds.), *Localist connectionist approaches to human cognition* (pp. 189–226). Mahwah, NJ: Erlbaum.

Dunn, L., & Dunn, L. (1997). *Peabody Picture Vocabulary Test—III.* Circle Pines, MN: American Guidance Service.

Durgunoglu, A. Y. (2002). Cross-linguistic transfer in literacy development and implications for language learners. *Annals of Dyslexia, 52,* 189–204.

Durgunoglu, A. Y., Nagy, W. E., & Hancin-Bhatt, B. J. (1993). Cross-language transfer of phonological awareness. *Journal of Educational Psychology, 85,* 453–465.

Durgunoglu, A. Y., & Oney, B. (1999). A cross-linguistic comparison of phonological awareness and word recog-nition. *Reading and Writing, 11,* 281–299.

Ehri, L. C. (1991). Development of the ability to read words. In R. Barr, M. Kamil, P. Mosenthal, & P. D. Pearson (Eds.), *Handbook of reading research* (Vol. II, pp. 383–417). New York: Longman.

Ehri, L. C. (1998). Grapheme-phoneme knowledge is essential for learning to read words in English. In J. L. Met-sala, & L. C. Ehri (Eds.), *Word recognition in beginning literacy* (pp. 3–40). Mahwah, NJ: Erlbaum.

Fleischman, H. L., & Hopstock, P. J. (1993). *Descriptive study of services to limited English proficient students, Vol. 1, Summary of findings and conclusions.* Arlington, VA: Development Associates Inc.

Frith, U., Wimmer, H., & Landerl, K. (1998). Differences in phonological recoding in German- and English-speak-ing children. *Scientific Studies of Reading, 2,* 31–54.

Frost, R. (1994). Prelexical and postlexical strategies in reading: Evidence from a deep and shallow orthography. *Journal of Experimental Psychology: Learning, Memory, and Cognition, 20,* 116–129.

Geva, E. (1995). Orthographic and cognitive processing in learning to read English and Hebrew. In I. Taylor, & D. R. Olson (Eds.), *Scripts and literacy: Reading and learning to read alphabets, syllabaries and character* (pp. 277–291). New York: Kluwer Academic/Plenum Publishers.

Geva, E., & Siegel, L. S. (2000). Orthographic and cognitive factors in the concurrent development of basic reading skills in two languages. *Reading and Writing, 12,* 1–31.

Goswami, U., & Bryant, P. (1990). *Phonological skills and learning to read.* New York: Psychology Press.

Goswami, U., Gombert, J. E., & de Barrera, L. F. (1998). Children's orthographic representations and linguistic transparency: nonsense word reading in English, French, and Spanish. *Applied Psycholinguistics, 19,* 19–52.

Gottardo, A. (2002). The relationship between language and reading skills in bilingual Spanish-English speakers. *Topics in Language Disorders, 22,* 46–71.

Hart, L. A., & Perfetti, C. A. (2000). Quality of lexical representations affects reading comprehension skills. Paper presented at the seventh annual meeting of the Society for the Scientific Study of Reading, Stockholm, July.

Haynes, M., & Carr, T. H. (1990). Writing system background and second language reading: A component skills analysis of English reading by native speaker-readers of Chinese. In T. H. Carr, & B. A. Levy (Eds.), *Reading and its development: Component skills approaches* (pp. 375–421). San Diego, CA: Academic Press.

Holm, A., & Dodd, B. (1996). The effect of first written language on the acquisition of English literacy. *Cognition, 59,* 119–147.

Hu, C.-F., & Catts, H. W. (1998). The role of phonological processing in early reading ability: What we can learn from Chinese. *Scientific Studies of Reading, 2,* 55–79.

Hulme, C., Hatcher, P. J., Nation, K., Brown, A., Adams, J., & Stuart, G. (2002). Phoneme awareness is a better pre-dictor of early reading skill than onset-rime awareness. *Journal of Experimental Child Psychology, 82,* 2–28.

Jackson, N. E., Lu, W. H., & Ju, D. (1994). Reading Chinese and reading English: Similarities, differences, and second-language reading. In V. W. Berninger (Ed.), *The varieties of orthographic knowledge 1: Theoretical and developmental issues. Neuropsychology and cognition* (Vol. 8, pp. 73–109). Norwell, MA: Kluwer Academic.

Katz, L., & Frost, R. (1992). The reading process is difference for difference orthographies: The orthographic depth hypothesis. In R. Frost, & L. Katz (Eds), *Orthography, phonology, morphology, and meaning* (pp. 67–84). Amsterdam: Elsevier Science Publishers.

Kim, S. Y., Wang, M., & Ko, I. Y. (2008). The processing of derivational morphology in Korean-English bilingual readers. Paper presented at the Biannual Conference of Mental Lexicon, Banff, Canada, October.

Koda, K. (1989). Effects of L1 orthographic representation on L2 phonological coding strategies. *Journal of Psycholinguistic Research, 18*, 201–222.

Koda, K. (1994). Second language reading research: Problems and possibilities. *Applied Psycholinguistics, 15*, 1–28.

Koda, K. (1999). Development of L2 intraword orthographic sensitivity and decoding skills. *Modern Language Journal, 83*, 51–64.

Koda, K. (2000). Cross-linguistic variations in L2 morphological awareness. *Applied Psycholinguistics, 21*, 297–320.

Kroll, J. F., & Curley, J. (1988). Lexical memory in novice bilinguals: The role of concepts in retrieving second language words. In M. Gruneberg, P. Morris, & R. Sykes (Eds.), *Practical aspects of memory* (Vol. 2, pp. 389–395). London: John Wiley & Sons, Ltd.

Kroll, J. F., & Stewart, E. (1994). Category interference in translation and picture naming: Evidence for asymmetric connections between bilingual memory representations. *Journal of Memory and Language, 33*, 149–174.

Kuo, L. J., & Anderson, R. C. (2007). Conceptual and methodological issues in comparing metalinguistic awareness across languages. In K. Koda, & A. Zehler (Eds.), *Learning to read across languages* (pp. 39–67). Mahwah, NJ: Erlbaum.

Lindsey, K. A., Manis, F. R., & Bailey, C. E. (2003). Prediction of first-grade reading in Spanish-speaking English-language learners. *Journal of Educational Psychology, 95*, 482–494.

Lundberg, I., Frost, J., & Petersen, O. (1988). Effects of an extensive program for stimulating phonological awareness in preschool children. *Reading Research Quarterly, 23*, 263–284.

Manis, F. R., Lindsey, K., A., & Bailey, C. E. (2004). Development of reading in grades K-2 in Spanish-speaking English-language learners. *Learning Disabilities Research & Practice, 19*, 214–224.

Mattingly, I. G. (1992). Linguistic awareness and orthographic form. In R. Frost, & L. Katz (Eds), *Orthography, phonology, morphology, and meaning* (Advances in Psychology, Vol. 94, pp. 11–26). Amsterdam: North-Holland.

McClelland, J. L., & Rumelhart, D. E. (1981). An interactive activation model of context effects in letter perception: Part 1. An account of basic findings. *Psychological Review, 88*, 375–407.

Muter, V., Hulme, C., Snowling, M., & Taylor, S. (1998). Segmentation, not rhyming, predicts early progress in learning to read. *Journal of Experimental Child Psychology, 71*, 3–27.

Nagy, W., Berninger, V., & Abbott, R. (2006). Contributions of morphology beyond phonology to literacy outcomes of upper elementary and middle-school students. *Journal of Educational Psychology, 98*, 134–147.

Nagy, W., Berninger, V., Abbott, R., Vaughan, K., & Vermeulen, K. (2003). Relationship of morphology and other language skills to literacy skills in at-risk second-grade readers and at-risk fourth grade writers. *Journal of Educational Psychology, 95*, 730–742.

Nicoladis, E. (2003). What compound nouns mean to preschool children. *Brain and Language, 84*, 38–49.

Nicoladis, E. (2006). Cross-linguistic transfer in adjective-noun strings by preschool bilingual children. *Bilingualism: Language and Cognition, 9*, 15–32.

Perfetti, C. A. (1991). Representations and awareness in the acquisition of reading competence. In L. Rieben, & C. A. Perfetti (Eds.), *Learning to read: Basic research and its implication* (pp. 33–44). Hillsdale, NJ: Erlbaum.

Perfetti, C. A. (1992). The representation problem in reading acquisition. In P. B. Gough, L. C. Ehri, & R. Treiman (Eds.), *Reading acquisition* (pp. 145–174). Hillsdale, NJ: Erlbaum.

Perfetti, C. A., Liu, Y., & Tan, L H. (2005). The lexical constituency model: Some implications of research on Chinese for general theories of reading. *Psychological Review, 12*, 43–59.

Perfetti, C. A., & Tan, L. H. (1998). The time course of graphic, phonological, and semantic activation in Chinese character identification. *Journal of Experimental Psychology: Learning, Memory, and Cognition, 24*, 101–118.

Perfetti, C.A., & Zhang, S. (1995). Very early phonological activation in Chinese reading. *Journal of Experimental Psychology: Learning, Memory, and Cognition, 21*, 24–33.

Plaut, D. C., McClelland, J. L., Seidenberg, M. S., & Patterson, K. (1996). Understanding normal and impaired word reading: Computational principles in quasi-regular domains. *Psychological Review, 103*, 56–115.

Potter, M. C., So, K-F., von Eckardt, B., & Feldman, L. B. (1984). Lexical and conceptual representation in beginning and proficient bilinguals. *Journal of Verbal Learning and Verbal Behavior, 23*, 23–38.

Seidenberg, M. S., & McClelland, J. L. (1989). A distributed, developmental model of word recognition and naming. *Psychological Review, 96*, 523–568.

Shimron, J. (1999). The role of vowel signs in Hebrew: Beyond word recognition. *Reading and Writing, 11*, 301–319.

Shu, H., McBride-Chang, C., Wu, S., & Liu, H. (2006). Understanding Chinese developmental dyslexia: Morphological awareness as a core cognitive construct. *Journal of Educational Psychology, 98*, 122–133.

Sun-Alperin, K., & Wang, M. (2008). Spanish-speaking children's spelling errors with English vowel sounds that are represented by different graphemes in English and Spanish words. *Contemporary Educational Psychology*, *33*, 932–948.

Sun-Alperin, K., & Wang, M. (in press). Cross-language transfer of phonological and orthographic processing skills from Spanish L1 to English L2. *Reading and Writing: An Interdisciplinary Journal.*

Sunderman, G., & Kroll, J. F. (2006). First language activation during second language lexical processing: An investigation of lexical form, meaning, and grammatical class. *Studies in Second Language Acquisition, 28*, 387–422.

Tan, L. H., Liu, H.-L., Perfetti, C. A., Spinks, J. A., Fox, P. T., & Cao, J.-H. (2001). The neural system underlying Chinese logographic reading. *NeuroImage, 13*, 836–846.

Tan, L. H., Spinks, J. A., Feng, C. M., Siok, W. T., Perfetti, C. A., Xiong, J., et al. (2003). Neural systems of second language reading are shaped by native language. *Human Brain Mapping, 18*, 158–166.

Treiman, R. (1993). *Beginning to spell: A study of first-grade children.* New York: Oxford University Press.

Treiman, R. (1995). Errors in short-term memory for speech: A developmental study. *Journal of Experimental Psychology: Learning, Memory, and Cognition, 21*, 1197–1208.

Treiman, R., & Cassar, M. (1997). Spelling acquisition in English. In C. A. Perfetti, L. Rieben, & M. Fayol (Eds.), *Learning to spell: Research, theory, and practices across languages* (pp. 61–80). Hillsdale, NJ: Erlbaum.

Treiman, R., Mullennix, J., Bijeljac-Babic, R., & Richmond-Welty, E. D. (1995). The special role of rimes in the description, use, and acquisition of English orthography. *Journal of Experimental Psychology: General, 124*, 107–136.

Van Orden, G. C. (1987). A rows is a rose: Spelling, sound, and reading. *Memory & Cognition, 15*, 181–198.

Verhoeven, L. T. (1990). Acquisition of reading in a second language. *Reading Research Quarterly, 25*, 90–114.

Wade-Woolley, L. (1999). First language influences on second language word reading: All roads lead to Rome. *Language Learning, 49*, 447–471.

Wang, M., Anderson, A., Cheng, C., Park, Y., & Thomas, J. (2008). General auditory processing, Chinese tone processing, English phonemic processing and English reading skill: A comparison between Chinese-English and Korean-English bilingual children. *Reading and Writing, 21*, 627–644.

Wang, M., Cheng, C., & Chen, S. (2006). Contribution of morphological awareness to Chinese–English biliteracy acquisition. *Journal of Educational Psychology, 98*, 542–553.

Wang, M., & Geva, E. (2003). Spelling performance of Chinese children using English as a second language: Lexical and visual-orthographic processes. *Applied Psycholinguistics, 24*, 1–25.

Wang, M., Ko, I. Y., & Choi, J. (2009). The importance of morphological awareness in Korean-English biliteracy acquisition. *Contemporary Educational Psychology, 34*, 132–142.

Wang, M., & Koda, K. (2005). Commonalities and differences in word identification skills among learners of English as a second language. *Language Learning, 55*, 71–98.

Wang, M., Koda, K., &, Perfetti, C. A. (2003). Alphabetic and nonalphabetic L1 effects in English word identification: A comparison of Korean and Chinese English L2 learners. *Cognition, 87*, 129–149.

Wang, M., Park, Y. J., & Lee, K. R. (2006). Korean-English biliteracy acquisition: Cross-language phonological and orthographic transfer. *Journal of Educational Psychology, 98*, 148–158.

Wang, M., Perfetti, C. A., & Liu, Y. (2005). Chinese-English biliteracy acquisition: Cross-language and writing system transfer. *Cognition, 97*, 67–88.

Williams, K, T. (2007). *Expressive vocabulary test* (2nd ed.). Bloomington, MN: Pearson Assessments.

Woodcock, R. W., McGrew, K. S., & Mather, N. (2001). *Woodcock-Johnson III.* Rolling Meadows, IL: Riverside Publishing.

Zhou, X., & Marslen-Wilson, W. (1996). Direct visual access is the only way to access the Chinese mental lexicon. In G. Cottrell (Ed.), *Proceedings of the 18th Annual Conference of the Cognitive Science Society* (pp. 714–719). Mahwah, NJ: Erlbaum.

Ziegler, J. C., & Goswami, U. (2005). Reading acquisition, developmental dyslexia, and skilled reading across languages: A psycholinguistic grain size theory. *Psychological Bulletin, 131*, 3–29.

8

LEARNING MOTOR SKILL IN PHYSICAL EDUCATION
Catherine D. Ennis and Ang Chen

Magill (2009) defined motor skill learning as "a change in the capability of a person to perform a skill that must be inferred from a relatively permanent improvement in performance" (p. 169). Research over three decades has provided evidence that practice is the single most important factor responsible in learning to perform a motor skill (Barnett, Ross, Schmidt, & Todd, 1973; Del Rey, Wughalter, & Whitehurst, 1982; Fitts, 1954; Guadagnoli, Holcomb, & Weber, 1999; Krigolson & Tremblay, 2009; Starkes, 2000; Swanson & Lee, 1992). Practice effectiveness, however, is related to how it is structured and the type, timing, and amount of feedback the learner receives while practicing (French et al., 1991). Maximizing the quality of the learner's skill practice opportunities is a primary goal of physical education teaching.

In this chapter, we will examine and critique research evidence from motor skill learning research. First, we will provide historical background documenting the evolution of motor skill learning research. We then will explain evidence-based research in motor skill learning, guided by the theoretical frameworks of information processing, expert–novice comparison, and dynamical systems theories. Today, because few physical education learning goals are oriented toward learning isolated motor skills, we will review research examining learners' tactical decision-making within complex games environments. In the final section, we examine the potential of conceptual change research to advance our understanding of motor skill learning in physical education.

HISTORICAL OVERVIEW

Beginning in the 1930s, research examining motor skill learning focused on the development of objective tests of motor ability and educability and the identification of critical variables that enhance learning and performance. Motor educability was defined as the strength, ability, and coordination necessary to perform motor skills effectively. For example, Minaert (1950) examined the effects of instruction in dry skiing on students' ability to perform basic skiing skills (e.g., snowplow, snowplow and stem turns) on learning to ski on the open slope.

Novice college women (N = 32) enrolled in a beginning skiing course were pre-tested on a motor educability test to equate the control and experimental groups. The control group received skiing instruction on the open slope while the experimental group received 30 min. of dry-skiing instruction each day for six days followed by open slope instruction. The dependent variable was the number of hours required to attain competency criteria based on performance tests for each skill. Minaert found a mean difference of 2.7 hrs between the experimental and control groups, with the experimental group reaching competency sooner than the control group. He concluded that dry skiing is advantageous for novices because it enhances motor educability. Although motor educability is no longer considered a valid construct, Minaert's research provided evidence that specific types of motor skill instruction were superior in decreasing learning time.

Early motor skill researchers focused on identifying skill components and effective practice contexts, like Minaert's (1950) dry skiing tasks, to increase students' learning and performance. Mortimer (1951), for example, conducted a descriptive study examining the basketball jump shot to determine the optimal arc of flight for shots from different distances from the basket. She emphasized the role of kinesthetic memory to reproduce the optimal angle and force for each shot.

Mortimer proposed several learning tasks using a horizontal bar suspended at various heights relative to the shooter's height and distance from the basket. Learners were instructed to direct the shot over the bar and toward the basket for optimal success. She calculated initial velocity and vertical angle of projection combinations for the 12-foot shot released 5 ft above the floor "to make the ball go through the center of the basket" (Mortimer, 1951, p. 237). Her results indicated that for a 12-foot shot, the vertical angle of projection should be 58° with an initial velocity of 24.009 ft per sec. The vertical height of the horizontal bar should be 11ft 5.8 in. to create the optimal arc (p. 239). Teachers were encouraged to use suspended horizontal bars or ropes as teaching tools and to formulate feedback in terms of these estimations to help learners master the skill.

In 1972, Gentile proposed a three-stage model of skill learning based, in part, on these early studies. In stage 1 of Gentile's theory, the learner acquires an "idea" of the movement in terms of skeletal-muscular relations of body parts as explained in teacher demonstrations and explanations. In stage 2, the learner's goals change to reflect the relation between the body movement and the environment in which the skill is performed. In stage 3, performance becomes "automatic" as the learner focuses attention on the continuous, rapidly changing temporal and spatial environmental conditions that develop with concomitant movements of the object and other players in relation to the goal. At this third automatic stage, the teacher/coach becomes peripheral to the skill learning process.

These stages differentiate between two types of skills: closed and open (Farrell, 1975). In closed skills, both performer and context are stationary at the beginning of the skill, such as in diving from a 3 m board. Conversely, in open skills both the performer and the context are moving, such as in dribbling against the press in basketball. Applying Gentile's (1972) skill acquisition theory to a closed skill, such as a golf swing, requires the learner to strive for "fixation" to perform the movement pattern consistently (stage 1; Del Rey, 1972, p. 42). The movement goal when executing the golf swing is to execute the swing essentially the same way whether using a driver or an iron. In stage 2, the learner continues to reduce the variability in the movement pattern or to bring the movement pattern into conformity with an externally imposed environment (distance to the hole, slope of the golf course). Because the environment is stable, the learner is able to determine the body–environment relations prior to skill execution. Stage 3 is rare in closed skill performance because of the absence of temporal and spatial changes at the moment of skill execution.

Conversely, when learning an open skill, the stages begin to differentiate after stage 1. In stage 2, the learning goal is motor pattern "diversification" (Del Rey, 1972, p. 42). Because the environment is changing moment by moment, the learner must rely on external feedback (knowledge of performance) to develop many diverse motor patterns, each one appropriate to a particular set of temporal and spatial conditions. Gentile (1972) emphasized that in open-skill tasks, no single motor pattern would accomplish the movement goal under all possible conditions. At stage 3, open skill performance becomes "automatic" as the learner internalizes knowledge of performance and focuses attention, instead, on environmental conditions that impact skill execution. Physical education research to enhance skill learning based on Gentile's model, therefore, focuses primarily on stage 2 as the learning stage in which teacher feedback is most useful. Feedback at this stage is critical because it informs the learner of relative body component positioning and environmental changes related to skill performance. To provide appropriate feedback, researchers and teachers need to understand the elements of each skill and how best to direct learner's attention and movement to enhance performance.

Consistent with these assumptions, researchers (e.g., Roberton, Halverson, Langendorfer, & Williams, 1979) examined the actions of specific body parts to analyze learners' skill development. To establish performance models for effective feedback, many isolated skills, such as the overarm throw, were analyzed using elite performers (professional baseball pitchers) to identify how each body component *should* move to meet criteria of distance or velocity, for example. The body-component model was based on the separation of skills into discrete parts conducive to corrective feedback applications. Roberton et al.'s (1979) research examined skill coordination and control variables of the overarm throw. They filmed children of different ages and abilities using the overarm throwing pattern to identify body component movements associated with the development of throwing speed and accuracy. They determined hierarchical stages of throwing efficiency using qualitative biomechanical analysis of high-speed film of student throwers at diverse stages of overarm throwing development.

Data from Roberton et al.'s (1979) study indicated that children's developing patterns reflected increases in both trunk and arm strength, contributing to balance and body stabilization during the throw. They concluded that overarm pattern efficiency depended on movements in each of the four body components involved: legs, trunk, humerus, and forearm. These components were most involved as learners performed the stepping, body rotation, humerus-lag, and arm-swing components, respectively, of the throwing motion. To assist learning, they advised physical educators to teach the throwing skill using a task sequence that induced changes in each body-component. For example, learners were instructed first to throw hard to develop the full range of motion and later to throw at a target for accuracy. Motion analysis, performed routinely today by television sport commentators, required considerable time and expertise to collect and analyze data in the mid-20th century prior to computer-assisted technologies. Research findings based on high-speed film analyses assisted physical educators to understand body component relations and sequences in complex skills necessary to provide learners with specific, corrective feedback to enhance learning.

Advocates of body-component analysis developed extensive cuing systems that focused learner attention on the relations of body parts, shaping movements to reflect a universal, ideal pattern. For example, Table 8.1 shows a cueing chart for teaching the overarm throwing pattern recommended by Knudson and Morrison (1996). In column 1, they listed the critical features or biomechanical characteristics of effective performance, while column 2 translated the biomechanical concepts into teaching cues reflecting a body component feedback model. When teaching from the body component model, teacher feedback emphasized the relative position of body parts to produce a developmentally appropriate overarm throw. Unlike the tasks developed by Mortimer (1951) to induce arc of flight, this cueing system did not focus on the throwing context. Instead, the teacher used cue words and phrases ("step as you throw") to focus learner attention on the body parts involved in the pattern. Less attention was given to context-based cues such as, "look at the target," or "point to the target" as the ball is released, all effective contextual cues to increase children's throwing accuracy.

The primary purpose of learning motor skills in physical education is to apply or transfer skills into effective game play and fitness activities (Stodden, Langendorfer, & Roberton, 2009). Learners, however, must have extensive experiences within increasingly more complex games to transfer skills successfully. Much of the early research examined isolated skills, such as the basketball jump shot or the overarm throw. Researchers assumed that ability to perform the skill in isolation would transfer into the complex game. Additionally, research subjects typically were advanced performers who provided ideal models of skillful performance. The goal was to teach novice adults and children to perform the skill within the adult expert model.

In physical education, however, many learners are child and adolescent novices. Understanding how adults or experts throw or hit the ball does not help the teacher know how children learn skills in complex social environments, such as team games. Like Minaert's (1950) and Mortimer's (1951) research, much of the early research in motor skill learning was conducted with novice college students enrolled in beginning sport courses. Among the initial challenges was the quest to describe variables that differentiated more versus less skilled performance. Tests of educability and gross motor ability, for example, were used to determine basic difference among performances in agility, speed, and coordination. These measures displayed limited validity and reliability when compared with more precise measures used today.

Additionally, early researchers' emphasis on description of isolated skills rather than the performance of skills in game contexts constrained teachers' understanding of context-focused (external) feedback necessary to increase the quality of game play. Finally,

Table 8.1 Features and cues for throwing

Critical features	Cues
Leg drive and opposition	Step with the opposite foot, turn your side to the target
Sequential coordination	Uncoil the body
Strong throwing position	Align arm with shoulders
Inward rotation of arm	Roll the arm and wrist at release
Relaxation	Relax your upper body
Angle of release	Throw up an incline; throw over the cutoff's head

Source: Adopted from Knudson and Morrison (1996).

because university professors with access to college-age populations conducted most research, there were few studies during this time other than those by Roberton and her colleagues examining children's movement patterns and development. Thus, children were taught to move based on elite, adult movement models rather than developmentally appropriate patterns such as those that Roberton (1982) described.

THEORETICAL FRAMEWORKS

Motor skill learning is characterized by incremental gains in performance on specific tasks (Schmidt & Lee, 2009). Success in learning relies on a process called neural and behavioral organization or neural-behavioral programming (Jeanerod, 1988; Schmidt & Lee, 2009). From this perspective (Jeanerod, 1988), learners complete a cognition-behavior loop through which a physical movement is planned and executed. Learning any motor skill is an effort with combined cognitive and physical involvement, advancing from the initial perceiving, coordinating, and receiving feedback, to coding and recoding a sequence, and finally controlling the movement to meet the goal of the action. The programming process is considered to be hierarchical, with the cognitive function of the brain constantly controlling the physical behavior. The influence of cognitive psychology on neural behavioral motor learning theories is evident. Under this influence, scholars have applied three models to explain and guide learning in the psychomotor domain: information processing, expert–novice comparison, and dynamical systems.

Information-Processing Frameworks

Beginning in the 1970s and continuing today, information processing theory has been used extensively to generate performance models examining variables and mechanisms relevant in motor skill learning. In this section we will describe several research studies examining two skill learning variables, feedback and contextual interference influential in motor skill learning.

Feedback

A very large body of research has examined feedback types, conditions and delivery systems within motor performance learning (Hebert & Landin, 1994). Feedback can be used to enhance particular types of motor skill learning within certain practice conditions (Magill, 2009). Feedback is defined as knowledge of results internally or externally focused to enhance motor skill learning. Feedback includes information from sources that are internal to the performer (sensory, kinesthetic) and typically available during the performance. Other forms of feedback from sources *not* usually available to the learner during the performance can be augmented or provided by an external source, such as the teacher or coach. Motor skill learners and sport performers actively seek information from internal and external sources to adjust movements based on the movement goal or problem to be solved within rapidly changing environments of differing complexity.

A fundamental assumption of learning in the psychomotor domain is that "learning is a problem-solving process in which the goal of an action represents the problem to be solved and the evolution of a movement configuration represents the performer's attempt to solve the problem" (Guadagnoli & Lee, 2004, p. 213). From this perspective, skills practiced in isolation within the laboratory or gymnasium reflect an overly simplified task without the complexity inherent in complex game, adventure, dance, or aquatic environments. For example, when the problem is associated with accuracy, the solution typically depends on external effect-related feedback rather than internal or body component feedback.

Research by Wulf, McConnel, Gärtner, and Schwarz (2002) demonstrated the value of effect-focused feedback to enhance learning and performance by comparing the effectiveness of two types of augmented feedback on performers' attention focus and performance accuracy. Augmented feedback consisted of specific feedback directed to body movements (internal-focus) or to movement-effects (external focus). In Experiment 1, groups of novices and advanced volleyball players (N = 48) practiced serves under the internal focus or the external focus feedback conditions in a 2 × 2 (Expertise × Feedback type) design. They found that although type of feedback did not affect movement quality, external-focus feedback resulted in greater serve accuracy than did internal-focus feedback during practice and retention conditions independent of performer skill level.

In Experiment 2, Wulf et al. (2002) examined the effects of relative feedback frequency as a function of attentional focus. In this experiment, a 2 × 2 (Feedback Frequency: 100% vs. 33% × Feedback Type) design was used. Experienced soccer players (N = 52) shot lofted passes at a target. Again the researchers concluded that external-focus feedback resulted in greater accuracy than internal-focus feedback. Additionally, reduced feedback frequency was beneficial under internal-focus feedback conditions whereas 100% and 33% feedback were equally effective under the external-focus conditions.

Wulf et al.'s (2002) research demonstrated the value of effect-related as opposed to movement-related feedback when learning to perform with greater accuracy. Researchers advised teachers to minimize use of body components feedback (internal), instead focusing learners' attention on the task or task goal. Wulf et al. (2002; Wulf & Su, 2007) also have provided evidence that effect-related feedback is effective when learning both open (skiing) and closed skills (golf). For example, learners performed a golf pitch shot more accurately when their attention was directed to the motion of the club head rather than the swinging motion of the arms (Wulf, Lauterbach, & Toole, 1999).

These research findings indicate that effect-focused models of feedback delivery could assist learners to perform with greater accuracy. Historically, teachers and coaches have emphasized movement-related feedback ("keep your arms straight") when learning accuracy related tasks, rather than directing the learners' attention to the movement outcome ("when putting, look at the hole, not the ball"). Much of the feedback research, however, has not been conducted in educational learning environments, but instead in laboratories with "novel" tasks in which reaction time, for example, is used as a measure of attentional demand (Wulf, McNevin, & Shea, 2001). In the laboratory, the less burdened the learner's autonomic system, the faster the reaction time and the greater degree of automaticity, reflecting Gentile's (1972) third stage of automatic performance.

Although applying feedback cues to whole-body movements with the appropriate timing and force production needed to perform with accuracy in open sport environments is challenging for adult experts, it is an overwhelmingly complex task for novice learners in physical education. Examination of children's motor skill learning in the gymnasium gains the advantage of authentic context, while losing the precision of novel laboratory tasks and controlled conditions. Additionally, because motor skill learning researchers often examine performance variables using adult or elite learners, we have less evidence-based research to confirm the generalizability of these findings to school-age populations in physical education.

Contextual Interference

Researchers studying motor skill learning have examined several practice variables in addition to feedback (motivation, attention, contextual interference) that influence this dynamic process. Contextual interference (CI) within practice situations involves measures of retention and transfer across different skills, contexts, and time frames. For example, researchers have focused on practice schedules that lead to initial learning and to skill retention within different sport contexts and over varying time periods (French, Rink, & Werner, 1990). Findings indicate that three practice conditions—blocked (BLO), alternating (ALT), and random (RAN)—lead to differences in transfer of isolated skills to complex game environments. In BLO schedules, the learner practices one skill, while ALT and RAN schedules require learners to practice two or more different skills in alternating or random order. Although ALT and RAN practice schedules more closely reflect game complexity, they may not permit novice learners to establish an initial consistent motor pattern. The ALT and RAN conditions are used to create "contextual interference" that can facilitate or disrupt transfer of motor skills to more complex situations.

Although many studies have examined practice schedules and contextual interference in the laboratory (Hall & Magill, 1995; Russell & Newell, 2007), research conducted to examine the effectiveness of contextual interference in physical education also can inform instruction. For example, Hebert, Landin, and Solmon (1996) examined the effects of practice schedule manipulation on the performance and learning of low and high skilled students. College undergraduates (N = 83) enrolled in five tennis classes performed a pre-test on the forehand and backhand basics such as the grip, preparation, and swing. They responded to a questionnaire to self-assess their experience level in tennis and in other open skills (racquetball, softball), and rated the perceived difficulty of learning to play tennis.

Following a skills pre-test, students were taught the skills during the first three class periods. Learners were categorized into high and low skill groups, and assigned to BLO and ALT practice schedules. Students began each of the next nine lessons by performing 30 ground strokes: 15 forehand and 15 backhand. High and low skilled students assigned to the BLO condition completed all forehand strokes followed by all backhand strokes, while the ALT condition group alternated forehand and backhand strokes on each trial. Trials were scored as successful when the ball was propelled over the net, landing in the backcourt. Students completed a post-test following the nine classes.

Practice success was analyzed using a 2 × 2 × 3 (Skill Level × Practice Schedule × Test) design with repeated measures on the last factor. Results indicated that high skilled students had significantly more success than low skilled students in both practice conditions. Low skilled learners assigned to the BLO schedule scored significantly higher on the post-test than low skilled students assigned to the ALT schedule. There were no differences in post-test performances of high skilled learners assigned to the BLO or ALT condition. The researchers concluded that low interference (BLO) practice enhanced the learning of low skilled students, while high skilled learners demonstrated no post-test difference regardless of practice condition. Magill and Hall (1990) argued that high interference conditions are too complex for novices who have not established a basic motor pattern and, thus, are unable to benefit from the ALT and RAN conditions. Some experience or expertise is a prerequisite for learners to benefit from high interference practice schedules.

Information-processing researchers have examined the dynamics of sensory and augmented feedback and practice schedules with college and adult learners. Most research studies involve feedback delivery systems in which knowledge of results or corrective feedback is provided by the researcher to a single learner immediately following the performance. This is an optimal feedback condition that often cannot be replicated in physical education where one teacher may observe 25 diverse learner performances. The generalizability of laboratory findings has not been confirmed in research conducted in physical education classes (Silverman, Woods, & Subramaniam, 1998). For example, Silverman, Tyson, and Krampitz (1992) investigated the relations between teacher feedback and middle school students' achievement. Students (N = 200) in 10 middle school physical education classes were pre-tested, received seven instructional lessons, and were post-tested on two volleyball skills, the serve and forearm pass. Instruction was videotaped and teacher feedback subsequently was coded using a validated six-category (type, form, time, referent, number of students, and quality) observation system. Data were analyzed to reveal the relations of various feedback patterns to achievement. Results indicated that most students received relatively little skill-related feedback (~ four times each lesson) and that total feedback, alone, did not relate to student achievement. Instead, the amount and practice quality proved to be more instrumental in student achievement of these two skills.

Teachers in these 10 middle school classes focused on internal-focused or body components (corrective, specifically descriptive and prescriptive) feedback, rather than external-related or context feedback. This may have been a factor in feedback effectiveness. The Silverman et al. (1992) research was a correlational study that monitored, but did not manipulate, the instruction and types of feedback used. Controlled experimental designs can provide a better understanding of these factors' contribution to motor skill learning.

Expert–Novice Comparison

Differences in sport skill execution are readily evident when comparing the performances of experts with those of novices (McPherson, 1999; McPherson & Thomas, 1989). Research examining low- and high-skilled learner differences in response to differing interference practice schedules has provided additional support for theories comparing novice and expert performance. Expert–novice frameworks that shift the research focus from expert performance to novice learning facilitate the search for neural-behavior determinants of performance excellence. In addition to laboratory examinations of skill programming mechanisms, researchers also studied field-based skill learning to define expertise as skill performance on more authentic performance tasks (Allard & Starkes, 1991).

It is well established that advanced performers are more capable of performing skillfully in isolated drill situations than their lesser skilled counterparts. Often the differences can be attributed to prior experience, superior strength, and greater coordination and control of physical movements. Based on findings from an extensive program of research, Ericsson (Ericsson & Kintsch, 1995; Ericsson, Krampe, & Tesch-Römer, 1993) argued that extended engagement with a particular domain leads to prior knowledge and the development of "memory skills that promote rapid encoding of information in long-term memory and afford selective access to that information when required" (Vaeyens, Lenoir, Williams, & Philippaerts, 2007, p. 395). Ericsson concluded that skilled performers develop more flexible and detailed memory representations than do less skilled individuals, permitting them to adapt more readily to changing situational demands. Expert–novice comparisons of key variables associated with learners' tactical decision-making can provide insight into superior playing ability in complex game environments.

Vaeyens and his colleagues (2007) investigated Ericsson's hypothesis in research to examine the complex interactions between perception, cognition, and expertise in novice and advanced youth soccer players. Previous research by Williams and his colleagues (Ward, Williams, & Bennett, 2002; Williams, Hodges, North, & Barton, 2006) found distinct differences in low and high skilled players' ability to recall patterns of play, use visual search patterns, monitor opponent's postural orientation prior to key events, and anticipate event outcomes (Ward & Williams, 2003). Vaeyens et al. (2007) investigated one hypothesized advantage that skilled performers appear to have when compared to less skilled opponents, namely that of superior visual search behaviors that precede tactical decisions. Specifically, they hypothesized that successful players would exhibit a higher search rate and more frequent alternations of fixation between display areas than would their less successful counterparts.

Vaeyens et al. (2007) examined visual search strategies in three groups (N = 65) of 14-year-old male soccer academy players, representing elite, sub-elite, and regional playing ability. Players were tested using film-based simulation sequences of offensive soccer plays. Simulations consisted of offensive patterns of play with variations in the positions and ratio of attackers to defenders (2 vs.1, 3 vs.1, 3 vs. 2, 4 vs. 3, and 5 vs. 2) and length of the play sequence. A panel of seven elite youth coaches determined the scoring system and later scored players' performances for the dependent variable, response accuracy

Visual scanning data were collected using an eye–head integration system with head tracker to measure and record eye line of gaze in relation to head movements as players scanned the "field" while viewing the simulation. Players viewed a near-life size image of each scenario projected on a wall and responded *physically* to the sequence by either passing the ball toward the player on the screen, shooting on goal, or moving to dribble around a defender. Players verbalized their intended responses immediately following each trial. Each player viewed 33 offensive patterns in a randomized order kept constant for each participant.

Results indicated that skillful learners were quicker to make decisions across all viewing conditions. Decision times for all learners were slower when responding to more complex situations involving multiple offensive and defensive players (3 vs. 2, 4 vs. 3). Further, analyses revealed that more skillful learners made more accurate decisions than their less skillful counterparts in all viewing conditions. Similarly, more skillful learners used a more exhaustive search pattern involving a higher number of fixations than did their less skillful counterparts. As situations increased in complexity, fixation and inter-fixation durations and decision times increased for both more and less skillful players. More skillful players alternated their gaze more frequently between the player in possession of the ball and other areas of the field than less skilled players. Further, more skillful players spent less time fixating on the ball, instead, fixating on the player in possession of the ball and on offensive players most closely marked by a defender.

One serious limitation of this research is the absence of a transfer test to determine if these results are applicable to actual playing settings. Expert–novice research also is limited by the opportunity to examine performances of established experts. In the Vaeyens et al. (2007) study it is questionable whether elite 14-year-old players are experts. It is likely that they would not be categorized in the expert group when competing against adult professional soccer players, for example. Additionally, it is unclear whether learners in physical education can be taught to use visual search techniques to improve their success in class games. Because learners in physical education typically reflect a wide range of technical skill and decision-making ability with a high preponderance of novice learners, effective instructional strategies should be examined with heterogeneous learners in modified and complex game situations. It is unclear at what point novice learners of any age can be taught to inhibit their tendency to focus on the ball and to employ more sophisticated visual strategies. Additionally, because expert–novice comparative research often is conducted with adolescents, it is not clear how visual search and decision-making strategies develop in children.

Vaeyens et al.'s (2007) research, however, does add support to the simple to complex instructional progression strategies advocated by many physical educators (Griffin & Butler, 2005; Griffin, Oslin, & Mitchell, 1997). One aspect of simple to complex game strategies is to begin with 2 vs. 1 and 3 vs. 1 modified games, adding offensive players first, and then defensive players, gradually increasing game complexity. Results from the Vaeyens et al. (2007) research are particularly informative for middle and high school physical education. Historically, many of these teachers have used large-sided games (11 vs. 11 soccer; 5 vs. 5 basketball) instead of using small numbers of players (small-sided games) and simple to complex instructional progressions as adolescent learners demonstrate their ability to transfer skills and decision-making ability from skill and tactical drills into small sided games. It is likely that most middle and high school learners are not as skilled as Vaeyens' lowest skilled group. Thus, based on findings from Vaeyens et al.'s (2007) research, low and moderately skilled adolescents in middle and high school physical education may be more successful in small-sided playing situations.

Dynamical Systems Perspective

Critics of the information-process and expert–novice comparison theories (e.g., Turvey, Fitch, & Tuller, 1982) argue that using pre-determined motor programs when executing motor tasks is inadequate. Like Gentile (1972), they emphasize that movement (i.e., open skill) is not a pre-programmed action sequence residing within an acquired knowledge structure or movement repertoire (Turvey et al., 1982). Thus, it is impossible for one to preselect a movement sequence from memory when facing novel or complex tasks. Instead, movements emerge from the constraints and affordances naturally occurring in the environment. Although laboratory-based studies attempt to recreate natural environments, the laboratory environment still may not be authentic. In laboratory situations, the fabricated variables can only mediate (Magill & Hall, 1990) rather than determine skill execution as in authentic performance settings. In dynamical systems theories, the individual learns or performs motor skills within the constraints of biological, physical, and social environments. From this ecological perspective, a motor sequence is hypothesized as an emergent consequence of action resulting from interactions between the biological system and environmental information.

A key concept in dynamical systems theory is that of constraints (Ko, Challis, & Newell, 2003; Newell & McDonald, 1994). Constraints arise from various sources within the human body itself (i.e., biological constraints), from the task (goals, rules, structure), and from the environment (i.e., contextual information/feedback received through perceptual/sensory channels, including physical and social elements). Research by Newell and Slifkin (1998) confirmed that these three constraint types influence the learning process simultaneously. They found that constraints for each skill are manifest in different ways in different individuals, even among performance experts.

The research, however, says little about how children actually learn the throwing pattern. Throwing, Roberton (1982) argued, is preliminary to catching in both isolated and more environmentally complex game situations. Additionally, there are a number of other environmental factors, such as object size and weight, playing field size and goal dimensions, and game rules that can facilitate or constrain skilled throwing. Supporting this principle, recent research by Breslin and his colleagues (2009) examined changes in the glenohumeral horizontal abduction angle (a relative angle greater than 180° between the humerus and the trunk) in novice throwers in response to different object weights. The researchers filmed 15 novice African American preschool-age children ($M = 4.69$ years; 7 girls) throwing baseballs and softballs each with a different mass, twice each.

Results indicated that novice throwers failed to achieve change in the glenohumeral horizontal abduction angle as a result of adjustments to changes in object weight. This is consistent with teachers' observations of novice throwers who are inclined to "push" the ball with a simultaneous motion "rather than the sequential whip like motion typically demonstrated with a temporal and spatial lag in the forward movement of the humerus" typically found in skilled baseball pitchers (Breslin et al., 2009, p. 377). Additionally, high standard deviations in the angle measurements indicated that these children had not yet developed a consistent throwing pattern. Thus, they demonstrated inconsistencies in throwing pattern attributable to ball size, grip size, and strength when attempting to perform an overarm throw under new task constraints. Findings from previous research (Southland, 1998) conducted with mature throwers found that throwing motion changes occurring with the addition of external mass cannot be generalized to novice throwers. Research with novice performers is subject to large performance variability. Novice throwers, such as those in this research, demonstrate an "extremely limited glenohumeral horizontal abduction angle suggesting that the cocking phase of the throw was not developed enough to generate the momentum required for increased inertia of the hand to draw the arm back" (Breslin et al., 2009, p. 378).

These findings provide additional support for the developmental nature of the overarm throwing pattern. It is likely that in most physical education classes, the heterogeneity of students' throwing patterns requires teachers to make significant adaptations within particular throwing tasks. Novices assessed on throwing tasks with different size and weight objects that require mature throwing patterns are unlikely to perform the task successfully. When children "lack the mechanical capability to exploit the inherent inertial properties of balls with increased size and mass," they are likely to fail regardless of the quality and nature of instruction and teacher feedback (Breslin et al., 2009, p. 378).

Understanding this variability explains, in part, why children learn the same skill in different ways and at different rates. Dynamical systems theory also describes how and why context-dependent skills taught within small-sided games, for example, may work to facilitate skill learning and more advanced game play in young learners (Kirk & Kinchin, 2003). MacPhail, Kirk, and Griffin (2008), building on the work of Nevett, Rovegno, Babiarz, and McCaughtry (2001), studied learning associated with throwing catchable passes in invasion games (e.g., territorial games with a goal at each end of the field or court: soccer, basketball). The term, *catchable pass*, in this case, is an environmental constraint for the overarm throwing skill. In the MacPhail et al. research, elementary school students (N = 29) participated in a six-week long learning unit.

Data consisted of video-recorded learning behaviors and semi-structured student interviews. Using the Game Performance Assessment Instrument (Griffin et al., 1997), the researchers analyzed the data in terms of decisions made, skills executed, on-ball support movements, and defensive moves. They concluded that learning to throw is constrained by the understanding of catching. Learning to execute throwing skills in a complex learning environment is coupled with both learning to catch and the understanding of catching in complex game environments.

In summary, these three major frameworks have been instrumental in explaining motor skill learning. The frameworks focus primarily on the neural-biological mechanism of the skill learning process. It was not until the advent of dynamical systems theory, however, that motor skill learning was studied in context. Empirical evidence strongly supports two conclusions. First, learning in the psychomotor domain requires high level cognitive functioning with a strong declarative knowledge of skill execution and performance base. Second, learning motor skills requires the learner to proceduralize declarative knowledge within the context in which the skills are performed. It is likely that skills are not pre-learned or pre-programmed, but emerge to address and overcome contextual constraints. Skill performances within complex game situations rely on the individual's richness of knowledge and skill repertoire developed through extensive, appropriate practice opportunities.

CURRENT TRENDS AND ISSUES: LEARNING TO MAKE TACTICAL DECISIONS IN COMPLEX GAMES

Physical education scholars and teachers value both the learning of physical skills and the application of those skills effectively in complex situations. Intricate, swiftly changing social situations, such as those found in team games, challenge learners to recognize complex patterns inherent in offensive and defensive tactics. Critical to team success is each learner's ability to anticipate the need to create and attack space or limit space and defend game territory. In so doing, they must both think and *move* temporally and spatially—at the right time, to the right place—and then effectively perform the right skill.

Cognitive knowledge of skill, sport, and fitness concepts and the social and cognitive processes that enhance or constrain individual and team skills and tactics is relevant in most physical education curricula. Research in physical education examining student learning as the cognitive understanding of what, how, and when to perform a skill has contributed a critical element to elaborate dynamical systems theories of motor skill learning. In this section, we discuss research examining student motor skill learning in complex social situations. In so doing, we summarize physical education research conducted within the Games for Understanding curriculum models (Gréhaigne, Wallian, & Godbout, 2005; Griffin & Butler, 2005).

Advocates of decision-making games curricula (Gréhaigne et al., 2005) view learning as an active, social process. They examine and value the relevance of prior knowledge in learning and utilize the social nature of games to enhance knowledge construction (Griffin & Butler, 2005). How students learn to perform skills within complex game environments is of particular importance in physical education where a significant allocation of instruction time is devoted to team games at elementary, middle, and high school levels. Students are required to apply or transfer isolated motor skills (e.g., throwing, kicking, catching, hitting) into the multifaceted, quickly evolving contexts of team games. Few other educational environments require learners to master their own cognitive and physical performances while simultaneously countering the decisions and skills of a crafty opponent.

Currently, researchers are examining learners' cognitive engagement as they learn game strategies and tactics within these models. Because of the cognitive complexity involved in successful performance, research designs often employ game scenarios to capture student learning. Blomqvist, Vänttinen, and Luhtanen (2005), for example, used a video-based test to evaluate 14–15-year-old students' understanding of soccer tactics. The video portrayed skillful boys playing a modified (3 vs. 3) soccer game. The video included 17 game sequences (9 offensive and 8 defensive) selected by expert coaches from 47 filmed sequences. Each sequence included lead-up play prior to the game situation to be evaluated, followed by the presentation of a still frame on which arrows were imposed representing three play, pass, or movement response options. Learners, first decided what to do, and then had 45 seconds to select two relevant arguments from a list of eight written arguments to explain their decision.

Blomqvist and her colleagues (2005) found that students made significantly more decisions related to the offensive tactic of "maintaining possession of the ball" than in other offensive or defensive situations. Learners scored on average 71% correct decisions in the game understanding video test in which they responded to offensive game situations (74.4% correct; with the ball 74%, off the ball, 63%) and defensive situations (67.3%). Again, this research was conducted in an experimental situation and not within the complexity of a physical education class. The extent to which these tactical decision-making skills transfer to physical education lessons is not known.

Physical educators strive to teach children to apply isolated motor skills effectively in game situations (French, Werner, Taylor, Hussey, & Jones, 1996). When teaching children, instructors simplify the environment and teach using game sequences that represent key parts of the game, such as maintaining possession of the ball, scoring, and defending. Nevett et al. (2001) for example, focused on passing and catching as key components of maintaining possession strategies that place throwing/catching skills within a social context. Nevett and his colleagues conducted research to describe changes in fourth grade students' use of basic tactics as a result of a 12-week unit on game tactics. Participants played a game of 3 vs. 3 aerial basketball pre and post-unit instruction. The object of the invasion or territorial game was to score goals by passing a ball to a teammate standing within one of two hoops in the attacking end. Additionally, they were required to defend these goals from attack by the opposing team. Hoops were placed so that players could attack the hoops from all directions. Players could advance the ball only by aerial passing; traveling with and stealing the ball were not permitted. Each 8-minute game was videotaped from the school roof to capture the overhead view of the playing area. The same teams were kept for the pre- and post-game situation, and players wore colored vests with numbers to facilitate identification.

The researchers used two coding instruments to examine decision-making and motor skill execution. The first instrument recorded children's passing decisions and passing-skill execution, while the second captured cutting or off the ball actions and catching-skill execution. Children's decision-making skills and actions were based on the overt behaviors they displayed during the games. Additionally, passing decisions and passing-skill-execution coding further evaluated the passer's actions. The researchers coded and evaluated the following actions: (a) passing decisions judged good or poor; (b) the type of good or poor decision (8 types considered); (c) the length of the pass (appropriate, too short, too far); and (d) the quality of the pass (seven levels). The second instrument was used to evaluate receivers' cutting actions and catching motor skill execution, specifically (a) cutting actions judged as good or poor; (b) the type of good or poor action (9 types); (c) the direction of the movement made to receive the pass (5 directions); (d) the distance from the passer to receiver (appropriate, too short, too long); and (e) catching ability (five levels). Data were analyzed as the percentage of each participant's total number of passing trials with good passing decisions and cutting actions. Because change in passing and cutting was the research focus, data were analyzed using two separate Gender × Skill Level × Test ANOVAs with repeated measures on the last factor.

Results indicated that children increased the number of effective passing and cutting decisions and quality of passes during the game tactics unit as reflected by the increase in the number of successful catches from pre- to post-test. There were no differences by gender or skill level. Specifically, the number of appropriate lead passes, held ball decisions, and successful catches increased significantly, reflecting improvement in receivers' number and quality of cuts. The results from this study indicated that effective passing and cutting tactics can be learned by fourth graders in a physical education school-based setting when simple tactics, such as throwing lead passes, are the focus of instruction. Catching a pass requires children to move into an open space rather than standing still and calling for the pass. Many invasion games require the use of effective lead passes and successful catches to advance the ball into opponent's territory.

Rovegno et al. (2001) further analyzed these data (Nevett et al., 2001) to provide clear descriptions of fourth grade children's developmental patterns when attempting to play throwing and catching games. The practical implications of this research are that teachers can readily observe these behaviors and teach directly to counter children's ineffective tactics. Specifically, Rovegno et al. (2001) found that fourth grade receivers tended to move or cut too slowly into a space using a curved (i.e., a banana cut) rather than a straight pathway. Receivers at this developmental level also tended to cut behind the defender and to reverse direction just as the ball was thrown or just as the receiver was about to evade the defender. Not only did the receiver not catch the ball, but these ineffective cutting patterns also were detrimental to the *passer's* learning of effective throwing practices. In this situation, the passer was reluctant to attempt effective passing strategies, such as leading the receiver and passing as the receiver was moving into an open space, and thus was less likely to throw a pass that the receiver could catch. Instead of passing ahead of the catcher's projected pathway (lead pass), throwers were more likely to send the pass behind the receiver, directly to the defender, or to the place where the receiver had been standing prior to cutting to receive the ball.

As a result of this analysis, Rovegno and her colleagues (2001) provided specific instructional tasks and teaching cues to assist fourth grade receivers learn to use quick, straight cuts into an open space, thus reinforcing the passer's attempts to throw lead passes into open spaces, learning to release the ball *before* the receiver reached the space. Although this simultaneous emphasis on the individual, task, and environment increases the complexity of the learning task, the authentic nature of the "catchable pass" context increases learners' understanding of temporal and spatial task dimensions. The situated nature of the catchable passing task enhances learners' understandings not only of how to perform a throw and a catch, but also when and where to pass, increasing students' opportunities for success in complex game situations (Rink, 2009).

FUTURE DIRECTIONS

Although there is a developing body of research in learner cognition in physical education (e.g., Lee, Landin, & Carter, 1992), research examining learners' beliefs and naïve conceptions that facilitate or constrain learning is just emerging as an area of study in physical education. Historically, physical educators have been aware of children's difficulties in learning to play complex games. Even pre-service teachers are quick to comment on the extensive amount of instructional time required for students to learn to play even simple games effectively. For example, when first learning to play territorial games, novices typically run directly to the ball in an attempt to gain possession. This naïve conception results in novice players congregating in a small space around the ball as they attempt to catch or kick the ball toward the goal. Griffin, Dodds, Placek, and Tremino (2001) described this as "bunching" and discussed learners' perceptions of bunching in research with middle-school students.

Game tactic learning provides a ripe area of study for researchers interested in conceptual change. Griffin et al. (2001), for example, conducted ethnographic research to examine sixth grade physical education students' understanding of soccer tactics. They used focused, structured interviews in which learners responded to seven basic tactical problems. During the interview, learners moved game pieces representing players on a soccer field game board and verbalized what those players should do in each situation and their rationale for each decision.

Researchers classified students' responses into four conceptual models or levels. A level 1 response described skills in isolation without identifying connections among skills, while responses categorized as level 2 described skills and gave reasons for using the skill in a game to score goals. Level 3 categorizations provided reasons for using skills in a game and possible consequences for particular actions. It was not until level 4, however, that learners could describe coherent sequences of actions, give reasons for those actions, and explain tactical options within condition-action (if–then) statements. As in the Blomqvist et al. (2005) study, middle schools learners could solve offensive tactical problems more accurately than defensive problems. The majority of these learners were categorized at level 2 (41%) and level 3 (32%). Girls' responses reflected levels 1–3, while boys' responses fit levels 2–4. None of the girls' responses was categorized at level 4. Boys reported more formal and informal soccer experiences than girls. The researchers concluded that soccer experience was more instrumental to soccer knowledge than was gender.

This research reflects limitations inherent in many physical education lessons. Although researchers collected data on students' authority source, they were not able to compare student knowledge with an objective knowledge standard such as found in detailed curricula or textbooks. Currently, few school districts provide physical education textbooks or other written material to establish detailed learning objectives and assessment criteria to structure the teaching-learning process. Most physical education teachers create curricula and design lessons for themselves, becoming familiar with students' knowledge and misconceptions as they search for reasons why students perform in ways counter to teacher instructions and or resist correction or change. Without objective sources of knowledge, it is more difficult to identify naïve theories or models of student conceptions. Griffin et al. (2001) also did not attempt to capture students' epistemic and ontological beliefs and theories about soccer knowledge, further limiting understanding of learners' naïve conceptions. Increased understanding of conceptual change processes in children's learning of physical education concepts and skills can lead to enhanced teacher training and improved curricular and instructional materials to target naïve, counter-intuitive, and resistant naïve conceptions or misconceptions (Vosniadou & Brewer, 1992). Future research in conceptual change associated with skill, sport, and fitness content can result in improved instruction and enhanced efforts to address students' naïve conceptions.

In conclusion, motor skill learning is a complex and time-consuming process. When the learning focus is on application or transfer of isolated skills to complex game environments in physical education settings, it is likely that the instructional time required to learn to perform effectively exceeds the instructional time allocated to K-12 physical education in most public schools. Additionally, because students are not grouped by prior knowledge, experience, or ability when assigned to physical education, the vast diversity of student skill and tactical prior knowledge and performance ability in most physical education classes makes each lesson its own unique expert–novice design. Thus, it is likely that most effective game players learn to become skillful *outside* of physical education in athletic and recreational settings where practice time is extensive, players are grouped by skill level (teams, leagues), and the coach is an expert teacher who focuses on skills and tactical game play within a particular sport (Ennis, 2006).

Physical educators are fortunate, however, to be able to draw on an array of evidence-based research studies examining motor skill learning. These studies have been conducted by scholars from a variety of research perspectives examining a number of critical variables in laboratory and instructional settings. Nevertheless, understanding and interpreting the findings for application in physical education is a challenge even for physical educators with advanced expertise. Continuing efforts to understand motor skill learning in complex sport environments should provide additional opportunities for enhanced instruction and student learning.

REFERENCES

Allard, F., & Starkes, J. L. (1991). Motor skill experts in sports, dance, and other domains. In K. A. Ericsson, & J. Smith (Eds.), *Toward a general theory of expertise: Prospects and limits* (pp. 126–152). Amsterdam: Elsevier.

Barnett, M. L., Ross, D., Schmidt, R. A., & Todd, B. (1973). Motor skills learning and the specificity of training principle. *Journal of Motor Behavior, 44,* 440–447.

Blomqvist, M., Vänttinen, T., & Luhtanen, P. (2005). Assessment of secondary school students' decision-making and game-play ability in soccer. *Physical Education and Sport Pedagogy, 10,* 107–120.

Breslin, C. M., Garner, J. C., Rudisill, M.E., Parish, L. E., St. Onge, P. M., Campbell, B. J., & Weimar, W. H. (2009). The influence of task constraints on the glenohumeral horizontal abduction angle of the overarm throw of novice throwers. *Research Quarterly for Exercise and Sport, 80,* 375–379.

Del Ray, P. (1972). Appropriate feedback for open and closed skill acquisition. *Quest, XVIII,* 42–45.

Del Rey, P., Wughalter, E. H., & Whitehurst, M. (1982). The effects of contextual interference on females with varied experience in one sport skills. *Research Quarterly for Exercise and Sport, 53,* 53–115.

Ennis, C. D. (2006). Curriculum: Forming and reshaping the vision of physical education in a high need, low demand world of schools. *Quest, 58,* 41–59.

Ericsson, K. A., & Kintsch, W. (1995). Long-term working memory. *Psychological Review. 102,* 211–245.

Ericsson, K. A., Krampe, R. T., & Tesch-Römer, C. (1993). The role of deliberate practice in the acquisition of expert performance. *Psychological Review, 100,* 363–406.

Farrell, J. E. (1975). The classification of physical education skills. *Quest, 24*, 63–68.

Fitts, P. M. (1954). The information capacity of the human motor system in controlling the amplitude of movement. *Journal of Experimental Psychology, 47*, 381–391.

French, K. E., Rink, J. E., Rikard, L., Mays, A., Lynn, S., & Werner, P. (1991). The effects of practice progressions on learning two volleyball skills. *Journal of Teaching in Physical Education, 10*, 261–274.

French, K. E., Rink, J. E., & Werner, P. H. (1990). Effects of contextual interference on retention of three volleyball skills. *Perceptual and Motor Skills, 71*, 179–186.

French, K. E., Werner, P. H., Taylor, K., Hussey, K., & Jones, J. (1996). The effects of a six-week unit of tactical, skill, or combined tactical and skill instruction on badminton performance of ninth-grade students. [Monograph] *Journal of Teaching in Physical Education, 15*, 439–463.

Gentile, A.M. (1972). A working model of skill acquisition with application to teaching. *Quest, XVII*, 3–23.

Gréhaigne, J. F., Wallian, N., & Godbout, P. (2005). Tactical-decision learning model and students' practices. *Physical Education and Sport Pedagogy, 10*, 255–269.

Griffin, L. L., & Butler, J. (2005). *Teaching games for understanding: Theory, research, and practice.* Champaign, IL: Human Kinetics.

Griffin, L. L., Dodds, P., Placek, J. H., & Tremino, F. (2001). Middle school students' conceptions of soccer: Their solutions to tactical problems. *Journal of Teaching in Physical Education, 20*, 324–340.

Griffin, L. L., Oslin, J. L., & Mitchell, S. A. (1997). *Teaching sports concepts and skills: A tactical games approach.* Champaign, IL: Human Kinetics.

Guadagnoli, M. A., Holcomb, W. R., & Weber, T. (1999). The relationship between contextual interference effects and performer expertise on the learning of a putting task. *Journal of Human Movement Studies, 37*, 19–36.

Guadagnoli, M. A., & Lee, T. D. (2004). Challenge point: A framework for conceptualizing the effects of various practice conditions in motor learning. *Journal of Motor Behavior, 36*, 212–224.

Hall, K. G., & Magill, R. A. (1995). Variability of practice and contextual interference in motor learning. *Journal of Motor Behavior, 27*, 299–309.

Hebert, E. P., & Landin, D. (1994). Effects of a learning model and augmented feedback on tennis skill acquisition. *Research Quarterly for Exercise and Sport, 65*, 250–257.

Hebert, E. P., Landin, D., & Solmon, M. A. (1996). Practice schedule effects on the performance and learning of low-and high-skilled students: An applied study. *Research Quarterly for Exercise and Sport, 67*, 52–58.

Jeanerod, M. (1988). *The neural and behavioral organization of goal-directed movements.* New York: Oxford University Press.

Kirk, D., & Kinchin, G. (2003). Situated learning as a theoretical framework for sport education. *European Physical Education Review, 9*, 221–235.

Knudson, D., & Morrison, C. (1996). An integrated qualitative analysis of the overarm throw. *Journal of Physical Education, Recreation & Dance, 67*(6), 17–22.

Ko, Y. G., Challis, J. H., & Newell, K. M. (2003). Learning to coordinate redundant degrees of freedom in a dynamic balance task. *Human Movement Science, 22*, 47–66.

Krigolson, O. E., & Tremblay, L. (2009). The amount of practice really matters: Specificity of practice may be valid only after sufficient practice. *Research Quarterly for Exercise and Sport, 80*, 197–204.

Lee, A.M., Landin, D. K., & Carter, J. A. (1992). Student thoughts during tennis instruction. *Journal of Teaching in Physical Education, 11*, 256–267.

MacPhail, A., Kirk, D., & Griffin, L. (2008). Throwing and catching as relational skills in game play: Situated learning in a modified game unit. *Journal of Teaching in Physical Education, 27*, 100–115.

Magill, R. A. (2009). *Motor learning: Concepts and applications* (8th ed.). Boston: McGraw-Hill.

Magill, R. A., & Hall, K. G. (1990). A review of the contextual interference effect in motor skill acquisition. *Human Movement Science, 9*, 241–289.

McPherson, S. L. (1999). Expert-novice differences in performance skills and problem representations of youth and adults during tennis competition. *Research Quarterly for Exercise and Sport, 70*, 233–251.

McPherson, S. L., & Thomas, J. R. (1989). Relation of knowledge and performance in boys' tennis: Age and expertise. *Journal of Experimental Child Psychology, 48*, 190–211.

Minaert, W. A. (1950). An analysis of the value of dry skiing in learning selected skiing skills. *The Research Quarterly, 21*, 47–52.

Mortimer, E. M. (1951). Basketball shooting. *The Research Quarterly, 22*, 234–243.

Nevett, M., Rovegno, I., Babiarz, M., & McCaughtry, N. (2001). Changes in basic tactics and motor skills in an invasion-type game after a 12-lesson unit of instruction. *Journal of Teaching in Physical Education, 20*, 352–369.

Newell, K. M., & McDonald, P. V. (1994). Learning to coordinate redundant biomechanical degrees of freedom. In S. Swinnen, J. Heuer, J. Massion, & P. Casaer (Eds.), *Interlimb coordination: Neural, dynamical and cognitive constraints* (pp. 515–536). San Diego, CA: Academic Press.

Newell, K. M., & Slifkin, A. B. (1998). The nature of movement variability. In J. P. Piek (Ed.), *Motor behavior and human skill: A multidisciplinary perspective* (pp. 143–160). Champaign, IL: Human Kinetics.

Rink, J. E. (2009). *Teaching physical education for learning* (6th ed.). Boston: McGraw-Hill.

Roberton, M. A. (1982). Changing motor patterns during childhood. In J. R. Thomas (Ed.), *Motor development during childhood and adolescence* (pp. 48–90). Minneapolis, MN: Burgess.

Roberton, M. A., Halverson, L. E., Langendorfer, S., & Williams, K. (1979). Longitudinal changes in children's overarm throw ball velocities. *Research Quarterly, 50,* 256–264.

Rovegno, I., Nevett, M., Brock, S., & Babiarz, M. (2001). Teaching and learning basic invasion game tactics in 4th grade: A descriptive study from situated and constraints theoretical perspectives. *Journal of Teaching in Physical Education, 20,* 370–388.

Russell, D. M., & Newell, K. M. (2007). How persistent and general is the contextual interference effect? *Research Quarterly for Exercise and Sport, 78,* 318–327.

Schmidt, R. A., & Lee, T. D. (2009). *Motor control and learning: A behavioral emphasis* (4th ed.). Champaign, IL: Human Kinetics.

Silverman, S., Tyson, L. A., & Krampitz, J. (1992). Teacher feedback and achievement in physical education: Interaction with student practice. *Teaching and Teacher Education, 8,* 333–344.

Silverman, S., Woods, A. M., & Subramaniam, P. R. (1998). Task structures, feedback to individual students, and student skill level in physical education. *Research Quarterly for Exercise and Sport, 69,* 420–424.

Southland, D. (1998). Mass and velocity: Control parameters for throwing patterns. *Research Quarterly for Exercise and Sport, 69,* 355–367.

Starkes, J. L. (2000). The road to expertise: Is practice the only determinant? *International Journal of Sport Psychology, 31,* 431–451.

Stodden, D., Langendorfer, S., & Roberton, M.A. (2009). The association between motor skill competence and physical fitness in young adults. *Research Quarterly for Exercise and Sport, 80,* 223–229.

Swanson, L. R., & Lee, T. D. (1992). The effects of aging and schedules of knowledge of results on motor learning. *Journal of Gerontology: Psychological Sciences, 47,* 406–411.

Turvey, M. T., Fitch, H. L., & Tuller, B. (1982). The Bernstein perspective: The problems of degrees of freedom and context-conditioned variability. In J. A. S. Kelso (Ed.), *Human motor behavior: An introduction* (pp. 239–252). Hillsdale, NJ: Lawrence Erlbaum.

Vaeyens, R., Lenoir, M., Williams, A. M., & Philippaerts, R. M. (2007). Mechanisms underpinning successful decision making in skilled youth soccer players: An analysis of visual search behaviors. *Journal of Motor Behavior, 39,* 395–408.

Vosniadou, S., & Brewer, W. F. (1992). Mental models of the earth: A study of conceptual change in childhood. *Cognitive Psychology, 24,* 535–585.

Ward, P., & Williams, A. M. (2003). Perceptual and cognitive skill development in soccer: The multidimensional nature of expert performance. *Journal of Sport and Exercise Psychology, 25,* 93–111.

Ward, P., Williams, A. M., & Bennett, S. J. (2002). Visual search and biological motion perception in tennis. *Research Quarterly for Exercise and Sport, 73,* 107–112.

Williams, A. M., Hodges, N. J., North, J. S., & Barton, G. (2006). Perceiving patterns of play in dynamic sport tasks: Investigating the essential information underlying skilled performance. *Perception, 35,* 317–332.

Wulf, G., Lauterbach, B., & Toole, T. (1999). Learning advantages of an external focus of attention in golf. *Research Quarterly for Exercise and Sport, 70,* 120–126.

Wulf, G., McConnel, N., Gärtner, M., & Schwarz, A. (2002). Enhancing the learning of sport skills through external-focus feedback. *Journal of Motor Behavior, 43,* 171–182.

Wulf, G., McNevin, H. N., & Shea, C. H. (2001). The automaticity of complex motor skill learning as a function of attentional focus. *Quarterly Journal of Experimental Psychology, 54A,* 1143–1154.

Wulf, G., & Su, J. (2007). An external focus of attention enhances golf shot accuracy in beginners and experts. *Research Quarterly for Exercise and Sport, 78,* 384–389.

9

LEARNING TO THINK CRITICALLY

Christina Rhee Bonney and Robert J. Sternberg

INTRODUCTION

One of the most important jobs teachers have in the classroom is not just imparting knowledge and facts to their students, but teaching them *how* to learn and how to become critical thinkers. As is often the case in social science research, several different terms are used to describe the same basic construct. What we refer to as "critical thinking" in this chapter has also been called higher-order thinking (Grant, 1988; Lipman, 1995), meta-cognition (Dean & Kuhn, 2003; Kuhn, 1999; Swartz, Costa, Beyer, Reagan, & Kallick, 2008), problem solving (Carlson & Bloom, 2005), evaluating (Anderson, Krathwohl, Airasian, Cruikshank, Mayer, et al., 2001; Krathwohl, 2002) or analytical thinking (Sternberg & Grigorenko, 2007; Sternberg, Torff, & Grigorenko, 1998). No matter what the name, the idea remains the same; in short, critical thinking makes use of cognitive skills and strategies in order to engage in thinking that is "purposeful, reasoned, and goal-directed" (Halpern, 2007, p. 6).

It is not necessarily enough simply to know the definition of critical thinking. In order to effectively teach students how to become critical thinkers, and for students to effectively learn how to think critically, it is important to be able to identify the features and steps involved in critical thinking; individual differences among students that may need to be taken into consideration when teaching critical thinking skills; the role of the student, teacher, and context in teaching critical thinking; and outcomes associated with critical thinking that impact teaching and learning. This chapter discusses the research done in each of these areas in greater detail, but also extends the discussion further by suggesting that although critical thinking is an important skill for students to have in their repertoire, teachers should also focus on students' creativity, practical skills, and the development of wisdom, for the purposes of encouraging and developing more well-rounded, successfully intelligent students.

HISTORICAL OVERVIEW AND THEORETICAL FRAMEWORK

The history of critical thinking can arguably be traced back to the days of Socrates, and his process of questioning and cross-examining ideas, known as the Socratic Method (Hoaglund, 1993). However, John Dewey's (1909) work on reflective thinking and inquiry has been generally viewed as the beginning of the modern critical thinking movement (Fisher, 2001; Streib, 1992). Over the past century, several researchers have continued to examine and develop the concept of critical thinking, including Edward M. Glaser (1941), who evaluated the importance of critical thinking skills or dispositions in examining evidence; Robert H. Ennis (1962, 1987, 1993), who built on Glaser's work and also looked at decision making as part of the critical thinking process; and Richard W. Paul (1989, 2005; Paul & Elder, 2008), who expanded critical thinking research to include aspects of problem solving (see Fisher, 2001; Streib, 1992, for a more detailed historical overview).

Those who engage in critical thinking do so in part to improve their thinking, generally leading to such positive outcomes as making sure one makes the right decisions or solves problems correctly. The process of studying and evaluating one's thoughts—which consequently improves them—is the essence of critical thinking (Elder & Paul, 2008; Paul, 2005). The first stage in critical thinking is the analysis stage. Although this stage—during which individuals deconstruct their thinking and ask questions targeted at clarifying the goals, data, concepts, assumptions, and implications of the thought process—is considered the first step, it does necessitate a relatively solid foundation in reasoning skills such that students can begin to reflect on the goals and purposes of thinking, as well as clarify the question that gave rise to the thinking process in the first place. To this end, students must be able to think purposefully; identify assumptions; use concepts, theories, and data; and be able to interpret information in order to understand the implications of their thoughts (Elder & Paul, 2008).

The second stage in critical thinking, according to Paul and his colleagues, is the assessment of thinking (Elder & Paul, 2008; Foundation for Critical Thinking, 2009). They argue that, ideally, critical thinkers assess their thinking based on universal intellectual standards of clarity, precision, accuracy, consistency, relevance, depth, breadth, logic, and fairness. In order to monitor whether thinking adheres to these standards, skilled critical thinkers will systematically ask questions to target these areas. For example, "Can you give me an example of your point?" (clarity); "How can we check that to see if it is true?" (precision); "Does this really make sense?" (logic). By analyzing and assessing thinking, a person is able to thereby improve thinking and make important distinctions between accurate and inaccurate thoughts, fair and unfair conclusions, and to develop ethical reasoning skills.

The stages of critical thinking proposed by Paul and his colleagues (Elder & Paul, 2008; Foundation for Critical Thinking, 2009) closely parallel a model of metacognition, defined as *thinking about thinking*. While a great deal of metacognition is involved in critical thinking, the critical thinking process also employs regular thought processes such as analysis, comparison, justification, critique, and application. Swartz et al. (2008) described the metacognitive process using the metaphor of climbing a ladder. The first rung of the ladder involves an awareness of *what* kind of thinking is being done; the second rung of the ladder involves describing *how* the thinking is being done from a procedural perspective (as opposed to an evaluative one); and the third rung of the metacognitive ladder involves thinking that becomes more evaluative, in terms of the student focusing on whether the way the thinking is being done is effective. Finally, the fourth (and final, or top) rung of the ladder involves metacognitive thinkers planning how they will engage in this same type of thinking in future situations, and utilize the previous rungs. The authors suggest that this type of deliberate commitment to think metacognitively eventually leads to a consistent habit of self-correcting one's thoughts and becoming a skillful thinker.

As Swartz et al. state, "The teaching of skillful thinking does not just help our students to learn some forms of skillful thinking, it is also a transformative process of developing independence of thought and continued reflection on the part of our students" (p. 101). Just as an athlete needs to practice to master his or her sport, metacognition—and simi-larly, critical thinking—takes effort, study, and reflection to be able to do so consistently and efficiently. The metacognitive ladder, as depicted by Swartz et al., may seem like an idealized depiction of the metacognitive process; as such, it should be considered more of a competence model rather than a performance model. A competence model gener-ally separates an idealized capacity (in this case, the gradually developed and honed mas-tery of skillful thinking strategies) whereas a performance model refers to real events, or the actual use of metacognitive strategies in a learning context.

It is important to note that critical thinking skills cannot be utilized, nor should they be considered, in the absence of knowledge; nor is just knowledge of facts and concepts necessarily sufficient. People must be able to *use* the knowledge in such a way as to make it effective and worthwhile (Halpern, 2007; Sternberg, 1987). They need something *about* which to think critically. Conversely, if an individual does not have a base of knowledge in the area about which he or she is trying to think critically, the analysis and assessment phases are unlikely to yield much, as novices in a given domain are much less likely to know even what questions to ask of their own thinking.

Developmental Considerations

When the topic of teaching critical thinking skills is discussed, it is important to take developmental considerations into account. Teaching critical thinking skills to elemen-tary school-aged children is necessarily different than teaching critical thinking skills in college classrooms. The following section reviews some of the research done on develop-mental considerations in teaching and learning critical thinking skills.

Elementary Education

For young children, critical thinking activities are necessarily different than for older children, adolescents, and adults. The process of inquiry generally focuses on simple descriptions, categorizations, and measurement. As students progress through elemen-tary school, they may be better equipped to move onto such tasks as identifying cause and effect (Kuhn, Black, Keselman, & Kaplan, 2000). Schauble (1990) conducted an experiment investigating the extent to which elementary school-aged children (10–12 years old) were able to set up a series of experiments testing five different design features on race cars through a computer module. Each car that was designed with varying fea-tures (e.g., various engines, wheels, tailfins, mufflers, and colors) could be "test-driven" on the computer, producing an outcome of the experiment. Most of the children were able to make some progress in drawing certain conclusions about the "microworld" of racecars; for example, that mufflers and color did not affect speed, but that engine and wheel size did matter.

Nevertheless, their methods of experimentation were rather haphazard, and did not usually follow a systematic pattern of using evidence from one experiment to inform the next experiment. Children often tested cars with the same features repeatedly, or designed experiments from which conclusions about design features could not necessarily be drawn. Piaget's (1952) theory of cognitive development asserted that children are not capable of the abstract and critical thinking skills necessary for such scientific inquiry before they reach the formal-operational stage of cognitive development. Piaget hypothesized that most children would reach this stage around 11 or 12 years of age, which falls within the age range of Schauble's (1990) subjects; consequently, this may explain why some of the students performed better than others with respect to experimental design. If the students in this study ranged in age from 10 to 12 years of age, it is possible that some of the children (i.e., those who performed better on the tasks) may have already reached the formal-operational stage whereas the others (i.e., those who performed poorly) may still have been in the concrete-operational stage. However, other researchers have reported success in teaching critical thinking skills to elementary school children and to those that Piaget (1952) would have argued could not grasp such skills and techniques (Chen & Klahr, 2008; Klahr & Nigam, 2004).

Lipman's (1995, 1998) *Philosophy for Children* program is one such example in which young children can be taught to engage in deliberative inquiry and reasoning. This program is a K-12 curriculum, in which "communities of inquiry" are utilized to foster critical, creative, and caring thinking, which results in better reasoning, comprehension, and evaluation. Instruction in critical thinking skills looks, out of necessity, qualitatively different for young children than for older children. Trying to provide direct instruction on inquiry styles is not necessarily developmentally appropriate for younger students (cf., Klahr & Nigam, 2004); therefore, the *Philosophy for Children* program engages models to *show* children what needs to be done (Lipman, 1998).

The use of scaffolding and modeling for strategy instruction can be an effective teaching tool for students as young as first graders learning to reflect, interpret, and elaborate on written responses (Wollman-Bonilla & Werchadlo, 1999). Once children have seen and heard examples of critical thinking, they are better equipped to emulate the kinds of thinking to which they have been exposed. The usual model used in *Philosophy for Children* instruction is a text-as-model. A narrative, whether a novel, short story, or even a comic strip, presents a fictional community of inquiry that parallels what the students themselves could and should be doing in their own learning community. The children in the narratives have various thinking styles, ask questions to clarify ambiguities, point out analogical relations, and listen to each other. Students, by modeling the children in the narratives, are eventually supposed to develop their own thinking style and critical thinking behaviors. They engage in thoughtful discussions within their own communities of inquiry. Engaging in philosophy is seen as the ideal tool in getting elementary-aged children to engage in critical thinking. Although philosophy is often viewed as an individual pursuit, the *Philosophy for Children* program is designed to encourage children not only to develop their own critical thinking skills, but it also teaches them how to think *with* others.

Trickey and Topping (2004) reviewed ten studies of the *Philosophy for Children* program, and found that on outcomes of reading, reasoning, cognitive ability, and other curriculum-related abilities, all studies showed positive outcomes with moderate effect sizes. Similarly, Fields (1995) reported that 7- and 8-year-old students involved in the *Philosophy for Children* program were able to engage in philosophical dialogue regarding cutting down the rainforests; what implications it may have on humans, animals, and the environment; and whether the intrinsic value of trees outweighed the lives of human beings. These students also engaged in discussions regarding when (if at all) it might be acceptable to tell a lie; none of the students took an absolutist viewpoint that it is never okay to lie, but instead reasoned that the individual's motives for lying would have to be taken into account. These exhibitions of logical thought, reasoning about hypothetical situations, and considerations of possible outcomes and consequences of actions are all characteristics of formal-operational thought, which Piaget argued would not have been possible before 11 or 12 years of age.

The need to learn critical evaluation skills in elementary schools is not limited just to science inquiry or philosophy. Brown and Campione (1990) also reviewed several studies in which they targeted reading comprehension and literacy skills in elementary school children. The authors argued that, whereas elementary school is the period when students learn how to read, they must also learn how to learn from reading. Students must be able to decode, comprehend, and critically evaluate the content of reading, as well as to be able to utilize the information they read in new and varied contexts. They used the term *intelligent novices*, defined as those who may not necessarily possess prior knowledge in a given field, but who know how to go about gaining that knowledge (Brown & Campione, 1990, p. 110). Intelligent novices possess the necessary skills to learn, and often utilize a wide variety of learning strategies, rather than just engaging in rote memorization when faced with a novel task (Brown, Bransford, Ferrara, & Campione, 1983). This can lead to learning at a faster rate, as well as performing better on tests of problem solving, conceptual understanding, transfer, and retention (Mathan & Koedinger, 2005).

Brown and Palincsar (1989) did extensive research involving reciprocal teaching to encourage reading comprehension. Reciprocal teaching involves guided practice in applying text comprehension strategies, during which an adult teacher and a group of students take turns "being the teacher" (i.e., leading discussions about material they have read, asking questions and summarizing what has been learned). Brown, Campione, Reeve, Ferrara, and Palincsar (1991) utilized reciprocal-teaching reading groups with at-risk third graders over a period of 20 days, during which they witnessed a dramatic improvement in students' reading comprehension (from 35% to 80% correct) compared to a variety of control groups, who did not witness significant improvements. These levels of improvement for students in the reciprocal reading groups were maintained even a year later. Students were able to transfer and apply knowledge and concepts from one reading passage to others, and retained the reciprocal teaching skills and *content* of lessons one year later.

More recently, several researchers have found evidence to suggest that young children can be taught strategies to monitor their comprehension and assess their own learning, both important components of critical thinking. LeFevre, Moore, and Wilkinson (2003) provided a reciprocal teaching intervention to 9-year-old students whose decoding skills were weak. Students receiving the intervention showed improved use of cognitive and metacognitive strategies, and increased comprehension, compared to students who did not receive the intervention.

In another study with third and sixth graders, Rubman and Waters (2000) taught students a technique for helping children perform the necessary integrations for detecting inconsistencies in stories. Children instructed in utilizing this technique, which involved creating storyboard representations of the story, were more likely to detect internal and external inconsistencies compared to children who simply read the stories. The researchers contend that explicitly instructing children how to integrate information from a story to create a coherent representation makes it more likely that they will attend to details in the text, reflect on those details, and evaluate the content for consistency.

Lederer (2000) conducted a study in which the reciprocal teaching technique was used with students with learning disabilities in fourth, fifth, and sixth grade inclusive classrooms during social studies lessons. Lederer found that not only did reciprocal teaching help improve students' reading comprehension, but that students in the fourth and sixth grade experimental conditions exhibited significant gains in comprehension after 30 days, compared to students in the comparison group. These findings suggest that reciprocal teaching methods can significantly improve the quality of students with learning disabilities' reading comprehension and monitoring skills, and not just in the content area in which reciprocal teaching was originally designed (language arts).

Anderson and his colleagues at the Center for the Study of Reading at the University of Illinois, Urbana-Champaign have developed a social-constructivist approach called *Collaborative Reasoning*, in which students take positions on issues raised in texts and engage in discussions on the issues using supporting evidence and reasoned argumentation (Anderson, Nguyen-Jahiel, McNurlen, Archodidou, Kim, et al., 2001; Waggoner, Chinn, Yi, & Anderson, 1995). "The discussion is a process of teasing out and working through 'big' issues; handling of ambiguity and opposing viewpoints; reasoning, exploring, evaluation and building of arguments; and holding one's own or letting go within a social context" (Collaborative Reasoning, n.d.). Anderson et al. (2001) discuss the social influences on the development of reasoning, such that people learn to reason from social interactions through the processes of modeling and imitation. The researchers investigated the extent to which norms for participation in a classroom impacted discussion, and compared teacher-controlled participation (e.g., students raising their hand and waiting to be called on before participating) and open participation (e.g., students can speak freely without raising their hands).

Four fourth grade classrooms participated in both types of collaborative reasoning discussion formats using issues raised in various stories. Qualitative and quantitative analyses were conducted on transcripts of discussions, specifically examining students' use of argument stratagems in their discussions (e.g., "I agree (or disagree) with [NAME]," "I got something [a challenge] for you, [NAME]," or "But [COUNTERARGUMENT]"). Researchers found that students participating in an open-format discussion were more susceptible to social influence, such that when argument stratagems were used early on in these discussions, students were more likely to continue using this stratagem, than if it occurred early on in a teacher-controlled discussion. These findings confirmed what the authors' referred to as the "snowball hypothesis" in that strategies used by students and directed at peers tended to spread to other students with increasing frequency. This held true not only for argument stratagems, but also for managing student participation, acknowledging hedges or uncertainties, using evidence to support arguments, etc.

Murphy, Wilkinson, Soter, Hennessey, and Alexander (2009) highlight the importance of discussion and discourse in the development of critical thinking skills for reading comprehension, which they refer to as *critical literacy*. The authors argue that high-level reasoning involves the ability to have several different perspectives represented in one's head on a particular issue, and that this ability to take more than one perspective into account arises from participating in discussions with others who hold different perspectives. To this end, Murphy et al. (2009) conducted a meta-analysis on studies—the majority of which were conducted on elementary-aged children—investigating the relationship between various discussion practices and students' critical thinking and text comprehension. The researchers found that although many of the studies they examined were effective at increasing students' literal and inferential comprehension of texts, not all discussion-based practices are equally effective at increasing students' critical literacy; in fact, very few of the approaches they investigated reported significant gains. Although an increase in student talk was related to increases in critical literacy, this relation was not automatic, and the *kind* of talk in which students engaged was important to consider. In other words, increasing the amount of student discussion is a means and not an end.

Specifically, the programs that Murphy et al. (2009) found to be most effective at increasing students' critical literacy (i.e., *Collaborative Reasoning, Philosophy for Children, Junior Great Books Shared Inquiry,* and *Questioning the Author*) took either a critical-analytic stance (encouraged discussion that prompts questions geared toward a more subjective response to the text) or an efferent stance (discussion was focused on reading as a way to acquire particular information about ideas, directions, or conclusions), as opposed to an expressive stance that focused on the reader's affective response to the text. *Collaborative Reasoning* and *Philosophy for Children* were categorized as taking a critical-analytic stance, and were discussed in greater detail earlier in this chapter.

The researchers suggest that the effects of the types of discussions were moderated by the study design (i.e., stronger effects were found in single-group design studies than in multiple-group design studies), and the nature of outcome measures (i.e., outcomes were weakened when researchers used commercially-available standardized measures compared to researcher-developed measures). The authors conclude that although discussion does appear to have a positive influence on developing students' critical literacy, teachers should pay close attention to the congruence between their instructional goals and the stated goals and outcomes of a particular program, and that researchers should consider designing future studies using multiple-group designs, commercially-available assessments of outcome measures, and as many indicators of text comprehension as possible.

Middle School Education

Critical thinking activities in middle school can continue to build on the skills learned in elementary school, such as identifying which variable is responsible for a particular outcome, or evaluating how changing one variable leads to changes in other variables (Kuhn et al., 2000). As discussed in the earlier section with Schauble and Glaser's (1990) research, students around this age may still be struggling with these types of scientific-reasoning skills.

Kuhn et al. (2000) advanced this argument by demonstrating how middle school students (sixth through eighth grade) may still be struggling with multivariable systems, and that such critical thinking and reasoning skills that might be required for successfully engaging in such activities cannot be assumed to be present. Researchers in this study randomly assigned classrooms to an experimental or control condition, in which students were asked to be builders for a construction company charged with building lakefront cabins. Students were informed that the area around the lake is prone to flooding, so the cabins must be built on supports that raise them above the ground. The students used a multimedia research program which helped them predict, based on several variables and outcomes, the optimal height for the supports to be built, so that costs would not be too high (i.e., supports were not built too high) nor would cabins be subject to flood damage (i.e., supports were not built too low). All students investigated the effects of the five variables (water pollution, water temperature, soil depth, soil type, and elevation) on flooding using the multimedia program; however, the students in the experimental condition also participated in paper-pencil exercises about the flood tasks with peers, focusing on controlled or confounded comparisons of variables.

Kuhn et al. (2000) found that students in the experimental condition exhibited greater improvement from the pretest to the posttest regarding multivariable systems (i.e., making appropriate inferences based on controlled comparisons of variables), but that a clear understanding of investigatory strategies were still lacking in several students, even if they were able to make correct inferences. The authors suggest that although "authentic" scientific inquiry is important for promoting good science education the skills required to engage in inquiry learning may not be assumed present in early adolescence.

However, Kuhn et al. (2000) are quick to dispel any notion that critical thinking and inquiry activities should therefore not be taught at the elementary and middle school levels. Instead, they propose that curricula should be designed with the incorporation of cognitive competencies that are necessary for learning how to think critically. In essence, critical thinking and strategy skills can be enhanced through explicit instruction (Bauman, 1984; Guthrie & Davis, 2003; Klahr & Nigam, 2004). By engaging students in roles that require critical-thinking skills to be used (e.g., continually asking them such questions as "Why are we doing this?" and "What did we gain from doing it?"), educators can help shift their thinking orientations from merely producing outcomes (e.g., complete this assignment) also to analysis and understanding (Kuhn, 2005).

Secondary Education

Teaching critical thinking skills in high school is challenging, even if students have already mastered basic cognitive skills and reasoning abilities that might prevent elementary and middle school students from doing so. As discussed, teaching critical thinking requires students to have prior knowledge in the domain in which they are to think critically. Students must have *something* to think about (Grant, 1988). High school teachers' content knowledge is often under scrutiny, especially under recent policy initiatives that differentiate "highly qualified" teachers from those without the requisite training and credentials to be labeled so. The content specialization of secondary school teachers usually necessitates extensive training and credentials in a specific subject area, which in turn, influence student achievement (Clotfelter, Ladd, & Vigdor, 2007; Noddings, 2006).

Grant (1988) contends that secondary school is essentially the only place that critical thinking skills are *expected* to be taught, because no other establishment in our society (i.e., peer groups, family, religion, work) systematically requires such thinking. "If higher-order thinking is not promoted in the course of learning to read, compose, and calculate, a student may never have an opportunity to move beyond the literal interpretation of information" (p. 3). Consequently, reform efforts are often aimed at improving students' higher-order processing and critical thinking skills, and for enhancing teachers' ability to teach these skills through pre-service teacher training or professional development.

Just as teachers' content knowledge influences the assignments and tasks they give to students, so does teachers' understanding of the critical thinking process influence their instruction (Grant, 1988). High school students are generally more cognitively advanced than middle school students, and are more likely to be able to comprehend abstract thoughts and metaphorical representations. Secondary school teachers can rely more heavily on different representations of content, such as visual imagery (drawings, charts) and numerical abstractions (models, graphs), in addition to linguistic representations of material (voice, narrative). By using multiple instructional methods that complement and capitalize on their students' cognitive development and capabilities, teachers can better facilitate student learning (Bonner, 1999; Francisco, Nicoll, & Trautmann, 1998; Harvey & Hodges, 1999).

For teachers to be aware of the cognitive level at which their students are functioning, and to be able to translate their own content knowledge into student understanding and achievement, they must have pedagogical content knowledge (PCK), or the combination of content knowledge and the awareness of *how* to teach the content to students (Gess-Newsome, 1999; Grant, 1988; Shulman, 1986). A teacher might be considered a genius in the field of mathematics, but this does not necessarily translate into an ability to *teach* mathematics to others. Similarly, even if teachers have a vast toolbox of teaching strategies, they are unlikely to get very far without an understanding of the subject matter they are teaching. PCK allows teachers to know where their students are in terms of background knowledge, what their preconceptions and misconceptions about a particular topic might be, and where they may struggle with both content and skills.

With respect to teaching critical thinking skills, content knowledge involves knowing the definition of critical thinking and what makes a good critical thinker. A teacher should be aware of factors that can influence students' learning of critical thinking skills. On the other hand, PCK means knowing what instructional strategies would be developmentally appropriate, having a repertoire of examples, metaphors, and analogies to which students might relate in order to help them learn the principles of critical thinking (Yeh, 2004; Zohar, 1999). Several researchers have examined the extent to which PCK for critical thinking instruction can be taught, as well as how it relates to teachers' existing content knowledge of thinking skills.

Zohar (1999) investigated Israeli middle and high school science teachers' content knowledge and PCK of thinking skills during in-service courses (held over a period of several months) for professional development. Through the use of audiotaped discussions, note-taking during in-service courses, and analysis of teachers' written work, the researcher found that although many teachers had "intuitive" notions of what critical thinking skills and metacognition were, their declarative knowledge of such concepts was lacking, and therefore their implementation of critical thinking instruction in their classes had been informal and unstructured. The in-service course—which consisted of discussions on basic theoretical concepts related to critical thinking, metacognition, and transfer; as well as workshops focused on creating new learning activities and reflecting on their teaching—not only highlighted to teachers the importance of teaching critical thinking as a distinct educational goal, but also helped develop teachers' declarative (or content) knowledge about critical thinking instruction and helped them develop more explicit critical thinking lessons and instructional strategies.

Although the initial goal of the study was to focus on teachers' PCK of critical thinking, it became clear to Zohar over the course of the in-service courses that teachers' declarative knowledge of critical thinking must be solidified before that knowledge can be effectively used for instruction. While it might be generally assumed that content knowledge must be in place before PCK, Zohar (1999) proposed that because teachers often have an intuitive and informal content knowledge base about critical thinking, it may be an effective training tool to draw upon teachers' PCK and *informal* content knowledge of critical thinking to help develop more formal, declarative knowledge of critical thinking. In other words, Zohar suggested utilizing teachers' prior informal content knowledge and pedagogical knowledge to strengthen and structure declarative and pedagogical content knowledge of critical thinking instruction.

Yeh (2004) developed a computer program called the *Computer Simulation for Teaching General Critical-Thinking Skills* (CS-TGCTS) to help cultivate reflective teachers and support critical thinking instruction, by guiding teachers through simulated critical thinking lessons. Yeh identified two types of professional knowledge (content knowledge and PCK) and three categories of effective teacher behavior for teaching critical thinking (increasing students' prior knowledge, enhancing students' critical thinking dispositions, and modeling and encouraging critical thinking skills and techniques), and assessed the extent to which the CS-TGCTS program helped increase this knowledge and behaviors. The study utilized a pre-test/post-test, random assignment, control group design, and found that while exposure to the CS-TGCTS program did in fact increase teachers' content knowledge for critical thinking instruction, there was no significant effect on PCK.

In this study, the researcher assumes that an increase in teachers' reflective teaching would manifest itself in enhanced teacher behaviors, which, in turn, would lead to increases in improved pedagogical development and PCK. Therefore, Yeh (2004) hypothesized that the CS-TGCTS program's focus on cultivating reflective teaching would result in enhanced content knowledge and PCK for critical thinking instruction; however, the number of intermediate steps assumed in this relationship between the computer program and PCK development may have been too large to yield significant results. As such, reflective teaching and content knowledge were directly addressed by the computer program, and teachers did indeed witness significant enhancements from pre- to post-test assessments. However, PCK was not directly addressed by the CS-TGCTS program and was not significantly improved over the course of the experiment. This may suggest that efforts to improve teachers' PCK for critical thinking instruction may need to be more explicit in terms of not just identifying good pedagogy and teacher behaviors, but *how* to select the most effective of these strategies for teaching specific groups of students.

Park and Oliver (2008) also propose a model of PCK which implies that a teacher develops PCK through reflection; however, they do not assume that reflective teaching necessarily results in PCK, or that it is the only component. They point out that teachers' abilities to recognize and identify students' misconceptions and confusions is also vital to the development of their PCK, and assert that "only when teachers grasp their students' cognitive and affective status with regard to the learning of a particular topic can they apply pedagogically adjusted procedures in order to facilitate learning" (p. 279). In other words, PCK should not be viewed simply as knowledge possessed by the teacher, but should also take into consideration the reciprocal influence of student learning on PCK and teacher reflections.

Higher Education

Valanides and Angeli (2005) investigated the effects of critical thinking instruction on college students' epistemological beliefs. Students were assigned to one of three experimental groups, each group receiving a different type of instruction on critical thinking. One group (general group) was asked to watch a lecture on the five general critical thinking principles, namely, "(a) Analyze the problem, (b) Generate solutions, (c) Develop the reasoning for your solutions, (d) Decide which is the best solution, and (e) Use criteria to evaluate your thinking" (p. 322). They were then paired off to develop an outline for a position paper on a given topic.

The second group (infusion group) was given time to work on their outline first, then watched a lecture on the critical thinking principles, and were engaged in a discussion by the researcher asking them to reflect on and evaluate their thinking for their position papers. Students were then given time to complete their outlines. The third condition (immersion group) was similar to the infusion condition, except that students were not necessarily given direct instruction on the critical thinking principles, but rather, were engaged in Socratic questioning by the researcher, which challenged them to reflect on and evaluate their reasoning for their point of view on the issue. Therefore, although they did not explicitly learn the five principles, students in the immersion condition were asked relevant questions such as, "Have you analyzed the problem in depth?" and "What are your reasons for supporting this view?" Student epistemological beliefs were assessed before and after these sessions.

Researchers found that students in the infusion group witnessed significantly higher improvements in their epistemological beliefs, compared to the general group. The authors conclude that critical thinking instruction in combination with a process by which students are given the opportunity to reflect upon, question, and evaluate their thinking based on explicitly-stated principles can have important effects on their epistemological beliefs. It is not enough simply to teach the critical thinking principles in a decontextualized setting; the sequence of instructional tasks can have an impact, especially with college students, whose epistemological beliefs may be strongly affected by educational experiences (Baxter Magolda, 1992; Kuhn, 1991; Perry, 1970).

The *ADAPT* (Accent on Developing Abstract Processes of Thought) program at the University of Nebraska, Lincoln, began in 1975 and was based on Piagetian principles of developing formal operational thought, or what the founding ADAPT faculty referred to as "scientific reasoning" (Fuller, 1998, p. 2). Freshmen were invited to enroll in the ADAPT curriculum, which incorporated critical thinking instruction across a variety of disciplines (e.g., anthropology, economics, literature, mathematics, sociology, etc.). Faculty teaching in the ADAPT program were volunteers interested in teaching students to develop their thinking skills. In order to teach critical thinking skills in college classrooms, some faculty found that they needed to decrease the amount of content they covered—some by as much as 40%—however, they also reported that seeing the measurable gains students made in critical thinking abilities outweighed the loss of content (Fuller, 1977). Specifically, one measure utilized by the ADAPT program to assess gains in critical thinking abilities was the Watson-Glaser Critical Thinking Appraisal Test. Pre- and post-tests were compared for students enrolled in the ADAPT curriculum and two control groups. ADAPT students improved as much as one standard deviation over the control groups in critical thinking abilities (Fuller, 1977). Cutting content by this much is clearly not an option for primary and secondary school teachers today, who have very strict curricula to follow in preparation for standardized exams; however, the implications for college faculty as suggested in these findings by the ADAPT program, who have considerably more leeway in what content is covered, are interesting to consider.

Motivational Considerations

There can be no mental development without interest. Interest is the *sine qua non* for attention and apprehension. You may endeavor to excite interest by means of birch rods, or you may coax it by the incitement of pleasurable activity. But without interest there will be no progress.

(Whitehead, [1929] 1967, p. 37)

Whitehead's assertion is indeed central to motivation; however, the question remains: *How* can teachers foster interest and motivation in their students? The best-intentioned and most-prepared teachers may still find challenges in educating their students when faced with structural obstacles (e.g., 50-minute lecture sessions, which rarely allow enough time for serious engagement in a topic), or obstacles presented by the students themselves (e.g., negative preconceptions about a particular topic or about their education in general; Meyers, 1986).

We will not necessarily go into particular strategies for motivated learning, as there is another chapter that addresses this topic (see Anderman & Dawson, this volume). Instead, we will discuss here some of the motivational implications for teaching and learning critical thinking. This is certainly not meant to be an exhaustive discussion of all motivational factors that have implications for critical thinking; however, we hope to address a few areas to which those teaching critical thinking, as well as those learning to think critically, should pay attention.

Whether students are intrinsically or extrinsically motivated, how interested they are in the topic or task, and whether they have a fear of failure or making mistakes will affect their willingness and ability to think critically. Sternberg (1988) points out that intrinsically motivated individuals, or those who work because they want to, or engage in a task for the sake of learning or enjoyment, are more likely to persist compared with extrinsically motivated individuals. These are the people who are motivated by external factors or rewards (e.g., grades, money, recognition); while they may perform as well as intrinsically motivated individuals, the performance and persistence often cease when the rewards stop, too.

The notion of intrinsic motivation is related to the idea of interest, such that individuals who are intrinsically motivated will engage in a task for no other reward than the interest and enjoyment of the activity (Frederickson, 1998; Malone & Lepper, 1987). In other words, interest is generally used as an indicator of intrinsic motivation, through its effect on sustained attention and effort (Renninger, 2000). For critical thinking to occur, students need time to thoroughly engage in the material, and if students are not interested or intrinsically motivated to engage in the material in the first place, critical thinking and inquiry is unlikely to occur (Meyers, 1986).

As mentioned, there may be structural obstacles like time-limited class formats, which may prevent providing enough time for thorough investigation of material; however, other student-driven obstacles must be overcome as well. Research on fostering student interest can be described as focusing on two types of interest: individual or personal interest, or an actualized state that develops slowly but tends to be long-lasting; and situational interest, or that which is triggered by something in the environment or situation and may or may not have a lasting impact on personal interest or learning (Hidi, 1990; Hidi & Anderson, 1992; Krapp, Hidi, & Renninger, 1992). For example, students may read a passage that has interesting qualities (e.g., a surprise ending or seductive details) and therefore may be situationally interested in the task; however, this does not necessarily mean that they are personally interested in the topic or find relevance or value in it as a learning tool. Nevertheless, situational interest may be used as a "hook" for getting students engaged in material in order to allow for critical thinking to occur, and possibly even leading to a more internalized state of personal interest in a task or topic (Hidi & Anderson, 1992; Krapp, 2002).

It is important to note that even if students have all the necessary dispositions and abilities to think critically, it is irrelevant if the student is not motivated or interested in using those skills. By incorporating critical thinking tasks into activities and topics that are interesting to children, teachers can thus ensure that those skills and abilities will indeed be used (Sternberg, 1987).

Fear of failure is another consideration when discussing motivational aspects of critical thinking (Sternberg, 1988). If people are afraid they will fail, they may avoid attempting any challenging tasks for fear that they will make a mistake, or not succeed in their attempt (Atkinson, 1964; Covington, 1998; Elliot & Harackiewicz, 1996; McClelland, Atkinson, Clark, & Lowell, 1953). Although people who do not have a fear of failure may also make a mistake or not succeed, the important distinction is that those with a fear of failure perceive that mistakes represent their incompetence, whereas others view making mistakes as part of the learning process and therefore, not necessarily detrimental to their sense of well-being (Dweck, 1986; Dweck & Elliott, 1983; Dweck & Leggett, 1988; Midgley et al., 2000; Nicholls, 1984; Sternberg, 1988). Critical thinking necessitates that students take risks by asking questions, generating ideas, and critically assessing their own thoughts and assumptions. If a student fears failure or fears making mistakes, the student may avoid the challenge of learning to think critically, and may view the critical thinking process as detrimental to his or her ego.

Role of the Student

The process of learning how to think critically must take into account the developmental and motivational considerations discussed earlier; however, the role that the students, teachers, and learning context play are also vital to the critical thinking process. With respect to the role of the student in the critical thinking process, Stout (2007) suggests that critical thinking may be viewed as requiring certain dispositions; that the critical thinker "must be *willing* to use appropriate reasons and principle and use them accordingly" (p. 45). Such principles include intellectual values of fairness, consistency, impartiality, desire for truth, acknowledging standards and criteria for evaluating arguments, and rejecting arbitrariness. Ennis (1987) provided a list of 14 critical thinking dispositions, in addition to five basic areas of critical thinking abilities, asserting that the ability to think critically is not enough, but that one must also possess critical thinking dispositions as well, in order to pursue clarity and criteria for evaluation.

Webster (1997) also describes critical thinking dispositions as "manifest in certain traits of minds—humility, empathy, integrity, fair-mindedness—and analytical and reasoning processes" (p. 187). Although the term *dispositions* lends itself to the idea of stable, internal traits, Stout (2007) acknowledged that critical thinking is not necessarily something that one with these qualities does in every situation. As she states, "Critical thinking may involve problem solving, assessing standards, applying principles—indeed a variety of skills, procedures, or attitudes—but these will likely differ qualitatively in each context" (p. 45). It is important to note that thinking *dispositions* focus on what an individual would tend to do in a given situation; whereas thinking *abilities* focus on what an individual is capable of doing (Perkins & Grotzer, 1997). Just because someone has a critical thinking disposition does not necessarily mean that they have the ability to do so, and vice versa (Facione, 2000; Facione & Facione, 1992; Stupnisky, Renaud, Daniels, Haynes, & Perry, 2008).

Not only will one person's critical thinking look differently in different contexts because of qualitative differences in what is required, but also because the individual's background knowledge and familiarity with necessary principles may differ by context as well. In order to engage in critical thinking, he or she must have prior knowledge in that area *about which* to think critically (Kuhn, 2005; Paul, 2005; Sternberg, Grigorenko, & Zhang, 2008; Stout, 2007). Therefore, before students can learn how to think critically in a given domain, they must first attain a certain level of background knowledge and understanding of the topic.

While prior knowledge is certainly an important factor in the learning of and instruction for critical thinking, there is some evidence to suggest that students' learning styles also play an important role (Kieft, Rijlaarsdam, & van den Bergh, 2008; Myers & Dyer, 2006; Sternberg, Grigorenko, Ferrari, & Clinkenbeard, 1999). Sternberg et al. (2008) discussed two types of learning and thinking styles, defined as "individual differences in approaches to tasks that can make a difference in the way in which and, potentially, in the efficacy with which a person perceives, learns, or thinks" (p. 486). First, people generally balance three kinds of abilities: analytical, creative, and practical thinking. Creative skills are needed to generate ideas, analytical skills are needed to assess whether they are good ideas, and practical skills are needed to implement the ideas and convince others of the value of the ideas. Ability-based styles, therefore, are learning and thinking styles based on the abilities or strengths of individuals in these areas. Personality-based styles, on the other hand, are not abilities themselves, per se, but individual *preferences* for how to use one's abilities. For example, there is a difference between how creative a student is (ability-based style) and how much the student likes to be creative (personality-based style). Although these learning styles can be assessed only at the level of the individual student, they have important implications for the role of the teacher, which will be further discussed in the next section.

Role of the Teacher

In teaching students how to think critically, teachers obviously play a vital role. They must not only have solid content knowledge in the area in which they are teaching, but they must also have a robust concept of critical thinking and of how critical thinking concepts can be integrated with teaching and learning concepts for their students' benefits (Paul, 2005). As Grant (1988) pointed out, teaching students to use higher-order thinking processes requires teaching students how to manipulate information, and not just to reproduce it upon request. "Students must think *about* something. Teaching critical thinking is, therefore, based on a teacher's broad and deep understanding of subject matter and a representation of that understanding in multiple forms of work activities for students" (p. 2). In other words, teachers must not only thoroughly know the content they are teaching, but must also be able to represent it in various ways for their students to be able to actively engage in the lessons.

There is a long-standing debate as to what role a teacher should play in the classroom, as well as how teachers are supposed to manage the numerous constraints on their time (Ben-Peretz, 2001; Cotton, 1991; Egan, 2000; Helsby, 1999; Smyth & Shacklock, 1998; Webster, 1997). Whether teachers, and the education of children in general, should focus on curriculum coverage, deeper understanding, learning strategies, or preparing competent citizens and productive workers for society, is certainly not a new debate. As discussed earlier, the balance between teaching content and teaching students thinking skills is a difficult one to achieve for many teachers. Although college faculty have considerably more leeway in the amount of content covered in their courses (e.g., what span of time is covered in an Introductory History course, or which concepts/theories are taught in an Introductory Psychology course), elementary, middle, and high school teachers do not necessarily have the same freedom, thanks to state standards and high-stakes accountability tests. The teacher, then, must decide how to incorporate critical thinking instruction into content lessons in such a way as to not sacrifice significant time. Specific strategies that teachers can use to this end will be discussed later in the chapter.

Once teachers have figured out what content they will teach, and how they will balance that with critical thinking instruction, another important step to consider is whether the teachers have a clear idea of what critical thinking is, and how they can teach it. Paul (2005) discussed the state of critical thinking instruction, lamenting findings from a study that revealed many college faculty lack a substantive concept of what critical thinking is, and could only provide vague responses when asked to elaborate on what critical thinking involved (Paul, Elder, & Bartell, 1997). Paul (2005) concludes that if faculty lack the proper conceptual framework, they cannot be expected to effectively teach their students critical thinking skills. Lipman (1988) agrees, asserting that critical thinking in schools cannot be fostered unless educators have a clear idea that critical thinking "is skillful, responsible thinking that facilitates good judgment because it (1) relies upon criteria, (2) is self-correcting, and (3) is sensitive to context" (p. 39). Lipman (1988, 1989) further argues that when teachers have a firm grasp of these concepts and can incorporate them into the classroom, the shift from learning to thinking at all levels—elementary, secondary, and higher education—will result not only in intellectual empowerment, but also in students who are able to make good judgments.

Role of Context

Context plays an important role in the teaching and learning of critical thinking skills. As already discussed, the student comes to the classroom with certain abilities, dispositions, and prior knowledge, which all play a role in learning to think critically in a given domain. Teachers further play a vital role in ensuring they themselves have the requisite content knowledge, pedagogical content knowledge, and conceptual framework for critical thinking, in order to effectively teach critical thinking skills. Nevertheless, there are factors within the environment that are not at the student- or teacher-level, which will affect children's classroom performance, and their abilities to transfer knowledge and skills from one context to another (Okagaki & Sternberg, 1990).

Okagaki and Sternberg (1990) defined context according to Bronfenbrenner's (1979) lifespan development model: that an individual's context consists of the "structures and processes in both the immediate and more remote environment [which shape] the course of human development throughout the lifespan" (p. 11). Therefore, in this domain of learning to think critically, relevant immediate environments might be considered the school or home, and the more remote environment might include societal and cultural influences on the individual.

Okagaki and Sternberg (1990) proposed a model depicting the way factors outside of school can influence children's development of thinking skills and school performance. They primarily focused on parental influence and the home environment; however, it is clear that even when looking only at how one factor, parental beliefs, can impact children's thinking and learning, the implications of examining how any potential number of environmental and contextual factors can influence critical thinking are nearly overwhelming. The authors therefore attempted to provide guidance on how we could be sensitive to contextual influences.

First, they argued that teachers must discern what prior ideas and beliefs students have regarding what is considered good problem solving and good thinking, in order to confirm how congruent students' and teachers' beliefs are. Students' beliefs are influenced by a variety of contexts that may or may not correspond with contexts to which their teachers have been exposed. Second, critical thinking skills and strategies must be explicitly taught, and no assumptions can be made about how students will approach various problems and tasks. Third, rules regarding social behavior and roles in the classroom must also be made explicit, because no assumptions can or should be made regarding students' prior understanding of the school learning context. Finally, it should be understood that the rules of "good thinking" may differ, and that there is not only one set of rules that can be applied. As Okagaki and Sternberg asserted, the focus in critical thinking instruction "should not be [on] a complete replacement of one set of rules for good thinking with another set. Rather, we should take advantage of the diversity in our school settings to stretch our concepts of good thinking" (p. 76).

The impact that contextual factors have on learning is important to consider, just as the impact that the context *in which learning occurs* is also important. The notion of transfer is an important one, such that learning that occurs in one context does not necessarily translate or carry over into other contexts or domains (Perkins & Grotzer, 1997). Lipman (2003) lamented the state of present-day education as teaching students isolated bits of knowledge that, "like ice cubes frozen in their trays, remain inert and incapable of interacting with one another" (p. 54). Consequently, in the realm of critical thinking, a student who engages in critical thinking in one subject area does not necessarily engage in critical thinking in other subjects as well, even if he/she possesses the necessary critical thinking dispositions and abilities. The challenge, then, becomes one in which teachers must not only teach students *how*, but also *when* to think critically and in what situations they can apply their critical thinking skills of analyzing, reasoning, and evaluating their thoughts. This is not an easy feat, and one that requires a solid foundation in reasoning, intellectual flexibility, and resourcefulness, for students to be able to make such connections from one domain to another (Lipman, 2003).

As we have already discussed, thinking skills are often tied to the context in which they were learned, and transfer to other contexts does not usually occur (Dean & Kuhn, 2003; cf. Halpern, 1998; Perkins & Salomon, 1989); therefore, teaching critical thinking must be done across subjects and in a variety of settings, to encourage transfer of skills (Meyers, 1986; Swartz, 1987; Swartz et al., 2008). For elementary school teachers who teach across the curriculum, this can be an easier task than for secondary school teachers, who may only teach one subject and must then coordinate with other teachers in different subject areas to continue critical thinking instruction. This type of follow-up instruction across subjects may include continued direct instruction on the critical thinking principles, using the same critical thinking language consistently to help students bridge the applications of critical thinking across subjects, and scaffolding students until they can demonstrate their ability to apply the critical thinking principles themselves (Swartz et al., 2008).

Meyers (1986) pointed out that critical thinking across contexts need not only be limited to different academic subjects, but ideally, would also extend into students' personal lives and their involvement with their communities and society in general. Historically speaking, the "brightest" individuals have not always been the "best think-ers," because while they might have possessed a vast array of knowledge, they lacked the ability to evaluate the best uses of that knowledge (p. 118). While Meyers cited such political examples as the Watergate scandal, the Vietnam War, and the threat of nuclear war in space to support his argument, the idea of transferring critical thinking skills to outside the classroom does not apply simply to politics. "While we may not be able to teach our students wisdom and virtue, we can at least—by openly incorporat-ing appropriate subjective elements of wonder, beauty, and passion in our courses—expose them to the caring side of knowledge" (p. 118). Meyers went on to suggest that teaching students to think critically about issues facing their communities may encourage them to find solutions to problems and empower them to make a differ-ence. Sternberg's (2001) balance theory of wisdom supports this argument, suggesting that implementing a wisdom-related curriculum in schools can help foster skills in students, such that "wisdom might bring us a world that would seek to better itself and the conditions of all the people in it" (p. 242).

CURRENT TRENDS AND ISSUES

Implications for Teaching and Learning

Now that we have discussed the definitions, features, developmental and motivational considerations, and roles of the student, teacher, and context in critical thinking, let us now look at what this all means for teaching and learning how to think critically. As Sternberg and Grigorenko (2007) stated: "The goal of teaching for analytical skills is to encourage students to formulate and ask questions, not just to answer them" (p. 40). However, the question becomes *how* can teachers encourage analytical skills and criti-cal thinking in their students? There are generally two models that educators employ to this end: stand-alone instruction, in which thinking skills are taught as a separate unit or course; and infused instruction, in which teaching thinking skills are integrated into the curriculum across subjects and lessons (Sternberg & Williams, 2010).

Stand-alone vs. Infused Instruction

One example of stand-alone instruction is Lipman's (1995, 1998) *Philosophy for Children* program. As described earlier, this K-12 curriculum teaches critical thinking skills and promotes discussion within communities of philosophical inquiry. Within this pro-gram, children learn specific sets of critical thinking skills through reading a narrative as a group, which serves as a model for how children should engage in thinking and discus-sions. Therefore, the children learn by modeling and "doing philosophy," and the cogni-tive skills they acquire (e.g., inquiry, reasoning, translating) help foster critical thinking dispositions, which influence learning across domains, and not just within philosophy

(Stout, 2007). As Lipman (1995) contended, "This is what makes philosophy the discipline that prepares children to think in the disciplines" (p. 69).

A typical *Philosophy for Children* session generally involves students reading aloud or acting out a story depicting fictional children exploring and reasoning out philosophical issues. Students then identify issues from the story that they find interesting, and purposefully and thoughtfully discuss these issues in a community of philosophical inquiry. This community of inquiry is viewed as one of the more effective methods for engaging students, because it encourages them to clarify their ideas and language, ask for and give good reasons for their arguments, question assumptions, and draw inferences. These discussions may culminate in tangible projects, but ultimately should at least result in students' self-correction of their previously-held beliefs, values, and attitudes.

Another example of stand-alone instruction is the *Instrumental Enrichment* (IE) program, which was developed by Reuven Feuerstein and his colleagues (Feuerstein, Hoffman, Rand, Jensen, Tzuriel, & Hoffman, 1986; Feuerstein, Rand, Hoffman, & Miller, 1980; Rand, Tannenbaum, & Feuerstein, 1979). The IE program stems from Feuerstein's structural cognitive modifiability theory, which assumes that peoples' levels of cognitive functioning are directly related to the types of mediated learning experiences (MLE) they have had. MLEs are defined as special interactions between learners and mediators. Mediators are not necessarily teachers, but are individuals who are mostly concerned with how a learner *approaches* solving a problem, as opposed to being concerned only with solving the problem itself. MLEs are focused on understanding and reflecting on the learning and thinking processes. Therefore, if a student has been deprived of sufficient MLEs because of low socioeconomic status, poverty, cultural differences, or other factors, his or her cognitive functions and intellectual abilities may be deficient. The IE curriculum is designed to act as a substitute for MLEs, thus compensating for any deficiencies in an individual's learning experiences.

The IE program consists of content-free exercises and tasks, which are generally presented concurrently with the student's regular curriculum for three to five hours a week, over a span of two years. A typical lesson involves an introduction to a problem that must be solved, independent work, a group discussion with peers, and a summary statement of what was accomplished during the lesson. Students are helped by a teacher to identify necessary vocabulary, concepts, and appropriate rules and strategies to help in their problem solving. Students are also asked to provide examples from other academic and non-academic areas that relate to the exercises and tasks they do, in order to demonstrate the particular concept in a variety of contexts. This "bridging" technique serves to encourage transfer, and bridges the IE learning to students' everyday lives. Throughout the lesson, the teacher serves as a mediator, providing feedback to students, modeling appropriate critical-thinking behavior, encouraging peer interaction, and guiding tasks to ensure various subgoals of the program are attained.

The program focuses on developing cognitive functions and skills necessary to complete various tasks, and the relatively "content-free" program is designed as a stand-alone program so that the lessons and strategies learned may be more easily generalizable to other academic, vocational, and personal areas (Feuerstein et al., 1986). In a review of the IE program, Shayer and Beasley (1987) found that among a group of 12–13-year-olds who all exhibited school performance in line with those of average 8- or 9-year-olds, fluid intelligence for students randomly placed in the experimental group showed an effect size of over one standard deviation—roughly equivalent to a difference of 20 months of development, compared to students in the control group that did not participate in the IE program. Also, the zone of proximal development (ZPD) for the experimental group increased from 9.5 years to 11.2 years at the post-test, compared to the ZPD of the control group increasing only from 10.5 to 10.7 years, reflecting a very large effect size. As Sternberg and Williams (2010) suggest, stand-alone instruction tends to be more intensive, and is taught in a more systematic and sequential manner, which positively influences students' skill building. The implications of the IE program on the teaching and learning of critical thinking skills are such that cognitive modifiability may be quite easy to achieve, allowing individuals to better cope with their ever-changing environments.

The second model that educators employ to teach critical thinking skills involves *infused instruction*, which integrates critical thinking instruction across the curriculum. Swartz (1987) described the instruction of teachers who restructured their classroom instruction to incorporate and infuse critical thinking lessons throughout. In one example, an American History teacher utilized conflicting eyewitness accounts of the Battle of Lexington to generate discussions about examining evidence, evaluating the reliability of sources of information, and evaluating criteria for making judgments. In another example, a social studies teacher used two contrasting accounts describing the role of women in the !Kung society. The influence of values, attitudes, and expectations on authors' frames of reference was explored by the students, such that they discussed in depth the implications of bias on the presentation of otherwise seemingly factual information.

Another example of infused instruction comes from the Cognition and Technology Group at Vanderbilt (CTGV) and their work on what is referred to as *anchored instruction* (e.g., Barron et al., 1995; Bransford et al., 1988). In several of their studies, researchers used video-based scenarios to encourage problem comprehension. For example, in a series of studies, students were shown clips of the film, *Raiders of the Lost Ark*, in which Indiana Jones travels to South America to retrieve the golden idol. Students are then asked to imagine that they are to return to the South American jungle to obtain some of the other artifacts left behind. In so doing, students must learn about potential obstacles and mathematically-based problems that could be derived from the film clip they observed. For example, the width of the pit they would have to jump, the height of a cave, the width of a river in relation to the size of the seaplane, etc., can all be estimated by studying freeze-frame shots from the movie and using known standards (e.g., the height of Indiana Jones) to deduce other pieces of information.

CTGV has also developed a series called *The Adventures of Jasper Woodbury*, consisting of 12 videodisc-based adventures that highlight mathematical problem finding and problem solving, geared toward students ages 10 and older (Barron et al., 1995; Cognition and Technology Group at Vanderbilt, 1992). Each videodisc contains a short video adventure that concludes with a complex challenge. All data needed to solve the adventure are contained within the video, as well as embedded models of teaching particular approaches to solving problems.

In both the stand-alone and infused instruction models, the process of examining and evaluating evidence, as well as identifying potential biases in thinking and writing, are important skills in critical thinking; however, they were embedded within the content lessons. Over the course of several lessons, consistent infusion of such critical thinking lessons into instruction will lead to a greater likelihood of students transferring the use of these skills across domains. Stout (2007) contended that critical thinking must be made a priority in classrooms, and that educators should employ a number of methods to encourage critical inquiry among their students, including encouraging both vertical (analytical) and lateral (creative) thinking, identifying assumptions in arguments, generating questions, and working on both open-ended and closed problems. These methods can all be utilized to infuse critical thinking skills with instruction.

It is difficult to evaluate whether stand-alone or infused instruction is "better" for teaching critical thinking skills, in large part because no studies have directly compared the two approaches in a controlled fashion. Williams and Worth (2001) conclude that "specialized courses in critical thinking have generally been successful in promoting this skill, but recent attempts to infuse critical thinking activities into subject-matter courses have yielded marginal results" (p. 13). Van Gelder's (2001) *Reason!* Project at the University of Melbourne developed the *Reason!Able* computer program as a stand-alone method of teaching and enhancing critical thinking skills. The software makes use of argument maps or trees (built up and manipulated by the user) to display and represent the relationships between claims and evidence. The "building" and "evaluation" modes of the program provide guidance and scaffolding for the user throughout the process. Students using the *Reason!Able* program exhibited improvement with large effect sizes from pre- to post-tests on critical thinking, and also demonstrated the largest gains when compared to other stand-alone methods or approaches; however, to our knowledge, there have been no controlled studies examining the impact of the *Reason!* method on critical thinking skills.

Hatcher (2006) attempted to investigate the question of whether stand-alone courses in critical thinking instruction or infused instruction were more effective, and found that college freshmen participating in a two-semester-long infused program performed significantly better on critical thinking assessments; however, his comparison groups were two stand-alone critical thinking and logic courses at other institutions. Other researchers have also found similar positive support for the infused instruction model, although their comparison/control groups received *no* critical thinking instruction (Reed & Kromrey, 2001; Solon, 2001, 2007). It should be noted that these comparison studies were all conducted with college-aged students; as such, not only should studies utilizing more controlled comparisons between stand-alone and infused instructional models be conducted, but also studies investigating students at different developmental stages.

Beyond Critical Thinking

While there does not seem to be much disagreement about the importance of students learning how to think critically, there is consideration of the idea that critical thinking instruction is simply one piece of the puzzle. Feuerstein et al. (1986) asserted that teaching critical thinking skills and employing *Instrumental Enrichment* to compensate for deficiencies in mediated learning experience is important for helping individuals to adapt within society; however, they also pointed out that "the acquisition of thinking skills is important, [but] it is not sufficient for adaptation to new and complex situations. Such adaptation requires an internal flexibility" (p. 76). Therefore, the goals of cognitive modifiability should be such that individuals should be enabled not only to think critically, but also flexibly in order to adapt and thrive. Stout (2007) agreed, as evidenced by her inclusion in her list of possible critical thinking infusing methods, "developing *lateral* as well as vertical thinking" (italics added, p. 57).

Successful Intelligence

Sternberg and his colleagues also agree, and have offered theoretical and empirical evidence that teaching for critical thinking, while important, is not enough, and that practical and creative skills, as well as wisdom, should be fostered in schools to ensure optimal student success (Stemler, Sternberg, Grigorenko, Jarvin, & Sharpes, 2009; Sternberg, 2003, 2008; Sternberg & Grigorenko, 2007; Sternberg et al., 1998, 2008). Sternberg's (1997, 1999) theory of successful intelligence proposes that an integrated set of abilities, namely critical thinking—which is generally referred to as analytical skills—creative, and practical skills, are needed to attain success. Successful intelligence is the result of recognizing and capitalizing on one's strengths, while identifying and compensating for one's weaknesses. This ability to adapt to or shape one's environments requires a balanced use of all three sets of abilities.

Schools have traditionally taught for and assessed analytical intelligence, since modern intelligence tests have focused primarily on this construct. However, the idea of intelligence and how it is conceived needs to be defined more broadly, so that success and intelligence take into account a greater range of criteria (Sternberg, 2003). Indeed, success in life requires not only the ability to think critically and analytically about one's own ideas and thoughts, but it is also necessary to think creatively in the generation of those ideas and thoughts, as well as to have the practical abilities to be able to implement those ideas and convince others of their value. For example, in the realm of education, a student must be able to think of an essay topic, and cogently write the essay arguing a particular point of view.

Successful intelligence entails not only balancing these three skills, but also recognizing where one's strengths and weaknesses are, and both capitalizing on strengths and compensating for or correcting any deficiencies. Adapting to the environment, as Feuerstein et al. (1986) proposed, is an important quality in society, and having the flexibility to modify oneself to suit the environment (adaptation), modify the environment to suit oneself (shaping), and finding a new environment that is more congruent with one's skills or desires (selection), are all indicators of successful intelligence (Sternberg, 2003; Sternberg & Grigorenko, 2007; Sternberg et al., 2008).

According to the theory of successful intelligence (Sternberg, 1997, 1999, 2003), a common set of universal mental processes underlies all aspects of intelligence. These processes are made up of metacomponents, performance components, and knowledge-acquisition components. *Metacomponents*, or executive processes, are used to plan, monitor, and evaluate problem solving. *Performance components* implement or execute the plans dictated by the metacomponents. *Knowledge-acquisition components* are the processes that are used to learn how to problem-solve in the first place. The three processes are interdependent, and all must be used depending on the situation or problem at hand, whether it requires analytical, creative, or practical thinking skills. For example, analytical thinking is appropriate for a situation in which the components are relatively familiar problems extracted from everyday life, whereas creative thinking skills may be better suited for novel problems or tasks. Practical skills are used when the components must be applied and implemented to adapt to, shape, and select one's environment.

The research that we have discussed thus far in this chapter on critical thinking draws a parallel to the metacomponential processes involved in problem solving. In learning how to analyze, assess, and evaluate their thinking, students are improving the facility of their metacomponential processes. Also, just as prior knowledge is vital for critical thinking, so are knowledge-acquisition components important for knowing what information is needed to solve problems, and how the information can be used. And while performance components are necessary to execute the instructions of the metacomponents, so are creative and practical intelligence needed to be able to effectively implement a sound solution.

Teaching triarchically, or infusing all three types of intelligence (analytical, creative, and practical) into instruction and assessment, has been found to be not only a valid and theoretically-sound method, but it has also been successful in improving students' abilities and achievement. In the context of the classroom, teaching for analytical intelligence manifests itself through tasks that involve analyzing, judging, evaluating, comparing and contrasting, and critiquing. Teaching for creative intelligence involves having students create, invent, discover, imagine, and speculate. Finally, teaching for practical intelligence involves having students implement, use, apply, and find relevance (Sternberg, 1994; Sternberg et al., 1998). Teaching and assessing should be done in a variety of ways, in order to capitalize on students' varying learning styles (Sternberg, 1997; Sternberg & Grigorenko, 2007; Sternberg et al., 2008). In order to maximize students' opportunities to showcase their skills and talents, teachers must value and incorporate ability-based styles other than the traditionally-highlighted analytical skills into their teaching and assessment.

Among 225 third graders and 142 eighth graders in science and social studies classes in North Carolina, students were assigned to one of three instructional conditions: (a) Students were taught in a way that emphasized analytical thinking; (b) students were taught in ways that emphasized analytical, creative, and practical thinking; and (c) students were not taught any differently than usual (i.e., the emphasis was mostly on memorization). Students in the successful intelligence condition (the group emphasizing all three ability-based styles) outperformed students in the other groups, even on memory-based multiple-choice assessments (Sternberg et al., 1998). Similar findings were found in middle and high school language arts classes (Grigorenko, Jarvin, & Sternberg, 2002); as well as in a sixth grade mathematics class for Alaskan Eskimos (Sternberg, Lipka, Newman, Wildfeuer, & Grigorenko, 2007).

These findings should serve to highlight the importance of using a wide variety of teaching methods and approaches to capitalize on students' strengths and compensate for their weaknesses, and allow them to learn and encode material in a variety of interesting ways. When students are taught in ways that highlight all ability-based styles, this method of teaching serves not only to create better thinkers, but also to help students perform better on assessments, no matter what form they take (Sternberg et al., 1998).

In another set of studies, researchers explored whether traditional schools and schooling favor students with analytical abilities at the expense of those with perhaps creative and practical abilities (Sternberg, Ferrari, Clinkenbeard, & Grigorenko, 1996; Sternberg et al., 1999). Students who were identified by their schools as gifted were given the Sternberg Triarchic Abilities Test (STAT; Sternberg, 1993), which measures students' analytical, creative, and practical skills in a variety of ways. Students who, based on their STAT performance, fell into one of five ability groupings (high-analytical, high-creative, high-practical, high in all three abilities, and low in all three abilities) were invited to a summer program at Yale University in college-level psychology, where they were divided into four instructional groups. All four groups used the same textbook and listened to the same lectures, but their afternoon discussion sections emphasized rote memory, analytical skills, creative skills, or practical skills, respectively. Student performance was evaluated the same across all students, regardless of the instructional group, and was based on homework, a midterm and final exam, and an independent project.

Several interesting findings resulted, supporting the utility of the theory of successful intelligence. First, when students first arrived at Yale, it was observed that those in the high-creative and high-practical groups were more ethnically, racially, socioeconomically, and educationally diverse than students in the high-analytical group. Therefore, while traditional conceptions of intelligence (i.e., focusing solely on analytical abilities) may have yielded low correlations with the demographic characteristics of these creative and practical students, expanding the range of abilities measured helped identify students that otherwise might not have been deemed as "intelligent."

In addition, all three ability tests significantly predicted student performance during the summer program, and there was an aptitude-treatment interaction, such that students who were assigned to an instructional group that matched their pattern of abilities were most advantaged and performed the best. For example, students who were identified as being high in creative skills and who were placed in the high-creativity instructional group outperformed other highly creative students who were placed in another instructional group. The relative lack of creative and practical instructional strategies in schools highlights the disadvantage that highly creative or practical students may be at, when they are never taught or assessed in a way that match their pattern of abilities.

It is not only important to teach in ways that emphasize all three types of abilities, but assessments that also focus on analytical, creative, and practical skills also allow students to maximally take advantage of their strengths while making up for their weaknesses. Stemler et al. (2009) worked with a group of Advanced Placement Physics teachers and readers to develop a series of AP Physics test items that assessed not only content knowledge, but also targeted memory, analytical, creative, and practical skills. The newly developed items were examined for validity and reliability, and were found to be statistically sound measures of physics knowledge, as well as measuring a broad range of cognitive skills.

Profiles of student achievement indicated that only 38% of students exhibited profiles associated with strong memory and analytical skills, meaning that many students' abilities are not necessarily assessed with traditional tests that focus only on these aspects of learning. By incorporating items that assessed creative and practical skills as well, ethnic differences in achievement on several subscales were witnessed, such that the usual achievement gap seen on such exams was reduced. Similar studies on other AP subject tests—psychology and statistics—have been conducted, with remarkably similar findings (e.g., Stemler, Grigorenko, Jarvin, & Sternberg, 2006), indicating the utility of expanding traditional assessments to include cognitive-processing areas that have been largely ignored. This expansion will allow educators and researchers to make more valid inferences about student learning and understanding, but will also allow students whose skills have largely been ignored and dismissed to demonstrate their particular patterns of abilities.

The Rainbow Project was a collaborative effort, in which analytical, creative, and practical measures were developed as a supplement to the SAT in predicting college success (as measured by grade point average [GPA]). Data were collected from 15 schools across the country (eight four-year colleges, five community colleges, and two high schools), including baseline standardized test scores (SAT) and high school GPA, as well as STAT scores to assess measures of successful intelligence. Researchers found that not only did Rainbow measures predict college freshman-year GPA, but they also roughly doubled the predictive power versus the SAT alone (Sternberg & The Rainbow Project Collaborators, 2006). In addition, the Rainbow measures appeared to reduce ethnic-group differences relative to those usually found with assessments such as the SAT. This research, like that done on AP tests (Stemler et al., 2009), has implications for reducing group differences in measures used to inform college admissions.

The WICS Theory—an Augmentation of the Theory of Successful Intelligence

Recently, Sternberg has augmented his theory by incorporating wisdom into the foundation of successful intelligence (Sternberg, 2003, 2005). The theory of Wisdom, Intelligence, and Creativity Synthesized (WICS) views intelligence (analytical and practical), creativity, and also wisdom as necessary components of successful intelligence. In the WICS model, analytical skills are equated with critical thinking skills. As we discussed earlier, while creative skills are needed to come up with new ideas and thoughts, analytical skills are necessary to evaluate whether those thoughts and ideas are good. Practical skills are needed to implement and execute such ideas, and wisdom is viewed as the essential component that allows one to determine whether and how the ideas can be implemented in the service of a common good, through the infusion of positive ethical values. This kind of thinking requires a balancing of intrapersonal, interpersonal, and extrapersonal interests over both the short and long term.

Therefore, a wise person often listens to others, weighs advice, and knows how to deal with a variety of people. "In seeking as much information as possible for decision making, the wise individual reads between the lines as well as making use of the obviously available information" (Sternberg, 2003, p. 180). Wise individuals learn not only from their own mistakes, but from the mistakes of others; and they are not afraid to change their minds as experience prescribes.

As a theory of educational leadership, WICS indeed has its roots in the theory for successful intelligence; however, it became clear that although a convergence of analytical, practical, and creative intelligence led to many positive academic outcomes for students, they were not necessarily enough for a happy and successful life (Sternberg, 2005). A person may be practically intelligent; however, he or she may use those practical skills toward selfish ends. Similarly, individuals with creative intelligence may not utilize their abilities for a common good.

The implications of the WICS theory for education are that schools should foster wisdom, in addition to knowledge and intelligence (Sternberg, 2008). Just as teaching students to think critically is not sufficient if they lack the ability to practically and creatively implement their critically-developed ideas and thoughts, so is their intelligence deficient if they lack the wisdom or ethical reasoning skills needed to put their ideas into practice in a manner that is for the common good. A wisdom-based approach to education would look similar to a constructivist approach in that students would take an active role in constructing their understanding; however, they would also be encouraged to construct knowledge from the point of view of others, in order to attain a more balanced comprehension.

For example, the American History teacher discussed earlier who provided his students with conflicting accounts of the Battle of Lexington was indeed using a wisdom-based approach to teaching his class. Not only was he encouraging his students to think critically about sources of information and the validity of evidence, but by presenting both the American and British perspectives on the battle, he exposed his students to the importance of balanced information and was supported in efforts to seek multiple points of view (Swartz, 1987).

Project Kaleidoscope at Tufts University examines the impact of the WICS theory on college admissions and success (Sternberg et al., 2008; Sternberg et al., 2010). Its roots stem from the Rainbow Project; however, the construct of wisdom was added to its measures. The Tufts admission application was amended to include optional essay questions designed to illicit analytical, creative, practical, or wise responses from applicants. Students have been encouraged to answer just one question out of a selection of 10–13 options. For example, a creative question asks students to write a short story with a title such as, "Seventeen Minutes Ago" or "No Whip Half-Caf Latte." A wisdom question might ask students to describe what inspires their original thinking or how they might apply their ingenuity to serve the common good and make a difference in society. Admissions officers are trained with rubrics to assess the Kaleidoscope essays as well as the rest of the application on measures of analytical skills, creativity, practical skills, and wisdom, and applications are rated on each dimension.

Since the integration of the Kaleidoscope framework with the existing Tufts admission process in 2006, the total number of applications to the school has increased. The quality of applicants has increased as well, both as a function of an increase in high-quality students applying and a decrease in low-quality students submitting applications. Acceptance rates have remained consistent; however, the percentage of ethnic minorities admitted to Tufts has increased dramatically (up 14% for Hispanic American students, and up 26% for African American students), suggesting that it is possible to increase academic quality and ethnic diversity on a large scale (Sternberg et al., 2008; Sternberg et al., 2010). Furthermore, when controlling for students' academic rating scores (SATs and high school GPAs), students who received a Kaleidoscope rating on their application performed significantly better than students who did not receive a Kaleidoscope rating, as measured by first-year college GPA.

It can be argued that college GPA is not the only measure of success or educational leadership that can or should be measured. Project Kaleidoscope has also conducted follow-up studies with students once they are enrolled at Tufts, in order to assess students' ratings of satisfaction with various aspects of their life during the school year; ratings of personal growth on different dimensions during the school year; listings and details of extracurricular activities with which they are involved, including the extent to which their involvement gave them the opportunity to cultivate wisdom, creativity, practical skills, analytical skills, and leadership skills; and ratings of the appropriateness of various descriptors of extracurricular experiences and what they gained from the experience. Students who received high ratings on Kaleidoscope measures on their admissions application reported greater satisfaction with their interactions with other students, reported becoming more socially active, reported more meaningful involvement in their extracurricular activities, and were more likely to describe their extracurricular experiences as enabling them to think practically, compared to students who received low ratings on Kaleidoscope measures (Sternberg et al., 2010). Further investigation is certainly warranted to examine the impact and implications of these subjective differences in experiences among individuals who are cultivating the qualities of successful leadership and preparing themselves for leadership roles in tomorrow's society.

FUTURE DIRECTIONS

According to Bloom's taxonomy, evaluation is the highest level of cognition, which involves making judgments based on criteria and standards through a process of monitoring and *critiquing* (Bloom & Krathwohl, 1956). Critical thinking indeed entails a high level of cognition, but as a recent revision to the taxonomy suggests, it is not necessarily the pinnacle of cognition (Anderson et al., 2001). The revised taxonomy now concludes with "creating," which entails putting together cognitive elements to form a functional whole, or reorganizing elements into a new model. This final step cannot be performed without the requisite evaluation or critical thinking process; however, this amendment recognizes the need for critical thinking instruction to be a means to a greater end, and not an end in and of itself.

The inclusion of a creative step in the taxonomy supports our proposition that not only is intelligence (analytical and practical) a necessary component of academic success and leadership, but also, perhaps, creativity and wisdom. Similarly, Stout (2007) proposed that imagination (which is associated with creativity) "allows us to hypothesize about what is possible; critical thinking helps us reason through those possibilities, and evaluation both helps us assess the quality of those processes and tells us whether our hypothesizing and reasoning are directed toward productive ends" (p. 58). Just as Stout called for an inclusion of imagination into the critical thinking model, so do we recommend a focus on critical and analytical thinking as being only the first step in maximizing student learning and understanding in the classroom, while simultaneously investigating and promoting the role of practical, creative, and wisdom skills.

REFERENCES

Anderman, E. M., & Dawson, H. (2011) Learning with motivation. In R. E. Mayer & P. A. Alexander (Eds.) *Handbook of research on learning and instruction* (pp. 219–241). New York: Routledge.

Anderson, L. W. (Ed.), Krathwohl, D. R. (Ed.), Airasian, P. W., Cruikshank, K. A., Mayer, R. E., Pintrich, P. R., et al. (2001). *A taxonomy for learning, teaching, and assessing: A revision of Bloom's Taxonomy of Educational Objectives* (Complete edition). New York: Longman.

Anderson, R. C., Nguyen-Jahiel, K., McNurlen, B., Archodidou, A., Kim, S.-Y., Reznitskaya, A., et al. (2001). The snowball phenomenon: Spread of ways of talking and ways of thinking across groups of children. *Cognition and Instruction, 19*, 1–46.

Atkinson, J. W. (1964). *An introduction to motivation*. Princeton, NJ: Van Nostrand.

Barron, B., Vye, N., Zech, L., Schwartz, D., Bransford, J., Goldman, S., et al. (1995). Creating contexts for community-based problem-solving: the Jasper Challenge Series. In C. N. Hedley, P. Antonacci, & M. Rabinowitz (Eds.), *Thinking and literacy: The mind at work*. Hillsdale, NJ: Lawrence Erlbaum.

Bauman, J. F. (1984). The effectiveness of a direct instruction paradigm for teaching main idea comprehension. *Reading Research Quarterly, 20*, 93–115.

Baxter Magolda, M. B. (1992). *Knowing and reasoning in college: Gender related patterns in students' intellectual development*. San Francisco, CA: Jossey-Bass.

Ben-Peretz, M. (2001). The impossible role of teacher educators in a changing world. *Journal of Teacher Education, 52*, 48–56.

Bloom, B. S., & Krathwohl, D. R. (1956). *Taxonomy of educational objectives: The classification of educational goals, by a committee of college and university examiners. Handbook 1: Cognitive domain*. New York: Longmans.

Bonner, S. E. (1999). Choosing teaching methods based on learning objectives: An integrative framework. *Issues in Accounting Education, 14*(1), 11–39.

Bransford, J., Hasselbring, T., Barron, B., Kulewicz, S., Littlefield, J., & Goin, L. (1988). Uses of macro-contexts to facilitate mathematical thinking. In R. Charles, & E. A. Silver (Eds.), *The teaching and assessment of mathematical problem solving* (pp. 125–147). Hillsdale, NJ: Lawrence Erlbaum.

Bronfenbrenner, U. (1979). *The ecology of human development*. Cambridge, MA: Harvard University Press.

Brown, A. L., Bransford, J. D., Ferrara, R. A., & Campione, J. C. (1983). Learning, remembering, and understanding.

In P. H. Mussen (Series ed.), J. H. Flavell, & E. M. Markman (Vol. eds.), *Handbook of child psychology: Vol. 3. Cognitive development* (4th ed., pp. 515–529). New York: Wiley.

Brown, A. L., & Campione, J. C. (1990). Communities of learning and thinking, or a context by any other name. In D. Kuhn (Ed.), *Developmental perspectives on teaching and learning thinking skills. Contributions to Human Development, 21* (pp. 108–126). Basel, Switzerland: Karger.

Brown, A. L., Campione, J. C., Reeve, R. A., Ferrara, R. A., & Palincsar, A. S. (1991). Interactive learning, individual understanding: The case of reading and mathematics. In L. T. Landsmann (Ed.), *Culture, schooling and psychological development* (pp. 136–170). Hillsdale, NJ: Erlbaum.

Brown, A. L., & Palincsar, A. S. (1989). Guided cooperative learning and individual knowledge acquisition. In L. B. Resnick (Ed.), *Knowing, learning, and instruction: Essays in honor of Robert Glaser* (pp. 393–451). Hillsdale, NJ: Erlbaum.

Carlson, M. P., & Bloom, I. (2005). The cyclic nature of problem solving: An emergent multidimensional problem-solving framework. *Educational Studies in Mathematics, 58*, 45–75.

Chen, Z., & Klahr, D. (2008). Remote transfer of scientific reasoning- and problem-solving strategies in children. In R. V. Kail (Ed.) *Advances in child development and behavior* (Vol. 36, pp. 419–470). Amsterdam: Elsevier.

Clotfelter, C. T., Ladd, H. F., & Vigdor, J. L. (2007). Teacher credentials and student achievement in high school: A cross-subject analysis with student fixed effects. NBER Working Paper series, w13617. Available at SSRN: http://ssrn.com/abstract=1033743.

Cognition and Technology Group at Vanderbilt (1992). The Jasper series as an example of anchored instruction: Theory, program description, and assessment data. *Educational Psychologist, 27*, 291–315.

Collaborative Reasoning (n.d.). On *Center for Study of Reading* website. Retrieved from http://csr.ed.uiuc.edu/CR/index.html.

Cotton, K. (1991). Close-Up #11: Teaching Thinking Skills. *Northwest Regional Educational Laboratory's School Improvement Research Series.* Retrieved from http://www.nwrel.org/scpd/sirs/6/cu11.html.

Covington, M. V. (1998). *The will to learn: A guide for motivating young people.* New York: Cambridge University Press.

Dean, D. W., & Kuhn, D. (2003). *Metacognition and critical thinking.* New York: Teachers College, Columbia University (ERIC Document Reproduction Service No. ED 477930).

Dewey, J. (1909). *How we think.* Boston: D.C. Heath and Co.

Dweck, C. S. (1986). Motivational processes affecting learning. *American Psychologist, 41*, 1040–1048.

Dweck, C. S., & Elliott, E. S. (1983). Achievement motivation. In E. M. Heatherington (Ed.), *Handbook of child psychology: Social and personality development* (Vol. 4, pp. 643–691). New York: Wiley.

Dweck, C. S., & Leggett, E. L. (1988). A social-cognitive approach to motivation and personality. *Psychological Review, 95*, 256–273.

Egan, K. (2000). Forward to the 19th century. *Teaching Education, 11*, 75–77.

Elder, L., & Paul, R. (2008). Critical thinking in a world of accelerated change and complexity. *Social Education, 72*, 388–391.

Elliot, A. J., & Harackiewicz, J. M. (1996). Approach and avoidance achievement goals and intrinsic motivation: A meditational analysis. *Journal of Personality and Social Psychology, 70*, 461–475.

Ennis, R. H. (1962). A concept of critical thinking. *Harvard Educational Review, 32*, 81–111.

Ennis, R. H. (1987). A taxonomy of critical thinking dispositions and abilities. In J. B. Baron, & R. J. Sternberg (Eds.), *Teaching thinking skills: Theory and practice* (pp. 9–26). New York: W. H. Freeman and Company.

Ennis, R. H. (1993). Critical thinking assessment. *Theory into Practice, 32*(3), 179–186.

Facione, P. A. (2000). The disposition toward critical thinking: Its character, measurement, and relationships to critical thinking skill. *Informal Logic, 20*, 61–84.

Facione, P., & Facione, N. (1992). *The California Critical Thinking Dispositions Inventory (CCTDI) and the CCTDI Test manual.* Millbrae, CA: California Academic Press.

Feuerstein, R. et al. (1986). Learning to learn: Mediated learning experiences and Instrumental Enrichment. *Special Services in the Schools, 3*(1–2), 49–82.

Feuerstein, R., Rand, Y., Hoffman, M., & Miller, R. (1980). *Instrumental enrichment: An intervention program for cognitive modifiability.* Baltimore, MD: University Park Press.

Fields, J. I. (1995). Empirical data research into the claims for using philosophy techniques with young children. *Early Child Development and Care, 107*, 115–128.

Fisher, A. (2001). *Critical thinking: An introduction.* Cambridge: Cambridge University Press.

Foundation for Critical Thinking (2009). *Defining critical thinking.* Retrieved from: http://www.criticalthinking.org/aboutCT/define_critical_thinking.cfm.

Francisco, J. S., Nicoll, G., & Trautmann, M. (1998). Integrating multiple teaching methods into a general chemistry classroom. *Journal of Chemical Education, 75*, 210–213.

Frederickson, B. L. (1998). What good are positive emotions? *Review of General Psychology, 2*, 300–319.

Fuller, R. G. (1977). *Multidisciplinary Piagetian-based programs for college freshmen.* Lincoln, NE: University of Nebraska at Lincoln Press.

Fuller, R. G. (1998). ADAPT: A multidisciplinary Piagetian-based program for college freshmen. Retrieved from http://digitalcommons.unl.edu/adaptessays/1.

Gess-Newsome, J. (1999). Pedagogical content knowledge: An introduction and orientation. In J. Gess-Newsome, & N. G. Lederman (Eds.), *Examining pedagogical content knowledge.* Dordrecht: Kluwer.

Glaser, E. M. (1941). An experiment on the development of critical thinking. *Teachers College Contributions to Education, No. 843.* New York: Bureau of Publications, Teachers College, Columbia University.

Grant, G. E. (1988). *Teaching critical thinking.* New York: Praeger.

Grigorenko, E. L., Jarvin, L., & Sternberg, R. J. (2002). School-based tests of the triarchic theory of intelligence: Three settings, three samples, three syllabi. *Contemporary Educational Psychology, 27,* 167–208.

Guthrie, J. T., & Davis, M. H. (2003). Motivating struggling readers in middle school through an engagement model of classroom practice. *Reading & Writing Quarterly, 19,* 59–85.

Halpern, D. F. (1998). Teaching critical thinking for transfer across domains. *American Psychologist, 53,* 449–455.

Halpern, D. F. (2007). The nature and nurture of critical thinking. In R. J. Sternberg, H. L. Roediger III, & D. F. Halpern (Eds.), *Critical thinking in psychology* (pp. 1–14). Cambridge: Cambridge University Press.

Harvey, L. C., & Hodges, L. C. (1999). The role of multiple teaching strategies in promoting active learning in Organic Chemistry. *The Chemical Educator, 4*(3), 89–93.

Hatcher, D. L. (2006). Stand-alone versus integrated critical thinking courses. *The Journal of General Education, 55,* 247–272.

Helsby, G. (1999). *Changing teachers' work.* Buckingham: Open University Press.

Hidi, S. (1990). Interest and its contribution as a mental resource for learning. *Review of Educational Research, 60,* 549–571.

Hidi, S., & Anderson, V. (1992). Situational interest and its impact on reading and expository writing. In K. A. Renninger, S. Hidi, & A. Krapp (Eds.), *The role of interest in learning and development* (pp. 215–238). Hillsdale, NJ: Erlbaum.

Hoaglund, J. (1993). Critical thinking: A Socratic model. *Argumentation, 7,* 291–311.

Kieft, M., Rijlaarsdam, G., & van den Bergh, H. (2008). An aptitude-treatment interaction approach to writing-to-learn. *Learning and Instruction, 18,* 379–390.

Klahr, D., & Nigam, M. (2004). The equivalence of learning paths in early science instruction: Effects of direct instruction and discovery learning. *Psychological Science, 15,* 661–667.

Krapp, A. (2002). Structural and dynamic aspects of interest development: Theoretical considerations from an ontogenetic perspective. *Learning and Instruction, 12,* 383–409.

Krapp, A., Hidi, S., & Renninger, K. A. (1992). Interest, learning and development. In K. A. Renninger, S. Hidi, & A. Krapp (Eds.), *The role of interest in learning and development* (pp. 3–26). Hillsdale, NJ: Erlbaum.

Krathwohl, D. R. (2002). A revision of Bloom's Taxonomy: An overview. *Theory into Practice, 41,* 212–218.

Kuhn, D. (1991). *The skills of argument.* Cambridge: Cambridge University Press.

Kuhn, D. (1999). A developmental model of critical thinking. *Educational Researcher, 28,* 16–26.

Kuhn, D. (2005). *Education for thinking.* Cambridge, MA: Harvard University Press.

Kuhn, D., Black, J., Keselman, A., & Kaplan, D. (2000). The development of cognitive skills to support inquiry learning. *Cognition and Instruction, 18,* 495–523.

Lederer, J. (2000). Reciprocal teaching of social studies in inclusive elementary classrooms. *Journal of Learning Disabilities, 33,* 91–106.

LeFevre, D. M., Moore, D. W., & Wilkinson, I. A. (2003). Tape-assisted reciprocal teaching: Cognitive bootstrapping for poor decoders. *British Journal of Educational Psychology, 73,* 37–58.

Lipman, M. (1988). Critical thinking – What can it be? *Educational Leadership, 46,* 38–43.

Lipman, M. (1989). *Misconceptions in teaching for critical thinking.* Institute for Critical Thinking Resource Publication, 2(3). Upper Montclair, NJ: Montclair State College.

Lipman, M. (1995). Moral education, higher-order thinking and philosophy for children. *Early Child Development and Care, 107,* 61–70.

Lipman, M. (1998). Teaching students to think reasonably: Some findings of the Philosophy for Children Program. *The Clearing House, 71,* 277–280.

Lipman, M. (2003). *Thinking in education* (2nd ed.). Cambridge: Cambridge University Press.

Malone, T. W., & Lepper, M. R. (1987). Making learning fun: A taxonomy of intrinsic motivations for learning. In R. E. Snow, & M. J. Farr (Eds.), *Aptitude, learning and instruction: III. Conative and affective process analyses* (pp. 223–253). Hillsdale, NJ: Erlbaum.

Mathan, S. A., & Koedinger, K. R. (2005). Fostering the intelligent novice: Learning from errors with metacognitive tutoring. *Educational Psychologist, 40,* 257–265.

McClelland, D. C., Atkinson, J. W., Clark, R. A., & Lowell, E. L. (1953). *The achievement motive.* New York: Appleton-Century-Crofts.

Meyers, C. (1986). *Teaching students to think critically.* San Francisco: Jossey-Bass Publishers.

Midgley, C. et al. (2000). *Manual for the Patterns of Adaptive Learning Scales (PALS).* Ann Arbor, MI: University of Michigan.

Murphy, P. K., Wilkinson, I. A. G., Soter, A. O., Hennessey, M. N., & Alexander, J. F. (2009). Examining the effects of classroom discussion on students' comprehension of text: A meta-analysis. *Journal of Educational Psychology, 101,* 740–764.

Myers, B. E., & Dyer, J. E. (2006). The influence of student learning style on critical thinking skills. *Journal of Agricultural Education, 47,* 43–52.

Nicholls, J. G. (1984). Achievement motivation: Conceptions of ability, subjective experience, task choice, and performance. *Psychological Review, 91,* 328–346.

Noddings, N. (2006). *Critical lessons: What our schools should teach.* New York: Cambridge University Press.

Okagaki, L., & Sternberg, R. J. (1990). Teaching thinking skills: We're getting the context wrong. In D. Kuhn (Ed.), *Developmental perspectives on teaching and learning thinking skills. Contributions to Human Development, 21* (pp. 63–78). Basel, Switzerland: Karger.

Park, S., & Oliver, J. S. (2008). Revisiting the conceptualization of pedagogical content knowledge (PCK): PCK as a conceptual tool to understand teachers as professionals. *Research in Science Education, 38,* 261–284.

Paul, R. (1989). Critical thinking in North America: A new theory of knowledge, learning, and literacy. *Argumentation, 3*(2), 197–235.

Paul, R. (2005). The state of critical thinking today. *New Directions for Community Colleges, 130,* 27–38.

Paul, R., & Elder, L. (2008). *The miniature guide to critical thinking: Concepts and tools.* Dillon Beach, CA: The Foundation for Critical Thinking.

Paul, R., Elder, L., & Bartell, T. (1997). *California teacher preparation for instruction in critical thinking: Research findings and policy recommendations.* Sacramento: California Commission on Teacher Credentialing.

Perkins, D. N., & Grotzer, T. A. (1997). Teaching intelligence. *American Psychologist, 52,* 1125–1133.

Perkins, D. N., & Salomon, G. (1989). Are cognitive skills context-bound? *Educational Researcher, 18,* 16–25.

Perry, W. G. (1970). *Forms of intellectual and ethical development in the college years: A scheme.* New York: Holt, Rinehart and Winston.

Piaget, J. (1952). *The origins of intelligence in children.* New York: International University Press.

Rand, Y., Tannenbaum, A. J., & Feuerstein, R. (1979). Effects of Instrumental Enrichment on the psychoeducational development of low-functioning adolescents. *Journal of Educational Psychology, 71,* 751–763.

Reed, J. H., & Kromrey, J. D. (2001). Teaching critical thinking in a community college history course: Empirical evidence from an infusion of Paul's model. *College Student Journal, 35,* 201–215.

Renninger, K. A. (2000). Individual interest and its implications for understanding intrinsic motivation. In C. Sansone, & J. M. Harackiewicz (Eds.), *Intrinsic motivation: Controversies and new directions* (pp. 373–404). San Diego, CA: Academic Press.

Rubman, C. N., & Waters, H. S. (2000). A, B, seeing: The role of constructive processes in children's comprehension monitoring. *Journal of Educational Psychology, 92,* 503–514.

Schauble, L. (1990). Belief revision in children: The role of prior knowledge and strategies for generating evidence. *Journal of Experimental Child Psychology, 49,* 31–57.

Schauble, L., & Glaser, R. (1990). Scientific thinking in children and adults. In D. Kuhn (Ed.), *Developmental perspectives on teaching and learning thinking skills. Contributions to Human Development, 21* (pp. 9–27). Basel, Switzerland: Karger.

Shayer, M., & Beasley, F. (1987). Does Instrumental Enrichment work? *British Educational Research Journal, 13,* 101–119.

Shulman, L. S. (1986). Those who understand: Knowledge growth in teaching. *Educational Researcher, 15,* 4–14.

Smyth, J., & Shacklock, G. (1998). *Re-making teaching: Ideology, policy and practice.* London: Routledge.

Solon, T. (2001). Improving critical thinking in an introductory psychology course. *Michigan Community College Journal: Research and Practice, 7*(2), 73–80.

Solon, T. (2007). Generic critical thinking infusion and course content learning in introductory psychology. *Journal of Instructional Psychology, 34,* 95–109.

Stemler, S. E., Grigorenko, E. L., Jarvin, L., & Sternberg, R. J. (2006). Using the theory of successful intelligence as a basis for augmenting AP exams in psychology and statistics. *Contemporary Educational Psychology, 31,* 75–108.

Stemler, S. E., Sternberg, R. J., Grigorenko, E. L., Jarvin, L., & Sharpes, K. (2009). Using the theory of successful intelligence as a framework for developing assessments in AP physics. *Contemporary Educational Psychology, 34,* 195–209.

Sternberg, R. J. (1987). Questions and answers about the nature and teaching of thinking skills. In J. B. Baron, & R. J. Sternberg (Eds.), *Teaching thinking skills: Theory and practice* (pp. 251–259). New York: W. H. Freeman and Co.

Sternberg, R. J. (1988). *The triarchic mind: A new theory of human intelligence.* New York: Penguin.

Sternberg, R. J. (1993). Sternberg triarchic abilities test. Unpublished manuscript.

Sternberg, R. J. (1994). Allowing for thinking styles. *Educational Leadership, 52,* 36–40.

Sternberg, R. J. (1997). *Successful intelligence.* New York: Plume.

Sternberg, R. J. (1999). The theory of successful intelligence. *Review of General Psychology, 3,* 292–316.

Sternberg, R. J. (2001). Why schools should teach for wisdom: The balance theory of wisdom in educational settings. *Educational Psychologist, 36,* 227–245.

Sternberg, R. J. (2003). *Wisdom, intelligence, and creativity synthesized.* Cambridge: Cambridge University Press.

Sternberg, R. J. (2005). WICS: A model of positive educational leadership comprising wisdom, intelligence, and creativity synthesized. *Educational Psychology Review, 17,* 191–262.

Sternberg, R. J. (2008). Schools should nurture wisdom. In B. Z. Presseisen (Ed.), *Teaching for intelligence* (2nd ed.). Thousand Oaks, CA: Corwin Press.

Sternberg, R. J., Bonney, C. R., Gabora, L., Jarvin, L., Karelitz, T. M., & Coffin, L. (2010). Broadening the spectrum of undergraduate admissions. *College & University, 86,* 2–17.

Sternberg, R. J., Ferrari, M., Clinkenbeard, P. R., & Grigorenko, E. L. (1996). Identification, instruction, and assessment of gifted children: A construct validation of a triarchic model. *Gifted Child Quarterly, 40,* 129–137.

Sternberg, R. J., & Grigorenko, E. L. (2007). *Teaching for successful intelligence: To increase student learning and achievement* (2nd ed.). Thousand Oaks, CA: Corwin Press.

Sternberg, R. J., Grigorenko, E. L., Ferrari, M., & Clinkenbeard, P. (1999). A triarchic analysis of an aptitude-treatment interaction. *European Journal of Psychological Assessment, 15,* 1–11.

Sternberg, R. J., Grigorenko, E. L., & Zhang, L.-F. (2008). Styles of learning and thinking matter in instruction and assessment. *Perspectives on Psychological Science, 3,* 486–506.

Sternberg, R. J., Lipka, J., Newman, T., Wildfeuer, S., & Grigorenko, E. L. (2007). Triarchically based instruction and assessment of sixth-grade mathematics in a Yup'ik cultural setting in Alaska. *International Journal of Giftedness and Creativity, 21,* 6–19.

Sternberg, R. J., & The Rainbow Project Collaborators (2006). The Rainbow Project: Enhancing the SAT through assessments of analytical, practical, and creative skills. In W. Camara, & E. Kimmel (Eds.), *Choosing students: Higher education admission tools for the 21st century* (pp. 159–176). Mahwah, NJ: Erlbaum.

Sternberg, R. J., Torff, B., & Grigorenko, E. L. (1998). Teaching triarchically improves school achievement. *Journal of Educational Psychology, 90,* 374–384.

Sternberg, R. J., & Williams, W. M. (2010). *Educational psychology* (2nd ed.). Upper Saddle River, NJ: Pearson/Merrill.

Streib, J. T. (1992). History and analysis of critical thinking. Dissertation, University of Memphis.

Stout, M. (2007). Critical thinking, imagination, and new knowledge in education research. In K. Egan, M. Stout, & K. Takaya (Eds.), *Teaching and learning outside the box: Inspiring imagination across the curriculum* (pp. 42–58). New York: Teachers College Press.

Stupnisky, R. H., Renaud, R. D., Daniels, L. M., Haynes, T. L., & Perry, R. P. (2008). The interrelation of first-year college students' critical thinking disposition, perceived academic control, and academic achievement. *Research in Higher Education, 49,* 513–530.

Swartz, R. J. (1987). Teaching for thinking: A developmental model for the infusion of thinking skills into mainstream instruction. In J. B. Baron, & R. J. Sternberg (Eds.), *Teaching thinking skills: Theory and practice* (pp. 106–126). New York: W. H. Freeman and Co.

Swartz, R. J., Costa, A. L., Beyer, B. K., Reagan, R., & Kallick, B. (2008). *Thinking-based learning: Activating students' potential.* Norwood, MA: Christopher-Gordon Publishers.

Trickey, S., & Topping, K. J. (2004). 'Philosophy for Children': A systematic review. *Research Papers in Education, 19,* 365–380.

Valanides, N., & Angeli, C. (2005). Effects of instruction on changes in epistemological beliefs. *Contemporary Educational Psychology, 30,* 314–330.

van Gelder, T. J. (2001). How to improve critical thinking using educational technology. In G. Kennedy, M. Keppell, C. McNaught, & T. Petrovic (Eds.), *Meeting at the crossroads: Proceedings of the 18th Annual Conference of the Australian Society for Computers In Learning In Tertiary Education (ASCILITE 2001)* (pp. 539–548). Melbourne: Biomedical Multimedia Unit, The University of Melbourne.

Waggoner, M., Chinn, C., Yi, H., & Anderson, R. C. (1995). Collaborative reasoning about stories. *Language Arts, 72,* 582–589.

Webster, Y. O. (1997). *Against the multicultural agenda: A critical thinking alternative.* Westport, CT: Praeger.

Whitehead, A. N. (1967). *The aims of education.* New York: Free Press. (Originally published 1929).

Williams, R. L., & Worth, S. L. (2001). The relationship of critical thinking to success in college. *Inquiry: Critical Thinking Across the Disciplines, 21*(1), *5–16.*

Wollman-Bonilla, J. E., & Werchadlo, B. (1999). Teacher and peer roles in scaffolding first graders' responses to literature. *The Reading Teacher, 52,* 598–607.

Yeh, Y.-C. (2004). Nurturing reflective teaching during critical-thinking instruction in a computer simulation program. *Computers & Education, 42,* 181–194.

Zohar, A. (1999). Teachers' metacognitive knowledge and the instruction of higher order thinking. *Teaching and Teacher Education, 15,* 413–429.

10

LEARNING TO SELF-MONITOR AND SELF-REGULATE

Marcel V. J. Veenman

INTRODUCTION

In the educational literature, the terms *metacognition* and *self-regulated learning* are often used interchangeably (Veenman, 2007), although their conceptual roots and theoretical perspectives are quite distinct (Dinsmore, Alexander, & Loughin, 2008; Fox & Riconscente, 2008). Metacognition theory originated from developmental psychology with Piaget (Inhelder & Piaget, 1958) and Flavell (1970) as progenitors. Metacognition initially focused on the "reflective abstraction of new or existent cognitive structures" (Dinsmore et al., 2008, p. 393), that is, on the developing person's thinking about cognition. Later, Brown and DeLoache (1978) affixed self-regulatory mechanisms to the conceptualization of metacognition.

Self-regulated learning (SRL), on the other hand, emerged from both metacognition theory and Bandura's self-regulation theory, however, with a strong emphasis on the regulation of learning processes and learning outcomes. SRL theory attempts to integrate cognitive, motivational and contextual factors of learning (Dinsmore et al., 2008; Zimmerman, 1995). Metacognition researchers consider self-regulation to be a subordinate component of metacognition, whereas SRL researchers regard self-regulation as a concept superordinate to metacognition, that is, cognitive regulation next to motivational and affective regulation (Veenman, van Hout-Wolters, & Afflerbach, 2006). Dinsmore et al. (2008) rightfully asserted that the boundaries between both theories have grown fuzzy over time and they plead for more clarity in conceptual and operational definitions.

In this chapter, a metacognitive perspective is taken. Hence, when referring to the SRL literature, only the cognitive self-regulatory aspects of SRL will be taken into account. Wang, Haertel, and Walberg (1990) concluded from their literature review that metacognition is the most important predictor of learning performance. More specifically, in an overview of studies with learners of different age, performing different tasks in various domains, Veenman (2008) estimated that metacognitive skillfulness accounted

198 • Marcel V. J. Veenman

for 40% of variance in learning outcomes. Therefore, the main focus is on metacognitive skills for the regulation of learning processes, although one cannot escape a discussion of the role of metacognitive declarative knowledge in the acquisition of metacognitive skills.

In conceptions of metacognition, a distinction is often made between knowledge of cognition and regulation of cognition (Brown, 1987; Schraw & Dennison, 1994). According to Schraw and Dennison (1994), knowledge of cognition consists of declarative knowledge about the cognitive system, procedural knowledge about how to execute cognitive strategies, and (declarative) conditional knowledge about the utility of strategies. Regulation of cognition refers to metacognitive skills for the control over one's strategy use, that is, to planning, monitoring, and evaluation. Procedural knowledge about how to execute cognitive strategies, however, essentially is cognitive knowledge (Anderson & Schunn, 2000). In order to avoid a circular reasoning of knowledge being cognitive and metacognitive at the same time, cognitive procedural knowledge should be excluded from a conception of metacognition. Thus, only two declarative components (i.e., declarative knowledge and conditional knowledge) remain in knowledge of cognition, referred to in the literature as *metacognitive knowledge* (Veenman et al., 2006). Regulation of cognition is the procedural component of metacognition, referred to as *metacognitive skills*.

This chapter starts out with defining the constructs of metacognitive knowledge and skills from a historical perspective. Next, a comprehensive model of the nature of metacognitive skills and the acquisition of those skills will be outlined. Consequences of this model for the assessment and instruction of metacognitive skills will be delineated. Finally, some new directions for metacognition research will be highlighted.

HISTORICAL OVERVIEW

Metacognitive Knowledge

Metacognitive knowledge refers to one's declarative knowledge about the interplay between person, task and strategy characteristics (Flavell, 1979). For instance, a learner may think that s/he (person characteristic) is not proficient in reading (task characteristic) and, therefore, that s/he should invest more effort in studying a textbook chapter (strategy characteristic). Conversely, another learner may more positively evaluate his/her reading proficiency, thus putting less effort into studying the same chapter. Some researchers implicitly assume that metacognitive knowledge only refers to correct knowledge, derived from earlier experiences (e.g., Schraw & Moshman, 1995; Simons, 1996). The assumption is that metacognitive knowledge can only be truly metacognitive by nature if it accurate and flawless.

However, metacognitive knowledge can be either correct or incorrect as learners may underestimate or overestimate their competences, relative to the subjectively perceived complexity of the task (Veenman et al., 2006). For instance, a student may erroneously think that s/he only needs to read a chapter once in preparation for an exam, despite repeated failure on earlier exams. In fact, this self-knowledge may prove quite resistant to change, especially when failure is misattributed to external causes such as poor teachers and unsound exams. Moreover, even correct metacognitive knowledge does not guarantee an adequate execution of appropriate strategies, as the learner may lack the motivation or capability to do so. For instance, Alexander, Carr, and Schwanenflugel (1995) found a discrepancy between children's knowledge about monitoring and application of monitoring skills during task performance. In a same vein, Winne (1996) stated that knowledge has no effect on behavior until it is actually being used. Consequently, metacognitive knowledge often poorly predicts learning outcomes (Veenman, 2005). A good deal of metacognitive knowledge has its roots in a person's belief system, which contains broad, often tacit ideas about the nature and functioning of the cognitive system (Flavell, 1979). Beliefs are personal and subjective by nature, and so remains metacognitive knowledge when it is not put to the test by the actual execution of strategies or skills.

Since researchers embarked on the study of metacognition in the 1970s, they have identified several subcomponents of metacognitive knowledge. The first component under study was metamemory (Flavell, 1970; Flavell & Wellman, 1977). Initially, metamemory only referred to the declarative knowledge about one's memory capabilities and about strategies that affect memory processes (Cavanaugh & Perlmutter, 1982). It was assumed that this factual knowledge of memory processes would affect memory performance. Later, especially within the study of Feeling of Knowing (FOK) and Judgment of Learning (JOL), the focus of metamemory research shifted from the knowledge product of metamemory to the process of metamemory (Nelson & Narens, 1990). Both FOK and JOL refer to a person's predictions about future test performance, either on items that are known (JOL), or on items that are not yet mastered (FOK). This process approach to metamemory stresses the role of monitoring or evaluation of memory contents. By including monitoring activities, metamemory research has crossed the border between metacognitive knowledge and metacognitive skills. Consequently, metacognitive knowledge about the memory system and monitoring skills for evaluating memory cannot be disentangled from the prediction of actual memory performance.

Another component of metacognitive knowledge is conditional knowledge (Schraw & Moshman, 1995). Conditional knowledge pertains to declarative knowledge about when a certain metacognitive strategy should be applied and to what purpose. Poor performers often do not know what strategy to choose, why they should use that strategy, and when to deploy that strategy. Even adequate conditional knowledge, however, does not guarantee the actual execution of a strategy as a learner may still miss the procedural knowledge for how the strategy should be enacted. In fact, conditional knowledge provides an entry to the first stage of skill acquisition, where a metacognitive strategy has to be consciously applied step-by-step and gradually transformed into a skill through proceduralization (Alexander & Jetton, 2000; Anderson & Schunn, 2000). Thus, conditional knowledge is a prerequisite, but not sufficient condition for the acquisition of metacognitive strategies or skills.

This is the very reason why Kuhn (1999) and Zohar and Ben-David (2009) postulated the notion of metastrategic knowledge, which encompasses both conditional knowledge and procedural knowledge for how to use a strategy. This concept of metastrategic knowledge, however, obscures the boundary between metacognitive knowledge and skills. It precludes the notion that metacognitive strategies may fail either due to incorrect and incomplete conditional knowledge, or due to lack of knowledge about how to execute a strategy.

Acquisition of Metacognitive Knowledge

Where does metacognitive knowledge come from? As noted, the belief system, which contains naïve theories and tacit ideas about cognitive functioning, provides a source of information from which metacognitive knowledge is built. Other information sources are judgments and feedback from other people, and metacognitive experiences (Efklides, 2006; Flavell, 1979). According to Efklides (2006), metacognitive experiences are non-analytic, non-conscious inferential processes that are driven by affective experiences, such as liking, interest, curiosity, disappointment, and being startled. Hence, metacognitive experiences are truly subjective by nature. For instance, while a task may have an externally defined objective level of difficulty or cognitive load (Sweller, 1994), feeling of difficulty is determined by subjective estimates of task difficulty, which depend on person characteristics, such as cognitive ability, and affective factors, such as mood and fear of failure, among others (Efklides, 2006). Metacognitive experiences may affect task performance directly through time on task and effort expenditure.

What metacognitive experiences and metacognitive knowledge have in common is that both originate from a monitoring process. Metacognitive knowledge, however, refers to memory-retrieved knowledge, whereas metacognitive experiences concern on-line feelings, judgments, estimates, and thoughts that people have during task performance. Although metacognitive experiences arise from unconscious inferential processes, as soon as learners become consciously aware of them, they may feed into the cognitive system and become more or less stable metacognitive knowledge. Thus, metacognitive experiences are a major source for building up metacognitive knowledge.

What is the developmental timeline of metacognitive knowledge? Flavell (1992) related his conceptualization of metacognition to Piaget's developmental stage of for-mal-operational thinking. At this stage children are capable of hypothetico-deductive reasoning, which requires a child to take a metacogitive perspective. Flavell indicated that Piaget would not expect metacognition to show up before the stage of formal-oper-ational thinking as "young children's egocentrism prevents them from being able to introspect or treat their own thought processes as an object of thought" (Flavell, 1992, p. 118; see also Fox & Riconscente, 2008; Inhelder & Piaget, 1958). Flavell further adhered to Piaget's theory by postulating an early developmental level of proto-metacognition, at which level children do acknowledge that different people may see different things, although they cannot handle the various perspectives other people may take. Therefore, metacognitive awareness may arise at the age of 4–6 years as an inclination that something is wrong (Blöte, Van Otterloo, Stevenson, & Veenman, 2004; Demetriou & Efklides, 1990; Istomina, 1975; Kluwe, 1987; Kuhn, 1999).

Indeed, recent research accounted for the missing link between Theory of Mind (TOM) and metamemory as a starting point of metacognitive development (Bartsch & Estes, 1996; Flavell, 2004; Kuhn, 1999; Larkin, 2006; Lockl & Schneider, 2006). TOM pertains to children's knowledge about the mind and, in particular, knowledge about the existence of mental states such as beliefs, desires, and intentions. Crucial to the development of TOM is the understanding of a child older than 4 years that another person may not know what the child knows. Longitudinal studies by Lockl and Schneider (2006) have shown that TOM at the age of 4 to 5 years is a precursor of later metamemory performance at the age of 5 to 6 years. Apparently, the development of metacognitive knowledge has its roots in earlier cognitive development. As the children's knowledge of cognitive processes, strategies, and task variables expands during the early school years, integration of this knowledge instigates the formation of metacognitive conditional knowledge (Alexander et al., 1995; Berk, 2003; Kuhn, 1999). A further growth of metacognitive knowledge occurs in the years thereafter. The formation of conditional knowledge is the overture to metacognitive skill development in successive years, though strategic behavior initially is impeded by the incompleteness and inappropriateness of conditional knowledge (Annevirta & Vauras, 2006; Kuhn, 1999).

Metacognitive Skills

Metacognitive skills pertain to the acquired repertoire of procedural knowledge for monitoring, guiding, and controlling one's learning and problem-solving behavior. There is some consensus of what learning activities are typical for metacognitive skills. The overview presented here is by no means exhaustive. For instance, Pressley and Afflerbach (1995) distinguished some 150 different metacognitive activities in detail for reading, while Meijer, Veenman, and Van Hout-Wolters (2006) drew up a list of 65 activities for solving physics problems. This chapter, however, merely presents a global description of what kind of activities are regarded as being representative of metacognitive skills.

Quite often, a distinction is made between activities at the onset of task performance, during task performance, and at the end of task performance (Meijer et al., 2006; Schraw & Moshman, 1995). At the onset of task performance one may find activities, such as reading and analyzing the task assignment, activating prior knowledge, goal setting, and planning (Brown, 1987; Van der Stel & Veenman, 2008). These activities are preparatory to actual task performance. Indicators of metacognitive skillfulness during task performance are systematically following a plan or deliberately changing that plan, monitoring and checking, note taking, and time and resource management (Brown, 1987; Veenman & Beishuizen, 2004). These activities guide and control the execution of the task at hand. At the end of task performance, activities such as evaluating performance against the goal, drawing conclusions, recapitulating, and reflection on the learning process may be observed (Butler, 1998; Veenman, Elshout, & Meijer, 1997). The function of these activities is to evaluate and interpret the outcome, and to learn from one's course of action for future occasions.

At first glance, the metacognitive activities of learners may vary from task to task, and from one domain to another. For instance, orienting activities for text studying include reading the title and subheadings, scanning the text to get an overview, activating prior knowledge, goal setting for reading, and getting hold of test expectations (Pressley & Afflerbach, 1995; Veenman & Beishuizen, 2004). Orientation during problem solving encompasses reading the problem statement, activating prior knowledge, goal setting, making a drawing representing the problem, establishing what is given and what is asked for, and predicting a plausible outcome (Meijer et al., 2006). Similarly, the process of planning in reading looks different from planning while solving physics problems. When studying a text, planning activities concern decisions about what to read first and how to navigate through the text (Veenman & Beishuizen, 2004). Planning in problem solving refers to the design of a step-by-step action plan of problem-solving activities (Mettes, Pilot, & Roossink, 1981). Monitoring in reading primarily pertains to text comprehension (Brown, 1987), while monitoring in problem solving mainly concerns the detection and repair of errors (Meijer et al., 2006).

Even when the same learner performs the same type of tasks, say problem solving, learner behavior may vary across content domains. For instance, Glaser, Schauble, Raghavan, and Zeitz (1992) found different patterns of learner activities for three discovery-learning tasks in the domains of physics and microeconomics. Glaser et al. argue that differences between tasks in the frequencies of predictions generated, controlled experiments, and notebook entries, among others, are due to differences in domain content and task demands. Since learners improved when moving from one learning task to the other, Glaser et al. did not rule out the role of general strategies of a larger grain size, such as planning and evaluation of activities. "However, these general skills take on specific value as they are differentially useful in varying contexts" (Glaser et al., 1992, p. 370).

Although specific overt activities are evoked by different task requirements, there is evidence that these activities spring from similar metacognitive grounds. In a longitudinal design, Van der Stel and Veenman (2008, 2010) followed 12-year-olds for three successive years, while they performed a reading task in history and a problem-solving task in mathematics each year. Principal component analysis on the metacognitive-skill measures, obtained from the separated analyses of think-aloud protocols for both tasks, revealed a steady general component over the years (accounting for 41% to 49% of variance) and a weaker domain specific component, fading out over the years (accounting for 22% down to 15% of variance). While contrasting discovery learning in biology with problem solving in mathematics, Veenman and Spaans (2005) found that metacognition skills for both tasks correlated .27 in 12-year-olds and .61 in 14-year-olds.

Consistent support for the general nature of metacognitive skills has been reported for learners in the age of 9 to 22 years performing four discovery-learning tasks in biology and geography (Veenman, Wilhelm, & Beishuizen, 2004), for undergraduate students performing three discovery-learning tasks in the domains of physics, statistics, and chemistry (Veenman et al., 1997), for undergraduates from a technical university who performed a mathematical model construction task and a discovery-learning task in chemistry (Veenman & Verheij, 2003), and for undergraduate students studying two texts about geography and criminology (Veenman & Beishuizen, 2004). In the latter four studies, principal component analysis yielded only a general component, accounting for 62–83% of variance, while correlations among measures of metacognitive skillfulness for different tasks and domains ranged between .67 and .86.

Finally, Schraw, Dunkle, Bendixen, and Roedel (1995) obtained support for a general monitoring skill in undergraduate students during test answering for five different content domains. Accuracy of students' confidence ratings on the five tests correlated on the average .19 and a principal component analysis yielded one general component that accounted for 37% of variance. In conclusion, the metacognitive skills of younger learners are general, as well as domain specific to a lesser extent. "[Their] metacognitive skills may initially develop on separate islands of tasks and domains that are very much alike" (Veenman & Spaans, 2005, p. 172). After the age of 12 years, metacognitive skills increasingly become more general, a transition process that is completed at the age of 14 years. Apparently, older learners have a personal repertoire of metacognitive skills that they tend to apply whenever they encounter a new learning task. This notion of general metacognitive skills has implications for the training and transfer of those skills across tasks and domains.

Contrary to metacognitive knowledge, metacognitive skills have a feedback mechanism built-in (Veenman et al., 2006). Either you are capable of planning and monitoring and, consequently, task performance progresses smoothly, or you do not and your actions are likely to go astray. Learners may notice the metacognitive nature of their failure, rather than attributing their failure to inadequate cognitive processing or task difficulty. This awareness would generate new metacognitive knowledge and, eventually, may lead to an adaptation of metacognitive skills. Skill acquisition and adaptation, however, take time and effort; they do not come quick and dirty.

Development of Metacognitive Skills

The development of metacognitive skills is generally thought of as commencing at the age of 8 to 10 years (Berk, 2003; Veenman et al., 2006). However, research by Whitebread et al. (2009) has shown that the behavior of young children may reveal elementary forms of planning, monitoring, and reflection if the task is appropriated to their interest and level of understanding. They observed 3- to 5-year-old children interact in playful situations, such as distributing dolls over a limited number of chairs. Children were capable of initiating an orderly sequence of actions (e.g., one doll per chair to start with), of self-correcting faulty actions (e.g., taking back an incorrectly placed doll), and of reviewing the outcome (e.g., noticing that the dolls are equally distributed over the chairs).

Similarly, Larkin (2006) observed elementary metacognitive strategy use in 5-year old children collaboratively performing age-appropriate tasks, such as sorting out buttons by shape. Protocols of two children showed that they could break the task down into steps, plan how to go about, monitor progress, and evaluate success or failure. According to Whitebread et al., earlier studies underestimated metacognitive processing in preschool children because assessment methods relied too much on children's verbal ability. Although metacognitive activities in the Whitebread et al. and Larkin studies had to be inferred from observed behavior, which in itself raises some methodological questions, their results may indicate that models of metacognitive development need some revision.

Most likely, metacognitive skills already develop alongside metacognitive knowledge during preschool or early-school years at a very basic level, but they become more sophisticated and academically oriented whenever formal educational requires the explicit utilization of a metacognitive repertoire (Veenman et al., 2006). Consequently, during primary and secondary education, learners reveal a steep incremental development in both frequency and quality of metacognitive skills (Alexander et al., 1995; Van der Stel & Veenman, 2010). Moreover, intelligence does not affect the development of metacognition, as correlations between intelligence and metacognition remain stable over the years (Veenman et al., 2004; Veenman & Spaans, 2005). In an overview of research with 439 learners from different age groups, performing different tasks in different domains, Veenman (2008) established that intelligence uniquely accounted for 10% of variance in learning performance, metacognitive skillfulness uniquely accounted for 18% of variance, while both predictors shared another 22% of variance in learning performance. Hence, metacognitive skills cannot be equated with intelligence. Even relatively low-intelligent learners spontaneously acquire metacognitive skills with age (Alexander et al., 1995; Van der Stel & Veenman, in press).

THEORETICAL FRAMEWORK

Metacognitive Skills and Cognitive Processing

A process model of metacognitive skills ought to make a distinction between meta-cognitive and cognitive activity. Incidentally, this distinction becomes manifest in the behavior of learners when they explicitly express their intention to apply a metacognitive skill. Most of the time, however, metacognitive skills remain covert mechanisms that take place inside the head. Consequently, these metacognitive skills cannot be directly assessed, but have to be inferred from their behavioral consequences (Veenman et al., 2006). For instance, when a learner spontaneously recalculates the outcome of a math problem, it is assumed that a monitoring or evaluation process must have preceded this overt cognitive activity of recalculation.

A perennial issue, then, is that higher-order metacognitive skills heavily draw on lower-order cognitive processes (Brown, 1987; Slife, Weiss, & Bell, 1985). A few examples may elucidate this tight connection between metacognitive and cognitive processes: Analysis of the task assignment requires reading and reasoning processes; activating prior knowledge is driven by memory processes; planning involves processes of serialization and sequencing; comprehension monitoring while reading relies on lexical access and other verbal processes; checking the outcome of a calculation requires numerical processes; note taking depends on writing processes; drawing conclusions entails inferential reasoning; both evaluation and reflection imply cognitive processes of making comparisons. Metaphorically speaking, metacognitive skills represent the driver, while cognitive processes form the vehicle for employing those metacognitive skills.

The problem of disentangling higher-order from lower-order skills is deeply rooted in psychological theory of human consciousness. Conceptualizations of metacognition have in common that they take the perspective of *higher-order cognition about cognition* (Flavell, 1979; Nelson, 1999). These conceptualizations stress the supervisory role of metacognition in the initiation of and control over cognitive processes. A higher-order agent is overlooking and governing the cognitive system, while simultaneously being part of it. This is the classical homunculus problem (Elshout, 1996), otherwise referred to as Comte's paradox (Nelson, 1996): One cannot split one's self in two, of whom one thinks while the other observes that thinking. What then is the higher-order nature of metacognitive skills? This issue will be addressed in the next section.

Metacognitive Skills as Self-Instructions

Nelson (1996; Nelson & Narens, 1990) gave an initial impetus to a unified theory of metacognition. Basically, he distinguished an "object level" from a "meta-level." At the object level, lower-order cognitive activities take place, usually referred to as *execution* processes. For instance, cognitive processes at the object-level for reading include decoding, lexical access, parsing, and relating concepts. The higher-order, *executive* processes of evaluation and planning at the meta-level govern the object level. Two general flows of information between both levels are postulated. Information about the state of the object level is conveyed to the meta-level through monitoring processes, while instructions from the meta-level are transmitted to the object level through control processes. Thus, if errors occur on the object level, monitoring processes will give notice of it to the meta-level, where the incoming information is evaluated and control processes are activated or planned to resolve the problem. This seems an elegant model, including both metacognitive knowledge through the information flows and metacognitive skills in subsequent processes of monitoring, evaluation, and planning.

According to Nelson's model, metacognition can be seen as a *bottom-up* process, where anomalies in task performance trigger monitoring activities, which in turn activate control processes on the meta-level. A limitation of this bottom-up model is that it does not clarify how monitoring processes themselves are triggered (Dunlosky, 1998). Moreover, the model does not account for spontaneous activation of control processes without prior monitoring activities, thus neglecting the goal directedness of problem-solving and learning behavior. As an extension to Nelson's model, metacognition could also take the perspective of a *top-down* process of self-instructions for the control over and regulation of task performance (Veenman, 2006). Apart from being triggered by task errors, the latter top-down process can also be activated as an acquired program of self-instructions whenever the learner is faced with performing a task the learner is familiar with to a certain extent. Either the task has been practiced before or the task resembles another familiar task. Such a program of self-instructions could be represented by a production system of condition-action rules (Anderson, 1996; Anderson & Schunn, 2000; Butler & Winne, 1995):

> IF you encounter a task, THEN look for the task assignment and take notice of it;
> IF you have an idea about the task assignment, THEN try to dig up from memory as much as you know about the subject matter;
> IF you understand the task assignment, THEN formulate the goal to be achieved;
> IF you have set your goal, THEN design an action plan for attaining that goal;
> IF you have an action plan, THEN follow that plan in a systematical way; or
> IF you are executing your action plan, THEN keep a close watch on what you are doing and detect any anomalies.
>
> (Veenman, 2006)

This production system embodies a set of self-induced metacognitive instructions to the cognitive system. Thus, in line with Nelson's model, self-instructions from the meta-level evoke various cognitive activities at the object level. The resulting cognitive activities can be very general (e.g., sorting out relevant information), or rather specific (e.g., looking for particular keywords that point to a certain theory), depending on the available prior knowledge.

How do humans acquire such a production system of metacognitive self-instructions? According to ACT-R theory (Anderson, 1996), skill acquisition passes through three successive stages. In the cognitive stage, *declarative* knowledge of condition and actions is interpreted and arranged in order to allow for a verbal description of a procedure (What to do, When, Why, and How; Veenman et al., 2006). The execution of the procedure progresses slowly because all activity needs to be consciously performed step-by-step, while being prone to error. During the acquisition of metacognitive skills at this stage, metacognitive knowledge, in particular conditional knowledge, is incorporated in a verbal description of the procedure. In fact, conditional knowledge contains information about the *Why* and *When* (Schraw, Crippen, & Hartley, 2006), defining the IF-side of a production rule. The *What* and *How* constitute the Then-side of a production rule. The conscious execution of the procedure at this stage explains why the initial acquisition of metacognitive skills through instruction or training requires extra effort, which may initially interfere with cognitive performance (Veenman et al., 2006).

In the second, associative stage, verbal descriptions of the procedure are transformed into a procedural representation through compilation. Errors in the procedure are eliminated, separate procedures are assembled into an organized set through composition, and references to declarative knowledge are removed through proceduralization. Consequently, the execution of procedures becomes faster and more accurate, requiring less effort.

Finally, in the autonomous stage, the execution of productions is fine-tuned and automated. Many metacognitive skills will never reach this stage, as they need to be consciously applied and tuned to the task at hand (Nelson, 1996). Monitoring processes, however, may run in the background until an error or anomaly is detected (Brown, 1987; Butler & Winne, 1995; Reder & Schunn, 1996). In the same vein, elements of the planning process may become automated, thus requiring less deliberate and conscious activity until an obstacle prevents a plan from being executed (Pressley, Borkowski, & Schneider, 1989). This is essentially the difference between a metacognitive strategy, which is always consciously executed, and a metacognitive skill that may be partly automated.

It is important to acknowledge that both the metacognitive self-instructions and the cognitive processes that are involved in the execution of those instructions are part of the same cognitive system. Metacognitive and cognitive activities, however, serve different goals and functions within the cognitive system (Brown, 1987; Butler, 1998; Veenman et al., 2006). Cognitive activities are needed for the *execution* of task-related processes on the object level, whereas metacognitive activity represents the *executive* function on the meta-level for regulating cognitive activity. Thus, metacognitive self-instructions are much like a general who cannot win a war without cognitive soldiers. On the other hand, an unorganized army will not succeed either. It is my experience from studying many thinking-aloud protocols that successful learners easily shift from a cognitive performance mode to a metacognitive self-instruction mode, and vice versa.

CURRENT TRENDS AND ISSUES

Assessment of Metacognitive Skills

In the assessment of metacognitive skills a distinction is made between off-line and on-line methods (Veenman et al., 2006). Off-line methods refer to questionnaires (e.g., MSLQ, Pintrich & De Groot, 1990; MAI, Schraw & Dennison, 1994) and interviews (Zimmerman & Martinez-Pons, 1990) that are administered to the learner either prior or retrospective to task performance. Off-line methods address the learner with questions about his/her (frequency of) strategy use and skill application. On-line methods, on the other hand, pertain to assessments during actual task performance, such as observations (Whitebread et al., 2009), think-aloud protocols (Azevedo, Greene, & Moos, 2007; Pressley & Afflerbach, 1995), and computer log-file registrations (Hadwin, Nesbit, Jamieson-Noel, Code, & Winne, 2007; Veenman et al., 2004). Recordings of the learner's behavior are then coded according to a standardized coding system. The essential difference between off-line and on-line methods is that off-line measures merely rely on self-reports from the learner, whereas on-line measures concern the coding of learner behavior on externally defined criteria.

Off-line methods have their pros and cons. Questionnaires are easy to administer in large groups, whereas interviews need to be administered on an individual basis, which is time-consuming. Off-line self-reports of metacognitive skills suffer from validity problems. The first problem relates to the nature of self-reports as response to questionnaires or interviews. In order to answer questions about the relative frequency of certain activities ("How often do/did you . . .?"), learners have to compare themselves to others (peers, teachers, parents). The individual reference point chosen, however, may vary from one learner to the other, or even within a particular learner from one question to the other (Prins, Busato, Elshout, & Hamaker, 1998; Veenman, Prins, & Verheij, 2003). Variation in the choice of reference points among learners may yield disparate data. Moreover, some learners may be prone to give socially desirable answers.

The second validity problem concerns the off-line nature of self-reports. While answering questions, learners have to consult their memory and reconstruct their earlier performance. This reconstruction process might suffer from memory failure and distortions (Ericsson & Simon, 1993; Nisbett & Wilson, 1977). In retrospective assessment, reconstructive interpretations may be elicited along with, or instead of correct recollections. Learners not only know more than they tell, they sometimes "tell more than [they] can know" (Nisbett & Wilson, 1977, p. 247). These memory problems can be partially relieved by means of stimulated recall. Learners are then prompted to reflect on their thoughts and behavior, while watching a video recording of their task performance (Artzt & Armour-Thomas, 1992; Peterson, Swing, Braverman, & Buss, 1982). Although supporting retrospective reconstruction, stimulated recall may still yield incomplete memory traces. Memory problems get even worse for off-line assessments administered prior to, or entirely separate from actual performance, as learners have to base their answers on earlier experiences in the past. In conclusion, off-line self-reports may not accurately reflect the learner's metacognitive skills.

On-line assessments of the learner's actual metacognitive behavior have their own merits and limitations. The think-aloud method differs from off-line self-reports or introspection in that learners are merely verbalizing their on-going thoughts during task performance. Learners do not reconstruct or interpret their thought processes. Merely verbalizing of one's thoughts does not interfere with thought processes in general (Ericsson & Simon, 1993) or, more specifically, with ongoing regulatory processes (Bannert & Mengelkamp, 2008; Veenman, Elshout, & Groen, 1993). Thinking aloud, however, may slightly slow down those processes. Nevertheless, the think-aloud method is neither suited for assessing highly automated processes (e.g., in expert performance), nor for processes that are extremely difficult or effortful. In these cases, learners fall silent and protocols are likely to be incomplete. This is referred to as the tip-of-the-iceberg phenomenon (Ericsson & Simon, 1993).

The think-aloud method requires learners to have an adequate level of verbal proficiency in order to avoid interference of the second, verbalization task with the target task (Cavanaugh & Perlmutter, 1982; Garner, 1988; Thorpe & Satterly, 1990). For instance, reading protocols of young children are likely to be incomplete or even distorted, because basic reading processes occupy all working memory available. Consequently, assessment of metacognition in younger, less verbally fluent children often relies on observational methods (Alexander et al., 1995; Whitebread et al., 2009). Observations only yield quantitative estimates of overt behavior, of which the metacognitive nature has to be inferred by the observers. Unless combined with thinking aloud, observations do not give access to mental processes underlying behavior. For instance, recalculation of a math problem may be due to different reasons. Either recalculation is a manifestation of metacognitive evaluation, or the outcome of an earlier calculation was not written down and forgotten (i.e., metacognitively sloppy). Observers need to scrutinize the learner's behavior in order to detect such subtle differences. Hence, coding from videotapes is preferred over direct on-line observations. Observation and think-aloud methods are both labor-intensive as they are administered on an individual basis, and the videotapes or transcribed protocols have to be coded by multiple judges.

More recently, researchers have advanced the on-line registration of metacognitive activities in computer logfiles (Hadwin et al., 2007; Kunz, Drewniak, & Schott, 1992; Veenman et al., 1993, 2004). Obviously, the task should lend itself to a computerized version, or otherwise it would impair the ecological validity of assessments. For instance, studying text from a computer screen may put demands on the learner, different from studying a hard copy. Logfile registration is restricted to concrete, covert behavior, without the learner's metacognitive deliberations. Prior to logfile registration, one has to select a restricted set of relevant metacognitive activities on rational grounds and to validate this potential set of activities against other on-line measures (Veenman, 2007). Validation is necessary because the coding of learner activities is automated during task performance. The advantage of logfile registration, however, is that the method in itself is minimally intrusive, and that it can be administered to large groups at the same time (Dinsmore et al., 2008; Veenman et al., 2006). In conclusion, the quality of on-line assessment depends on the adequacy of the coding system.

Studies with multi-method designs have shown that off-line measures hardly correspond to on-line measures (Veenman, 2005). In a study of Veenman et al. (2003) the Inventory Learning Styles questionnaire (ILS) was administered to 30 students from a technical university, prior to studying a text about earth sciences while thinking aloud. The Self-Regulation scale from the ILS correlated .22 with think-aloud measures of activities corresponding to the ILS scale. Cromley and Azevedo (2006) compared another off-line self-report measure, the Metacognitive Awareness of Reading Strategies Inventory (MARSI), with think-aloud measures of studying a text about the Civil War, and with an on-line test where respondents had to apply reading strategies to text fragments. The strategies involved in all three measures were the activation of prior knowledge, generating hypotheses, self-questioning, summarizing, and making inferences. MARSI scores of 30 secondary-school students correlated −.02 with scores obtained from the think-aloud protocols, and .18 with scores from the on-line questionnaire.

In a study with 66 undergraduates studying an electronic text on meteorology, Winne and Jamieson-Noel (2002) found that retrospective self-reports of students overestimated their actual strategy use, which was assessed with logfile registrations of goal setting, planning, and reviewing activities in the electronic environment. Moreover, self-reports were poorly calibrated with the logfile measures. In the same vein, Hadwin et al. (2007) showed that self-reports on MSLQ items were not well calibrated with logfile traces of eight students studying an electronic text on educational psychology. On the average, MSLQ items only had 27% in common with specific activities in the logfile traces that pertained to those items.

From a study with 48 graduate students who studied a hypertext on operant conditioning, Bannert and Mengelkamp (2008) concluded that think-aloud measures of orientation, planning, and monitoring were not significantly correlated to retrospective self-reports of the same activities. So far, the evidence is limited to text studying. Veenman and Van Cleef (2007) administered the MSLQ and ILS to 30 secondary-school students, prior to mathematical problem solving while thinking aloud. The Cognitive Strategy Use and Self-Regulation scales from the MSLQ and the Self-regulation scale from the ILS correlated .11 on the average with measures for metacognitive skillfulness, rated from think-aloud protocols. As one could argue, the MSLQ and ILS are more appropriate to text-studying tasks, a retrospective questionnaire was administered immediately after solving the math problems. Scores on this retrospective questionnaire correlated .28 with protocol measures, although both instruments addressed the same broad set of metacognitive skills for problem solving in mathematics. Apparently, learners do not actually do what they say they will do, nor do they recollect accurately what they have done.

Moreover, correlations among off-line measures are often low to moderate (Artelt, 2000; Peterson et al., 1982; Sperling, Howard, Miller, & Murphy, 2002; Veenman, 2005), whereas correlations among on-line measures usually are moderate to high (Cromley & Azevedo, 2006; Veenman, 2005). Apparently, off-line measures yield diverging results, while on-line measures converge in their assessments of metacognitive skills. Finally, off-line and on-line measures differ with respect to their external validity for learning performance. External validity is an important issue as metacognitive skills are expected to predict learning performance according to metacognition theory (Veenman, 2007). On the average, off-line measures are poor predictors of learning outcomes, relative to on-line measures (Bannert & Mengelkamp, 2008; Cromley & Azevedo, 2006; Sperling et al., 2002). In a review study, Veenman (2005) found that correlations with learning performance range from slightly negative to .36 for off-line measures, and from .45 to .90 for on-line measures.

What is there to be learned from this overview of assessment methods? It appears that off-line methods do not adequately assess learners' metacognitive skills. Perhaps, off-line measures capture elements of metacognitive knowledge or metacognitive conditional knowledge, but that remains to be ascertained in further research. As stated, even though learners may report to acknowledge the relevance of using certain metacognitive skills, this does not imply that learners have those skills on an operational level at their disposal, or that they will actually apply those skills when appropriate. Someone can tell you perfectly well how to prepare a meal, but that does not necessarily make this person a perfect cook. With on-line methods, the proof of the pudding is in the eating. On-line measures are based on actual learner behavior. They show concurrent validity with other on-line measures, and they substantially predict learning outcomes. For these reasons, the utility of off-line methods for the assessment of metacognitive skills should be reconsidered (cf. Dinsmore et al., 2008) and, for the time being, on-line methods should be preferred over off-line methods.

Instruction and Training of Metacognitive Skills

There are three principles fundamental to effective instruction of metacognitive skills: (1) the synthesis position; (2) informed training; and (3) prolonged instruction (Veenman et al., 2006). According to the *synthesis position* (Volet, 1991), metacognitive instruction should be embedded in the context of the task at hand in order to relate the execution of metacognitive skills to specific task demands. In fact, embedded instruction will enable the learner to connect task-specific conditional knowledge of which skill to apply when (the IF-side) to the procedural knowledge of how the skill is applied in the context of the task (the THEN-side of production rules).

The second principle is *informed instruction* (Campione, Brown, & Ferrara, 1982). Learners should be informed about the benefit of applying metacognitive skills in order to make them exert the initial extra effort. When learners do not spontaneously utilize metacognitive skills, the execution of the instructed skills initially requires effort and occupies working-memory space. This may result in cognitive overload, especially if the task at hand is demanding. Learners may be inclined to abandon the instructed skills, unless they appreciate why the application of metacognitive skills facilitates task execution.

Finally, the third principle refers to *prolonged instruction*. Instruction and training should be stretched over time, thus allowing for the formation of production rules and ensuring smooth and maintained application of metacognitive skills. Opinions differ about the preferred length of instruction. The instruction period may be relatively short for mastering a limited set of metacognitive skills (Kramarski & Mevarech, 2003; Veenman, Kok, & Blöte, 2005). For establishing enduring effects on spontaneous metacognitive functioning, however, the instruction period may cover a year or more, especially for learners with a learning disability (Mettes et al., 1981; Pressley & Gaskin, 2006). Any successful instructional program abides with these three principles.

Veenman (1998) refers to these principles as the WWW&H rule for complete instruction of metacognitive skills, meaning that learners should be instructed, modeled and trained *when* to apply *what* skill, *why* and *how* in the context of a task. Not all learners, however, are alike in their need for instruction. Learners who exhibit a poor level of metacognitive skillfulness may suffer from either an availability deficiency or a production deficiency (Brown & DeLoache, 1978; Flavell, 1976; Mayer, 1992; Veenman et al., 2005). Learners with an availability deficiency do not have metacognitive skills at their disposal. For instance, they do not know how to plan or monitor their actions.

Cues or prompts that merely remind these learners of applying metacognitive skills during task performance neither affect their metacognitive behavior, nor result in enhanced learning performance (Veenman, Kerseboom, & Imthorn, 2000). Learners with an availability deficiency need to receive complete instruction and training of metacognitive skills from scratch. Learners with a production deficiency, on the other hand, have metacognitive skills at their disposal but they do not spontaneously execute the available skills for some reason. For instance, they do not know when to plan or monitor their actions, they do not recognize the relevance of those skills for a particular task, or test anxiety prevents them from applying those skills (Veenman et al., 2000). Metacognitive cues may help these learners to overcome their production deficiency, reminding them of what to do when during task performance (Connor, 2007; Muth, 1991; Veenman et al., 2000, 2005). Production-deficient learners need not be fully instructed and trained in how to apply those skills.

For the implementation of metacognitive instruction often step-by-step action plans are used. Such a step-by-step plan contains a series of questions or keywords, addressing metacognitive actions that should be undertaken in the course of task performance. Typically, activities of task analysis, activating prior knowledge, goal setting, and planning are promoted at the onset of task performance. Orderly execution of plans, monitoring, and note taking are encouraged during task performance, while evaluation, recapitulation, reflection are endorsed at the end of task performance. As these descriptions of activities are rather abstract to learners, they need to be translated into concrete activities that apply to the task at hand. For instance, goal setting and planning require different concrete activities for problem-solving and text-studying tasks. The application of such a concrete step-by-step plan is explained, modeled, and practiced with the learner according to the principles delineated above.

One of the first successful step-by-step plans was the Systematical Approach to Problem solving in physics (Mettes et al., 1981), although metacognition was not explicitly referred to at the time. SAP instruction provided students with an orderly sequence of problem solving activities, which sequence was broken down into three successive stages of orientation, execution, and evaluation. During orientation, students carefully read the problem, made a drawing or scheme of the problem including the relevant data and the unknown, used prior knowledge to determine whether it was a known problem, used multiple strategies to convert a complex problem to a known problem, and estimated the outcome. In the execution phase standard operations were carried out, of which the outcome was checked in the evaluation phase against the problem statement and the earlier estimation. Throughout SAP, checks were built in, which could lead to backtracking. After implementation of SAP in an existing thermodynamics course at a technical university, average course grades went up from 5.8 to 6.8 (on a 10-point scale).

IMPROVE (Kramarski & Mevarech, 2003; Mevarech & Fridkin, 2006) is a more recent program for teaching learners to address themselves with metacognitive questions during problem solving in mathematics. These self-questions pertain to understanding the nature of the problem, relating the problem to prior knowledge, planning solution steps, and evaluating outcomes. In a study by Mevarech and Fridkin (2006) pre-college students, who failed on a mathematical entry test for university, followed a 50-hrs course on mathematical functions. The group receiving the IMPROVE training significantly enhanced their mathematical knowledge and reasoning from pretest to posttest with 18% on the average, whereas the control group did not improve despite the content instruction. Kramarski and Mevarech (2003) further showed that IMPROVE training in a cooperative setting of small workgroups yielded better mathematics results, relative to individualized IMPROVE training.

Veenman et al. (2005) asked 12–13-year-old secondary-school students to solve a series of mathematical word problems without support and, subsequently, another series with metacognitive cueing. Cues prompted students to set goals, to select relevant data, to plan problem-solving steps, to monitor progress, to check outcomes, and to draw conclusions related to the problem statement. Students displayed significantly better metacognitive skills and mathematics performance on cued problems, relative to non-cued problems, even after correction for a learning curve over the two series of problems.

In a study by Azevedo et al. (2007), undergraduate students learned about the blood circulatory system with hypermedia. Half of them received metacognitive prompts from a human tutor who encouraged them to set goals, to activate prior knowledge, to plan time and effort, to monitor comprehension and progression towards the learning goals, and to apply strategies such as summarizing, hypothesizing, and drawing diagrams. Compared to the control group without prompts, the prompted group employed more self-regulatory activities and showed higher gains in content knowledge from pretest to posttest. The prompted group also attained a higher level of sophistication in their mental model of the circulatory system.

What these studies have in common is that they promoted proper metacognitive activities at the right time in the context of a given task. With the introduction of computers in education, computer programs have also been used for metacognitive instruction during task performance (Winters, Greene, & Costich, 2008). Most computer programs provide a fixed array of metacognitive scaffolds, much like the step-by-step plans (e.g., Kapa, 2001; Kramarski & Hirsch, 2003; Manlove, Lazonder, & de Jong, 2007; Teong, 2003; Veenman, Elshout, & Busato, 1994). Scarcely out of the egg are attempts to provide scaffolds adapted to the learner's needs through an intelligent tutoring system, so far with mixed results (Puntambekar & Stylianou, 2005; Roll, Aleven, McLaren, & Koedinger, 2007).

Teachers can also provide for metacognitive instruction in natural classroom settings. Teachers, however, tend to give implicit instruction rather than explicit instruction. That is, they spontaneously use examples of metacognitive activity in their lessons, but they are not inclined to explain the metacognitive nature of these activities and the benefit of using these activities. After observing 17 lessons of various teachers, Veenman, de Haan, and Dignath (2009) concluded that metacognitive instruction was given, but that 96% concerned implicit instruction and only 4% was explicit. By doing so, teachers unintentionally violate the principle of informed instruction. There are, however, successful programs for classroom settings (Dignath & Büttner, 2008; Stoeger & Ziegler, 2008; Zohar & Ben-David, 2008). The metacognitive scaffolding of peer-questioning in small-group online discussions (Choi, Land, & Turgeon, 2005) is reminiscent of reciprocal teaching (Brown & Palincsar, 1987).

More recently, Pressley and Gaskins (2006; Pressley, Gaskins, Solic, & Collins, 2006) described the teaching method of a special Benchmark school for students with a very low reading ability, where teachers of all school disciplines address the students with a broad array of metacognitive reading instructions throughout the day. Teachers incessantly explain, model, and prompt the use of comprehension strategies, such as determining the purpose for reading, grasping the theme and main ideas of the text, making predictions about further developments in the text, relating new information to prior knowledge, monitoring understanding through self-questioning, resolving incomprehension by re-reading or looking for additional information sources, summarizing the text, and reviewing the reading process. Instruction explicitly addresses when and how strategies are to be used. After spending 4 to 8 years at Benchmark school, students typically return to regular education with "scores in the upper end of the distribution of [reading] achievement for same-age students" (Pressley & Gaskins, 2006, p. 103).

Many studies on the effectiveness of metacognitive instruction fall short of a complete design. Either they lack a measure for learning outcomes (Winters et al., 2008), or they fail to report the effects of instruction on the actual metacognitive behavior (Veenman, 2007). In order to account for the effectiveness of metacognitive instruction, a causal chain of instruction leading to improved metacognitive behavior and, thus, leading to better learning outcomes should be established. When the mediating metacognitive behavior is not assessed, attribution of instructional effects on learning outcomes to various confounding variables cannot be excluded, such as extended time-on-task due to compliance with the instructions or enhanced motivation due to extra attention. When learning outcomes are not assessed, on the other hand, it remains unclear whether the intended metacognitive behavior actually supports the learning process. As discussed, metacognitive instruction might sometimes have detrimental effects on learning performance, either because initial compliance with instruction may yield a temporary cognitive overload, or simply because instruction may divert the learner's attention from the task at hand (Puntambekar & Stylianou, 2005).

PRACTICAL IMPLICATIONS

First, we should ask what the benefit is of the present theoretical framework for meta-cognitive skills. Obviously, Nelson's model helps us to understand how learners react to errors and anomalies in task performance. Errors trigger monitoring processes, which in turn activate the selection of control processes for dealing with errors. The present extension of Nelson's model with a top-down program of self-instructions, appreciates that learners are not passively waiting for an error or anomaly to occur. They actively employ their acquired repertoire of metacognitive skills whenever appropriate. Moreover, linking metacognitive self-instructions to Anderson's ACT-R theory provides us with a framework for the acquisition and instruction of metacognitive skills. Complete metacognitive instruction should address the What, When, Why and How of metacognitive skills (WWW&H).

The cognitive phase of metacognitive-skill acquisition initially draws on declarative conditional knowledge of WWW&H. Metacognitive knowledge, however, is fallible, which raises two questions. The first question pertains to the issue of how to assess conditional knowledge. Earlier the limitations of off-line methods have been discussed. For instance, the MAI (Schraw & Dennison, 1994) has a separate subscale for assessing conditional knowledge. The score on the MAI subscale, however, does not provide us with sufficient and sufficiently correct information for entry into the cognitive phase of skill acquisition. Therefore, the question should be rephrased to how it can be determined whether the learner's conditional knowledge is correct and sufficient enough for the acquisition of a specific metacognitive skill?

The second question is related to the first one: How can we remedy incorrect or incomplete conditional knowledge *upon* entry into the cognitive stage? In fact, ACT-R (Anderson, 1996; Anderson & Schunn, 2000) has a feedback loop for repairing flawed skills. Once a skill has been proceduralized, however, the correction of errors requires the cumbersome process of skill decompilation, which means that the tags of declarative knowledge need to be reinstated. Learners spontaneously acquiring metacognitive skills cannot but rely on this feedback loop, but to learners receiving metacognitive instruction this feedback loop comes a day after the fair. They need to be provided with correct conditional knowledge from the start. The answer to both questions lies in the responsiveness of instructors and teachers. They have to set the example in an early stage of skill acquisition, and they have to do so explicitly. In order to remedy incorrect or incomplete conditional knowledge during the cognitive stage, they have to be sensitive of its presence in learners.

Earlier the general nature of metacognitive skills was discussed. The implication is that metacognitive instruction preferably should be given by all teachers from all school disciplines simultaneously in order to achieve transfer across tasks and domains (Veenman et al., 2004). The Benchmark school of Pressley and Gaskins (2006) shows what such a synchronized teaching program may achieve. Certainly, it requires teacher commitment and administrative coordination, but the long-term results are precious.

FUTURE DIRECTIONS

Most studies on metacognitive instruction or training investigate the effects of a relatively short instruction on one single task, only measuring near transfer if any. Given the general nature of metacognitive skills, we are awaiting research that establishes to what extent prolonged metacognitive training on one task might transfer to metacognitive behavior on another task, and under what conditions (Salomon & Perkins, 1989). Adequate identification of the causal pathways of instructional effects would then require the assessment of metacognitive skills and learning performance for both tasks.

Veenman et al. (2006) and, more recently, Dinsmore et al. (2008) have pleaded in favor of using multi-method designs for the assessment of metacognitive skills. During the past decade a number of multi-method studies has been carried out and results have been overly negative for off-line assessment methods. Nevertheless, off-line methods are still predominantly used for the assessment of metacognitive skills (or strategy use in terms of SRL). In a review of about 200 studies, Dinsmore et al. (2008) established that for the assessment of metacognition 37% relied on off-line measures (24% self-reports and 13% interviews), while for the assessment of SRL 68% relied on off-line measures (59% self-reports and 9% interviews). There is still a world to win for multi-method designs.

Neuropsychological research has shown that the development of the pre-frontal lobe in the brain is related to an increase of executive functioning during childhood and adolescence (Crone, Donohue, Honomichl, Wendelken, & Bunge, 2006). Executive functions, such as planning processes and inhibitory processes, are closely related to metacognitive skills. Earlier this kind of research had to rely on patients with brain damage or dementia (Pinon, Allain, Kefi, Dubas, & Le Gall, 2005), but now researchers can *in vivo* look into the brain of normally functioning people. We are far from connecting specific cognitive processes to specific brain activities, as the disparity between fine-grained cognitive processes and more global brain activity is still huge. Therefore, it is an understatement to say that it will take a while before neuropsychological methods will be available for the assessment of metacognitive skills as a diagnostic instrument. Although this kind of research is still in its infancy, we should not ignore its potential role in the future.

REFERENCES

Alexander, J. M., Carr, M., & Schwanenflugel, P. J. (1995). Development of metacognition in gifted children: Directions for future research. *Developmental Review, 15*, 1–37.

Alexander, P. A., & Jetton, T. L. (2000). Learning from text: A multidimensional and developmental perspective. In M. L. Kamil, P. B. Mosenthal, P. D. Pearson, & R. Barr (Eds.), *Handbook of reading research* (Vol.III, pp. 285–310). Mahwah, NJ: Erlbaum.

Anderson, J. R. (1996). *The architecture of cognition*. Mahwah, NJ: Erlbaum.

Anderson, J. R., & Schunn, C. D. (2000). Implications of the ACT-R learning theory: No magic bullets. In R. Glaser (Ed.), *Advances in instructional psychology* (Vol. 5, pp. 1–33). Mahwah, NJ: Erlbaum.

Annevirta, T., & Vauras, M. (2006). Developmental changes of metacognitive skill in elementary school children. *Journal of Experimental Education, 74*, 197–225.

Artelt, C. (2000). Wie prädiktiv sind retrospektive Selbstberichte über den Gebrauch von Lernstrategien für strategisches Lernen? *German Journal of Educational Psychology, 14*, 72–84.

Artzt, A. F., & Armour-Thomas, E. (1992). Development of a cognitive-metacognitive framework for protocol analysis of mathematical problem solving in small groups. *Cognition and Instruction, 9*, 137–175.

Azevedo, R., Greene, J. A., & Moos, D. C. (2007). The effect of a human agent's external regulation upon college students' hypermedia learning. *Metacognition and Learning, 2*, 67–87.

Bannert, M., & Mengelkamp, C. (2008). Assessment of metacognitive skills by means of instruction to think aloud and reflect when prompted. Does the verbalization method affect learning? *Metacognition and Learning, 3*, 39–58.

Bartsch, K., & Estes, D. (1996). Individual differences in children's developing theory of mind and implications for metacognition. *Learning and Individual Differences, 8*, 281–304.

Berk, L. E. (2003). *Child development*. Boston: Pearson Education.

Blöte, A. W., Otterloo, S. G. van, Stevenson, C. E., & Veenman, M. V. J. (2004). Discovery and maintenance of the many-to-one counting strategy in 4-year-olds: A microgenetic study. *British Journal of Developmental Psychology, 22*, 83–102.

Brown, A. (1987). Metacognition, executive control, self-regulation, and other more mysterious mechanisms. In F. E. Weinert, & R. H. Kluwe (Eds.), *Metacognition, motivation and understanding* (pp. 65–116). Hillsdale, NJ: Erlbaum.

Brown, A. L., & DeLoache, J. S. (1978). Skills, plans, and self-regulation. In R. S. Siegel (Ed.), *Children's thinking: What develops?* (pp. 3–35). Hillsdale, NJ: Erlbaum.

Brown, A. L., & Palincsar, A. S. (1987). Reciprocal teaching of comprehension skills: a natural history of one program for enhancing learning. In J. D. Day, & J. G. Borkowski (Eds.). *Intelligence and exceptionality: New directions for theory, assessment, and instructional practices* (pp. 81–131). Norwood, NJ: Ablex.

Butler, D. L. (1998). Metacognition and learning disabilities. In B. Y. L. Wong (Ed.), *Learning about learning disabilities* (2nd ed., pp. 277–307). San Diego: Academic Press.

Butler, D. L., & Winne, P. H. (1995). Feedback and self-regulated learning: A theoretical synthesis. *Review of Educational Research, 65*, 245–281.

Campione, J. C., Brown, A. L., & Ferrara, R. A. (1982). Mental retardation and intelligence. In R. J. Sternberg (Ed.), *Handbook of human intelligence* (pp. 392–490). Cambridge: Cambridge University Press.

Cavanaugh, J. C., & Perlmutter, M. (1982). Metamemory: A critical review. *Child Development, 53*, 11–28.

Choi, I., Land, S. M., & Turgeon, A. J. (2005). Scaffolding peer-questioning strategies to facilitate metacognition during online small group discussion. *Instructional Science, 33*, 483–511.

Connor, L. N. (2007). Cueing metacognition to improve researching and essay writing in a final year high school biology class. *Research in Science Education, 37*, 1–16.

Cromley, J. G., & Azevedo, R. (2006). Self-report of reading comprehension strategies: What are we measuring? *Metacognition and Learning, 1*, 229–247.

Crone, E. A., Donohue, S. E., Honomichl, R., Wendelken, C., & Bunge, S. A. (2006). Brain regions mediating flexible rule use during development. *Journal of Neuroscience, 26*, 11239–11247.

Demetriou, A., & Efklides, A. (1990). The objective and subjective structure of problem-solving abilities: Metacognitive awareness from early adolescence to middle age. In H. Mandl, E. de Corte, S. N. Bennett, & H. F. Friedrich (Eds.), *Learning and instruction in an international context*. Vol. 2.1. *Social and cognitive aspects of learning and instruction* (pp. 161–179). Oxford: Pergamon.

Dignath, C., & Büttner, G. (2008). Components of fostering self-regulated learning among students. A meta-analysis on intervention studies at primary and secondary school level. *Metacognition and Learning, 3*, 231–264.

Dinsmore, D. L., Alexander, P. A., & Loughlin, S. M. (2008). Focusing the conceptual lens on metacognition, self-regulation, and self-regulated learning. *Educational Psychology Review, 20*, 391–409.

Dunlosky, J. (1998). Epilogue. Linking metacognitive theories to education. In D. J. Hacker, J. Dunlosky, & A. C. Graesser (eds.), *Metacognition in educational theory and practice* (pp. 367–381). Mahwah, NJ: Erlbaum.

Efklides, A. (2006). Metacognition and affect: What can metacognitive experiences tell us about the learning process? *Educational Research Review, 1*, 3–14.

Elshout, J. J. (1996). Architecture of cognition. In E. de Corte, & F. E. Weinert (Eds.), *International encyclopedia of developmental and instructional psychology* (pp. 369–372). Oxford: Pergamon.

Ericsson, K. A., & Simon, H. A. (1993). *Protocol analysis*. Cambridge, MA: MIT Press.

Flavell, J. H. (1970). Developmental studies of mediated memory. In H. W. Reese, & L. P. Lipsitt (Eds.), *Advances in child development and behavior* (Vol. 5, pp. 181–211). New York: Academic Press.

Flavell, J. H. (1976). Metacognitive aspects of problem solving. In L. B. Resnick (Ed.), *The nature of intelligence* (pp. 231–235). Hillsdale, NJ: Erlbaum.

Flavell, J. H. (1979). Metacognition and cognitive monitoring: A new area of cognitive-developmental inquiry. *American Psychologist, 34*, 906–911.

Flavell, J. H. (1992). Perspectives on perspective taking. In H. Beilin, & P. Pufall (Eds.), *Piaget's theory: Prospects and possibilities* (pp. 107–141). Hillsdale, NJ: Erlbaum.

Flavell, J. H. (2004). Theory-of-Mind development: Retrospect and prospect. *Merrill-Palmer Quarterly, 50*, 274–290.

Flavell, J. H., & Wellman, H. M. (1977). Metamemory. In R. V. Kail, & J. W. Hagen (Eds.), *Perspectives on the development of memory and cognition* (pp. 3–33). Hillsdale, NJ: Erlbaum.

Fox, E., & Riconscente, M. (2008). Metacognition and self-regulation in James, Piaget, and Vygotsky. *Educational Psychology Review, 20*, 373–389.

Garner, R. (1988). Verbal-report data on cognitive and metacognitive strategies. In C. E. Weinstein, E. T. Goetz, & P. A. Alexander (Eds.), *Learning and study strategies: Issues in assessment, instruction, and evaluation* (pp. 63–76). San Diego: Academic Press.

Glaser, R., Schauble, L., Raghavan, K., & Zeitz, C. (1992). Scientific reasoning across different domains. In E. de

Corte, M. C. Linn, H. Mandl, & L. Verschaffel (Eds.), *Computer-based learning environments and problem solving* (NATO ASI series F, Vol. 84, pp. 345–371). Heidelberg: Springer Verlag.

Hadwin, A. F., Nesbit, J. C., Jamieson-Noel, D., Code, J., & Winne, P. H. (2007). Examining trace data to explore self-regulated learning. *Metacognition and Learning, 2,* 107–124.

Inhelder, B., & Piaget, J. (1958). *The growth of logical thinking from childhood to adolescence.* London: Routledge & Kegan Paul.

Istomina, Z. M. (1975). The development of voluntary memory in children of preschool age. *Soviet Psychology, 13,* 5–64.

Kapa, E. (2001). A metacognitive support during the process of problem solving in a computerized environment. *Educational Studies in Mathematics, 47,* 317–336.

Kluwe, R. H. (1987). Executive decisions and regulation of problem solving behavior. In F. E. Weinert, & R. H. Kluwe (Eds.), *Metacognition, motivation, and understanding* (pp. 31–64). Hillsdale, NJ: Erlbaum.

Kramarski, B., & Hirsch, C. (2003). Using computer algebra systems in mathematical classrooms. *Journal of Computer Assisted Learning, 19,* 35–45.

Kramarski, B., & Mevarech, Z. R. (2003). Enhancing mathematical reasoning in the classroom: The effects of cooperative learning and metacognitive training. *American Educational Research Journal, 40,* 281–310.

Kuhn, D. (1999). Metacognitive development. In L. Balter, & C. S. Tamis-LeMonda (Eds.), *Child psychology: A handbook of contemporary issues* (pp. 259–286). Philadelphia. PA: Psychology Press.

Kunz, G. C., Drewniak, U., & Schott, F. (1992). On-line and off-line assessment of self-regulation in learning from instructional text. *Learning and Instruction, 2,* 287–301.

Larkin, S. (2006). Collaborative group work and individual development of metacognition in the early years. *Research in Science Education, 36,* 7–27.

Lockl, K., & Schneider, W. (2006). Precursors of metamemory in young children: The role of theory of mind and metacognitive vocabulary. *Metacognition and Learning, 1,* 15–31.

Manlove, S., Lazonder, A. W., & De Jong, T. (2007). Software scaffolds to promote regulation during scientific inquiry learning. *Metacognition and Learning, 2,* 141–155.

Mayer, R. E. (1992). *Thinking, problem solving, cognition.* New York: Freeman.

Meijer, J., Veenman, M. V. J., & van Hout-Wolters, B. H. A. M. (2006). Metacognitive activities in text-studying and problem-solving: Development of a taxonomy. *Educational Research and Evaluation, 12,* 209–237.

Mettes, C. T. C. W., Pilot, A., & Roossink, H. J. (1981). Linking factual and procedural knowledge in solving science problems: A case study in a thermodynamics course. *Instructional Science, 10,* 333–361.

Mevarech, Z., & Fridkin, S. (2006). The effects of IMPROVE on mathematical knowledge, mathematical reasoning and meta-cognition. *Metacognition and Learning, 1,* 85–97.

Muth, K. D. (1991). Effects of cuing on middle-school students' performance on arithmetic word problems containing extraneous information. *Journal of Educational Psychology, 83,* 173–174.

Nelson, T. O. (1996). Consciousness and metacognition. *American Psychologist, 51,* 102–116.

Nelson, T. O. (1999). Cognition versus metacognition. In R. J. Sternberg (Ed.), *The nature of cognition* (pp. 625–641). Cambridge, MA: MIT Press.

Nelson, T. O., & Narens, L. (1990). Metamemory: A theoretical framework and new findings. In G. Bower (Ed.), *The psychology of learning and motivation* (pp. 125–173). New York: Academic Press.

Nisbett, R. E., & Wilson, T. D. (1977). Telling more than we know: Verbal reports on mental processes. *Psychological Review, 84,* 231–259.

Peterson, P. L., Swing, S. R., Braverman, M. T., & Buss, R. (1982). Students' aptitudes and their reports of cognitive processes during direct instruction. *Journal of Educational Psychology, 74,* 535–547.

Pinon, K, Allain, P., Kefi, M. Z., Dubas, F., & Le Gall, D. (2005). Monitoring processes and metamemory experience in patients with dysexecutive syndrome. *Brain and Cognition, 57,* 185–188.

Pintrich, P. R., & De Groot, E. V. (1990). Motivational and self-regulated leaning components of classroom academic performance. *Journal of Educational Psychology, 82,* 33–40.

Pressley, M., & Afflerbach, P. (1995). *Verbal protocols of reading: The nature of constructively responsive reading.* Hillsdale, NJ: Erlbaum.

Pressley, M., Borkowski, J. G., & Schneider, W. (1989). Good information processing: What it is and how education can promote it. *International Journal of Educational Research, 13,* 866–878.

Pressley, M., & Gaskins, I. (2006). Metacognitive competent reading is constructively responsive reading: How can such reading be developed in students? *Metacognition and Learning, 1,* 99–113.

Pressley, M., Gaskins, I. W., Solic, K., & Collins, S. (2006). A portrait of a benchmark school: How a school produces high achievements in students who previously failed. *Journal of Educational Psychology, 98,* 282–306.

Prins, F. J., Busato, V. V., Elshout, J. J., & Hamaker, C. (1998). A new contribution to the validation of the (meta)cognitive part of the Inventory Learning Styles (ILS). *Pedagogische Studien, 75,* 73–93.

Puntambekar, S., & Stylianou, A. (2005). Designing navigation support in hypertext systems based on navigation patterns. *Instructional Science, 33,* 451–481.

Reder, L. M., & Schunn, C. D. (1996). Metacognition does not imply awareness: Strategy choice is governed by implicit learning and memory. In L. M. Reder (Ed.), *Implicit memory and metacognition* (pp. 45–77). Mahwah, NJ: Erlbaum.

Roll, I., Aleven, V., McLaren, B. M., & Koedinger, K. R. (2007). Designing for metacognition—applying cognitive tutor principles to the tutoring of help seeking. *Metacognition and Learning, 2,* 125–140.

Salomon, G., & Perkins, D. N. (1989). Rocky roads to transfer: Rethinking mechanisms of a neglected phenomenon. *Educational Psychologist, 24,* 113–142.

Schraw, G., Crippen, K. J., & Hartley, K. (2006). Promoting self-regulation in science education: Metacognition as part of a broader perspective on learning. *Research in Science Education, 36,* 111–139.

Schraw, G., & Dennison, R. S. (1994). Assessing metacognitive awareness. *Contemporary Educational Psychology, 19,* 460–475.

Schraw, G., Dunkle, M. E., Bendixen, L. D., & Roedel, T. D. (1995). Does a general monitoring skill exist? *Journal of Educational Psychology, 87,* 433–444.

Schraw, G., & Moshman, D. (1995). Metacognitive theories. *Educational Psychology Review, 7,* 351–371.

Simons, P. R. J. (1996). Metacognition. In E. de Corte, & F. E. Weinert (Eds.), *International encyclopedia of developmental and instructional psychology* (pp. 436–441). Oxford: Pergamon.

Slife, B. D., Weiss, J., & Bell, T. (1985). Separability of metacognition and cognition: Problem solving in learning disabled and regular students. *Journal of Educational Psychology, 77,* 437–445.

Sperling, R. A., Howard, B. C., Miller, L. A., & Murphy, C. (2002). Measures of children's knowledge and regulation of cognition. *Contemporary Educational Psychology, 27,* 51–79.

Stoeger, H., & Ziegler, A. (2008). Evaluation of a classroom based training to improve self-regulation in time management tasks during homework activities with fourth graders. *Metacognition and Learning, 3,* 207–230.

Sweller, J. (1994). Cognitive load theory, learning difficulty, and instructional design. *Learning and Instruction, 4,* 295–312.

Teong, S. K. (2003). The effects of mathematical training on mathematical word-problem solving. *Journal of Computer Assisted Learning, 19,* 46–55.

Thorpe, K. J., & Satterly, D. J. H. (1990). The development and inter-relationship of metacognitive components among primary school children. *Educational Psychology, 10,* 5–21.

Van der Stel, M., & Veenman, M. V. J. (2008). Relation between intellectual ability and metacognitive skillfulness as predictors of learning performance of young students performing tasks in different domains. *Learning and Individual Differences, 18,* 128–134.

Van der Stel, M., & Veenman, M. V. J. (2010). Development of metacognitive skillfulness: A longitudinal study. *Learning and Individual Differences, 20,* 220–224.

Veenman, M. V. J. (1998). Kennis en vaardigheden; Soorten kennis een vaardigheden die relevant zijn voor reken-wiskunde taken. [Knowledge and skills that are relevant to math tasks]. In A. F. Duinmaijer, J. E. H. van Luit, M. V. J. Veenman, & P. C. M. Vendel (Eds.), *Hulp bij leerproblemen; Rekenen-wiskunde* (pp. G0050.1–13). Zoetermeer: Betelgeuze.

Veenman, M. V. J. (2005). The assessment of metacognitive skills: What can be learned from multi-method designs? In C. Artelt, & B. Moschner (Eds), *Lernstrategien und Metakognition: Implikationen für Forschung und Praxis* (pp. 75–97). Berlin: Waxmann.

Veenman, M.V.J. (2006). Metacognitive skills as self-instructions. Paper presented at the second bi-annual conference Metacognition SIG 16, University of Cambridge.

Veenman, M. V. J. (2007). The assessment and instruction of self-regulation in computer-based environments: A discussion. *Metacognition and Learning, 2,* 177–183.

Veenman, M. V. J. (2008). Giftedness: Predicting the speed of expertise acquisition by intellectual ability and metacognitive skillfulness of novices. In M. F. Shaughnessy, M. V. J. Veenman, & C. Kleyn-Kennedy (Eds.), *Meta-cognition: A recent review of research, theory, and perspectives* (pp. 207–220). Hauppage: Nova Science Publishers.

Veenman, M. V. J., & Beishuizen, J. J. (2004). Intellectual and metacognitive skills of novices while studying texts under conditions of text difficulty and time constraint. *Learning and Instruction, 14,* 619–638.

Veenman, M. V. J., Elshout, J. J., & Busato, V. V. (1994). Metacognitive mediation in learning with computer-based simulations. *Computers in Human Behavior, 10,* 93–106.

Veenman, M. V. J., Elshout, J. J., & Groen, M. G. M. (1993). Thinking aloud: Does it affect regulatory processes in learning? *Tijdschrift voor Onderwijsresearch, 18,* 322–330.

Veenman, M. V. J., Elshout, J. J., & Meijer, J. (1997). The generality vs. domain-specificity of metacognitive skills in novice learning across domains. *Learning and Instruction, 7,* 187–209.

Veenman, M. V. J., de Haan, N., & Dignath, C. (2009). An observation scale for assessing teachers' implicit and explicit use of metacognition in classroom settings. Paper presented at the 13th Biennial Conference for Research on Learning and Instruction, EARLI. Amsterdam.

Veenman, M. V. J., Kerseboom, L, & Imthorn, C (2000). Test anxiety and metacognitive skillfulness: Availability versus production deficiencies. *Anxiety, Stress, and Coping, 13*, 391–412.

Veenman, M. V. J., Kok, R., & Blöte, A. W. (2005). The relation between intellectual and metacognitive skills at the onset of metacognitive skill development. *Instructional Science, 33*, 193–211.

Veenman, M. V. J., Prins, F. J., & Verheij, J. (2003). Learning styles: Self-reports versus thinking-aloud measures. *British Journal of Educational Psychology, 73*, 357–372.

Veenman, M. V. J., & Spaans, M. A. (2005). Relation between intellectual and metacognitive skills: Age and task differences. *Learning and Individual Differences, 15*, 159–176.

Veenman, M. V. J., & Van Cleef, D. (2007). Validity of assessing metacognitive skills for mathematic problem solving. In A. Efklides, & M.H. Kosmidis (Eds.), *9th European Conference on Psychological Assessment. Program and abstracts* (pp. 87–88). Thessaloniki: Aristotle University of Thessaloniki.

Veenman, M. V. J., Van Hout-Wolters, B. H. A. M., & Afflerbach, P. (2006). Metacognition and learning: Conceptual and methodological considerations. *Metacognition and Learning, 1*, 3–14.

Veenman, M. V. J., & Verheij, J. (2003). Identifying technical students at risk: Relating general versus specific metacognitive skills to study success. *Learning and Individual Differences, 13*, 259–272.

Veenman, M. V. J., Wilhelm, P., & Beishuizen, J. J. (2004). The relation between intellectual and metacognitive skills from a developmental perspective. *Learning and Instruction, 14*, 89–109.

Volet, S. E. (1991). Modelling and coaching of relevant metacognitive strategies for enhancing university students' learning. *Learning and Instruction, 1*, 319–336.

Wang, M. C., Haertel, G. D., & Walberg, H. J. (1990). What influences learning? A content analysis of review literature. *Journal of Educational Research, 84*, 30–43.

Whitebread, D., Coltman, P., Pasternak, D. P., Sangster, C. Grau, V., Bingham, S., Almeqdad, Q., & Demetriou, D. (2009). The development of two observational tools for assessing metacognition and self-regulated learning in young children. *Metacognition and Learning, 4*, 63–85.

Winne, P. H. (1996). A metacognitive view of individual differences in self-regulated learning. *Learning and Individual Differences, 8*, 327–353.

Winne, P. H., & Jamieson-Noel, D. (2002). Exploring students' calibrations of self reports about study tactics and achievement. *Contemporary Educational Psychology, 27*, 551–572.

Winters, F. I., Greene, J. A., & Costich, C. M. (2008). Self-regulation of learning with computer-based learning environments: A critical analysis. *Educational Psychology Review, 20*, 429–444.

Zimmerman, B. J. (1995). Self-regulation involves more than metacognition: A social cognitive perspective. *Educational Psychologist, 30*, 217–221.

Zimmerman, B. J., & Martinez-Pons, M. (1990). Student differences in self-regulated learning: Relating grade, sex, and giftedness to self-efficacy and strategy use. *Journal of Educational Psychology, 82*, 51–59.

Zohar, A., & Ben-David, A. (2008). Explicit teaching of meta-strategic knowledge in authentic classroom situations. *Metacognition and Learning, 3*, 59–82.

Zohar, A., & Ben-David, A. (2009). Paving a clear path in a thick forest: A conceptual analysis of a metacognitive component. *Metacognition and Learning, 4*, 177–195.

11

LEARNING WITH MOTIVATION

Eric M. Anderman and Heather Dawson

The study of academic motivation has blossomed during the past 30 years. Although motivation has been recognized as an important construct in both the fields of psychology and education for many years, it has recently become a major focus of research on academic learning. There is a vast array of empirical data and theory that readily inform both learning and instruction. In the present chapter, we examine some of the most prominent current research on academic motivation. In particular, we discuss the major theoretical perspectives, as well as the empirical research that supports these perspectives. We also demonstrate that motivation theory and research can be applied to instructional contexts at all levels (i.e., kindergarten through adult learning) in order to improve student learning.

In their classic text, Pintrich and Schunk defined motivation as "the process whereby goal-directed activity is instigated and sustained" (2002, p. 5). This definition reflects a social-cognitive perspective on motivation, wherein academic motivation is determined both by social (contextual) factors, as well as by the cognitions (thoughts) of learners. For example, a student who is reading a book can be "motivated" to read the book in many different ways. For some students, the goal may be to complete the book because the book is enjoyable; for others, the goal may be to complete the book in order to earn a good grade on a test about the book. From a motivation perspective, the *processes* by which reading is initiated and continued are the focus of interest; these processes are reviewed in the present chapter.

Our major goal is to demonstrate that motivation is a complex topic with a rich research base; however, at the same time, we also demonstrate that motivation theory can be readily applied to educational practice. The results of many empirical studies examining both predictors of academic motivation and outcomes that are predicted *by* academic motivation are quite consistent, and many of these results can be applied to practice. We first provide a brief historical overview of the study of academic motivation. We then discuss some of the currently popular and empirically supported theoretical frameworks. Then, we examine current trends and issues in the study of motivation.

Next, we present practical implications of motivation research, and we end by discussing future directions for the field.

HISTORICAL OVERVIEW

An historical overview of the study of motivation could encompass an entire book. Detailed reviews have been provided by others (Heckhausen, 2008; Schunk, Pintrich, & Meece, 2008; Weiner, 1990). Nevertheless, there are important trends that have occurred, particularly during the last century, that have shaped current theory and research in the field. These trends include the shift from behavioral to cognitive conceptions of motivation, as well as subtle and major developments within specific theories.

There are several different ways to examine developments in motivation research. One manner is simply to examine chronologically the various theories and perspectives that developed; another way is to examine these developments thematically. In the present chapter, we have chosen the latter approach, so that we can more readily point out the links between programmatic developments over the past century to current models of academic motivation.

From Behaviorism and Drives to Cognitivism

Probably the most obvious and often discussed shift in motivational theorizing over time is the general movement from behavioral views of motivation to more cognitive and particularly social-cognitive views of academic motivation.

Behavioral Theories

Most research on academic motivation prior to the 1970s emanated from a behavioral perspective (E. Anderman, 2010). These theoretical perspectives generally did not acknowledge the cognitive components involved in motivated behaviors. The two most prominent theories that have framed this argument are operant conditioning and classical conditioning. Operant theorists argue that motivated behaviors are shaped by reinforcers and by punishments (Skinner, 1953, 1954). In operant conditioning terms, a child would become more "motivated" to read books if the child were rewarded with a new toy upon completion of each book; receipt of the new toy would increase reading behavior. In contrast, if a teacher wants a student to stop reading aloud during silent reading time, then the teacher might punish the child (e.g., give the student a "time out"). Thus various environmental reinforcers and punishers are seen as being the determinants of motivated behaviors from an operant perspective.

Classical conditioning represents a somewhat different but important behavioral framework for explaining motivated behaviors. In classical conditioning, motivation arises from individuals' reactions to various stimuli; those stimuli can be both unconditioned (e.g., salivation at the sight of food), or conditioned (e.g., salivation upon hearing a bell that has been associated with food; Pavlov, 1927). Thus individuals may appear to be motivated to engage in certain behaviors (or to avoid engaging in certain behaviors) as a result of reactions to such stimuli. Classical conditioning is related to motivation in important ways. For example, a student who experiences difficulties learning math may ultimately become conditioned to experience unpleasant anxious reactions at the mere sight of mathematical problems in the future.

Drive theories also played an important role in early motivation research. Drive theories are based on individuals' needs (e.g., the need for sleep or food). Individuals' "drives" become salient when a "need" must be satisfied. The individual is thus motivated to engage in certain behaviors in order to reduce the drive (and satisfy the need). Drive theory originated in early writings by Watson and Morgan (Remley, 1980), and was described in detail in theories developed by scholars such as Hull (1943) and Mowrer (1960).

Although behavioral theories have had an important impact on education, many motivation researchers grew dissatisfied with behavioral perspectives. Specifically, these theories do not account for the fact that learners' beliefs at times override previously learned reinforcement patterns in determining motivated behaviors (Dember, 1974). In addition, over time researchers became more cognizant of the fact that learning and motivation involved cognitive components (Bandura, 1986, 1997; Bruning, Schraw, & Ronning, 1999). Theoretical perspectives that focused on drives and conditioned behaviors did not acknowledge the important role that cognition plays in determining motivated behavior.

Early Cognitive Theories

Although many of the cognitive theories of motivation that are prominent in contemporary research can be perceived as having developed as reactions to behavioral theories, it is important to note that many cognitive motivation theories developed at the same time that behavioral theories were in vogue. For example, volition, or "will" has been acknowledged as being related to beneficial educational outcomes (Corno, 1994). Nevertheless, volition originally was acknowledged as an important cognitive motivation construct in early studies by researchers such as Wundt (Blumenthal, 1998; Danziger, 2001) and James (1890; Rychlak, 1993).

Freud's theory of psychoanalysis also became prominent early in the 20th century (Freud, 1966). Freud's views on motivation stood in sharp contrast to behavioral views. Freud argued that motivation emanates from the satisfaction of needs. If an individual has a particular need, that individual tries to have that need met. In Freud's theory, the cognitive components of motivation are primarily unconscious in nature, but they are cognitive and not simply reactions to reinforcers or stimuli. As the individual channels psychological energy into meeting needs, the diminution of energy is experienced as satisfaction, ultimately increasing motivation. Freud's work was the impetus for other needs-based theories, such as Maslow's Hierarchy of Needs (Maslow, 1987).

Social Cognitive Theories

Most contemporary theories of academic motivation have moved toward a social cognitive perspective. Social cognitive theories acknowledge that motivation is determined by beliefs about the self, cognitions, and social contexts (Alderman, 2008; Bandura, 1997). There are a number of contemporary motivation theories that have emerged in recent decades, and each of these theories feature both cognitive and social components.

Contemporary social cognitive theories, which are discussed in this chapter, include expectancy-value theory (Eccles & Wigfield, 1995), social learning theory (including self-efficacy; Bandura, 1986; Pajares, 1996; Schunk & Pajares, 2002), self-determination theory (Deci, 1980; Ryan, Connell, & Deci, 1985) and goal orientation theory (Ames, 1992b; Dweck & Leggett, 1988; Pintrich, 2000a; Thorkildsen & Nicholls, 1998). Although these theories differ, all of them acknowledge that self-beliefs (i.e., beliefs about one's own competencies), individual cognitions (i.e., how we think and self-regulate in academic situations), and social contexts (i.e., the nature of schools, classrooms, and cultures) affect academic motivation in important ways.

Changes within Theories

Another way to examine trends in the field of motivation is to consider developments within individual theories. Such changes are important, but also are often complex and slowly developed. Whereas some developments in theories have been large-scale revisions, other changes have been minute. Next we provide a few examples of major changes in theories, in order to demonstrate that shifts in thinking about motivation have at times had profound effects on how motivation is studied, and on the implications of motivation research for practice.

One major historical change occurred within the expectancy-value framework. Specifically, original conceptions of the theory suggested that expectancies for success at tasks and the value held for those tasks are inversely related (Atkinson, 1957). However, later research suggested that expectancy and value beliefs are positively related (i.e., individuals expect to be successful at tasks they value; Eccles et al., 1983; Eccles & Wigfield, 1995). For example, Wigfield et al. (1997) examined the relations between expectancies and values in elementary school children ranging from grades 1 through 6. Results indicated that the constructs were correlated positively in math, reading, music, and sports, and that these correlations were stronger for older compared to younger children.

Another more recent historical change occurred in the literature on goal theory. Prior to the mid-1990s, most researchers discussed mastery goals and performance goals (Ames, 1992a; Dweck & Leggett, 1988). However, in the mid-1990s, researchers argued that performance goals reflect both approach and avoidance goals; thus performance goals were reconceptualized as performance-approach goals (i.e., the goal of demonstrating one's ability relative to others), and performance-avoid goals (i.e., the goal of avoiding appearing incompetent; Elliot & Harackiewicz, 1996; Middleton & Midgley, 1997). More recently, researchers have argued that mastery goals can be characterized both by approach and avoid qualities (Conroy, Elliot, & Hofer, 2003; Elliot & McGregor, 2001). These changes in the theory occurred because empirical research in both laboratory settings and using survey instruments confirmed that these constructs could be conceptualized in terms of both approach and avoid tendencies (Elliot, 2005). For example, Elliot and Harckiewicz (1996) compared the effects of performance-approach and performance-avoid goals on completion of word puzzles; results indicated that performance-avoid goals in particular undermined intrinsic motivation (compared to performance-approach), thus demonstrating that the approach-avoid distinction led to different types of outcomes.

In summary, motivation research has a rich history. The methodologies, constructs, and levels of specificity used to study motivation have changed greatly over the past century. Conceptualizations of motivation have evolved from theoretical perspectives solely concerned with unconscious motives, drives, and rote behaviors to current theories that acknowledge cognitive, social, and developmental aspects of motivation.

THEORETICAL FRAMEWORK

It is important to note that motivation is not a "one size fits all" term; rather, motivation is complex and consists of an array of components, and these various components are more readily explained with distinct theories. We prefer not to look at theories of motivation as competitive; rather, each theory addresses distinct aspects of academic motivation. In addition, each theory has both strengths and weaknesses that must be considered.

In this section, we review four of the most prominent current theoretical perspectives on achievement motivation. These include: goal orientation theory, social cognitive theory, self-determination theory, and expectancy-value theory. We describe the general tenets of each theory, and review empirical studies that support each framework.

Achievement Goal Theory

Achievement Goal Theory (also known as Goal Orientation Theory) focuses on the reasons that students choose to engage in some tasks, and not others. We review below the basic tenets of this framework, and their relations to educational outcomes. Two primary goal orientations are considered in this theory: mastery goals and performance goals. Depending on a variety of other factors, the orientation that students adopt is central to many motivational and academic outcomes (Ames, 1992b; Kaplan, Middleton, Urdan, & Midgley, 2002; Pintrich, 2000a).

Goal orientations have been measured across several levels: the types of goals that individuals adopt are known as *personal goal orientations*; the goals that are perceived as being emphasized in classroom settings are known as *classroom goal structures* (Ames, 1992b; Midgley, 2002). The addition, the goals that are perceived as being emphasized at the school-level are referred to as *school goal structures* (E. Anderman & Maehr, 1994; Maehr & Midgley, 1996). Most research on goal orientations has used survey methodologies, wherein students report self-perceptions; however, some researchers have used experimental methodologies in which goal orientations have been induced by manipulations (e.g., Elliot & Harackiewicz, 1996).

Students who endorse mastery goals (also referred to as task goals and learning goals) are invested in tasks for the sake of learning. Mastery-oriented students refer to their own past performance as a point of comparison, instead of comparing their performance to that of other students. Students who endorse performance goals (also referred to as ability goals, relative ability goals, competitive goals, and ego-involved goals) are concerned with demonstrating their ability relative to others. Students who adopt performance goals are concerned about appearing competent, and compare their performance with that of other students. Demonstrating ability, rather than learning the material, is the central focus of the performance-oriented student (see E. Anderman & Wolters, 2006, for a review).

It is also important to distinguish between the *performance-approach* and *performance-avoid* goals (Elliot & Church, 1997; Middleton & Midgley, 1997). Students who adopt performance-approach goals seek to appear more competent than others; in contrast, students who adopt *performance-avoid goals* seek to avoid appearing incompetent, often by attempting to achieve only what is minimally required. Recent work also distinguishes between *mastery-approach* goals (i.e., the goal is to master the task) and *mastery-avoid* goals (i.e., the goal is to avoid misunderstanding the task; Conroy, et al., 2003; Elliot & McGregor, 2001).

Classroom goal structures were introduced later by such theorists as Ames (1984) and Midgley (2002). These are defined as "goal-related messages that are made salient in the achievement setting (i.e., the laboratory, classrooms, schools) that are related to, and most likely influence, the personal goals that individuals pursue in those settings" (Kaplan et al., 2002, p. 24). Classroom goal structures reflect the purposes for learning that students perceive in classrooms. If a student perceives a mastery goal structure, the student believes that instruction emphasizes learning, improvement, and effort; if a student perceives a performance goal structure, the student believes that instruction focuses on relative ability, outperforming others, and grades. Goal structures are communicated to students through assessments, daily tasks, and discourse and instruction (Kaplan et al., 2002; Midgley, 2002).

Research generally indicates that mastery goals and perceptions of mastery goal structures are related to adaptive educational outcomes. For example, Archer (1994) used three independent large samples of university students to examine the relations between mastery goals and a variety of outcomes. Results indicated that mastery goals were related positively to the use of effective learning strategies, enjoyment of learning, and likelihood of choosing challenging academic tasks.

Performance-avoid goals are generally related to maladaptive outcomes, whereas results for performance-approach goals are mixed. Middleton and Midgley (1997), using a large sample of early adolescents, found that performance-avoid goals were related to maladaptive outcomes such as text anxiety, the avoidance of help-seeking, and lower levels of achievement; in contrast, the relations of performance-approach goals to various outcomes are somewhat inconsistent. Elliot, McGregor, and Gable (1999) found that performance-approach goals are related positively to examination scores and to the use of deep processing strategies using a sample of college-aged students; in contrast, using a sample of middle school students, Middleton and Midgley (1997) found that a performance-approach goal orientation was unrelated to self-regulation and self-efficacy, and was related positively to test anxiety.

In summary, goal orientation theorists conceptualize motivation in terms of the goals that students have when they are engaged with academic tasks. These goals are related to a variety of educational outcomes. Goals are determined both by students' individual cognitive beliefs, as well as by contextual influences.

Social Cognitive Theory

Social cognitive theory is a term that is used to describe several related constructs. Among these are *self-efficacy, reciprocal determinism*, and *social learning*. Aspects of these various concepts and constructs all emphasize the social nature of learning, and are focused on how social interactions influence learning. Social cognitive theorists examine the interactions between the learner, the environment, and others. In this section, we focus specifically on self-efficacy, since much research indicates that it is related in important ways to educational outcomes (Bandura, 1997; Pajares, 1996).

Self-efficacy was put forth by Bandura in the 1970s, and became popular among researchers in education. *Self-efficacy* is defined as a person's beliefs about his or her ability to complete a task (Bandura, 1997). Self-report is the primary method used to assess efficacy beliefs (Pajares, 1996). Self-efficacy beliefs are dependent upon the task they are associated with, and as a result, a microanalytic assessment is needed (Pajares, 1996). Thus general efficacy beliefs are occasionally measured, but such measures may be less accurate than more specific measures (Pajares, 1996).

Self-efficacy is critical to educators because of the empirical connection to outcomes for students. For example, research indicates that self-efficacy beliefs are related to the types of choices that students make. Betz and Hackett (1983) examined the relations between mathematics self-efficacy college major choices; results indicated that students with higher math self-efficacy were more likely to report choosing a science major. Self-efficacy also has been shown to relate positively to effort, persistence, and achievement (Bandura, 1997; Pajares, 1996).

Individuals acquire efficacy for a task from four potential sources (Bandura, 1997). The mastery experience, or actually completing the task, is the most potent source. A successful mastery experience increases self-efficacy whereas an unsuccessful mastery experience causes efficacy to drop. The second source is vicarious experience, or being present while another individual engages with the task. The importance of the task and closeness of the relationship to the person completing the task are related the development of self-efficacy from a vicarious experience. The third is social persuasion, which includes being convinced by another individual that one is capable of completing a task. The significance of the relationship with the other individual is also critical to the potency of this source. The final source of efficacy is physiological, which refers to the human body's reaction to the task. For example, sweating while giving a speech may cause self-efficacy for public speaking to diminish.

Self-Determination Theory (SDT)

Deci, Connell, and Ryan (1989) defined *self-determination* as "experiencing a sense of choice in initiating and regulating one's own actions" (p. 580). Self-determination focuses on three basic human needs: *the need for competence* (i.e., the need to experience success and mastery), *the need for autonomy* (i.e., the need to experience control over outcomes in one's life), and *the need for relatedness* (i.e., the need for feeling a sense of social belonging; Deci & Ryan, 2000). According to SDT, it is particularly important to satisfy the needs for competence and autonomy to become intrinsically motivated (Deci & Moller, 2005).

The basic tenets of SDT, as described in Deci and Ryan's (1985) more specific Cognitive Evaluation Theory, are *intrinsic* and *extrinsic* motivation. Although controversial among some scholars, these two constructs represent parts of a continuum that consists of (a) amotivation (i.e., a complete lack of motivation), (b) four levels of extrinsic motivation (external, introjected, identified, and integrated), and (c) intrinsic motivation (Ryan & Deci, 2000a). Intrinsic motivation is defined as engagement with a task fully and freely, without the necessity of material rewards or constraints (Deci & Ryan, 1985); extrinsic motivation refers to varying degrees of engagement with a task in order to receive an external reward. The four types of extrinsic motivation describe the extent to which an individual internalizes motivation for the task; through this process, learners begin to transform their reasons for engaging with tasks from extrinsic to intrinsic (Deci & Ryan, 1991).

External regulation describes how motivation originates outside a person. For example, a student who engages in academic tasks for the sole purpose of receiving a reward, or for the sole purpose of avoiding an unpleasant consequence such loss of recess is *externally regulated* (Deci et al., 1991). *Introjected regulation* is a type of extrinsic motivation in which behavior is largely determined by one's feelings; an individual who is regulated by introjection may behave in ways that the individual feels are appropriate (i.e., socially acceptable); however, such individuals are not motivated by their own volition (Deci et al., 1991). *Identified regulation* describes a person who values to some extent the task, and has accepted the process of regulation. Students who spend extra time studying because they genuinely feel their skill level may improve, even if they do not enjoy the task, fall into the category of *identified regulation* (Deci et al., 1991). Finally, *integrated regulation* is very similar to intrinsic motivation: *integrated regulation* toward an activity suggests that a learner has internalized information and integrated involvement with specific tasks into one's self-schema, whereas purely *intrinsic motivation* refers to a situation in which a person is interested in the activity itself.

Research supports the relation of SDT to adaptive motivational outcomes. Specifically, when social contexts support meeting individuals' needs for autonomy, those individuals experience a variety of positive outcomes. For example, in one study, Deci and colleagues (1993) examined the relations between mothers' vocalizations and intrinsic motivation of 6–7-year-old children. Results indicated that when mothers' vocalizations were perceived as *controlling*, their children reported lower levels of intrinsic motivation. In another study in an organizational setting, Deci et al. (1989) examined the relations of managerial styles to workers self-determined motivation. Using a sample of over 1000 employees from a large cooperation, Deci and colleagues found that when extrinsic stressors were addressed in an organization (e.g., when salary issues were addressed), there was a strong relation between provision of an autonomy-supportive work context with workers' satisfaction with their jobs.

Although research on SDT supports individual facets of the theory, much additional research is warranted. In particular, future research that examines multiple aspects of the theory simultaneously should be extremely beneficial.

Expectancy-Value Theory

Expectancy-value theory originally was described mathematically as the product of one's expectancy of attaining a given outcome and the value one placed on that outcome (hence Expectancy * Value, often shortened to EV; Atkinson, 1957). These expectancies and values were originally thought to be inversely related; that is, the more challenging the task, the lower the value, and vice versa. This idea has since been invalidated empirically (Eccles et al., 1983; Wigfield & Eccles, 1992). For example, Wigfield et al. (1997) examined the relations between expectancies and values in math, reading, music, and sports, using a longitudinal sample of over 600 children. Results indicated that expectancies and values were correlated positively in all domains, across grades 1 through 6.

More recent developments have included the identification a number of sub-components of achievement values (Eccles et al., 1983; Wigfield & Eccles, 1992). Eccles and Wigfield (1995) examined the structure of achievement values using confirmatory factor analysis. Data from a longitudinal sample of adolescents indicated that values separated into three distinct factors (interest, perceived importance, and perceived utility). In a subsequent study, Battle and Wigfield (2003) examined the factor structure of achievement values using a sample of female undergraduates, and developed a measure of cost, which is the fourth component; cost refers to the sacrifices the student must accept in order to engage in the task.

Summary

To summarize, motivation is complex, in that there are numerous theoretical perspectives that are used by researchers to explain the reasons why students engage with academic tasks. Motivation researchers are concerned with students' goals, the intrinsic and extrinsic nature of motivation, students' beliefs about their competence, and students' perceived valuing of tasks.

For most motivation researchers, the specific motivational issue that is being examined determines the theoretical perspective that is most useful in a given situation. For example, if a motivation researcher is interested in examining students' long-term likes and dislikes in a particular subject (e.g., mathematics), then the researcher might examine the question using an expectancy-value perspective. Thus specific motivational questions are the best determinants of the theory that should be employed.

CURRENT TRENDS AND ISSUES

As indicated, motivation theory and research has developed and changed over time, with many substantive changes occurring during the past 30 years. Today, there are trends and issues in the study of academic motivation that remain particularly salient, and that are vigorously debated among researchers. Here, we discuss a few of those salient and contested issues. Specifically, we examine some of the issues related (a) intrinsic verses extrinsic motivation; and (b) the debate about the costs and benefits of performance-approach goals.

The Intrinsic/Extrinsic Motivation Debate

One of the most vocal debates among motivation researchers in recent years concerns the benefits verses potential problems associated with the use of extrinsic rewards. This has become particularly salient in the United States, given the *No Child Left Behind* legislation, which affords states the opportunity to implement high-stakes rewards (e.g., money) and high-stakes punishments (e.g., changing the leadership of a school) based on students' test scores (Mathis, 2003; U.S. Department of Education, 2003).

The debate among researchers has focused mostly on the potential benefits versus harmful effects of extrinsic rewards on intrinsic motivation. The effects of rewards on motivation can be examined in terms of effects on students (e.g., in terms of student motivation), as well as in terms of the effects on teachers (e.g., in terms of teachers' motivation toward their jobs, and the selection of instructional practices to be used with students).

Some researchers argue that the extensive use of extrinsic rewards ultimately undermines intrinsic motivation (Deci, Koestner, & Ryan, 1999a, 1999b, 2001; Kohn, 1993; Ryan & Deci, 2000b), whereas others argue that the use of extrinsic rewards does not undermine intrinsic motivation (Cameron & Pierce, 1994; Eisenberger, Pierce, & Cameron, 1999). Specifically, those who argue that extrinsic rewards are problematic contend that if individuals are offered rewards for activities that they would do regardless of whether or not a reward is available, intrinsic motivation declines. In a classic study, Lepper, Greene, and Nisbett (1973) provided preschool children with the opportunity to draw freely with magic markers. Children were assigned to either receive an expected reward, an unexpected reward, or no reward. Results indicated that children's intrinsic motivation to draw was lower for students in the expected reward condition than for the other two conditions.

The phenomenon of intrinsic motivation declining in the presence of rewards has been explained by the overjustification hypothesis (Lepper et al., 1973; Lepper & Henderlong, 2000). When students perceive that a reward is available for their participation in a given activity, the students' participation in the activity is in essence overjustified (since they would have participated in the activity anyway). Once the reward is no longer available, the "justification" for engaging with the task is gone, and consequently intrinsic motivation to subsequently engage with the task decreases. More specifically, students reason that their participation is no longer justified, given the loss of the possibility of receiving the reward.

A debate has ensued over the past decade regarding the undermining effects of extrinsic rewards on intrinsic motivation. Cameron and Pierce (1994) presented results of a meta-analysis and concluded that although researchers often argue that extrinsic rewards undermine intrinsic motivation, this finding actually is not empirically supported. In response, a variety of researchers argued that Cameron and Pierce's meta-analysis was methodologically problematic, and that their conclusions were not warranted (Kohn, 1996; Lepper, Keavney, & Drake, 1996; Ryan & Deci, 1996). Deci and his colleagues conducted their own independent meta-analysis, and came to the opposite conclusion (Deci et al., 1999a). Lepper, Henderlong, and Gingras (1999) argue that these different results are due to differing approaches to meta analysis; specifically, they argue that meta analyses may not be accurate when the studies incorporated use highly diverse samples and procedures, and contain extensive moderator variables. Although the debate has continued (Deci et al., 1999b; Eisenberger et al., 1999; Lepper et al., 1996), researchers generally do acknowledge that extrinsic rewards can be harmful if used inappropriately. However, extrinsic incentives do not have to be harmful, if they are used in ways that provide students with information about their learning, and if the rewards are perceived as non-controlling (Deci, 1975). Pittman, Davey, Alafat, Wetherill, and Kramer (1980) compared the effects of informational and controlling rewards on intrinsic motivation. Undergraduate college students were asked to complete puzzles. Participants who received informational verbal rewards displayed greater intrinsic motivation than did participants who received controlling rewards or no rewards; specifically, during a free-time period, participants who had received informational feedback were more likely to continue to voluntarily work on the puzzles than were the others.

The Performance-Approach Goal Debate

Another contemporary debate among motivation researchers is the debate over the benefits and problems associated with performance-approach goals. Recall that in goal orientation theory, there are two primary goals: *mastery goals* (where the goal is to truly master the task at hand), and *performance goals* (where the goal involves demonstration of one's ability).

In the mid-1990s, researchers argued and demonstrated that performance goals can be broken down into performance-approach and performance-avoid goals (Elliot & Harackiewicz, 1996; Middleton & Midgley, 1997). A student who endorses performance-approach goals engages with a task in order to demonstrate that the student is more competent than others; in contrast, a student who endorses performance-avoid goals engages with a task in order to avoid appearing "dumb" or incompetent. Thus when presented with a challenging math problem, a student with performance-approach goals would be focused on demonstrating that she is better than others at solving the problem, whereas a student with performance-avoid goals would be focused on avoiding being seen as unable to solve the problem.

Prior to the mid-1990s, measures of performance-approach and avoid goals often were confounded, in that measures often contained items reflecting both the approach and avoid aspects of these constructs (E. Anderman & Wolters, 2006). Now that more appropriate measures exist, researchers have been able to more carefully address the relations between performance-approach and performance-avoid goals with other important educational outcomes.

Research indicates that performance-avoid goals are maladaptive. When students approach their academic work with the goal of avoiding appearing unable or incompetent, few benefits arise (Pintrich, 2000a). For example, research indicates that performance avoid goals are inversely related to grades and performance (Elliot & Church, 1997; Elliot & McGregor, 2001; Roney & O'Connor, 2008; Skaalvik, 1997), and positively related to the use of self-handicapping strategies (Midgley & Urdan, 2001). Although most of this research has been conducted using self-report survey measures, some experimental studies also support the negative effects of performance-avoid goals. For example, Elliot and Harackiewicz (1996) conducted an experiment in which undergraduate students were randomly assigned to one of four conditions: performance-approach, performance-avoid, performance-neutral, and mastery. In the performance-avoid condition, students were instructed to solve a puzzle in order to demonstrate that they were not poor puzzle solvers; results indicated that intrinsic motivation to solve puzzles was undermined for participants in the performance-avoid condition.

In contrast, there are mixed results regarding the benefits of performance-approach goals. Some research indicates that the adoption of performance-approach goals is related to maladaptive educational outcomes, such as the avoidance of help-seeking (Ryan, Hicks, & Midgley, 1997) and the avoidance of challenge (Middleton & Midgley, 1997). However, other studies indicate that performance-approach goals may be beneficial. For example, among college students, the adoption of performance-approach goals is related positively to achievement (Church, Elliot, & Gable, 2001; Elliot & McGregor, 1999; Harackiewicz, Barron, Carter, Lehto, & Elliot, 1997).

An interesting debate has emerged in recent years regarding the potential benefits of performance-approach goals. Midgley, Kaplan, and Middleton (2001) argued that results of studies examining relations of performance-approach goals to various adaptive educational outcomes are at best inconsistent. Midgley et al. (2001) argued that goal theory should not be "revised" to indicate that both mastery and performance goals are universally beneficial, given the mixed evidence surrounding performance-approach goals. They cautioned that future research is needed explain inconsistent findings about the relations of performance-approach goals to various outcomes. In addition, they argued that a revision of goal orientation theory with a greater emphasis on the benefits of performance-approach goals might lessen the emphasis placed in classrooms on mastery goals, which are known to be beneficial.

In contrast, Harackiewicz and colleagues (Harackiewicz, Barron, Pintrich, Elliot, & Thrash, 2002) have argued that achievement goal theory should be reconceptualized. Specifically, they have argued that given the empirical evidence for the existence of both performance-approach and avoid goal orientations, it is sensible to revise goal orientation theory to reflect this distinction. In addition, they argue that the evidence regarding the beneficial effects of performance goals is quite robust.

The debate about the costs and benefits of performance-approach goals is important, because the types of goals that students adopt are related to the types of instructional practices that teachers use in classrooms (E. Anderman & L. Anderman, 2010; E. Anderman & Maehr, 1994). For example, E. Anderman, Maehr, and Midgley (1999) examined student motivation in two middle schools: one that was characterized as emphasizing performance goals, and one that emphasized mastery goals. Results indicated that although there were no significant differences in motivation prior to transitioning into those schools, after the transition the students in the "performance" school reported higher performance and extrinsic goals. Thus the contrasting instructional practices in the two schools may have produced these different outcomes.

The debate about the costs verses benefits of performance-approach goals continues to be a salient issue for motivation researchers. Nevertheless, there are other issues that need to also be considered in this argument; this is not a simple question of "good" verses "bad" goals. For example, Bouffard and her colleagues (Bouffard, Bouchard, Goulet, Denocourt, & Couture, 2005) have suggested that the nature of a goal may not matter as much as the personal significance of the goal to the individual students. Roeser (2004) argued that the debate about performance-approach goals actually represents a larger debate regarding science (i.e., theory-building) and application (i.e., applying theory to practice). The Harackiewicz et al. argument represents the perspective of motivation theorists who are mostly concerned with theory-building, whereas the Midgley et al. argument represents the perspective those who are primarily concerned with educational applications. For example, Elliot and his colleagues have spent much time in recent years conducting empirical research to validate a theoretical model of achievement goals that includes mastery-approach and avoid goals, as well as performance-approach and avoid goals (e.g., Elliot & McGregor, 2001), whereas Maehr, Midgley, and their colleagues have focused on the roles of goal orientations in school settings (e.g., E. Anderman et al., 1999; Maehr & Midgley, 1996). Clearly both perspectives are important, and when viewed in this way, both sides of the issue can be better appreciated (Roeser, 2004).

Practical Implications

The practical implications of motivation research are plentiful. Of particular importance are the daily decisions that teachers make in classrooms and their powerful effects on students' motivation. Whereas expensive, large-scale interventions can certainly be delivered to enhance achievement motivation, simple changes in daily instructional practices can also have profound effects on students, both positively and negatively. For example, E. Anderman et al. (2001) found that in classrooms where teachers used performance-oriented instructional practices (e.g., displaying the work of the best students), children's valuing of math and reading declined over the course of a year.

Reviews of the implications of motivation research for practice have been presented elsewhere (Ames, 1992b; E. Anderman & L. Anderman, 2010; Brophy, 2004; Maehr & Midgley, 1996). In the following sections, we briefly examine some of the daily decisions that teachers make, and how these decisions affect student motivation. In particular, we examine decisions regarding (a) selection of academic tasks; (b) evaluation of achievement; and (c) grouping students for instruction.

Selection of Academic Tasks

Every day in classrooms, teachers choose the types of tasks and activities that they present to students. Although standards and curricula often are set by districts and states, the ways in which curricula are presented varies. Teachers make choices about how curricula are presented, and those decisions can affect student motivation both in the short and long term.

Classification of Tasks

Academic tasks can be classified in a number of different ways. The way that a task is classified and ultimately presented to students can affect motivation. For example, tasks are classified by teachers in terms of whether the task represents (a) seatwork; (b) homework; (c) group work; or (d) assessments. These terms have different connotations and applied meanings for students; when a student hears that a task is going to be "seatwork," the student may express different types of motivation, compared to when the task is presented as an assessment.

Researchers tend to classify academic tasks somewhat differently, but these classifications nevertheless may affect student motivation. Doyle (1983) described four types of tasks that are presented in classrooms. These include (a) *memory tasks* (i.e., recalling information that has been learned previously); (b) *procedural/routine tasks* (i.e., applying an algorithm to solve a problem); (c) *comprehension/understanding tasks* (i.e., recognizing that an article about outer space is referring to possible voyage to Mars); and (d) *opinion tasks* (i.e., giving opinions about the performance of nationally elected government officials; Doyle, 1983).

Another common classification system is Bloom's Taxonomy. The original taxonomy for the classification of cognitive learning objectives included six categories: (a) knowledge; (b) comprehension; (c) application; (d) analysis; (e) synthesis; and (f) evaluation (Bloom, Engelhart, Furst, Hill, & Krathwohl, 1956). The taxonomy was revised several years ago; this revision was undertaken in order to better reflect the actual cognitive processes that students use when engaging with academic tasks. The revised taxonomy includes the following cognitive functions: (a) remember; (b) understand; (c) apply; (d) analyze; (e) evaluate; and (f) create (Anderson et al., 2001). Bümen (2007) conducted an experimental study in which preservice teachers were taught either the original taxonomy, or both the original and revised taxonomies. Results indicated that teachers who also learned the revised version produced lesson plans that were rated as being of higher quality than those of the group that was only exposed to the original taxonomy.

Motivation and Tasks

As mentioned, the choice of task is related to student motivation. Thus if a teacher chooses a task that focuses on *analysis*, this task may be motivational for some students, but not for others. Indeed, the task may be exciting to students who enjoy analyzing complex phenomena, whereas the same task may induce anxiety in a student who either does not enjoy analytic tasks or has had unpleasant experiences in the past with such tasks.

Depending on the type of task that is selected, the context of the classroom environment, and the students' prior experiences and beliefs about the nature of the task, the specific task that students are asked to complete affects their motivation (E. Anderman & L. Anderman, 2010). Most theories of achievement motivation can be used to explain how task choice affects student motivation; however, research from goal orientation and from expectancy-value theories in particular have focused on how tasks affect motivation.

Goal Orientation Theory and Task Choice

Goal orientation theorists argue that students' goals are determined by several factors, including the classroom context, as well as the specific task. In most cases (although certainly not all), the teacher determines the types of tasks that students encounter. From a goal theory perspective, the student can adopt mastery goals, performance-approach goals, or performance-avoid goals for the task; in addition, the student can adopt several of these goals simultaneously (Linnenbrink & Pintrich, 2001; Pintrich, 2000b).

The instructions that teachers provide to students upon receipt of the task can determine the types of goals that students adopt. Both experimental research (Elliot & Harackiewicz, 1996) and descriptive research (E. Anderman et al., 1999) indicate that students' adoption of goals for particular tasks can be induced by the context. More specifically, when teachers focus students on issues related to relative ability or social comparison, performance goals may be induced, whereas when teachers focus students on effort, improvement, and using oneself as a point of reference, mastery goals may be induced. For example, Patrick et al. (2001) examined teachers' specific behaviors in fifth-grade classrooms that were perceived by students as emphasizing a variety of goal structures. Classroom observations indicated that teachers utilized distinct behaviors across these classrooms. Although teachers in both high and low performance-focused classrooms publicly provided feedback about task performance and rewards during instruction, the emphasis on the *importance* of feedback and rewards was much greater in the high-performance classrooms. Results also indicated that teachers in high mastery classrooms emphasized creativity and deep understanding. Those teachers also were noted as being particularly enthusiastic and encouraging verbal participation from their students.

Expectancy-Value Theory and Task Choice

Recall that Eccles and Wigfield's expectancy-value theory of motivation focuses on four core achievement values (attainment value, utility value, intrinsic value, and cost). Research indicates that values develop over time, and that students are able to think about achievement values in a more complex manner as they move from childhood into adolescence (Eccles, 1993; Eccles, Wigfield, Harold, & Blumenfeld, 1993; Wigfield & Eccles, 1992). The development of positive achievement values in students is important, because valuing an academic subject is predictive of subsequent involvement with that subject (e.g., enrollment in future courses in that subject; Wigfield & Eccles, 1992) and of later life-choices, including career-related decisions (Durik, Vida, & Eccles, 2006).

Teachers communicate achievement values to students by the ways in which they present academic tasks. Many times, students engage in academic tasks without understanding why the task is important. However, educators can easily affect student motivation by helping students to value certain tasks. Specifically, it is incumbent upon educators to choose tasks that perceive as being important, interesting, useful, and worthy of one's time.

Evaluation of Student Achievement

Most education involves the assessment of achievement. From pre-school through graduate-level education, there is an implicit expectation that students' work will be evaluated. The motivational consequences of evaluation are important. Indeed, receipt of a "good grade" or a "bad grade" can have profound effects on subsequent motivation. In addition, a forthcoming assessment may produce debilitating anxiety in some students, which can adversely affect performance. On a larger scale, policy in the United States such as the *No Child Left Behind* legislation mandates that high-stakes assessments are given in all states (Linn, Baker, & Betebenner, 2002).

Intrinsic/Extrinsic Motivation and Evaluation

Students' intrinsic motivation and extrinsic motivation are related to assessment practices. When a student is intrinsically motivated, the receipt of a grade may ultimately lower the students' intrinsic motivation to learn (Deci et al., 1999b, 2001; Freedman, Cunningham, & Krismer, 1992; Ryan et al., 1985). This may be particularly true in schools or classrooms that stress the importance of testing. When the teacher persistently talks about the importance of extrinsic outcomes such as grades, students may become highly focused on obtaining those outcomes. In such contexts, students ultimately may come to believe that the grade is more important than the actual material that is being learned; this in turn can lead to decrements in intrinsic motivation. For example, a student who truly loves reading mystery novels may experience decrements in intrinsic motivation to read such novels, if the student is enrolled in an English class in which the students are persistently tested on the novels. This may be particularly true if the assessments focus on factual recall of somewhat trivial details in the novel.

Testing and assessment are not going to be eliminated in schools. However, the emphasis on testing can be diminished. First, teachers can be better educated to use discourse that does not focus on evaluation; rather, teachers can be better trained to communicate about the intrinsic value of the material, rather than simply focusing on the importance of a forthcoming test. Second, teachers also can be better educated regarding to the proper way to present grades to students. The negative effects of grades on intrinsic motivation can be lessened if grades are presented as informational and non-controlling in nature (Deci, Spiegel, Ryan, Koestner, & Kauffman, 1982; Pittman et al., 1980). Thus rather than simply writing "A" on a student's paper, optimal motivation may be achieved if an additional personal comment is written to the student; such comments should indicate that the student earned the "A" grade because she truly mastered the material. In addition, the comment should indicate that the student earned the grade, rather than indicating that the teacher "gave" the student the grade (which could be perceived as controlling).

Grouping Students for Instruction

The ways that teachers organize groups for instruction can affect student motivation (Linnenbrink, 2005). Children recognize that they often receive differentiated instruction based on ability (Weinstein, Marshall, Brattesani, & Middlestadt, 1992). Thus students who are placed in lower ability groups are aware of such placements. Such grouping practices often are inevitable, but they do impact academic motivation.

A student who is put in the "low" ability reading group during the first grade may develop a poor self-concept of ability at reading; that low self-concept of ability may perpetuate if the student consistently is placed in low-ability reading groups throughout the elementary school years. In contrast, a student who moves from a low ability group into a higher ability or heterogenous group at a later time may not experience the same decrements in motivation (E. Anderman & L. Anderman, 2010). Low achieving students in particular may benefit from participation in mixed-ability groups. For example, Saleh, Lazonder, and De Jong (2005) randomly assigned fourth graders to either homogeneous or heterogeneous groups. Students all received identical instruction on plant biology. Results indicated that low ability students displayed greater learning when they were assigned to the heterogeneous groups.

Grouping of students by ability is very popular among educators, particularly because it is easier for a teacher to prepare instruction for a more homogeneous group of students. Nevertheless, the evidence about the effectiveness of ability grouping on achievement is limited. Indeed, research indicates that between-class ability grouping is largely unrelated to achievement, except for the highest ability students (Fuligni, Eccles, & Barber, 1995; Gamoran, 1992; Slavin, 1990). Other research indicates that teachers of low ability groups focus less on students' individual interests and use less cognitively demanding tasks than do teachers of higher ability groups (Borko & Eisenhart, 1986; Oakes & Lipton, 1990).

Cooperative learning has been demonstrated to be a viable alternative to grouping students by ability (Johnson, Johnson, & Smith, 2007; Johnson, Maruyama, Johnson, Nelson, & Skon, 1981; Slavin, 1996, 1983, Chapter 17 in this volume). Most cooperative grouping techniques have several common characteristics: (a) success of the group is dependent on mutual success among group members; (b) groups are heterogeneous in composition; and (c) students must still demonstrate individual learning.

Research on cooperative learning indicates that it is effective both at producing achievement gains and at maintaining students' motivation to learn (Qin, Johnson, & Johnson, 1995; Slavin, 1990, 1992). A number of explanations have been posited to explain the benefits of cooperative learning. For example, Webb and her colleagues have argued that in classrooms where cooperative groups are used effectively, students communicate better with each other, and offer each other help that students ordinarily might not receive (Webb, 1982, Webb, Nemer, & Ing, 2006). From a Vygotskian perspective, when students learn in cooperative groups, the social interaction among the students facilitates cognitive growth, since higher achieving students can scaffold learning and lure lower achieving students into their zones of proximal development (Palincsar, 1986; Vygotsky, 1978).

Educators can effectively use groups for instruction without harming students' intrinsic motivation. In particular, groups can be organized around students' interests instead of around abilities. Motivation is enhanced when students are allowed to examine areas of personal interest (Hidi, 1990; Renninger, 2000; Schiefele, Krapp, & Winteler, 1992; Schraw, Flowerday, & Lehman, 2001). Thus an alternative to assigning students to reading groups that are organized in terms of students' abilities is to organize the groups around various topics. For example, teachers could arrange groups so that one group is reading a mystery, another is reading science fiction, another is reading an adventure, and another is reading a tragedy. Such arrangements afford all students the opportunity to engage in reading with peers around mutually interesting topics.

FUTURE DIRECTIONS

In this chapter, we have reviewed developments in research on academic motivation. Although motivation research has exhibited important and significant theoretical and applied developments in recent years, there is still much that needs to be pursued. In the next section, we suggest some areas in which motivation research has shown some initial promise, and in which further research is needed.

Motivation-Based Interventions

Motivational issues have not been the focus of many intervention studies. Maehr (1976) noted over 30 years ago that motivation often is neglected as a valued outcome variable. Although motivation often has been included as a predictor variable in educational interventions, it for the most part has not been identified as a valued outcome worthy of study.

A recent issue of *Educational Psychologist* focused on educational interventions that are designed to enhance student motivation (Wentzel & Wigfield, 2007). Whereas that issue featured several important and promising interventions, it also served as an important reminder about the limited amount of intervention-based work that has occurred in the study of motivation. Indeed, the majority of studies over the past 30 years have been descriptive. Such studies are important and have helped us to identify how motivation constructs are related to other important outcomes (e.g., achievement). However, few studies have experimentally evaluated programmatic efforts (i.e., programs that are well grounded in motivation theory) aimed directly at enhancing academic motivation. This is a fruitful area for future research.

Developmental Studies

Another important area for future research is in the area of longitudinal/developmental studies of motivation. Some longitudinal studies examining changes in motivation constructs over time have been conducted. For example, some studies have examined changes in expectancies and values (Eccles et al., 1993; Wigfield & Eccles, 1992, 2002; Wigfield, et al., 1991); other studies have examined changes in achievement goal orientations (E. Anderman & Midgley, 1997; L. Anderman & E. Anderman, 1999); and some studies have investigated changes in intrinsic motivation over time (Gottfried, Fleming, & Gottfried, 2001). However, developmental studies are still relatively rare in the motivation field.

Longitudinal studies are particularly difficult to conduct because of problems with participant attrition. First, it is very time-consuming to collect large-scale longitudinal data. Families often move to new neighborhoods, and it becomes quite difficult and expensive to track students over time. Second, it often is difficult to get participants to agree to remain in studies over extended periods of time. Even though a study participant may remain in the viable sample pool, it may be difficult to convince all participants to remain in the study.

Nevertheless, there is a need for additional studies examining how motivational beliefs develop over time. In particular, the field is lacking in studies that examine motivation in both very young children (i.e., preschool and the lower grades), and in studies examining older adolescents (i.e., after the transition into high school; Wigfield & Eccles, 2002). In addition, there is a need for studies that examine the development of motivational beliefs across diverse populations and from varied socioeconomic backgrounds. Finally, there is a need for developmental studies that are framed in other theoretical frameworks. For example, the field would benefit from additional studies examining developmental changes using self-determination theory.

Qualitative Studies

Most motivation research has been conducted using survey-based designs and quantitative methods. Whereas researchers have learned much about the relations of motivation constructs to a host of variables, quantitative studies have not provided researchers or practitioners with more nuanced studies of how students think about motivation, and how social contexts and social interactions affect motivation. In particular, many of the quantitative studies that have been conducted in the field of motivation have relied on self-report data, provided by students via survey instruments. Turner and Meyer (2009) recently re-examined one of their survey-based studies of motivation in math classrooms, and concluded that the results of self-report measures about math are quite generic in nature. Specifically, they noted that whereas students responded to items about math, the researchers really did not know about the specific aspects of math that students were thinking about when responding to the survey items.

Qualitative studies allow motivation researchers to delve more deeply into the ways in which students truly think about motivation. Some qualitative studies have been conducted in recent years. These studies have provided the motivation community with important insights into the relations of motivation to learning in classrooms. For example, the previously mentioned study by Patrick and colleagues (L. Anderman, Patrick, Hruda, & Linnenbrink, 2002; Patrick et al., 2001) examined the ways that elementary school teachers communicate mastery and performance goal structures to their students. Classroom observations indicated that teachers who communicated a mastery goal structure to their students engaged in specific instructional behaviors, such as communicating the importance of effort, encouraging student interaction, and demonstrating a concern for student learning. In comparison, teachers who communicated the presence of a performance goal structure emphasized grades, tests, and ability differences among students.

In another study, L. Anderman and her colleagues (L. Anderman, Andrzejewski, & Allen, in press) conducted an observational study in high school classrooms. Surveys were used to identify a small set of teachers who were perceived by students as communicating a strong mastery goal structure, high academic press, high social support, and a low performance-avoid goal structure. Observations were then conducted in order to identify and describe the instructional practices of those teachers. The authors proposed a grounded model that included three intersecting themes: supporting understanding, building and maintaining rapport, and managing the classroom.

CONCLUSION

Motivation affects learning in important ways. As we have reviewed in this chapter, motivation is related to how students learn in classrooms; to ways in which students approach academic tasks; to the development of interest in certain domains; to students' beliefs about their abilities and their weaknesses; to the activities in which students choose to participate during their free time; and to numerous other outcomes, including career choices.

Although student motivation is affected by numerous entities (e.g., parents or communities), motivation is communicated to students daily and consistently by their teachers. The interactions that students have with their teachers have powerful effects on motivation; thus the practical implications of motivation research are profound. Educators make both small and large instructional decisions that affect students' motivation. The selection of tasks, the manner in which assessments are delivered, the ways that instructional groups are formed, and the discourse that teachers use in class all are related to students' motivational beliefs.

Finally, we must reiterate that motivation is a complex topic. Many educators have a simplistic view of motivation, and many assume that motivation solely resides within the student, and that the teacher does not have any responsibility in determining student motivation. In the present chapter, we have tried to communicate that motivation is complex; it involves students' goals, values, ability beliefs, and numerous other variables. Although at some level motivation does emanate from the student, motivation also is largely determined by the instructional practices and social contexts of schools and classrooms. The instructional decisions made by teachers everyday strongly influence students' beliefs about their abilities, their goals, their values, and ultimately their educational and vocational choices.

REFERENCES

Alderman, M. K. (2008). *Motivation for achievement: Possibilities for teaching and learning* (3rd ed.). New York: Routledge.

Ames, C. (1984). Achievement attribution and self-instructions under competitive and individualistic goal structures. *Journal of Educational Psychology, 76,* 478–487.

Ames, C. (1992a). Achievement goals and the classroom motivational climate. In D. H. Schunk, & J. L. Meece (Eds.), *Student perceptions in the classroom* (pp. 327–348). Hillsdale, NJ: Lawrence Erlbaum Associates, Inc.

Ames, C. (1992b). Classrooms: Goals, structures, and student motivation. *Journal of Educational Psychology, 84,* 261–271.

Anderman, E. M. (2010). Reflections on Wittrock's Generative Model of Learning: A motivation perspective *Educational Psychologist, 45,* 55–60.

Anderman, E. M., & Anderman, L. H. (2010). *Classroom motivation.* Upper Saddle River, NJ: Pearson.

Anderman, E.M., Eccles, J.S., Yoon, K.S., Roeser, R.W., Wigfield, A., & Blumenfeld, P. (2001). Learning to value mathematics and reading: Relations to mastery and performance-oriented instructional practices. *Contemporary Educational Psychology, 26,* 76–95.

Anderman, E. M., & Maehr, M. L. (1994). Motivation and schooling in the middle grades. *Review of Educational Research, 64,* 287–309.

Anderman, E. M., Maehr, M. L., & Midgley, C. (1999). Declining motivation after the transition to middle school: Schools can make a difference. *Journal of Research and Development in Education, 32,* 131–147.

Anderman, E. M., & Midgley, C. (1997). Changes in achievement goal orientations, perceived academic competence, and grades across the transition to middle-level schools. *Contemporary Educational Psychology, 22,* 269–298.

Anderman, E. M., & Wolters, C. (2006). Goals, values, and affect: influences on student motivation. In P. Alexander, & P. Winne (Eds.), *Handbook of educational psychology* (2nd ed., pp. 369–389). Mahwah, NJ: Lawrence Erlbaum Associates.

Anderman, L. H., & Anderman, E. M. (1999). Social predictors of changes in students' achievement goal orientations. *Contemporary Educational Psychology, 25,* 21–37.

Anderman, L. H., Andrzejewski, C.E., & Allen, J. (in press). How do teachers support students' motivation and learning in their classrooms? *Teachers' College Record.*

Anderman, L. H., Patrick, H., Hruda, L. Z., & Linnenbrink, E. A. (2002). Observing classroom goal structures to clarify and expand goal theory. In C. Midgley (Ed.), *Goals, goal structures, and patterns of adaptive learning* (pp. 243–278). Mahwah, NJ: Lawrence Erlbaum Associates.

Anderson, L. W., Krathwohl, D. R., Airasian, P. W., Cruikshank, K. A., Mayer, R. E., Pintrich, P. R., et al. (2001). *A taxonomy for learning, teaching, and assessing.* New York: Longman.

Archer, J. (1994). Achievement goals as a measure of motivation in university students. *Contemporary Educational Psychology, 19,* 430–446.

Atkinson, J. W. (1957). Motivational determinants of risk taking behavior. *Psychological Review, 64,* 359–372.

Bandura, A. (1986). *Social foundations of thought and action: A social cognitive theory.* Englewood Cliffs, NJ: Prentice-Hall.

Bandura, A. (1997). *Self-efficacy: The exercise of control.* New York: W.H. Freeman and Company.

Battle, A., & Wigfield, A. (2003). College women's value orientations toward family, career, and graduate school. *Journal of Vocational Behavior, 62,* 56–75.

Betz, N.E., & Hackett, G. (1983). The relationship of mathematics self-efficacy expectations to the selection of science-based college majors. *Journal of Vocational Behavior, 23,* 329–345.

Bloom, B. S., Engelhart, M. D., Furst, E. J., Hill, W. H., & Krathwohl, D. R. (Eds.). (1956). *Taxonomy of educational objectives: Handbook I, Cognitive domain.* New York: David McKay.

Blumenthal, A. L. (1998). *Leipzig, Wilhelm Wundt, and psychology's gilded age.* Washington, DC: American Psychological Association.

Borko, H., & Eisenhart, M. (1986). Students' conceptions of reading and their reading experiences in school. *The Elementary School Journal, 86*, 589–611.

Bouffard, T., Bouchard, M., Goulet, G., Denocourt, I., & Couture, N. (2005). Influence of achievement goals and self-efficacy on students' self-regulation and performance. *International Journal of Psychology, 40*, 373–384.

Brophy, J. (2004). *Motivating students to learn* (2nd ed.). Mahwah, NJ: Lawrence Erlbaum Associates.

Bruning, R. H., Schraw, G. J., & Ronning, R. R. (1999). *Cognitive psychology and instruction* (3rd ed.). Upper Saddle River, NJ: Merrill.

Bümen , N.T. (2007). Effects of the original verses revised Bloom's taxonomy on lesson planning skills: A Turkish study among pre-service teachers. *Review of Education, 53*, 439–455.

Cameron, J., & Pierce, W. D. (1994). Reinforcement, reward, and intrinsic motivation: A meta-analysis. *Review of Educational Research, 64*, 363–423.

Church, M. A., Elliot, A. J., & Gable, S. L. (2001). Perceptions of classroom environment, achievement goals, and achievement outcomes. *Journal of Educational Psychology, 93*, 43–54.

Conroy, D. E., Elliot, A. J., & Hofer, S. M. (2003). A 2 x 2 Achievement goals questionnaire for sport: evidence for factorial invariance, temporal stability, and external validity. *Journal of Sport & Exercise Psychology, 25*, 456–476.

Corno, L. (1994). Student volition and education: Outcomes, influences, and practices. In D. H. Schunk, & B. J. Zimmerman (Eds.), *Self-regulation of learning and performance: Issues and educational applications* (pp. 229–251). Hillsdale, NJ: Erlbaum.

Danziger, K. (2001). *The unknown Wundt: Drive, apperception, and volition.* New York: Kluwer Academic/Plenum.

Deci, E. (1975). *Intrinsic motivation.* New York: Plenum.

Deci, E. (1980). *The psychology of self-determination.* Lexington: D.C. Heath.

Deci, E.L., Connell, J.P., & Ryan, R.M. (1989). Self-determination in a work organization. *Journal of Applied Psychology, 74*, 580–590.

Deci E.L., Driver, R.E., Hotchkiss, L., Robbins, R.J., & Wilson, I.M. (1993). The relation of mothers' controlling vocalizations to children's intrinsic motivation. *Journal of Experimental Child Psychology, 55*, 151–162.

Deci, E. L., Koestner, R., & Ryan, R. M. (1999a). A meta-analytic review of experiments examining the effects of extrinsic rewards on intrinsic motivation. *Psychological Bulletin, 125*, 627–668.

Deci, E. L., Koestner, R., & Ryan, R. M. (1999b). The undermining effect is a reality after all–Extrinsic rewards, task interest, and self-determination: Reply to Eisenberger, Pierce, and Cameron (1999) and Lepper, Henderlong, and Gingras (1999). *Psychological Bulletin, 125*, 692–700.

Deci, E.L., Koestner, R., & Ryan, R. M. (2001). Extrinsic rewards and intrinsic motivation in education: Reconsidered once again. *Review of Educational Research, 71*, 1–27.

Deci, E.L., & Moller, A.C. (2005). The concept of competence: A starting place for understanding intrinsic motivation and self-determined extrinsic motivation. In A. J. Elliot, & C. S. Dweck (Eds.), *Handbook of competence and motivation* (pp. 579–597). New York: The Guilford Press.

Deci, E. L., & Ryan, R. M. (1985). *Intrinsic motivation and self-determination in human behavior.* New York: Plenum.

Deci, E. L., & Ryan, R. M. (1991). A motivational approach to self: Integration in personality. In R. A. Dienstbier (Ed.), *Nebraska Symposium on Motivation, 1990: Perspectives on motivation* (pp. 237–288). Lincoln: University of Nebraska Press.

Deci, E. L., & Ryan, R. M. (2000). The "what" and the "why" of goal pursuits: Human needs and the self-determination of behavior. *Psychological Inquiry, 11*, 227–268.

Deci, E. L., Spiegel, N. H., Ryan, R. M., Koestner, R., & Kauffman, M. (1982). Effects of performance standards on teaching styles: Behavior of controlling teachers. *Journal of Educational Psychology, 74*, 852–859.

Deci, E. L., Vallerand, R. J., Pelletier, L. G., & Ryan, R. M. (1991). Motivation and education: The self-determination perspective. *Educational Psychologist, 26*, 325–346.

Dember, W. N. (1974). Motivation and the cognitive revolution. *American Psychologist, 29*, 161–168.

Doyle, W. (1983). Academic work. *Review of Educational Research, 53*, 159–199.

Durik, A. M., Vida, M., & Eccles, J. S. (2006). Task values and ability beliefs as predictors of high school literacy choices: A developmental analysis. *Journal of Educational Psychology, 98*, 382–393.

Dweck, C. S., & Leggett, E. L. (1988). A social-cognitive approach to motivation and personality. *Psychological Review, 95*, 256–273.

Eccles (Parsons), J., Adler, T. F., Futterman, R., Goff, S. B., Kaczala, C. M., Meece, J. L., et al. (1983). Expectancies, values, and academic behaviors. In J. T. Spence (Ed.), *Achievement and achievement motivation* (pp. 75–146). San Francisco: Freeman.

Eccles, J. S. (1993). School and family effects on the ontogeny of children's interest, self-perceptions, and activity choices. In J. E. Jacobs (Ed.), *Developmental perspectives on motivation* (Vol. 40, pp. 145–208). Lincoln: University of Nebraska Press.

Eccles, J. S., & Wigfield, A. (1995). In the mind of the actor: The structure of adolescents' achievement task values and expectancy-related beliefs. *Personality and Social Psychology Bulletin, 21*, 215–225.

Eccles, J. S., Wigfield, A., Harold, R. D., & Blumenfeld, P. (1993). Age and gender differences in children's self- and task perceptions during elementary school. *Child Development, 64*, 830–847.

Eisenberger, R., Pierce, W. D., & Cameron, J. (1999). Effects of reward on intrinsic motivation–Negative, neutral, and positive: Comment on Deci, Koestner, and Ryan (1999). *Psychological Bulletin, 125*, 677–691.

Elliot, A .J. (2005). A conceptual history of the achievement goal construct. In A. J. Elliot & C. S. Dweck (Eds.), *Handbook of competence and motivation* (pp. 52–72). New York: Guilford.

Elliot, A. J., & Church, M. A. (1997). A hierarchical model of approach and avoidance achievement motivation. *Journal of Personality and Social Psychology, 72*, 218–232.

Elliot, A. J., & Harackiewicz, J. M. (1996). Approach and avoidance achievement goals and intrinsic motivation: A meditational analysis. *Journal of Personality and Social Psychology, 70*, 461–475.

Elliot, A. J., & McGregor, H. A. (1999). Test anxiety and the hierarchical model of approach and avoidance achievement motivation. *Journal of Personality and Social Psychology, 76*, 628–644.

Elliot, A. J., & McGregor, H. A. (2001). A 2 * 2 achievement goal framework. *Journal of Personality and Social Psychology, 80*, 501–519.

Elliot, A. J., McGregor, H. A., & Gable, S. (1999). Achievement goals, study strategies, and exam performance: A meditational analysis. *Journal of Educational Psychology, 91*, 549–563.

Freedman, J., Cunningham, J., & Krismer, K. (1992). Inferred values and the reverse-incentive effect in induced compliance. *Journal of Personality and Social Psychology, 62*, 357–368.

Freud, S. (1966). *The complete introductory lectures on psychoanalysis* (J. Strachey, Trans.). New York: Norton.

Fuligni, A. J., Eccles, J. S., & Barber, B. L. (1995). The long-term effects of seventh-grade ability grouping in mathematics. *Journal of Early Adolescence, 15*, 58–89.

Gamoran, A. (1992). Is ability grouping equitable? *Educational Leadership, 50*, 11–17.

Gottfried, A. E., Fleming, J. S., & Gottfried, A. W. (2001). Continuity of academic intrinsic motivation from childhood through late adolescence: A longitudinal study. *Journal of Educational Psychology, 93*, 3–13.

Harackiewicz, J. M., Barron, K. E., Carter, S. M., Lehto, A. T., & Elliot, A. J. (1997). Predictors and consequences of achievement goals in the college classroom: Maintaining interest and making the grade. *Journal of Personality and Social Psychology, 73*, 1284–1295.

Harackiewicz, J. M., Barron, K. E., Pintrich, P. R., Elliot, A. J., & Thrash, T. M. (2002). Revision of achievement goal theory: Necessary and illuminating. *Journal of Educational Psychology, 94*, 638–645.

Heckhausen, H. (2008). Historical trends in motivation research. In J. Heckhausen, & H. Heckhausen (Eds.), *Motivation and action* (2nd ed., pp. 10–41). New York: Cambridge University Press.

Hidi, S. (1990). Interest and its contribution as a mental resource for learning. *Review of Educational Research, 60*, 549–571.

Hull, C. L. (1943). *Principles of behavior.* New York: Appleton-Century-Crofts.

James, W. (1890). *The principles of psychology* (Vol. 2). New York: Henry Holt.

Johnson, D. W., Johnson, R. T., & Smith, K. (2007). The state of cooperative learning in postsecondary and professional settings. . *Educational Psychology Review, 19*, 15–29.

Johnson, D. W., Maruyama, G., Johnson, R., Nelson, D., & Skon, L. (1981). Effects of cooperative, competitive, and individualistic goal structures on achievement: A meta-analysis. *Psychological Bulletin, 89*, 47–62.

Kaplan, A., Middleton, M. J., Urdan, T., & Midgley, C. (2002). Achievement goals and goal structures. In C. Midgley (Ed.), *Goals, goal structures, and patterns of adaptive learning* (pp. 21–53). Mahwah, NJ: Lawrence Erlbaum Associates.

Kohn, A. (1993). *Punished by rewards: The trouble with gold stars, incentive plans, A's, praise, and other bribes.* Boston, MA: Houghton Mifflin Co.

Kohn, A. (1996). By all available means: Cameron and Pierce's defense of extrinsic motivators. *Review of Educational Research, 66*, 1–4.

Lepper, M. R., Greene, D., & Nisbett, R. E. (1973). Undermining children's intrinsic interest with extrinsic reward: A test of the "overjustification" hypothesis. *Journal of Personality and Social Psychology, 28*, 129–137.

Lepper, M. R., & Henderlong, J. (2000). Turning "play" into "work" and "work" into "play:" 25 years of research on intrinsic versus extrinsic motivation. In C. Sansone, & J. Harackiewicz (Eds.), *Intrinsic and extrinsic motivation: The search for optimal motivation and performance* (pp. 257–307). San Diego: Academic Press.

Lepper, M. R., Henderlong, J., & Gingras, I. (1999). Understanding the effects of extrinsic rewards on intrinsic motivation: Uses and abuses of meta-analysis: Comment on Deci, Koestner, and Ryan (1999). *Psychological Bulletin, 125*, 669–676.

Lepper, M. R., Keavney, M., & Drake, M. (1996). Intrinsic motivation and extrinsic rewards: A commentary on Cameron and Pierce's meta analysis. *Review of Educational Research, 66*, 5–32.

Linn, R. L., Baker, E. L., & Betebenner, D. W. (2002). Accountability systems: implications of requirements of the No Child Left Behind Act of 2001. *Educational Researcher, 31*, 3–16.

Linnenbrink, E. A. (2005). The dilemma of performance-approach goals: The use of multiple goal contexts to promote students' motivation and learning. *Journal of Educational Psychology, 97,* 197–213.

Linnenbrink, E. A., & Pintrich, P. R. (2001). Multiple goals, multiple contexts: The dynamic interplay between personal goals and contextual goal stresses. In S. Volet, & S. Jaervelae (Eds.), *Motivation in learning contexts: Theoretical advances and methodological implications. Advances in learning and instruction series* (pp. 251–269). Elmsford, NY: Pergamon Press, Inc.

Maehr, M. L. (1976). Continuing motivation: An analysis of a seldom considered educational outcome. *Review of Educational Research, 46,* 443–462.

Maehr, M. L., & Midgley, C. (1996). *Transforming school cultures.* Boulder, CO: Westview Press.

Maslow, A. (1987). *Motivation and personality* (3rd ed.). New York: Harper & Row.

Mathis, W. J. (2003). No Child Left Behind: Costs and benefits. *Phi Delta Kappan, 84,* 679–686.

Middleton, M. J., & Midgley, C. (1997). Avoiding the demonstration of lack of ability: An underexplored aspect of goal theory. *Journal of Educational Psychology, 89,* 710–718.

Midgley, C. (Ed.). (2002). *Goals, goal structures, and patterns of adaptive learning.* Mahwah, NJ: Lawrence Erlbaum Associates.

Midgley, C., Kaplan, A., & Middleton, M. J. (2001). Performance-approach goals: Good for what, for whom, under what circumstances, and at what cost? *Journal of Educational Psychology, 93,* 77–86.

Midgley, C., & Urdan, T. (2001). Academic self-handicapping and achievement goals: A further examination. *Contemporary Educational Psychology, 26,* 61–75.

Mowrer, O.H. (1960). *Learning theory and behavior.* New York: Wiley.

Oakes, J., & Lipton, M. (1990). Tracking and ability grouping: A structural barrier to access and achievement. In J. I. Goodlad, & P. Keating (Eds.), *Access to knowledge: An agenda for our nation's schools* (pp. 187–204). New York: College Entrance Examination Board.

Pajares, F. (1996). Self-efficacy beliefs in academic settings. *Review of Educational Research, 66,* 543–578.

Palincsar, A. S. (1986). The role of dialogue in providing scaffolded instruction. *Educational Psychologist, 21,* 73–98.

Patrick, H., Anderman, L. H., Ryan, A. M., Edelin, K. C., & Midgley, C. (2001). Teachers' communication of goal orientations in four fifth-grade classrooms. *Elementary School Journal, 102,* 35–58.

Pavlov, I. P. (1927). *Lectures on conditioned reflexes* (G. V. Anrep, Trans.). London: Oxford University Press.

Pintrich, P. R. (2000a). An achievement goal theory perspective on issues in motivation terminology, theory, and research. *Contemporary Educational Psychology, 25,* 92–104.

Pintrich, P. R. (2000b). Multiple goals, multiple pathways: The role of goal orientation in learning and achievement. *Journal of Educational Psychology, 92,* 544–555.

Pintrich, P.R., & Schunk, D.H. (2002). *Motivation in education: Theory, research, and applications* (2nd ed.). Upper Saddle River, NJ: Merrill/Prentice Hall.

Pittman, T. S., Davey, M. E., Alafat, K. A., Wetherill, K. V., & Kramer, N. A. (1980). Informational versus controlling verbal rewards. *Personality and Social Psychology Bulletin, 6,* 228–233.

Qin, Z., Johnson, D. W., & Johnson, R. T. (1995). Cooperative versus competitive efforts and problem solving. *Review of Educational Research, 65,* 129–143.

Remley, N.R. (1980). J.B. Watson and J.J.B. Morgan: The original drive theory of motivation. *Bulletin of the Psychonomic Society, 16,* 314–316.

Renninger, K. A. (2000). Individual interest and its implications for understanding intrinsic motivation. In J. M. Harackiewicz, & C. Sansone (Eds.), *Intrinsic and extrinsic motivation: The search for optimal motivation and performance* (pp. 373–404). San Diego: Academic Press.

Roeser, R. W. (2004). Competing schools of thought in achievement goal theory? In P. R. Pintrich, & M. L. Maehr (Eds.), *Motivating students, improving schools: The legacy of Carol Midgley* (pp. 265–300). San Diego: Elsevier.

Roney, C. J. R., & O'Connor, M. C. (2008). The interplay between achievement goals and specific target goals in determining performance. *Journal of Research in Personality, 42,* 482–489.

Ryan, A. M., Hicks, L. H., & Midgley, C. (1997). Social goals, academic goals, and avoiding seeking help in the classroom. *Journal of Early Adolescence, 17,* 152–171.

Ryan, R., Connell, J., & Deci, E. (1985). A motivational analysis of self-determination and self-regulation. In C. Ames, & R. Ames (Eds.), *Research on motivation in education.* Vol. 2: *The classroom* (pp. 13–51). New York: Academic Press.

Ryan, R. M., & Deci, E. L. (1996). When paradigms clash: Comments on Cameron and Pierce's claim that rewards do not undermine intrinsic motivation. *Review of Educational Research, 66,* 33–38.

Ryan, R.M., & Deci, E.L. (2000a). Intrinsic and extrinsic motivations: Classic definitions and new directions. *Contemporary Educational Psychology, 25,* 54–67.

Ryan, R. M., & Deci, E. L. (2000b). When rewards compete with nature: The undermining of intrinsic motivation and self-regulation. In C. Sansone, & J. M. Harackiewicz (Eds.), *Intrinsic and extrinsic motivation: The search for optimal motivation and performance* (pp. 13–54). San Diego, CA: Academic Press, Inc.

Rychlak, J. E. (1993). William James and the concept of free will. In M. E. Donnelley (Ed.), *Reinterpreting the legacy of William James* (pp. 323–338). Washington, DC: American Psychological Association.

Saleh, M., Lazonder, A. W., & De Jong, T. (2005). Effects of within-class ability grouping on social interaction, achievement, and motivation. *Instructional Science, 33,* 105–119.

Schiefele, U., Krapp, A., & Winteler, A. (1992). Interest as a predictor of academic achievement: A meta-analysis of research. In K. A. Renninger, S. Hidi, & A. Krapp (Eds.), *The role of interest in learning and development* (pp. 183–212). Hillsdale, NJ: Lawrence Erlbaum Associates.

Schraw, G., Flowerday, T., & Lehman, S. (2001). Increasing situational interest in the classroom. *Educational Psychology Review, 13,* 211–224.

Schunk, D. H., & Pajares, F. (2002). The development of academic self-efficacy. In A. Wigfield, & J. S. Eccles (Eds.), *Development of achievement motivation* (pp. 15–31). San Diego, CA: Academic Press.

Schunk, D. H., Pintrich, P. R., & Meece, J. (2008). *Motivation in education: Theory, research, and applications* (3rd ed.). Upper Saddle River, NJ: Pearson.

Skaalvik, E. M. (1997). Self-enhancing and self-defeating ego orientation: Relations with task and avoidance orientation, achievement, self-perceptions, and anxiety. *Journal of Educational Psychology, 89,* 71–81.

Skinner, B. F. (1953). *Science and human behavior.* New York: Macmillan.

Skinner, B. F. (1954). The science of learning and the art of teaching. *Harvard Educational Review, 24,* 86–97.

Slavin, R. E. (Ed.). (1983). *Cooperative learning.* New York: Longman.

Slavin, R. E. (1990). Ability grouping and student achievement in secondary schools. *Review of Educational Research, 60,* 417–499.

Slavin, R. E. (1992). When and why does cooperative learning increase achievement? Theoretical and empirical perspectives. In R. Hertz-Lazarowitz, & N. Miller (Eds.), *Interaction in cooperative groups: The theoretical anatomy of group learning* (pp. 145–173). Cambridge: Cambridge University Press.

Slavin, R. E. (1996). Research on cooperative learning and achievement: What we know, what we need to know. *Contemporary Educational Psychology, 21,* 43–69.

Thorkildsen, T. A., & Nicholls, J. G. (1998). Fifth graders' achievement orientations and beliefs: Individual and classroom differences. *Journal of Educational Psychology, 90,* 179–201.

Turner, J. C., & Meyer, D. K. (2009). Understanding motivation in mathematics: What is happening in classrooms? In K. R. Wentzel, & A. Wigfield (Eds.), *Handbook of motivation at school* (pp. 527–552). New York: Routledge.

U.S. Department of Education. (2003). *No Child Left Behind: A toolkit for teachers.* Retrieved April 20, 2009, from U.S. Department of Education web site: http://www.ed.gov/teachers/nclbguide/nclb-teachers-toolkit. pdf.

Vygotsky, L. S. (1978). *Mind in society: The development of higher psychological processes* (M. Cole, V. John-Steiner, S. Scribner & E. Souberman, Trans.). Cambridge, MA: Harvard University Press.

Webb, N. M. (1982). Student interaction and learning in small groups. *Review of Educational Research, 52,* 421–445.

Webb, N. M., Nemer, K. M., & Ing, M. (2006). Small-group reflections: Parallels between teacher discourse and student behavior in peer-directed groups. *The Journal of the Learning Sciences, 15,* 63–119.

Weiner, B. (1990). History of motivational research in education. *Journal of Educational Psychology, 82,* 616–622.

Weinstein, R. S., Marshall, H., Brattesani, K., & Middlestadt, S. (1992). Student perceptions of differential teacher treatment in open and traditional classrooms. *Journal of Educational Psychology, 74,* 678–692.

Wentzel, K. R., & Wigfield, A. (2007). Motivational interventions that work: Themes and remaining issues. *Educational Psychologist, 42,* 261–271.

Wigfield, A., & Eccles, J. S. (1992). The development of achievement task values: A theoretical analysis. *Developmental Review, 12,* 265–310.

Wigfield, A., & Eccles, J. S. (2002). The development of competence beliefs, expectancies for success, and achievement values from childhood through adolescence. In A. Wigfield, & J. S. Eccles (Eds.), *Development of achievement motivation* (pp. 91–120). San Diego, CA: Academic Press.

Wigfield, A., Eccles, J. S., MacIver, D., Reuman, D. A., & Midgley, C. (1991). Transitions during early adolescence: Changes in children's domain-specific self-perceptions and general self-esteem across the transition to junior high school. *Developmental Psychology, 27,* 552–565.

Wigfield, A., Eccles, J.S., Yoon, K.S., Harold, R.D., Arbreton, A.J.A., Freedman-Doan, C., & Blumenfeld, P.C. (1997). Change in children's competence beliefs and subjective task values across the elementary school years: A 3-year study. *Journal of Educational Psychology, 89,* 451–469.

Part II
Research on Instruction

12

INTRODUCTION TO RESEARCH ON INSTRUCTION
Patricia A. Alexander and Richard E. Mayer

In the opening pages of *Talks to Teachers*, William James ([1899] 1979) contrasted the science of psychology with the art of teaching. As the fore-runner of educational psychology wrote:

> To know psychology, therefore, is absolutely no guarantee that we shall be good teachers. To advance to that result, we must have an additional endowment altogether, a happy tact and ingenuity to tell us what definite things to say and do when the pupil is before us. That ingenuity in meeting and pursuing the pupil, that tact for the concrete situation, though they are the alpha and omega of the teacher's art, are things to which psychology cannot help us in the least.
>
> (p. 7)

Thankfully, since James gave those groundbreaking lectures that put our discipline on its current course, many educational psychologists have set aside the belief that teaching must be relegated only to art or that "psychology cannot help us in the least." As the ensuing chapters strongly establish, educational psychology has a great deal to say to those concerned with the academic development of students. Even more importantly, the mission of this collection of exceptional chapters is to demonstrate there are critical processes and techniques that have been shown—through science—to contribute to the learning of students. Our commitment in developing this section of the handbook was to set aside the "arts" of teaching when those arts have not been put to empirical test or when they operate solely at the level of pedagogical intuition. What we can see in the pages that follow is that science has so very much to contribute to teachers and about teaching and about the interactions between teacher and students. These chapters are aimed at, in essence, science *in* teaching.

Thus, we begin this scientific exploration of instruction with a detailed consideration of the nature and influence of feedback on student learning by John Hattie and Mark Gan (Chapter 13). What these researchers allow us to appreciate is not only how complex and varied this seemingly commonplace process of giving feedback can be, but also how very powerful the effects can be on all those who populate the classroom community. Indeed, the evidence that Hattie and Gan present positions feedback among the top 10 influences on student achievement. However, as they also caution, "merely prescribing lots of feedback does not imply that learning will take place" (p. 24). Instead, it is understanding how to craft and deliver feedback effectively.

Like feedback, examples are commonplace components of instruction that we all may have come to take for granted. As with feedback, Alexander Renkl (Chapter 14) takes care to remind us that examples *per se* do not produce the thinking and performance desired. Rather, evidence points us in a direction as to the more effective use of examples. What do good examples look like and when should they be introduced into the instructional context? Renkl's detailed analysis helps us understand why well-crafted and well-positioned examples translate into positive learning.

According to Renkl, one of the reasons that examples can facilitate the deeper processing of content has to do with the self-explanations that they promote. The chapter by Brenda Fonseca and Michelene Chi (Chapter 15) goes far to illuminate the facilitative nature of self-explanations, especially when this reflective, analytic process is raised to the level of a learning strategy. In effect, when individuals intentionally and purposefully engage in self-explanation to augment problem-solving, the outcome can be significantly better than when such analytic self-talk does not occur or remains in the mental shadows. Fonseca and Chi position effective self-explanation within a theoretical framework that entails *passive-active-constructive-interactive* learning activities.

While the chapters by Hattie and Gan, Renkl, and Fonseca and Chi demonstrate how common pedagogical and cognitive processes can be effectively re-cast to extend and deepen human learning, the next collection of chapters deals more expressly with human relations and verbal exchanges. For example, the chapter on peer interactions by Kathryn Wentzel and Deborah Watkins (Chapter 16) turns our attention to student-to-student relations and the significance of those relations to learning and development. Drawing on the extensive literature in educational and social psychology, the authors set out to establish that "this body of work illustrates how learning is inextricably linked to the social contexts within which children learn, and highlights the notion that intellectual development is highly dependent on the characteristics of and opportunities provided by peers within learning contexts." We could not agree more.

The power of social relations that Wentzel and Watkins established for peers is further evidenced in Robert Slavin's consideration of cooperative learning (Chapter 17). As a leading authority in cooperative learning, Slavin articulates a particular configuration of social relations where there is an expressed and shared purpose of learning or academic performance. Through his detailed and well-substantiated presentation, Slavin examines cooperative learning from four theoretical perspectives that differ in their goals and underlying processes. He also offers a characterization of various forms of cooperative learning that have been empirically tested. One of those characterizations is the role of the teacher in not only forming these cooperative groups, but also in systematically monitoring their progress toward mutual learning and performance goals.

What the chapters on peer interactions and cooperative learning share is a systematic exploration of learning and cognitive processing as it takes place within groups. In the chapter on inquiry-based instruction by Sofie Loyens and Remy Rikers (Chapter 18), this investment in co-constructed understanding or enhanced performance continues, but at the level of the class. Through a broad consideration of inquiry-based instruction, the authors allow us to ponder *if, when,* or *how* the joint pursuit of understanding between teachers and students translates into better learning. As we learn from the authors, the answers to those questions are not simple or straightforward. Rather, they demand a systematic consideration of many factors within the learning environment, including the background of the students and the guidance afforded by teachers. Loyens and Rikers provide just such a consideration and the results should prove invaluable for educators and educational researchers looking to share instructional responsibility within the learning environment.

Across many of the chapters in this section, there is the shared recognition that words matter. Whether those words come in the form of feedback, self-explanations, or peer interactions, what is said and how it is said are core to human learning. With the chapter entitled, "Instruction Based on Discussion" (Chapter 19), Karen Murphy, Ian Wilkinson, and Anna Soter take on the topic of one specific form of verbal exchange that has had a presence in human learning long before Socrates engaged in pointed dialogues with young Greek students. What these researchers effectively argue by means of empirical evidence is that all discussions are not equal. In fact, there are many instances when the inclusion of discussion does little more than increase talk—not achievement. With that awareness, Murphy et al. specify the forms or characteristics of discussion that are, in fact, related to higher levels of student learning. Among those characteristics are efforts to promote critical analysis and evidentiary-based responses; getting beyond simple talk to argument and justification.

The final grouping of chapters in our Research on Instruction section have the shared attribute of examining instructional methods that are often implemented with computer-based technologies that are part and parcel of students' lives not only in school but in the world outside the classroom. Although these chapters highlight computer-based media, the authors are careful to note that it is instructional methods—involving tutoring, graphics, and simulations—that cause learning. In short, effective instructional methods implemented by computer-based media can also be effective in face-to-face learning environments, and vice versa.

For instance, in their chapter on tutoring (Chapter 20), Arthur Graesser, Sidney D'Mello, and Whitney Cade remind us that the value of shared thinking and learning described by Robert Slavin (Chapter 17) is very evident when there is someone within a pairing who has particular knowledge or expertise to support the learning of the other. This is the foundation of tutoring, which is a special case of one-to-one instruction. Several aspects of the Graesser et al. chapter are unique. For one, the authors explain how the relationship between tutor and tutee is not necessarily fixed. Rather, as the nature of the task or content shifts, so too can the roles and responsibilities of the pair; that is, the tutor can become the tutee. Further, tutoring need not come just in the form of direct human-to-human contact. Intelligent tutors, which are technology-based systems, have been shown to be very effective in supporting the learning of students employing them. Graesser et al. provide an excellent overview of such intelligent tutoring systems that have strong records of promoting students' comprehension and domain learning.

According to Richard Mayer (Chapter 21), instructional visualizations are visual-spatial representations intended to promote understanding and contribute to learning. Such visualizations fill the multimedia landscape in which we live and work, but do such visualizations actually have the desired effects? That is the first of several critical questions that Mayer explores in this richly substantiated chapter. Once the potential value of instructional visualizations has been empirically established, the author turns to other equally critical questions including when, how, and where visualizations give rise to greater comprehension, higher recall, and better achievement. Building on the extensive literature he has helped to forge, Mayer puts forward five instructional design principles that should result in positive effects on cognitive performance. Such principles also have implications for instructional practice as students increasingly engage in multimedia learning.

In the final contribution to this investigation of evidenced-based instructional processes and technique, Ton de Jong (Chapter 22) delves into the realm of computer simulations, which have become viable forms of instruction because of continued advances in computer-based learning. As de Jong makes clear, there are important learning experiences that occur in the real world that cannot be simply, safely, or effectively brought into the classroom. Computer simulations that are well crafted according to design principles can make that possible through *simplification*, which entails the reduction and abstraction of those real-world phenomena.

All the contributions in Part II of the Handbook stand as testament to the fact that effective instruction cannot be and must not be divorced from science—regardless of James's claim to the contrary. These chapters also argue strongly that there are any number of processes or techniques that teachers can apply with the assurance that their pedagogical decisions come with the backing of empirical evidence that such processes and techniques work to the betterment of learning and achievement.

Another important lesson to be learned from all these chapters is that these effective processes and techniques can be based on acts and materials that already populate learning environments—from verbal exchanges to well-chosen examples and from shared learning to self-explanations. Further, these evidence-based processes and techniques embrace the hypermedia and multimedia world in which we all live and learn. But, as with inquiry or cooperative learning, these researchers remind us that simply infusing intelligent tutoring systems, visualizations, and simulations into the curriculum does not guarantee better learning. To paraphrase Mayer, research is needed to determine how, when and where instructional methods work, including those afforded by hypermedia and multimedia environments.

REFERENCE

James, W. ([1899] 1979). Talks to teachers on psychology. In G. E. Myers (Gen. Ed.), *William James: Writings 1878–1899*. New York: The Library of America.

13

INSTRUCTION BASED ON FEEDBACK

John Hattie and Mark Gan

There is a preponderance of evidence that feedback is a powerful influence in the development of learning outcomes. Two findings from the many meta-analyses of the effects of feedback are most fascinating—the average effects of feedback are among the highest we know in education, and feedback effects are among the most variable in their influences. From a review of 12 meta-analyses that have included specific information on feedback in classrooms (based on 196 studies and 6972 effect-sizes), the average effect-size was $d = .79$, which is twice the average effect (Hattie, 2009). This places feedback among the top 10 influences on achievement. The variance of effects, however, was considerable, indicating that some types of feedback are more powerful than others (Kluger & DeNisi, 1996). It appears that merely prescribing lots of feedback does not imply that learning will take place, as one has to take into consideration the differential effects of feedback on learning as well as learners.

An accompanying finding is that although feedback is frequently provided in typical classrooms, much of this information is poorly received and hardly used in revision of work (Carless, 2006). Most teacher feedback is presented to groups and so often students do not believe that such class feedback is relevant to them. Carless (2006) also has shown that teachers consider their feedback far more valuable than the students do—students often find teachers' feedback confusing, non-reasoned, and not understandable. Sometimes students think they have understood the teachers' feedback when they have not, and even when they do understand, they claim to have difficulties in applying it to their learning (Goldstein, 2006; Nuthall, 2007).

The research on feedback has focused predominantly on findings about its effects, whereas it is time to see *how* feedback makes a difference in classrooms. Although researchers are beginning to see the impact of feedback from a multidimensional perspective, more work needs to be done to explore effective feedback strategies in relation to individual learner characteristics (e.g., learner dispositions at the early learning, proficiency, or expert stage of learning); the active engagement of feedback with learners in terms of cognitive, metacognitve and motivational variables; as well as the nature, frequency and timing of feedback (Narciss, 2008). It seems we know much about the power of feedback, but too little about how to harness this power and make it work more effectively in the classroom.

The first part of this chapter outlines four major learning perspectives that can help frame research in feedback and provides key studies to illustrate how different assumptions of learning and learners can influence the way feedback is construed and incorporated into the teaching and learning process. This sets the scene for the second part of the chapter, which considers feedback as helping make teaching and learning "visible." In particular, the second section highlights the power of peer feedback; the mind sets of teachers when giving feedback, and particularly when they are receiving and seeking feedback; as well as the mechanism of developing teacher–student relationships that led to trust in students acknowledging error and misunderstandings, which then permits feedback to be effective. Central to this chapter is the observation that: (a) feedback is a consequence of instruction and it is more productive to consider when and how it is received rather than when or how it is given; (b) feedback is powerful when it makes the criteria of success in reaching learning goals transparent to the learner; (c) feedback is powerful when it cues attention of the learner to the learning task, task processing strategies and self-regulation strategies instead of attention to the self; (d) feedback should be calibrated to engage learners with the learning task at, or just above, the level where the learner is currently functioning; (e) feedback should challenge the learner to invest effort in setting and monitoring learning goals; (f) the learning environment should be open to errors and disconfirmation; (g) peer feedback provides a platform for engaging students in interactive and elaborative feedback discourse as well as taking ownership of their learning; and (h) feedback should also cue teachers' attention to errors in their own instruction so that modifications can be made to improve teaching and learning.

THEORETICAL PERSPECTIVES OF LEARNING AND THEIR RELATION TO FEEDBACK

Feedback can serve different functions depending on the particular learning perspective under which it is viewed and the underlying assumptions about the learning context on which research in these areas are based. This part of the review considers four major psychological perspectives—objectivism, information processing, sociocultural, and visible learning theory—that provide the frameworks for describing different views of learning and the nature of feedback. The features of these four theoretical perspectives are summarized in Table 13.1.

Objectivism

Objectivism takes the view that "reliable knowledge about the world" exists (Jonassen, 1991, p. 8) and instruction based on this assumption is seen as predominantly "receptive-transmission" (Askew & Lodge, 2000). From an epistemological view, objectivism is a mirror image or reality created by the mind and these representations of the real world constitute the way of knowing (Lakoff, 1987). The traditional learning theory paradigm of behaviorism adopts this objectivist perspective and most feedback studies in the earlier literature have examined feedback within this philosophical viewpoint (Mory, 2004).

From a behaviorist perspective, learning is viewed as conditioning where behavior that is followed by a reinforcer will increase in frequency or probability (i.e., Skinner's operant conditioning). Learning is seen as a process of reinforcing knowledge acquired

Table 13.1 Perspectives of learning and the nature of feedback

Philosophical perspective	Assumptions	View of learning	Nature of feedback
Objectivism – Reliable knowledge of the world exist	• All reality consists of entities • The entities, their properties & their relations made up our world • This reality exists outside of the individual • The mind functions to create representations of these entities and learning involves knowing these correct representations	• Behaviorist • 3 types of learning: respondent learning, operant conditioning & observational learning • Social-behavioral	• Feedback is external response which may contain symbols that match an external entity • Feedback reinforces current representations or corrects misrepresentations of this external entity (by providing corrective information)
Information processing each learner constructs his or her own reality through processing and interpretation of experiences of the external world	• Reality is an interpretation based on an individual's experiences • Learning takes place through individual meaning construction or cognitive activity when an individual tries to make sense of the world	• Cognitive elaboration • Self-regulated learning	• Feedback helps learners in processing information and meaning construction • Feedback is used to build internal understanding through connections with learner's prior experiences, mental structures and beliefs
Socioculturalism – knowledge creation is a shared rather than an individual experience	• Reality exists through individual as well as being shaped by society and an individual's relationship with society • Learning involves social negotiation of meaning	• Vygotsky's zone of proximal development	• Feedback is a social negotiation through the meaningful use of language • Feedback involves a reciprocal and dialogic process of co-construction of meaning • Feedback quality depends on the interaction process of peers and not just the person providing feedback
Visible learning and teaching – knowledge creation is based on developing strategies of learning used to regulate understandings	• Knowledge creation is an individual, shared, and interactive process • Reality exists through developing evaluative criteria as the veracity, worthwhileness, or integrity of the individual's experiences • Learning involves social and evaluative negotiation of meaning	• Hattie & Timperley's levels of feedback	• Feedback is a social negotiation through the development of cognitive and evaluative skills in developing understanding • Feedback involves an explicit and conscious discourse with attention to assimilation, accommodation, and evaluation • Feedback quality depends on the changes to teaching and learning strategies of the teacher, learner, and peers to effect the learning goals

in a sequenced and hierarchical fashion and learning tasks can be preplanned, organized, and programmed with specific outcomes defined. The learning task is analyzed to identify the components that must be acquired in order to complete the task and the most appropriate sequence of learning is prescribed based on observable learning outcomes. Feedback is usually seen as reinforcement, aimed at helping the learner to progress from a hierarchy of simple to more complex task performance. The objectivist roots are evident, with feedback provided from an external source (usually from the teacher who is viewed as an expert) in order to match an external learning outcome to the learner's current observable performance on the prescribed task. The dominant feedback discourse is one of receptive-transmission (Askew & Lodge, 2000) and a prevalent view of feedback is that it serves as a motivator or incentive for increasing response rate and/or accuracy (Kulhavy & Wager, 1993).

A classical example of this instructional approach is the programmed instruction of the 1960s—depending on the answer to a question the student is directed to remediation or to more difficult questions. Although it can be argued that feedback as reinforcement is beneficial to novice learners on new learning tasks, its effects are limited and at times confusing (Kulhavy & Wager, 1993). The focus on incentives may distract learners from the instructional content of feedback and results in little effort used to interpret feedback for learning (Kulhavy & Wager, 1993). Anderson and his colleagues (1972) found that students usually bypass the feedback if the answer is readily available in the learning task and when feedback is provided prior to completion of the task, students tend to copy their answers from the feedback instead of processing the feedback information meaningfully. This finding points to the importance of providing feedback as a "consequence" of performance and not before completion of any learning task.

The view that feedback serves as a motivator or incentive for learning is still prevalent in the classrooms of today and there remains a perpetual confusion between praise and content-related feedback (Hattie & Timperley, 2007). Deci, Koestner, and Ryan (1999) found that when teachers provide tangible rewards as a form of feedback, intrinsic motivation is significantly undermined and students are less inclined to take responsibility for motivating or regulating themselves. Feedback as extrinsic rewards often led students to place more emphasis on incentives, which result in greater surveillance, evaluation and competition, rather than enhanced engagement in learning. Kulhavy and Wager (1993) suggested that motivational variables be separated from the feedback message, in order to focus on the instructional content of feedback.

Information Processing Perspective

The information-processing perspective of learning may be seen as a transition phase from behaviorism to socioculturalism and represents a shift in emphasis from an external view toward an internal view. An important feature of information-processing theories is that they recognize the cognitive ability of individuals to use information actively when engaging with the learning task. This suggests that feedback functions not only to reinforce correct answers but also as corrective information to help learners to correct his or her errors. The feedback-as-information position asserts that correction and analysis of errors is a crucial component of learning and feedback acts as verification of a learner's response certitude or level of certainty (Kulhavy & Stock, 1989).

For example, Kulhavy and Stock's (1989) Response Certitude model suggested that instructional feedback message contains two important components: verification and elaboration. Verification is stated as a *dichotomous judgment* to indicate that a response is right or wrong. Elaboration is the component of the feedback message, which contains relevant information to help the learner in error correction. Feedback elaboration can be classified based on the type of information included: (a) task-specific; (b) instruction-based; and (c) extra-instructional. Task-specific elaborations include restatement of the correct answer, or inclusion of multiple-choice alternatives as part of item feedback. Instruction-based elaborations provide explanations of why a certain response is correct, or re-presentation of the instructional text in which the right answer was contained. Extra-instructional elaboration refers to new examples or analogies not found in the instructional text. Besides the type of information, elaboration can take different forms, which refer to changes in stimulus structure between instruction and the feedback message. The load of an elaborative feedback is the total amount of information contained in the feedback message.

In this model, the feedback process is composed of three cycles, in which each cycle involves an external stimulus, learner comparison of the input to a reference standard, followed by a resultant response. The first cycle describes the learner as comparing the perceived task demand against previous experience and evaluates various response possibilities. The second cycle involves feedback processing by the learner. Here the learner's level of certainty (response certitude) is argued to be related to the discrepancy between perceived stimulus and reference standard results. According to the authors, when learners are certain their answer is correct (high certitude correct with low discrepancy), they will spend little time analyzing feedback, and verification feedback is sufficient. When learners are certain their answer is correct but it was in reality an incorrect response (high certitude correct with high discrepancy), elaborate information in feedback is useful to the learner, who will spend more time reviewing feedback. For learners with low-certitude responses, they would more likely to benefit from feedback that acts as new instruction. Cycle three involves the learner responding to the same task after processing the feedback, and it is the aim that the corrective feedback now leads to a correct response (see also Kulhavy et al., 1990). Heubusch and Lloyd (1998) reviewed 24 studies on the effect of corrective feedback on reading comprehension. They found that there were some common characteristics such as correcting errors immediately, requiring students to repeat the correct response, and interrupting the reading process to provide effective correction. Although this model is built around experimental testing environments that are unlike the typical classroom-learning situation, it supports the notion of learner involvement in the feedback process and highlights the need for adaptive use of feedback information with consideration to learner characteristics, in this case, high or low confidence in responding to questions.

Taking a step further, Bangert-Drowns et al. (1991) proposed a five-stage model of mindful feedback. This model suggests that feedback that encourages learner's mindful reflection is beneficial to learning. Although the model explicates the need for reflection on the part of the learner, the main focus of feedback is to change the current behavioral and cognitive state of the learner. For feedback to promote learning, it has to be designed to bring about mindfulness and to minimize mindlessness, such as providing feedback before learners begin their memory search for an answer.

Another feedback framework that takes an information processing perspective is the feedback intervention theory by Kluger and DeNisi (1996). This theory suggests that feedback intervention that focuses the learner on the learning task results in a larger learning gain than feedback that draws attention to the self, which, on the contrary, can be detrimental to learning. It follows that when norm-referenced feedback that compares the individual's performance to lower achieving learners may attribute their poor performance to a lack of ability, for example, this leads to decreased expectancies in future performance and lower motivation on future tasks. Kluger and DeNisi (1996) argued that there were three classes of variables, which determined the effect of feedback on performance: the cues of the feedback message, the nature of the task performed, and situational and personality variables. Feedback can provide cues that capture a person's attention. The central assumption is that feedback information gets a person's attention, and that *attention* is hierarchical in nature.

Of the many goals of feedback, it certainly can direct attention to the processes to accomplish the task, provide information about erroneous hypotheses, and motivate students to invest more effort or skill in the task. Feedback effectiveness decreases as attention moves up the hierarchy closer to the self and away from the task. Therefore, feedback that directs its attention to the meta-task goals may lead to disengagement from the task even when the feedback is positive. A major key to unlocking the power of feedback is to ensure the cues are responsive to the task performed and that any provision of these cues considers the situational and personality attributes of the receiver.

Butler and Winne (1995) proposed an examination of feedback that takes into account how internal and external feedback affects self-regulated cognitive engagement with tasks and how different forms of engagement relates to achievement. They argued that feedback serves a multidimensional role in knowledge construction, which translates into a model involving self-regulation. This helps to extend the traditional view of feedback as predominantly seeking a set of correct responses or error-correction to one in which feedback is seen as a function of regulative cognitive process of the learner and is both dependent and a resultant of self-regulated learning. Internal feedback is generated when self-regulated learners monitor their processes of task engagement (e.g., setting goals, applying strategies or reviewing products of learning). This internal feedback provides information for the learner to regulate his or her task engagement and may be further influenced by external feedback, motivational beliefs, and affective reactions. When there is a perceived discrepancy between a current state and the desired goals, internal feedback allows the learner to decide whether to invest further effort, modify their plan or abandon the task completely. The result of this cognitive monitoring and processing is the possible change in knowledge and beliefs, which, in turn, might further influence subsequent self-regulation (Butler & Winne, 1995).

Feedback as self-regulation recognizes the importance of interaction between feedback information and the receiver, and further emphasizes the active engagement of the learners in cue-seeking as well as monitoring and evaluating their own performance. For example, Butler and Winne (1995, p. 251) postulated that "several elaborated forms of feedback that may support self-regulated engagement in tasks by enhancing the learner's calibration." *Calibration* describes the "accurate associations between cues and achievement" by the learner, and the learner is said to be *well calibrated* when he or she is able to "self-regulate by recursively adjusting approaches based on perceived task cues in relation to achievement" (p. 251). Citing the study by Balzer et al. (1989), Butler and Winnie argued that cognitive feedback may enhance learners' calibration by monitoring cues such as task features or cognitive activities, which is a necessary part of self-regulation.

Butler and Winne (1995, p. 250) further asserted that learners' "beliefs about learning affect self-regulation by influencing the nature of and interpretation of feedback." Explicating from two lines of research—Schommer and her colleagues' (1992) research on learners' epistemological views about learning and Chinn and Brewer's (1993) review that identified seven ways that learners respond to anomalous information—Butler and Winne acknowledged the need to interpret feedback in light of the learners' beliefs and knowledge domains. In summary, Butler and Winne (1995) concluded that the learner's prior knowledge, beliefs, and thinking act as a filter to mediate the effects of externally provided feedback as well as internal feedback. This mediation, in turn, influences the learner's monitoring of task engagement and progress, which is an inherent part of self-regulated learning. The explicit emphasis on the role of monitoring and feedback within a self-regulated learning framework broadens the objectivist conception of feedback to include the viewpoint of information processing, and hence, "integrates instruction, self-regulation, feedback, and knowledge construction" (p. 275). What is also evident from this synthesis is the acknowledgement that learners are not passive receivers of feedback but actively interpret feedback information through self-regulatory processes and have the capacity to be responsible for their own learning.

Narciss and Huth (2004) suggested a content-related classification of feedback in terms of the instructional context that is addressed by simple or elaborated information. In general, they claimed that designing and developing effective formative feedback needs to take into consideration the instructional factor or context (e.g., instructional objectives, tasks, and errors), learner characteristics (e.g., learning objectives and goals, prior knowledge, skills, abilities, and academic motivation), as well as feedback elements (e.g., content of feedback, function and presentation). The informative value of the feedback can be enhanced by combining elaborated feedback, tutoring, and mastery learning strategies. Narciss (2008) used the term *informative tutoring feedback* to refer to feedback strategies that provide elaborated feedback components to guide learners toward successful task completion. The elaborated feedback information may take the form of: (a) task rules, task constraints, and task requirements; (b) conceptual knowledge; (c) errors or mistakes; (d) procedural knowledge; and (e) metacognitive knowledge. Feedback as tutoring is focused on guiding students in error detection, overcoming obstacles, and applying more efficient strategies for completing the learning tasks (Narciss, 2008).

Socioculturalism

Feedback may be seen as performing a wider function in helping learners when viewed from a sociocultural perspective. The sociocultural view derives from the work of Vygotsky (1978, 1986), who advanced a view that knowledge and understanding are socially constructed through interactions with others. For Vygotsky, the learner's interactions with other people, preferably a more competent member of the society in which the learner is growing up, initiates the learner into the social, linguistic practices and artifacts of the society. Through participating in the cultural life of the community, the learner is seen as engaging in a kind of cognitive apprenticeship, which helps him/her to acquire the *cultural tools* that permit the learner to develop more a advanced level of thinking and conscious control over his or her mental processes. According to Vygotsky, the processes of interaction between the learner and others become internalized as the basis for *intramental* reflection and logical reasoning. Thus, learning and development are seen as mediated by the dialectical relationship between interpersonal and intrapersonal processes (Mercer & Littleton, 2007).

The notion of constructivism postulates that learners actively construct their reality or knowledge based on their prior experiences, mental structures, and beliefs. This firmly places constructivism as a theory of learning and *not* a theory of teaching (Bereiter, 2002; Hattie, 2009). In contrast to objectivism, which views knowledge as existing independently of learners, constructivism considers knowledge as constructed by learners as they attempt to make sense of their experiences. Instead of learning as transfer of knowledge from outside to within the learner, constructivist theory assumes that learners are not empty vessels waiting to be filled but rather active participants in the meaning-making process. The constructive process usually involves the learner forming, elaborating, and testing mental structures until a satisfactory one emerges, which undergoes further changes when the learner experiences conflicting new information which may lead to more restructuring.

Research conducted by Villamil and de Guerrero (2006) provides some insights into situating feedback within a sociocultural framework. Through a long-term study of peer feedback and revision, the authors found that individual development in second language could be enhanced by the social experience of talking about writing, as well as writing and revising with a partner. Five classes were taught how to revise their writing. The first drafts were collected and then randomly paired. Next, students in pairs were asked to revise these drafts with one working as the writer the other as the reader.

Villamil and Guerrero analyzed the interactions and found that the peers needed to be at similar stages of self-regulation and shared control, as well have high levels of empathy when listening to the partner's comments. Then they could discuss textual problems, acquire strategic competence in revising a text, acquire a sense of audience, and develop their own sense of regulation about their own writing. Although the study recognized the beneficial effect of peer interaction in learning, the authors noted the necessity to prepare and instruct learners on desirable behaviors such as maintaining mutual cognitive engagement and minimize negative behaviors that would impede collaborative learning. The authors recommended the need for educators to be aware of the learners' strategic behaviors that may influence the success of scaffolding during peer feedback and to explicitly address the learners' sociocultural contexts and learning backgrounds to enhance collaborative learning in the classroom. They concluded that the exchange of ideas among peers resulted in consolidating, reorganizing and making knowledge explicit for the development of writing skills and discourse strategies. An important implication for feedback is the need to address the sociocultural differences of learners, which may take the form of social relationships, cultural norms, and behavioral expectations (see Pryor & Crossouard, 2008). For example, the nature of the teacher–student and student–student relationships may influence the level of acceptance of feedback by students as well as their involvement in seeking feedback (Bell & Cowie, 2001).

VISIBLE TEACHING AND LEARNING MODELS OF FEEDBACK

The above perspectives suggest that there is need to understand the underlying assumptions that educators make about learning and how such assumptions impact on the way feedback is delivered and used. In classrooms, there may be a need to move from seeing the teacher as giver and learner as receiver of feedback, to also accounting for the social context of learning—particularly the ways peers provide feedback. Thus, feedback needs to move from a predominantly transmissive and verification process to a dialogic and elaborative process in a social context. Then feedback can be seen in a context of students' learning (with peers, with adults, alone), at varying stages of proficiency (novice, proficient, expert) and understanding (surface, deep, conceptual), with differing levels of regulation (by others, with others, self), and with differing levels of information and focus to the feedback information.

An important question is whether the feedback provided is meaningfully received, and then interpreted by a learner to some effect or not. Building on these three models, we advance a further model based on making the visibility of the teaching and learning apparent to both the teacher and learner (or to the same person when the teacher and the learner are one). This model not only critically notes the social context of this visibility and the powerful part peers can play in the learning and feedback process, but sees the most impact relating to when the teacher (a more experienced person who could be adult or peer) receives feedback and thence changes or supports his or her teaching strategies with the resultant effect of improving learning.

The premise of the visibility model is that feedback is most powerful when it makes learning visible to the teacher (who could also be the learner). The notion is that the teacher needs to construct environments and activities that optimize making the learning of the student visible to the teacher (and preferably also to the student). This means that the teacher needs to invest, modify, or enhance their probability of succeeding to making the intentions and success of the learning transparent to the learner, as well as where on this trajectory the student is relative to the success of the learning goal. The key notions are that feedback is enhanced when the criteria of success in reaching the learning goal are most transparent, when students and teacher see sufficient challenge to invest in seeking and using the feedback to assist in reaching success, and when the feedback is sufficiently at or ahead of where the cognitive nature of the task is focused, and it addresses three major questions—Where am I going?, How am I going?, Where to next?

Such feedback often has to compete with many other cues for the student (e.g., completing the task with minimum effort, alternative cues from peers about how to reach success, not realizing the nature of what success in the task looks like, or even knowing when it is achieved). Hence, the social context can be critical when students interpret feedback. Most importantly, feedback is something that has its powers not so much when it is given or how it is given, but when and how it is received—it does not enter a vacuum but enters into a cycle of learning (e.g., from novice, proficiency, expert; from surface, deep, or conceptual; from being passively received to activity regulated into learning). I have outlined the evidence for this model, based on a synthesis of 800 meta-analyses elsewhere (Hattie, 2009).

CURRENT ISSUES AND TRENDS

The Goal Nature of Feedback

Following Sadler (1989), Hattie and Timperley (2007) considered feedback to be information that aims to reduce the gap between what is now and what should/could be. Specifically, we claimed that feedback is information provided by an agent (e.g., teacher, peer, book, parent, and self/experience) regarding aspects of one's performance or understanding that reduces the discrepancy between what is understood and what is aimed to be understood. When a teacher or peer provides information about a student's work or query (e.g., in spoken or printed form) that helps the student move from where they are in their knowledge or understanding closer to what is considered success at the task then there is evidence of feedback. This feedback information could aid the student to increase effort, motivation or engagement in the task, could indicate the correct or incorrectness of the students responding, could indicate that more information is available or needed, could point to directions that the students could pursue, or could indicate alternative strategies to understand particular information. Some key considerations are that feedback comes second—after instruction—and thus is limited in effectiveness when provided in a vacuum; that feedback works optimally when there is a clear appreciation of where the student is currently at and where they need to be; that appropriately challenging tasks optimize the probability that feedback can be valuable; and feedback works best when the current status and goals, the challenge and success criteria of the learning intention are transparent to the teacher and the learner.

The Three Feedback Questions

Hattie and Timperley (2007) argued that feedback can be considered to relate to three major questions and four major dimensions of learning and learners. Effective feedback needs to address one of three major questions asked by the teacher and/or by the student: Where am I going? (What are the goals?), How am I going? (What progress is being made toward the goal?), Where to next? (What activities need to be undertaken to make better progress?). The four dimensions are task performance, processes of understanding a task, the regulatory or meta-cognitive process dimension, and/or the self or person (unrelated to the specifics of the task). Feedback has differing effects across these levels.

The first question relates to goals or "Where am I going?" When students understand their goals and what success at those goals look like, then the feedback provided is more powerful. Without such an understanding (and even better commitment to attaining these goals) feedback is often confusing, disorienting, and interpreted as something about the student not their tasks/work; or worse, seen as irrelevant, not understood, and ignored. The second question is more related to progress feedback "How am I going?" This entails feedback (about past, present or how to progress) relative to the starting or finishing point and is often expressed in relation to some expected standard, to prior performance, and/or to success or failure on a specific part of the task. The third question is more consequential, "Where to next?" Such feedback can assist in choosing the next most appropriate challenges, more self-regulation over the learning process, greater fluency and automaticity, different strategies and processes to work on the tasks, deeper understanding, and more information about what is and what is not understood.

For example, feedback can be provided about "where the student is going" via clear learning intentions and an outline of what success looks like when a student attains these intentions (at varying levels of success, e.g., not achieved, achieved, with merit, with excellence). This would require the teacher and learner understanding "where the student is" currently in the learning process and the aim of feedback is to reduce the gap between where they are and where they need to be. Feedback about "How am I going" relates to where on the path the student is placed on this process of learning, to the success and gaps in the learning, can involve comparative feedback (both normative and criterion referenced), can invoke personal bests, and typically requires a reasonably well understood sense of curriculum progression. Feedback relating to "where to next" could lead to more challenging intentions, lead to greater fluency and automaticity, invoke different strategies and processes to work on the tasks, and lead to deeper understanding.

There is little research on how students set academic goals, and less on how to teach the setting of these goals. This is not to say they cannot set goals, indeed, many school-age students often set goals in their sport or social endeavors. When they do set academic goals, these tend to be more performance or social than mastery oriented (Hastie, 2009); such as completion of work, being on time, or trying harder. Similarly, the setting of more specific targets for academic goals is often done at the class but rarely at the student level. Smith (2009) asked teachers to set specific targets for secondary students based on students' past performance and many teachers were reluctant to set goals as they claimed attaining them was not in their control (it was student effort and commitment that led to attaining goals not their teaching). Smith provided teachers with a trajectory of each student's achievement over the past four years and then asked the teachers at the beginning of the year to set specific targets for each student at the end of the year. Those who set the targets compared to those who refused had greater success in academic achievement for their students (on an externally set of examinations), had different (more academic) conversations with students throughout the year, revised the targets upward with their students, and had a greater sense of agency in their teaching.

Along with appropriateness (i.e., relative to student's past performance and attainable future), there are two further attributes of goals, challenge and commitment. Challenge relates to feedback in two major ways. First, they inform individuals

as to what type or level of performance is to be attained so that they can direct and evaluate their actions and efforts accordingly ... Feedback allows students to set reasonable goals and to track their performance in relation to their goals so that adjustments in effort, direction, and even strategy can be made as needed.

(Locke & Latham, 1990, p. 23)

Second, feedback allows students (or their teachers) to set *further* appropriately challenging goals as the previous ones are attained, thus establishing the conditions for ongoing learning. By having clear goals, students are more likely to attend to reducing the gap instead of overstating their current status, or claiming various attributions that reduce effort and engagement. Goal commitment, which refers to one's attachment or determination to reach a goal, has a direct and often secondary impact on goal performance. There are many mediators that can affect goal commitment such as authority figures, peers, peer pressure, role models, valence, public nature of goals, and ego involvement. Peers influence goal commitment through pressure, modeling, and competition, and particularly during adolescence the reputation desired by the student can very much affect the power of this peer influence (Carroll, Houghton, Durkin, & Hattie, 2009). A further consideration in the power of goals is the intention to initiate goal directed behaviors. Gollwitzer and Sheeran (2006) have shown how those students who have a planning mindset toward their goals are more open-minded, more successful, and have a more accurate analysis of information needed to achieve the goal. From a meta-analysis of 63 studies (N = 8461 participants) their overall effect was $d = .65$ of the existence of an implementation intention on the outcome, which is quite substantial. When forming implementation intentions students are more open to feedback as to how to achieve the goals, particularly in an efficient, self-regulatory manner and are able to reduce unnecessary disruptions.

Four Feedback Levels

Hattie and Timperley (2007; see also Hattie, 2010) proposed that feedback may help learners to "reduce discrepancies between current understandings and performance and a learning intention or goal" (p. 6) by engaging learners at four different levels in which feedback operates: task level, process level, self-regulation level, and self level.

First, feedback can engage learners at the *task* level, such as providing information on correct response (e.g., "You explained the limitations but could have said why they were not reliable"). Such feedback can be about the task or product, and in this case feedback is powerful if it is more information focused (e.g., correct or incorrect), leads to acquiring more or different information, and builds more surface knowledge. This type of feedback is most common (Sheen, 2004), many teachers and students see feedback primarily in these terms (Peterson & Irving, 2008), and it is often termed corrective feedback or knowledge of results. It is constantly given in classrooms via teacher questions (as most are at this information level), it is often specific and not generalizable, and it can be powerful particularly when the learner is a novice (Heubusch & Lloyd, 1998).

When there is low task complexity, then Kluger and DeNisi (1996) argued that motivation increases performance particularly when lower cognitive resources are needed, and if motivation is directed to external factors to the task this may debilitate performance. Thus, reducing cognitive load when completing a task can allow for feedback to be more influential (positively or negatively). When task feedback moves from simple to more complex, provides additional information, and comes from a perceived reputable source then it is more powerful. Most class group feedback is of this task type, and most individuals do not consider such feedback as pertinent to them (so it can be given by the teacher and not received by the student). Having correct information is a pedestal on which the processing (level 2) and self-regulation (level 3) can be effectively built.

Second, feedback can be aimed at the *process* level, such as providing task processing strategies and cues for information search (e.g., "You could show more why the test was fair by highlighting the control variables"). This second level is feedback aimed at the processes used to create the product or complete the task. Such feedback can lead to alternative processing, reduction of cognitive load, providing strategies for error detection, reassessment of approach, cueing to seek more effective information search and employment of task strategies. Feedback at this process level appears to be more effective than at the task level for enhancing deeper learning, and there can be a powerful interactive effect between feedback aimed at improving the strategies and processes, and feedback aimed at the more surface task information.

In a series of studies where the clarity of goals and nature of process feedback was manipulated, Earley, Northcraft, Lee, and Lituchy (1990) concluded that "process feedback interacted with goal setting to strongly affect the quality of people's task strategies and information search" (p. 101). Feedback provided a "cueing device" about which decisions are made as to whether strategies are effective or not to attain the goal, and the more specific and challenging the goal the greater the effectiveness of process feedback. This kind of feedback can assist in improving task confidence and self-efficacy, which in turn provides resources for more effective and innovative information and strategy searching. Chan (2006) induced a failure situation and then found that self-efficacy was best enhanced by formative more than summative feedback, and self-referenced more than comparative to other peer's feedback.

Third, feedback at the *self-regulation* level, including skills on self-evaluation, expanding effort in task engagement or seeking further feedback information (e.g., "What would happen if you chose a different temperature range for your experiment"). Such feedback can boost confidence to engage further on the task, assist in seeking, accepting, and accommodating feedback information, provide conditional knowledge in the form of reflective or probing questions, help increase the capability to create internal feedback and to self-assess, and lead to internal more than external attributions about success or failure. At this level there can be more direct links to self-as-learner, information to guide the learner when and where to select and employ task and process level strategies, and this can be done via developing attributes of self-assessment, self-help seeking, self-appraisal, and self-management.

Fourth, feedback can be seen as directed to the "*self*" that, in most occasions, does not provide information on how to improve performance on the task (e.g., "well done"), and so often directs attention away from the task, processes, or self-regulation. Such praise can comfort and support, is ever-present in many classrooms, is welcomed and expected by students, but rarely does it enhance achievement or learning. When Kessels, Warner, Holle, and Hannover (2008) provided students with feedback with and without the addition that teachers were proud of them, this led to lower engagement and effort. Hyland and Hyland (2006) noted that almost half of teachers' feedback was praise, and premature and gratuitous praise can confuse students and discourage revisions. Most often teachers used praise to mitigate critical comments, which indeed dilutes the effect of such comments. Praise usually contains little task-related information and is rarely converted into more engagement, commitment to the learning goals, enhanced self-efficacy, or understanding about the task. By incorporating self with other forms of feedback, the information is often diluted, uninformative about performance on the task, and provides little assistance to answering the three feedback questions. Wilkinson (1981) found a low effect-size for praise ($d = .12$), as did Kluger and DeNisi (1998; $d = .09$), and no praise has a greater impact on achievement ($d = .34$).

These four levels are an expansion of the model developed by Kluger and DeNisi (1996). They argued that the highest level *meta-task processes* involves "self" feedback; their *task-motivation processes* is akin to the self-regulation level; and their third, *task-learning processes* has been separated into task and learning processes. Feedback is explicated to be powerful when it engages the learner with the learning task or goal at, or just above, the level where the learner is currently functioning. Thus, the challenge for educators is to provide *calibrated* feedback that is designed to function at the appropriate operational level of the learner.

One instructional approach for promoting the awareness of different feedback levels and their appropriate use in learning is to support the feedback process (between peers or teacher-student) through the use of a graphic organizer (see Figure 13.1). The graphic organizer incorporates the three feedback levels to provide visual scaffolding that facilitates explicit and meaningful feedback discourse. Learners may use this organizer to formulate feedback, interpret the feedback received and extend the use of feedback information to further their understanding. This graphic organizer provides a common platform for teachers and learners to engage in feedback discussion and elaboration, and may create opportunities for a more dialogic and visible feedback process.

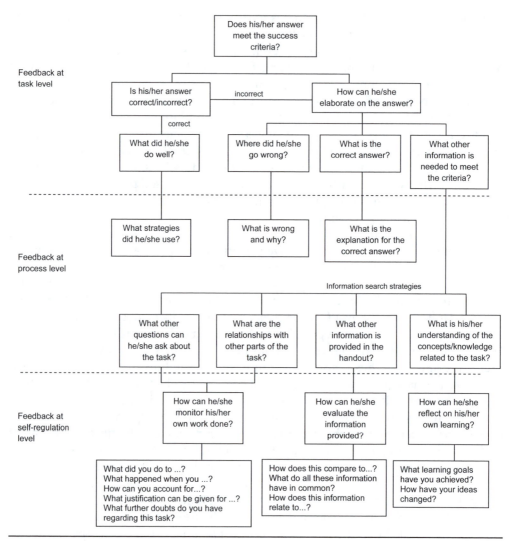

Figure 13.1 Graphic organizer on feedback levels and question prompts

The Interaction of Feedback and Student Dispositions

Feedback is not only differentially given but also differentially received, and thus it is important to consider various interactions with person characteristics such as culture, influence of peers, and classroom climate.

Luque and Sommer (2000) found that students from collectivist cultures (e.g., Confucian-based Asia, South Pacific nations) preferred indirect and implicit feedback, more group-focused feedback and no self-level feedback. Students from individualist/Socratic cultures (e.g., the USA) preferred more direct feedback particularly related to effort, were more likely to use direct inquiry to seek feedback, and preferred more individual focused self-related feedback. Kung (2008) found that while both individualistic and collectivist students sought feedback to reduce uncertainty, collectivist students were more likely to welcome self-criticism "for the good of the collective" and more likely seek developmental feedback, whereas individualistic students decreased such feedback to protect their ego. Individualistic students were more likely to engage in self-helping strategies, as they aim to gain status and achieve outcomes (Brutus & Greguras, 2008). Hyland and Hyland (2006) argued that students from cultures where teachers are highly directive, generally welcome and expect teachers to notice and comment on their errors and feel resentful when they do not. This differential effect relating to the cultural attributes of the students can be used to optimize instruction, as Bishop (2003) has so successfully demonstrated. He and his team have developed specific models and methods for changing teacher mind frames, strategies to acknowledge the cultural attributes of students within a class. They have used observation schedules of the teachers' interactions with students and visibly shown the teachers the nature, frequency and success of their interactions with students and how the feedback provided has or has not been received differentially by majority and minority students in the classes.

Feedback is often considered as something that occurs between teacher and student, but the influence of peers in the feedback cycle is often critical. Nuthall (2007), for example, conducted extensive in-class observations and noted that 80% of verbal feedback comes from peers and most of this feedback information is incorrect. There is a need for much more research about how to teach and involve peers in the feedback and teaching process, and therefore ensure that their feedback is correct and assisting to close the gap between current status and desired outcomes. Teachers who do not acknowledge the importance of peer feedback can be most handicapped in their effects on students, and interventions that aim at fostering peer feedback are needed particularly as many teachers seem reluctant to involve peers as agents of feedback.

Nuthall (1999) argued that students' learning in the classroom is shaped by their experiences within the context of three different worlds—the public world structured by the learning activities and routines the teacher designs and manages; the semiprivate world of ongoing peer relationships; and the private world of the child's own mind. He demonstrated that the assumption that "all students experience essentially the same activities in the classroom when carefully planned by teachers and thus, all students will translate these experiences into expected learning outcomes" does not hold true to the research findings (2007, p. 160). Instead, learner differences as well as peer relationships and status strongly influence their opportunities for more engaging learning experiences. Thus, teachers should consider the differences in background knowledge of learners, the power of peer relationships and status, and the need to constantly monitor students' learning progress—and to respond accordingly. More importantly, because much of what students learn comes from their peers, teachers need to become "involved with the peer culture and to work with it to manage our students' learning" and build a culture of learning in the classroom that entails "mutual respect and co-operation—a culture where everyone feels he or she has something to contribute to classroom activities, where everyone takes responsibility for learning" (Nuthall, 2007, p. 162).

One method to understand the importance of peer feedback is via investigating the collaborative discourse between peers (e.g., Nussbaum, 2008; O'Donnell, 2006; O'Donnell & King, 1998). Such discourse highlights that the one-way transmission model of teaching is not evident for most students, as they make emotional and social investments in learning, interact as much if not more with peers during the learning, and build understandings about what it is they are supposed to be learning/doing, how they are going, and where they go next in their learning (or not). For example, Webb and colleagues (2008) found that the levels and elaborate nature of explanations among students in collaborative groups predicted individual learning in mathematics, with the highest growth associated with those generating explanations. In a recent review on collaborative discourse and argumentation, Nussbaum (2008, p. 345) coined the term "critical, elaborative discourse" to emphasize the importance of students "considering different viewpoints" as well as "generating connections among ideas and between ideas and prior knowledge"—much coming from peer discussions (see Chapter 20 in this volume). Peers thus provide much feedback to each other by such elaborations and critical discourse; they are not merely providers of right/wrong feedback but interpreters of the usefulness of feedback.

Of course, not all students provide such elaborations or quality feedback (Lockhart & Ng, 1995; Strijbos et al., 2010). Often the more able, the more committed, and the more verbal students provide greater elaboration and critical feedback and thus, are more advantaged in peer interactions. Teachers may need to deliberately teach some students these skills, structure classrooms to share this expertise, and make specific interventions to ensure all students can benefit from these peer interactions. Even though, when ignored the elaborations and feedback often are incorrect or misleading, the effects are still powerful and teachers have an even more difficult task of moving students to the desired success outcomes (e.g., Ballantyne et al., 2002; Topping, 1998).

One method for peers to provide feedback is via assessment of others' work, and there has been a recent resurgence in research relating to the positive effects of peer assessment (PA) on student learning (e.g., Dochy et al., 1999; Falchikov & Goldfinch, 2000; Topping, 2010; Van Zundert et al., 2010). Peer assessment involves students assessing the quality of their fellow students' work and providing one another with feedback (Dochy et al., 1999). The important elements of peer assessment are that it involves students engaging in reflective criticism of the products of other students, providing constructive feedback using previously defined criteria, and consisting of one or more cycles of feedback with opportunities for revisions. It certainly can be plentiful. Ngar-Fun and Carless (2006) argued that involving students in peer assessment and peer feedback enables students to take an active role in the management of their own learning, helps to enhance students' self-assessment skills, and can improve learning of subject matter (see also Boud et al., 1995; Boud et al., 1999). In contrast to comments provided by teachers, students can receive more feedback from peers and more quickly (Gipps, 1999).

There can be resistance to using students to provide feedback in peer assessment; for example, teachers may have concerns about the reliability of students grading or marking; power relations among peers and with teachers; that some students can fail to participate (social loafing), freeload off others, be impacted by friendship bonds, power relations, or collusion. Hence, the most effective use of peer assessment often occurs following deliberate training of students in providing peer feedback, ensuring that peer feedback is integrated into the lesson in a deliberative and transparent manner, and when rubrics are provided to the students that outline the success criteria of the lesson (Cho & MacArthur, 2010; Lundstrom & Baker, 2009; Min, 2005; Prins et al., 2006; Rollinson, 2005; Zhu, 1995).

For example, Sluijsmans et al. (2002) found that students who received training that involved providing feedback were more likely to use the criteria and to give more constructive comments (specific, direct, accurate, achievable, practicable, and comprehensible to the peer) than the students in the control group who did not receive training.

Similarly, Min (2005) indicated that students with extensive coaching in peer reviewing, generated more specific and relevant written feedback on global features of their peer's writing. Students were trained by observing an instructor demonstrate how to comment on a peer's draft following a four-step strategy (i.e., ask for clarification, identify a problem, explain the problem, and suggest possible revisions) and thereafter, encouraged to apply the strategy in commenting on their peer's writing. The analysis of a peer's draft before and after training showed that students made more comments explaining problems (see also Van Steendam et al., 2010).

Nelson and Schunn (2009) investigated the effect of feedback features (e.g., type-praise, summary, identifying problem/solution, scope of problem/solution, localization of problem/solution, explanation of problem/solution) on mediators (e.g., understanding feedback and agreement with feedback) that were proposed to affect feedback implementation behavior (revision of draft writing). The authors analyzed 1,073 feedback segments from writing assessed by peers from an online peer review system and found that understanding the problem has a significant effect on implementation. The student was more likely to understand the problem if a solution was offered, the location of the problem or solution was given, or a summary of the problem was included. Tseng and Tsai (2007) conducted a web-based peer assessment with tenth grade students (16-year-olds) involving three rounds of peer feedback and two rounds of modifications on their projects for a computer course. Peer feedback was coded based on Chi's (1996) framework: corrective, reinforcing, didactic, and suggestive. Tseng and Tsai found that online peer assessment significantly enhanced students' quality of projects and concluded that the learning in the peer assessment process comes from both students' adaptation of peers' feedback and their assessment of peers' project. Reinforcing feedback was found to be most helpful to promote quality student projects but the reasons behind this were not provided by the authors (see also Gielen, 2007).

CONCLUSION AND FUTURE DIRECTIONS

The major claim is that feedback is related to the assumptions teachers have about the nature of feedback (often it is correct/incorrect), its purpose (learning, motivation), and degree of visibility that feedback plays in the learning process (by teachers and by students). Feedback can indeed make the learning visible (e.g., via noting errors in thinking or fact), lead to error detection, and enhance students' assessment capabilities about their learning. Central to these notions is a teacher–student relationship that not only permits but also fosters errors and the seeking of feedback, and classroom climates where peer assessment/feedback is a visible and important part of the learning for all students. Feedback is successful when it is aimed at or slightly above where the student is performing on the learning curve from novice to proficiency to be accomplished. There is a need to move from considering feedback as something that is "given" to something that is "received" which means that more research is needed on how students understand and process feedback and less on finding ways for teachers to increase the amount of feedback they give. Feedback not received is unlikely to have any effect on learning.

We outlined four major perspectives of learning and their relation to feedback. While not unique, the point of elaborating these perspectives is that teachers (and also students) can hold these views as if they are unique and thus restrict the power of feedback.

Each of the four perspectives build on each other, although the Visible Learning mind set uses the notions from the objectivist models of feedback as reinforcer, motivator, verifier and elaborator; from the information processing models of feedback as modifier of the students understandings of their reality and knowledge, cognitive monitoring and self-regulation; and from the socioculturalism model of feedback in a sociocultural context, the potential power of peer feedback, and understanding the gap between current and a more advanced or desired level.

The Visible Learning model places more emphasis on the mind sets that the teacher and student bring to the learning process, the importance for teachers to see their effects on the learning process and learner, and the value of encouraging students to see the power of teaching from others (e.g., expert or peers) and thus seek or receive feedback in their own learning. Feedback can serve all the above roles, but more importantly, the concern with feedback should be less whether it is given and more how it is received (by students and teachers). There is increasing evidence of the interactions between the type of feedback (task, process, regulation) and the level of proficiency of the student (novice, proficient, mastery); we are understanding the importance of studying the receiving more than the giving of feedback; and it is becoming clear that the transparency and challenge of the goal are important for the effectiveness of feedback. The climate of the class is critical particularly when there is high trust and a climate where being wrong is seen as a positive part of the learning—and thence feedback can be sought when a student does not attain a goal.

The Visible Learning model, building particularly on Kluger and DeNisi's (1996) seminal work, sees feedback as purposive (re. the three feedback questions), operating at different levels for different purposes, and being most effective when there is a high degree of transparency between the current status and the desired outcome to both teacher and student. Thus, there is a need to understand feedback within the context of students' learning (with peers, with adults, alone), at varying stages of proficiency (novice, proficient, expert) and understanding (surface, deep, conceptual), with differing levels of regulation (by others, with others, self), and with differing levels of information and focus in the feedback information. The aim is to make learning (and feedback) as visible as possible in the classroom, acknowledging the dispositions of students, and the power of peers in the feedback process. Indeed, more research on peer feedback (e.g., their discourse in class, peer assessment) could open up many exciting ways to maximize the power of feedback in classrooms.

The current interest in teacher reflection often fails to take into account that so much in the learning process is not seen by teachers and thus difficult to reflect about. Nuthall's claim about the hidden lives in the classroom and his findings that about 70% of classrooms are not seen by teachers means that many teachers may not be aware of student error, whether feedback is being sought or received, or its effects particularly when provided by peers. Errors need to be welcomed in classrooms by teachers, student, *and* peers. Feedback is most effective when we do not have proficiency or mastery; thus it thrives when there is error or incomplete knowing and understanding (i.e., often there is little information value in providing task level feedback when the student is mastering the content). This means there need to be classroom climates where there is minimum peer reactivity to not welcoming errors, when evaluative salience of the self is low, and when there is low personal risk involved in responding publicly and failing (Alton-Lee & Nuthall, 1990).

Table 13.2 Possible research questions derived from the evidence provided in this chapter

How feedback makes a difference in learning

What are the most effective ways (and conditions) to provide feedback?

What are the factors that affect the variability of the influence of feedback?

Why do students not see feedback as powerful in their learning as do the teachers?

How do students receive, understand and use feedback in their learning?

How can we use theories and research from the past 100 years to build more successful models of the how and why of feedback on learning?

How to use feedback more as reinforcement, cues for attention, and a motivator of learning?

What is the role of learner certainty in their response, reactions to error, and open-mindedness to receiving feedback?

The multidimensional role of feedback in instruction

Should feedback be differently provided according to the three fundamental feedback questions?

How to most effectively make the learning goals and success criteria transparent and realizable to students so as to maximize the effects of feedback?

What is the role that feedback takes relative to other learning dimensions (e.g., the role of cognitive load, cueing, attention, levels of understanding)?

What is the role of appropriate challenge in learning goals so that the influence of feedback is maximized?

Feedback to teachers

What is the role of feedback in changing teacher behaviors and expectations?

How do teachers use feedback about the effects of their teaching to then alter their instruction?

What are the effects of target setting on the basis of prior achievement on teachers' expectations and success in their teaching?

Feedback to students

What are students' beliefs about feedback and how do these affect the power and direction of influence on learning?

How do students set performance and mastery goals in classes, and how then do these affect how they seek or receive feedback?

What is the role of goal specification, challenge, commitment, and implementation intention on the role and power of feedback?

What is the influence of culture on how feedback should be provided, and how it is received?

Types of feedback

Is there a typology of feedback that can best relate to the differential effects on learning?

What are the effects of different forms and intensity of feedback relative to the varying stages of proficiency (novice, proficient, expert), understanding (surface, deep, conceptual), with differing levels of regulation (by others, with others, self), and with differing levels of information and focus to the feedback information?

Can we devise effective methods to assess the frequency, nature, and value of feedback in classrooms?

The four feedback levels

What is the differential impact of feedback relative to the four feedback levels (task, process, regulation, self)?

Is there an optimal balance of feedback relative to the four levels of feedback?

Why is praise so present, and are there ways to combine praise and feedback to have a positive effect on learning?

The influence of peers in feedback

How to use peers to provide correct feedback to others in the classroom?

How to provide prompts to make peer feedback more reliable and frequent?

How to use peers in elaborating the meaning of feedback in classrooms?

How to involve peers in assessment of others' work in a positive and efficient manner such that there are benefits to all? How to teach reflective criticism?

Too often, students only respond when they are fairly sure that they can respond correctly, which often indicates they have already learned the answer to the question being asked or when they are not fearful of their peers' reactions. Heimbeck, Frese, Sonnentag, and Keith (2003) noted the paucity of research on errors in classrooms, and they recommended that rather than being error-avoidant, training that increases the exposure to errors in a safe environment can lead to higher performance. Such an environment requires high levels of self-regulation or safety (e.g., explicit instructions that emphasizes the positive function of errors) for errors to be valuable, and it is necessary to deal primarily with errors as potentially avoidable deviations from goals.

Another major conclusion relates to the mind frame that teachers need to develop that they may be making "errors"; that is, their methods, strategies, and involvement in classrooms may not be assisting in student learning. Seeking feedback about their effects can be among the more critical methods for enhancing student learning. There is much still too understand, and Table 13.2 provides a compendium of questions that arise from this review. It is not that we do not know a lot, indeed the research on feedback is now growing, but Table 13.2 is an attempt to outline the questions that derive from this review that can help move the field forward.

REFERENCES

Alton-Lee, A., & Nuthall, G. (1990). Research on teaching and learning: Thirty years of change. *The Elementary School Journal, 90*(5), 547–570.

Anderson, R. C., Kulhavy, R. W., & Andre, T. (1972). Conditions under which feedback facilitates learning from programmed lessons. *Journal of Educational Psychology, 63*, 186–188.

Askew, S., & Lodge, C. (2000). Gifts, ping-pong and loops – linking feedback and learning, in S. Askew (Ed.), *Feedback for learning*. London: Routledge Falmer.

Ballantyne, R., Hughes, K., & Mylonas, A. (2002). Developing procedures for implementing peer assessment in large classes: Using an action research process. *Assessment & Evaluation in Higher Education, 27*(5), 427–441.

Balzer, W. K., Doherty, M. E., & O'Connor, R. (1989). Effects of cognitive feedback on performance. *Psychological Bulletin, 106*, 410–433.

Bangert-Drowns, R. L., Kulik, C.-L. C., & et al. (1991). The instructional effect of feedback in test-like events. *Review of Educational Research, 61*(2), 213.

Bereiter, C. (2002). *Education and mind in the knowledge age*. Mahwah, NJ: Lawrence Erlbaum Associates.

Bell, B., & Cowie, B. (2001). *Formative assessment and science education*. London: Kluwer.

Bishop, R. (2003). Changing power relations in education: Kaupapa M ori Messages for "Mainstream" education in Aotearoa/New Zealand. *Comparative Education, 39*(2), 221–238.

Boud, D., Cohen, R., & Sampson, J. (1999). Peer learning and assessment. *Assessment & Evaluation in Higher Education, 24*(4), 413.

Boud, D., Keogh, R., & Walker, D. (1985). What is reflection in learning? In D. Boud, R. Keogh, & D. Walker (Eds.), *Reflection: Turning experience into learning* (pp. 85–90). New York: Nichols Publishing Company.

Brutus, S., & Greguras, G. J. (2008). Self-construals, motivation, and feedback-seeking behaviors. *International Journal of Selection and Assessment, 16*(3), 282–291.

Butler, D. B. (1998). The strategic content approach to promoting self-regulated learning: a report of three studies. *Journal of Educational Psychology, 90*, 682–697.

Butler, D., & Winne, P. (1995). Feedback and self-regulated learning: A theoretical synthesis. *Review of Educational Research, 65*(3), 245–281.

Carless, D. (2006). Differing perceptions in the feedback process. *Studies in Higher Education, 31*(2), 219–233.

Carroll, A., Houghton, S., Durkin, K., & Hattie, J. A. C. (2009). *Adolescent reputations and risk: Developmental trajectories to delinquency*. New York: Springer.

Chan, C. Y. J. (2006). The effects of different evaluative feedback on students' self-efficacy in learning. Unpublished PhD, University of Hong Kong.

Chi, M. T. H. (1996). Constructing self-explanations and scaffolded explanations in tutoring. *Applied Cognitive Psychology, 10*, 33–49.

Chi, M. T. H., Siler, S. A., Jeong, H., Yamauchi, T., & Hausmann, R. G. (2001). Learning from human tutoring. *Cognitive Science, 25,* 471–533.

Chinn, C. A., & Brewer, W. F. (1993). The role of anomalous data in knowledge acquisition: A theoretical framework and implications for science instruction. *Review of Educational Research, 63,* 1–49.

Cho, K., & MacArthur, C. (2010). Student revision with peer and expert reviewing. *Learning and Instruction, 20*(4), 328–338.

Deci, E. L., Koestner, R., & Ryan, R. M. (1999). A meta-analytic review of experiments examining the effects of extrinsic rewards on intrinsic motivation. *Psychological Bulletin, 125*(6), 627–668.

Dochy, F., Segers, M., & Sluijsmans, D. (1999). The use of self-, peer and co-assessment in higher education: A review. *Studies in Higher Education, 24,* 331–350.

Earley, P. C., Northcraft, G. B., Lee, C., & Lituchy, T. R. (1990). Impact of process and outcome feedback on the relation of goal setting to task performance. *Academy of Management Journal, 33*(1), 87–105.

Falchikov, N., & Goldfinch, J. (2000). Student peer assessment in higher education: A meta-analysis comparing peer and teacher marks. *Review of Educational Research, 70,* 287–322.

Gielen, S. (2007). Peer assessment as a tool for learning. Unpublished doctoral dissertation, Leuven University, Leuven, Belgium.

Gipps, C. (1999). *Beyond testing: Towards a theory of educational assessment.* London: Falmer Press.

Goldstein, L. (2006). Feedback and revision in second language writing: Contextual, teacher, and student variables. In K. Hyland, & F. Hyland (Eds.), *Feedback in second language writing: Contexts and issues* (pp. 185–205). Cambridge: Cambridge University Press.

Gollwitzer, P. M., & Sheeran, P. (2006). Implementation intentions and goal achievement: A meta-analysis of effects and processes. *Advances in Experimental Social Psychology, 38,* 69–119.

Hastie, S. (2009). Teaching students to set goals: Strategies, commitment, and monitoring. Unsubmitted doctoral dissertation, University of Auckland. New Zealand.

Hattie, J. A.C. (2009). *Visible learning: A synthesis of 800+ meta-analyses on achievement.* Abingdon: Routledge.

Hattie, J.A.C. (in press). The power of feedback in school settings. In R. Sutton, M. Hornsey, & K. Douglas (Eds.), *Feedback: The handbook of praise, criticism, and advice.*

Hattie, J., & Timperley, H. (2007). The power of feedback. *Review of Educational Research, 77*(1), 81–112.

Heimbeck, D., Frese, M., Sonnentag, S., & Keith, N. (2003). Integrating errors into the training process: The function of error management instructions and the role of goal orientation. *Personnel Psychology, 56,* 333–362.

Heubusch, J., & Lloyd, J. W. (1998). Corrective feedback in oral reading. *Journal of Behavioral Education, 8,* 63–79.

Hyland, K., & Hyland, F. (Eds.). (2006). *Feedback in second language writing: Contexts and issues.* Cambridge: Cambridge University Press.

Jonassen, D. (1991). Objectivism vs. constructivism: Do we need a new philosophical paradigm? *Educational Technology, Research and Development, 39*(3), 5–13.

Kessels, U., Warner, L. M., Holle, J., & Hannover, B. (2008). Threat to identity through positive feedback about academic performance. *Zeitschrift für Entwicklungspsychologie und Pädagogische Psychologie, 40*(1), 22–31.

Kluger, A. N., & DeNisi, A. (1996). The effects of feedback interventions on performance: A historical review, a meta-analysis, and a preliminary feedback intervention theory. *Psychological Bulletin, 119*(2), 254–284.

Kluger, A. N., & DeNisi, A. (1998). Feedback interventions: Towards the understanding of a double-edged sword. *Current Directions in Psychological Science, 7,* 67–72.

Kulhavy, R. W., & Stock, W. (1989). Feedback in written instruction: The place of response certitude. *Educational Psychology Review, 1*(4), 279–308.

Kulhavy, R. W., Stock, W. A., Hancock, T. E., Swindell, L. K., & Hammrich, P. L. (1990). Written feedback: Response certitude and durability. *Contemporary Educational Psychology, 15*(4), 319–332.

Kulhavy, R. W., & Wager, W. (1993). Feedback in programmed instruction: Historical context and implications for practice. In V. Dempsey, & G. C. Sales (Eds.), *Interactive instruction and feedback* (pp. 3–20). Englewood Cliffs, NJ: Educational Technology Publications.

Kung, M. C. (2008). Why and how do people seek success and failure feedback? A closer look at motives, methods and cultural differences. Unpublished doctoral dissertation, Florida Institute of Technology.

Lakoff, G. (1987). *Women, fire, and dangerous things.* Chicago: University of Chicago Press.

Locke, E. A., & Latham, G. P. (1990). *A theory of goal setting and task performance.* Englewood Cliffs, NJ: Prentice Hall.

Lockhart, C., & Ng, P. (1995). Analyzing talk in ESL peer response groups: stances, functions and content. *Language Learning, 45,* 605–655.

Lundstrom, K., & Baker, W. (2009). To give is better than to receive: The benefits of peer review to the reviewer's own writing. *Journal of Second Language Writing, 18*(1), 30–43.

Luque, M. F., & Sommer, S. M. (2000). The impact of culture on feed-back-seeking behavior: An integrated model and propositions. *The Academy of Management Review, 25*(4), 829–849.

Mercer, N., & Littleton, K. (2007). *Dialogue and the development of children's thinking: A sociocultural approach.* London: Routledge.

Min, H. T. (2005). Training students to become successful peer reviewers. *System, 33,* 293–308.

Mory, E. H. (2004). Feedback research review. In D. Jonassen (Ed.), *Handbook of research on educational communications and technology* (pp. 745–783). Mahwah, NJ: Lawrence Erlbaum.

Narciss, S. (2008). Feedback strategies for interactive learning tasks. In J. M. Spector, M. D. Merrill, J. J. G. Van Merrienboer, & M. P. Driscoll (Eds.), *Handbook of research on educational communications and technology* (3rd ed., pp. 125–143). Mahwah, NJ: Lawrence Erlbaum Associates.

Narciss, S., & Huth, K. (2004). How to design informative tutoring feedback for multi-media learning. In H. M. Niegemann, D. Leutner, & R. Brünken (Eds.), *Instructional design for multimedia Learning* (pp. 181–195). Münster: Waxmann.

Nelson, M., & Schunn, C. (2009). The nature of feedback: how different types of peer feedback affect writing performance. *Instructional Science, 37*(4), 375–401.

Ngar-Fun, L., & Carless, D. (2006). Peer feedback: the learning element of peer assessment. *Teaching in Higher Education, 11*(3), 279–290.

Nussbaum, E. M. (2008). Collaborative discourse, argumentation, and learning: Preface and literature review. *Contemporary Educational Psychology, 33*(3), 345–359.

Nuthall, G. A. (1999). Learning how to learn: The evolution of students' minds through the social processes and culture of the classroom. *International Journal of Educational Research, 31*(3), 141–156.

Nuthall, G. A. (2007). *The hidden lives of learners.* Wellington, New Zealand: New Zealand Council for Educational Research.

O'Donnell, A. M. (2006). The role of peers and group learning. In P. H. Winne, & P. A. Alexander (Eds.), *Handbook of educational psychology* (pp. 781–802). Mahwah, NJ: Erlbaum.

O'Donnell, A. M., & King, A. (Eds.). (1998). *Cognitive perspectives on peer learning.* Mahwah, NJ: Erlbaum.

Peterson, R., & Irving, I (2008). Secondary school students' conceptions of assessment and feedback *Learning and Instruction, 18*(3), 238–250.

Prins, F., Sluijsmans, D., & Kirschner, P. (2006). Feedback for general practitioners in training: Quality, styles and preferences. *Advances in Health Sciences Education, 11,* 289–303.

Pryor, J., & Crossouard, B. (2008). A socio-cultural theorization of formative assessment. *Oxford Review of Education, 34*(1), 1–20.

Rollinson, P. (2005). Using peer feedback in the ESL Writing class. *ELT Journal: English Language Teachers Journal, 59*(1), 23–30.

Sadler, R. (1989). Formative assessment and the design of instructional systems. *Instructional Science, 18,* 119–144.

Schommer, M., Crouse, A., & Rhodes, N. (1992). Epistemological beliefs and mathematical text comprehension: Believing it is simple does not make it so. *Journal of Educational Psychology, 84,* 435–443.

Sheen, Y. H. (2004). Corrective feedback and learner uptake in communicative classrooms across instructional settings. *Language Teaching Research, 8(3),* 263–300.

Sluijsmans, D. M. A., Brand-Gruwel, S., van Merriënboer, J. J. G., & Bastiaens, T. J. (2002). The training of peer assessment skills to promote the development of reflection skills in teacher education. *Studies in Educational Evaluation, 29*(1), 23–42.

Smith, S. L. (2009). Academic target setting: Formative use of achievement data. Unpublished doctoral thesis, University of Auckland.

Strijbos, J. W., Narciss, S., & Dünnebier, K (2010). Peer feedback content and sender's competence level in academic writing revision tasks: Are they critical for feedback perceptions and efficiency?, *Learning and Instruction , 20*(4), 291–303.

Topping, J. K. (2010). Methodological quandaries in studying process and outcomes in peer assessment. *Learning and Instruction, 20*(4), 339–343.

Topping, K. (1998). Peer assessment between students in colleges and universities. *Review of Educational Research, 68,* 249–276.

Tseng, S.-C., & Tsai, C.-C. (2007). On-line peer assessment and the role of the peer feedback: A study of high school computer course. *Computers & Education, 49*(4), 1161–1174.

Van Steendam, E., Rijlaarsdam, G., Sercu, L., & Van den Bergh, H. (2010). The effect of instruction type and dyadic or individual emulation on the quality of higher-order peer feedback in EFL. *Learning and Instruction, 20*(4), 316–327.

Van Zundert, M., Sluijsmans, D., & van Merrienboer, J. (2010). Effective peer assessment processes: Research findings and future direction. *Learning and Instruction, 20*(4), 270–279.

Villamil, O. S., & de Guerrero, M. C. M. (2006). Sociocultural theory: A framework for understanding the social-cognitive dimensions of peer feedback. In K. Hyland, & F. Hyland (Eds.), *Feedback in second language writing: Contexts and issues* (pp. 23–41). New York: Cambridge University Press.

Vygotsky, L. S. (1978). *Mind in society: The development of higher mental processes.* Cambridge, MA: Harvard University Press.

Vygotsky, L. S. (1986). *Thought and language.* (A. Kozulin, Trans. and Ed.). Cambridge, MA: The MIT Press.

Webb, N. M., Franke, M. L., Ing, M., Chan, A., De, T., Freund, D., et al. (2008). The role of teacher instructional practices in student collaboration. *Contemporary Educational Psychology, 33*(3), 360–381.

Wilkinson, S. S. (1981). The relationship of teacher praise and student achievement: A meta-analysis of selected research. *Dissertation Abstracts International, 41*(9-A), 3998. US: University Microfilms International.

Zhu, W. (1995). Effects of training for peer response on students' comments and interaction. *Written Communication, 12*, 492–528.

14

INSTRUCTION BASED ON EXAMPLES
Alexander Renkl

The path of precept is long, that of example short and effectual.
(Seneca, about 4 BC–AD 65)

Often in school, at university, or in further education abstract concepts and principles are taught without providing the opportunity to elaborate on how to apply this abstract knowledge. For example, in university lectures, principles of scientific argumentation are explained without the opportunity to learn how to apply them. In such cases, often just *inert knowledge* (Whitehead, 1929) is acquired (Renkl, Mandl, & Gruber, 1996). The learners can state the relevant concepts and principles but they cannot or, at least, do not apply them when solving complex problems. In other cases, such as project-based learning, the learners may encode concrete problem solutions, however, this is often of little help when solving subsequent related problems. This deficient knowledge use is mainly due to two factors. For one, the learners may not have encoded the general rules or principles behind the previously encountered problem solutions. For another, the learners may not have noticed the relevance of the known problem solutions (e.g., Reeves & Weisberg, 1993; Renkl, 2009). In order to best enhance cognitive skills, instruction should encourage learners to encode and interconnect both abstract concepts as well as abstract principles and concrete cases in which it is shown how this abstract knowledge is applied. In order to achieve such interconnected knowledge structures, instruction by examples, especially as specified in research on worked examples, is an appropriate instructional method.

Figure 14.1 shows an example in a double sense. This is taken from an example-based learning environment by Hilbert, Renkl, Schworm, Kessler, and Reiss (2008) in which teachers learn how to design worked examples for high-school students. In this environment, it is argued that at first formulas that are computationally efficient but difficult to understand (the left side of Figure 14.1) should be avoided (the general rule). Instead, the design should use solution procedures that are easy to understand (the right side of Figure 14.1). The teachers learned about principles of example design (i.e., the general rule) and were shown two concrete examples, one in accord with and one in contrast to

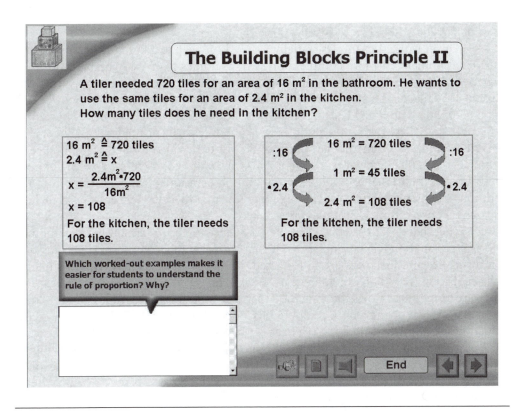

Figure 14.1 A worked example in a "double sense": Screenshot from an example-based learning program for teachers that shows two versions of a worked example for high-school students

Source: Taken from a learning program by Hilbert, Renkl, Schworm et al. (2008).

this rule. In addition, they were also requested to explain why the given examples were in accordance with or in contrast to the rule. By explaining the "why?" (see Figure 14.1), teachers should connect the general rule with the concrete examples, which should lead to an integrated representation. To fully exploit the potential of example-based instruction, it is necessary to elicit explanations from the learners. As these explanations are provided by the learners themselves and not in an interactive setting with a communication partner, such explanations are called self-explanations (Chi, Bassok, Lewis, Reimann, & Glaser, 1989; Renkl, 1997; see also Chapter 15 in this volume).

Proponents of teaching and learning by examples propose that after the explicit introduction of one or more domain principles (e.g., mathematical theorem, physics laws, or design principles for worked examples), learners should be presented with *several* examples rather than a single example, as is commonly the case. The basic argument is that learners should first gain an understanding of the abstract principles and their application in problem solving before solving problems on their own. Otherwise they engage—due to their lack of understanding—in superficial strategies that do not deepen understanding (e.g., Renkl, 2010). Despite this emphasis on examples, these proponents also acknowledge the importance of solving problems later on in cognitive skill acquisition in order to achieve proficiency (e.g., Kalyuga, Ayres, Chandler, & Sweller, 2003; Renkl, 2009; Renkl & Atkinson, 2003).

Research on worked examples initially focused on well-structured domains. Recent research also analyzed more complex forms of examples from ill-structured domains such as identifying designer styles (Rourke & Sweller, 2009), collaborating productively (Rummel, Spada, & Hauser, 2009), engaging in scientific argumentation (Schworm & Renkl, 2007), and applying learning strategies in journal writing (Hübner, Nückles, & Renkl, 2010). In these cases, the examples were not necessarily printed pieces, like typical worked examples from mathematics or physics. In part, video models were used (e.g., Rummel et al., 2009; Schworm & Renkl, 2007). This development blurred the boundaries between traditional example research and observational learning research in the tradition of Bandura's (1986) socio-cognitive learning theory. Hence, we also include research on observational learning in this chapter.

Researchers have proposed that example-based instruction, especially when combined with self-explanation elicitation, has the advantage for initial cognitive skill acquisition that principles and instances are interrelated. However, does it really lead to superior skill acquisition? Based on our analysis of research literature, the answer is a clear "yes." There are numerous studies showing the superiority of example-based learning as compared to problem solving (e.g., Carroll, 1994; Cooper & Sweller, 1987; Eysink et al., 2009; Hilbert, Renkl, Kessler, & Reiss, 2008; Paas & van Merriënboer, 1994; Sweller & Cooper, 1985; Zhu & Simon, 1987). Learning by examples is even superior when learning by problem solving is well supported (Salden, Aleven, Schwonke, & Renkl, 2010; Schwonke et al., 2009).

Against the background of the effectiveness of example-based instruction, it is worth considering this type of instruction in detail. In the following, an historical sketch of the roots of instruction by examples will be provided. Second, important theoretical foundations of this approach will be discussed. Third, evidence-based principles for instructional design will be presented. Finally, fruitful lines of further research will be outlined.

HISTORICAL SKETCH

The quote of Seneca that opened this chapter shows that the appreciation of examples as a means of learning and teaching has a very long tradition. This section, however, adopts a more short-term perspective, in which four important roots of research on example-based instruction are considered: research on concept formation, research on social-cognitive theory, research on analogical reasoning, and research on cognitive load theory.

Research on Concept Formation

From the mid-1950s on, cognitive and educational psychologists examined how concepts are formed by the provision of examples (e.g., Bruner, Goodnow, & Austin, 1956; Tennyson & Cocchiarella, 1986). Merrill and Tennyson (1977) formulated a concept-teaching model that contains four main elements: (a) the provision of a verbal rule; (b) expository instances (i.e., examples and non-examples of a concept); (c) interrogatory examples, which means that the learners have to answer questions on critical attributes of instances in order to determine whether it is an example or a non-example of a category; and (d) attribute elaboration (i.e., learners reflect on the critical attributes of examples). It is not too difficult to map these instructional design elements to the features of "modern" worked examples approach (see also Figure 14.1): Introduction of a principle (a), provision of a series of examples (b and c), and self-explaining these examples (c and d; see the questions in Figure 14.1).

Research on Social-Cognitive Theory

Bandura (1971) made the following statement in the Introduction to his book *Psychological Modeling*: "This volume is principally concerned with learning by example" (p. 1). In accord with worked examples research, Bandura advocated using multiple examples or models (e.g., Bandura, 1986). He emphasized that models are examples instantiating rules, especially in what he calls "abstract modeling." This type of modeling refers to the acquisition of cognitive skills that are based on underlying abstract rules or principles (in contrast to models that can be more or less mimicked, e.g., motor skills). Bandura's approach led to social-cognitive research programs on teaching by modeling on academics skills such as reading and writing (for overviews of their research programs, see, e.g., Braaksma, Rijlaarsdam, van den Bergh, & van Hout-Wolters, 2006; Schunk & Zimmerman, 2007).

Research on Analogical Reasoning

The topic of analogical reasoning became an intensively researched area in the 1980s (e.g., Gentner, 1989; Gick & Holyoak, 1983; Ross, 1987). In this research tradition, typically four phases are distinguished (Holyoak, 2005; Reeves & Weisberg, 1993). First, examples are encoded that are presented as sources of transfer or learning; a schema might already be constructed (phase 1). When a transfer problem is to be solved, potentially relevant analogs are activated and selected (phase 2). The problem to be solved is mapped onto the analog (phase 3), that is, the learners determine the communalities and differences between a known problem (analog) and the new problem at hand. Finally, the induction of an abstract schema might arise out of this mapping process (or the modification of a schema when it has been already constructed in phase 1) because the learners notice that some superficial features (e.g., concrete numbers and objects in a mathematics word problem) are not relevant with respect to the appropriate solution method. Thus, the relevant structural features are encoded in the form of a schema (phase 4). Analogical reasoning research also led to instructional approaches. For example, Gentner and colleagues (e.g., Gentner, Loewenstein, & Thompson, 2003; Thompson, Gentner, & Loewenstein, 2000) successfully taught negotiation strategies by analogical encoding, that is, by having learners compare exemplified strategy applications.

Research on Cognitive Load Theory

Cognitive load theory—a theory based on assumptions on working memory capacity—began to emerge in the mid-1980s. One of the instructional effects of this theory is the worked example effect. In their seminal studies, Sweller and Cooper (1985; Cooper & Sweller, 1987) compared learning by problem solving with example-based learning. For example, in Sweller and Cooper (Exp. 3), ninth grade students learned to solve algebraic equations under two conditions. First, all students saw worked examples as part of the introduction to the learning contents. Then, in the conventional problem-solving condition, the students worked on eight problems representing four problem types. In the worked example condition, the students worked on the same eight problems, except that the first problem of each structurally identical problem pair was worked out. In a post-test including four structurally identical problems, the example condition produced fewer errors than the conventional condition. In addition, learners in the example condition spent less time on the acquisition phase well as on the post-test problems. The findings of additional experiments by Sweller and Cooper (1985; Cooper & Sweller, 1987) showed that the positive effect of examples is restricted to similar (i.e., isomorphic) test problems. Example-based instruction brought no advantages for dissimilar problems.

On the theoretical level, Sweller and Cooper (1985) argued that the usual method of problem solving directs attention to search processes but not to aspects that are directly relevant for schema acquisition (i.e., learning). Hence, problem solving induces learning-irrelevant (i.e., extraneous) cognitive load. Worked examples, in contrast, leave cognitive capacities for learning-relevant (i.e., germane) load (Paas & van Gog, 2006; Sweller, van Merriënboer, & Paas, 1998). Examples allow the learners to acquire knowledge about problem states, about operators, and about the consequences of the application of certain operators. These knowledge components are, in turn, organized into schemas that can be used for later problem solving. As Sweller and Cooper (1985) expected motivational problems with worked examples because they do not induce activity, they used isomorphic example-problem pairs. If the learners know that a similar problem is to be solved afterwards, they should be motivated to process the preceding example.

Since the emergence of these historical roots, which have especially shown that examples are an important source of learning, research has made significant progress. The advances relate especially to theory and to instructional guidelines that allow for optimizing the potential of instruction by examples. These advances are discussed in the following sections.

THEORETICAL FOUNDATIONS

Renkl (2010) has recently proposed a theory of example-based learning. In this section, two important building blocks of this theory are presented: (1) the appropriate place of example-based instruction in the course of skill acquisition; and (2) explanations of the effectiveness of instruction by examples.

The Appropriate Place of Example-Based Instruction in the Course of Skill Acquisition

There are a number of skill acquisition models in which example-based learning plays a significant role (Anderson, Fincham, & Douglass, 1997; Schunk & Zimmerman, 2007; VanLehn, 1996). As each of these models makes sensible assumptions that are not included in other models, Renkl (2010) formulated an integrative model including four stages.

In the first stage (*principle encoding*), learners acquire some basic declarative knowledge about a domain and in particular about the domain principles that should later guide problem solving (VanLehn, 1996). For example, they may learn about Kuhn's (1991) theory of scientific argumentation (Schworm & Renkl, 2007). In this stage, the learner does not yet know how to apply principles. In the second stage (*relying on analogs*), learners turn their attention to problem solving (VanLehn, 1996). They may first encounter examples printed in a textbook—as is often the case in mathematics textbooks after introducing a topic—or presented "live" by a teacher or, in a classroom, by a peer student.

To take up the example of argumentation, students may observe instantiations, such as exemplary models of proper scientific argumentation. These examples are encoded by the learners, but the quality of this encoding depends on the quality of the learners' self-explanations (Chi et al., 1989). If problems or just part of a problem have to be solved, this is primarily done by analogy (Ross, 1987, 1989; VanLehn, 1998). Hence, problems are solved not solely on the basis of applying general principles (e.g., theorems, laws) but (also) by referring to concrete examples (see Reeves & Weisberg, 1993). Learners do not necessarily disregard principles, but they are nevertheless first guided by analogs that are checked for suitability (Holyoak, 2005; VanLehn, 1998). Analogs can then remind learners of the relevant underlying principles if the analog is encoded with references to the underlying domain principles. Learners differ to the extent which they rely on abstract principles or case information (Didierjean & Cauzinille-Marmèche, 1998). Successful problem solving with reference to analogs leads to generalized schemas, at least if the initial encoding of multiple examples has not yet resulted in generalized schemas (Ross, 1987, 1989). Both initial example encoding and later retrieval for problem solving contribute to schema formation.

When the learners develop declarative rules of action in a content area (Anderson et al., 1997), they have entered the third stage (*forming declarative rules*). They have acquired verbalizable rules on how to act or to solve (parts of) problems. For example, a learner having observed an argumentation model might be able to state the rule "if considering counterarguments against my position, I will (try to) disconfirm them." Ideally, such rules are embedded in schemas that allow for categorizing problem cases irrespective of their superficial features (e.g., about what topic is argued). In both the second and the third phases, the learners typically correct their still partly faulty declarative knowledge when they encounter difficulties in problem solving (cf. VanLehn's, 1996, 1998, impasse-driven learning).

In the fourth and final stage (*fine tuning: automation and flexibilization*), the learners have already learned to solve structurally identical problems because they have acquired schemas that allow them to correctly identify certain problem categories and to apply corresponding solution procedures. There are, however, two ways in which skills can be optimized during problem solving. First, single solution steps can be chunked into one step. The procedures involved in the skill can become automatic (i.e., proceduralized rules are formed), resulting in faster performance and minimal working memory demands. If certain problems are recurrent, the solution can also be directly retrieved from memory (Anderson et al., 1997). Second, according to Schunk and Zimmerman (2007), the learners might adapt their skill to changes in contextual conditions or even changes in the structural features of the problems to be solved. Learners gain flexibility. These two aspects of improvement (i.e., automation and flexibility) are not independent. If working memory resources are saved by automation, more capacity is left for engaging in reasoning processes that render a skill more flexible.

As is the case with the phase models proposed by Anderson et al. (1997), VanLehn (1996), and Schunk and Zimmerman (2007), there are no strict boundaries between these stages. Particularly when learners acquire complex skills, they might be in an early stage with respect to some sub-skills whereas other sub-skills might already be automatized.

Instruction should especially emphasize examples in the second phase (*relying on analogs*). The learners are shown how principles are applied, concrete examples are encoded, and ideally related to principles in generalized schemas. In the next phase (*forming declarative rules*), teaching by examples is still relevant when a learner acquires declarative rules on when a certain principle should be applied (e.g., in the case of a certain problem category) and when it should not be applied (e.g., in the case of a related, but different problem category). In advanced skill acquisition, when automation and flexible application are the main goals, teaching by examples is not considered the best option.

Explanations of the Effectiveness of Instruction by Examples

If problem solving, instead of example study, is required in the very beginning of skill acquisition, the learners typically lack understanding of the domain principles and their application (Renkl, 2009). Hence, they use shallow strategies, for example, a key word strategy (i.e., selecting a procedure by a key word in the cover story of a problem; Clement & Bernhard, 2005), a copy-and-adapt strategy (i.e., copying the solution procedure from a presumably similar problem and adapting the numbers in the procedure; VanLehn, 1998), or a means–ends analysis focusing on superficial problem features. Due to their lack of understanding, they cannot rely on domain strategies in their problem solving efforts that refer to the principles to be learned (VanLehn et al., 2005). However, employing general or shallow strategies for problem solving does not deepen domain understanding and can therefore be classified as activities inducing extraneous load. Worked examples free learners from such extraneous activities. They leave cognitive resources for self-explanation, that is, for explicating the rationale of the solution for oneself, especially under reference to the underlying domain principles. Once the learners have understood the domain principles and their applications, it is sensible to encourage them to solve problems requiring the application of these principles. In short, learning from example is only sensible for initial skill acquisition.

Note that self-explaining is regarded as a crucial factor of example-based instruction. However, not all learners actively self-explain given examples. For them, this learning approach is only effective when self-explaining is supported by prompting or training. Self-explaining examples is also of special importance because abstract principles and concrete exemplars become interrelated and the learners gain understanding on how to apply principles in problem solving.

Whereas the preceding mechanisms focused on example encoding, another important learning mechanism, revealed by analogical reasoning research (e.g., Ross 1989), is related to the later use of encoded examples. When a transfer problem is to be solved, potentially relevant analogs are activated and selected. The problem to be solved is mapped onto the analog. If the learner identifies common structural features of the problem and the analog (e.g., common domain rule), a schema that abstracts from surface features (e.g., objects and numbers) can result from such a mapping process (e.g., Ross, 1989; Ross & Kennedy, 1990).

Whereas Sweller and Cooper (1985) provided example-problem pairs in order to heighten the motivation to study the example, analogical reasoning research shows that such an arrangement is also fruitful because students rely on the preceding example when trying to solve a problem, map the problem to example, and, thereby, construct generalized knowledge structures that can be used for later problem solving. It is important to note that the construction of generalized schemas can occur during example encoding as well as during subsequent problem solving.

In summary, examples relieve the learners from problem-solving demands that are mainly driven by superficial problem-solving strategies, especially during initial skill acquisition when learners lack understanding. In particular, the latter strategies do not really deepen understanding. When studying examples, the learners have enough capacity for gaining understanding by self-explanations that interrelate abstract principles and concrete exemplars. Finally, generalized schemas are constructed when the learners refer to examples in later problem solving.

EVIDENCE-BASED PRINCIPLES FOR INSTRUCTION DESIGN

In this section, I condense the huge body of research findings on factors that moderate the effectiveness of example-based instruction by clustering them into nine instructional guidelines. For that purpose, I consider only findings that do not come merely from one research group relying on one experimental paradigm and using one learning domain. The nine guidelines discussed are: self-explanation guideline, help guideline, example-set guideline, easy-mapping guideline, meaningful-building-blocks guideline, learning by errors guideline, similarity guideline, interleaving by fading guideline, and imagery guideline. It is important to note that some qualifications have to be made with all these guidelines because they are moderated by other factors or are not directly applicable to certain domains or certain types of examples. Hence, the boundary conditions of the guidelines are also discussed.

Self-Explanation Guideline

As the learners' self-explanation activities are crucial in order to fully exploit the potential of example-based instruction, this concept has already been mentioned (Chi et al., 1989; Renkl, 1997; see also Chapter 15 in this volume). In this section, self-explanations are discussed in detail.

In order to achieve transfer to novel problems, learners have to intensively process the presented examples so that they gain profound understanding. However, most learners do not do so spontaneously (Renkl, 1997). In their seminal study on the *self-explanation effect*, Chi et al. (1989) found individual differences in how intensively learners self-explained the solution steps of worked physics examples. Successful learners studied the examples longer and explained them more actively to themselves, that is, they tried to figure out the rationale of the solution procedure. Renkl (1997) showed that even when the example study time was held constant, self-explanation activity is related to learning outcomes.

Self-explanations fall into two main categories (Gerjets, Scheiter, & Schuh, 2008; Nokes & VanLehn, 2008): (1) elaborating on examples in order to foster their understanding; and (2) comparing examples, which typically helps to form or differentiate abstract problem categories.

Elaborating on Examples

Learners can in particular engage in two types of self-explanations in order to assign meaning to examples (see Conati & VanLehn, 2000): Principle-based explanations and goal-operator elaborations.

Principle-based explanations refer to relating problem solutions to abstract domain principles (e.g., mathematics theorem, physics law; Renkl, 1997). Such an activity fosters a principle-based understanding of examples. Figure 14.1 provides a prompt (see lower left corner, above the note box) that asks for an instructional design principle that explains why one example version is superior to the other, which in the case is the principle of meaningful building blocks (Hilbert, Renkl, Schworm, et al., 2008). Atkinson, Renkl, and Merrill (2003) experimentally tested the effects of principle-based self-explanations in probability. These authors compared conditions, in which the learners had to justify worked solution steps in terms of the underlying probability principle. More specifically, they selected a probability principle from a menu of potentially relevant principles. In the conditions without elicited self-explanations, the learners studied the worked solution steps without the requirement to select a principle. In two experiments, elicited self-explanations led to superior later problem-solving performance with respect to structurally identical problems (i.e., just new surface features such as numbers and objects) as well as to novel transfer problems (i.e., principles had to be applied in sequences not seen in the learning phase).

Goal-operator elaborations are also a way by which learners can assign meaning to operators by identifying the subgoals achieved by these operators (e.g., in a probability example, the elaboration might be, "By subtracting the probability of red items from 1, we get the probability of non-red items"). This activity fosters the representation of goals to be achieved and of knowledge about operators for achieving these goals. There is rich evidence that such elaborations foster transfer to novel problems (Catrambone, 1996; Chi et al., 1989; Conati & VanLehn, 2000; Renkl, 1997; Renkl, Stark, Gruber, & Mandl, 1998).

There are two main ways to foster principle-based self-explanations and operator-goal elaborations: Training and prompting. A *training approach* specifically tailored to example-based learning was employed, for example, by Renkl et al. (1998). These authors analyzed the effects of a short self-explanation training (10–15 min.) focusing mainly on goal-operator elaborations in interest calculation. This intervention included the following components: (a) information on the importance of self-explanations (i.e., *informed training*); (b) modeling self-explanations (one worked example from interest calculation); and (c) coached practice (with another worked example). This intervention had a strong effect on self-explanation activities and on transfer on similar problems as well as on novel problems (Stark, Mandl, Gruber, & Renkl, 2002).

Prompting interventions were employed in most of the studies designed to experimentally test the effects of self-explanation activities. Such a study (Atkinson et al., 2003) was discussed previously (see also Schworm & Renkl, 2006, 2007). As in many studies where computer-based learning environments were employed, the learners typically had to type their self-explanations into text boxes (see Figure 14.1). Sometimes, as already detailed for Atkinson et al. (2003), self-explanation activity is supported by menus that provide a list of potential principles or goals (e.g., Conati & VanLehn, 2000).

Comparing Examples

The potential of comparing examples is in particular emphasized by analogical reasoning research (e.g., Holyoak, 2005). Comparing examples can induce an abstract schema that includes a general principle (e.g., Gick & Holyoak, 1983). In the future, such a schema can be used to solve transfer problems. It is important to note that the two types of self-explanations (i.e., example elaboration and example comparison) can actually serve the same function. Principle-based self-explanations relate concrete examples or worked steps to abstract principles; the same effect might result from comparing two (or more) examples or steps and notifying that they instantiate the same principle (Nokes & VanLehn, 2008).

Such example comparisons are typically *within-category comparisons* (Gerjets et al., 2008). A category relates to a set of problems that can be solved by applying the same set and sequence of principle(s). For example, when learners compare probability examples of a certain type (e.g., order relevant, without replacement), they can see that the numbers and objects used are irrelevant for selecting the appropriate solution procedure and that these features can vary between problems from the same category. Ideally, the learners' attention is directed to the structural features (e.g., whether the order is relevant or not) that remain constant across problems of the same category (see, e.g., Berthold & Renkl, 2009; Gerjets et al., 2008). Hence, when learners compare examples they can understand that the constant (i.e., structural) features determine the appropriate solution procedure and that there can be a variety of surface features (e.g., cover stories) that are irrelevant for selecting the solution procedure.

Beyond correlational evidence that learners who induce the correct principles by example comparisons show better transfer performance (e.g., Catrambone & Holyoak, 1989; Gick & Holyoak, 1983; Thompson et al., 2000), there are a number of studies providing experimental evidence for the effectiveness of prompts (i.e., request to identify communalities and differences) or aids, for example comparison (e.g., more scripted procedures) (e.g., Catrambone & Holyoak, 1989; Cummins, 1992; Gentner et al., 2003; Gerjets et al., 2008; Nokes & VanLehn, 2008).

Besides comparing isomorphic examples, there are types of comparisons that can be labeled as *critical-feature comparisons*. In these cases, comparisons are guided in a way that specific aspects that differ between examples should become salient and be encoded as important features (cf. the contrasting cases model by Bransford & Schwartz, 1999). For example, probability examples from different, but easily mixed-up categories such as "order relevant" and "order irrelevant" are presented so that the learners can notice that it is important when solving probability problems to check whether the order is relevant or not (between-category comparison; Gerjets et al., 2008). In this case, the critical feature is the "relevance of order."

Sometimes within-category and between-category comparisons are combined so that learners can see that seemingly similar problems (i.e., same cover story) can require different solution procedures and that seemingly dissimilar problems (i.e., different cover story) can require the same solution procedure (structure-emphasizing example set; see Quilici & Mayer, 1996). Scheiter, Gerjets, and Schuh (2003) found that it is important to instruct the learners to compare the examples with respect to similarities and differences. Without such instructions, they failed to detect positive effects of a structure-emphasizing example set (see also Scheiter & Gerjets, 2005).

Braaksma et al. (2006; Braaksma, Rijlaarsdam, & van den Bergh, 2002) instructed the learners in their observational learning conditions to compare poor and well performing writing models. Such contrasting was recommended by Bandura (1986) in order to make the important aspects (i.e., critical features) of good performance more salient; in addition, what should be avoided can also become more obvious.

Rittle-Johnson, Star, and colleagues (Rittle-Johnson & Star, 2009; Rittle-Johnson, Star, & Durkin, 2009) guided their learners to explain the difference between two worked solution methods to the same problem and the conditions which must be met so that the more parsimonious method can be applied. In this case, the critical feature are the conditions that must be met to apply the easier solution method. Flexible problem solving was taught by this comparison procedure.

From an instructional point of view on comparing examples, typical prompts that worked well in the within-category comparison studies are the ones that ask for communalities and differences of the examples to be compared. In some cases, prompts ask the learner to identify the principle that applies to all examples (e.g., Thompson et al., 2000). The prompts for critical-feature comparisons are formulated quite diversely and have been tailored to the specific learning goal (i.e., the critical features to be identified). For example, Rittle-Johnson and Star (2009) asked their learners to compare two solutions of two fictitious students (Patrick and Nathan) by the following prompt: "What must be true about an equation for Patrick's ways to be easier than Nathan's way?" (p. 533).

Boundary Conditions

Beyond numerous positive findings on eliciting self-explanations, there are several studies which did not find corresponding positive effects (e.g., Gerjets, Scheiter, & Catrambone, 2006; Große & Renkl, 2006; Mwangi & Sweller, 1998). In recent years, a number of authors (e.g., Kalyuga, 2010; Sweller, 2006) have proposed converging explanations for lacking or negative effects of elicited self-explanations. If cognitive load on working memory is high—due to complex learning tasks (i.e., intrinsic load) and/or to suboptimal instructional design (i.e., extraneous load)—explicit prompts to generate self-explanations might impose too much processing demands (i.e., cognitive overload), which hinders learning. However, against the background of the present literature, this hypothesis remains tentative and has to be tested in studies explicitly designed to do so.

Help Guideline

Relying solely on self-explanations might be sub-optimal. At times learners are not able to self-explain a solution step or their self-explanations will be incorrect which can hinder learning (e.g., Berthold & Renkl, 2009). Hence, help in the form of instructional explanations that supports self-explanation activity is sensible. Note that in this context, help means the provision of instructional explanation as a supplement to self-explanations.

In Renkl's (2002) experiment on help, the learners studied probability examples with the opportunity to click on an "Explanation" button. In this case, a "minimalist" explanation of a solution step that just contained the underlying principle was provided. When the learners deemed this form of help as sufficient in order to continue in their self-explanations, they could click on a "Back" button to return to the example. The other possibility was to request more extensive support ("More help" button). In this case, it was shown how the elements of the worked examples matched the formula elements and how the probability could be determined. In the condition without help it was not possible to request any explanation or help. The learners with the possibility to request help outperformed the learners without help in a subsequent post-test with transfer problems.

There are a number of additional studies showing positive effects of help in the form of instructional explanations added to examples. In some studies such help was obligatorily provided, in other studies, learners could demand help (e.g., Atkinson, 2002; Myers, Hanson, Robson, & McCann, 1983; Ross & Kilbane, 1997; Schworm & Renkl, 2006).

There are, however, some *boundary conditions* for the help guideline. Besides positive evidence there are also many studies that failed to show positive effects of instructional explanations (as help) or that found even detrimental effects (e.g., Brown & Kane, 1988; Große & Renkl, 2006; Hoogveld, Paas, & Jochems, 2005; Schworm & Renkl, 2006; van Gog, Paas, & van Merriënboer, 2006). In their meta-analysis, Wittwer and Renkl (in press) found three factors that moderate the effects of instructional explanations as help. Positive effects can be found in the following cases: (1) Help is effective when conceptual understanding is tested as learning outcome. In contrast, there were no effects on problem solving performance, perhaps because instructional explanations primarily provide conceptual information. (2) Help fosters learning when there was no simultaneous self-explanation elicitation (typically by prompts). Two types of support, prompts and instructional explanations, are redundant. (3) Help was effective with mathematical content. A tentative, yet to be tested explanation is that learners perceive mathematics as particularly difficult and they are unsure when they are left to their own devices (Wittwer & Renkl, in press).

In summary, instructional explanations as help have often restricted or even negative effects in example-based instruction. However, under certain circumstances (e.g., conceptual understanding as learning goal; no self-explanation prompting), they can sensibly supplement self-explanation activities and thereby foster learning outcomes.

Example-Set Guideline

One possibility to direct learners' attention to specific aspects (e.g., structural aspects of problem categories) is to assemble sets of examples in specific ways. As mentioned, Quilici and Mayer (1996) used structure-emphasizing example sets. Such sets arrange examples in a way that (1) each problem category is exemplified by a set of different cover stories (i.e., surface); and (2) the same set of cover stories is used across the problem categories. The learners can see that cover stories and structure do not necessarily co-vary and relying on surface features does not necessarily help to find the correct solution procedure. Two experiments showed positive effects of structure-emphasizing sets with respect to sorting problems according to their structure and solving transfer problems (compared to a control condition receiving very similar surface stories for all examples of a given category). Quilici and Mayer (2002) replicated the positive effects of such example sets.

Paas and van Merriënboer (1994) presented six geometry examples to their learners. These examples belonged to three problem categories that varied with regard to the types of values to be determined. In a low-variability condition with respect to the problem sequence, pairs of isomorphic worked examples were presented so that within each pair just the numerical values differed. In the high variability condition, the types of values to be determined varied from example to example. High variability was assumed to foster comparison processes of subsequent examples with respect to relevant and irrelevant features. As predicted, high variability led to superior transfer performance.

There is some evidence that *boundary conditions* must be met for the effectiveness of example sets. Positive effects are not stable if the self-explanations directed to example comparison are not explicitly fostered. As already mentioned, Scheiter et al. (2003) found positive effects of structure-emphasizing example sets only when the learners were instructed to compare the examples with respect to similarities and differences. There is also ample evidence from analogical reasoning research that the provision of sets of multiple examples is not sufficient for transfer. Instead the learner must be prompted to compare the examples (e.g., Catrambone & Holyoak, 1989; Gentner et al., 2003; Gerjets et al., 2008). In addition, more support as compared to little support in example comparison leads to better outcomes (e.g., Gentner et al., 2003: prompts to compare versus training package).

In summary, example sets—typically designed to make structural aspects more salient—can have positive effects on learning outcomes. However, this is not necessarily the case. In order to assure positive effects of example sets, prompts or training interventions can be used to foster example comparison processes.

Easy-Mapping Guideline

The positive effects of worked examples are lost when the learners have difficulties in mapping different information sources onto each other, such as figures and arithmetical equations in geometry problems (Tarmizi & Sweller, 1988). In an effort to map the different information sources, such difficulties can lead to an extensive visual search that requires so much cognitive capacity (i.e., induce extraneous load) that productive self-explanations are more or less blocked. One possibility to make it easier to interrelate different information sources is to physically integrate them (e.g., writing the size of an angle in a geometry example directly into the figure). Such mapping facilitation makes cognitive resources available so that self-explanations can occur. Hence, facilitating mapping substantially enhances learning outcomes (Mwangi & Sweller, 1998; Tarmizi & Sweller, 1988; Ward & Sweller, 1990; see also Mayer & Moreno, 2003, for similar results in their research program).

An integrated format is not the only possibility to facilitate mapping between information sources. The capacity for initial information processing is distributed over several sensory subsystems (e.g., Mayer & Moreno, 2003; Rummer, Schweppe, Scheiter, & Gerjets, 2008). Hence, information processing can be facilitated by providing spoken text together with a figure instead of presenting both types of information visually (i.e., printed text). For example, Mousavi, Low, and Sweller (1995) compared in several experiments two conditions: (1) geometry proof examples were presented visually only (i.e., figure and written proof statements); and (2) geometry proof examples were presented in mixed modality, that is, the figure was printed and the proof statements were provided by a tape recorder. In six experiments, Mousavi et al. showed that in the mixed presentation mode, learners solved the post-test problem more quickly (with low overall failure rates in both conditions). Jeung, Chandler, and Sweller (1997) qualified these findings. In three experiments, in which the difficulty of mapping between information sources was varied, they showed that for visually complex, unfamiliar materials the superiority of auditory explanations on visually presented examples disappeared. It only reappeared when electronic flashing was additionally used showing to which part of the diagram the spoken text was referring.

Atkinson (2002) also showed that an animated agent supporting mapping by gaze and gestures enhances learning. Berthold and Renkl (2009) used a combined color coding and flashing procedure in order to facilitate mapping when learning from examples containing solution procedure in a graphical and an arithmetical representation format (see Figure 14.2). They found that this procedure fostered conceptual understanding.

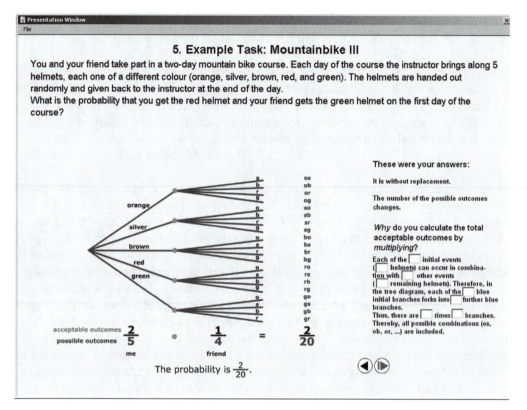

Figure 14.2 A worked example with color coding in order to facilitate mapping between different representations (Berthold & Renkl, 2009)

What are the *boundary conditions* of this guideline? An open question that cannot be answered on the basis of available empirical evidence is when to integrate, when to use dual-mode and signaling, or when to used color coding and/or flashing. Pragmatic answers suggest using an integrated format in the cases where an auditory presentation is not or hardly possible, due to technical restrictions. Integrated format cannot be used if elements in one representation mode do not correspond to certain, well-circumscribed parts in the other representation mode. For example, in Figure 14.2, the "20" in the denominator of the resulting probability corresponds to the 20 branches of the tree-like structure. In these cases, a "classical" integrated format is hardly possible. However, there is no principled guideline when to use which support procedure.

In a nutshell, in order to support the learners during the study of examples with different information sources (e.g., geometry examples with figures and arithmetical equations), it is sensible to facilitate mapping. Such facilitation can be accomplished by several instructional procedures such as integrated format, color coding, or combining auditory and visual presentation formats.

Meaningful-Building-Blocks Guideline

Learners can encounter novel problems for which known solution procedures do not work. A modified solution procedure has to be constructed. Sometimes, however, students have encoded solution procedures for certain problem types as a "fixed chain" of steps. For example, a student might have worked on the following problem:

> Jonathan has recently bought a new camera. Independently of each other he frequently makes two errors when he takes a picture. He manages to blur the image in 40% of his photos (p = 2/5) and he forgets to activate the flash in 10% of the photos (p = 1/10) so that the pictures end up too dark. If you randomly choose one of Jonathan's pictures, what is the probability that it will be flawless?
>
> (Renkl, Atkinson, Maier, & Staley, 2002)

The student might have learned the "fixed" solution procedure: "first multiply the probabilities, second, add them, and subtract the product determined in the first step, third, subtract the outcome of step 2 from '1'." If the students does not understand the meaning of, for example, the third step (i.e., determining the complementary probability), s/he will probably have difficulties to determine whether the last solution step can be simply left out if the problem question was modified: "If you randomly choose one of Jonathan's pictures, what is the probability that it will have a flaw?" In other words, transfer is likely to fail if the learners have not encoded the single steps of a chain as meaningful building blocks (e.g., a certain type of subgoal, here the complementary probability, is achieved by a certain operator). They cannot flexibly reassemble them for a novel problem in which, for example, the sequence of the steps has to be changed or steps have to be left out. Against this background, it is favorable to present examples in a way that subcomponents can easily be identified as meaningful building blocks (cf. also the previous discussion about goal-operator elaborations).

Catrambone (e.g., 1996, 1998) has shown in a series of experiments that the ability to assemble new procedures can be fostered by making subgoals in a worked solution salient, either by visually isolating them (e.g., making circles around them) or by assigning a label to them. Catrambone (1996) also showed that salient subgoals lead to self-explanations about what these steps accomplished. As a result, learning outcomes were enhanced.

A further possibility to make subgoals salient is to use a step-by-step presentation of a worked solution. This procedure clearly marks the single subgoals. Actually, Atkinson and Derry (2000) found a stepwise presentation to be more effective than a simultaneous presentation of the solution. Schmidt-Weigand, Hänze, and Wodzinski (2009) also found positive effects of a step-by-step presentation, especially when learners were prompted to think about the next step before its presentation.

In some cases, learners can hardly identify meaningful building blocks of worked solutions because the instructional materials use formulas that are computationally efficient but opaque. Beginning learners can hardly understand—and later re-construct if necessary—such *molar* formulas. For example, the problem in Figure 14.1 is efficiently solved by the formula shown on the left side. The formula is called molar because it synthesizes a number of more fine-grained *modular* steps (see Figure 14. 1 on the right side). The rationale of the solution can be understood much better when learning from the solution on the right side. Several experimental studies have shown that breaking the *molar* solutions into *modular* units (as shown in Figure 14.1) leads to better performance on isomorphic and novel problem (Atkinson, Catrambone, & Merrill, 2003; Gerjets, Scheiter, Catrambone, 2004, 2006). Hence, computationally not so efficient modular solution procedures are more favorable for beginners (of course, the efficient molar solutions might be more convenient for advanced learners).

Boundary conditions refer to the type of content area. The relevant findings were all obtained in mathematical content areas. If examples consist, for example, of realistic video models (e.g., Rummel et al., 2009; Schworm & Renkl, 2007), it also seems plausible that making building blocks salient helps learners to parse the complex examples and to learn about the sub-components of cognitive skills. However, there is little direct evidence. In addition, there is no straightforward way to transfer the procedures used for mathematic examples to examples provided by realistic video models. For example, is it best to use headings or subtitles in videos for different sections of the model behavior or should the model articulate the subgoals?

In summary, it is recommended to design examples, especially if they are very complex, in a way that the single building blocks of skills become salient. Emphasizing meaningful building blocks is in particular important for the ability of the learners to rearrange single moves in order to solve novel problems. How to make building blocks salient is best known for mathematics.

Learning by Errors Guideline

Typical examples show correct performance or solutions. As errors can be a productive element in learning, it might, nevertheless, be fruitful to include errors in example-based instruction (e.g., impasse-driven learning, VanLehn, 1999). Actually, Siegler (2002) found that self-explaining correct and incorrect worked solutions is more favorable than self-explaining correct worked solutions only. Siegler assumed that explaining incorrect solutions ("corrective self-explanations") helps to avoid these errors later on.

There are corresponding findings from modeling research. A number of studies compared mastery models that showed smooth performance and coping models that initially showed difficulties (i.e., made errors) and how they can be overcome. Learners usually profit from coping models (Kitsantas, Zimmerman, & Cleary, 2000; Schunk, Hanson, & Cox, 1987). For example, Zimmermann and Kitsantas (2002) taught college students writing skills by models demonstrating a revision strategy. The mastery model performed this strategy flawlessly with nine training problems. The coping model made and corrected errors on the initial revision problems but gradually reduced them. In a post-test with three revision problems, students who had observed the coping model outperformed their counterparts who had observed a mastery model.

Of course, coping and mastery models differ in more than whether or not errors or sub-optimal moves are shown. In particular, a coping model also demonstrates how to cope with difficulties. Nevertheless, these findings are in line with the previously mentioned studies on the effects of errors in examples.

The findings of Große and Renkl (2007) show that there are *boundary conditions* for this guideline. In two experiments a mixture of correct examples and examples with errors, as compared to correct examples only, helped learners with good prior knowledge, but impeded learners with poor prior knowledge. Providing errors in worked examples too early in the learning process (i.e., when prior knowledge is too low) might overwhelm learners. A possibility is to provide more support for weaker learners. Große and Renkl found that explicitly marking errors (versus not doing so) especially supported learners with low prior knowledge.

In summary, including errors in examples can foster learning. Less advanced learners, however, can be overwhelmed by the demands to process erroneous examples. In this case, help such as marking the errors is necessary.

Similarity Guideline

In social-cognitive theorizing about cognitive skill acquisition from exemplary models, one of the classical moderators of model effects is the similarity of the model and the observer (e.g., Bandura, 1986; Schunk, 1987, 1999; Schunk & Zimmerman, 2007). If the model that shows that a problem solution to be learned is too dissimilar, in particular, too advanced, the observer might not realize that s/he is able to show the appropriate behavior by herself/himself (i.e., lack of self-efficacy; Schunk & Hanson, 1985). For example, Ryalls, Gul, and Ryalls (2000) found that 14–18-month-old children learned three-step sequences better from peer models than from adult models.

Braaksma et al. (2002) provided both a competent and a non-competent model to students in order to learn argumentative writing in their observational conditions. In one condition the learners were instructed to especially focus on the competent model and in one condition on the non-competent model when comparing both models. Weak students profited more from focusing on the non-competent model than on the competent model. Stronger students profited more from focusing on the competent model. This pattern of findings was interpreted as a similarity effect in observational learning.

In addition, the coping model effect, already discussed, was interpreted as the similarity effect in the literature on socio-cognitive learning (e.g., Schunk, 1999). However, it is not clear whether the similarity and/or the shown errors (and how they are overcome) are crucial. In this context, the findings of Schunk and Hanson (1985) are interesting: They showed that elementary students learning subtraction skills profited more from (same sex) peer models, either coping or mastery, than from an adult teacher model (mastery). Obviously, similarity plays a role beyond the learning by errors effect.

What are the *boundary conditions* of this effect? In particular, when examples in the form of realistic models are employed it is highly plausible that the similarity is an important factor. If the competence level is far below or above the learner, little learning can be expected. Beyond that, it is, up to now, unclear which type of similarity is important and which features of potential similarity are more or less irrelevant (e.g., age, gender, language accent, ethnicity). In addition, it might be that different similarity features influence learning by different mechanism. For example, similarity in ethnicity might primarily enhance motivation, whereas competence-level similarity might also influence cognitive aspects such as the possibility to assimilate the modeled behavior.

On the whole, the available empirical evidence makes it very probable that model-observer similarity is a crucial factor of the effectiveness of example-based learning. However, further research has to determine which specific aspects of similarity are crucial.

Interleaving by Fading Guideline

In the classical studies on the worked example effect by Sweller and colleagues (e.g., Cooper & Sweller, 1987; Sweller & Cooper, 1985), the example condition included a combination of example study and problem solving. More specifically, isomorphic example-problem pairs were employed, in an attempt to motivate example processing. Trafton and Reiser (1993) found that example-problem pairs are more effective than a blocked series of examples and problems.

Analogical reasoning research shows that solving a problem isomorphic to a preceding analog fosters schema induction (see Holyoak, 2005; Ross, 1989). Bandura (1986) claimed that learners need practice between observations of models. The resulting difficulties show the learners what they have to attend to, specifically in subsequent models to repair their deficits.

Pashler et al. (2007) recommended in their evidence-based practice guide to interleave worked solutions with problem solving, as one of seven central recommendations. Such interleaving is to be implemented by problem-example pairs. Although there can be little doubt about the benefits of interleaving example and problems as compared to pure example study, pairing is not the best method of interleaving.

Many experiments have shown that gradually fading worked solution steps leads to better learning outcomes than example-problem pairs (Atkinson et al., 2003; Kissane, Kalyuga, Chandler, & Sweller, 2008; Renkl, Atkinson & Große, 2004; Renkl et al., 2002; Schwonke et al., 2009). In such a fading procedure a complete example is presented first; second, an isomorphic example is presented in which one single step is omitted; after trying to supplement the faded step, the learner receives feedback about the correct solution. Then, in the following examples, the number of blanks is increased step by step until just the problem formulation is left, that is, a problem to be solved. Such fading is also important as it provides an answer to the question of how to structure the transition from worked examples in earlier stages of skill acquisition to problem solving in later stages (cf. the expertise-reversal effect by Kalyuga et al., 2003).

It is important to emphasize that fading also leads to interleaving. For example, if learners come to a worked example with one step to be determined (and two steps worked out), they will encounter again worked steps after the first problem-solving demand. The main difference between fading and example-problem pairs is constant versus increasing problem-solving demands over time.

In order to optimize fading, it might be sensible to adapt the rate of introducing problem-solving elements to the individual learner's progress, instead of using a fixed fading procedure for all learners. Salden et al. (2010) assumed that studying and self-explaining worked solution steps prepare learners to deal with subsequent problem-solving demands in a principle-based way. A learner who has not yet gained a basic understanding of a principle and its application should not be exposed to the corresponding problem-solving demands. Once the student shows such understanding, s/he should try to apply this knowledge in problem solving. Salden et al. implemented a corresponding adaptive fading procedure for geometry learning on the basis of Cognitive Tutors' intelligent tutoring technology (Koedinger & Corbett, 2006). In short, if a learner could provide correct self-explanations on a type of worked step—relating to a certain underlying geometry principles—then the worked solution was faded in the next instance of such a step. Salden et al. compared such an adaptive fading procedure with a fixed fading procedure which was the same for every learner in the respective condition. In addition, there was a pure problem-solving condition, which represents the standard procedure of Cognitive Tutor lessons. In two experiments (laboratory and field), learners in the adaptive fading condition performed best in a delayed post-test.

Similar *boundary conditions* as in the case of the meaningful-building-blocks guideline apply. When learning from complex examples such as video models, it also seems sensible to gradually fade worked parts of skills. Nevertheless, there is little corresponding evidence, and it is unclear how to best implement fading with such complex models (e.g., stopping the video model and having the learners to determine the next model move?).

To sum up, a fading procedure is the most favorable way to interleave example study and problem solving. Such fading also structures the transition from example study in earlier stages of skill acquisition to problem solving in later stages in a sensible way. Adapting fading to the individual progress is especially effective. Implementing effective fading procedures on the basis of available evidence can best be achieved in areas with mathematical solution procedures.

Imagery Guideline

Sweller and colleagues have conducted a number of experiments on the effects of imagery in example-based instruction (Cooper, Tindall-Ford, Chandler, & Sweller, 2001; Ginns, Chandler, & Sweller, 2003; Leahy & Sweller, 2004; Tindall-Ford & Sweller, 2006). The imagery procedure included first reading a worked solution, second, turning away from the screen, and, third, imagining performing the solution procedure. Similarly, Scheiter, Gerjets, and Catrambone (2006) had some of their learners imagine the event flow described in the worked examples. Empirical evidence clearly shows that imagery can foster learning. Some studies—although in the area of perceptual and motor skills— have shown that mental imagery can have effects comparable to actually performing (e.g., Corriss & Kose, 1998). This finding raises the question whether the imagery effect is tightly related to the interleaving effect when example-problem pairs are presented.

Studies by Sweller and colleagues (Cooper et al., 2001; Ginns et al., 2003; Leahy & Sweller, 2004; Tindall-Ford & Sweller, 2006) have shown that the imagery effect has *boundary conditions*. It does not come into effect when the learners are not familiar with the learning contents. A lack of prior knowledge prevents the learners actually being able to comply with the imagining instruction. They simply cannot imagine the solution when looking away from the example. Hence, imagery instructions should be not given too early in the course of skill acquisition. A solution is to first provide an example for pure study and then an example for imagery (Ginns et al., 2003).

FURTHER RESEARCH

Three issues in particular need further analyses in order to advance the theoretical foundation and the practical relevance of example-based instruction:

1 The dominant *explanation of the effectiveness of example-based instruction* is based on cognitive load theory and its extensions. Salden, Koedinger, Renkl, Aleven, and McLaren (in press) recently challenged in particular a central assumption of the cognitive load account. They raised the question whether the reduction of learning-irrelevant (extraneous) cognitive load is actually the cause of the example effect. It might well be that the avoidance of superficial learning strategies and the facilitation of productive self-explanations is the cause, whereas the type and amount of cognitive load resulting from superficial strategies or self-explanations, respectively, are just an epiphenomenon. As the worked examples effect can be seen as one of the best established effects in the field of learning and instruction, it is important that future studies shed further light on the exact reasons, especially with respect to the status of cognitive load (i.e., cause or epiphenomenon).

2 *Diverse research traditions* are relevant when considering example-based instruction. Although the main reference point of this chapter was the research on worked examples, findings from research on analogical reasoning and on abstract modeling in the sense of Bandura (1986) were included (see also Renkl, 2010). However, a more complete integration of the three mentioned lines of research (i.e., worked examples, analogical reasoning, and modeling) and potentially of additional related areas such as case-based reasoning (e.g., Kolodner, 1993; Schank, Berman, & Macpherson, 1999) or cognitive apprenticeship (Collins, Brown, & Newman, 1989) is surely desirable. Each research tradition should not have to "reinvent the wheel."

3 The relations between the different *instructional guidelines* discussed in the chapter are not well understood. There is evidence that some of the discussed effects are independent and, hence, additively affect learning outcomes. For example, Atkinson et al. (2003) found additive effects for interleaving by fading and prompting for self-explanations. Nevertheless, it would be naïve to assume full additivity of the single effects (i.e., the more the better). Some effects depend inherently on each other, such as example sets and self-explanations with respect to example comparisons. For example, Rittle-Johnson and Star (2009) could not encourage their learners to compare solution methods without providing sets of different example solutions. For other effects, it has been empirically shown that they interact. For example, Wouters, Paas, and van Merriënboer (2009) found an interaction between easy-mapping in terms of a dual-mode arrangement and self-explanation prompts (i.e., no dual-mode effect under prompting conditions). More theoretical and empirical analyses are necessary to understanding the interplay between the discussed effects in a principled way. Such understanding is probably only possible when more is known about the specific knowledge construction processes that are involved in the diverse effects.

In examining reviews of example-based instruction over the decade, such as articles from 2000 (Atkinson, Derry, Renkl, & Wortham, 2000) and from 2005 (Renkl, 2005) as well as considering this chapter, it becomes clear that research has substantially progressed and improved the knowledge base. This development justifies an optimistic forecast on how profoundly the three suggested issues for further research will be addressed in the upcoming years.

REFERENCES

Anderson, J. R., Fincham, J. M., & Douglass, S. (1997). The role of examples and rules in the acquisition of a cognitive skill. *Journal of Experimental Psychology: Learning, Memory, and Cognition, 23*, 932–945.

Atkinson, R. K. (2002). Optimizing learning from examples using animated pedagogical agents. *Journal of Educational Psychology, 94*, 416–427.

Atkinson, R. K., Catrambone, R., & Merrill, M. M. (2003). Aiding transfer in statistics. Examining the use of conceptually oriented equations and elaborations during subgoal learning. *Journal of Educational Psychology, 95*, 762–773.

Atkinson, R. K., & Derry, S. J. (2000). Computer-based examples designed to encourage optimal example processing: A study examining the impact of sequentially presented, subgoal-oriented worked examples. In B. Fishman, & S. F. O'Connor-Divelbiss (Eds.), *Proceedings of the Fourth International Conference of Learning Sciences* (pp. 132–133). Hillsdale, NJ: Erlbaum.

Atkinson, R. K., Derry, S. J., Renkl, A., & Wortham, D. W. (2000). Learning from examples: Instructional principles from the worked examples research. *Review of Educational Research, 70*, 181–214.

Atkinson, R. K., Renkl, A., & Merrill, M. M. (2003). Transitioning from studying examples to solving problems: Combining fading with prompting fosters learning. *Journal of Educational Psychology, 95*, 774–783.

Bandura, A. (1971). *Psychological modeling: Conflicting theories.* Chicago, IL: Aldine Atherton.

Bandura, A. (1986). *Social foundations of thought and action: A social cognitive theory.* Englewood Cliffs, NJ: Prentice Hall.

Berthold, K., & Renkl, A. (2009). Instructional aids to support a conceptual understanding of multiple representations. *Journal of Educational Psychology, 101*, 70–87.

Braaksma, M. A. H., Rijlaarsdam, G., & van den Bergh, H. (2002). Observational learning and the effects of model-observer similarity. *Journal of Educational Psychology, 94*, 405–415.

Braaksma, M. A. H., Rijlaarsdam, G., van den Bergh, H., & Van Hout Wolters, B. H. A. M. (2006). What observational learning entails: A case study. *L1-Educational Studies in Language & Literature, 1*, 31–62.

Bransford, J. D., & Schwartz, D. L. (1999). Rethinking transfer: A simple proposal with multiple implications. *Review of Research in Education, 24*, 61–100.

Brown, A. L., & Kane, M. J. (1988). Preschool children can learn to transfer: Learning to learn and learning from examples. *Cognitive Psychology, 20*, 493–523.

Bruner, J. S., Goodnow, J., & Austin, G. (1956). *A study of thinking.* New York: Wiley.

Carroll, W. M. (1994). Using worked examples as an instructional support in the algebra classroom. *Journal of Educational Psychology, 86*, 360–367.

Catrambone, R. (1996). Generalizing solution procedures learned from examples. *Journal of Experimental Psychology: Learning, Memory, and Cognition, 22*, 1020–1031.

Catrambone, R. (1998). The subgoal learning model: Creating better examples so that students can solve novel problems. *Journal of Experimental Psychology: General, 127*, 355–376.

Catrambone, R., & Holyoak, K. J. (1989). Overcoming contextual limitations on problem-solving transfer. *Journal of Experimental Psychology: Learning, Memory, and Cognition, 15*, 1147–1156.

Chi, M. T., H., Bassok, M., Lewis, M. W., Reimann, P., & Glaser, R. (1989). Self-explanations: How students study and use examples in learning to solve problems. *Cognitive Science, 13*, 145–182.

Clement, L. L., & Bernhard, J. Z. (2005). A problem-solving alternative to using key words. *Mathematics Teaching in the Middle School, 10*, 360–365.

Collins, A., Brown, J. S., & Newman, S. E. (1989). Cognitive apprenticeship: Teaching the crafts of reading, writing, and mathematics. In L. B. Resnick (Ed.), *Knowing, learning, and instruction* (pp. 453–494). Hillsdale, NJ: Erlbaum.

Conati, C., & VanLehn, K. (2000). Toward computer-based support of meta-cognitive skills: A computational framework to coach self-explanation. *International Journal of Artificial Intelligence in Education, 11*, 398–415.

Cooper, G., & Sweller, J. (1987). Effects of schema acquisition and rule automation on mathematical problem-solving transfer. *Journal of Educational Psychology, 79*, 347–362.

Cooper, G., Tindall-Ford, S., Chandler, P., & Sweller, J. (2001). Learning by imagining procedures and concepts. *Journal of Experimental Psychology: Applied, 7*, 68–82.

Corriss, D., & Kose, G. (1998). Action and imagination in the formation of images. *Perceptual and Motor Skills, 87*, 979–983.

Cummins, D. D. (1992). Role of analogical reasoning in the induction of problem categories. *Journal of Experimental Psychology: Learning, Memory, and Cognition, 18*, 1103–1124.

Didierjean, A., & Cauzinille-Marmèche, E. (1998). Reasoning by analogy: Is it schema-mediated or case-based? *European Journal of Educational Psychology, 13*, 385–398.

Eysink, T. H. S., de Jong, T., Berthold, K., Kolloffel, B., Opfermann, M., & Wouters, P. (2009). Learner performance in multimedia learning arrangements: An analysis across instructional approaches. *American Educational Research Journal, 46*, 1107–1149.

Gentner, D. (1989). The mechanisms of analogical learning. In S. Vosniadou, & A. Ortony (Eds.), *Similarity and analogical reasoning* (pp. 199–241). New York: Cambridge University Press.

Gentner, D., Loewenstein, J., & Thompson, L. (2003). Learning and transfer: A general role for analogical encoding. *Journal of Educational Psychology, 95*, 393–408.

Gerjets, P., Scheiter, K., & Catrambone, R. (2004). Designing instructional examples to reduce intrinsic cognitive load: Molar versus modular presentation of solution procedures. *Instructional Science, 32*, 33–58

Gerjets, P., Scheiter, K., & Catrambone, R. (2006). Can learning from molar and modular worked-out examples be enhanced by providing instructional explanations and prompting self-explanations? *Learning and Instruction, 16*, 104–121.

Gerjets, P., Scheiter, K., & Schuh, J. (2008). Information comparisons in example-based hypermedia environments: Supporting learners with processing prompts and an interactive comparison tool. *Educational Technology Research and Development, 56*, 73–92

Gick, M. L., & Holyoak, K. J. (1983). Schema induction and analogical transfer. *Cognitive Psychology*, *15*, 1–38.

Ginns, P., Chandler, P., & Sweller, J. (2003). When imagining information is effective. *Contemporary Educational Psychology*, *28*, 229–251.

Große, C. S., & Renkl, A. (2006). Effects of multiple solution methods in mathematics learning. *Learning & Instruction*, *16*, 122–138.

Große, C. S., & Renkl, A. (2007). Finding and fixing errors in worked examples: Can this foster learning outcomes? *Learning & Instruction*, *17*, 612–634.

Hilbert, T. S., Renkl, A., Kessler, S., & Reiss, K. (2008). Learning to prove in geometry: Learning from heuristic examples and how it can be supported. *Learning & Instruction*, *18*, 54–65.

Hilbert, T. S., Renkl, A., Schworm, S., Kessler, S., & Reiss, K. (2008). Learning to teach with worked-out examples: A computer-based learning environment for teachers. *Journal of Computer-Assisted Learning*, *24*, 316–332.

Holyoak, K. J. (2005). Analogy. In K. J. Holyoak, & R. G. Morrison (Eds.), *The Cambridge handbook of thinking and reasoning* (pp. 117–142). New York: Cambridge University Press.

Hoogveld, A. W. M., Paas, F., & Jochems, W. M. G. (2005). Training higher education teachers for instructional design of competency-based education: Product-oriented versus process-oriented worked examples. *Teaching and Teacher Education*, *21*, 287–297.

Hübner. S., & Nückles, M., & Renkl, A. (2010). Writing learning journals: Instructional support to overcome learning-strategy deficits. *Learning & Instruction*, *20*, 18–29.

Jeung, H., Chandler, P., & Sweller, J. (1997). The role of visual indicators in dual sensory mode instruction. *Educational Psychology*, *17*, 329–433.

Kalyuga, S. (2010). Schema acquisition and sources of cognitive load. In J. Plass, R. Moreno, & R. Brünken (Eds.), *Cognitive load theory and research in educational psychology* (pp. 48–64). New York: Cambridge University Press.

Kalyuga, S., Ayres, P., Chandler, P., & Sweller, J. (2003). The expertise reversal effect. *Educational Psychologist*, *38*, 23–31.

Kissane, M., Kalyuga, S., Chandler, P., & Sweller, J. (2008). The consequences of fading instructional guidance on delayed performance: The case of financial services training. *Educational Psychology*, *28*, 809–822.

Kitsantas, A., Zimmerman, B. J., & Cleary, T. (2000). The role of observation and emulation in the development of athletic self-regulation. *Journal of Educational Psychology*, *92*, 811–817.

Koedinger, K. R., & Corbett, A. T. (2006). Cognitive tutors: Technology bringing learning sciences to the classroom. In R. K. Sawyer (Ed.), *The Cambridge handbook of the learning sciences* (pp. 61–78). New York: Cambridge University Press.

Kolodner, J. L. (1993). *Case-based reasoning*. San Mateo, CA: Morgan Kaufmann.

Kuhn, D. (1991). *The skills of argument*. New York: Cambridge University Press.

Leahy, W., & Sweller, J. (2004). Cognitive load and the imagination effect. *Applied Cognitive Psychology*, *18*, 857–875.

Mayer, R. E., & Moreno, R. (2003). Nine ways to reduce cognitive load in multimedia learning. *Educational Psychologist*, *38*, 43–52.

Merrill, M. D., & Tennyson, R. D. (1977). *Concept teaching: An instructional design guide*. Englewood Cliffs, NJ: Educational Technology Publications.

Mousavi, S. Y., Low, R., & Sweller, J. (1995). Reducing cognitive load by mixing auditory and visual presentation modes. *Journal of Educational Psychology*, *87*, 319–334.

Mwangi, W., & Sweller, J. (1998). Learning to solve compare word problems: The effect of example format and generating self-explanations. *Cognition and Instruction*, *16*, 173–199.

Myers, J. L., Hanson, R. S., Robson, R. C., & McCann, J. (1983). The role of explanation when learning elementary probability. *Journal of Educational Psychology*, *75*, 374–381.

Nokes, T. J., & VanLehn, K. (2008). Bridging principles and examples through analogy and explanation. In P. A. Kirschner, F. Prins, V. Jonker, & G. Kanselaar (Eds.), *Proceedings of the 8th International Conference of the Learning Sciences 2008* (Vol. 3, pp. 100–102). Utrecht, NL: ICLS.

Paas, F., & van Gog, T. (2006). Optimising worked example instruction: Different ways to increase germane cognitive load. *Learning and Instruction*, *16*, 87–91.

Paas, F, & van Merriënboer, J. J. G. (1994). Variability of worked examples and transfer of geometrical problem solving skills: A cognitive load approach. *Journal of Educational Psychology*, *86*, 122–133.

Pashler, H., Bain, P. M., Botge, B. A., Graesser, A., Koedinger, K., McDaniel, M., & Metcalfe, J. (2007). *Organizing instruction and study to improve student learning: IES practice guide*. Washington, DC: US Department of Education.

Quilici, J. L., & Mayer, R. E. (1996). Role of examples in how students learn to categorize statistics word problems. *Journal of Educational Psychology*, *88*, 144–161.

Quilici, J. L., & Mayer, R. E. (2002). Teaching students to recognize structural similarities between statistics word problems. *Applied Cognitive Psychology, 16*, 325–342.

Reeves, L. M., & Weisberg, R. W. (1993). On the concrete nature of human thinking: Content and context in analogical transfer. *Educational Psychology, 13*, 245–258.

Renkl, A. (1997). Learning from worked-out examples: A study on individual differences. *Cognitive Science, 21*, 1–29.

Renkl, A. (2002). Learning from worked-out examples: Instructional explanations supplement self-explanations. *Learning & Instruction, 12*, 529–556.

Renkl, A. (2005). The worked-out-example principle in multimedia learning. In R. Mayer (Ed.), *Cambridge handbook of multimedia learning* (pp. 229–246). New York: Cambridge University Press.

Renkl, A. (2010). Towards an instructionally oriented theory of example-based learning. (Manuscript submitted for publication.)

Renkl, A., & Atkinson, R. K. (2003). Structuring the transition from example study to problem solving in cognitive skills acquisition: A cognitive load perspective. *Educational Psychologist, 38*, 15–22.

Renkl, A., Atkinson, R. K., & Große, C. S. (2004). How fading worked solution steps works – a cognitive load perspective. *Instructional Science, 32*, 59–82.

Renkl, A., Atkinson, R. K., Maier, U. H., & Staley, R. (2002). From example study to problem solving: Smooth transitions help learning. *Journal of Experimental Education, 70*, 293–315.

Renkl, A., Mandl, H., & Gruber, H. (1996). Inert knowledge: Analyses and remedies. *Educational Psychologist, 31*, 115–121.

Renkl, A., Stark, R., Gruber, H., & Mandl, H. (1998). Learning from worked-out examples: The effects of example variability and elicited self-explanations. *Contemporary Educational Psychology, 23*, 90–108.

Rittle-Johnson, B., & Star, J. R. (2009). Compared with what? The effects of different comparisons on conceptual knowledge and procedural flexibility for equation solving. *Journal of Educational Psychology, 101*, 529–544.

Rittle-Johnson, B., Star, J. R., & Durkin, K. (2009). The importance of prior knowledge when comparing examples: Influences on conceptual and procedural knowledge of equation solving. *Journal of Educational Psychology, 101*, 836–852.

Ross, B. H. (1987). This is like that: The use of earlier problems and the separation of similarity effects. *Journal of Experimental Psychology: Learning, Memory, and Cognition, 13*, 629–639.

Ross, B. H. (1989). Distinguishing types of superficial similarities: Different effects on the access and use of earlier problems. *Journal of Experimental Psychology: Learning, Memory, and Cognition, 15*, 456–468.

Ross, B. H., & Kennedy, P. T. (1990). Generalizing from the use of earlier examples in problem solving. *Journal of Experimental Psychology: Learning, Memory, and Cognition, 16*, 42–45.

Ross, B. H., & Kilbane, M. C. (1997). Effects of principle explanation and superficial similarity on analogical mapping in problem solving. *Journal of Experimental Psychology: Learning, Memory, & Cognition, 23*, 427–440.

Rourke, A. J., & Sweller, J. (2009). The worked-example effect using ill-defined problems: Learning to recognise designers' styles. *Learning and Instruction, 19*, 185–199.

Rummel, N., Spada, H., & Hauser, S. (2009). Learning to collaborate while being scripted or by observing a model. *International Journal of Computer-Supported Collaborative Learning, 4*, 69–92.

Rummer, R., Schweppe, J., Scheiter, K., & Gerjets, P. (2008). Lernen mit Multimedia: Die kognitiven Grundlagen des Modalitätseffekts [Learning with multimedia: The cognitive basis of the modality effect]. *Psychologische Rundschau, 59*, 98–107.

Ryalls, B. O., Gul, R. E., & Ryalls, K. R. (2000). Infant imitation of peer and adult models: Evidence for a peer model advantage. *Merrill-Palmer Quarterly, 46*, 188–202.

Salden, R., Aleven, V., Schwonke, R., & Renkl, A. (2010). The expertise-reversal effect and worked examples in tutored problem solving. *Instructional Science, 38*, 289–307.

Salden, R., Koedinger, K, Renkl, A., Aleven, V., & McLaren, B. M. (in press). Accounting for beneficial effects of worked examples in tutored problem solving. *Educational Psychology Review*.

Schank, R., Berman, T. R., & Macpherson, K. A. (1999). Learning by doing. In C. M. Reigeluth (Ed.), *Instructional design theories and models* (Vol. II, pp. 161–181). Mahwah, NJ: Erlbaum.

Scheiter, K., & Gerjets, P. (2005). When less is sometimes more: Optimal learning conditions are required for schema acquisition from multiple examples. In B. G. Bara, L. Barsalou, & M. Bucciarelli (Eds.), *Proceedings of the 27th Annual Conference of the Cognitive Science Society* (pp. 1943–1948). Mahwah, NJ: Erlbaum.

Scheiter, K., Gerjets, P., & Catrambone, R. (2006). Making the abstract concrete: Visualizing mathematical solution procedures. *Computers in Human Behavior, 22*, 9–26.

Scheiter, K., Gerjets, P., & Schuh, J. (2003). Are multiple examples necessary for schema induction? In F. Schmalhofer, R. Young, & G. Katz (Eds.), *Proceedings of EuroCogSci 03. The European Cognitive Science Conference 2003* (pp. 283–288). Mahwah, NJ: Erlbaum.

Schmidt-Weigand, F., Hänze, M., & Wodzinski, R. (2009). Complex problem solving and worked examples: The role of prompting strategic behavior and fading-in solution steps. *German Journal of Educational Psychology*, *23*, 129–138.

Schunk, D. H. (1987). Peer models and children's behavioral change. *Review of Educational Research*, *57*, 149–174.

Schunk, D. H. (1999). Social-self interaction and achievement behavior. *Educational Psychologist*, *34*, 219–227.

Schunk, D. H., & Hanson, A. R. (1985). Peer models: Influence on children's self-efficacy and achievement. *Journal of Educational Psychology*, *77*, 313–322.

Schunk, D. H., Hanson, A. R., & Cox, P. D. (1987). Peer model attributes and children's achievement behaviors. *Journal of Educational Psychology*, *79*, 54–61.

Schunk, D. H., & Zimmerman, B. J. (2007). Influencing children's self-efficacy and self-regulation of reading and writing through modeling. *Reading & Writing Quarterly*, *23*, 7–25.

Schwonke, R., Renkl, A., Krieg, K., Wittwer, J., Aleven, V., & Salden, R. (2009). The worked-example effect: Not an artefact of lousy control conditions. *Computers in Human Behavior*, *25*, 258–266.

Schworm, S., & Renkl, A. (2006). Computer-supported example-based learning: When instructional explanations reduce self-explanations. *Computers & Education*, *46*, 426–445.

Schworm, S., & Renkl, A. (2007). Learning argumentation skills through the use of prompts for self-explaining examples. *Journal of Educational Psychology*, *99*, 285–296.

Siegler, R. S. (2002). Microgenetic studies of self-explanation. In N. Granott, & J. Parziale (Eds.), *Microdevelopment. Transition processes in development and learning* (pp. 31–58). New York: Cambridge University Press.

Stark, R., Mandl, H., Gruber, H., & Renkl, A. (2002). Conditions and effects of example elaboration. *Learning & Instruction*, *12*, 39–60.

Sweller, J. (2006). The worked example effect and human cognition. *Learning and Instruction*, *16*, 165–169.

Sweller, J., & Cooper, G. A. (1985). The use of worked examples as a substitute for problem solving in learning algebra. *Cognition and Instruction*, *2*, 59–89.

Sweller, J., van Merriënboer, J. J. G., & Paas, F. G. (1998). Cognitive architecture and instructional design. *Educational Psychology Review*, *10*, 251–296.

Tarmizi, R. A., & Sweller, J. (1988). Guidance during mathematical problem solving. *Journal of Educational Psychology*, *80*, 424–436.

Tennyson, R. D., & Cocchiarella, M. J. (1986). An empirically based instructional design theory for teaching concepts. *Review of Educational Research*, *56*, 40–71.

Thompson, L., Gentner, D., & Loewenstein, J. (2000). Avoiding missed opportunities in managerial life: Analogical training more powerful than individual case training. *Organizational Behavior and Human Decision Processes*, *82*, 60–75.

Tindall-Ford, S., & Sweller, J. (2006). Altering the modality of instructions to facilitate imagination: Interactions between the modality and imagination effects. *Instructional Science*, *34*, 343–365.

Trafton, J. G., & Reiser, B. J. (1993). The contributions of studying examples and solving problems to skill acquisition. In M. Polson (Ed.), *The Proceedings of the Fifteenth Annual Conference of the Cognitive Science Society* (pp. 1017–1022). Hillsdale, NJ: Erlbaum.

Van Gog, T., Paas, F., & Van Merriënboer, J. J. G. (2006). Effects of process-oriented worked examples on troubleshooting transfer performance. *Learning and Instruction*, *16*, 154–164.

VanLehn, K. (1996). Cognitive skill acquisition. *Annual Review of Psychology*, *47*, 513–539.

VanLehn, K. (1998). How examples are used during problem solving. *Cognitive Science*, *22*, 347–388.

VanLehn, K. (1999). Rule-learning events in the acquisition of a complex skill: An evaluation of CASCADE. *The Journal of the Learning Sciences*, *8*, 71–125.

VanLehn, K., Lynch, C., Schulze, K. Shapiro, J. A., Shelby, R., Taylor, L., Treacy, D., Weinstein, A., & Wintersgill, M. (2005). The Andes physics tutoring system: Lessons learned. *International Journal of Artificial Intelligence and Education*, *15*, 1–47.

Ward, M., & Sweller, J. (1990). Structuring effective worked examples. *Cognition and Instruction*, *7*, 1–39.

Whitehead, A. N. (1929). *The aims of education.* New York: Macmillan.

Wittwer, J., & Renkl, A. (in press). How effective are instructional explanations in example-based learning? A meta-analytic review of literature. *Educational Psychology Review*.

Wouters, P., Paas, F., & Van Merriënboer, J. J. G. (2009). Observational learning from animated models: Effects of modality and reflection on transfer. *Contemporary Educational Psychology*, *34*, 1–8.

Zhu, X., & Simon, H. A. (1987). Learning mathematics from examples and by doing. *Cognition & Instruction*, *4*, 137–166.

Zimmerman, B. J., & Kitsantas, A. (2002). Acquiring writing revision and self-regulatory skill through observation and emulation. *Journal of Educational Psychology*, *94*, 660–668.

15

INSTRUCTION BASED ON SELF-EXPLANATION
Brenda A. Fonseca and Michelene T.H. Chi

INTRODUCTION

Over twenty years of research has documented the fact that explaining a concept aloud to oneself enhances learning and aids in comprehension monitoring. How powerful is this technique and to what extent is it superior to many other, more commonly employed learning strategies? The goal of this chapter is to review the literature on the self-explanation effect in the context of a theoretical framework based on the overt activities of the learner. We begin with a discussion of the self-explanation effect, followed by a brief description of the *passive-active-constructive-interactive* theoretical framework. Then we compare self-explaining with other learning strategies in the context of this framework.

HISTORICAL OVERVIEW

Research across a variety of domains has consistently supported the finding that students learn better when they explain to themselves the material they are studying. Known as the *self-explanation effect* (Chi, Bassok, Lewis, Reimann, & Glaser, 1989), the phenomenon has been studied across age groups, domains, and instructional formats (Bielaczyc, Pirolli, & Brown, 1995; Chi, de Leeuw, Chiu, & LaVancher,1994; Ferguson-Hessler & de Jong, 1990; Hausmann & Chi, 2002; McNamara, O'Reilly, Best, & Ozuru, 2006; Renkl, Stark, Gruber, & Mandl, 1998; Siegler, 1995; Wong, Lawson, & Keeves, 2002) and research studies have repeatedly found that attempting to clarify an idea by explaining to oneself leads to enhanced learning, more accurate self-assessments, and more effective problem-solving. The purpose of this review is to demonstrate that the process of self-explaining is a *constructive* learning activity and the effectiveness of self-explaining compared to other learning activities can be understood within a framework of *passive-active-constructive-interactive* learning strategies.

The goal of the learner is to convert information into usable skills and knowledge. Within a classroom context, that information often comes in the form of words and examples generated from a teacher or text. Successful learning strategies should assist the student in his or her attempt to construct this new knowledge. Self-explaining is a learning strategy in which a learner elaborates upon the presented sentences or example lines by relating them to prior knowledge, making inferences from them, and integrating them with prior text sentences or example lines. For example, if two text sentences about the human circulatory system say that:

The septum divides the heart lengthwise into two sides.
The right side pumps blood to the lungs, and the left side pumps blood to the other parts of the body

then a student can self-explain by saying aloud "So the septum is a divider so that *the blood doesn't get mixed up*. So the right side is to the lungs and the left side is to the body. So the *septum is like a wall . . . separates it*" (Chi, 2000). In this self-explanation, the student is inferring that the septum is a solid divider and its function is to prevent the blood from mixing. Note that self-explanations are the generated inferences (italicized) that go beyond the text sentences. Moreover, self-explanations do not have to be generated overtly; the processes of generating inferences and integrating new information with prior knowledge can be done covertly. Experimentally, in order to collect data, we requested that students self-explain aloud.

Chi et al. (1989) observed students studying worked-out solution examples of physics problems and found that the most successful performers generated more self-explanations than the less successful performers. In addition, they found that the self-explanations from the successful students were more principle-based than those generated by the poorer performing students. Numerous studies in the domain of procedural learning have replicated the relation between the generation of self-explanations and enhanced learning outcomes. For example, increases in self-explanations have been associated with learning gains in the areas of computer programming (Pirolli & Recker, 1994), applications of principles of electricity and magnetism to Aston mass spectrometry (Ferguson-Hessler & de Jong, 1990), and solving algebra word problems (Nathan, Mertz, & Ryan, 1994). The positive impact of self-explanation on problem-solving ability has been replicated under a variety of conditions (Bielaczyc, Pirolli, & Brown, 1995; Chi et al., 1994; Neuman & Schwarz, 1998; Renkl, 1997, 2002; Renkl, Stark, Gruber, & Mandl, 1998).

To investigate if this learning strategy could be experimentally manipulated and to explore the impact of self-explanations in a conceptual domain, Chi et al. (1994) compared learning of the circulatory system between a group of eighth grade students prompted to self-explain with a control group instructed to read the same text twice. The researchers found that the self-explanation group showed greater gains in learning from the pre-test to the post-test and furthermore, the students that generated the largest number of explanations showed the greatest gains in learning.

Subsequent research proceeded to test specific instructional regimens for the subjects to be trained in self-explanation procedures (Bielaczyc et al., 1995). A number of successful training programs have been designed to teach students self-explanation on a large scale. For example, McNamara (2004b) developed a self-explanation reading training program (SERT) and found that training significantly improved text-based comprehension during training compared to reading aloud alone for a group of psychology undergraduate students studying science-based text passages. When the researchers examined post-training comprehension, they found that the high knowledge readers did not show a benefit of the SERT training but low knowledge readers in the SERT condition doubled their comprehension scores when compared to the control read-aloud condition. Following the success of the human one-to-one training program of SERT, a web-based application called the Interactive Strategy Training for Active Reading and Thinking (iSTART) was developed and has also been shown to improve both high and low prior knowledge students' reading comprehension scores when compared to students who did not receive iSTART training (McNamara, Levinstein, & Boonthum, 2004; McNamara, O'Reilly, Best, & Ozuru, 2006). The research studies overwhelmingly demonstrated that self-explanation could be taught and that subjects in the self-explanation groups generated a higher number of self-explanations and performed better on a variety of learning outcomes across multiple domains.

Other research has focused on the optimal conditions under which self-explanation is found to have a beneficial learning impact. For example, does self-explanation work better for students with high or low prior knowledge? Are there specific prompts that elicit more or less self-explanations? And does the self-explanation technique work for all age groups? The following studies described below were designed to address these questions.

With regard to high and low prior knowledge, the self-explanation effect has been demonstrate in both group and even in subjects where the learner has little to no prior knowledge of the topic (de Bruin, Rikers, & Schmidt, 2007). Further, Ferguson-Hessler and de Jong (1990) found that although good and poor performers did not differ in the number of study processes they engaged in during a problem solving task, they did differ in the type of study process used, with good performers using a greater number of integrative study processes and poor performers more likely to engage in superficial processing. For example, in a study of the effects of self-explanation training and worked-out examples in bank tellers' learning about compound and real interest (Renkl et al., 1998), it was found that training on self-explanation primarily benefited low prior topic knowledge subjects, especially on a near-transfer task. In this study, the self-explanation training consisted of modeling self-explanation behavior for one example and coaching the learner in a second example. All learners were instructed to "think aloud" throughout the entire experiment. The benefit for the low prior knowledge learners may have arisen from the fact that self-explanation allowed them to fill in gaps in their knowledge.

Further investigations into the optimal conditions on self-explanation found that prompted self-explanation improved problem-solving scores in a far-transfer test (e.g., see Wong, Lawson, & Keeves, 2002). The findings of Wong et al. suggest that prior knowledge also interacts positively with the self-explanation effect in that the greater the existing knowledge base, the more advantage of the self-explanations. Although there is some inconsistency in the findings of several studies with respect to whether self-explaining benefits the low or high prior knowledge learners more, one interpretation of such mixed results is that it can benefit both low and high prior knowledge learners for different reasons. For individuals with high prior knowledge, the act of self-explaining may allow them to repair their existing mental models and thus improve learning outcomes, whereas for individuals with low prior knowledge, the act of self-explaining may allow them to generate inferences to fill gaps of missing knowledge (Chi, 2000).

Other studies examined whether the format of the study material had an impact on learning from self-explanation. For example, Ainsworth and Loizou (2003) found that students presented with diagrams generated significantly more self-explanations and showed greater learning outcomes than students presented with the material in a text-only format. Further, Butcher (2006) found that simple diagrams led to more inference generation in college students studying the circulatory system when compared with students presented with text only or complex diagrams.

With regard to age, the self-explanation effect has been found in subjects as young as 5-year-olds. Siegler (1995) found that 5-year-old children asked to explain an expert's reasoning performed significantly better than those asked to explain their own reasoning or those not asked to explain at all. Siegler proposed that much of children's learning in general comes from trying to explain other people's reasoning.

However, there have also been reported instances in which self-explanation did not lead to greater learning (e.g., Hausmann & Chi, 2002; Mwangi & Sweller, 1998). There are generally two explanations for such failed results. One explanation is that a large number of self-explanations were not generated. For example, when students were asked to type their explanations, the number of self-explanations generated reduced significantly along with the positive learning gains from this learning strategy (Hausmann & Chi, 2002). However, this smaller quantity can be increased by increasing the number of prompts, even for typed explanations (Aleven & Koedinger, 2002). Another explanation is that sometimes what is generated are not self-explanation inferences, but merely paraphrases (Teasley, 1995). In these cases, essentially no self-explanations were produced, therefore it is not surprising that no increased learning took place.

What is it about self-explanation that has made it such a successful learning strategy? Several cognitive mechanisms underlying the self-explanation effect have been proposed. The two mechanisms with the greatest amount of empirical support are that self-explanations allow learners to identify and fill in knowledge gaps, and that self-explanations aid learners in the construction and repairing of their mental models (Chi, 2000). In support of the dual underlying cognitive mechanisms mediating the self-explanation effect, Ainsworth and Burcham (2007) manipulated the coherence of an expository text about the circulatory system and measured learning in groups of university students who received self-explanation training and those who did not. The researchers found that the greatest learning occurred with the maximally coherent text, suggesting that self-explanations are not only used to fill in missing information or knowledge gaps, but also may support knowledge revision and mental model repair. For minimally coherent texts, self-explanation seems to be used primarily to generate inferences and fill in the missing information.

THEORETICAL FRAMEWORK: PASSIVE-ACTIVE-CONSTRUCTIVE-INTERACTIVE

To improve learning, it has been widely proposed in the literature that students engage in active learning, as opposed to passive learning. *Active learning* is broadly defined as encouraging learners to pay "attention to relevant information, organizing it into coherent mental representations, and integrating representations with other knowledge" (Mayer, 2008, p. 17). However, many learning activities have been proposed that encourage students to pay attention, organize, and integrate new information with knowledge, and it is not clear which activities are superior for learning. Chi (2009) provided a framework for active learning by differentiating students' learning activities into four types: *passive, active, constructive,* and *interactive.* The framework classifies the four types according to the observable overt activities that occur during learning along with the hypothesized underlying learning processes. In addition, the framework suggests a testable hypothesis with regard to the type of learning activities that should lead to the greatest learning outcomes.

In the following section, we first more clearly delineate the framework for classifying *passive*, *active*, *constructive*, and *interactive* learning activities, and then we briefly discuss the testable hypothesis specifically in relation to the self-explanation effect. The remainder of the chapter consists of direct comparisons between self-explanation learning conditions and groups engaged in either passive, active, constructive, or interactive activities. For the framework outlined below and first proposed by Chi (2009), a learning activity is classified by observable, overt actions on the part of the learner. The actions can be manipulated by the researcher or instructor and can be assessed, coded, and analyzed in a variety of ways as evidence of learning.

Passive Learning Activities

A *passive* learning activity is defined as any learning situation in which the learner is essentially not engaging in any overt activity related to the learning task. Some examples of passive activities include listening to a lecture, watching a video, or reading a text without engaging in any additional activity such as note-taking, highlighting, or underlining. Of course, it is always possible that the learner's attention may be engaged in the learning task but without overt confirmation of such engagement, the conservative approach is to classify this level of behavior as a passive learning situation since the learner may be zoning out a large proportion of the time. It is also entirely possible of course that an overtly passive learner is processing deeply, but merely does not exhibit any observable behavior. For example, it is possible that an individual is engaged in a passive behavioral activity, such as reading silently without taking notes or underlining the text passages, and yet is employing deep underlying comprehension processes. However, for the purpose of comparing different overt activities that can be manipulated, say, by a teacher in a classroom, we can only rely on a single metric for classification purposes, and the metric is the amount of learning activities that are directly observable. For example, Williams and Lombrozo (in press) tested subjects' abilities to recognize underlying patterns of category membership under two different conditions. The first group was instructed to self-explain aloud and the second group was not prompted to engage in any specific learning strategy. According to our classification scheme, the second "unprompted" group would be labeled as passive, since they did not engage in any overt activity related to the learning task. Clearly, the possibility exists that the individual learners were engaged in a variety of covert study strategies, however, we would still classify this as passive since the subjects were not being forced to engage in an overt learning activity. Our theoretical framework assumes that if subjects are forced to do something overtly, then they are more likely to learn. This is in fact what Williams and Lombrozo found, with the self-explain group performing significantly better than the unprompted study group on a number of learning outcome measures. In fact, the self-explain group showed superior learning even though approximately one-third of the subjects in the unprompted group reported covertly trying to explain during the study session of the experiment, supporting our hypothesis that subjects are more likely to learn if they are required to engage in an overt learning strategy. Moreover, our assumptions pertain to relative differences. That is, we are assuming that a learner who overtly undertakes some learning behavior is more likely to be cognitively engaged than a learner who does not behaviorally exhibit any learning activities. Therefore, we assume the overt behavioral activity corresponds to the minimum underlying cognitive processes required to produce the behavior. The cognitive processes proposed for the passive level of the taxonomy can be thought of as at best direct storing of the presented information, in sort of an episodic memory way as to be able to repeat it back verbatim. Or at worst, the learner is not engaged in any learning processes and is zoning out.

Active Learning Activities

In order to categorize a learning activity as an *active* activity, the learner must be engaged in doing something physical while learning. A simple contrast would be between the passive activity of reading a text versus the active activity of highlighting while reading a text. The difference is that in the latter, the learner is performing a physical task that provides an overt measurement of paying attention. Numerous examples exist in the literature of active learning activities including pointing or gesturing, underlining a text, copying and pasting, repeating sentences verbatim, copying problem solution steps, delete-and-substitute summarizing, clicking on the screen in a computer environment, navigating a website, selecting an answer from a list of choices, and matching two columns of concepts and their definitions.

As can be seen from the list, the criterion for active activities is that the learner is visibly engaged with the learning materials thereby increasing the likelihood for learning to occur. The underlying cognitive processes that may be mediating this learning can be thought of as assimilating processes and could include attending to the presented materials, thereby activating and strengthening relevant knowledge, searching for related knowledge, and encoding new information in the context of the relevant activated knowledge or instantiating new information in the context of an existing schema (Chi, 2009). These processes have the potential to enhance learning by strengthening existing knowledge and adding the newly presented knowledge among other possibilities. The difference between direct storing in the case of passive activity and assimilating in the case of active activity is that in assimilating, the learner is not only paying attention to the materials that are being actively manipulated (such as the underlined sentences), but the activity (of underlining, for example) often involves selecting parts of the materials so that it enhances the potential of activating prior knowledge pertaining to the material that is being attended to, therefore the new information is more likely to be assimilated into a relevant context. If passive learners are storing any new information at all, it is done mindlessly in an episodic way without a consideration of its proper context.

Constructive Learning Activities

When a learner goes one step further than simply engaging in a physical activity and produces some additional output that contains information beyond that provided in the original material, then we can classify this behavior as a *constructive* learning activity. Specific examples of constructive learning activities include generating self-explanations, constructing a concept map, asking questions, drawing a diagram, comparing and contrasting cases or examples, and constructing a timeline. As is illustrated by the examples, constructive activities require the learner to produce some overt output (e.g., an explanation, a map, a question, a diagram, a timeline, etc.) and the output must go beyond the given information. As the case for classifying a learner as passive or active, a learner of course can be constructive without exhibiting any overt behavior. However, for the purpose of classification, we can rely on a single metric in order to infer learning using the same observable dimension of behavior.

It is also important to note that in order to verify that a learner's overt activity is truly constructive, the researcher or instructor needs to examine the generated output to confirm that it does indeed go beyond the provided information. For example, if a student is asked to "think aloud" during a learning task, the verbal protocols would need to be analyzed to determine if the articulations fall into the active or constructive categories. Articulations that would place the learning activity in the active category would include items such as verbatim repetitions, nonsense phrases, or paraphrases, while statements defined as elaborations or inferences would place the learning activity in the constructive category since such statements demonstrate that the learner produced output beyond the original material, such as descriptions of new spatial relations.

The creating processes required for constructive learning activities may mediate learning through the underlying cognitive mechanisms of inference generation and mental model repair as proposed for the self-explanation effect (Chi, 2000). These mechanisms may work by enriching existing knowledge, along with repairing existing knowledge to make it more coherent, accurate or better structured.

Interactive Learning Activities

The final category in the learning activity taxonomy is that of *interactive* learning activity. This final category is inherently more complex than the three preceding classifications in many ways. For one thing, a learner can interact either with a peer, an expert, or a system such as a computer-tutoring program. As a starting point to classify interactive learning activities, Chi (2009) focused solely on dialoguing among dyads as a form of overt interactive activities. In order to be classified as interactive, the dialogue must include substantive contributions from both partners with neither partner's contributions being ignored. The dialogue can be between an expert and a novice and would be characterized by activities such as responding to scaffoldings, revising errors based on feedback, and responding to the expert's questions. In addition, the dialogue can be between two peers and would contain dialogue patterns that build on each other's contributions, confronts or challenges the partner's statements, argues and defends the learner's own case, and ask or answer each other's questions. Again, it is critical that the verbal protocols of the partners be analyzed to ensure that an interactive learning strategy is actually in place. If the analysis finds that only one partner is making substantive contributions or the partners are ignoring each other's contributions and simply taking turns speaking, then those activities would not be categorized as an interactive learning event.

In sum, an interactive learning situation includes the cognitive mechanisms of creating and assimilating that have been proposed to mediate learning in the constructive and active learning activities respectively. From the perspective of the individual learner, the creating and assimilating processes appear to be similar in interactive and constructive activities, the question arises as to why being interactive would lead to enhanced learning more so than merely being constructive. One explanation may be that in an interactive environment, the learner has the additional advantage of a partner's contributions that can be a valuable source of additional information, a new perspective, or corrective feedback to name a few possibilities. In addition, a dyad has the potential of creating a shared understanding together that may be more novel or deeper than either could create in isolation. Thus, for our current discussion here, we expand interaction to include

Table 15.1 Characteristics of the passive-active-constructive-interactive theoretical framework

	Passive	Active	Constructive	Interactive
Observable overt learning activity	No physical activity	Doing something physically	Producing novel outputs	Dialoguing with substantive contributions
Examples of overt learning activities	Listening to a lecture, watching a video, reading a text	Highlighting a text, pointing or gesturing, underlining a text, copying and pasting, clicking on a computer screen	Generating self-explanations, creating a concept map, asking questions, drawing a diagram, comparing and contrasting cases	Responding to scaffolding, responding to expert's questions, challenging a partner's statements, asking and answering each other's questions
Possible underlying cognitive processes	Direct-storing processes	Assimilating processes	Creating processes	Jointly creating and assimilating processes
Expected cognitive learning outcomes	Storing information in an "episodic" manner without regard to context	Activating and strengthening prior knowledge, storing information in a meaningful way	Generating inferences, repairing mental models	Encoding corrective feedback, taking new perspectives, creating novel understanding
Expected overt learning outcomes	Minimal	Greater than passive	Greater than passive or active	Greater than passive, active, or constructive

dialoguing with any kind of a system (such as an Intelligent Tutoring System), and thus the commonality of interaction more broadly includes additional information that is provided in the form of feedback, elaboration, critiques, questions, and challenges, among other possibilities. Table 15.1 provides a summary of the passive-active-constructive-interactive theoretical framework along with examples of overt learning activities and possible underlying cognitive mechanisms.

CURRENT TRENDS AND ISSUES: A TESTABLE HYPOTHESIS WITH REGARDS TO SELF-EXPLANATION

The framework described above along with the possible underlying cognitive processes suggest the testable hypothesis that active learning activities produce greater learning outcomes (especially on measures of deep learning) than passive, constructive is better than active, and interactive is better than constructive. Evidence in the literature testing this hypothesis has been presented by Chi (2009). The purpose of the present chapter is to examine this hypothesis within the specific context of the self-explanation effect. According to the proposed taxonomy, self-explaining would fall under the category of constructive activity since by definition, self-explanations include inferences beyond the presented materials (Chi, 2000).

Accordingly, research studies comparing self-explanation to passive or active learning activities, should find that the self-explanation groups exhibit the greatest learning, particularly on measures of deep learning. Additionally, studies in which self-explanation is contrasted with another constructive activity should find minimal differences in learning outcomes. Any differences that do exist between the constructive activities would need to be explained, perhaps in terms of the task demands. Finally, the interactive activities between peers or between peers and experts should yield greater gains than subjects engaged in self-explaining alone. Again, it is important to note that the taxonomical classification of the learning activities of the research studies to be examined are based on the overt learning activities as described in the study and thus may differ from the authors' original categorizations and descriptions.

The following section examines the available literature on the self-explanation effect in comparison with passive, active, other constructive, and interactive learning activities. The illustrative studies we cite are based on the learners' overt activities (not necessarily the authors' intent), are limited to those that manipulated only one activity in a given condition, and when possible, focus on measures of deep learning. In addition, we provide systemic labels for the conditions in a way that makes them more easily compared, and calculate effect sizes for significant finding. The effect sizes, when not stated in the research study, were calculated as *Cohen's d* by dividing sample mean differences by pooled variances using either stated means and standard deviations, *t*-test values or *F*-test values according to the formulas defined in Thalheimer and Cook (2002) and based on the procedures originally detailed by Rosnow and Rosenthal (1996) and Cohen (1992).

Self-Explanation versus Passive Learning Activities

As a *constructive* activity, self-explaining should show clear learning outcome advantages when compared to *passive* learning strategies such as reading a text, listening to a lecture, or watching a video (again, assuming that passive learners are less likely to be engaged fully in appropriate cognitive processing relative to constructive learners). Studies comparing self-explanation to passive activities are prevalent in the literature and we have selected five studies to illustrate this contrast below.

In one of the original studies investigating the effectiveness of self-explanation as a learning strategy, Chi et al. (1994) tested eighth-grade students' declarative knowledge of the circulatory system under two different learning conditions. In the self-explain text condition, the students were prompted to generate explanations after reading each sentence of the text, thus this condition consists of a constructive activity requiring the subjects to generate output that goes beyond the provided information. In contrast, under the read-twice condition, the students were instructed to read the same text passage twice, so the read-twice group would fall into a passive learning activity as they were not engaged in doing something physical and also did not generate any additional overt output. An examination of post-test scores found that the self-explain text group significantly outperformed the read-twice condition. In particular, for the two categories of questions that were designed to assess deeper levels of understanding by requiring use of prior knowledge and knowledge inferences, the self-explain text group showed a 22.6% gain while the scores for the subjects in the read-twice condition only improved by 12.5%, $t(22) = 2.64$, $p < 0.01$, with a large effect size of $d = 1.14$.

Similarly, in a study of novice chess players, de Bruin et al. (2007) compared learning outcomes for a group of college students instructed to predict the next move of a computer opponent and self-explain why that was the correct move (self-explain + predict group) with a group instructed only to predict the next move by physically placing the chess piece in the predicted location (predict group) and with a third group instructed to simply observe the moves made by the computer (observe group). The comparison of interest for this section is between the self-explain + predict group with the observe group. The self-explain + predict group was not only required to do something physical (i.e., make a prediction in terms of placing a chess piece), they were also required to produce some additional output that was not contained in the original material (i.e., to generate explanations as to why the predicted move was the correct move to make).

According to the taxonomy detailed in the previous section, the self-explain + predict group clearly falls into the constructive learning activity category. On the other hand, the observe group was instructed to simply watch the computer as the simulated chess game progressed. The subjects were not asked to perform any manipulations or generate any outputs and thus this group falls into the passive category of learning activities. The researchers then looked at the number of checkmates achieved for each group in the test phase. As the framework predicted, the self-explain + predict condition attained significantly more checkmates ($M = 3.00$, $SD = 1.77$) than the observe group ($M = 1.33$, $SD = 1.68$). This difference was significant with a large effect size of $d = 0.97$. In fact, the subjects in the constructive condition achieved twice as many checkmates as the subjects in the passive condition, providing further support for our hypothesis that the success of the self-explanation effect may be attributed to the constructive nature of the learning activity.

In another study that looked at the effectiveness of reading as a learning activity, Griffin, Wiley, and Thiede (2008) divided college undergraduates into three groups: one group was instructed to read the text only once as if they were to be tested on the material (read-once group), the second group was instructed to read the text once quickly and then a second time more thoroughly as if they were to be tested on the material (read-twice group) and the third group was instructed to read the text once and then a second time during which they should try to explain the material to themselves (self-explain text group). This study provides a clear contrast between the constructive activity of self-explaining and the potentially more passive activity of reading and re-reading. Again, the researchers found that the constructive learning activity of self-explanation significantly improved accuracy over the passive learning activities of reading once and of reading twice ($M = 0.63$, $SD = 0.38$ for the self-explain text group versus $M = 0.21$, $SD = 0.49$, $d = 0.95$ for the read-once group and $M = 0.39$, $SD = 0.38$, $d = 0.63$ for the read-twice group).

In a study investigating children's learning abilities, Pine and Messer (2000) investigated 5–9-year-old children's performance on a balance beam task before and after a demonstration by the instructor. In the self-explanation condition, the children were asked to explain how the instructor was able to balance the beam (self-explain expert condition) while in the observe condition the children were instructed to just watch and were not invited to make comments. This study represents an example of a constructive learning strategy (self-explanation) compared directly to a passive learning strategy (sit and watch the instructor). This study is particularly interesting, since this specific passive strategy is commonly employed in the classroom—even with the seemingly more involved activities such as classroom demonstrations. Pine and Messer found that significantly more children improved in the self-explain expert condition (70%) when compared with the observe condition (50%) and in addition, the amount of improvement as measured by gain in mental model shift was significantly greater for the self-explanation condition than for the observe condition $F(1,74) = 8.96$, $p = 0.003$, $d = 0.61$.

Although the passive learning strategy of simply listening to a teacher explain a concept may be one of the most commonly employed strategies in the classroom, only a limited number of studies have compared the effectiveness of this technique to self-explanations. In one study, Pillow, Mash, Aloian, and Hill (2002) investigated the effects of self-explanation on 4- and 5-year-olds' ability to predict misinterpretations of ambiguous pictures. The training conditions in this study consisted of having the children explain their own misinterpretations (self-explain own), explain the misinterpretations of a puppet viewing similar drawings (self-explain puppet), or simply view the drawings while the experimenter discussed the drawings (observe).

The first training condition, self-explain own, clearly fits the definition of self-explanation and thus provides a direct comparison between the constructive learning activity of self-explaining and the passive activity of watching the drawings and listening found in the third condition of observe. In addition, the second training condition (self-explain puppet) also fits into the definition of self-explanation and is similar to the task of self-explaining a text or instructor. The researchers' findings were as anticipated with a significant effect between both explaining groups (self-explain own and self-explain puppet) versus the passive no explaining group (observe). Specifically, the researchers measured the percentage of trials in which the children correctly identified the misinterpretation between what they or the puppet "thought" the drawing was and what the picture really was in "reality." This measure was labeled the "think-reality contrast" score and the group found that 4-year-olds in the self-explain own condition displayed a post-test think-reality contrast score of 65% ($SD = 33.60$) and the self-explain puppet condition had a score of 79% ($SD = 45.03$) while the same age group in the observe condition had a "think-reality contrast" score of only 48% ($SD = 38.43$). This difference was significant with moderate to large effect sizes of $d = 0.46$ and $d = 0.73$, respectively.

In summary, all five studies described above illustrate the advantage of the constructive strategy of self-explanation over passive learning activities commonly used in the classroom. Table 15.2 summarizes the five studies of this section and shows that self-explanation is superior to a variety of passive activities, with an overall mean effect size of $d = 0.78$, which is close to being a large effect.

Table 15.2 Summary of studies: self-explaining (SE) versus passive

Study	Age group	Text/task	Results	Effect size
Chi et al. (1994)	Children (eighth grade students)	Read circulatory system text	SE text > Read-twice	$d = 1.14$
De Bruin et al. (2007)	College students	Predict computer chess moves	SE + Predict > Observe	$d = 0.97$
Griffin et al. (2008)	College students	Read natural and social sciences text	SE text > Read-once SE text > Read-twice	$d = 0.95$ $d = 0.63$
Pine & Messer (2000)	Children (5–9-year-olds)	Solve balance beam task	SE expert > Observe	$d = 0.61$
Pillow et al. (2002)	Children (4–5-year-olds)	Predict misinterpretations	SE own > Observe SE puppet > Observe	$d = 0.46$ $d = 0.73$
			Mean Effect Size	$d = 0.78$

Self-Explanation versus Active Learning Activities

An active learning strategy is an activity that asks the learner to become physically involved in some activity so that it engages the learner's attention but does not require the learner to generate any additional output than that provided to the learner. The difference between active and constructive learning activities is whether or not the learner produced additional information. Learning is expected to be greater when a student is engaged in a constructive activity and thus generating their own additional knowledge compared to learning in an active activity where the student is focused and engaged but does not produce any additional output. The following five studies represent an illustrative sample of the studies in the literature comparing self-explanation with a variety of active learning tasks, perhaps the most popular comparison found in the literature.

In the de Bruin et al. (2007) study described above, they compared learning outcomes for a group instructed to predict the next chess move of a computer opponent and explain why (self-explain + predict group) with a group instructed only to predict the next move (predict group). The self-explain + predict group provides an excellent example of a constructive activity compared with an active activity (predicting the next move). Predicting the next move can be categorized as active and not constructive since the subjects had been exposed to many possible computer moves in the learning phase and therefore were basically selecting the next move since they did not have to generate any novel moves. The researchers found that the self-explain + predict condition performed significantly better than the predict condition. For example, when compared with the predict group, the self-explain + predict group showed higher percentages of correct predictions ($M = 66\%$, $SD = 8.7$ versus $M = 59\%$, $SD = 9.2$), correct applications of chess principles ($M = 63\%$, $SD = 10.5$ versus $M = 50\%$, $SD = 10.6$), and a higher number of checkmates in the test phase ($M = 3.0$, $SD = 1.77$ versus $M = 0.87$, $SD = 0.92$ with a very large effect size of $d = 1.51$).

In an investigation of problem-solving skills, Aleven and Koedinger (2002) compared two different versions of a computer-based tutoring program on problem-solving and transfer outcome measures for tenth grade high school geometry students. The self-explain + solve group was prompted to solve the geometry problem and required to type a reason for their solution. This activity would be classified as a constructive learning activity due to the fact that the students had to generate new output via their self-explanations. The solve group was prompted to solve the geometry problem but was not required to enter a reason for their answer. This was the only difference between the two groups. The solve group would be considered active since the students engaged in a physical activity of generating steps that they had seen before but they did not have to produce output that contained ideas going beyond the information presented. Since feedback was comparable across both conditions, we can hold the feedback as a constant and compare the constructive versus the active nature of the student activities as opposed to the interactive aspect of the Intelligent Tutoring System. The researchers found that students in the self-explain + solve group improved significantly more that those in the solve condition in all three post-test measures, $F(1,22) = 10.3$, $p < 0.005$, with a very large effect size of $d = 1.37$.

Kastens and Liben (2007) examined spatial task abilities of fourth graders by requiring them to place stickers on a map corresponding to the real-world locations of flags placed around an outdoor park area. The researchers divided the children into two groups. One group was given a map and told to explore the area and place stickers on the map corresponding to the flag locations as they discovered them (place-sticker group). This task clearly qualifies as an active learning activity as the children are so obviously engaged in doing something physical (i.e., exploring the park area and physically placing the stickers on the map) but are not required to generate any novel output. The second group of children received the exact same instructions as the first group with one modification. The students in the second group were told that after they found the flag and placed their sticker on the map, they were to write down the clues they had used to decide where to place the sticker on the map (self-explain + place-sticker group). This group constitutes the self-explanation group and the fact that they generated additional output than that provided to them originally (specifically, their explanations as to sticker placement) places this learning task in the constructive category. As predicted by the passive-active-constructive-interactive framework, the self-explanation group performed significantly better than the active group who placed the stickers on their maps without explanation. The main measure of learning was how far off the sticker was placed from the true location on the map, measured in units of sticker diameter. This measure was called the sticker offset and the researchers found an average sticker offset of 4.9 ($SD =$ 3.1) in the active learning condition and only 2.2 ($SD = 1.5$) in the constructive, self-explanation condition, $F(1,29) = 23.20$, $p < 0.001$, $d = 0.96$.

O'Reilly, Symons, and MacLatchy-Gaudet (1998) tested college students' recall and recognition ability for factual knowledge of the human circulatory system under three different learning conditions: repetition, elaborative interrogation, and self-explanation. For the purposes of the comparisons in this section of the chapter, we will examine the repetition and the self-explanation groups. Although the researchers did not record or analyze the subjects' verbal protocol, the two learning strategies can be categorized within the passive-active-constructive-interactive framework by examining the overt activities the subjects were instructed to engage in. The prompt for the repetition group was to "repeat each sentence until the next fact appears on the computer screen" thus placing this group in the active learning category. The self-explanation group was prompted with the instructions, "Explain what the sentence means to you. That is, what new information does the sentence provide for you? And how does it relate to what you already know?" This activity requires the subject to generate additional output and places the self-explanation condition into a constructive learning activity. As predicted, the researchers found that cued recall and recognition were higher for the self-explanation group ($M = 18.36$, $SD = 5.21$) when compared to the repetition group ($M = 14.04$, $SD = 4.46$), $F(2, 52) = 4.89$, $p < 0.05$, $d = 0.92$.

In a study by King (1992), learning outcomes were compared across three groups of underprepared college students. The students were trained in techniques of self-questioning, summarizing, or note-taking and presented with a traditional lecture. Learning was measured after the lecture through assessments of comprehension, retention, and idea units listed in the students' lecture notes. The self-questioning group can be classified as self-explaining and thus constructive on the basis of the prompts used to guide the student learning strategy. The prompts for the self-questioning group included statements such as "What is the main idea of . . .?", "How does . . . relate to . . .?", and "What conclusions can I draw about . . .?" Previous studies on self-questioning have proposed that such prompts facilitate learning by inducing cognitive activities including the integration of new information with existing knowledge (Palincsar & Brown, 1984).

In essence, the self-questioning group is being taught to self-explain through the use of generic question-stem prompts. After being trained with the question-stem prompts, the students in the self-questioning group then generated and answered their own questions, thus providing explanations for their self-generated prompts. The summarizing group is discussed in the next section of this chapter. The third group of students was instructed to simply take notes during the lecture and, assuming that student notes tend to be verbatim copying, can thus be classified as an active learning strategy at best. The researchers found that the constructive activity of self-explaining was superior to the active learning task of note-taking for retention ($M = 51.05$, $SD = 12.87$ versus $M = 33.88$, $SD = 19.75$), comprehension ($M = 67.74$, $SD = 11.16$ versus $M = 59.90$, $SD = 12.06$), and number of important idea units in the post-test lecture notes ($M = 17.70$, $SD = 4.80$ versus $M = 13.30$, $SD = 4.80$, with a large effect size of $d = 0.92$).

As can be seen in all five studies described above, the constructive strategy of self-explanation consistently results in higher learning outcomes when compared with a diverse set of active learning activities commonly used in the classroom. Table 15.3 summarizes the five studies described in this section and illustrates the advantages of self-explanation over a variety of active activities with an overall mean effect size of $d = 1.14$.

Self-Explanation versus Other Constructive Learning Activities

According to the passive-active-constructive-interactive framework, a comparison of self-explanation with other constructive types of learning strategies should result in similar learning outcomes since one constructive learning activity should not in principle be better than another constructive learning activity. Surprisingly, there are relatively few experimental studies comparing self-explanation with alternative constructive activities. The most commonly used constructive activities in addition to self-explanation include compare-and-contrast, concept mapping, drawing diagrams, and generative summarizing. The following two studies provide an illustration of equivalent learning outcomes between two constructive activities.

In the King (1992) study cited in the section above in which she compared learning outcomes across three groups of underprepared college students, the self-questioning group, the generative summary group, and the note-taking group, we had determined that the self-questioning group is essentially a self-explanation group.

Table 15.3 Summary of studies: self-explaining (SE) versus active

Study	Age Group	Text/Task	Results	Effect Size
De Bruin et al. (2007)	College students	Predict computer chess move	SE + Predict > Predict	$d = 1.51$
Aleven & Koedinger (2002)	Adolescents (tenth graders)	Solve math problems with computer tutor	SE + Solve > Solve	$d = 1.37$
Kastens & Liben (2007)	Children (fourth graders)	Place stickers on field map	SE + Place-sticker > Place-sticker	$d = 0.96$
O'Reilly et al. (1998)	College students	Read circulatory system text	SE > Repeat Sentence	$d = 0.92$
King (1992)	College students	Listen to a lecture	SE > Take notes	$d = 0.92$
			Mean Effect Size	$d = 1.14$

The generative summary group was trained to create what King referred to as a generative summary as opposed to the select-delete-modify approach that many students commonly use when attempting to summarize a lecture or text. The students in the generative summary group were trained to use their own words to construct novel sentences that make connections between the existing material and the students' own prior knowledge. Assuming that the students were able to implement the training correctly, this activity would be classified as a constructive learning activity and thus this study provides a direct comparison between two different constructive learning activities.

The third group was instructed to simply take notes during the lecture and as described in the preceding section, can be classified as an active learning strategy at best. As predicted by our hypothesis, there were no significant differences found between the self-explanation group and the generative summary group in lecture comprehension ($M = 67.74$, $SD = 11.16$ versus $M = 74.68$, $SD = 9.41$, respectively) or retention ($M = 51.05$, $SD = 12.87$ versus $M = 44.74$, $SD = 25.25$, respectively). In addition, no significant differences were found between the self-explanation group and the generative summary group in the deeper learning measure of percentage of important idea units in the post-test lecture notes ($M = 17.7\%$, $SD = 4.8$ versus $M = 17.2\%$, $SD = 5.2$ with a negligible effect size of $d = 0.10$).

The Pillow et al. (2002) study described in a preceding section and shown in Table 15.2, also compared two conditions that were both constructive. Recall that their task was to investigate the effects of explanation on 4- and 5-year-olds' ability to predict misinterpretations of ambiguous pictures. The first condition prompted the children to explain their own misinterpretations (self-explain own), the second condition prompted the children to explain the misinterpretations of a puppet viewing similar drawings (self-explain puppet), and the third condition instructed the children to simply view the drawings while the experimenter discussed the drawings (observe). The first training condition falls under the realm of self-explanation and should be classified as a constructive activity since the children were required to produce output beyond that provided to them. The second condition, explaining someone else's misinterpretation (in this case, a puppet), also falls under the category of constructive since the children once again had to generate novel output to complete the task. The final group required no action or output on the part of the children, that makes it a passive activity and has already been discussed earlier and shown in Table 15.2. We would anticipate that learning outcomes between the first two training conditions would be fairly equivalent since they both fall into the constructive category. The researchers' findings were as anticipated with no significant differences between the two explanation conditions. For example, the 5-year-olds in the self-explain own group scored an average of 65% correct ($SD = 33.6\%$) on the think-reality contrast questions in the study compared to 79% correct ($SD = 45\%$) for the self-explain puppet group on the same task. The difference between the conditions was not significant, $F(1, 85) = 0.02$ with a small effect size of $d = 0.35$.

Although the passive-active-constructive-interactive framework predicts equivalent learning outcomes between two constructive learning activities, surprisingly, three of the five studies we examined yielded significantly higher learning outcomes for the self-explanation condition when compared to other constructive learning activities. For example, a study by Roscoe and Chi (2008) clearly illustrates the superiority of self-explanation as a constructive learning activity. In that study, college undergraduates were asked to read a text on the human eye and retina and then were assigned to one of three experimental conditions. The first group was given 30 minutes to explain the text to a peer tutee (explain-to-other group), the second group was given 30 minutes to create a tutorial videotape about the text that would be shown to a future student (explain-to-video group), and the third group was given 30 minutes to review the text and explain aloud to themselves as they read (self-explain text group). All groups were encouraged to "go beyond what the text says." The first (explain-to-other) condition falls into the category of interactive and will be discussed in the next section.

On the surface, it appears that the last two conditions (explain-to-video and self-explain text) would both satisfy the criteria of the constructive category as it seems that the subjects produced additional novel output. We would predict that the two conditions would produce similar learning outcomes, however, the researchers found that the self-explainers seemed to gain a deeper understanding of the material than the tutorial (explain-to-video) explainers. For example, post-test scores on the questions test (a measure of deeper learning than the definitions test given in the study) found that the self-explain text group had a mean score of 32.4 ($SD = 4.9$) while the explain-to-video group showed a mean score of only 24.1 ($SD = 5.3$). This difference was significant with a large effect size of $d = 1.64$. A closer analysis can provide some insight into the advantages gained by the self-explanation condition.

A detailed protocol analysis was conducted for each condition examining the types of activities in which the subjects engaged. The researchers found that if the activities were broken down into knowledge-telling versus knowledge-building activities, then the explain-to-video group engaged in a significantly higher proportion of knowledge-telling episodes ($M = 0.87$, $SD = 0.11$) than the self-explain text group ($M = 0.60$, $SD = 0.16$). On the other hand, the self-explain text group engaged in almost four times as many knowledge-building episodes as the explain-to-video group ($M = 13.6$, $SD = 5.1$ compared to $M = 3.7$, $SD = 3.3$). Knowledge-telling activities consisted primarily of paraphrase statements and were essentially unelaborated summaries of the text while knowledge-building activities were defined as verbal episodes involving the integration of concepts and the generation of knowledge through inferences (Scardamalia & Bereiter, 1994). In other words, knowledge-telling episodes included active learning activities while knowledge-building required constructive activity on the part of the learner. Thus, the fact that the self-explain text group outperformed the explain-to-video group is consistent with the prediction of our framework and may be attributed to the greater degree of inference generation and knowledge integration observed in the self-explain text condition. The question remains as to why the self-explain group was more likely to engage in knowledge-building than knowledge-telling.

In addition to the Roscoe and Chi (2008) findings just described, several researchers have found a clear advantage for one type of self-explain condition when compared to an alternative self-explain group. Siegler (1995) asked 5-year-old children to participate in a Piagetian number conservation task under one of three different conditions. The control group simply performed the task and was given feedback on the correctness of their answer (solve group), the second group performed the task, was asked to explain how they knew that was the answer and were then given feedback on the correctness of their own answer (self-explain own + solve group), and finally, the third group performed the task, was given feedback on the correctness of their answer and then was asked to explain how the researcher knew that was the correct answer (self-explain expert + solve group).

The researchers found that the self-explain expert group displayed a significantly higher percentage of correct answers ($M = 62\%$) when compared to the self-explain own group ($M = 48\%$). This difference was significant, however, not enough data were presented in the article to estimate effect size. Since self-explain own and self-explain expert seem to be the only activity that differed between the second and third condition, and since both activities (self-explain self and self-explain expert) appear to fall under the category of constructive, a closer examination of the children's verbal protocols is required in order to understand the differential learning outcomes.

One interpretation is that self-explaining an expert's solution is analogous to the traditional self-explaining a text condition wherein the text contains correct information. In this case, the contrast is between self-explaining an expert's correct solution versus one's own imperfect solution. It is not surprising that one might learn more information from a correct solution. Moreover, it turns out that Siegler (1995) found the self-explain expert group to be engaged in generating a greater number of explanations and also generated a greater diversity of explanation types. We know that the number of self-explanations generated typically predicts the amount of learning (Chi et al., 1994).

To further examine the difference between a self-explain own versus a self-explain expert condition, a study by Calin-Jageman and Ratner (2005) instructed children to solve addition problems and after receiving feedback on the correct answer, they were asked to explain "How did I [the researcher] know that?" (self-explain expert group) or "How did you know that?" (self-explain own group). Again, the researchers found that the self-explain expert group displayed significantly more improvement in their scores than the self-explain own group and was much more likely to use the strategy of the researcher (i.e., "count-all strategy") than the self-explain own condition as revealed through the degree to which they encoded the expert's behavior, referred to as the "encoding score" and measured in the last testing session. The self-explain expert group had an average encoding score of 1.67 ($SD = 0.90$) while the self-explain own group had an average encoding score of only 0.89 ($SD = 0.90$). This difference was significant with a large effect size of $d = 0.87$. An analysis of the types of explanations provided between the two groups showed that the self-explain expert group produced significantly more "what + why" explanations versus the simple "what" explanations provided by the self-explain own group. Again, generating more "what + why" explanations indicate that the self-explain expert condition led to more constructive activity on the part of the children. Of course we still need to understand why self-explain expert leads to the generation of more "what + why" explanations.

In summary, two of the five studies described above found no differences between learning outcomes in a self-explanation condition compared to an alternative constructive activity, as predicted by our theoretical framework. The overall mean effect size for the studies with equivalent learning outcomes was small with $d = 0.23$. Surprisingly, three of the five studies comparing self-explanation to other constructive learning activities resulted in superior learning outcomes among the self-explanation groups when compared to alternative constructive activities, with a large effect size, $d = 1.26$. Since the passive-active-constructive-interactive framework predicted equivalent results, obtaining non-equivalent learning results needs to be accounted for by the specific task demands of the contrasting constructive activities.

A variety of reasons in the task demands could account for the superior learning outcomes of the self-explaining group (including self-explaining a text, or self-explaining an expert's solution), such as more knowledge-building activities in a self-explain versus explain-to-a-video group, and an increased generative activity of the subjects in the self-explain expert conditions when compared to the self-explain own condition. However, additional explanations need to be provided for why self-explaining has more favorable task demands than other constructive activities. For example, why does self-explaining generate more knowledge-building than explaining-to-a-video? One post-hoc explanation is that explaining-to-a-video is like teaching to an audience, in which a teacher prefers to explain what she or he already knows, thus restricting what she or he can learn from explaining. Similar other post-hoc explanations can be given for why self-explaining expert is superior to self-explaining own. One reason is that an expert's solution contains more correct information; therefore explaining a correct solution allows one to learn more than explaining one's own erroneous solution. Therefore, although self-explaining should in principle produce equivalent learning outcomes as other constructive learning activities, the task demands of self-explaining show it often to be a superior constructive activity as compared with others. A summary of the findings from this section can be found in Table 15.4.

Self-Explanation versus Interactive Learning Activities

From a learning perspective, the critical components of interactive situations beyond the advantage of construction, is receiving additional information in the form of feedback, elaborations, questions, and so forth. Our framework predicts that interactive activities should, in general, lead to better learning outcomes than the constructive activity of self-explaining. However, it will be important to examine the precise nature of the interactions as they can vary in degree of exchanges as well as the level of constructive engagement. Most of the studies comparing self-explanation to an interactive learning condition are fairly recent. We have selected five studies to demonstrate this contrast below.

One of the clearest comparisons between the individual constructive activity of self-explanation and an interactive learning task can be found in a study conducted

Table 15.4 Summary of studies: self-explaining (SE) versus constructive

Study	Age group	Text/task	Results	Effect size
King (1992)	College students	Listen to a lecture	SE lecture= Generative summary	$d = 0.10$
Pillow et al. (2002)	Children (4–5-year-olds)	Predict misinterpretations	SE own = SE puppet	$d = 0.35$
			Mean Effect Size	$d = 0.23$
Roscoe & Chi (2008)	College students	Read a text on the human eye	SE text > Explain-to-video	$d = 1.64$
Siegler (1995)	Children (5-year-olds)	Solve a number conservation task	SE expert + solve > SE own + solve	$d = *$
Calin-Jageman & Ratner (2005)	Children (5-year-olds)	Solve addition problems	SE expert > SE own	$d = 0.87$
			Mean Effect Size	$d = 1.26$

Note: * Not enough data provided to calculate effect size.

by Hausmann, van de Sande, and VanLehn (2008). College students were assigned the task of alternating between solving physics problems with the aid of a computer-based intelligent tutoring program and explaining worked-out physics problems presented by the tutoring program in video format. The researchers divided the students into two groups. In the self-explain group, students worked alone at the computer to solve the problems and were prompted to generate explanations to the solution steps presented in the video examples. In the joint-explain group, students worked in dyads at the computer to solve the physics problems and then generated joint explanations to the video presented solution steps. The critical difference between the two conditions is whether the individual was working alone or with a partner. The results of the study clearly show the advantages of an interactive environment. The dyads answered faster, finished more problems in the allotted time, entered more correct entries, displayed a lower error rate and requested fewer hints when solving problems in the computer program. Specifically, on one measure of learning outcome, the individuals requested an average of 2.26 hints ($SD = 1.52$) while the dyads requested an average of only 0.99 hints ($SD = 0.82$). Requesting more hints means the individuals cannot figure out how to solve the problem, therefore they needed more help as provided in the hints. This difference was statistically significant with a large effect size, $d = -1.13$. We report the effect size as negative because of the direction of the comparison, in that self-explaining condition was worse than the joint-explaining condition. While both conditions engaged in the constructive task of explaining, the results clearly show the advantage of interactions over working alone.

To illustrate the importance of the nature of the interactive activity on learning outcomes, Kramarski and Dudai (2009) assigned one hundred ninth grade students to one of three instructional conditions. In the first two conditions, the students worked in groups of four to solve mathematical problems at a computer screen. The students solved the problems individually and interacted with the others in their group via an online forum. The self-explain own group was trained to generate self-explanations to prompts such as "What is my conclusion?" and "Is my explanation clear?" as they solved math problems. The feedback group was trained to generate explanations utilizing prompts that focused on responding to the other members' contributions, such as "How can I respond to my friend regarding the correctness of his/her explanation?" and "How can I modify my friend's solution and explanation?" A third control group did not receive any training on using prompts while solving the math problems. The level of interaction should be highest among the feedback group and, based on our theoretical framework, we would expect this group to demonstrate the highest learning gains. In fact, the researchers did find that the feedback group scored significantly higher in their mathematical accuracy than the self-explain own group and also scored higher in the deeper measure of problem-solving transfer scores ($M = 86.43$, $SD = 19.9$ for feedback group versus $M = 71.39$, $SD = 26.20$ for self-explain own group) with a medium effect size of $d = -0.65$.

In another study demonstrating the advantages of an interactive learning activity over an individual constructive learning task, Coleman, Brown, and Rivkin (1997) assigned college undergraduates to two different interactive conditions and compared the learning outcomes with a group of undergraduates assigned to a constructive self-explain condition. The students in the two interactive groups were instructed to study a text on natural selection and to either teach the contents through explanation (explain-to-other) or through summary to their partners (summarize-to-other). The self-explanation group was instructed to study the same material and explain the material aloud to themselves (self-explain text).

As predicted, the researchers found that both interactive conditions (explain-to-other and summarize-to-other) outperformed the constructive activity of self-explanation, F $(2, 77) = 9.74$, $p < 0.001$. For example, the explain-to-other and summarize-to-other conditions scored an average of 7.36 ($SD = 0.44$) and 7.07 ($SD = 0.44$) respectively on a near-transfer task, while the self-explain text condition only scored an average of 6.78 ($SD = 0.44$) on the same task. This difference was significant with small effect sizes of $d = -0.35$ and $d = -0.18$ respectively. These results are consistent with our hypothesis that interactive learning activities should yield greater learning outcomes than constructive activities.

The three studies described in this section so far have demonstrated that the constructive activity of self-explaining is worse than interactive learning activities, with the interactive learning activity having an overall clear advantage with an effect size of $d = -0.58$. However, not all studies have followed our predicted direction and these studies need to be examined more closely to understand why. The two following studies illustrate our point. Moreno (2009) investigated whether college undergraduates engaged in two types of interactions (cooperative or jigsaw) would learn more than students working alone using a self-explanation technique. The students worked with an agent-based computer instructional program to learn about botany. The cooperative condition consisted of students working together at the computer throughout the entire learning phase to solve the problems as a team while the jigsaw condition involved each student working individually at the computer to learn their piece of the material and then coming back together as a group to teach each other what they had learned individually. The self-explanation condition consisted of students working alone at the computer and then after finishing their tasks with the computer program, generating self-explanations to the solutions they had produced earlier.

Looking only at the more important deep learning measures of a problem-solving transfer test, Moreno found no differences between the self-explanation ($M = 17.7$, $SD = 4.05$) and the cooperative groups ($M = 18.7$, $SD = 3.84$), $d = 0.25$, but a significant advantage of the self-explanation group compared to the jigsaw group ($M = 15.11$, $SD = 3.81$), with a medium effect size of $d = 0.66$.

These findings at first seem surprising as they contradict our prediction, since both jigsaw and cooperative activities would seem to fit into the interactive category while self-explanation is clearly constructive. A more detailed analysis of the methodology is required to understand the apparent contradictions. First, we would expect that the cooperative (interactive) group would score higher than the self-explanation (constructive) group, however, no significant differences in transfer scores were found. One possible explanation for the null finding is that the self-explanation group actually had the benefit of additional information over the cooperative group. At the end of the computer program session, the self-explanation group was given a four-page review sheet to facilitate the generation of self-explanations. In addition, although the self-explanation group did work individually on the learning task, the agent-based computer program provided feedback to both the cooperative and self-explanation group. This human–computer interaction could have strengthened learning in the self-explanation group and helped contribute to the null results between the cooperative and self-explanation learning strategies.

The second finding is even more surprising in that the constructive activity of self-explanation was actually superior to the interactive jigsaw condition. If we look only at the learning phase of the study, the cooperative group learned in pairs, while both the jigsaw and the self-explanation group learned alone. In this way, the jigsaw group was not interactive in the learning phase and was not even constructive, but was merely active because the students were not required to generate any novel output as they worked through the computer program alone. Thus, it makes sense that this active learning condition did not score higher than the constructive activity of self-explanation. Another way to show that the jigsaw group may have only been active is that the jigsaw group made a significantly higher proportion of retention statements than the cooperative group ($M = 0.68$, $SD = 0.10$ versus $M = 0.56$, $SD = 0.06$, respectively). Retention statements represent a knowledge-telling approach to teaching a peer or explaining a concept and do not require the generation of any new novel output, suggesting that the jigsaw group was engaged only in a more active type of interaction in which they were involved in a physical activity but were not producing any novel output. Thus, if the jigsaw group was only active, then it makes sense that they learned less than the self-explaining constructive group.

A similar result to the study described above was found by Roscoe and Chi (2008) comparing the effects of peer tutoring with self-explanation. The study, described in a previous section of this chapter, consisted of giving college undergraduates a text to learn about the human eye and then instructing them to either teach the information to a peer tutee (explain-to-other), teach the information to a video (explain-to-video), or self-explain the information to themselves (self-explain text). Contrast between the latter two groups was reported in Table 15.4. Here, an examination of the first and last groups allows a comparison between an interactive condition (explain-to-other) and a constructive self-explanation condition (self-explain text). Both groups were instructed to "go beyond what the text says" and thus were encouraged to engage in constructive activities either alone (self-explain text group) or with a partner (explain-to-other group). The researchers found no difference between the two groups on a shallow definitions post-test ($M = 37.6$, $SD = 11.4$ for self-explanation, and $M = 33.3$, $SD = 10.2$ for explain-to-other). However there was a significant difference in the deeper learning outcome of a questions post-test and unexpectedly, the self-explain text group performed better than the explain-to-other group ($M = 32.4$, $SD = 4.9$ versus $M = 26.9$, $SD = 4.9$. respectively). The difference between the groups was significant with a large effect size, $d = 1.13$. An examination of the verbal protocols reveals one possible explanation for this apparent discrepancy.

We expected that an interactive learning activity should yield greater learning outcomes than a constructive learning. Looking at the articulations of the subjects in the explain-to-other group, it can be seen that the subjects were engaged in some constructive activity (for example, 28% of their statement episodes consisted of knowledge-building, a constructive type of activity), however, they were primarily engaged in the more active task of knowledge-telling. This type of activity made up 72% of their verbal interactions. On the other hand, an investigation of the statements made by the self-explain group revealed that this group spent 40% of their time in the constructive task of knowledge-building and only 60% of their time engaged in knowledge-telling activities. One explanation for why students engaged mostly in knowledge-telling when they are teaching a peer is that the explainers tend to teach only what they already know.

Thus, they are basically regurgitating existing knowledge instead of being constructive by building new knowledge. It seems that one goal in designing an effective interactive learning situation is to ensure that the students engage in constructive and not merely active tasks during their interactions together.

In summary, in comparing interactive tasks with self-explaining, four comparison conditions in three of the five studies presented found that the interactive condition resulted in significantly greater learning gains, with an average effect size of $d = -0.58$, as predicted by our theoretical framework. Two other studies actually found self-explaining (a constructive activity) to be as good as or better than interactive activities. We surmise that the task demands of self-explaining led to studies with mixed or equivalent outcomes. Table 15.5 provides a summary of the results described in this section.

DISCUSSION AND PRACTICAL IMPLICATIONS

The illustrative examples presented in the preceding sections provide strong support for a passive-active-constructive-interactive theoretical framework for learning strategies. It is hoped that such comparisons will not only help to simplify the numerous studies conducted to date on self-explanations, but also help to guide future research on the effectiveness and implementation of self-explanation to aid learners' success. Comparisons between self-explanation and passive learning activities consistently showed that self-explanation, as a constructive strategy, led to greater learning outcomes, especially when looking at measures of deep learning. The overall average effect size was large with $d = 0.78$. In addition, an overview of research studies comparing active learning activities with self-explanation also consistently showed greater learning gains among the self-explanation experimental groups, with a very large overall average effect size of $d = 1.14$.

As expected, for two of the studies, the comparisons among self-explanations and other constructive activities found no differences and showed a small overall average effect size of $d = 0.23$. However, for three of the five studies reviewed, self-explaining was actually superior, with an average effect size of $d = 1.26$.

Table 15.5 Summary of studies: self-explaining (SE) versus interactive

Study	Age group	Text/task	Results	Effect size
Hausmann, van de Sande, & VanLehn (2008)	College students	Solve physics problems	SE < Joint-explain	$d = -1.13$
Kramarski & Dudai (2009)	Adolescents (ninth graders)	Solve math problems	SE own < Feedback	$d = -0.65$
Coleman et al. (1997)	College students	Read a text on natural selection	SE text < Explain-to-other	$d = -0.35$
			SE text < Summarize-to-other	$d = -0.18$
			Mean Effect Size	$d = -0.58$
Moreno (2009)	College students	Interact with computer botany program	SE = Cooperative group SE > Jigsaw group	$d = 0.25$ $d = 0.66$
Roscoe & Chi (2008)	College students	Read a text on the human eye	SE text > Explain-to-other	$d = 1.13$

When the comparisons did not yield the predicted equivalent outcomes, more detailed analyses of the research designs and of the subject verbal protocols, when available, allowed us to identify the probable explanations of the findings within the theoretical framework of our hypothesis. The unexpected results were explained based on factors such as task demands and methodological design that either encouraged or suppressed explanations. For example, self-explaining a correct solution or a correct text was often better than explaining-to-video or explaining one's own incorrect solution because feedback is provided in self-explaining a correct solution or text. Similarly, although we expected self-explaining to be inferior to interactive activities that benefitted from additional information (e.g., feedback, elaborations, questions, etc.), the difference was not as large as might be expected, with an overall average effect size of $d = 0.58$. Moreover, we found mixed results among the comparisons of other self-explanation studies and interactive learning activities. However, again these findings could be fairly easily resolved to understand why they were not in the predicted direction, via a more thorough examination of the methods and results and in particular, by looking more closely at the precise nature of the interaction.

Overall, we can conclude that self-explaining consistently led to higher learning gains when compared to passive or active tasks. Among the five studies that contrasted self-explaining with other constructive tasks, self-explaining yielded equivalent or superior learning gains in all five of the studies. Finally, we predicted that self-explaining, being a constructive activity, ought to be consistently worse than other interactive activities and found that to be the case in four comparison conditions among three of the five studies. Surprisingly, self-explaining was equal or better than interactive activities in two of the studies, perhaps due to the fact that self-explaining is inherently constructive in nature, while the level of constructive engagement varies in an interactive learning environment depending on the nature of the task.

What are the practical implications for such findings in the actual classroom and even if self-explanation is the better technique in the research environment, is it always the best choice for the classroom? As an instructor, perhaps the most straightforward implementation to make in the classroom is to move across the categories of our theoretical framework. That is to say, for example, to take an activity from an active format into a constructive format. For instance, instead of having students underline a text (active), ask the students to generate explanations for each idea unit (constructive). Or, for example, instead of asking students to read aloud (active), have them engage in a "questioning the author" (constructive) activity (McKeown & Beck, 1999). Even moving from passive to active should increase learning gains for the student and should be fairly easy to implement on a daily basis. The greatest success will most likely come from picking activities that are more active, constructive, or interactive in nature and that are also easy to implement.

A more challenging task is selecting the right activity within a specific category. For example, even if self-explanation is superior in a research study, other constructive activities might be more straightforward to implement for both the students and the teacher, such as, for example, compare and contrast or concept-mapping. Again, in practical terms, the most important deciding factor is most likely the ease of implementation in the actual classroom.

FUTURE DIRECTIONS

An interesting direction for the implementation of our theoretical framework is in the area of online learning. The computer–student relationship of any online class is inherently interactive, but that does not necessarily make the student activity itself interactive. A student could easily sit in front of a computer and engage in a passive learning activity such as reading a text. This is commonly seen in many online learning classes. An opportunity exists to move the student–computer interaction to a more active, constructive or interactive level. For example, instead of just having the student read a text for an online class, ask the student to underline key words (active) or explain key concepts when given a prompt (constructive) or generate joint explanations with another student in a web-based chat situation (interactive). It is the responsibility of the instructor to structure the student–computer interaction in a way that maximizes learning outcomes. Instructors and researchers both need to look at what the student is doing—is it passive (just reading on the text screen), active (e.g., clicking on pages, opening and playing videos), or constructive (e.g., generating novel output through compare/contrast, generative summaries, self-explanations, and creating concept maps)? And if the experience is supposed to be an interactive one, then it is important to make sure that the interactions are not empty, in that the students are in fact making substantive contributions and experiencing true interactions in terms of receiving and providing feedback, defending and challenging positions, and so forth. Other motivational factors, such as the presence or absence of an on-screen agent, may also need to be considered in order to design the most effective future learning environments in the ever-increasing online learning community.

ACKNOWLEDGMENTS

In preparation of this chapter, funding from the National Science Foundation (Grant Award No. 0935235) is greatly appreciated. We are grateful to Yuning Xu for her editorial help.

REFERENCES

Ainsworth, S., & Burcham, S. (2007). The impact of text coherence on learning by self-explanation. *Learning and Instruction, 17,* 286–303.

Ainsworth, S., & Loizou, A. T. (2003). The effects of self-explaining when learning with text or diagrams. *Cognitive Science: A Multidisciplinary Journal, 27*(4), 669–681.

Aleven, V. A. W. M. M., & Koedinger, K. R. (2002). An effective metacognitive strategy: Learning by doing and explaining with a computer-based Cognitive Tutor. *Cognitive Science, 26*(2), 147–179.

Bielaczyc, K., Pirolli, P. L., & Brown, A. L. (1995). Training in self-explanation and self-regulation strategies: Investigating the effects of knowledge acquisition activities on problem solving. *Cognition and Instruction, 13*(2), 221–252.

Butcher, K. R. (2006). Learning from text with diagrams: Promoting mental model development and inference generation. *Journal of Educational Psychology, 98*(1), 182–197.

Calin-Jageman, R.J., & Ratner, H.H. (2005). The role of encoding in the self-explanation effect. *Cognition and Instruction, 23*(4), 523–543.

Chi, M. T. H. (2000). Self-explaining expository texts: The dual processes of generating inferences and repairing mental models. In R. Glaser (Ed.). *Advances in Instructional Psychology* (pp. 161–238). Mahwah, NJ: Lawrence Erlbaum Associates.

Chi, M. T. H. (2009). Active-constructive-interactive: A conceptual framework for differentiating learning activities. *Topics in Cognitive Science, 1,* 73–105.

Chi, M. T. H., Bassok, M., Lewis, M., Reimann, P., & Glaser, R. (1989). Self-explanations: How students study and use examples in learning to solve problems. *Cognitive Science, 13,* 145–182.

Chi, M. T. H., de Leeuw, N., Chiu, M., & LaVancher, C. (1994). Eliciting self-explanations improves understanding. *Cognitive Science, 18*, 439–477.

Chi, M. T. H., Lewis, M. W., Reimann, P., & Glaser, R. (1989). Self-explanations: How students study and use examples in learning to solve problems. *Cognitive Science, 13*, 145–182.

Cohen, J. (1992). A power primer. *Psychological Bulletin, 112*, 155–159.

Coleman, E. B., Brown, A. L., & Rivkin, I. D. (1997). The effect of instructional explanations on learning from scientific texts. *The Journal of the Learning Sciences, 6*(4), 347–365.

de Bruin, A., Rikers, R., & Schmidt, H. (2007). The effect of self-explanation and prediction on the development of principled understanding of chess in novices. *Contemporary Educational Psychology, 32*(2), 188–205.

Ferguson-Hessler, M. G. M., & de Jong, T. (1990). Studying physics texts: Differences in study processes between good and poor performers. *Cognition and Instruction, 7*(1), 41–54.

Griffin, T. D., Wiley, J., & Thiede, K. W. (2008). Individual differences, rereading, and self-explanation: Concurrent processing and cue validity as constraints on metacomprehension accuracy. *Memory & Cognition, 36*(1), 93–103.

Hausmann, R. G. M., & Chi, M. T. H. (2002). Can a computer interface support self-explaining? *Cognitive Technology, 7*(1), 4–14.

Hausmann, R. G., van de Sande, B., & VanLehn, K. (2008). Are self-explaining and coached problem solving more effective when done by pairs of students than alone? In B. C. Love, K. McRae, & V. M. Sloutsky (Eds.), *Proceedings of the 30th Annual Conference of the Cognitive Science Society*. (pp. 2369–2374). New York: Erlbaum.

Kastens, K. A., & Liben, L. S. (2007). Eliciting self-explanations improves children's performance on a field-based map skills task. *Cognition and Instruction, 25*(1), 45–74.

King, A. (1992). Comparison of self-questioning, summarizing, and notetaking-review as strategies for learning from lectures. *American Educational Research Journal, 29*(2), 303–323.

Kramarski, B., & Dudai, V. (2009). Group-metacognitive support for online inquiry in mathematics with differential self-questioning. *Journal of Educational Computing Research, 40*(4), 377–404.

Mayer, R. E. (2008). *Learning and instruction* (2nd ed.). Upper Saddle River, NJ: Pearson Merrill Prentice Hall.

McKeown, M.G., & Beck, I. L. (1999). Getting the discussion started. *Educational Leadership, 57*, 25–28.

McNamara, D. S. (2004a). iSTART: Interactive strategy training for active reading and thinking. *Behavior Research Methods, Instruments & Computers, 36*(2), 222–233.

McNamara, D. S. (2004b). SERT: Self-explanation reading training. *Discourse Processes, 38*(1), 1–30.

McNamara, D. S. Levinstein, I. B., & Boonthum, C. (2003). iSTART: Interactive Strategy Trainer for Active Reading and Thinking. *Behavioral Research Methods, Instruments, and Computers, 36*, 222–233.

McNamara, D. S., O'Reilly, T. P., Best, R. M., & Ozuru, Y. (2006). Improving adolescent students' reading comprehension with iSTART. *Journal of Educational Computing Research, 34*(2), 147–171.

Moreno, R. (2009). Constructing knowledge with an agent-based instructional program: A comparison of cooperative and individual meaning making. *Learning and Instruction, 19*, 433–444.

Mwangi, W., & Sweller, J. (1998). Learning to solve compare word problems: The effect of example format and generating self-explanations. *Cognition and Instruction, 16*(2), 173–199.

Nathan, M. J., Mertz, K., & Ryan, R. (1994). Learning through self-explanation of mathematics examples: Effects of cognitive load. Paper presented at the annual meeting of the American Educational Research Association, New Orleans.

Neuman, Y., & Schwarz, B. (1998). Is self-explanation while solving problems helpful? The case of analogical problem-solving. *British Journal of Educational Psychology, 68*, 15–24.

O'Reilly, T., Symons, S., & MacLatchy-Gaudet, H. (1998). A comparison of self-explanation and elaborative interrogation. *Contemporary Educational Psychology, 23*, 434–445.

Palincsar, A. S., & Brown, A. L. (1984). Reciprocal teaching of comprehension fostering and comprehension monitoring activities. *Cognition and Instruction, 1*(2), 117–175.

Pillow, B. H., Mash, C., Aloian, S., & Hill, V. (2002). Facilitating children's understanding of misinterpretation: Explanatory efforts and improvements in perspective taking. *The Journal of Genetic Psychology, 163*(2) 133–148.

Pine, K. J., & Messer, D. J. (2000). The effect of explaining another's actions on children's implicit theories of balance. *Cognition and Instruction, 18*(1) 35–51.

Pirolli, P., & Recker, M. (1994). Learning strategies and transfer in the domain of programming. *Cognition and Instruction, 12*(3), 235–275.

Renkl, A. (1997). Learning from worked-out examples: A study on individual differences. *Cognitive Science: A Multidisciplinary Journal, 21*(1), 1–29.

Renkl, A. (2002). Worked-out examples: Instructional explanations support learning by self-explanations. *Learning and Instruction, 12*(5), 529–556.

Renkl, A., Stark, R., Gruber, H., & Mandl, H. (1998). Learning from worked-out examples: The effects of example variability and elicited self-explanations. *Contemporary Educational Psychology, 23*, 90–108.

Roscoe, R.D., & Chi, M.T.H. (2008). Tutor learning: The role of explaining and responding to questions. *Instructional Science, 36*, 321–350.

Rosnow, R. L., & Rosenthal, R. (1996). Computing contrasts, effect sizes, and counternulls on other people's published data: General procedures for research consumers. *Psychological Methods, 1*, 331–340.

Scardamalia, M., & Bereiter, C. (1994). Computer support for knowledge building communities. *Journal of the Learning Sciences, 3*, 265–283.

Siegler, R. S. (1995). How does change occur?: A microgenetic study of number conservation. *Cognitive Psychology, 28*, 225–273.

Teasley, S. (1995). The role of talk in children's peer collaborations. *Developmental Psychology, 31*(2), 207–220.

Thalheimer, W., & Cook, S. (2002). *How to calculate effect sizes from published research articles: A simplified methodology.* Retrieved January 12, 2010 from http://work-learning.com/effect_sizes.htm.

Williams, J. J., & Lombrozo, T. (in press). The role of explanation in discovery and generalization: evidence from category learning. *Cognitive Science.*

Wong, R. M. F., Lawson, M. J., & Keeves, J. (2002). The effects of self-explanation training on students' problem solving in high-school mathematics. *Learning and Instruction, 12*, 233–262.

16

INSTRUCTION BASED ON PEER INTERACTIONS
Kathryn R. Wentzel and Deborah E. Watkins

Peers are of central importance to children throughout childhood and adolescence. They provide companionship and entertainment, help in solving problems, personal validation, and emotional support. In turn, children who engage in positive activities with peers also tend to experience levels of emotional well-being, positive beliefs about the self, and values for prosocial forms of behavior and social interaction that are stronger and more adaptive than children who do not (see Rubin, Bukowski, & Parker, 2006). In addition, children who enjoy positive interactions and relationships with their peers also tend to be engaged in and even excel at academic tasks more than those who experience problems with peers (see Wentzel, 2003). For example, numerous studies have documented that children's interactions and personal relationships with peers are associated with a range of academically-related outcomes at school, including goals and values, skills related to self-regulation and problem-solving, grades, and test scores (Wentzel, 2005).

This body of work illustrates how learning is inextricably linked to the social contexts within which children learn, and highlights the notion that intellectual development is highly dependent on the characteristics of and opportunities provided by peers within learning contexts (see Bronfenbrenner, 1989). In light of this evidence that links children's adaptive functioning across social and academic domains, a central question that will be addressed in this chapter is how students' involvement with peers might be related to academic motivation and accomplishments. To this end, peer-related activities will be discussed in terms of children's interactions and interpersonal relationships with classmates as they occur within the broader social structures of school settings. We first summarize the evidence that links involvement with peers at school to learning and intellectual outcomes. We discuss peer involvement within structured learning contexts and within informal day-to-day relationships. Next, we present theoretical and conceptual models that might explain these links. Finally, we close with a discussion of ways in which evidence and theory can be applied to classroom instruction and school-based practices, and suggest future directions for this field of work.

STUDENTS' INTERACTIONS WITH PEERS AND SCHOOL-RELATED COMPETENCE

Researchers typically study children's involvement with peers at school in two ways. First, peer interactions are examined within the context of informal relationships, as defined by the degree of social acceptance by the larger peer group, membership in specific peer groups, and dyadic friendships. Second, they are examined within more formal, structured contexts designed specifically for learning (see Slavin, Chapter 17 in this volume). In this section, we first describe students' informal interactions with peers and provide evidence of positive associations between these types of interactions and students' motivation and academic outcomes. We then review briefly findings relating interactions in more structured learning contexts to learning outcomes. Theoretical perspectives that provide insights into why associations between peer interactions and academically-related outcomes exist are then considered.

Evidence Linking Informal Peer Interactions to Motivation and Learning

Students interact with each other within the context of social relationships on a daily basis. Relationships with peers are typically studied in terms of peer acceptance or sociometric status, peer groups and crowds, and friendships. Research that establishes causal relations between informal peer interactions and academic outcomes is rare. However, a growing body of work indicates that the quality of these relationships has implications for understanding students' academic competencies, including motivation and engaged effort as well as performance outcomes (see Wentzel, 2005). The evidence linking these various aspects of peer relationships to academically-related motivation and achievement is summarized in the following sections.

Peer Acceptance

Although the vast majority of studies have utilized correlational designs and therefore, do not support causal conclusions, an extensive body of work supports the notion that being socially accepted by one's classmates is related to children's motivation and academic functioning at school. Research indicates that sociometrically popular children (groups of children who are well-liked and not disliked by peers) tend to be academically proficient, whereas sociometrically rejected children (those who are not liked and highly disliked) experience academic difficulties; social preference for individual students (scores are on a continuum ranging from well-accepted to rejected) yield highly similar findings. Results are most consistent with respect to classroom grades, although peer acceptance has been related positively to standardized test scores as well as to IQ. These findings are robust for elementary-aged children as well as adolescents, and longitudinal studies document the stability of relations between peer acceptance and academic accomplishments over time (e.g., Gest, Domitrovich, & Welsh, 2005; Parker & Asher, 1993; Wentzel & Caldwell, 1997). Sociometric status and peer preference also have been related to positive aspects of academic motivation, including satisfaction with school, pursuit of goals to learn, interest in school, and perceived academic competence (Wentzel, 1991; Wentzel & Asher, 1995).

Peer Groups and Crowds

Students' membership in specific peer groups has been studied most frequently in adolescent samples. Research on peer group membership has been mostly descriptive, identifying the central norms and values that uniquely characterize various adolescent school-based groups and crowds (e.g., Brown, 1989). The power of crowd influence is reflected in relations between crowd membership and adolescents' attitudes toward academic achievement. Typical adolescent crowds include "Populars," students who engage in positive forms of academic as well as social behavior but also in some delinquent activities; "Jocks," students characterized by athletic accomplishments but also relatively frequent alcohol use; more alienated groups (e.g., "Druggies") characterized by poor academic performance and engagement in delinquent and other illicit activities; and "Normals," who tend to be fairly average students who do not engage in delinquent activities. Clasen and Brown (1985) found that adolescent peer groups differ in the degree to which they pressure members to become involved in academic activities, with "Jocks" and "Popular" groups providing significantly more pressure for academic involvement than other groups.

Researchers who identify friendship-based peer groups using statistical procedures also have found relations between group membership and academic effort (Kindermann, 1993) and academic outcomes such as grades (Kurdek & Sinclair, 2000; Wentzel & Caldwell, 1997). Membership in friendship-based groups in elementary school and middle school also have been related to changes in academic performance over the course of the school year (Kindermann, 1993; Kindermann, McCollam, & Gibson, 1996; Ryan, 2001; Wentzel & Caldwell, 1997).

Friendships

Finally, peer relationships are studied with respect to dyadic friendships. The central distinction between friendships and involvement with the broader peer group is that friendships reflect relatively private, egalitarian relationships often formed on the basis of idiosyncratic criteria. In contrast, peer groups are defined by publicly acknowledged and therefore, easily identified and predictable characteristics that are valued by the group. Larger peer groups often are comprised of students who have formed close dyadic friendships with each other. However, friendships are enduring aspects of children's peer relationships at all ages, whereas peer groups and crowds emerge primarily in the middle school years, peak at the beginning of high school, and then diminish in prevalence as well as influence by the end of high school (Brown, 1989).

Similar to other types of peer relationships, having friends also has been related positively to grades and test scores (Berndt & Keefe, 1995; Wentzel, Barry, & Caldwell, 2004; Wentzel & Caldwell, 1997), and to positive aspects of motivation and engagement in school-related activities (e.g., Berndt & Keefe, 1995; Ladd, 1990; Wentzel et al., 2004; Wentzel & Caldwell, 1997) in elementary school and middle school. Of special interest is that students making transitions to new school settings (e.g., into Kindergarten and middle school) with existing friends appear to make better social and academic adjustments to school than those who do not (Ladd, 1990; Ladd & Price, 1987; Wentzel et al., 2004). During adolescence, friends are likely to support academic engagement in the form of studying and making plans for future educational engagement in college (e.g., Berndt, Laychak, & Park, 1990; Epstein, 1983).

Peer Interactions in Formal Learning Activities

Connections between peer involvement and learning also have been studied within the context of structured learning activities that require collaborative and cooperative interactions (see Slavin, Chapter 17 in this volume). For the purposes of the following discussion, we consider these activities at two levels, those that require dyadic interactions and those that require interactions among members of a larger group. Dyadic learning activities typically involve the joint structuring of an activity with shared participation of two students in which outcomes for each individual are typically documented (Radiszewska & Rogoff, 1991). In contrast, group activities typically involve four to six members; outcomes can be gauged by group-level as well as individual-level performance (Damon, 1984; Phelps & Damon, 1989). While both of these approaches to peer learning appear to promote individual learning outcomes, they do so under different task and partner conditions. In the following sections, evidence linking participation in each of these formal peer learning activities to learning outcomes is described briefly (see Slavin, Chapter 17 in this volume, for a more detailed review of this literature).

Dyadic Learning

Learning in dyads is a well-established educational practice that has been linked to learning outcomes in specific ways (e.g., Azmitia, 1988; Blaye, Light, Joiner, & Sheldon, 1991; Gauvain & Rogoff, 1989; Watkins & Wentzel, 2008). In general, reviews of these studies indicate that dyadic peer interactions contribute most (albeit modestly) to learning outcomes for minority, urban-dwelling, and young children, and when dyads are homogeneous with respect to gender (e.g., Rohrbeck, Ginsburg-Block, Fantuzzo, & Miller. 2003). However, experimental laboratory studies of peers working in dyads have documented that active discussion, problem solving, and elaborative feedback among peers are associated with advances in a range of cognitive competencies including problem solving skills, conceptual understanding, and metacognitive reasoning; samples range from preschool to high school students (see Gauvain & Perez, 2007; Rogoff et al., 2007, for reviews). In the domain of mathematics, experimental studies also have shown peer dyadic collaboration to improve problem solving and planning, resulting in more accurate solutions to problems (Ginsburg-Block & Fantuzzo, 1998). Understanding of science concepts also has been shown to be stronger when learned in dyadic settings than in non-dyadic settings (Golbeck, 1998), especially when the quality of peer interactions is high (Webb, Nemer, & Zuniga, 2002).

At a more general level, experimental evidence has linked dyadic problem solving to high levels of intellectual engagement, use of advanced strategic thinking skills, and specific academic gains (Radziszewska & Rogoff, 1991; Tudge & Winterhoff, 1993; Tudge, Winterhoff, & Hogan, 1996). Research also has demonstrated that dyadic problem solving with a peer often leads to greater task engagement and understanding than does problem solving done individually or within the context of traditional classroom instruction. These latter findings are qualified, however, by strong evidence that positive outcomes occur for less competent students when they have peer partners who are competent in the task, have good communication skills, provide ability-related positive feedback, and who clearly articulate problem-solving strategies (Azmitia, 1988; Fuchs, Fuchs, Bentz, Phillips, & Hamlett, 1994; Tudge & Winterhoff, 1993).

In contrast to findings from more controlled experimental studies conducted in laboratory settings, results of classroom intervention studies on dyadic learning have been less conclusive. However, specific dyadic peer tutoring programs have yielded promising results (see Graesser, Olney, & Cade, Chapter 20 in this volume for an extended discussion of tutoring). Dyadic peer tutoring has been used effectively in teaching basic skills such as math, reading and spelling (Mastropieri et al., 2001), and has been particularly effective with students of varying cognitive and academic abilities (e.g., Greenwood, Carta, Maheady, 1991). Peer tutoring is particularly efficacious with students who have attention deficits because it incorporates active responding to academic material under conditions of frequent, immediate feedback using individualized academic content presented at the student's level and pace (DuPaul, Henningson, & North, 1993).

Group Learning

The effects of peers working together in small groups on academic outcomes also appear to be generally positive (see Slavin, Chapter 17 in this volume). Results of quasi-experimental and experimental studies suggest that the most successful group learning activities are those that require positive interdependence among group members, individual accountability, face-to-face interactions among students, and learning social skills necessary to work cooperatively. Effects on academic achievement and cognitive outcomes (e.g., creative problem solving, knowledge retention) are consistently positive when students work toward group goals while individual group members are simultaneously held accountable for progress (i.e., individual testing).

Positive increases in motivational outcomes in the form of intrinsic motivation, positive attitudes toward school, persistence, sense of efficacy, and self-esteem also have been documented, especially when group approaches are structured, cultivate informational interdependence such as in a jigsaw arrangement (Aronson & Patnoe, 1997), and combine group goals and individual accountability (Buchs, Butera, Mugny, & Darnon 2004). Group learning also tends to be largely unsuccessful in producing cognitive gains when group members differ as a function of ability, race, ethnicity, and SES (Cohen, 1986; McMaster & Fuchs, 2002, 2005). Moreover, direct pathways from dyadic and group forms of learning to cognitive gains rarely have been established when accounting for the complex social and motivational aspects of peer interactions in groups.

Summary

The literature on peer relationships and interactions provides strong and convincing evidence that peer interactions within informal relationships and more structured learning activities are related positively to a wide range of academic competencies at school. Although findings often are robust across samples and age groups, the evidence linking peer relationships and academic outcomes is based almost entirely on correlational studies lacking strong bases for drawing causal inferences. Similarly, experimental work on dyadic and group learning often has not included important controls. Therefore, it is not clear whether positive academic outcomes reported in these studies are the direct result of interactions with peers, or the result of other outcomes associated with peer interactions such as behavioral styles and social skills that are conducive to classroom learning or the motivational benefits of having positive relationships with peers that also are beneficial to learning.

Despite these methodological drawbacks, however, it is reasonable to assume that for many children, peers have the power to influence the development and demonstrations of academic competencies in positive ways. Theoretical perspectives on why and how such positive influence might take place are discussed in the following section.

THEORETICAL PERSPECTIVES ON PEER INTERACTIONS AND ACADEMIC COMPETENCE

How and why might students' relationships with peers be related to positive school-related accomplishments? Traditionally, theoretical explanations have focused on the broad notion that positive interactions with peers contribute directly to intellectual and social functioning (e.g., Piaget, 1965; Vygotsky, 1978). A more recent approach to answering these questions has been to consider how students' positive relationships with each other provide important opportunities for motivating and facilitating academic accomplishments (Wentzel, 2005). A final explanation for positive associations between peer interactions and achievement outcomes is that peer interactions might not influence academic accomplishments directly but that functioning in the two domains might be linked to each other by way of factors that contribute to positive outcomes in each. In the following sections, each of these perspectives will be described.

Interactions in Informal Peer Contexts and Academic Accomplishments

What do positive relationships and interactions with peers provide to students that enable or facilitate positive academic outcomes? With respect to informal peer contexts, most researchers agree that at the core of positive peer relationships and interactions are the benefits they provide in the form of social supports (Bukowski, Motzoi, & Meyer, 2009; Parker & Asher, 1993). These supports serve a range of functions, including maintenance of the peer group by promoting socially valued goals and social cohesion, as well as facilitating the development of individual outcomes such as social skills and psychological well-being. At a general level, dimensions of support that promote allegiance to the broader group and to engagement in group-valued activities take the form of expectations for the pursuit of and achievement of specific outcomes, help to achieve these outcomes, a safe environment, and emotional nurturance (see Wentzel, 2004, for a review). These dimensions reflect essential components of social support in that if present: (a) information is provided concerning what is expected and valued by the group; (b) attempts to achieve these valued outcomes are met with help and instruction; (c) attempts to achieve outcomes can be made in a safe, non-threatening environment; and (d) individuals are made to feel like a valued member of the group.

These dimensions also have been identified as essential characteristics of contexts that promote positive individual outcomes (Bronfenbrenner, 1989; Ford, 1992; Wentzel, 2004), including academic engagement and achievement (Connell & Wellborn, 1991). For example, Ford has argued that beliefs about social relationships and settings can play an influential role in decisions to engage in the pursuit of personal goals. Specifically, individuals evaluate the correspondence between their personal goals and those of others, the degree to which others will provide access to information and resources necessary to achieve one's goals, and the extent to which social relationships will provide an emotionally supportive environment for goal pursuit. Applied specifically to peer activities as they occur in classroom and school settings, this perspective suggests that students will engage in the pursuit of academic goals in part, when their peers communicate positive expectations and standards for achieving academic goals; provide direct assistance and help in achieving them; and create a climate of emotional support that facilitates positive engagement in valued classroom activities, including protection from physical threats and harm (see Ford, 1992; Wentzel, 2004). In this manner, peer supports can play a powerful role in motivating academic pursuits.

In line with this proposal, a growing body of research supports the notion that social supports enjoyed within the informal context of peer relationships at school reflect these four dimensions. As outlined in the following sections, empirical evidence also suggests that these multiple supports are associated with students' school-related competencies in meaningful ways.

Communicating Goals and Expectations for Performance

Teachers and parents are obvious socializers of students' goals and values (see Grusec & Goodnow, 1994). Although not well documented, it is reasonable to assume that students also communicate to each other specific academic values and expectations for performance (e.g., Altermatt, Pomerantz, Ruble, Frey, & Greulich, 2002). During early adolescence, students report that their classmates expect them to perform well academically at school; for example, approximately 80% of students from three predominantly middle-class middle schools reported that their peers strongly valued academic learning (Wentzel, Battle, Russell, & Looney, 2100). However, as students advance through their middle school and high school years, the degree to which their goals and values support positive academic accomplishments can become fairly attenuated. In samples of high school students, only 40% of adolescents report similar levels of peer academic expectations (Wentzel, Monzo, Williams, & Tomback, 2007).

In addition to general expectations concerning academic achievement, peers also provide proximal input concerning reasons for engaging in academic tasks. In support of this notion, students who perceive relatively high expectations for academic learning and engagement from their peers also report that they pursue goals to learn for internalized reasons (e.g., because it is important or fun) significantly more often than for more extrinsic reasons (e.g., because they believe they will get in trouble or lose social approval if they do not; Wentzel, 2004). Similarly, in the social domain, perceived expectations from peers for behaving prosocially are significant predictors of internalized values for prosocial behavior as well as displays of prosocial behavior in the classroom (Wentzel, Filisetti, & Looney, 2007). Therefore, peers who convey expectations that others are likely to experience a sense of importance or enjoyment with regard to academic engagement and positive social interactions are likely to lead others to form similar positive attitudes (Bandura, 1986).

Although children articulate sets of goals that they would like and expect each other to achieve, specific aspects of informal peer relationships that lead children to adopt these academic goals and values are not well understood. However, the larger peer group can be a source of behavioral standards, and group pressures can provide a mechanism whereby adherence to group standards and expectations is monitored and enforced. Students also have been observed to monitor each other by ignoring non-instructional behavior and responses during group instruction and by the private sanctioning of inappropriate conduct (Eder & Felmlee, 1984). It should be noted that peer monitoring of behavior will contribute to positive motivational orientations only insofar as the peer group has adopted adult standards for achievement and norms for conduct. As children enter middle school and establishing independence from adult influence becomes a developmental task, they are less likely to acknowledge the legitimacy of adult-imposed norms (Smetana & Bitz, 1996) or automatically enforce adult-imposed classroom rules (Eccles & Midgley, 1989).

A second way that peers contribute to students' goals and expectations for performance is by way of influence on perceptions of ability; students' beliefs about their academic efficacy are powerful predictors of academic values and goal pursuit as well as actual performance (Schunk & Pajares, 2005). Children utilize their peers for comparative purposes as early as four years of age (see Butler, 2005 for a review). As children work on academic tasks that require fairly specific skills and that are evaluated with respect to clearly defined standards, they use each other to monitor and evaluate their own abilities. Experimental work also has shown that peers serve as powerful models that influence the development of academic self-efficacy (see Schunk & Pajares, 2005), especially when children observe similar peers who demonstrate successful ways to cope with failure. These modeling effects are especially likely to occur when students are friends (Crockett, Losoff, & Petersen, 1984), although students who have higher-achieving friends tend to have lower levels of self-efficacy than those with lower-achieving friends (Altermatt & Pomerantz, 2005).

Providing Help and Assistance

Perhaps the most explicit and obvious way in which peers can have a direct influence on students' academic competence is by way of help giving. Indeed, students who enjoy positive relationships with their peers will also have greater access to resources and information that can help them accomplish academic tasks than those who do not. These resources can take the form of information and advice, modeled behavior, or experiences that facilitate learning specific skills (e.g., Cooper, Ayers-Lopez, & Marquis, 1982; Schunk, 1987). Although teachers play the central pedagogical function of transmitting knowledge and training students in academic subject areas, at least during adolescence, students report that their peers are as, or more, important sources of instrumental aid than are their teachers (Lempers & Lempers-Clark, 1992).

Developmental research on peer help giving is rare. However, findings on middle school students making the transition into high school suggest that receiving academic help from familiar peers tends to increase over the course of the transition (Wentzel, Monzo, Williams, & Tomback, 2007). One reason for this growing dependence on peers is that when adolescents enter new high school structures, the relative uncertainty and ambiguity of having multiple teachers and different sets of classmates for each class, new instructional styles, and more complex class schedules necessitate that students turn to each other for social support, ways to cope, and academic help.

Providing Emotional Support

Feelings of emotional security and being socially connected are believed to facilitate the adoption of goals and interests valued by others, and desires to contribute in positive ways to the overall functioning of the social group (Connell & Wellborn, 1991; see also Ryan & Deci, 2000). Therefore, differences in the degree to which students believe that their peers accept and care about them might also account for significant relations between the nature of peer relationships at school and competent academic functioning. In support of this notion is an extensive literature relating positive academic outcomes to perceived emotional support from peers. Specifically, perceiving that peers are supportive and caring has been related positively to interest and engagement in positive aspects of classroom life, whereas perceiving relationships with peers in a negative light has been related to motivational and academic problems (e.g., Goodenow, 1993; Wentzel, 1998; Wentzel, Battle, Russell, & Looney, 2010).

One explanation for these findings is that exclusion from caring peer relationships can result in negative outcomes in the form of emotional distress. Children without friends or who are socially rejected often report feeling lonely, emotionally distressed and depressed (Buhs & Ladd, 2001; Flook, Repetti, & Ullman, 2005; Wentzel & Caldwell, 1997; Wentzel et al., 2004). Of central concern is evidence documenting significant relations between psychological distress and depression and a range of achievement-related outcomes including interest in school (Wentzel, Weinberger, Ford, & Feldman, 1990), negative attitudes toward academic achievement, actual levels of performance (Dubow & Tisak, 1989; Wentzel et al., 1990), school avoidance and low levels of classroom participation (Buhs & Ladd, 2001), and ineffective cognitive functioning (Jacobsen, Edelstein, & Hofmann, 1994). Therefore, students' affective functioning is likely to be an important outcome that links peer-related activity in informal settings to academic outcomes (e.g., Juvonen, Nishina, & Graham, 2000).

Providing a Safe Environment

Of final interest is that students who are accepted by their peers and who have established friendships with classmates also are more likely to enjoy a relatively safe school environment and are less likely to be the targets of peer-directed violence and harassment than their peers who do not have friends (Hodges, Boivin, Vitaro, & Bukowski, 1999; Pellegrini, Bartini, & Brooks, 1999; Schwartz et al., 2000). The general effects of peer harassment on other aspects of school-related functioning such as student motivation and academic competence have not been studied frequently. However, threats to physical safety at school can have a significant impact on students' academic self-concept and emotional well-being (e.g., Buhs & Ladd, 2001). Students who are frequently victimized also tend to report higher levels of distress and depression than those who are not routinely victimized (e.g., Boivin & Hymel, 1997; Kochenderfer-Ladd & Waldrop, 2001; Olweus, 1993). Few studies have identified pathways whereby peer victimization and harassment affect academic outcomes. However, as with perceived support, peer abuse and exclusion are likely to be associated with academic achievement by way of emotional distress (Buhs, 2005; Flook, Repetti, & Ullman, 2005). Therefore, although indirect, having supportive peers in these negatively charged situations can have positive effects on a wide range of social, motivational, and academic outcomes.

Interactions in Formal Peer Contexts and Cognitive Gains

Theories of cognitive development have a longstanding tradition of relying on social interaction to explain cognitive growth and learning. As constructivists, both Piaget and Vygotsky proposed that children are active participants in their own development and that they acquire knowledge about their world through activity and social interactions. For example, Piaget (e.g., 1965) proposed that mutual discussion, perspective taking, and conflict resolution with peers can motivate the accommodation of new and more sophisticated approaches to intellectual problem solving, including social problem solving. This conflict facilitates an awareness of differences in perspectives and fosters the evaluation and development of each partner's own beliefs. For Piaget, development was contingent on the relatively symmetrical nature of same-aged peer interactions that allowed conflict resolution within the context of mutual reciprocity.

Piaget's notion of symmetrical interaction among peers is found most often in collaborative learning contexts. The nature of these collaborative problem solving contexts orients children toward discovery and reflection rather than practice and implementation (Phelps & Damon, 1989). Collaborative learning is unique, in that by definition, it encourages discovery learning by incorporating co-construction of knowledge from the original learning situation and always involves retaining each partner's perspective to some degree. Therefore, the resulting cognitive representation involves an integration of multiple perspectives. In support of this notion is evidence that problem solving tasks which demand the acquisition of basic reasoning skills have been found to occur best in peer collaborative contexts rather than other forms of peer learning contexts such as tutoring (Sharan, 1984; Slavin, 1980). Cognitive gains attributed to participation in cooperative learning activities also have been explained with respect to mechanisms associated with symmetrical peer interactions (Slavin, Chapter 17 in this volume).

The social activity on which Vygotsky (1981) placed primary importance involves small groups, often pairs of individuals, who also engage in social interactions. However, Vygotsky suggested that within these peer groupings, social interactions can contribute directly to the development of academic and social skills when competent students teach specific strategies and standards for performance to peers who are less skilled. Therefore, in contrast to Piaget's theory, Vygotsky proposed that asymmetrical interactions contributed to competent development.

Of interest for making a distinction between the influence of asymmetrical versus symmetrical peer interactions within structured learning contexts is the notion of scaffolding. Vygotsky was clear in his suggestion that not only is a difference in the level of expertise between partners necessary, but also an understanding by the more advanced partner of the abilities of the less advanced child so that information can be presented at a developmentally-appropriate level (Tudge & Rogoff, 1989). Therefore, the challenge for the advanced partner is to find a technique that will facilitate as well as motivate positive social interactions and communication with the less advanced partner. This process of scaffolding extends the range of the less advanced child by bridging the gap between current skill and desired skill, thereby allowing him or her to accomplish a task not otherwise possible. From an instructional perspective, scaffolding requires deliberate decision-making and choice of peer partners in order to create the optimal learning environment for students.

Summary

In this section, we have argued that peers have the potential to influence students' intellectual development and academic accomplishments by way of interactions in informal as well as formal contexts. Informal contexts as defined by various types of interpersonal relationships can provide students with essential supports in the form of expectations and values, instrumental help, emotional support and safety from physical threats and harm. In turn, these supports can be instrumental in terms of helping students learn (e.g., provisions of help and communication of expectations and values). These positive relationships also can support positive psychological functioning and emotional well-being, aspects of interpersonal competence frequently associated with motivation and engagement as well as performance outcomes such as classroom grades and test scores (Wentzel, 2003, 2005). Formal peer contexts such as dyadic and group learning activities are believed to foster intellectual development by way of interactive problem solving. Such development is typically explained by constructivist perspectives, based on the assumption that cognitive gains are made when peers collaborate while engaging in fairly structured tasks. These perspectives describe cognitive gains in fairly narrow terms, that is, as the development of specific cognitive structures and intellectual skills.

Although discussion of ways in which these two perspectives on peer learning might be synergistic is rare, it is useful to think about ways in which peer interactions in one type of context might influence interactions in the other. For example, the same supports that are afforded by informal peer contexts also are likely to facilitate the types of positive interactions that are related to cognitive gains within more structured peer learning contexts (see Wentzel & Watkins, 2002). The fact that collaborating on academic tasks with friends tends to yield more predictable cognitive advances than does collaboration with non-friends (e.g., Fonzi, Schneider, Tani, & Tomada, 1997) provides support for this notion. Therefore, it is reasonable to assume that the specific supports provided within the context of informal peer relationships can partly explain successful learning in formal peer learning activities, especially if the students know each other well. In the same vein, it is likely that successful peer collaborations can enhance the quality of peer relationships by providing opportunities for students to strengthen interpersonal ties and therefore, the likelihood that positive peer supports will become available during other forms of classroom instruction.

An additional way to think about connections between students' interactions in informal and formal peer contexts is to consider basic underlying skills that might facilitate competent functioning in both types of settings. Specifically, behaving in socially competent ways can contribute to the development of positive relationships with peers (Fabes, Martin, & Hanish, 2009), which in turn provide students with a range of positive supports. Socially competent behavior also can provide a foundation for the types of positive peer interactions in formal settings that are necessary for cognitive gains to occur.

In support of the notion that social skills and behavior are competencies important for developing successful peer relationships as well as for positive interactions in structured learning settings is empirical work documenting associations between peer relationships and social behavioral outcomes, and between positive forms of social behavior and successful peer collaborations. For example, when compared to their average status peers, popular students tend to be more prosocial and sociable and less aggressive, whereas rejected students are less compliant, less self-assured, less sociable and more aggressive (Newcomb, Bukowski, & Pattee, 1993; Parkhurst & Asher, 1992; Wentzel, 1991; Wentzel & Asher, 1995). Ethnographic studies describe how behaviors and interaction styles that are characteristic of a crowd are modeled frequently so that they can be learned easily and adopted by individuals (Brown, Morey, & Kinney, 1984). In addition, children with friends tend to be more sociable, cooperative, altruistic and prosocial, and less aggressive when compared to their peers without friends (Aboud & Mendelson, 1996; Newcomb & Bagwell, 1995; Wentzel et al., 2004). The quality of friendships also has been related to school-based behavioral outcomes such as truancy and fighting (Crosnoe & Needham, 2004).

Research relating socially competent behaviors to successful collaborative efforts has been less frequent. However, research on collaborative peer learning has confirmed that most children do not naturally develop constructive interaction patterns without specific training in social skills. Without explicit preparation, more competent children collaborating with less competent peers tend to offer help in the form of lectures and demonstrations, rarely elaborate their explanations or allow their partner to apply new information on their own, and often ignore their less competent partners altogether (e.g., Fuchs et al., 1994). Collaborative interaction skills, however, can be enhanced by training higher-achieving peers to interact constructively, develop conceptually rich explanations, and to engage their less competent peers in strategic behavior (Fuchs, Fuchs, Hamlett, Phillips, Karns, & Dutka, 1997). When this takes place, less competent peers demonstrate increases in verbal communication skills, more collaborative social interactions, and more positive learning outcomes (Swing & Peterson, 1982).

In short, numerous studies provide evidence in support of strong associations between peer relationships and social behavior. Work on peer collaborative learning also has documented the important role of social skills in facilitating the positive effects of peer interactions on cognitive gains. From a theoretical perspective, examining the extent to which behavioral styles and social skills account for positive associations between peer relationships, collaborative interactions, and academic outcomes is a critical next step in understanding the role of peers in facilitating intellectual growth and academic accomplishments. From a practical perspective, it is important to understand the role that adults can play in promoting positive peer relationships and interactions at school, as well as supporting positive displays of behavior. Indeed, teachers and administrators are the primary architects of the classroom and school contexts where students interact with each other. In the following section, we describe the potential impact that teachers and the broader school context can have on students' ability to provide positive resources and supports to each other, to interact with each other in positive ways within structured learning activities, and to behave in socially appropriate ways.

LINKING EVIDENCE AND THEORY TO PRACTICE

Given the potentially powerful and positive role that peers can have on student learning and achievement, it becomes important to understand the role of teachers and the broader school context in promoting successful interactions and personal relationships among peers. There is evidence that teachers' beliefs and behaviors, classroom organization and instructional practices, and school-wide structure, composition, and climate affects students' ability to interact successfully in peer learning activities, students' peer choice and general propensity to make friends, and levels of peer acceptance and friendship networks in classrooms. In the following sections, relevant research on teachers and classroom contexts, and then on school-level influences is described.

Teachers and Informal Peer Relationships

Although the nature of causal connections between teacher–student and peer relationships is unclear, it is reasonable to assume that the development of positive relationships with peers might be due in large part to teachers' communications of specific expectations for behavior and achievement, and to systematic regulation of student behavior through instruction-related activities. To illustrate, young students appear to be aware of the academic and behavioral expectations their teachers hold for their fellow classmates, and tend to reject or accept their peers based on these perceived expectations. In elementary classrooms, students perceived to be intelligent by their teachers are consistently viewed in a more positive light by their peers, while those viewed by teachers as trouble makers are likely to be rejected (Hughes & Zhang, 2007). Teachers' perceptions and beliefs concerning students' aptitude and performance also have been related to student friendship choice (Donohue, Perry, & Weinstein, 2003).

Teachers' verbal and nonverbal behavior toward certain children also has been related to how these children are treated by their peers. For instance, teacher praise directed at specific groups of elementary school-aged students has been related to increased peer preference for those students (e.g., Flanders & Havumaki, 1960). In addition, teachers' positive feedback in response to appropriate behavior has been related to students' positive evaluations of and peer preference for students exhibiting that behavior, whereas negative and critical feedback for disruptive and off-task behavior has been related to negative evaluations of and peer disliking of students exhibiting such behavior (White & Kistner, 1992). Finally, teachers can contribute to the formation of social norms that can impact the nature of peer interactions. For example, teachers vary in the behaviors they consider to be appropriate and inappropriate when children are interacting with each other, especially with regard to aggression; in turn, teachers' perspectives on the appropriateness of behaviors are adopted by their students (Craig, Henderson, & Murphy, 2000; Smith, 2007).

The instructional approach that a teacher adopts also can have an impact on students' opportunities to make friends (Epstein, 1983). Adolescents with teachers who employ learner-centered practices (e.g., involve students in decision-making, emphasize the importance of building positive social relationships) as opposed to those who experience teacher-centered practices (e.g., focus on rote learning, norm-referenced evaluation), report having more close friends and a greater number of friends in general. Additionally, learner-centered practices have been related to lower rates of peer rejection, fewer student displays of anger, and more instances of peer-directed empathy than other types of practices (Donohue et al., 2003; Gadeyne, Ghesquière, & Onghena, 2006). Middle and high school students in classrooms where frequent interactions with classmates are condoned, that is, where students are encouraged to talk to each other about class assignments, to work in small groups, and to move about while working on activities, also are less likely to be socially isolated or rejected by their classmates, enjoy greater numbers of friends, and experience more diversity and stability in their friendships (e.g., Epstein, 1983).

Teachers and Formal Peer Learning Activities

Teachers play a critical role in the success of formal peer-learning activities in that the implementation of these activities, and particularly of peer tutoring techniques, requires that students have partners who can benefit from the interactions as well as contribute to the learning of their peer partners. Therefore, when implementing peer-assisted learning structures, teachers cannot just place students together and hope for the best. These activities require explicit planning and training that will prepare peer partners in academic as well as social skill areas. Indeed, the Vygotskian model presumes that a measure of assistance and feedback will typically be provided by the more competent partner in collaborative learning contexts and that peers will interact with each other in socially competent ways.

Probably one of the greatest advances in research on peer-assisted learning has been the increased awareness of the link between partner training in task and mentoring skills, and positive achievement outcomes. Research on peer learning has confirmed that children do not necessarily develop the constructive interaction patterns or the ability to scaffold that are required for productive engagement to occur without explicit preparation. As Person and Graesser (1999) note, tutoring behaviors tend to be primitive and are often characterized by questioning limited in frequency and level of cognitive demand, coupled with infrequent correction of errors, and the giving of positive feedback at inappropriate times. Moreover, students do not necessarily have the ability to engage in positive social interactions that are necessary for successful collaborations with one another (Peterson, Wilkinson, Spinelli, & Swing, 1984).

The positive effects of training students to work with peers have been demonstrated. Specifically, evidence suggests that higher-achieving partners who offer positive constructive feedback and guided direction can enhance the quality of social interactions and cognitive functioning of lower-achieving students (Fuchs et al., 1996; Tudge, 1992; Tudge & Winterhoff, 1993; Tudge, Winterhoff, & Hogan, 1996; Webb, 1983). In contrast, researchers who have not explicitly prepared higher-achieving partners to work collaboratively and constructively have shown these partners to display less adaptive interactions with their less competent peers (Mugny & Doise, 1978; O'Connor & Jenkins, 1996).

Of particular importance to teachers in inclusive educational settings is the use of peer contexts as vehicles for increasing learning or for ameliorating academic problems for diverse groups of students. Training peer partners to work with these students also is especially important for obtaining positive results (e.g., DuPaul et al., 1998; Pfiffner & Barkley, 1998). A case in point is found with children diagnosed with Attention Deficit Hyperactivity Disorder (ADHD) who are being educated in regular classroom settings. These children typically exhibit characteristic behaviors of inattention, overactivity, and impulsivity in the classroom and often are perceived as annoying and intrusive, disruptive, and overtly domineering by their peers (Clark, Cheyne, Cunningham, & Siegel, 1988). Their social difficulties are intensified by deficits in communication and social reciprocity skills (Cunningham & Siegel, 1987), negative social feedback, and low rates of peer acceptance (Whalen & Henker, 1985).

Given the success of collaborative interaction training studies, however, it is reasonable to assume that preparing higher-achieving partners to engage and encourage peers with ADHD to participate in the problem-solving process might improve the quality of their social interactions, and ultimately foster an opportunity for children with ADHD to profit from collaborative peer learning. For example, in a study by Watkins and Wentzel (2008), high-achieving females were trained in specific social interaction and communication skills such as: (a) reflective listening (i.e., clarifying and summarizing their partner's ideas by paraphrasing the suggestion or restating his/her feelings); (b) providing positive feedback (i.e., giving constructive, positive ability-related statements that reinforce the partner's ideas); (c) avoiding criticism (i.e., avoiding negative comments to the partner even if an illogical suggestion is offered); (d) providing advance organizers (i.e., describe a proposed method of solving the task through thoughtful planning); (e) providing strategies by thinking aloud (i.e., convey to the partner the reasons underlying one's decisions by allowing the partner to share in the thinking process); (f) giving elaborate explanations (i.e., giving clear, explicit, step-by-step explanations and answers to the partner); and (g) reciprocal questioning (i.e., elicit explanatory replies and engage the partner in verbal participation). Observations of interactions between the trained high-achieving female partners and their male partners with ADHD documented that a positive significant increase in the use of these skills over the course of a session was associated with significant increases in joint participation and advanced strategic problem solving and significant decreases in inappropriate behavior and immature social interaction patterns for the male partners. This work suggests that collaborative settings can benefit children with ADHD when their peer partners are prepared to elaborate explanations, reflect and validate their partner's explanations, verbalize their thoughts (think-aloud), give positive, constructive feedback, and engage the participation of their partner.

Teachers and Student Behavior

Research on classroom management has provided a vast literature on ways in which teacher practices can influence student behavior in positive ways. Although a review of this literature is beyond the scope of this chapter, it is important to note that certain basic practices have been linked causally and strongly to improved student behavior over time. These include consistent implementation and reinforcement of classroom rules, ample opportunities for students to engage in meaningful and challenging learning activities, and peer tutoring (see Epstein, Akins, Cullinan, Kutash, & Weaver, 2008). Therefore, in light of evidence that positive behavior predicts positive peer relationships (reviewed in previous sections), this work suggests that teachers can have a powerful impact on informal peer relationships by way of their impact on student behavior via classroom management practices. Moreover, the fact that participating in formal peer learning activities also can lead to improvements in students' classroom behavior supports an indirect pathway from these formal activities to the formation of positive peer relationships.

School-Level and Structural Influences

Evidence of ways in which school structures and school-level characteristics can influence peer interactions and relationships has been less forthcoming. However, variations in the social, academic, ethnic, and gender composition of classrooms are known to influence friendship dynamics. Specifically, homogenous classroom composition can be deleterious to the formation and maintenance of positive, high quality, peer relationships over time (Barth, Dunlap, Dane, Lochman, & Wells, 2004). The gender composition of a classroom can influence the relationships students form with each other in that elementary-aged boys who transition to same-sex classrooms tend to develop more friendships than do girls (Barton & Cohen, 2004). Similarly, African-American students in classrooms that are ethnically diverse tend to report having more high quality friendships than those in less diverse classrooms (Jackson, Barth, Powell, & Lochman, 2006). Finally, the degree to which middle schools and high schools are ethnically diverse, as opposed to having clear majority and minority groupings, also can influence the nature and stability of students' friendships, with greater diversity resulting in students who have more friends and more extensive social networks than those in less diverse schools (Urberg, Degirmencioglu, Tolson, & Halliday-Scher, 1995).

On a positive note, universal school-wide policies and programs that accentuate the importance of students' prosocial behavior also tend to create environments where more positive peer relationships are likely to be formed (Gresham, Van, & Cook, 2006). In this regard, proactive efforts to promote social skill development and positive social interactions among students have had some success in reducing the frequency of maladaptive social skills, thus enabling the formation of better relationships with peers (for a review, see Ang & Hughes, 2001; Epstein et al., 2008). In general, the best outcomes have been observed when programs involve more than 30 hours of instruction over the course of several weeks, and use a variety of instructional methods and treatment approaches. Whole-school approaches also tend to be more effective than classroom-level or individual interventions (Hughes, Cavell, Meehan, Zhang, & Collie, 2005).

Other structured efforts to enhance prosocial behavior and corresponding peer interactions are exemplified by the Child Development Project (CDP; Developmental Studies Center). The CDP curriculum provides cooperative learning activities and class meetings designed to communicate and reinforce positive behavioral and social norms of the classroom, foster cognitive and social problem-solving, and to build classroom unity and a sense of community. Formal evaluations (Developmental Studies Center) have documented that CDP schools out-perform comparison schools on a multitude of factors, including increased levels of positive behavioral outcomes, lower levels of negative behaviors, and academic outcomes. Similarly, the Fast Track Program (Bierman et al., 1999), designed in part to promote friendship building skills and social problem solving strategies, has documented improvements in the quality of elementary-aged students' peer relationships and social interactions (Lavallee, Bierman, & Nix, 2005).

From a developmental perspective, improving the quality of peer relationships should be of special concern for teachers and administrators who work with students during transitions to new schools. For example, many young adolescents enter new middle school structures that necessitate interacting with larger numbers of peers on a daily basis. In contrast to the greater predictability of self-contained classroom environments in elementary school, the relative uncertainty and ambiguity of multiple classroom environments, new instructional styles, and more complex class schedules often result in middle school students turning to each other for information, social support, and ways to cope. Students who have access to positive peer supports are likely to adapt to the demands of middle school transition more quickly and in more positive ways than those without such supports (Wentzel et al., 2004).

Finally, although the literature implies that peers might be the primary source of threats to students' physical safety and well-being, of central importance to understanding this process is that teachers and school administrators can play a central role in creating schools that are free of peer harassment and in alleviating the negative effects of harassment once it has occurred (e.g., Olweus, 1993). Interventions designed to offset the often negative influence of peer groups and gangs on behavior and school attendance are especially successful if students have access to adults who provide them with warmth and strong guidance (Chaskin, 2010; Heath & McLaughlin, 1993; Larson & Rumberger, 1995). There also is evidence that schools which stress intergenerational bonding (i.e., closeness between students and teachers) support the development of teacher–student relationships that can act as buffers against the potentially negative effects of aggressive peers on behavior (Crosnoe & Needham, 2004).

CONCLUSION AND FUTURE DIRECTIONS

In this chapter, we addressed the question of how and why students' social interactions and relationships with peers might be related to learning and intellectual development. Toward this end, we provided evidence that links involvement with peers at school to learning and intellectual outcomes, defining peer involvement with respect to interactions in structured learning contexts and as it plays out in interpersonal relationships on a daily basis. Theoretical and conceptual models that might explain these links also were described, and we presented ways in which evidence and theory can be applied to classroom instruction and school-based practices.

In general, theory and research provide a strong foundation for concluding that students' involvement with their peers provides multiple opportunities and resources for the development of intellectual competencies and positive motivational orientations toward learning. Structured learning contexts such as collaborative or cooperative learning activities can provide a context where basic skills necessary for later achievement in content areas can be learned and practiced. These types of peer learning structures also provide students with an equal opportunity to participate in ways that eliminate the possibility that students will become passive learners. Formal as well as informal peer interactions also foster working relationships which emphasize mutual assistance and relatedness, shared goals, emotional support and safety, interdependency and group cohesion. All of these elements of peer involvement have the potential to make learning with peers highly motivating, to promote personal responsibility for learning, to utilize intellectual and interpersonal strengths, and to challenge the development of more sophisticated approaches to learning.

As the field moves forward, well-controlled experimental studies will be needed to understand the true causal impact of peer involvement on learning. At the same time, more sophisticated models that include mediating and moderating pathways are needed to understand specific processes that enhance (or detract from) the positive impact of peers on learning. For example, to what extent does the development of motivational processes such as goal setting, efficacy, and self-determination explain positive associations between peer interactions and academic outcomes? The moderating effects of gender, race/ethnicity, and age in relations between peer interactions and achievement also deserve further study.

Similarly, models that identify ways in which classroom settings and instructional practices might modify the influence of peers on learning are lacking. In this regard, explanatory models must be developed with specific types of social configurations in mind (e.g., learning in dyads versus groups; learning with friends versus acquaintances), and perhaps modified depending on whether the target student is in elementary, middle, or high school, or has special needs. Integration of research on classroom reward structures (Slavin, Chapter 17 in this volume), organizational culture and climate (Maehr & Midgley, 1991), and person–environment fit (Eccles & Midgley, 1989) into models of peer learning also can inform our understanding of how the social institutions and contexts within which learning takes place can facilitate the positive impact of peer involvement in learning. We look forward to these advances in the field.

REFERENCES

Aboud, F. E., & Mendelson, M. J. (1996). Determinants of friendship selection and quality: Developmental perspectives. In W. M. Bukowski, A. F. Newcomb, & W. W. Hartup (Eds.), *The company they keep: Friendship during childhood and adolescence* (pp. 87–112). New York: Cambridge University Press.

Altermatt, E. R., & Pomerantz, E. M. (2005). The implications of having high-achieving versus low-achieving friends: A longitudinal analysis. *Social Development, 14,* 61–81.

Altermatt, E. R., Pomerantz, E. M., Ruble, D. N., Frey, K. S., & Greulich, F. K. (2002). Predicting changes in children's self-perceptions of academic competence: A naturalistic examination of evaluative discourse among classmates. *Developmental Psychology, 38,* 903–917.

Ang, R., & Hughes, J. (2001). Differential benefits of skills training with antisocial youth based on group composition: A meta-analytic review. *School Psychology Review, 31*, 164–185.

Aronson, E., & Patnoe, S. (1997). *The jigsaw classroom: Building cooperation in the classroom* (2nd ed.). New York: Addison Wesley Longman.

Azmitia, M. (1988). Peer interactions and problem solving: When are two heads better than one? *Child Development, 59*, 87–96.

Bandura, A. (1986). *Social foundations of thought and action: A social cognitive theory.* Englewood Cliffs, NJ: Prentice-Hall.

Barth, J., Dunlap, S., Dane, H., Lochman, J., & Wells, K. (2004). Classroom environment influences on aggression, peer relations, and academic focus. *Journal of School Psychology, 42*, 115–133.

Barton, B., & Cohen, R. (2004). Classroom gender composition and children's peer relations. *Child Study Journal, 34*, 29–45.

Berndt, T. J., & Keefe, K. (1995). Friends' influence on adolescents' adjustment to school. *Child Development, 66*, 1312–1329.

Berndt, T. J., Laychak, A. E., & Park, K. (1990). Friends' influence on adolescents' academic achievement motivation: An experimental study. *Journal of Educational Psychology, 82*, 664–670.

Bierman, K., Coie, J., Dodge, K., Greenberg, M., Lochman, J., McMahon, R., & Pinderhughes, E. (1999). Initial impact of the Fast Track Prevention Trial for conduct problems: II. Classroom effect. *Journal of Consulting and Clinical Psychology, 67*, 648–657.

Blaye, A., Light, P., Joiner, R., & Sheldon, S. (1991). Collaboration as a facilitator of planning and problem solving on a computer-based task. *British Journal of Developmental Psychology, 9*, 471–483.

Boivin, M., & Hymel, S. (1997). Peer experiences and social self-perceptions: A sequential model. *Developmental Psychology, 33*, 135–145.

Bronfenbrenner, U. (1989). Ecological systems theory. In R. Vasta (Ed.), *Annals of child development* (Vol. 6, pp. 187–250). Greenwich, CT: JAI.

Brown, B. B. (1989). The role of peer groups in adolescents' adjustment to secondary school. In T. J. Berndt, & G. W. Ladd (Eds.), *Peer relationships in child development* (pp. 188–215). New York: Wiley.

Brown, B. B., Mory, M. S., & Kinney, D. (1994) Casting adolescent crowds in a relational perspective: Caricature, channel, and context. In R. Montemayor, G. R. Adams, & T. P. Gullotta (Eds.), *Personal relationships during adolescence* (pp. 123–167). Newbury Park, CA: Sage.

Buchs, C., Butera, F., Mugny, G., & Darnon C. (2004). Conflict elaboration and cognitive outcomes. *Theory into Practice, 43*, 23–30.

Buhs, E. (2005). Peer rejection, negative peer treatment, and school adjustment: Self-concept and classroom engagement as mediating processes. *Journal of School Psychology, 43*, 407–424.

Buhs, E. S., & Ladd, G. W. (2001). Peer rejection as an antecedent of young children's school adjustment: An examination of mediating processes. *Developmental Psychology, 37*, 550–560.

Bukowski, W. M., Motzoi, C., & Meyer, F. (2009). Friendship as process, function, and outcome. In K. Rubin, W. Bukowski, & B. Laursen (Eds.), *Handbook on peer relationships* (pp. 217–231). New York: Guilford.

Butler, R. (2005). Competence assessment, competence, and motivation between early and middle childhood. In A. Elliot, & C. Dweck (Eds.), *Handbook of competence and motivation* (pp. 202–221). New York: Guilford.

Chaskin, R. J. (2010). *Youth gangs and community intervention: Research, practice, and evidence.* New York: Columbia University Press.

Clark, M. L., Cheyne, J. A., Cunningham, C. E., & Siegel, S. (1988). Dyadic peer interactions and task orientation in attention-deficit disordered children. *Journal of Abnormal Child Psychology, 16*, 1–15.

Clasen, D. R., & Brown, B. B. (1985). The multidimensionality of peer pressure in adolescence. *Journal of Youth and Adolescence, 14*, 451–468.

Cohen, E. G. (1986). *Designing group work: Strategies for the heterogeneous classroom.* New York: Teachers College Press.

Connell, J., & Wellborn, J. (1991). Competence, autonomy, and relatedness: A motivational analysis of self-system processes. *Self processes and development* (pp. 43–77). Hillsdale, NJ: Lawrence Erlbaum.

Cooper, C. R., Ayers-Lopez, S., & Marquis, A. (1982). Children's discourse during peer learning in experimental and naturalistic situations. *Discourse Processes, 5*, 177–191.

Craig, W., Henderson, K., & Murphy, J.G. (2000). Prospective teachers' attitudes toward bullying and victimization. *School Psychology International, 21*, 5–21.

Crockett, L., Losoff, M., & Petersen, A. C. (1984). Perceptions of the peer group and friendship in early adolescence. *Journal of Early Adolescence, 4*, 155–181.

Crosnoe, R., & Needham, B. (2004). Holism, contextual variability, and the study of friendships in adolescent development. *Child Development, 75*, 264–279.

Cunningham, C. E., & Siegel, S. (1987). Peer interactions of normal and attention-deficit disordered boys during free-play, cooperative task, and simulated classroom situations. *Journal of Abnormal Child Psychology, 15,* 247–268.

Damon, W. (1984). Peer education: The untapped potential. *Journal of Educational Psychology, 5,* 331–343.

Developmental Studies Center (n.d.). Retrieved August 2, 2007, from www.devstu.org/.

Donohue, K., Perry, K., & Weinstein, R. (2003). Teachers' classroom practices and children's rejection by their peers. *Journal of Applied Developmental Psychology, 24,* 91–118.

Dubow, E. F., & Tisak, J. (1989). The relation between stressful life events and adjustment in elementary school children: The role of social support and social problem-solving skills. *Child Development, 60,* 1412–1423.

DuPaul, G. J., Ervin, R. A., Hook, C. L., & McGoey, K. E. (1998). Peer tutoring for children with attention deficit hyperactivity disorder: Effects on classroom behavior and academic performance. *Journal of Applied Behavior Analysis, 3,* 579–592.

DuPaul, G., Henningson, J., & North, P. (1993). Peer tutoring effects on the classroom performance of children with attention deficit hyperactivity disorder, *School Psychology Review, 22*(1), 43–53.

Eccles, J. S., & Midgley, C. (1989). Stage-environment fit: Developmentally appropriate classrooms for young adolescents. In C. Ames, & R. Ames (Eds.), *Research on motivation in education* (Vol. 3, pp. 139–186). New York: Academic Press.

Eder, D. E., & Felmlee, D. (1984). The development of attention norms in ability groups. In P. L. Peterson, L. C. Wilkinson, & M. Hallinan (Eds.), *The social context of instruction: Group organization and group processes* (pp. 189–225). New York: Academic Press.

Epstein, J. L. (1983). The influence of friends on achievement and affective outcomes. In J. L. Epstein, & N. Karweit (Eds.), *Friends in school* (pp. 177–200). New York: Academic Press.

Epstein, M., Atkins, M., Cullinan, D., Kutash, K., & Weaver, R. (2008). *Reducing behavior problems in the elementary school classroom: A practice guide* (NCEE #2008–012). Washington, DC: National Center for Education Evaluation and Regional Assistance, Institute of Education Sciences, U.S. Department of Education. Retrieved from: http://ies.ed.gov/ncee/wwc/publications/practiceguides.

Fabes, R. A., Martin, C. L., & Hanish, L. D. (2009). Children's behaviors and interactions with peers. In K. Rubin, W. Bukowski, & B. Laursen (Eds.), *Handbook on peer relationships* (pp. 45–62). New York: Guilford.

Flanders, N. A., & Havumaki, S. (1960). The effect of teacher–pupil contacts involving praise on the sociometric choices of students. *Journal of Educational Psychology, 51,* 65–68.

Flook, L., Repetti, R. L., & Ullman, J. B. (2005). Classroom social experiences as predictors of academic performance. *Developmental Psychology, 41,* 319–327.

Fonzi, A., Schneider, B. H., Tani, F., & Tomada, G. (1997). Predicting children's friendship status from their dyadic interaction in structured situations of potential conflict, *Child Development, 68,* 496–506.

Ford, M. E. (1992). *Motivating humans: Goals, emotions, and personal agency beliefs.* Newbury Park, CA. Sage.

Fuchs, L. S., Fuchs, D., Bentz, J., Phillips, N. B., & Hamlett, C. L. (1994). The nature of student interactions during peer tutoring with and without prior training and experience. *American Educational Research Journal, 31,* 75–103.

Fuchs, L. S., Fuchs, D., Hamlett, C. L., Phillips, N. B., Karns, K., & Dutka, S. (1997). Enhancing students' helping behavior during peer-mediated instruction with conceptual mathematical explanations. *The Elementary School Journal, 97,* 223–249.

Fuchs, L. S., Fuchs, D., Karns, K., Hamlett, C. L., Dutka, S., & Katzaroff, M. (1996). The relation between student ability and the quality and effectiveness of explanations. *American Research Journal, 33,* 631–664.

Gadeyne, E., Ghesquière, P., & Onghena, P. (2006). Psychosocial educational effectiveness criteria and their relation to teaching in primary education. *School Effectiveness and School Improvement, 17*(1), 63–85.

Gauvain, M., & Perez, S. M. (2007). The socialization of cognition. In J. E. Grusec, & P. Hastings (Eds.), *Handbook of socialization: Theory and research* (pp. 588–613). New York: Guilford.

Gauvain, M., & Rogoff, B. (1989). Collaborative problem solving and children's planning skills. *Developmental Psychology, 25,* 139–151.

Gest, S. D., Domitrovich, C. E., & Welsh, J. A. (2005). Peer academic reputation in elementary school: Associations with changes in self-concept and academic skills. *Journal of Educational Psychology, 97,* 337–346.

Ginsburg-Block, M. D., & Fantuzzo, J. W. (1998). An evaluation of the relative effectiveness of NCTM standards-based interventions for low-achieving urban elementary students. *Journal of Educational Psychology, 90,* 560–569.

Golbeck, S. L (1998). Peer collaboration and children's representation of the horizontal surface of liquid. *Journal of Applied Developmental Psychology, 19,* 571–592.

Goodenow, C. (1993). Classroom belonging among early adolescent students: Relationships to motivation and achievement. *Journal of Early Adolescence, 13,* 21–43.

Greenwood, C. R., Carta, J. J., & Maheady, L. (1991). Peer tutoring programs in the regular education classroom. In G. Stoner, M. Shinn, & H. Walker (Eds.), *Interventions for achievement and behavior problems* (pp. 179–200). Washington, DC: National Association of School Psychologists.

Gresham, F., Van, M., & Cook, C. (2006). Social-skills training for teaching replacement behaviors: Remediating acquisition in at-risk students. *Behavioral Disorders, 31*, 363–377.

Grusec, J. E., & Goodnow, J. J. (1994). Impact of parental discipline methods on the child's internalization of values: A reconceptualization of current points of view. *Developmental Psychology, 30*, 4–19.

Heath, S. B., & McLaughlin, M. W. (1993). *Identity and inner-city youth.* New York: Teachers College Press.

Hodges, E. V., Boivin, M., Vitaro, F., & Bukowski, W. M. (1999). The power of friendship: Protection against an escalating cycle of peer victimization. *Developmental Psychology, 35*, 94–101.

Hughes, J., Cavell, T., Meehan, B., Zhang, D., & Collie, C. (2005). Adverse school context moderates the outcomes of selective interventions for aggressive children. *Journal of Consulting and Clinical Psychology, 73*, 731–736.

Hughes, J., & Zhang, D. (2007). Effects of the structure of classmates' perceptions of peers' academic abilities on children's perceived cognitive competence, peer acceptance, and engagement. *Contemporary Educational Psychology, 32*, 400–419.

Jackson, M., Barth, J., Powell, N., & Lochman, J. (2006). Classroom contextual effects of race on children's peer nominations. *Child Development, 77*, 1325–1337.

Jacobsen, T., Edelstein, W., & Hofmann, V. (1994). A longitudinal study of the relation between representations of attachment in childhood and cognitive functioning in childhood and adolescence. *Developmental Psychology, 30*, 112–124.

Juvonen, J., Nishina, A., & Graham, S. (2000). Peer harassment, psychological adjustment, and school functioning in early adolescence. *Journal of Educational Psychology, 92*, 349–359.

Kindermann, T. A. (1993). Natural peer groups as contexts for individual development: The case of children's motivation in school. *Developmental Psychology, 29*, 970–977.

Kindermann, T. A., McCollam, T. L., & Gibson, E. (1996). Peer networks and students' classroom engagement during childhood and adolescence. In J. Juvonen, & K. R. Wentzel (Eds.), *Social motivation: Understanding children's school adjustment* (pp. 279–312). New York: Cambridge University Press.

Kochenderfer-Ladd, B., & Waldrop, J. L. (2001). Chronicity and instability of children's peer victimization experiences as predictors of loneliness and social satisfaction trajectories. *Child Development, 72*, 134–151.

Kurdek, L. A., & Sinclair, R. J. (2000). Psychological, family, and peer predictors of academic outcomes in first-through fifth-grade children. *Journal of Educational Psychology, 92*, 449–457.

Ladd, G. W. (1990). Having friends, keeping friends, making friends, and being liked by peers in the classroom: Predictors of children's early school adjustment. *Child Development, 61*, 1081–1100.

Ladd, G. W., & Price, J. M. (1987). Predicting children's social and school adjustment following the transition from preschool to kindergarten. *Child Development, 58*, 1168–1189.

Larson, K. A., & Rumberger, R. W. (1995). ALAS: Achievement for Latinos through academic success. In H. Thornton (Ed.), *Staying in school: A technical report of the dropout prevention projects for junior high school students with learning and emotional disabilities.* Minneapolis, MN: University of Minnesota, Institute on Community Integration.

Lavallee, K. L., Bierman, K. L., & Nix, R. L. (2005). The impact of first-grade "friendship group" experiences on child social outcomes in the Fast Track Program. *Journal of Abnormal Child Psychology, 33*, 307–324.

Lempers, J. D., & Lempers-Clark, D. S. (1992). Young, middle, and late adolescents' comparisons of the functional importance of five significant relationships. *Journal of Youth and Adolescence, 21*, 53–96.

Maehr, M. L., & Midgley, C. (1991). Enhancing motivation: A schoolwide approach. *Educational Psychologist, 26*, 399–427.

Mastropieri, M. A., Scruggs, T. E., Mohler, L., Beranek, M., Spencer, V., Boon, R. T., & Talbot, E. (2001). Can middle school students with serious reading difficulties help each other and learn anything? *Learning Disabilities Research & Practice, 16*(1), 18–27.

McMaster, K. N., & Fuchs, D. (2002). Effects of cooperative learning on the academic achievement of students with learning disabilities: An update of Tateyama-Sniezek's review. *Learning Disabilities Research and Practice, 17*, 107–117.

McMaster, K. N., & Fuchs, D. (2005). Cooperative learning for students with disabilities. *Current Practice Alerts, 11*.

Mugny, G., & Doise, W. (1978). Socio-cognitive conflict and structure of individual and collective performances. *European Journal of Social Psychology, 8*, 181–192.

Newcomb, A. F., & Bagwell, C. L. (1995). Children's friendship relations: A meta-analytic review. *Psychological Bulletin, 117*, 306–347.

Newcomb, A. F., Bukowski, W. M., & Pattee, L. (1993). Children's peer relations: A metanalytic review of popular, rejected, neglected, and controversial sociometric status. *Psychological Bulletin, 113*, 99–128.

O'Connor, R. E., & Jenkins, J. R. (1996). Cooperative learning as an inclusion strategy: A closer look. *Exceptionality*, 6, 29–51.

Olweus, D. (1993). Victimization by peers: Antecedents and long-term outcomes. In K. Rubin, & J. B. Asendorf (Eds.), *Social withdrawal, inhibition, and shyness in childhood* (pp. 315–341). Chicago: University of Chicago Press.

Parker, J. G., & Asher, S. R. (1993). Friendship and friendship quality in middle childhood: Links with peer group acceptance and feelings of loneliness and social dissatisfaction. *Developmental Psychology*, 29, 611–621.

Parkhurst, J., & Asher, S. R. (1992). Peer rejection in middle school—subgroup differences in behavior, loneliness, and interpersonal concerns. *Developmental Psychology*, 28, 231–241.

Pellegrini, A. D., Bartini, M., & Brooks, F. (1999). School bullies, victims, and aggressive victims: Factors relating to group affiliation and victimization in early adolescence. *Journal of Educational Psychology*, 91, 216–224.

Person, N. K., & Graesser, A. G. (1999). Evolution of discourse during cross-age tutoring. In A. M. O'Donnell, & A. King (Eds.), *Cognitive perspectives on peer learning* (pp. 69–86). Mahwah, NJ: Lawrence Erlbaum.

Peterson, P. L., Wilkinson, L. C., Spinelli, F., & Swing, S. R. (1984). Merging the process-product and sociolinguistic paradigms: Research on small-group processes. In P.L. Peterson, L. C. Wilkinson, & M. Hallinan (Eds.), *The social context of instruction: Group organization and group processes* (pp. 126–152). New York: Academic Press.

Pfiffner, L. J., & Barkley, R. A. (1998). Treatment of ADHD in school settings. In R. A. Barkley (Ed.), *Attention-deficit hyperactivity disorder: A handbook for diagnosis and treatment* (2nd ed., pp. 458–490). New York: Guilford Press.

Phelps, E., & Damon, W. (1989). Problem-solving with equals: Peer collaboration as a context for learning mathematics and spatial concepts. *Journal of Educational Psychology*, 81, 639–646.

Piaget, J. (1965). *The moral judgment of the child.* New York: The Free Press (Originally published, 1932).

Radziszewska, B., & Rogoff, B. (1991). Children's guided participation planning imaginary errands with skilled adult or peer partners. *Developmental Psychology*, 27, 381–389.

Rogoff, B., Moore, L., Najafi, B., Dexter, A., Correa-Chavez, M., & Solis, J. (2007). Children's development of cultural repertoires through participation in everyday routines and practices. In J. E. Grusec, & P. Hastings (Eds.), *Handbook of socialization: Theory and research* (pp. 490–515). New York: Guilford Press.

Rohrbeck, C. A., Ginsburg-Block, M. D, Fantuzzo, J. W., & Miller, T. R. (2003). Peer-assisted learning interventions with elementary school students: A meta-analytic review. *Journal of Educational Psychology*, 95, 240–257.

Rubin, K. H., Bukowski, W., & Parker, J. (2006). Peer interactions, relationships, and groups. In N. Eisenberg (Ed.), *Handbook of child psychology* (6th ed.) *Social, emotional, and personality development* (pp. 571–645). New York: Wiley.

Ryan, A. (2001). The peer group as a context for the development of young adolescent motivation and achievement. *Child Development*, 72, 1135–1150.

Ryan, R.M., & Deci, E.L. (2000). Self-determination theory and the facilitation of intrinsic motivation, social development, and well-being. *American Psychologist*, 55, 68–78.

Schunk, D. H. (1987). Peer models and children's behavioral change. *Review of Educational Research*, 57, 149–174.

Schunk, D. H., & Pajares, F. (2005). Competence perceptions and academic functioning. In A. Elliot, & C. Dweck (Eds.), *Handbook of competence and motivation* (pp. 85–104). New York: Guilford Press.

Schwartz, D., Dodge, K. A., Pettit, G. S., Bates, J. E., & The Conduct Problems Prevention Research Group (2000). Friendship as a moderating factor in the pathway between early harsh home environment and later victimization in the peer group. *Developmental Psychology*, 36, 646–662.

Sharan, S. (1984). *Cooperative learning.* Hillsdale, NJ: Erlbaum.

Slavin, R. E. (1980). A review of peer tutoring and cooperative learning projects in twenty-eight schools. *Review of Educational Research*, 11, 315–342.

Smetana, J., & Bitz, B. (1996). Adolescents' conceptions of teachers' authority and their relations to rule violations in school. *Child Development*, 67, 1153–1172.

Smith, J. (2007). "Ye've got to 'ave balls to play this game sir!"—Boys, peers and fears: the negative influence of school-based "cultural accomplices" in constructing hegemonic masculinities. *Gender and Education*, 19, 179–198.

Swing, S. R., & Peterson, P. L. (1982). The relationship of student ability and small-group interaction to student achievement. *American Educational Research Journal*, 19, 259–274.

Tudge, J. R. H. (1990). Vygotsky, the zone of proximal development, and peer collaboration: Implications for classroom practice. In L. C. Moll (Ed.), *Vygotksy and education: Instrumental implications and applications of sociohistorical psychology* (pp. 155–172). Cambridge: Cambridge University Press.

Tudge, J. R. H. (1992). Processes and consequences of peer collaboration: A Vygotskian analysis. *Child Development*, *63*, 1364–1379.

Tudge, J. R. H., & Rogoff, B. (1989). Peer influences on cognitive development: Piagetian and Vygotskian perspectives. In M. H. Bornstein, & J. S. Bruner (Eds.), *Interaction in human development* (pp. 17–40). Hillsdale, NJ: Erlbaum.

Tudge, J., & Winterhoff, P. (1993). Can young children benefit from collaborative problem solving? Tracing the effects of partner competence and feedback. *Social Development*, *2*, 242–259.

Tudge, J. R. H., Winterhoff, P. A., & Hogan, D. M. (1996). The cognitive consequences of collaborative problem solving with and without feedback. *Child Development*, *67*, 2892–2909.

Urberg, K., Degirmencioglu, S., Tolson, J., & Halliday-Scher, K. (1995). The structure of adolescent peer networks. *Developmental Psychology*, *31*, 540–547.

Vygotsky, L. S. (1978). *Mind in society: The development of higher psychological processes.* Cambridge, MA: MIT Press.

Vygotsky, L. S. (1981). The genesis of higher mental functions. In J. V. Wertsch (Ed.), *The concept of activity in Soviet psychology* (pp. 144–188). Armonk, NY: Sharpe.

Watkins, D. E., & Wentzel, K. R. (2008). Training boys with ADHD to work collaboratively: Social and learning outcomes. *Contemporary Educational Psychology*, *33*, 625–646.

Webb, N. M. (1983). Predicting learning from student interaction: Defining the interaction variables. *Educational Psychologist*, *18*, 33–41.

Webb, N.M., Nemer, K.M., & Zuniga, S. (2002). Short circuits or superconductors? Effects of group composition on high-achieving students' science assessment performance. *American Educational Research Journal*, *39*, 943–989.

Wentzel, K. R. (1991). Relations between social competence and academic achievement in early adolescence. *Child Development*, *62*, 1066–1078.

Wentzel, K. R. (1998). Social support and adjustment in middle school: The role of parents, teachers, and peers. *Journal of Educational Psychology*, *90*, 202–209.

Wentzel, K. R. (2003). School adjustment. In W. Reynolds, & G. Miller (Eds.), *Handbook of psychology*, Vol. 7: *Educational psychology.* New York: Wiley.

Wentzel, K. R. (2004). Understanding classroom competence: The role of social-motivational and self-processes. In R. Kail (Ed.), *Advances in child development and behavior* (Vol. 32, pp. 213–241). New York: Elsevier.

Wentzel, K. R. (2005). Peer relationships, motivation, and academic performance at school. In A. Elliot, & C. Dweck (Eds.), *Handbook of competence and motivation* (pp. 279–296). New York: Guilford Press.

Wentzel, K. R., & Asher, S. R. (1995). Academic lives of neglected, rejected, popular, and controversial children. *Child Development*, *66*, 754–763.

Wentzel, K. R., Barry, C., & Caldwell, K. (2004). Friendships in middle school: Influences on motivation and school adjustment. *Journal of Educational Psychology*, *96*, 195–203.

Wentzel, K. R., Battle, A., Russell, S., & Looney, L. (2010). Teacher and peer contributions to classroom climate in middle school. *Contemporary Educational Psychology.*

Wentzel, K. R., & Caldwell, K. (1997). Friendships, peer acceptance, and group membership: Relations to academic achievement in middle school. *Child Development*, *68*, 1198–1209.

Wentzel, K. R., Filisetti, L., & Looney, L. (2007). Adolescent prosocial behavior: The role of self-processes and contextual cues. *Child Development*, *78*, 895–910.

Wentzel, K. R., Monzo, J., Williams, A. Y., & Tomback, R. M. (2007). Teacher and peer influence on academic motivation in adolescence: A cross-sectional study. Paper presented at the biennial meeting of the Society for Research in Child Development, Boston, April.

Wentzel, K. R., & Watkins, D. E. (2002). Peer relationships and collaborative learning as contexts for academic enablers. *School Psychology Review*, *31*, 366–377.

Wentzel, K. R., Weinberger, D. A., Ford, M. E., & Feldman, S. S. (1990). Academic achievement in preadolescence: The role of motivational, affective, and self-regulatory processes. *Journal of Applied Developmental Psychology*, *11*, 179–193.

Whalen, C. K., & Henker, B. (1985). The social worlds of hyperactive (ADHD) children. *Clinical Psychology Review*, *5*, 447–478.

White, K. J., & Kistner, J. (1992). The influence of teacher feedback on young children's peer preferences and perceptions. *Developmental Psychology*, *28*, 933–940.

17

INSTRUCTION BASED ON COOPERATIVE LEARNING
Robert E. Slavin

OVERVIEW OF COOPERATIVE LEARNING

Cooperative learning refers to instructional methods in which teachers organize students into small groups, which then work together to help one another learn academic content. Cooperative learning methods are extensively researched and under certain well-specified conditions, they are known to substantially improve student achievement in most subjects and grade levels, yet the structured forms of cooperative learning that have proven to be effective are not used as often as more informal forms. Further, there remains considerable debate about the theoretical basis for achievement outcomes of cooperative learning. This chapter reviews and integrates evidence on the theoretical mechanisms relating to learning outcomes of cooperative learning, and presents evidence on the most widely used practical applications of cooperative methods.

Cooperative learning methods vary widely in their details. Group sizes may be from two to several. Group members may have individual roles or tasks, or they may all have the same task. Groups may be evaluated or rewarded based on group performance or the average of individual performances, or they may simply be asked to work together.

In one form or another, cooperative learning has been used and studied in every major subject, with students from preschool to college, and in all types of schools. Cooperative learning is used at some level by hundreds of thousands of teachers. One national survey in the 1990s found that 79% of elementary teachers and 62% of middle school teachers reported regular use of cooperative learning (Puma, Jones, Rock, & Fernandez, 1993). Antil, Jenkins, Wayne, and Vadasy (1998) found that 93% of a sample of U.S. teachers reported using cooperative learning, with 81% reporting daily use.

There have been hundreds of studies of cooperative learning focusing on a wide variety of outcomes, including academic achievement in many subjects, second language learning, attendance, behavior, intergroup relations, social cohesion, acceptance of classmates with handicaps, attitudes toward subjects, and more (see Johnson & Johnson, 1998; Rohrbeck et al., 2003; Slavin, 1995; Webb, 2008). Reviews of research on a wide variety of innovations in curriculum, technology, and professional development have consistently found certain forms of cooperative learning to be among the most effective of all strategies for elementary and secondary reading (Slavin et al., 2008, 2009a) and mathematics (Slavin & Lake, 2008; Slavin et al., 2009b).

THEORETICAL PERSPECTIVES ON COOPERATIVE LEARNING

Although there is a fair consensus among researchers about the positive effects of cooperative learning on student achievement, there remains a controversy about why and how cooperative learning methods affect achievement and, most importantly, under what conditions cooperative learning has these effects. Different groups of researchers investigating cooperative learning effects on achievement begin with different assumptions and conclude by explaining the achievement effects of cooperative learning in quite different theoretical terms. In earlier work, Slavin (1995) identified motivationalist, social cohesion, cognitive-developmental and cognitive-elaboration theories as the four major perspectives on the achievement effects of cooperative learning.

The motivationalist perspective presumes that task motivation is the single most impactful part of the learning process, asserting that the other processes such as planning and helping are driven by individuals' motivated self interest. Motivationalist-oriented scholars focus more on the reward or goal structure under which students operate, even going so far as to suggest that under some circumstances, interaction may not be necessary for the benefits of cooperative goal structures to manifest (Slavin, 1995). By contrast, the social cohesion perspective (also called social interdependence theory) suggests that the effects of cooperative learning are largely dependent on the cohesiveness of the group. This perspective holds that students help each other learn because they care about the group and its members and come to derive self-identity benefits from group membership (Johnson & Johnson, 1998).

The two cognitive perspectives focus on the interactions among groups of students, holding that, in themselves, these interactions lead to better learning and thus better achievement. Within the general cognitive heading, developmentalists attribute these effects to processes outlined by scholars such as Piaget (1926) and Vygotsky (1978). Work from the cognitive elaboration perspective asserts that learners must engage in some manner of cognitive restructuring (or elaboration) of new materials in order to learn them. Cooperative learning is said to facilitate that process. One reason for the continued lack of consensus among cooperative learning scholars is that adherents of each perspective tend to approach the topic without reference to the body of similar work from other perspectives.

This chapter offers a theoretical model of cooperative learning processes that acknowledges the contributions of work from each of the major theoretical perspectives. It places them in a model that suggests the likely role each plays in cooperative learning processes. This work further explores conditions under which each may operate, and suggests research and development needed to advance cooperative learning scholarship so that educational practice may truly benefit from the lessons of thirty years of research.

The alternative perspectives on cooperative learning may be seen as complementary, not contradictory. For example, motivational theorists would not argue that the cognitive theories are unnecessary. Instead, they assert that motivation drives cognitive process, which in turn produces learning (Slavin, 1995). They would argue that it is unlikely over the long haul that students would engage in the kind of elaborated explanations found by Webb (2008) and others to be essential to profiting from cooperative activity without a goal structure designed to enhance motivation. Similarly, social cohesion theorists might hold that the utility of extrinsic incentives must lie in their contribution to group cohesiveness, caring, and pro-social norms among group members, which could in turn affect cognitive processes.

A simple path model of cooperative learning processes, adapted from Slavin (1995), is shown in Figure 17.1. It depicts the main functional relationships among the major theoretical approaches to cooperative learning.

Figure 17.1 begins with a focus on group goals or incentives based on the individual learning of all group members. That is, the model assumes that motivation to learn and to encourage and help others to learn activates cooperative behaviors that will result in learning. This would include both task motivation and motivation to interact in the group. In this model, motivation to succeed leads to learning directly, and also drives the behaviors and attitudes that lead to group cohesion, which in turn facilitates the types of group interactions that yield enhanced learning and academic achievement. The relationships are conceived to be reciprocal, such that as task motivation leads to the development of group cohesion, that development may reinforce and enhance task motivation. By the same token, the cognitive processes may become intrinsically rewarding and lead to increased task motivation and group cohesion.

Each aspect of the diagrammed model is well represented in the theoretical and empirical cooperative learning literature. All have well-established rationales and some supporting evidence. What follows is a review of the basic theoretical orientation of each perspective, a description of the cooperative learning strategies each prescribes, and a discussion of the empirical evidence supporting each.

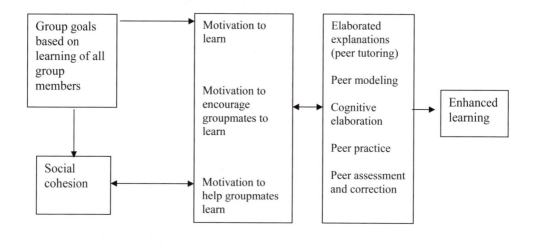

Figure 17.1 Integration of theoretical perspectives on cooperative learning effects on learning

FOUR MAJOR THEORETICAL PERSPECTIVES ON COOPERATIVE LEARNING AND ACHIEVEMENT

Motivational Perspective

The motivational perspective on cooperative learning posits that task motivation is the most important part of the process, believing that the other processes are driven primarily by motivation. From a motivationalist perspective (e.g., Johnson & Johnson, 1998; Slavin, 1983, 1995, 2009), cooperative incentive structures create a situation in which the only way group members can attain their own personal goals is if the group is successful. Therefore, to meet their personal goals, group members must both help their groupmates to do whatever enables the group to succeed, and, perhaps even more importantly, to encourage their groupmates to exert maximum efforts. In other words, rewarding groups based on group performance (or the sum of individual performances) creates an interpersonal reward structure in which group members will give or withhold social reinforcers (e.g., praise, encouragement) in response to groupmates' task-related efforts.

The motivationalist critique of traditional classroom organization holds that the competitive grading and informal reward system of the traditional classroom creates peer norms opposing academic efforts (see Coleman, 1961). Since one student's success decreases the chances that others will succeed, students are likely to express norms that high achievement is for "nerds" or "teacher's pets." However, by having students work together toward a common goal, they may be motivated to express norms favoring academic achievement, to reinforce one another for academic efforts.

Not surprisingly, motivational theorists build group rewards into their cooperative learning methods. In methods developed at Johns Hopkins University (Slavin, 1994, 1995), students can earn certificates or other recognition if their average team scores on quizzes or other individual assignments exceed a pre-established criterion. Methods developed by David and Roger Johnson (1998) and their colleagues at the University of Minnesota often give students grades based on group performance, which is defined in several different ways. The theoretical rationale for these group rewards is that if students value the success of the group, they will encourage and help one another to achieve.

Empirical Support for the Motivational Perspective

Considerable evidence from practical applications of cooperative learning in elementary and secondary schools supports the motivationalist position that group rewards are essential to the effectiveness of cooperative learning, with one critical qualification. Use of group goals or group rewards enhances the achievement outcomes of cooperative learning if and only if the group rewards are based on the individual learning of all group members (Slavin, 1995). Most often, this means that team scores are computed based on average scores on quizzes which all teammates take individually, without teammate help. For example, in Student Teams-Achievement Divisions, or STAD (Slavin, 1994), students work in mixed-ability teams to master material initially presented by the teacher. Following this, students take individual quizzes on the material, and the teams may earn certificates based on the degree to which team members have improved on their own past records. The only way the team can succeed is to ensure that all team members have learned, so the team members' activities focus on explaining concepts to one another, helping one another practice, and encouraging one another to achieve. In contrast, if group rewards are given based on a single group product (for example, the team completes one worksheet or solves one problem), there is little incentive for group members to explain concepts to one another, and one or two group members may do all the work (see Slavin, 1995).

In assessing the empirical evidence supporting cooperative learning strategies, the greatest weight must be given to studies of longer duration. Well executed, these are bound to be more realistically generalizable to the day-to-day functioning of classroom practices. A review of 99 studies of cooperative learning in elementary and secondary schools that involved durations of at least four weeks compared achievement gains in cooperative learning and control groups. Of 64 studies of cooperative learning methods that provided group rewards based on the sum of group members' individual learning, 50 (78%) found significantly positive effects on achievement, and none found negative effects (Slavin, 1995). The median effect size for the studies from which effect sizes could be computed was $d = +0.32$ (32% of a standard deviation separated cooperative learning and control treatments).

In contrast, studies of methods that used group goals based on a single group product or provided no group rewards found few positive effects, with a median effect size of only $d = +0.07$. Comparisons of alternative treatments within the same studies found similar patterns; group goals based on the sum of individual learning performances were necessary to the instructional effectiveness of the cooperative learning models (e.g., Fantuzzo, Polite, & Grayson, 1990; Fantuzzo, Riggio, Connelly, & Dimeff, 1989).

Why are group goals and individual accountability so important? To understand this, consider the alternatives. In some forms of cooperative learning, students work together to complete a single worksheet or to solve one problem together. In such methods, there is little reason for more able students to take time to explain what is going on to their less able groupmates or to ask their opinions. When the group task is to *do* something, rather than to *learn* something, the participation of less able students may be seen as interference rather than help. It may be easier in this circumstance for students to give each other answers than to explain concepts or skills to one another.

In contrast, when the group's task is to ensure that every group member *learns* something, it is in the interests of every group member to spend time explaining concepts to his or her groupmates. Studies of student behavior within cooperative groups have consistently found that the students who gain most from cooperative work are those who give and receive elaborated explanations (Webb, 1985, 2008). In contrast, giving and receiving answers without explanations were *negatively* related to achievement gain. Group goals and individual accountability motivate students to give elaborated explanations and to take one another's learning seriously, instead of simply giving answers.

Social Cohesion Perspective

A theoretical perspective somewhat related to the motivational viewpoint holds that the effects of cooperative learning on achievement are strongly mediated by the cohesiveness of the group. The quality of the group's interactions is thought to be largely determined by group cohesion. In essence, students will engage in the task and help one another learn because they identify with the group and want one another to succeed. This perspective is similar to the motivational perspective in that it emphasizes primarily motivational rather than cognitive explanations for the instructional effectiveness of cooperative learning. However, motivational theorists hold that students help their groupmates learn primarily because it is in their own interests to do so. Social cohesion theorists, in contrast, emphasize the idea that students help their groupmates learn because they care about the group. A hallmark of the social cohesion perspective is an emphasis on team-building activities in preparation for cooperative learning, and processing or group self-evaluation during and after group activities. Social cohesion theorists have historically tended to downplay or reject the group incentives and individual accountability held by motivationalist researchers to be essential. They emphasize, instead, that the effects of cooperative learning on students and on student achievement depend substantially on the quality of the group's interaction (Battisch, Solomon, & Delucchi, 1993).

For example, Cohen (1986, pp. 69–70) stated:

> If the task is challenging and interesting, and if students are sufficiently prepared for skills in group process, students will experience the process of groupwork itself as highly rewarding . . . never grade or evaluate students on their individual contributions to the group product.

Cohen's (1994) work, as well as that of Shlomo and Yael Sharan (1992) and Elliot Aronson and his colleagues (Aronson, Blaney, Stephan, Sikes, & Snapp, 1978), may be described as social cohesiveness theories. Cohen, Aronson, and the Sharans all prescribe forms of cooperative learning in which students take on individual roles within the group, which Slavin (1983) calls *task specialization methods*.

In Aronson's Jigsaw method, students study material on one of four or five topics distributed among the group members. They meet in *expert groups* to share information on their topics with members of other teams who had the same topic, and then take turns presenting their topics to the team. In the Sharans' Group Investigation method, groups take on topics within a unit studied by the class as a whole, and then further subdivide the topic into tasks within the group. The students investigate the topic together and ultimately present their findings to the class as a whole. Cohen's Finding Out/Descubrimiento program has students play different roles in discovery-oriented science activities.

One main purpose of the task specialization used in Jigsaw, Group Investigation, and Finding Out/Descubrimiento is to create interdependence among group members. In the Johnsons' methods, a somewhat similar form of interdependence is created by having students take on roles as "checker," "recorder," "observer," and so on. The idea is that if students value their groupmates (as a result of teambuilding and other cohesiveness-building activities) and are dependent on one another, they are likely to encourage and help one another to succeed.

Empirical Support for the Social Cohesion Perspective

There is some evidence that the achievement effects of cooperative learning depend on social cohesion and the quality of group interactions (Battisch et al., 1993). The achievement outcomes of cooperative learning methods that emphasize task specialization are less clear. Research on the original form of Jigsaw has not generally found positive effects of this method on student achievement (Slavin, 1995). One problem with Jigsaw is that students have limited exposure to material other than that which they studied themselves, so learning gains on their own topics may be offset by losses on their groupmates' topics. In contrast, there is evidence that when it is well implemented, Group Investigation can significantly increase student achievement (Sharan & Shachar, 1988). In studies of at least four weeks' duration, the Johnsons' (1998) methods have not been found to increase achievement more than individualistic methods unless they incorporate group rewards (in this case, group grades) based on the average of group members' individual quiz scores (see Slavin, 1995). Studies of forms of Jigsaw that have added group rewards to the original model have found positive achievement outcomes (Mattingly & Van Sickle, 1991).

Research on practical classroom applications of methods based on social cohesion theories provide inconsistent support for the proposition that building cohesiveness among students through teambuilding alone (i.e., without group incentives) will enhance student achievement. In general, methods which emphasize teambuilding and group process but do not provide specific group rewards based on the learning of all group members are no more effective than traditional instruction in increasing achievement (Slavin, 1995), although there is evidence that these methods can be effective if group rewards are added to them.

Cognitive Perspectives

The major alternative to the motivationalist and social cohesiveness perspectives on cooperative learning, both of which focus primarily on group norms and interpersonal influence, is the cognitive perspective. The cognitive perspective holds that interactions among students will in themselves increase student achievement for reasons which have to do with mental processing of information rather than with motivations. Cooperative methods developed by cognitive theorists involve neither the group goals that are the cornerstone of the motivationalist methods nor the emphasis on building group cohesiveness characteristic of the social cohesion methods. However, there are several quite different cognitive perspectives, as well as some which are similar in theoretical perspective, but have developed on largely parallel tracks. The two most notable of these are described in the following sections—the developmental perspective and the cognitive elaboration perspective.

Developmental Perspective

One widely researched set of cognitive theories is the developmental perspective (e.g., Damon, 1984). The fundamental assumption of the developmental perspective on cooperative learning is that interaction among children on appropriate tasks increases their mastery of critical concepts. Vygotsky (1978, p. 86) defines the zone of proximal development as "the distance between the actual developmental level as determined by independent problem solving and the level of potential development as determined through problem solving under adult guidance or in *collaboration with more capable peers*" (emphasis added). In his view, collaborative activity among children promotes growth because children of similar ages are likely to be operating within one another's proximal zones of development, modeling in the collaborative group behaviors more advanced than those they could perform as individuals.

Similarly, Piaget (1926) held that social-arbitrary knowledge—language, values, rules, morality, and symbol systems—can only be learned in interactions with others. Peer interaction is also important in logical-mathematical thought in upsetting the child's egocentric conceptualizations and in providing feedback to the child about the validity of logical constructions.

There is a great deal of empirical support for the idea that peer interaction can help non-conservers become conservers. Many studies have shown that when conservers and nonconservers of about the same age work collaboratively on tasks requiring conservation, the nonconservers generally develop and maintain conservation concepts (see Bell, Grossen, & Perret-Clermont, 1985). From the developmental perspective, the effects of cooperative learning on student achievement would be largely or entirely due to the use of cooperative tasks. In this view, opportunities for students to discuss, to argue, and to present and hear one another's viewpoints are the critical element of cooperative learning with respect to student achievement.

Empirical Evidence for the Developmental Perspective

Despite considerable support from theoretical and laboratory research, there is little evidence from classroom experiments conducted over meaningful time periods that pure cooperative methods, which depend solely on interaction, produce higher achievement. However, it is likely that the cognitive processes described by developmental theorists are important mediating variables that can help explain the positive outcomes of effective cooperative learning methods (Slavin, 1995).

Cognitive Elaboration Perspective

A cognitive perspective on cooperative learning quite different from the developmental viewpoint is one which might be called the cognitive elaboration perspective. Research in cognitive psychology has long held that if information is to be retained in memory and related to information already in memory, the learner must engage in some sort of cognitive restructuring, or elaboration, of the material (Wittrock, 1986). One of the most effective means of elaboration is explaining the material to someone else. Research on peer tutoring has long found achievement benefits for the tutor as well as the tutee (Devin-Sheehan, Feldman, & Allen, 1976). In such methods, students take roles as recaller and listener. They read a section of text, and then the recaller summarizes the information while the listener corrects any errors, fills in any omitted material, and helps think of ways both students can remember the main ideas. The students switch roles on the next section.

Empirical Evidence for the Cognitive Elaboration Perspective

Dansereau and his colleagues have found in a series of brief studies that college students working on structured cooperative scripts can learn technical material or procedures better than can students working alone (O'Donnell, 1996). While both the recaller and the listener learned more than did students working alone, the recaller learned more (O'Donnell & Dansereau, 1992). This mirrors both the peer tutoring findings and the findings of Webb (2008), who discovered that the students who gained the most from cooperative activities were those who provided elaborated explanations to others. In this research as well as in Dansereau's, students who received elaborated explanations learned more than those who worked alone, but not as much as those who served as explainers. Studies of Reciprocal Teaching, in which students learn to formulate questions for each other, have generally supported its positive effects on student achievement (O'Donnell, 2000; Palincsar, Brown, & Martin, 1987; Rosenshine & Meister, 1994).

STRUCTURING GROUP INTERACTIONS

There is some evidence that carefully structuring the interactions among students in cooperative groups can be effective, even in the absence of group rewards. For example,

Meloth and Deering (1992) compared students working in two cooperative conditions. In one, students were taught specific reading comprehension strategies and given *think sheets* to remind them to use these strategies (e.g., prediction, summarization, character mapping). In the other group, students earned team scores if their members improved each week on quizzes. A comparison of the two groups on a reading comprehension test found greater gains for the strategy group.

However, there is also evidence to suggest that a combination of group rewards and strategy training produces much better outcomes than either alone. The Fantuzzo et al. (1992) study, cited earlier, directly made a comparison between rewards alone, strategy alone, and a combination, and found the combination to be by far the most effective. Further, the outcomes of dyadic learning methods, which use group rewards as well as strategy instruction, produced some of the largest positive effects of any cooperative methods, much larger than those found in studies that provided groups with structure but not rewards. As noted earlier, studies of scripted dyads also find that adding incentives adds to the effects of these strategies (O'Donnell, 1996). The consistent positive findings for Cooperative Integrated Reading and Composition (CIRC) (Stevens et al., 1987), which uses both group rewards and strategy instruction, also argue for this combination.

RECONCILING THE FOUR PERSPECTIVES

The model shown previously in Figure 17.1 illustrates how group goals might operate to enhance the learning outcomes of cooperative learning. Provision of group goals based on the individual learning of all group members might affect cognitive processes directly, by motivating students to engage in peer modeling, cognitive elaboration, and/or practice with one another. Group goals may also lead to group cohesiveness, increasing caring and concern among group members and making them feel responsible for one another's achievement, thereby motivating students to engage in cognitive processes that enhance learning.

Finally, group goals may motivate students to take responsibility for one another independently of the teacher, thereby solving important classroom organization problems and providing increased opportunities for cognitively appropriate learning activities. Scholars whose theoretical orientations de-emphasize the utility of extrinsic rewards attempt to intervene directly on mechanisms identified as mediating variables in the model described earlier. For example, social cohesion theorists intervene directly on group cohesiveness by engaging in elaborate teambuilding and group processing training. Cognitive theorists would hold that the cognitive processes that are essential to any theory relating cooperative learning to achievement can be created directly, without the motivational or affective changes discussed by the motivationalist and social cohesion theorists.

From the perspective of the model diagrammed in Figure 17.1, starting with group goals and individual accountability permits students in cooperative learning groups to benefit from the full range of factors that are known to affect cooperative learning outcomes. While group goals and individual accountability may not always be absolutely necessary, to ignore them would be to ignore the tool with the most consistent evidence of positive effects on student achievement.

RESEARCH ON PRAGMATIC APPROACHES TO COOPERATIVE LEARNING

Research and development over the years have led to the creation and evaluation of several practical approaches to cooperative learning. The most widely used and extensively researched of these programs are described in the following sections.

Cooperative learning methods fall into two main categories. One set, *Structured Team Learning*, involves rewards to teams based on the learning progress of their members, and individual accountability, which means that team success depends on individual learning, not group products. A second set, *Informal Group Learning Methods*, includes methods more focused on social dynamics, projects, and discussion than on mastery of well-specified content.

STRUCTURED TEAM LEARNING METHODS

Student Team Learning

Student Team Learning (STL) techniques were developed and researched at Johns Hopkins University (see Slavin, 1994, 1995). More than half of all experimental studies of practical cooperative learning methods involve STL methods.

All cooperative learning methods share the idea that students work together to learn and are responsible for one another's learning as well as their own. STL methods also emphasize the use of team goals and team success, which can only be achieved if all members of the team learn the objectives being taught. That is, in Student Team Learning the students' tasks are not to *do* something as a team but to *learn* something as a team.

Four concepts are central to all Student Team Learning methods: *team rewards, individual opportunities, individual accountability,* and *equal opportunities* for success. Using STL techniques, teams earn certificates or other team rewards if they achieve above a designated criterion. *Individual accountability* means that the team's success depends on the individual learning of all team members. This focuses the activity of the team members on explaining concepts to one another and making sure that everyone on the team is ready for a quiz or other assessment that they will take without teammate help. *Equal opportunities for success* means that students contribute to their teams by improving over their past performances. This ensures that high, average, and low achievers are equally challenged to do their best and that the contributions of all team members will be valued.

Four principal Student Learning methods have been extensively developed and researched. Two are general cooperative learning methods adaptable to most subjects and grade levels: Student Team-Achievement Divisions (STAD) and Teams-Games-Tournament (TGT). The remaining two are comprehensive curricula designed for use in particular subjects at particular grade levels: Team Assisted Individualization (TAI) for mathematics in Years 3–6 and Cooperative Integrated Reading and Composition (CIRC) for reading and writing instruction in Years 3–5.

Student Teams-Achievement Divisions (STAD)

In STAD (Slavin, 1994), students are assigned to four-member learning teams mixed in performance level, sex and ethnicity. The teacher presents a lesson, and the students work within their teams to make sure that all team members have mastered the lesson.

Finally, all students take individual quizzes on the material, at which time they may *not* help one another.

Students' quiz scores are compared to their own past averages, and points are awarded based on the degree to which students can meet or exceed their own earlier perform-ances. These points are then summed to form team scores, and teams that meet certain criteria earn certificates or other rewards. The whole cycle of activities, from teacher presentation to team practice to quiz, usually takes three to five class periods.

STAD has been used in a wide variety of subjects, including mathematics, language arts, and social studies. It has been used from grade 2 through college. STAD is most appropriate for teaching well-defined objectives, such as mathematical computations and applications, language usage and mechanics, geography and map skills, and science facts and concepts. In STAD, students work in four-member heterogeneous teams to help each other master academic content. Teachers follow a schedule of teaching, team work, and individual assessment. The teams receive certificates and other recognition based on the average scores of all team members on weekly quizzes.

Numerous studies of STAD have found positive effects of the program on traditional learning outcomes in math, language arts, science, and other subjects (Barbato, 2000; Mevarech, 1985; Reid, 1992; Slavin, 1995; Slavin & Karweit, 1984). For example, Slavin and Karweit (1984) carried out a large, year-long randomized evaluation of STAD in Math 9 classes in Philadelphia. These were classes for students not felt to be ready for Algebra I, and were therefore the lowest-achieving students. Overall, 76% of students were African American, 19% were White, and 6% were Hispanic. Forty-four classes in 26 junior and senior high schools were randomly assigned within schools to one of four conditions: STAD, STAD plus *Mastery Learning, Mastery Learning,* or control. All classes, including the control group, used the same books, materials, and schedule of instruction, but the control group did not use teams or mastery learning. In the *Mas-tery Learning* conditions, students took formative tests each week, students who did not achieve at least an 80% score received corrective instruction, and then students took summative tests.

Shortened versions of the standardized Comprehensive Test of Basic Skills (CTBS) in mathematics served as pre-test and post-test. The four groups were very similar at pre-test. On 2×2 nested analyses of covariance, there was a significant effect of a teams factor ($d = +0.21$). The effect size comparing STAD + *Mastery Learning* to control was $d = +0.24$, and that for STAD without *Mastery Learning* was $d = +0.18$. There was no significant *mastery learning* main effect or teams by mastery interaction either in the random effects analysis or in a student-level fixed effects analysis. Effects were similar for students with high, average, and low pre-test scores.

Teams-Games-Tournament (TGT)

Teams-Games-Tournament (Slavin, 1994) uses the same teacher presentations and teamwork as in STAD, but replaces the quizzes with weekly tournaments. In these, stu-dents compete with members of other teams to contribute points to their team score. Students compete at three-person tournament tables against others with a similar past record in mathematics. A procedure changes table assignments to keep the competition fair. The winner at each tournament table brings the same number of points to his or her team, regardless of which table it is; this means that low achievers (competing with other low achievers) and high achievers (competing with other high achievers) have equal opportunity for success. As in STAD, high performing teams earn certificates or other forms of team rewards. TGT is appropriate for the same types of objectives as STAD. Several studies of TGT have found positive effects on achievement in math, science, and language arts (Slavin, 1995).

Team Assisted Individualization (TAI)

Team Assisted Individualization (TAI) (Slavin et al., 1986) shares with STAD and TGT the use of four-member mixed ability learning teams and certificates for high-performing teams. However, where STAD and TGT use a single pace of instruction for the class, TAI combines cooperative learning with individualized instruction. Also, where STAD and TGT apply to most subjects at grade levels, TAI is specifically designed to teach mathematics to students in grades 3–6 (or older students not ready for a full algebra course).

In TAI, students enter an individualized sequence according to a placement test and then proceed at their own rates. In general, team members work on different units. Teammates check each other's work against answer sheets and help one another with any problems. Final unit tests are taken without teammate help and are scored by student monitors. Each week, teachers total the number of units completed by all team members and give certificates or other team rewards to teams that exceed a criterion score based on the number of final tests passed, with extra points for perfect papers and completed homework.

Because students take responsibility for checking each other's work and managing the flow of materials, the teacher can spend most of the class time presenting lessons to small groups of students drawn from the various teams who are working at the same point in the mathematics sequence. For example, the teacher might call up a decimals group, present a lesson, and then send the students back to their teams to work on problems. Then the teacher might call the fractions group, and so on. Several large evaluations of TAI have shown positive effects on math achievement in the upper-elementary grades (e.g., Slavin & Karweit, 1985; Stevens & Slavin, 1995b).

Cooperative Integrated Reading and Composition (CIRC)

A comprehensive program for teaching reading and writing in the upper elementary grades is called Cooperative Integrated Reading and Composition (CIRC) (Stevens et al., 1987). In CIRC, teachers use reading texts and reading groups, much as in traditional reading programs. However, all students are assigned to teams composed of two pairs from two different reading groups. While the teacher is working with one reading group, the paired students in the other groups are working on a series of cognitively engaging activities, including reading to one another, making predictions about how narrative stories will come out, summarizing stories to one another, writing responses to stories, and practicing spelling, decoding, and vocabulary. Students work as a total team to master main idea and other comprehension skills. During language arts periods, students engage in writing drafts, revising and editing one another's work, and preparing for publications of team books.

In most CIRC activities, students follow a sequence of teacher instruction, team practice, team pre-assessments and quizzes. That is, students do not take the quiz until their teammates have determined that they are ready. Certificates are given to teams based on the average performance of all team members on all reading and writing activities.

Research on CIRC and similar approaches has found positive effects in upper-elementary and middle school reading (Stevens & Durkin, 1992; Stevens, Madden, Slavin, & Farnish, 1987; Stevens & Slavin, 1995a, 1995b). CIRC has been adapted as the upper-elementary and middle school component of the Success for All comprehensive reform model and is currently disseminated under the name *Reading Wings* by the Success for All Foundation (see Slavin & Madden, 2009).

Peer-Assisted Learning Strategies (PALS)

Peer Assisted Learning Strategies (PALS) is a dyadic learning approach in which pairs of children take turns as teacher and learner. The children are taught simple strategies for helping each other, and are rewarded based on the learning of both members of the pair. Research on PALS in elementary and middle school math and reading has found positive effects of this approach on student achievement outcomes (e.g., Calhoon, 2005; Calhoon et al., 2006; Fuchs, Fuchs, & Karns, 2001; Fuchs, Fuchs, Kazden, & Allen, 1999; Mathes & Babyak, 2001). Positive effects of a similar program called Classwide Peer Tutoring (Greenwood, Delquadri, & Hall, 1989) have also been found, and another similar approach has been found to be effective in two Belgian studies (Van Keer & Verhaeghe, 2005, 2008).

IMPROVE

IMPROVE (Mevarech, 1985) is an Israeli mathematics program that uses cooperative learning strategies similar to those used in STAD but also emphasizes teaching of metacognitive skills and regular assessments of mastery of key concepts and re-teaching of skills missed by many students. Studies of IMPROVE have found positive effects on the mathematics achievement of elementary and middle school students in Israel (Mevarech & Kramarski, 1997; Kramarski, Mevarech, & Lieberman, 2001).

For example, Mevarech and Kramarski (1997, Study 1) evaluated IMPROVE in four Israeli junior high schools over one semester. Three seventh grade classes used IMPROVE and five served as matched controls, using the same books and objectives. The experimental classes were selected from among those taught by teachers with experience teaching IMPROVE, and matched control classes were selected as well. Students were pre- and post-tested on tests certified by the Israeli superintendent of mathematics as fair to all groups. Pre-test scores were similar across groups. On analyses of covariance with classes nested within treatments, treatment effects significantly favored the IMPROVE classes on scales assessing introduction to algebra ($d = +0.54$) as well as mathematical reasoning ($d = +0.68$), for an average effect size of $d = +0.61$. Effects were similar for low, average, and high achievers.

Informal Group Learning Methods

Jigsaw

Jigsaw was originally designed by Elliot Aronson and his colleagues (1978). In Aronson's Jigsaw method, students are assigned to six-member teams to work on academic material that has been broken down into sections. For example, a biography might be divided into early life, first accomplishments, major setbacks, later life, and impact on history. Each team member reads his or her section. Next, members of different teams who have studied the same sections meet in expert groups to discuss their sections. Then the students return to their teams and take turns teaching their teammates about their sections. Since the only way students can learn sections other than their own is to listen carefully to their teammates, they are motivated to support and show interest in one another's work.

Slavin (1994) developed a modification of Jigsaw at Johns Hopkins University and then incorporated it in the Student Team Learning program. In this method, called Jigsaw II, students work in four-or five-member team as in TGT and STAD. Instead of each student being assigned a particular section of text, all students read a common narrative, such as a book chapter, a short story, or a biography. However, each student receives a topic (such as "climate" in a unit on France) on which to become an "expert." Students with the same topics meet in expert groups to discuss them, after which they return to their teams to teach what they have learned to their teammates. Then students take individual quizzes, which result in team scores based on the improvement score system of STAD. Teams that meet pre-set standards earn certificates. Jigsaw is primarily used in social studies and other subjects where learning from text is important (Mattingly & Van Sickle, 1991).

Learning Together

David Johnson and Roger Johnson at the University of Minnesota developed the Learning Together models of cooperative learning (Johnson & Johnson, 1998). The methods they have researched involve students working on assignment sheets in four- or five-member heterogeneous groups. The groups hand in a single sheet and receive praise and rewards based on the group product. Their methods emphasize team-building activities before students begin working together and regular discussions within groups about how well they are working together. Numerous relatively brief experiments have shown positive effects of these approaches (see Johnson & Johnson, 1998).

Group Investigation

Group Investigation, developed by Shlomo Sharan and Yael Sharan (1992) at the University of Tel-Aviv, is a general classroom organization plan in which students work in small groups using cooperative inquiry, group discussion, and cooperative planning and projects. In this method, students form their own two-to-six-member groups. After choosing subtopics from a unit being studied by the entire class, the groups further break their subtopics into individual tasks and carry out the activities necessary to prepare group reports. Each group then makes a presentation or display to communicate its findings to the entire class. A study in Israel by Sharan and Shachar (1988) found positive effects of Group Investigation on achievement in language and literature.

CONCLUSION AND FUTURE DIRECTIONS

Learning environments for the 21st century must be ones in which students are actively engaged with learning tasks and with each other. Today, teachers are in competition with television, computer games, and all sorts of engaging technology, and the expectation that children will learn in a passive way, which was never very realistic, is becoming even less so. Cooperative learning offers a proven, practical means of creating exciting social and engaging classroom environments that can help students master traditional skills and knowledge as well as develop the creative and interactive skills needed in today's economy and society.

Cooperative learning has been established as a practical alternative to traditional teaching, and specific forms of cooperative learning have been proven effective in hundreds of studies throughout the world. Yet many observational studies (e.g., Antil, Jenkins, Wayne, & Vadasy, 1998) find that most use of cooperative learning is informal, and does not incorporate the group goals and individual accountability that research has found to be essential to producing positive achievement outcomes. Clearly, cooperative learning can be a powerful strategy for increasing student achievement, but fulfilling this potential depends on the provision of professional development for teachers that is focused on the forms of cooperative learning that are most likely to make a difference.

In comparison to schooling practices that are often supported by government, such as tutoring, technology use, and school restructuring, cooperative learning is relatively inexpensive and easily adopted. Yet 30 years after much of the foundational research was completed, cooperative learning remains at the edge of school policy. This does not have to remain the case, and it may be that as governments begin to support the larger concept of evidence-based reform, the strong evidence base for the forms of cooperative learning that have been found to be effective will lead to a greater focus on this set of approaches to the core of instructional practice.

ACKNOWLEDGMENTS

Portions of this chapter are adapted from Slavin (1995). It was written under funding from the Institute of Education Sciences, U.S. Department of Education. However, any opinions expressed are those of the author and do not necessarily represent Department of Education positions or policies.

REFERENCES

Antil, L. R., Jenkins, J. R., Wayne, S., & Vadasy, P. F. (1998) Cooperative learning: Prevalence, conceptualizations, and the relation between research and practice. *American Educational Research Journal, 35*(3), 419–454.

Aronson, E., Blaney, N., Stephan, C., Sikes, J., & Snapp, M. (1978). *The jigsaw classroom.* Beverly Hill, CA: Sage.

Barbato, R. (2000). Policy implications of cooperative learning on the achievement and attitudes of secondary school mathematics students. Unpublished doctoral dissertation, Fordham University, New York.

Battisch, V., Solomon, D., & Delucci, K. (1993). Interaction process and student outcomes in cooperative learning groups. *The Elementary School Journal, 94*(1), 19–32.

Bell, N., Grossen, M., & Perret-Clermont, A-N. (1985). Socio-cognitive conflict and intellectual growth. In M. Berkowitz (Ed.), *Peer conflict and psychological growth.* San Francisco: Jossey-Bass.

Calhoon, M. (2005). Effects of a peer-mediated phonological skill and reading comprehension program on reading skill acquisition for middle school students with reading disabilities. *Journal of Learning Disabilities, 38*(5), 424–433.

Calhoon, M., Otaiba, S., Greenberg, D., King, A., & Avalos, A (2006). Improving reading skills in predominately Hispanic Title I first grade classrooms: The promise of Peer-Assisted Learning Strategies. *Learning Disabilities Research and Practice, 21*(4), 261–272.

Cohen, E. G. (1986). *Designing groupwork: Strategies for the heterogeneous classroom.* New York: Teachers College Press.

Cohen, E. G. (1994). *Designing groupwork: Strategies for the heterogeneous classroom* (2nd ed.). New York: Teachers College Press.

Coleman, J. (1961). *The adolescent society.* New York: Free Press.

Damon, W. (1984). Peer education: The untapped potential. *Journal of Applied Developmental Psychology, 5,* 331–343.

Devin-Sheehan, L., Feldman, R., and Allen, V. (1976). Research on children tutoring children: A critical review. *Review of Educational Research, 46*(3), 355–385.

Fantuzzo, J. W., King, J. A., & Heller, L. R. (1992). Effects of reciprocal peer tutoring on mathematics and school adjustment: A component analysis. *Journal of Educational Psychology, 84,* 33–39.

Fantuzzo, J. W., Polite, K., & Grayson, N. (1990). An evaluation of reciprocal peer tutoring across elementary school settings. *Journal of School Psychology, 28*, 309–323.

Fantuzzo, J. W., Riggio, R. E., Connelly, S., & Dimeff, L. A. (1989). Effects of reciprocal peer tutoring on academic achievement and psychological adjustment: A component analysis. *Journal of Educational Psychology, 81*, 173–177.

Fuchs, L., Fuchs, D., & Karns, K. (2001). Enhancing kindergarteners' mathematical development: Effects of peer-assisted learning strategies. *Elementary School Journal, 101*(5), 495–510.

Fuchs, L. S., Fuchs, D., Kazden, S., & Allen, S. (1999). Effects of peer-assisted learning strategies in reading with and without training in elaborated help giving. *The Elementary School Journal, 99*(3), 201–221.

Greenwood, C. R., Delquadri, J. C., & Hall, R. V. (1989). Longitudinal effects of classwide peer tutoring. *Journal of Educational Psychology, 81*, 371–383.

Johnson, D. W., & Johnson, R. T. (1998). *Learning together and alone: Cooperative, competitive, and individualistic learning* (5th ed.). Boston: Allyn & Bacon.

Johnson, D. W., & Johnson, R. T. (1999). *Learning together and alone* (6th ed.). Englewood Cliffs, NJ: Prentice-Hall.

Kramarski, B., Mevarech, Z.R., & Lieberman, A. (2001). Effects of multilevel versus unilevel metacognitive training on mathematical reasoning. *Journal of Educational Research, 54*(5), 292–300.

Mathes, P. G., & Babyak, A. E. (2001). The effects of peer-assisted literacy strategies for first-grade readers with and without additional mini-skills lessons. *Learning Disabilities Research & Practice, 16*(1), 28–44.

Mattingly, R. M., & Van Sickle, R. L. (1991). Cooperative learning and achievement in social studies: Jigsaw II. *Social Education, 55*(6), 392–395.

Meloth, M. S., & Deering, P. D. (1992). The effects of two cooperative conditions on peer group discussions, reading comprehension, and metacognition. *Contemporary Educational Psychology, 17*, 175–193.

Mevarech, Z. R. (1985). The effects of cooperative mastery learning strategies on mathematics achievement. *Journal of Educational Research, 78*, 372–377.

Mevarech, Z. R., & Kramarski, B. (1997). IMPROVE: A multidimensional method for teaching mathematics in heterogeneous classrooms. *American Educational Research Journal, 34*(2), 365–394.

O'Donnell, A. M. (1996). The effects of explicit incentives on scripted and unscripted cooperation. *Journal of Educational Psychology, 88*(1), 74–86.

O'Donnell, A. M. (2000). Interactive effects of prior knowledge and material format on cooperative teaching. *Journal of Experimental Education, 68*(2), 101–108.

O'Donnell, A.M., & Dansereau, D.F. (1992). Scripted cooperation in student dyads: A method for analyzing and enhancing academic learning and performance. In R. Hertz-Lazarowitz, & N. Miller (Eds.), *Interaction in cooperative groups: The theoretical anatomy of group learning* (pp. 120–144). New York: Cambridge University Press.

Palincsar, A. S., Brown, A. L., & Martin, S. M. (1987). Peer interaction in reading comprehension instruction. *Educational Psychologist, 22*, 231–253.

Piaget, J. (1926). *The language and thought of the child.* New York: Harcourt Brace.

Puma, M. J., Jones, C. C., Rock, D., & Fernandez, R. (1993). *Prospects: The congressionally mandated study of educational growth and opportunity. Interim Report.* Bethesda, MD: Abt Associates.

Reid, J. (1992). *The effects of cooperative learning with intergroup competition on the math achievement of seventh grade students.* (ERIC Document Reproduction Service No. ED355106.)

Rohrbeck, C. A., Ginsburg-Block, M. D., Fantuzzo, J. W., & Miller, T. R. (2003). Peer-assisted learning interventions with elementary school students: A meta-analytic review. *Journal of Educational Psychology, 94*(20), 240–257.

Rosenshine, B., & Meister, C. (1994). Reciprocal teaching: A review of research. *Review of Educational Research, 64*, 4788–5306.

Sharan, S., & Shachar, C. (1988). *Language and learning in the cooperative classroom.* New York: Springer-Verlag.

Sharan, Y., & Sharan, S. (1992). *Expanding cooperative learning through group investigation.* New York: Teachers College Press.

Slavin, R. E. (1983). When does cooperative learning increase student achievement? *Psychological Bulletin, 94*, 429–445.

Slavin, R. E. (1994). *Using student team learning* (2nd ed.). Baltimore, MD: Johns Hopkins University, Center for Social Organization of Schools.

Slavin, R.E. (1995). *Cooperative learning: Theory, research, and practice* (2nd ed.). Boston: Allyn & Bacon.

Slavin, R.E. (2009). Cooperative learning. In G. McCulloch & D. Crook (Eds.) *International encyclopedia of education.* Abingdon: Routledge.

Slavin, R. E., Cheung, A., Groff, C., & Lake, C. (2008). Effective reading programs for middle and high schools: A best-evidence synthesis. *Reading Research Quarterly, 4*(3), 290–322.

Slavin, R. E., & Karweit, N. (1984). Mastery learning and student teams: A factorial experiment in urban general mathematics classes. *American Educational Research Journal, 21*, 725–736.

Slavin, R. E., & Karweit, N. (1985). Effects of whole-class and ability group instruction on math achievement. *American Educational Research Journal, 22*, 351–367.

Slavin, R. E., & Lake, C. (2008). Effective programs in elementary mathematics: A best-evidence synthesis. *Review of Educational Research, 78*(3), 427–515.

Slavin, R. E., Lake, C., Chambers, B., Cheung, A., & Davis, S. (2009a). Effective reading programs for the elementary grades: A best-evidence synthesis. *Review of Educational Research. 79*(4), 1391–1465.

Slavin, R.E., Lake, C., & Groff, C. (2009b). Effective programs in middle and high school mathematics: A best-evidence synthesis. *Review of Educational Research, 79*(2), 839–911.

Slavin, R. E., Leavey, M. B., & Madden N. A. (1986). *Team accelerated instruction mathematics*. Watertown, MA: Mastery Education Corporation.

Slavin, R. E., Madden, N. A., Chambers, B., & Haxby, B. (Eds.). (2009). *Two million children: Success for All*. Thousand Oaks, CA: Corwin.

Stevens, R. J., & Durkin, S. (1992). *Using student team reading and student team writing in middle schools: Two evaluations*. Baltimore, MD: Johns Hopkins University, Center for Research on Effective Schooling for Disadvantaged Students, Report No. 36.

Stevens, R. J., Madden, N. A., Slavin, R. E., & Farnish, A. M. (1987). Cooperative integrated reading and composition: Two field experiments. *Reading Research Quarterly, 22*, 433–454.

Stevens, R. J., & Slavin, R. E. (1995a). Effects of a cooperative learning approach in reading and writing on handicapped and nonhandicapped students' achievement, attitudes, and metacognition in reading and writing. *Elementary School Journal, 95*, 241–262.

Stevens, R. J., & Slavin, R. E. (1995b). The cooperative elementary school: Effect on student achievement and social relations. *American Educational Research Journal, 32*, 321–351.

Van Keer, H., & Verhaeghe, J. (2005). Comparing two teacher development programs for innovating reading comprehension instruction with regard to teachers' experiences and student outcomes. *Teaching and Teacher Education, 21*, 543–562.

Van Keer, H., & Verhaeghe, J. (2008). Strategic reading in peer tutoring dyads in second and fifth-grade classrooms. Unpublished report. Ghent University, Belgium.

Vygotsky, L. S. (1978). *Mind in society* (M. Cole, V. John-Steiner, S. Scribner, & E. Souberman, Eds.). Cambridge, MA: Harvard University Press.

Webb, N. (1985). Student interaction and learning in small groups: A research summary. In R. Slavin, S. Sharan, S. Kagan, R. Hertz-Lazarowitz, C. Webb, and R. Schmuc (Eds.) *Learning to cooperate, cooperating to learn*. New York: Plenum.

Webb, N. M. (2008). Learning in small groups. In T. L. Good (Ed.), *21st Century education: A reference handbook* (pp. 203–211). Los Angeles: Sage.

Wittrock, M. C. (1986). Students' thought processes. In M. C. Wittrock (Ed.), *Handbook of research on teaching* (3rd ed.). New York: Macmillan.

18

INSTRUCTION BASED ON INQUIRY
Sofie M. M. Loyens and Remy M. J. P. Rikers

Every day we struggle to understand the reality we live in. Sometimes we are able to unravel the mechanisms behind the things that happen around us, but more often we have to rely on parents, teachers or peers to reach a better understanding. Over many centuries our educational system has developed into a system in which the teacher plays a pivotal role. The teacher is the source of information and the student is the receiver. In this exchange between student and teacher, there has always been a strong emphasis on the reproduction of knowledge. An early study by Stevens (1912) demonstrated that two-thirds of classroom questions required students to accurately recite textbook information. Sixty years later, Gall's (1970) research still showed that 60% of the questions asked in the classroom required factual answers.

Even though teachers have always recognized the importance of actively involving students by asking them probing questions, researchers have observed that it was not until the 1960s that the teachers' role gradually changed (e.g., Bransford, Franks, Vye, & Sherwood, 1989). Instead of providing students with the question and the answer, teachers created more room for students to formulate and explore their answers to the posed question. This approach crystallized into several teaching strategies that place emphasis on the learner as an active agent in his or her learning process instead of the learner as a passive receiver of information. These instructional formats have been labeled *student-centered* and employ classroom practices such as observations, generating questions, discovering gaps in one's knowledge base, and studying resources to try to overcome these gaps. Often they are also labeled as *inquiry* (or *enquiry* in British English) *based instruction.*

Besides being a teaching approach, inquiry also refers to the process of knowledge building within the learner or, in other words, the process of doing scientific investigations (Justice, Rice, Roy, Hudspith, & Jenkins, 2009; Olsen & Loucks-Horsley, 2000; Sandoval, 2005). Anderson (2007) has therefore made the distinction between *inquiry learning*, which refers to engagement in the process of inquiry, and *inquiry teaching*, which comprises a whole spectrum of instructional techniques that make, to a varying degree, use of inquiry practices such as generating questions and formulating and evaluating explanations. This chapter will focus on the process of inquiry from a pedagogical perspective and will hence treat inquiry as a method to structure activities in the classroom (Sandoval, 2005). Inquiry-based learning, problem-based learning, project-based learning, and case-based learning are discussed.

It has been argued that inquiry is inherent to scientific research: "Beginning in the 17th century, when Galileo rolled balls down ramps, scientific research has been based on inquiry; experimental investigations that attempt to answer questions about the natural world" (Pine et al., 2006, p. 468). Generally stated, inquiry is thus based on a scientific investigation through classroom practices such as posing questions and it is aimed at knowledge acquisition and development (e.g., Blanchard, Southerland, & Granger, 2008). Instruction based on inquiry is most strongly advocated in science education by, for example, the National Research Council (NRC, 2000) and the American Association for the Advancement of Science (AAAS, 1993). Being a student-centered approach, it also originated as a reaction to the traditional classroom, which was believed to be too occupied with the teaching of facts (Schwab, 1962).

The prominent role given to inquiry at the policy level was prompted because it was believed to promote a deeper understanding of the subject matter as well as to facilitate transfer (i.e., the application of knowledge outside the classroom, Blanchard et al., 2008). In addition, it is argued that with inquiry, students learn the ins and outs of scientific processes and they reach an understanding of how these processes are related to each other (Singer, Marx, Krajcik, & Clay-Chambers, 2000). Whether these claims can be supported by research findings will be discussed later in this chapter. First, a brief historical overview is given on student-centered learning, followed by a description of the constructivist view of learning, which is often associated with student-centered learning environments.

HISTORICAL PERSPECTIVE ON STUDENT-CENTERED INSTRUCTION

Educational methods that try to involve learners in their own learning processes can be found in the early history of didactics. The ancient Greeks used the *dialogos*, the method of the dialogue, in their education. In essence, a teacher proposes a problem and helps the learner solving this problem by asking questions. This method can be found in the work of Plato (427–347 BC) where he describes how Socrates helps a slave boy solve Pythagoras' theorem (Plato, 1949). It was based on the assumption that the learner possessed all the necessary knowledge, which just had to be activated. Further, the works of Socrates, Plato, and Aristotle (ranging from 470–320 BC) all include ideas about epistemology, i.e., the branch of philosophy that studies the nature and scope of knowledge.

The epistemology of later philosophers such as Immanuel Kant (late 18th to early 19th centuries) also stresses the role of the learner. Kant mentions the faculty of knowledge that people have, which refers to the influence of people's own experiences in making sense of the environment around them. Therefore, he argues: "But though all our knowledge begins with experience, it does not follow that it all arises out of experience" (Kant, 1959, p. 25). Some form of mental activity is required from the one who experiences: People need to generate or construct knowledge on the basis of their individual experiences.

In the late 19th century, the American philosopher and educator John Dewey (1859–1952) reacted against passive teaching in a rote manner, which was common practice in the late 19th to early 20th centuries. He believed that the child is an active learner who learns best by doing. He argued for constructive activities in the classroom that were meaningful and interesting for children (i.e., connecting with the child's social environment). Education should not be about becoming narrowly educated in academic topics; it should be pragmatic and should teach children how to think and adapt to a world outside (Dewey, 1902, 1929).

In sum, ascribing an active role to the learner is not a new idea in education. However, in recent years, it has gained renewed attention in educational research because of the increased consideration of a learning view that starts from the idea that knowledge and understanding are actively constructed by the learner: *constructivism* (Birenbaum, 2003; Eberlein et al., 2008; Harris & Alexander, 1998; Tobias & Duffy, 2009).

THE LEARNING VIEW RELATED TO INQUIRY: CONSTRUCTIVISM

Constructivist theories are concerned with how people make sense of situations or, more generally, with how people create meaning and construct knowledge out of experiences. A clear, unambiguous definition of constructivism is hard to find, but many writings in educational psychology (e.g., Mayer, 1996; Parsons, Lewis Hinson, & Sardo-Brown, 2001; Woolfolk, 2004) explain constructivism as a response to cognitivism, or more broadly, information processing theories. Cognitivism is a theoretical approach to understand the mind. This view argues that the teacher disseminates knowledge, which students absorb. The aim of instruction, according to the cognitivists, is an increase in knowledge in students' memory systems. Constructivism reacted against the traditional classroom that focused on the transmission of knowledge and a classroom in which teachers were the conveyors of meaning. Transferring knowledge from a knowledgeable person to someone who lacks specific knowledge, does not work according to a constructivist view of learning, since "wisdom cannot be told" (Bransford et al., 1989, p. 470). When constructivism is explained in terms of a reaction against cognitivism, it is seen as a theory of learning, concentrating on the question "How do learners acquire knowledge?" Although most cognitive views of learning agree with the concept of active learners, constructivism focuses more on learners constructing their own understanding. In this respect, constructivism could also be considered a rising paradigm in the field of cognitive psychology instead of a reaction against it (Duffy, 2009; Gijbels & Loyens, 2009; Sinatra & Mason, 2007).

Instruction based on inquiry is often related to constructivist views on learning because of the emphasis on classroom practices that involve the active participation of the learner as well as a prominent role for questions and issues generated by the learner. However, caution is needed when instruction is labeled constructivist, because constructivism is situated on the *prescriptive* level in that case. Constructivism as a learning theory, on the other hand, is situated on the *descriptive* level (Mayer, 2009; Renkl, 2009). In other words, a theory of learning/knowing is then confused with a theory of pedagogy (Eggen & Kauchak, 2006). The question that arises in this respect is: What makes classroom practices constructivist? Bridging the gap between educational theory and practice is a challenge for all learning theories (Bednar, Cunningham, Duffy, & Perry, 1992; De Corte, 2000; Kennedy, 1997), but the many faces of constructivism have made it particularly difficult to narrow this gap.

Some educators believe that knowledge construction can occur, irrespective of instructional methods. By listening to a lecture, one can be involved in active attempts to construct new knowledge (Bransford, Brown, & Cocking, 2000). Von Glasersfeld (1993) argued that all mental activity is constructive because that is the way the mind operates. Even when learners are engaged in rote learning, they are still constructing knowledge. Therefore, all teaching can be considered constructivist (Windschitl, 2002). According to others, specific constructivist operationalizations can be identified in education and they are typically student-centered.

As mentioned, instructional formats based on inquiry are examples of student-centered approaches to teaching. It is important to note that instruction based on inquiry is not *by definition* constructivist. It is, however, often related to and discussed within this framework and it does carry several constructivist elements in it.

Constructivist Elements in Inquiry-Based Instruction

Although constructivism is an ill-defined concept with many flavors and colors and although some researchers view it differently (e.g., Colliver, 2002), constructivist views on learning share some principles that can foster learning (e.g., Driscoll, 2005; Marshall, 1992; Slavin, 2006).

First, the emphasis lies on the construction of knowledge, which forms the essence of constructivist views on learning. In this process, the learner tries to integrate new information with prior knowledge (Blumenfeld, 1992). Second, constructivists are of the opinion, although to a varying degree, that one can learn a lot from fellow-students and that learning involves social negotiation (Savery & Duffy, 2001; Scardamalia & Bereiter, 1991). Communication of ideas about subject matter is believed to be facilitated by working together with fellow-students, because of similar levels of understanding among them. Further, student discussions can serve as a gauge of prior knowledge and understanding (Slavin, 2006). Third, goal setting, plan making, and monitoring one's learning process (i.e., self-regulated learning), are important foci of constructivist learning views. Self-regulated learning yields benefits for one's learning (e.g., Boekaerts, 1999; Winne, 1995). Fourth, constructivist learning approaches use meaningful tasks in education to make learning situations similar to future professional situations (Loyens, Rikers, & Schmidt, 2007).

These four elements—prior knowledge, social negotiation, self-regulation, and meaningful tasks—can be found in many instructional methods based on inquiry as discussed next. The challenge for constructivist and, in fact, for all views on learning is to apply the elements they describe in educational practice. A constructivist view brings the students, their interests, and previous experiences and knowledge to the fore, which has consequences for instruction.

INSTRUCTIONAL METHODS BASED ON INQUIRY

As mentioned earlier, inquiry comprises a broad range of educational approaches and formats that are student-centered as opposed to teacher-centered. Within these student-centered, inquiry approaches to teaching, we can identify considerable differences. According to Barrows (1986), three important variables can vary in different student-centered approaches: (1) the design and format of the problem, project or case; (2) the degree to which learning is teacher-centered or learner-centered; and (3) the sequence in which problems or tasks are offered and information is acquired. Based on these three dimensions, we will compare inquiry-based learning (IBL), problem-based learning (PBL), project-based learning (PjBL), and case-based learning (CBL).

Inquiry-Based Learning (IBL)

In IBL, learning is propelled by the process of inquiry, which allows students to become familiar with particular subject matter that is introduced in the presented situation, but also to learn more about the inquiry process itself. Students are confronted with or generate themselves a question or puzzling situation that is open-ended to allow several responses or solutions (Savery, 2006). An example of a question in IBL is: In what ways does the moon's shape and position in the sky change over the course of a month (Bell, Smetana, & Binns, 2005, p. 31)? The core elements of IBL have been described by the NRC (2000) and consist of engaging in scientifically oriented questions, seeking evidence to find answers to these questions, developing explanations/answers to the questions that were posed, evaluating these explanations as well as the probability of alternative explanations, and communicating and clarifying their own conclusions. In the example of the moon shapes, students can observe the moon during a month (Bell et al., 2005). Hence, questioning, critical thinking (i.e., students are forced to think about the data they have collected and try to understand their implications), problem-solving, and communication are important activities within IBL.

Windschitl, Thompson, and Braaten (2008) have proposed a cycle with the key intellectual activities in which students are engaged in IBL. The cycle starts with learners making an inventory of what is known and what they would like to know about the situation or phenomenon at hand. Next, students generate testable hypotheses for which they will seek evidence. In seeking evidence, many roads can lead to Rome. Finally, students construct an argument, which describes potential explanations and takes into account the evidence found. If needed, the cycle can be repeated, but eventually students will reach the goal of IBL: "to develop defensible explanations of the way the natural world works" (Windschitl et al., 2008, p. 955). A student can take part in the IBL process as a group member, but can also individually be involved in the process, supported by fellow-students (Kahn & O'Rourke, 2005).

Whether instruction is inquiry-based depends on whether it starts with a research question that students need to investigate and answer by means of data analysis. This question can be generated by the students themselves (i.e., the most authentic form of inquiry as explained in the next paragraph), but an instructional approach can still be inquiry-based when research questions and data are already available to the students. In that case, it is essential that students analyze the data themselves and construct their own arguments based on their analyses. Solely gathering information by searching literature resources or the internet is not considered IBL (Bell et al., 2005).

The instructor's role is primarily that of a facilitator of the inquiry process. Students can ask the instructor questions throughout the cycle. However, the role of the instructor varies depending on the amount of scaffolding that is needed and provided to the students. For example, with younger learners, the instructor has an important role in defining the boundaries of what will be studied. The instructor will choose a key scientific phenomenon that can be explored, taking into account students' interest. Besides being central to science, this phenomenon needs to contain comprehensible underpinnings (Windschitl et al., 2008). Learners of this age are not yet ready to independently generate scientific questions and collect data. Ideally, the instructor helps students to progress to more autonomy in the inquiry process (Bell et al., 2005). Differences in the amount of guidance have led to the distinction of three subtypes of IBL: (a) *structured inquiry* in which the question is given and the procedure to investigate is prescribed; (b) *guided inquiry* in which the question is presented, but students have to work out for themselves a procedure to answer the question; and (c) *open inquiry*, also referred to as *authentic inquiry*, in which the students also formulate topic-related questions themselves, besides coming up with possible procedures. The latter is the kind of research scientists are involved in (Bell et al., 2005; Chinn & Malhorta, 2002; Colburn, 2000).

Problem-Based Learning (PBL)

In PBL, small groups of 10–12 students learn in the context of meaningful problems that describe observable phenomena or events (Barrows, 1996). It was first developed in medical education to show medical students the relevance of the subject matter by putting it in a realistic context (Barrows & Tamblyn, 1980; Schmidt, 1983). Therefore, the problems used in PBL often originate from professional practice. However, in other cases, PBL problems tackle problems or events typical for a particular domain of study (Barrows, 1996; Norman & Schmidt, 1992; Schmidt, Loyens, Van Gog, & Paas, 2007). In either case, the problems need to be understood in terms of their underlying theoretical explanations. Consider the following example of a problem from an educational psychology course (Loyens, Kirschner, & Paas, 2010):

> You work as a school psychologist and your task is to diagnose children's learning disorders, consult parents, and give them advice about proposed possible treatments. On a Monday morning, you see Harry (7 years old) in your office. Harry seems an intelligent and spontaneous child. Harry's teacher told you that Harry has no trouble understanding things. He is good at mathematics and does not seem to have any problems in social contacts, either at school or at home. An eye doctor has determined that Harry's eyes are ok. Harry has great difficulty with learning to read. He often confuses the letters b and d, reverses words, and even writes some words backwards. The teacher told you that Harry has some trouble with his speech as well, but she could not give any specific examples.

After reading the problem, students discuss possible explanations for the problem. With respect to the problem example, students might come up with the diagnosis of dyslexia and subsequently will try to explain the different elements in the problem (e.g., language understanding, making contact, or findings of an eye doctor) in the light of this diagnosis. They will talk about Harry's possible problem(s), the signs and symptoms, and, most importantly, how he can be treated, since this was the school psychologist's task. It is important to note in this respect that PBL students discuss the problem *before* they have received any other curriculum input. The initial discussion of the problem is meant to evaluate one's prior knowledge about the topic (e.g., What do I know about dyslexia?, Are alternative explanations possible for Harry's symptoms?), as well as to discover one's knowledge gaps (e.g., How can dyslexia be treated?).

This awareness of one's knowledge gaps is believed to trigger interest in the subject matter that will motivate students to find out the state of affairs with respect to dyslexia. The issues that are still unclear after the initial discussion of the problem are formulated as questions, so-called learning issues (e.g., "What is dyslexia?" and "What are possible treatments for dyslexia?"). The self-generation of learning issues is believed to create a perception of autonomy in students (e.g., Deci & Ryan, 2008), through which they experience agency. The learning issues direct students' self-directed learning activities during the period of self-study in-between tutorial meetings. Students' self-study activities consist of selecting relevant literature resources from such sources as the library, the electronic learning environment, or Internet, and studying them. The fact that students have a certain degree of freedom in selecting and studying the literature resources adds to the experience of autonomy and agency as well. During the next tutorial meeting, students share their findings with each other and critically evaluate the answers to the learning issues (Barrows, 1996; Hmelo-Silver, 2004; Schmidt, 1983). Tutorial meetings last for two or three hours and are held once or twice a week (Schmidt, Van der Molen, Te Winkel, & Wijnen, 2009).

Tutorial meetings in PBL are guided by a tutor who stimulates the discussion, provides students (if necessary) with just-in-time content information, evaluates the progress, and monitors the extent to which each group member contributes to the group's work (Schmidt et al., 2007). A tutor can be an instructor or a senior student, and guides both the PBL process and students' learning (Hmelo-Silver & Barrows, 2006).

Besides via the tutor, guidance is also provided in PBL through the problems and the sequence in which they are presented to the students. The problem example about dyslexia is presented to first-year psychology students, after they have studied the topic of learning to read. In this way it can build on students' prior knowledge, since they first learned the normal development of learning to read before tackling specific problems in the reading process (Loyens et al., 2010).

Not surprisingly, also within PBL, different formats can be distinguished. Unlike IBL, those formats do not differ in the amount of guidance that is offered, but in the aimed outcome of PBL. Based on the outcome, three different types of PBL can be distinguished: a type that stresses the construction of flexible knowledge bases (Type 1); a type that emphasizes the development of inquiry skills (Type 2); and a type that perceives PBL primarily as a tool for 'learning how to learn' (Type 3; Schmidt et al., 2009). The Type 1 PBL accounts for the most PBL curricula and is most often researched.

Project-Based Learning (PjBL)

In Project-Based Learning or Project-Centered Learning (often also abbreviated to PBL, but to avoid confusion with problem-based learning, PjBL is used), the learning process is organized around projects, which drive students' activities (Blumenfeld et al., 1991). Students learn central concepts and principles of a discipline through the projects. Therefore, projects are central in PjBL or, in other words, "projects *are* the curriculum" (Thomas, 2000, p. 3). In general, students have a significant voice in selecting the content areas and nature of the projects they do, although not necessarily. In any case, students have a significant degree of control of the project they will work on and what they will do in the project. The projects are hence student-driven and, similar to PBL, try to create agency within learners. Specific end products need to be reached and those are clearly defined, while the processes to get to the end product can vary. The end products (e.g., a computer animation, thesis, website, presentation, report) serve as the basis for discussion, feedback, and revision (Blumenfeld et al., 1991; David, 2008; Helle, Tynjälä, & Olkinuora, 2006; Tal, Krajcik, & Blumenfeld, 2006). They are believed to reflect a learner's knowledge in information search, knowledge related to the project's topic, and metacognitive knowledge (i.e., knowledge about one's own cognition, Grant & Branch, 2005). A project can be a problem to solve (e.g., How can we reduce the pollution in the schoolyard pond?), a phenomenon to investigate (e.g., Why do you stay on your skateboard?), a model to design (e.g., Create a scale model of an ideal high school) or a decision to make (e.g., Should the school board vote to build a new school?; Yetkiner, Anderoglu, & Capraro, 2008). Contextualization is crucial in this respect; projects are designed to be realistic and meaningful for students (Helle et al., 2006; Thomas, 2000). Students engage in different activities while working on the project such as problem-solving, design, decision making, argumentation, using and weighing different pieces of knowledge, explanation, investigation, and modeling (Krajcik, McNeill, & Reiser, 2007; Thomas, 2000). Students can work individually or together and projects last for considerable periods of time (Helle et al., 2006; Thomas, 2000).

The role of the instructor consists of facilitating the project. That is, the instructor helps with framing and structuring the projects, monitors the development of the end product, and assesses what students have learned (David, 2008; Helle et al., 2006).

Case-Based Learning (CBL)

CBL is a form of collaborative learning where learners are presented with a case. For example, in a teacher education course, students can be presented with a case on classroom management in which the teacher wants to change the arrangement of children's desks because two boys are constantly talking and interrupting the class instruction. However, one of the two boys seems to have few friends, and is experiencing problems adjusting to school and the boy next to him seems to be the only one he is close with (Choi & Lee, 2009, p. 104). Cases are similar to problems in PBL. However, in Barrows's terms (1986), the sequence of the problem and gathered information is different. In PBL, the problem is the starting point. In CBL, students need to prepare in advance for the group session and can ask questions during the session, when the case is discussed under the guidance of a facilitator (Srinivasan, Wilkes, Stevenson, Nguyen, & Slavin, 2007; Williams, 2005). Therefore, CBL can be considered a special form of PBL.

Differences between IBL, PBL, PjBL, and CBL

All the instructional formats just described carry the constructivist elements that were mentioned earlier. They all are based on the idea that students need to be actively engaged in the subject matter by investigations and discussions. Therefore, students construct knowledge in an active way. Although IBL and PjBL can also be carried out individually, all formats usually imply working together with fellow-students. Next, all methods require student control and students taking responsibility for their learning process. Students need to plan activities, monitor progress, and evaluate at regular times. Finally, all inquiry-based instructions work with meaningful tasks, whether they are questions, problems, projects or cases. Learning activities are therefore put in a realistic context for students.

Despite this common ground, the methods do differ from each other on one or multiple aspects. The difference between IBL on the one hand, and PBL and CBL on the other, lies in the role of the teacher. In PBL and CBL, the teacher's (i.e., tutor's) task is to facilitate the group discussion. While this is also true for IBL, here the teacher also acts as the expert, since s/he provides information to the students based on their questions. In PBL and CBL, students have to rely more on their own resources to find information about the problem (Savery, 2006). In addition, the range of learning activities is usually more diverse in IBL and PjBL compared to PBL and CBL. For example, students may be asked to reflect on a question or puzzling situation or identify research questions, but can also be asked to interview persons or visit specific locations related to task (Feletti, 1993). Besides more diverse learning activities, IBL and PjBL also have more diverse end products compared to PBL and CBL. Depending on the amount of guidance given, IBL and PjBL can be more student-centered compared to PBL and CBL, since on some occasions, students come up with their own questions and projects. As noted, the difference between PBL and CBL lies in the moment the discussion of the problem or case takes place. In PBL, this is before any other curriculum input, while in CBL, students need to be prepared when they come to the group session (Srinivasan et al., 2007; Williams, 2005).

A Note: Discovery Learning

An instructional format that is not discussed in this chapter is *discovery learning*. Discovery learning, advocated by Bruner (1961), can be seen as a very open form of inquiry-based instruction. It is a learning format in which students work on examples presented by the teacher, in order to discover the relations among the examples and to formulate general principles that apply to them. These inductive reasoning activities are said to trigger students' curiosity and make students persistent to find answers. In addition, the conceptions learned through discovery learning were believed to be better remembered (Bruner, 1961). However, it has been argued that inquiry-learning and discovery should not be lumped together, since inquiry implies more activities than solely discovery (Edelson, Gordin, & Pea, 1999). In addition, inquiry implies more guidance compared to pure discovery learning. Although more guided forms of discovery exist as well, discovery in its pure form should be considered different from inquiry-based instruction.

Apples and Oranges

As a final note in this section, it is important to acknowledge that, apart from the fact that there are several forms of student-centered learning using different labels (i.e., IBL, PBL, PjBL, and CBL) differences may also exist *within* these separate approaches. Different types of IBL and PBL were already indicated. Differences within each approach exist primarily in terms of implementation and focused elements (Lloyd-Jones, Margetson, & Bligh, 1998). This can be ascribed to various reasons such as modifications because of the target group (e.g., K-12 versus higher education), but also because of the so-called *coverage virus*; the fear of teachers that subject-matter is insufficiently covered, leading to the incorporation of more teacher-centered practices and less student autonomy (Moust, van Berkel, & Schmidt, 2005). In addition, hybrid forms have emerged throughout the years, combining student-centered with teacher-led formats (e.g., Kwan, 2008).

Whatever the method used, conceptual clarity and a clear description of the elements constituting a particular method are indispensable. For example, in the PBL context, Lloyd-Jones and colleagues (1998, p. 494) argued: "For the purposes of research, evaluation and educational development the brevity of the 'PBL' label is an inadequate description." Fair comparisons with traditional, teacher-centered methods can only follow out of careful descriptions and explanations of the method under study. Even with clear descriptions, examining the effectiveness of multifaceted approaches is challenging

(Cobb, Confrey, diSessa, Lehrer, & Schauble, 2003). Some researchers have even considered it impossible to compare inquiry methods with direct instruction, as reflected in this quote from Jonassen (2009, p. 29):

> I am not able to identify "high-quality research studies comparing the effectiveness of inquiry methods and direct instruction" because it probably does not exist and cannot exist. Researchers examining the effectiveness of direct instruction begin with fundamentally different assumptions, evoke significantly different theory bases, and use different research methods than researchers examining informal or inquiry learning. Therefore the questions they ask, the learning outcomes they seek and the research tools and methods they use are also quite different. We cannot compare apples with oranges. Each relies on intellectual biases that would leave the other at a disadvantage were we to compare results.

Although direct comparisons between inquiry-based instruction and direct instruction might not always be possible or reported in the research literature, the next section gives an overview of empirical studies on the different forms of inquiry-based instruction. Nevertheless, we do reckon with the caveats just mentioned.

A REVIEW OF THE RESEARCH OF INSTRUCTION BASED ON INQUIRY

Generally, research on instructional methods based on inquiry can be divided into three categories. First, several studies describe students' and teacher' perceptions of a specific method and their experiences with working with it. Although valuable for those who plan to implement a specific method, this line of research is mainly exploratory and descriptive. Therefore, these studies do not give a decisive answer about the effectiveness of the method under investigation. However, a great deal of studies conducted in the field of inquiry-based instruction could be categorized here (Helle et al., 2006; Park Rogers & Abell, 2008).

A second line of research investigates specific elements of an inquiry-based method of instruction. For example, one might manipulate the size of the tutorial group in PBL in an experimental study to discover the ideal group size. Similarly, one can vary end products in PjBL to determine whether these variations lead to different ways of dealing with the project. In a way, this second line of studies searches for improvements in the existing methods by scrutinizing their constituting elements. Here, effectiveness should be considered in the light of the specific element under investigation, not in terms of the method as a whole.

Finally, the third line of research investigates the effectiveness of an instructional method as a whole. Often, a comparative approach is used, contrasting a student-centered format with a control group or investigating changes before and after a curriculum shift. Certainly, great disparities of outcome variables exist, since one can argue about the question: "What makes an instructional method effective?" Usually, effectiveness is measured in terms of knowledge (i.e., student performance on knowledge tests), skills/competencies, and/or affective variables such as motivation. Effects on student satisfaction should be more considered as an example of the first line of research. The research review presented in this chapter is focused on this third line of research. Thus, for articles in which both self-reported ratings and non-self-reported learning outcomes were investigated, only the findings that were not based on self-report measures were included, since the self-report data can be seen as an instance of the first line of research. Further, we focused on knowledge and skills in this review, since those are often considered most revealing in terms of effectiveness. However, we do acknowledge that effects on affective variables can be insightful as well.

In our search for research articles investigating inquiry methods, we employed several criteria. First, investigation of the instructional method needed to be the focus of the article. Studies investigating variables solely *within* an inquiry-based environment, but not dealing with the learning environment in itself were not included. Second, we limited our search to studies that have been published during the past five years (i.e. 2005–2010). Besides the fact that our intent was to give a state-of-the-art review, this decision was also due to the publication of several meta-analyses and review articles before or around that time.

For example, a meta-analysis of experimental and quasi-experimental US research studies on teaching strategies published between 1980 and 2004, included inquiry strategies as one of the teaching strategies. They reported an average effect size of .65 of inquiry strategies on student achievement (Schroeder, Scott, Tolson, Huang, & Lee, 2007).

For PBL, comprehensive reviews by Dochy, Segers, Van den Bossche, and Gijbels (2003), Hmelo-Silver (2004), and Gijbels, Dochy, Van den Bossche, and Segers (2005) were published. Strobel and Van Barneveld (2009, p. 53) summarized the findings of all meta-analyses on PBL effects conducted before 2005 in two trends:

> The first general tendency of noted in the research was that traditional learning approaches tended to produce better outcomes on assessment of basic science knowledge but, according to Albanese and Mitchell (1993), not always. A second trend noted was that a PBL approach tended to produce better outcomes for clinical knowledge and skills.

For PjBL, a qualitative review of studies can be found in the article of Helle and colleagues (2006). For CBL, Williams (2005) gave a literature overview. It was concluded that students enjoyed their CBL experience, but a shortcoming of the research in this area is the limited set of studies that examine actual changes in students' learning and practice.

Several literature searches in PsycINFO, ERIC, and MEDLINE were carried out using the terms inquiry, inquiry-based, problem-based, project-based, and case-based (with and without hyphen). Only empirical and review articles in peer-reviewed journals and edited books were considered. Dissertations as well as conference papers were excluded from examination.

Research on the Effects of IBL

Casotti, Rieser-Danner, and Knabb (2008) compared undergraduate students' performance on show and tell presentations before and after a curriculum shift towards IBL. These presentations were part of the physiology curriculum's assessment. Students' performance on three learning outcomes was measured: understanding of physiological concepts, understanding of the scientific approach, and creative and critical thinking. Significant changes were found for the understanding of the scientific approach and creative and critical thinking. Students' scores for the understanding of physiological concepts approached significance ($p < .06$).

A study, in which the effects of IBL were also measured in an undergraduate course, was performed by Lewis and Lewis (2008). Students of chemistry classes taught with IBL were compared to students in classes that received traditional, lecture-based instruction. The analyses span three years of implementation in a college general chemistry course. They found that IBL was associated with improved performance on the American Chemistry Society exam given at the end of the semester, regardless of student SAT sub-scores or class SAT average. In addition, the effects of IBL in reducing the achievement gap by SAT sub-scores were investigated as well. No significant differences were found in this respect.

Another study used a randomized controlled approach to establish the effects of IBL among 14–16-year-old students. Students were randomly assigned to either the IBL group or the so-called commonplace teaching group. Both groups were taught based on the same learning goals by the same teacher. Students' scores on knowledge, reasoning through the application of models, and construction and critique of scientific explanations were measured. Pre- and post-tests were administered immediately before and after the instruction. Students in the IBL group outperformed the students in the commonplace group, controlled for variances in students' pre-test scores. Cohen's d effect size was .47. In addition, interviews were held after four weeks in which students' explanations were tested and scored on the quality of their claim, evidence, and reasoning. Again, scores of the IBL group were significantly higher on all three dimensions with effect sizes of $d = .58$, .74, and .59 respectively. Finally, an achievement gap by race was discovered for the commonplace, but not for the IBL group (Wilson, Taylor, Kowalski, & Carlson, 2010).

Taraban, Box, Myers, Pollard, and Bowen (2007) tested high school students on their content knowledge and knowledge of science skills (i.e., factual recall, critical thinking, and process skills) in a biology class. Six classes of two different cohorts were tested on two topics (i.e., microscopy and biotechnology) in two different instructional methods: traditional (i.e., more direct transmission of information and prescribed laboratory activities) and IBL. A within-subject, cross-over design was employed. The IBL group obtained significantly higher overall test scores irrespective of the topic that was learned. Analysis of the question types demonstrated significant differences for factual recall and process skills. The IBL scores were slightly better on the critical thinking questions as well, but this difference was not statistically significant.

Houle and Barnett (2008) investigated middle school students' understanding of sound, their misconceptions about sound, and their conceptual understanding of the scientific problem addressed in the IBL module. Comparisons were made pre- and post-enactment of the IBL module in the curriculum. Students' scores on state and national exams (e.g., National Assessment of Educational Progress, NAEP) were investigated with respect to their understanding of and misconceptions about sound. To measure conceptual understanding of the problem, students' answers on multiple choice questions and short answer questions that measured knowledge relevant to the curriculum were analyzed. These measures were only gathered post-enactment. Results showed no significant changes in students' understanding and misconceptions of sound. To some degree, students did show conceptual understanding of the problem, but could not give a complete explanation of the problem. The authors plead for a significant rethinking of how to design inquiry based science activities.

Similar results were found by Wolf and Fraser (2008), who compared inquiry and non-inquiry laboratory activities of middle school students' achievement on a test measuring basic physical science concepts. Groups were selected in order to rule out the effects of differences in prior knowledge. Over eight weeks, two teachers taught four classes: two IBL and two non-IBL. Both groups learned about the topic of static electricity and except for the method of instruction, all other activities (i.e., homework assignments and examinations) were kept consistent. They found that students in the IBL group obtained slightly higher scores on the test, but this difference was not statistically significant.

Pine and colleagues (2006) studied the effects of IBL on inquiry abilities. Four performance assessments (two on one-period investigations and two on three-period investigations, all including a cognitive abilities test) were used to investigate six aspects of scientific investigation skills (i.e., planning an inquiry, observation, data collection, graphical and pictorial presentation, inference, and explanation based on evidence). Two groups of fifth-grade students participated: one IBL group and one textbook-based group. On three of the four assessments, no significant differences in scientific investigations skills were found between both groups. On one task, the IBL group performed 11% better than text students, which was labeled as a small effect.

In sum, effect studies show mixed results with some studies reporting benefits for IBL, while others did not find significant differences in outcome measures.

Research on the Effects of PBL

A recent review of PBL effect studies (Loyens et al., 2010) included studies published from 2004 to 2010 that investigated the effects of PBL on knowledge, skills, and competencies. Furthermore, articles that studied the PBL curriculum as a whole were included. These articles did not study the effects of PBL on knowledge or skills, but compared PBL and traditional, lecture-based curricula in terms of graduation rates and study duration as a measure of how successful a particular curriculum was.

For PBL's effects on knowledge it could be concluded that the results were mixed: some studies found effects, although small, and others failed to find effects. No negative effects were reported either. A recent meta-analysis of curricular comparisons, using a single PBL medical school in the Netherlands found similar results. The overall weighted effect size averaged over the 90 comparisons involving the PBL curriculum under study and various Dutch medical schools was equal to $d = .07$ (Schmidt et al., 2009), which is considered less than even a small effect.

For skills, it seemed warranted to conclude that PBL graduates have some advantages in social skills compared to graduates from a traditional curriculum. There is some evidence for beneficial effects of PBL students in medical curricula on medical skills compared to medical students in traditional curricula, although not all studies endorse this. For critical thinking skills, the conclusion seemed positive. However, a remark on this conclusion is the limited number of studies in this area.

With respect to graduation and retention rates and students' study progress, all studies indicated positive effects for PBL curricula. Interestingly, an often-heard criticism of PBL is that it requires fairly large initial investments, financial and otherwise. Higher retention and graduation rates, however, are exactly those components that can bring in financial resources for programs.

Research on the Effects of PjBL

Geier and colleagues (2008) investigated the effects of PjBL on standardized science test (i.e., Michigan Educational Assessment Program, MEAP) outcomes of two cohorts of seventh and eighth graders from public schools. One group of students received a PjBL intervention, while the other group did not. MEAP scores reflected science content understanding and process skills. Significant differences in favor of the PjBL group were found on both content understanding and process skills (standardized effect size of $d = .44$). These differences between both groups also translated into significant differences in passing rates of MEAP.

Chu (2009) found similar results among primary school children. In this study, project grades of children that were taught with PjBL were compared with children's project grades of the previous year, when a traditional approach was followed. The PjBL group significantly outperformed the traditional teaching group.

Three experimental, PjBL high-achieving high-school classes were compared with three high-achieving control high-school classes in technology education. Learning achievements of the students in both groups were measured by means of the standardized matriculation exam administered as pre- and post-tests. After the learning process both groups performed significantly better, but the gain for the experimental group was significantly higher (84%) compared to the control group (52%; Mioduser & Betzer, 2007).

Another study investigated the implementation of a PjBL approach on pre-service teachers' understanding and application of problem solving skills within the domain of technology. Significant differences were found between pre- and posttests that measured problem identification, design briefs with the main requirements for construction, specification of the projects (e.g., costs, production time, and safety), problem investigation, alternative solutions, and tests and evaluations (Mettas & Constantinou, 2007).

Pre-service teachers were also tested in a study by Wilhelm, Sherrod, and Walters (2008). These teachers' understanding of concepts related to lunar phases as well as mathematical concepts underlying them (e.g., periodic patterns and geometric spatial visualization) was examined pre- and post-enactment of a PjBL unit. Results revealed a significant increase in the mean overall test scores. The effect size of $d = .44$ demonstrated an educationally significant gain in lunar-related understanding that could be attributed to the project-enhanced unit.

In sum, studies published on the effectiveness of PjBL during the past five years seem to reflect a positive image. All five studies included in this review found favorable effects of this approach, although methodological flaws must temper any conclusions.

Research on the Effects of CBL

Two groups of medical students (i.e., one CBL group and one traditional, lecture-based group) were compared in a study by Jamkar, Yemul, and Singh (2006). Factual knowledge was evaluated by students' scores on a test. Further, students needed to create a concept map in response to a question regarding differential diagnoses. The CBL group obtained significantly higher test scores compared to the control group. They also received higher evaluations of their concept maps compared to the control group, although it is not mentioned in the article whether this difference was statistically significant.

Choi and Lee (2009) used a single-group repeated-measures design to study whether CBL could improve students' ill-structured problem-solving skills during their case activity and whether the overall learning experience with CBL could improve students' ill-structured problem-solving skills in a transfer test. Ill-structured problem-solving skills were measured with an open-ended questions test reflecting seven sub-skills in two main phases of problem-solving (i.e., problem identification and solution generation): considering multiple perspectives in problem identification, justification skills (i.e., developing a sound argument for one's claim) in problem identification, critical thinking in problem identification, linking to theory (i.e., understand what they read and apply the knowledge to particular problems) in problem identification, generating solutions and evaluating them, critical thinking in solution generation, and linking to theory in the solution generation phase. Transfer was measured by the same questions, but related to a new case. Undergraduate teacher education students were tested three times during the three weeks that the CBL format was implemented and on two different cases. Results revealed significant time effects on all of the seven sub-skills for ill-structured problem-solving with effect sizes ranging from .67 to .87. For the transfer test, a pre- and post-test on a case problem were implemented before and after the review of two cases. The results indicated that the students' consideration of multiple perspectives in problem identification was significantly improved from the pre-test (effect size of $d =$ .42). However, justification, critical thinking, and linking to theory in problem identification did not show any statistically significant improvement from the pre- to post-test. In contrast, two of the sub-skills solution generation showed a statistically significant improvement: solution and justification.

Another study tested an undergraduate CBL group and an undergraduate, traditional, lecture-based group on: (a) knowledge gains; (b) misconception clarification; and (c) data analysis skills between pre- and post-tests with respect to the topic of cellular respiration. Pre- and post-tests measured comprehension of content and processes related to cellular respiration. Results demonstrated similar scores on the pre-test for all three dependent variables. Differences from pre- to post-test were significant for knowledge gains (effect size $d = .98$) and data analysis skills, but not for misconception clarification (Rybarczyk, Baines, McVey, Thompson, & Wilkins, 2007).

Cliff (2006) examined students' understanding of blood oxygen transport in a CBL environment. He found that high percentages of students could correctly use the oxygen-hemoglobin saturation curve as a measure for blood oxygen transport understanding after the CBL approach. However, a control group is missing in this study and hence no conclusions can be drawn with respect to the relative effects of CBL.

Dupuis and Persky (2008) compared examination scores of pharmacy students enrolled in a partial CBL course with control students of the previous year that were exclusively taught with a traditional, lecture-based approach. A pharmacokinetics course consisted of three content sections of which the first was modified to CBL, the second remained lecture-based, and the third section was a mix of CBL and lectures. Scores on three examinations with a different format were compared. The first examination was case-based, similar to the cases completed during class. The second examination was similar in format to that used in previous years, with a combination of short answer, multiple choice questions, and open-ended problems. The final examination included case-based and multiple-choice questions. When comparing examination scores to control students from previous years, scores on the first and the third examinations, which corresponded to sections of the course where case-based learning was used, were significantly higher than historical controls. Scores on the second examination, which covered information presented using the standard class format used in previous years were significantly lower than historical controls. CBL lead to higher scores compared to the control group of the previous year, but only when the assessment matched the instructional approach.

Finally, one study compared CBL to a human patient simulation (HPS) approach in medical education. HPS is an upcoming approach in medical education utilizing computerized, physiologically responding mannequins. Students were randomly assigned to either CBL or HPS and clinical examination (i.e., OSCE) scores were analyzed. Examination scores did not differ significantly between both groups. The authors conclude that CBL is as effective as HPS for students' learning (Schwartz, Fernandez, Kouyoumjian, Jones, & Compton, 2008).

Altogether, the CBL studies show superiority of CBL on knowledge measures as well as several, though not all, measured skills. However, conclusions must be tempered in light of methodological issues, including lack of control groups.

CONCLUSION AND FUTURE DIRECTIONS

What can be concluded from this review of studies on inquiry-based instruction? In order to draw appropriate conclusions, several points of attention should be put forward.

First, some methodological issues can be raised with respect to the studies. For example, it should be noted that not all studies in this review included a control group. Sometimes, significant improvements were found on several learning outcomes from pre- to post-test, but it still remains unclear whether and if so, how much students would have gained from the implementation of a different (e.g., lecture-based) instructional method in these studies. Also, effect sizes are regularly missing in the studies. This makes it difficult to evaluate the scope of a difference that was found. In addition, some studies had relatively small sample sizes and time periods in which a specific instructional method was implemented could vary from three weeks to complete curricula. All these issues ask for caution in interpreting the results.

Second, not all studies provided a clear and detailed description of the instructional approach used. Given that all approaches fall under the umbrella term of inquiry-based instruction, overlap could be observed in several articles. For example, some studies on PjBL cited PBL literature in their theoretical framework. Although we attempted to carefully categorize the different studies into IBL, PBL, PjBL, and CBL, the information needed to make these categorizations was restricted to the descriptions given in the articles.

In summary, the review of articles on the effectiveness of inquiry-based instruction in terms of knowledge and skills showed mixed results for IBL and PBL and predominantly positive results for PjBL and CBL. For knowledge, IBL had positive effects on some tests, but not on others. Also for standardized exams and skills, results are inconclusive for IBL. PBL seems to foster the development of several skills, but has mainly advantages compared to lecture-based curricula in terms of less student drop-out and a shorter study duration for students. Effects for knowledge were absent or small. All studies on PjBL reported positive effects and the same can be concluded for CBL. All in all, taking into account the aforementioned points of attention, inquiry-based instruction seems to hold some benefits for students' learning outcomes. Further, the review's studies report effects of inquiry in different populations, justifying the claim that inquiry-based instruction might work for learners of a different age and background. Evidence could be found for the absence of an achievement gap by race in IBL (Wilson et al., 2010), but not by SAT sub-scores (Lewis & Lewis, 2008).

In a way, we have provided a limited review of studies, since we only focused on studies that included knowledge and skills measures and discarded other variables that might influence students' learning. But as mentioned before, these are the variables that are often valued most in the context of effectiveness. However, in the next section, suggestions are made for other lines of research on inquiry-based instruction.

Future Directions: If, Why, When, and For Whom?

If we want a decisive answer about the effectiveness of inquiry-based instruction above direct instruction, future research should focus on randomized controlled studies such as the study of Wilson and colleagues (2010). As mentioned previously, the number of controlled studies comparing inquiry-based instruction with more direct instruction is rather limited. These studies are, however, crucial to determine *if* inquiry-based instruction is effective.

Nevertheless, future studies should not be limited to the if-question, but should also take into account *why* a specific inquiry-based method yields benefit for students' learning. In other words, more emphasis should be laid on crucial elements and activities. Although this was not the focus of their study, Wilson and colleagues (2010) also tested whether both instructional methods that were compared had the intended outcome in the classroom. Each class session was observed by three external researchers, who took notes and completed the Reformed Teaching Observation Protocol (RTOP) for each unit. In addition, classroom sessions were videotaped and activities in the class were coded to map differences between both enactments. Similarly, a recent study looked closely into why students benefit from group discussion in a PBL context by analyzing video footage of tutorial groups. Results demonstrated that actively providing explanations during a discussion appeared crucial and resulted in benefits for long-term memory performance (Van Blankenstein, Dolmans, Van der Vleuten, & Schmidt, 2009). Studies like these are crucial for unraveling reasons behind students' differences in different instructional approaches.

Finally, a lot is still to be explored with respect to *when* inquiry-based instruction is effective. Hmelo-Silver, Duncan, and Chinn (2007, p. 105) state in this respect:

> But we would argue that "Does it work?" is the wrong question. The more important questions to ask are under what circumstances do these guided inquiry approaches work, what are the kinds of outcomes for which they are effective, what kinds of valued practices do they promote, and what kinds of support and scaffolding are needed for different populations and learning goals.

The issue of the different populations in this quote addresses yet another question: *for who?* Effects of instructional approaches cannot make claims about individual students' learning. It should be taken into account that "a curriculum is a potpourri of individual components, making it difficult to establish links between specific aspects of the curriculum and student behavior" (Norman, Wenghofer, & Klass, 2008, p. 795). Although our review included different populations (i.e., K-16, higher education, and high achieving students), future research should investigate interactions between aptitude and instructional approach in greater detail. Irrespective of whether a learning environment or educational practice is labeled as inquiry-based or direct instruction, educators' main challenge still remains to foster and promote meaningful learning and understanding within *all* learners.

REFERENCES

Albanese, M. A. & Mitchell S. (1993) Problem-based learning: A review of literature on its outcomes and implementation issues. *Academic Medicine, 68*(1), 52–81.

American Association for the Advancement of Science (1993). *Benchmarks for science literacy.* New York: Oxford University Press.

Anderson, R. D. (2007). Inquiry as an organizing theme for science curricula. In S. K. Abell, & N. G. Lederman (Eds.), *Handbook of research on science education* (pp. 807–830). Abingdon: Taylor & Francis.

Barrows, H. S. (1986). A taxonomy of problem-based learning methods. *Medical Education, 20,* 481–486.

Barrows, H. S. (1996). Problem-based learning in medicine and beyond: A brief overview. In W. H. Gijselaers (Ed.), New directions for teaching and learning (Vol. 68, pp. 3–11). San Francisco: Jossey-Bass.

Barrows, H. S., & Tamblyn, R. (1980). *Problem-based learning: An approach to medical education.* New York: Springer.

Bednar, A. K., Cunningham, D. J., Duffy, T. M., & Perry, J. D. (1992). Theory into practice: How do we link? In T. M. Duffy, & D. H. Jonassen (Eds.), *Constructivism and the technology of instruction* (pp. 17–34). Hillsdale, NJ: Lawrence Erlbaum Associates.

Bell, R. L., Smetana, L., & Binns, I. (2005). Simplifying inquiry instruction. *The Science Teacher, 72*(7), 30–33.

Birenbaum, M. (2003). New insights into learning and teaching and their implications for assessment. In M. Segers, F. Dochy, & E. Cascallar (Eds.), *Optimising new modes of assessment: In search for qualities and standards* (pp. 13–36). Dordrecht: Kluwer Academic Publishers.

Blanchard, M. R., Southerland, S. A., & Granger, E. M. (2008). No silver bullet for inquiry: Making sense of teacher change following an inquiry-based research experience for teachers. *Science Teacher Education, 93,* 322–360.

Blumenfeld, P. C. (1992). Classroom learning and motivation: Clarifying and expanding goal theory. *Journal of Educational Psychology, 84,* 272–281.

Blumenfeld, P. C., Soloway, E., Marx, R. W., Krajcik, J. S., Guzdial, M., & Palincsar, A. (1991). Motivating project-based learning: Sustaining the doing, supporting the learning. *Educational Psychologist, 26,* 369–398.

Boekaerts, M. (1999). Self-regulated learning: where we are today. *International Journal of Educational Research, 31,* 445–457.

Bransford, J. D., Brown, A. L., & Cocking, R. R. (Eds.). (2000). *How people learn: Brain, mind, experience, and school.* Washington, DC: National Academy Press.

Bransford, J. D., Franks, J. J., Vye, N., & Sherwood, R. D. (1989). New approaches to instruction: Because wisdom can't be told. In S. Vosniadou, & A. Ortony (Eds.), *Similarity and analogical reasoning* (pp. 470–491). Cambridge, MA: Harvard University Press.

Bruner, J. S. (1961). The act of discovery. *Harvard Educational Review, 31,* 21–32.

Casotti, G., Rieser-Danner, L., & Knabb, M. T. (2008). Successful implementation of inquiry-based physiology laboratories in undergraduate major and nonmajor courses. *Advances in Physiology Education, 32,* 286–296.

Cobb, P., Confrey, J., diSessa, A., Lehrer, R., & Schauble, L. (2003). Design experiments in educational research. *Educational Researcher, 32,* 9–13.

Chinn, C. A., & Malhorta, B. A. (2002). Epistemologically authentic inquiry in schools: A theoretical framework for evaluating inquiry tasks. *Science Education, 86,* 175–218.

Choi, I., & Lee, K. (2009). Designing and implementing a case-based learning environment for enhancing ill-structured problem solving: classroom management problems for prospective teachers. *Educational Technology Research and Development, 57,* 99–129.

Chu, K. W. S. (2009). Inquiry project-based learning with a partnership of three types of teachers and the school librarian. *Journal of the American Society for Information Science and Technology, 60,* 1671–1686.

Cliff, W. H. (2006). Case-based learning of blood oxygen transport. *Advances in Physiology Education, 30,* 224–229.

Colburn, A. (2000). An inquiry primer. *Science Scope, 23,* 42–44.

Colliver, J. A. (2002). Constructivism: The view of knowledge that ended philosophy or a theory of learning and instruction? *Teaching and Learning in Medicine, 14,* 49–51.

David, J. L. (2008). Project-based learning. *Educational Leadership, 65,* 80–82.

Deci, E. L., & Ryan, R. M. (2008). Facilitating optimal motivation and psychological well-being across life's domains. *Canadian Psychology, 49,* 14–23.

De Corte, E. (2000). Marrying theory building and the improvement of school practice: A permanent challenge for instructional psychology. *Learning and Instruction, 10,* 249–266.

Dewey, J. (1902). *The child and the curriculum.* Chicago: The University of Chicago Press.

Dewey, J. (1929). *The quest for certainty.* New York: Minton.

Dochy, F., Segers, M., Van den Bossche, P., & Gijbels, D. (2003). Effects of problem-based learning: a meta-analysis. *Learning and Instruction, 13,* 533–568.

Driscoll, M. (2005). *Psychology of learning for instruction.* Needham Heights, MA: Allyn & Bacon.

Duffy, T. M. (2009). Building lines of communication and a research agenda. In S. Tobias, & T. M. Duffy (Eds.), *Constructivist instruction: Success or failure?* (pp. 351–367). New York: Routledge.

Dupuis, R. E., & Persky, A. M. (2008). Use of case-based learning in a clinical pharmacokinetics course. *American Journal of Pharmaceutical Education, 72* (article 29), 1–7.

Eberlein, T., Kampmeier, J., Minderhout, V., Moog, R. S., Platt, T., Varma-Nelson, P., & White, H. B. (2008). Pedagogies of engagement in science. *Biochemistry and Molecular Biology Education, 36*, 262–273.

Edelson, D., Gordin, D. N., & Pea, R. D. (1999). Addressing the challenges of inquiry-based learning through technology and curriculum design. *The Journal of the Learning Sciences, 8*, 391–450.

Eggen, P., & Kauchak, D. (2006). Interpretations of constructivism: Clarifying issues and implications for instruction. Paper presented at the Annual Meeting of the American Educational Research Association, San Francisco, CA, April.

Feletti, G. (1993). Inquiry based and problem based learning: How similar are these approaches to nursing and medical education? *Higher Education Research and Development, 12*, 143–156.

Gall, M. (1970). The use of questions in teaching. *Review of Educational Research, 40*, 707–720.

Geier, R., Blumenfeld, P. C., Marx, R. W., Krajcik, J. S., Fishman, B., Soloway, E., & Clay-Chambers, J. (2008). Standardized test outcomes for students engaged in inquiry-based science curricula in the context of urban reform. *Journal of Research in Science Teaching, 45*, 922–939.

Gijbels, D., Dochy, F. Van den Bossche, P., & Segers, M. (2005). Effects of problem-based learning: a meta-analysis from the angle of assessment. *Review of Educational Research, 75*, 27–61.

Gijbels, D., & Loyens, S. M. M. (2009). Constructivist learning (environments) and how to avoid another tower of Babel: Reply to Renkl. *Instructional Science, 37*, 499–502.

Grant, M. M., & Branch, R. M. (2005). Project-based learning in a middle school: Tracing abilities through the artifacts of learning. *Journal of Research on Technology in Education, 38*, 65–98.

Harris, K. R., & Alexander, P. A. (1998). Integrated, constructivist education: Challenge and reality. *Educational Psychology Review, 10*, 115–127.

Helle, L., Tynjälä, P., & Olkinuora, E. (2006). Project-based learning in secondary education: Theory, practice and rubber sling slots. *Higher Education, 51*, 287–314.

Hmelo-Silver, C. E. (2004). Problem-based learning: What and how do students learn? Educational Psychology Review, 16, 235–266.

Hmelo-Silver, C. E., & Barrows, H. S. (2006). Goals and strategies of a problem-based learning facilitator. *The Interdisciplinary Journal of Problem-Based Learning, 1*, 21–39.

Hmelo-Silver, C. E., Duncan, R. G., & Chinn, C. A. (2007). Scaffolding and achievement in problem-based and inquiry-based learning: A response to Kirschner, Sweller, and Clark (2006). *Educational Psychologist, 42*, 99–107.

Houle, M. E., & Barnett, G. M. (2008). Students' conceptions of sound waves resulting from the enactment of a new technology-enhanced inquiry-based curriculum on urban bird communication. *Journal of Science Education and Technology, 17*, 242–251.

Jamkar, A., Yemul, V., & Singh, G. (2006). Integrated teaching programme with student-centred case-based learning. *Medical Education, 40*, 466–467.

Jonassen, D. (2009). Reconciling a human cognitive architecture. In S. Tobias, & T. M. Duffy (Eds.), *Constructivist instruction: Success or failure?* (pp. 13–33). New York: Routledge.

Justice, C., Rice, J., Roy, D., Hudspith, B., & Jenkins, H. (2009). Inquiry-based learning in higher education: Administrators' perspectives on integrating inquiry pedagogy into the curriculum. *Higher Education, 58*, 841–855.

Kahn, P., & O'Rourke, K. (2005). Understanding enquiry-based learning. In T. Barrett, I. Mac Labhrainn, & H. Fallon (Eds.), *Handbook of enquiry and problem-based learning* (pp. 1–12). Galway: CELT.

Kant, I. (1959). *Critique of pure reason.* London: Dent/Everyman (Original work published in 1787).

Kennedy, M. M. (1997). The connection between research and practice. *Educational Researcher, 26*, 4–12.

Krajcik, J., McNeill, K. L., & Reiser, B. J. (2007). Learning-goals-driven design model: Developing curriculum materials that align with national standards and incorporate project-based pedagogy. *Science Education, 92*, 1–32.

Kwan, T. Y. L. (2008). Student-teachers' evaluation on the use of different modes of problem-based learning in teacher education. *Asia-Pacific Journal of Teacher Education, 36*, 323–343.

Lewis, S., & Lewis, J. (2008). Seeking effectiveness and equity in a large college chemistry course: An HLM investigation of peer-led guided inquiry. *Journal of Research in Science Teaching, 45*, 794–811.

Lloyd-Jones, G., Margetson, D., & Bligh, J. G. (1998). Problem-based learning: A coat of many colours. *Medical Education, 32*, 492–494.

Loyens, S. M. M., Kirschner, P. A., & Paas, F. (in press). Problem-based learning. In S. Graham, A. Bus, S. Major, & L. Swanson (Eds.), *APA Educational Psychology Handbook: Vol 3. Application to learning and teaching*. Washington, DC: American Psychological Association.

Loyens, S. M. M., Rikers, R. M. J. P., & Schmidt, H. G. (2007). Students' conceptions of distinct constructivist assumptions. *European Journal of Psychology of Education, 12*, 179–199.

Marshall, H. H. (Ed.). (1992). *Redefining student learning: Roots of educational change*. Norwood, NJ: Ablex.

Mayer, R. E. (1996). Learners as information processors: Legacies and limitations of educational psychology's second metaphor. *Journal of Educational Psychology, 31*, 151–161.

Mayer, R. E. (2009). Constructivism as a theory of learning versus constructivism as a prescription for instruction. In S. Tobias, & T. M. Duffy (Eds.), *Constructivist instruction: Success or failure?* (pp. 184–200). New York: Routledge.

Mettas, A. C., & Constantinou, C. C. (2007). The technology fair: a project-based learning approach for enhancing problem solving skills and interest in design and technology instruction. *International Journal of Technology and Design Education, 18*, 79–100.

Mioduser, D., & Betzer, N. (2007). The contribution of project-based learning to high achievers' acquisition of technological knowledge and skills. *International Journal of Technology and Design Education, 18*, 59–77.

Moust, J. H. C., van Berkel, H. J. M., & Schmidt, H. G. (2005). Signs of erosion: Reflections on three decades of problem-based learning at Maastricht University, *Higher Education, 50*, 665–683.

National Research Council (2000). *Inquiry and the National Science Education Standards*. Washington, DC: National Academy Press.

Norman, G. R., & Schmidt, H. G. (1992). The psychological basis of problem-based learning: A review of the evidence. *Academic Medicine, 67*, 557–565.

Norman, G. R., Wenghofer, E., & Klass, D. (2008). Predicting doctor performance outcomes of curriculum interventions: problem-based learning and continuing competence. *Medical Education, 42*, 794–799.

Olson, S., & Loucks-Horsley, S. (2000). *Inquiry and the national science education standards: A guide for teaching and learning*. Washington, DC: National Academy Press.

Park Rogers, M. A., & Abell, S. K. (2008). The design, enactment, and experience of inquiry-based instruction in undergraduate science education: a case study. *Science Education, 92*, 591–607.

Parsons, R. D., Lewis Hinson, S., & Sardo-Brown, D. (2001). *Educational psychology: A practitioner-researcher model of teaching*. Toronto: Wadsworth.

Pine, J., Aschbacher, P., Roth, E., Jones, M., McPhee, C., Martin, C., Phelps, S., Kyle, T., & Foley, B. (2006). Fifth graders' science inquiry abilities: A comparative study of students in hands-on and textbook curricula. *Journal of Research in Science Teaching, 43*, 467–484.

Plato (1949). *Meno*. Indianapolis, IN: Bobbs-Merrill.

Renkl, A. (2009). Why constructivists should not talk about constructivist learning environments: A commentary on Loyens and Gijbels (2008). Instructional Science, 37, 495–498.

Rybarczyk, B. J., Baines, A. T., McVey, M., Thompson, J. T., & Wilkins, H. (2007). A case-based approach increases student learning outcomes and comprehension of cellular respiration concepts. Biochemistry and Molecular Biology Education, 35, 181–186.

Sandoval, W. A. (2005). Understanding students' practical epistemologies and their influence on learning through inquiry. Science Education, 89, 634–656.

Savery, J. R. (2006). Overview of problem-based learning: Definitions and distinctions. *The Interdisciplinary Journal of Problem-Based Learning, 1*, 9–20.

Savery, J. R., & Duffy, T. M. (2001). *Problem based learning: An instructional model and its constructivist framework*. CRLT Technical Report No. 16-01. Indiana University: Center for Research on Learning and Technology.

Scardamalia, M., & Bereiter, C. (1991). Higher levels of agency for children in knowledge building: A challenge for the design of new knowledge media. *Journal of the Learning Sciences, 1*, 37–68.

Schmidt, H. G. (1983). Problem-based learning: Rationale and description. *Medical Education, 17*, 11–16.

Schmidt, H. G., Loyens, S. M. M., Van Gog, T., & Paas, F. (2007). Problem-based learning is compatible with human cognitive architecture: Commentary on Kirschner, Sweller, and Clark (2006). *Educational Psychologist, 42*, 91–97.

Schmidt, H. G., Van der Molen, H. T., Te Winkel, W. W. R., & Wijnen, W. H. F. W. (2009). Constructivist, problem-based learning does work: A meta-analysis of curricular comparisons involving a single medical school. *Educational Psychologist, 44*, 1–23.

Schroeder, C. M., Scott, T. P., Tolson, H., Huang, T. Y., & Lee, Y. H. (2007). A meta-analysis of national research: Effects of teaching strategies on student achievement in science in the United States. *Journal of Research in Science Teaching, 44*, 1436–1460.

Schwab, J. J. (1962). The teaching of science as inquiry. In J. J. Schwab, & P. F. Brandwein (Eds.), *The teaching of science* (pp. 3–103). Cambridge, MA: Harvard University Press.

Schwartz, L. R., Fernandez, R., Kouyoumjian, S. R., Jones, K.A., & Compton, S. (2008). A randomized comparison trial of case-based learning versus human patient simulation in medical student education. *Academic Emergency Medicine, 14*, 130–137.

Sinatra, G. M., & Mason, L. (2007). Beyond knowledge: Learner characteristics influencing conceptual change. In S. Vosniadou (Ed.), *Handbook on conceptual change* (pp. 560–582). Mahwah, NJ: Lawrence Erlbaum Associates.

Singer, J., Marx, R. W., Krajcik, J., & Clay-Chambers, J. (2000). Constructing extended inquiry projects: Curriculum materials for science education reform. *Educational Psychologist, 35*, 165–178.

Slavin, R. E. (2006). *Educational psychology: Theory and practice* (8th ed.). Needham Heights, MA: Allyn and Bacon.

Srinivasan, M., Wilkes, M., Stevenson, F., Nguyen, T., & Slavin, S. (2007). Comparing problem-based learning with case-based learning: Effects of a major curricular shift at two institutions. *Academic Medicine, 82*, 74–82.

Stevens, R. (1912). The question as a measure of efficiency in instruction: A critical study of classroom practice. *Teachers College Contributions to Education, 48*, 95.

Strobel, J., & Van Barneveld, A. (2009). When is PBL more effective? A meta-synthesis of meta-analyses comparing PBL to conventional classrooms. *The Interdisciplinary Journal of Problem-Based Learning, 3*, 44–58.

Tal, T., Krajcik, J. S., & Blumenfeld, P. C. (2006). Urban schools' teachers enacting project-based science. *Journal of Research in Science Teaching, 43*, 722–745.

Taraban, R., Box, C., Myers, R., Pollard, R., & Bowen, C. W. (2007). Effects of active-learning experiences on achievement, attitudes, and behaviors in high school biology. *Journal of Research in Science Teaching, 44*, 960–979.

Thomas, J. W. (2000). *A review of research on project-based learning.* Retrieved April 1, 2010, from http://www.bie.org/files/researchreviewPBL.pdf.

Tobias, S., & Duffy, T. M. (2009). The success or failure of constructivist instruction: An introduction. In S. Tobias, & T. M. Duffy (Eds.), *Constructivist instruction: Success or failure?* (pp. 3–10). New York: Routledge.

Van Blankenstein, F. M., Dolmans, D. H. J. M., Van der Vleuten, C. P. M., & Schmidt, H. G. (2009). Which cognitive processes support learning during small-group discussion? The role of providing explanations and listening to others. *Instructional Science.* DOI 10. 1007/s11251–009–9124–7.

von Glasersfeld, E. (1993). Questions and answers about radical constructivism. In K. Tobin (Ed.), The practice of constructivism in science education (pp. 23–38). Hillsdale, NJ: Lawrence Erlbaum.

Wilhelm, J., Sherrod, S., & Walters, K. (2008). Project-based learning environments: Challenging pre-service teachers to act in the moment. *Journal of Educational Research, 101*, 220–233.

Williams, B. (2005). Case based learning – a review of the literature: Is there scope for this educational paradigm in prehospital education? *Emergency Medical Journal, 22*, 577–581.

Wilson, C. D., Taylor, J. A., Kowalski, S. M., & Carlson, J. (2010). The relative effects and equity of inquiry-based and commonplace science teaching on students' knowledge, reasoning, and argumentation. *Journal of Research in Science Teaching, 47*, 276–301.

Windschitl, M. (2002). Framing constructivism in practice as the negotiation of dilemmas: An analysis of the conceptual, pedagogical, cultural, and political challenges facing teachers. Review of Educational Research, 72, 131–175.

Windschitl, M., Thompson, J., & Braaten, M. (2008). Beyond the scientific method: Model-based inquiry as a new paradigm of preference for school science investigations. Science Education, 92, 941–967.

Winne, P. H. (1995). Self-regulation is ubiquitous but its forms vary with knowledge. *Educational Psychologist, 30*, 217–221.

Wolf, S. J., & Fraser, B. J. (2008). Learning environment, attitudes and achievement among middle-school science students using inquiry-based laboratory activities. *Research in Science Education, 38*, 321–341.

Woolfolk, A. E. (2004). Educational psychology (9th ed.). Needham Heights, MA: Allyn and Bacon.

Yetkiner, Z. E., Anderoglu, H., & Capraro, R. M. (2008). *Research summary: Project-based learning in middle grades mathematics.* Retrieved April 2, 2010, from http://www.nmsa.org/Research/ResearchSummaries/ProjectBasedLearninginMath/tabid/1570/Default.aspx.

19

INSTRUCTION BASED ON DISCUSSION

P. Karen Murphy, Ian A. G. Wilkinson, and Anna O. Soter

Discussion is . . . bringing various beliefs together; shaking one against another and tearing down their rigidity. It is conversation of thoughts; it is dialogue—the mother of dialectic in more than the etymological sense.

(Dewey, 1916, pp. 194–195)

Discussion is an integral part of our lived experiences. Whether one is sharing a story with a friend, inquiring with the principal about the school's discipline policy, or debating the reality of the normal distribution with future researchers, individuals are involved in discussion. *Discussions* in classrooms are fairly open-ended and collaborative episodes of talk among teachers and students, or among students, for the purpose of fostering student thinking, learning, problem-solving, comprehension, or literary appreciation (Wilkinson, 2009). Broadly conceived, classroom discussions can take many forms including sharing time, content lessons, or even interactions with computers (Cazden & Beck, 2003), and they can involve differing numbers of individuals such as pairs, small groups, or a whole class, with or without a teacher present (Murphy, Wilkinson, & Soter, 2004).

Different approaches to classroom discussion are structured to serve diverse purposes. Some discussions are focused on a text where the purpose of the talk can vary from the development of critical thinking skills through the sharing of their lived experiences (e.g., *Book Club*, Raphael & McMahon, 1994) to the thoughtful engagement about a text so as to create a meaningful mental representation (e.g., *Questioning the Author*, Beck & McKeown, 2006). Other approaches to text-based discussion seek to bridge the sharing of lived-through experiences with a text with the seeking of information, where the purpose of the discussion is to enable students to think critically and analytically about, around, and with a given text (e.g., *Quality Talk*, Wilkinson, Soter, & Murphy, 2010). Still other discussions do not directly involve text at all, but are focused on critically analyzing information encountered as part of a class activity (e.g., discussion of observations during a science experiment, Mason, 2001). The aforementioned examples all assume mutual interest in the content, allow for give and take, foster probing and exploration, and encourage the collaborative and maternal "giving birth" to newly formed understandings (Dewey, 1916, p. 195).

As Dewey (1916) suggested in *Essays in Experimental Logic*, discussion also plays a very important role in the development of logical thought. Discussion embodies the very process whereby ideas are brought together and shaken-up and their viability is tested (Dewey, 1916). This testing of ideas encourages doubt and inquiry on the part of discussion participants. Almasi (1996) describes this type of productive discussion as an *interactive event* in which individuals arrive at new understandings through a collaborative construction of meaning where multiple viewpoints are considered and explored. In such discussions, students have considerable interpretive authority for evaluating the validity and plausibility of individual perspectives as well as any co-constructed understandings (Soter et al., 2008).

What is more, Dewey held that participants—as a consequence of participating in this meaning-making experience—internalize the process, and thereafter are be able to have such discussions within their own consciousness. As Dewey states: "The discussion which at first took place by bringing ideas from different persons into contact . . . became a habit of the individual with himself. He became a miniature social assemblage" (1916, pp. 194–195). Similar theoretical perspectives were forwarded by Vygotsky (1978) regarding the development of language and thought.

Specifically, Vygotsky theorized that children developed language as a mechanism for communicating and becoming enculturated into their environment. As children develop physically, cognitively, and socially, the language, tools, and signs of the culture are internalized. Speech that was once external now becomes internal, and language becomes mentally represented as thought. Like Dewey, Vygotsky also contended that along with language, the audience or discourse community is also internalized. Consequently, older learners are able to have internal debates about topics and ideas—debates that were once only possible in the presence of a discourse community. Support for this theoretical position can be found in the research on *Collaborative Reasoning* (CR; Chinn, Anderson, & Waggoner, 2001) where students' ability to write persuasive arguments independently improves after participation in CR discussions.

The following excerpt is taken from a discussion among a small group of middle-school students and a teacher who are discussing the moral ambiguities in *To Kill a Mockingbird* (see Applebee, Langer, Nystrand, & Gamoran, 2003, p. 711). In this excerpt, the teacher asks a pointed question regarding how Bob Ewell is killed:

Teacher: How does Bob Ewell get killed?
Student: Boo Radley [did it].
Teacher: How did you figure out that Boo killed him?
Student: . . . But I guess that I thought that the knife . . . I really didn't understand this [part]. I thought it was Boo at the beginning, but then I was not sure.

At this point, the teacher intervenes with some scaffolding to help students understand what actually happened in the story. The students turn the focus of the discussion to the issue of the cover-up that follows Ewell's death (Applebee et al., 2003, pp. 711–712).

Student: It said that he doesn't want to reveal it to the [sheriff] because . . . it would ruin, you know, Boo's life.
Student: Right.
Student: Even if he totally [did it].
Student: He'd get all this attention and he couldn't obviously . . .
Student: No, he wouldn't be able to [continue to live as before] if they all found out that he did it.
Teacher: Why not?
Student: Well, he's going to have to go to trial, and uhh, . . . all this stuff, and everyone will know about what he has.
Student: I think it's worth it . . .
Teacher: So you think that Heck Tate was wrong in covering up?

In this excerpted discussion, the many interchanges among students are immediately apparent. Students appear to control the turn taking and the flow of the discussion topic, and manifest the authority to explore varied interpretations of the moral conundrum present in the text. The teacher's questions are understood by students to be open-ended and authentic. Indeed, following the teacher's question, the students immediately launch into exploration, probing, and considering possibilities. Also striking in this example is that student talk is more syntactically complete and complex (Applebee et al., 2003). As in a genuine dialogic interchange, the students' responses build on each another by taking up previous remarks although not necessarily in the form of a question. The students appear to be genuinely interested in exploring the issue of a cover-up, and the discourse nicely illustrates a situation in which students are exercising interpretive authority. Moreover, the teacher's response reinforces the authority of the students in interpreting and making meaning of the text (e.g., "So you think that Heck Tate was wrong in covering up?").

The previous exchange is very different from traditional recitation where the teacher recites what is known about a particular topic or what can be gleaned from a given text (Wilkinson, 2009). In recitation, the teacher holds interpretive authority and controls the talk. In recitation, the teacher typically talks almost 70% of the time (Cazden, 2001) and exchanges between the teacher and the students follow an IRE (Mehan, 1979) or IRF (Sinclair & Coulthard, 1975) pattern in which the teacher *initiates* a topic by asking a question; the student *responds*; and, the teacher *evaluates* or gives *feedback* regarding the students response. The IRE or IRF pattern of discourse is often portrayed as counterproductive to student learning or comprehension (e.g., Almasi & Garas-York, 2009; Nystrand, 2006).

In this chapter, rather than portray a given approach as always good or always bad or pit one theoretical perspective against another theoretical perspective, our goal is to take a more pragmatic approach to discussion as an instructional method—an approach in keeping with the writings of early 20th-century American philosophers like William James, John Dewey, or Charles Peirce. In short, our goal is to offer an integrative overview of the theoretical and empirical literature pertaining to classroom discussion with an eye toward the enhancement of student learning. Moreover, given that closely related instructional methods such as collaboration (Slavin, Chapter 17 in this volume), feedback (Hattie and Gan, Chapter 13 in this volume), or questioning and self-explanation (Fonseca and Chi, Chapter 15 in this volume) are being covered in other chapters within this volume, we have chosen to narrow our focus primarily to classroom discussion about, around, or with text. That is, our focus is on text-based discussions, though research and theory on classroom discussions in general are referenced, as needed, to situate this work. The remainder of this chapter is comprised of four major sections including: (a) a philosophical and sociological history of discussion in which we overview some of the major forces that have helped to shape discussion as an instructional tool; (b) a contemporary theoretical framework where we outline some of the predominant models of classroom discussion about text; (c) current trends and issues pertaining to key findings in the relevant empirical literature on approaches to classroom discussion; and (d) future directions in which we consider next steps for teachers and researchers in this important area.

PHILOSOPHICAL AND SOCIOLOGICAL OVERVIEW OF THE HISTORY OF DISCUSSION

The centrality of talk in teaching and learning is as old as language itself. Arguably, what has changed or evolved over time is the emphasis placed on various features of the talk, as well as our understanding of the role that talk plays in student learning. Indeed, there are likely as many perspectives on talk in the annals of history as there are individuals who have written about the topic. Our purpose herein is not to offer a detailed or complete genealogy of the history of discussion as an instructional tool. The exact genealogy of classroom discussion is not overtly clear in the extant literature. This lack of genealogical clarity is likely due to the pervasiveness of talk in every aspect of life, as well as the shared lineages of constructs such as dialogue, dialectic, discourse, rhetoric, and discussion.

Our intention is to highlight philosophers and theorists from history whom we have judged to be key theoretical ancestors of classroom discussion. To us, the theoretical leanings and writings of these ancestors are readily apparent in contemporary theories and models of classroom discussion. Certainly, our selection is not exhaustive nor is it meant to be irrefutable. The forbearers of discussion that we selected include: ancient and medieval philosophers, 16th-century empiricists, and late 19th-century German and American social theorists.

Ancient and Medieval Thinkers: The Birth of Dialectical Reasoning

Explorations of the various types of talk and their role in learning, understanding, and remembering are evident in the texts of ancient Greek philosophers circa 350 BC (e.g., Cornford, 1935). The Socratic method or elenchus, often illustrated in Plato's dialogues such as the *Meno* or the *Symposium*, is perhaps the paragon discussion method. An elenchus discussion is one in which an individual poses an initial or primary question (e.g., What is knowledge?) to another individual who responds to the question usually with a statement. In most of the Platonic dialogues, Socrates serves as the questioner and some less knowledgeable individual (e.g., Theatetus) serves as the responder. After this initial exchange, the questioner asks a series of follow-up or secondary questions in order to test the truth value of the responder's initial statement. In essence, the elenchus is a form of intricate refutation or cross-examination (Robinson, 1953). In many of Plato's dialogues (e.g., *Meno*), the primary question aligns very much with what Nystrand (1997) refers to as an authentic question pertaining to an issue of genuine interest and importance, whereas the secondary questions appear much more in line with test questions where there is a predetermined answer.

The overarching purpose of the discourse in these early dialogues is to lay bare the ignorance of the responder regarding the topic—a topic that the responder initially answered with some assurance. Importantly, however, Socrates thought of himself as midwife to the intellectual progeny of those whom he engaged in dialogue (Woods & Murphy, 2001). In the *Theatetus*, Socrates states that through his intellectual exchange he could, "prove by every test whether the offspring of a young man's thought [was] a false phantom or instinct with life and truth" (Bostock, 1988, 150c). Socrates maintained that only by realizing one's ignorance could the individual have any hope of gaining a true understanding of the topic.

One of the primary criticisms levied against this type of discussion is that the refutation illuminates that the initial statement of the responder is incorrect but fails to explain *why* the reasoning is flawed (Robinson, 1953). In the later dialogues, Plato alters his method of elenchus to be more integrated into the dialectic, the exchanges were friendlier, and both members of the discussion exhibited increased participation. The questioners more readily acknowledged their attempts to refute the initial claim and the responders attempted to defend their claims (e.g., Gadamer, 1980).

This more open type of discussion laid the groundwork for Aristotle's syllogistic rules in *Topics* and his notions of proofs in *Rhetoric*. Aristotle defined rhetoric as "the faculty of discovering in the particular case what are the available means of persuasion" (Cooper, 1932, p. 7). Although persuasion is often construed as outside the purview of educational settings and classroom discussions, Aristotle considered persuasion to be a particularly effective means of instruction particularly when individuals failed to be convinced by scientific arguments (Cooper, 1932). In *Rhetoric*, Aristotle explained that the essence of persuasion lies in the nature of the arguments or proofs forwarded in the text (i.e., oral or written). He described two types of proofs: artistic proofs (i.e., evidence or arguments created by the author) and nonartistic proofs (e.g., laws, witnesses, or contracts). Whereas personal testimony, written contracts, laws, and the like (i.e., nonartistic proofs) are present at the outset of any oratory, artistic proofs must be supplied or invented by the speaker. Artistic proofs must appeal to the knowledge and beliefs of the audience. This can be accomplished in a number of ways. A speaker might gain the confidence of the listener based on personal characteristics as portrayed in speech or text (i.e., ethos) or the speaker may choose to elicit a particular attitude in the listener (i.e., pathos). Still another approach by the speaker would be to present a strong, cogent argument that taps into the present knowledge and beliefs of the receiver.

Heavily influenced by Aristotle's writings, St. Thomas Aquinas was a key figure in the 13th-century Scholastic method of teaching as is evidenced in the *Summa Theologica* (1947). The Scholastic method of teaching emphasized dialectical reasoning where the primary activity was to find answers to important questions by scouring multiple, usually conflicting, texts and seeking to resolve differences in the texts through philosophical and logical analysis. It is this style of teaching that formed the basis of Aquinas's philosophy of education, and provided the template for his written arguments. Rather than laying the truth out for the students, Aquinas thought that the process of presenting the question, then introducing arguments for and against, not only would provide a model of academic reasoning for the students, but also strengthen the listeners' understanding of all facets of the issue raised.

Whether it be the elenchus enacted by Socrates in Plato's later dialogues, Aristotle's artistic proofs, or the scholasticism of St. Aquinas, these scholars laid the groundwork for later discussion models that emphasize critical and analytic analyses of talk and text. These ancient scholars encouraged those they taught to grapple with difficult questions and conflicting positions and sources, and talk was one of the primary mechanisms through which students were encouraged to consider multiple perspectives and the truth value of what was commonly accepted.

17th-Century Empiricists: Sense Experiences Precede Reasoning

The theoretical roots of much of the research on classroom discourse (e.g., Graesser, Gernsbacher, & Goldman, 2003; Kintsch, 2005), particularly cognitively oriented investigations, can be traced to 17th-century British empiricists. Similarly, a number of approaches to text-based discussion (e.g., *Instructional Conversations*, Goldenberg, 1993) emphasize the need for students' to build accurate mental models of the text, and classroom discussion is seen an a mechanism for enhancing students' ability to build accurate mental representations. As such, we think it is important to look to the philosophical past in order to explore the theoretical roots of these more cognitively oriented, knowledge-focused models.

In the broadest sense, empiricism refers to a philosophical position in which *a posteriori* reasoning (i.e., reasoning from sense experience or observation) provides a mechanism for obtaining substantive knowledge and truths about the world (Locke, 1917). Radical empiricists understand sense experience to be our sole source of knowledge when it comes to the nature of the world (Hume, 1748/1910). It is not that such knowledge is automatic, but rather that deductions or inferences must be based in sensory experience. Empiricism found strong supporters among anti-rationalists of the 17th century including John Locke, George Berkeley, and David Hume. Among Locke's (1917) many contributions to empiricism is the notion that children are born without innate ideas and that "perception is the inlet to all knowledge" (p. 72). That is, the mind is a *tabula rasa* or blank slate on which sensory experiences are imprinted for future reflection (Locke, 1917). In a text-based discussion, the discussion itself would serve as a sensory experience that can be imprinted.

In his essays on human understandings, particularly Essays IX and X, Locke argued that ideas are actual sense perceptions in the mind. Imprinting or stamping is a process that proceeds from sensation to reflection, and potentially, retention. Like modern information processing models (Baddeley, 2003), Locke suggests that there are two routes to retention: (1) contemplation (i.e., keeping the perception active); and (2) memory (i.e., stored for later retrieval). Moreover, retention or "fixing" in memory is mediated by attention, repetition, pleasure, and pain (Locke, 1917, pp. 75–76). Locke also claimed that remembering or reviving memories requires active processing, and that the building of complex or compound ideas involves discerning and clarifying among many perceptions. Without the refreshing of both simple and complex ideas, these understandings will decay and be forgotten. Classroom discussion of a text allows students to both revisit the perceptions they acquired during reading, and allows them to gain additional relevant perceptions from the other members of the discussion.

Although contemporary research in educational and cognitive psychology has questioned the notion of pure sensory imprinting, the fact remains that much of what Locke (1917) proposed in his essays on human understanding served to undergird positivistic and post-positivistic research in various realms of psychology. Moreover, as we have illustrated above, some of the basic tenets of Locke's perspectives on human learning also undergird aspects of contemporary models of classroom discussion about text, particularly those approaches emphasizing the building of mental models of text through discourse (e.g., Beck & McKeown, 2006).

19th-Century Philosophers and Sociologists: The Social Awakening

Although the literatures from the late 19th and early 20th centuries are replete with the writings of scholars who have likely influenced the nature of contemporary models of classroom discussion of text, we have chosen to highlight just a few individuals that we feel brought the importance of the social and cultural condition to the forefront. In turn, the writings of these individuals radically influenced approaches to classroom talk about text. Among those individuals are Karl Marx, noted author of the *Communist Manifesto* (Marx & Engels, 2004), and Charles Cooley most known for his concept of the looking-glass self (1902/1922). Both in their native countries and abroad, these individuals shed light on the interplay between the individual and society and culture. Arguably, one of the basic tenets underlying text-based discussion models is that students' benefit from talk about text because it exposes students to diverse perspectives on a given text. That is, students' interpretations, explanations, and understandings are colored by the social and cultural experiences that they bring to the reading of the text.

Indeed, the rise of sociocultural theory, which serves as a backbone of many contemporary classroom discussion models in the late 20th century, has been attributed to pragmatist philosophers and anthropologists such as Dewey and Mead, as well as Marxist social theory through the work of Soviet scholars like Vygotsky and Luria (Cole, 1996; Giddens, 1979). Marxist social theory held that the existence of humans is fundamentally based on the ways that humans and nature interact; it is an intricate dance in which the knower and what is to be known mutually adapt. In *Grundrisse*, Marx (1973) states: "Society does not consist of individuals but expresses the sum of interrelations, the relations within which these individuals stand" (p. 265). What matters most in the Marxist paradigm is not society or the individual, but the relations between individuals.

Sociocultural theory has also been traced to Cooley's writings on human nature and the social order. In fact, Cooley (1902/1922) has been credited as introducing one of the primary tenets of sociocultural theory; that is, the claim of inseparability of the individual and society (Sawyer, 2002). Cooley (1902), in his classic treatise on human nature and the social order, wrote: "*Society* and *individuals* do not denote separable phenomena" (pp. 1–2). It is from this notion of the collective that the idea of co-construction of meaning emerges, and upon which the role of the community as the repository of legitimate cultural practices takes form (Lave & Wenger, 1991). Indeed, as Marx (1973) suggests, the same object can appear very different and necessarily hold a differential value for individuals from varying social classes.

It is this diversity of thinking that is reflective of one's unique life experiences that is often manifested during discussions of text. In fact, some researchers of text-based discussion would contend that the understandings of a text that emerge from a group discussion are representative of this inseparability. That is, the meanings cannot be ascribed to any single individual because individual and social thinking are indivisible in a classroom discussion. Indeed, although neither Marx nor Cooley wrote explicitly about classroom discussion, the emphasis that these scholars placed on the social and cultural aspects of human existence is reflected in contemporary models of classroom discussion. This is particularly the case for those approaches to discussion of text that privilege students' aesthetic and emotive responses to the text and emphasize the importance of breaking down the traditional classroom power structure where the teacher is the gatekeeper to knowledge (e.g., *Book Club*, Raphael & McMahon, 1994).

CONTEMPORARY THEORETICAL FRAMEWORKS

The theory underlying the use of discussions as an instructional tool to improve learning from text derives from cognitive, social constructivist, sociocultural, and dialogic perspectives on learning and teaching. Historically, cognitive theory preceded social constructivist and sociocultural theory so we have chosen to present the theoretical frameworks in that order. Order is in no way meant to imply importance, as our perspective is that there is much to be gleaned from the extant literatures in each of these areas.

Cognitive Theory

Although many contemporary researchers emphasize the sociocognitive and sociocultural theoretical underpinnings of classroom discussion (e.g., Almasi & Garas-York, 2009; Cazden & Beck, 2003), there also exists a rich cognitive theoretical literature pertaining to the ways students process and make meaning from discourse and text (Graesser, Gernsbacher, & Goldman, 2003). Cognitive-based theoretical models such as the Construction-Integration model (Kintsch, 1988, 1998) or the Concurrent, Capacity-Constrained Activation-Based Production System (3CAPS, Carpenter, Miyake, & Just, 1994; Just & Carpenter, 1992) are being applied to classroom discourse to better understand the mechanisms at play when students attempt to mentally represent and process the various forms of discourse and text present within a classroom environment.

Such cognitive models are also being employed to examine how various mechanisms and processes can be used to predict or explain student learning and change (Graesser, Swamer, Baggett, & Sell, 1996). Indeed, the purpose of these models is to understand the ways in which social interaction promotes individual reasoning and knowledge acquisition (Piaget, 1928/1967) by accounting for both learner characteristics such as prior knowledge, working memory capacity, or beliefs, *and* features of the discourse or text including source credibility, coherence, or rhetorical structure (e.g., Kintsch, 1988; Goldman, Varma, & Coté 1996; Murphy & Alexander, 2004). Although it is beyond the scope of the present chapter to overview all of the various cognitive discourse models, it is important nonetheless to examine some common themes and assumptions across many cognitive models of discourse.

There are a number of commonalities across the more prominent models of discourse and text comprehension (Foltz, 2003). One key commonality is the assumption that discourse comprehension requires that the message be perceived and internalized by the receiver in the form of mental representations (e.g., propositions, semantic networks, or scripts). Discourse researchers have embraced propositional representations more than other representational possibilities (e.g., Kintsch, 1998). In discourse and text models, propositions are the smallest unit assumed to contain meaning and are usually comprised of a predicate (i.e., verb or adjective) and at least one argument (e.g., a noun or another proposition; van Dijk & Kintsch, 1983).

Because propositions are the smallest, meaningful unit of discourse, they can be incorporated through processing into other forms of representations including scripts or schemas. Moreover, although propositional representations capture the meaning of a discourse segment, they do no retain the surface or sentence structure of the message (see Kintsch, 1998). Studies have shown that when cued to a given proposition, individuals are more likely to remember information from within that proposition than information from other propositions from the same sentence.

A second commonality across many cognitive, discourse models is that during the encoding of discourse or text, individuals construct increasingly complex levels of cognitive representation (Zwaan & Singer, 2003). At least three levels of increasingly complex representation are widely accepted in the field of cognitive models of discourse comprehension (van Dijk & Kintsch, 1983). Among the levels of discourse processing are the *surface form* or surface code that refers to a record of the exact wording and syntax of the discourse or text. Generally, the surface form remains in memory for only a few seconds (Gernsbacher, 1985; Jarvella, 1971). Research indicates that retention can be mediated by expectations or pragmatic content like a joke (e.g., Zwaan, 1996). For example, in hearing or reading a song, the actual words are of particular importance and listeners generally retain the actual text longer than would be expected for other text genres (Rubin, 1995).

The next level of representation is the *textbase*, which contains the semantic meaning or explicit propositions from the text. These propositions are generally understood to be networked into a simplified form that retains meaning but loses the surface code syntactic details. As more text is read, the individual adds to the propositional network in working memory (Fletcher & Bloom, 1988). Given the initial processing, the textbase has been shown to be retained in memory for several minutes. Of note is that while van Dijk and Kintsch (1983) separated these first two levels of representation, other researchers have chosen to collapse across these levels (e.g., Johnson-Laird's 1996 propositional representation).

The final level proposed by van Dijk and Kintsch (1983) is the *situation model* or the mental model. In creating the situation model, the individual combines the textbase propositions with propositions from long-term memory that serve to provide a fuller and richer understanding of the situation portrayed in the discourse or text (Foltz, 2003). The construction of a sufficient situation model requires an adequate level of prior knowledge or world knowledge pertinent to the message being comprehended. This deeper level of processing also results in longer retention of the situation model in memory. Shallow comprehension requires only the surface code and textbase, whereas deeper comprehension requires the creation of a cohesive, situation model of the text (e.g., Coté, Goldman, & Saul, 1998; Verhoeven & Graesser, 2008; Zwaan et al., 1995). Of importance is the caveat that there remains some debate concerning the extent to which situational models are comprised primarily of propositions or of some combination of propositions and images (Paivio, 2008).

The final commonality across many cognitive models employed to understand text and discourse comprehension pertains to the mechanisms involved in students' processing of what they hear and read. That is, how exactly are students able to assign meaning to discourse or text? Until more recently, there were at least two competing perspectives on this issue. In the memory-based view of comprehension, it was assumed that the memory-based processes associated with reading took place autonomously and passively, and that activation was the result of the signaling from the discourse or text input and its association to other information such as prior knowledge (e.g., McKoon, Gerrig, & Greene, 1996).

In stark contrast, the constructionist perspective assumed that learners must actively engage in the search for meaning while participating in discourse or reading a text (Graesser, Singer, & Trabasso, 1994). During the activity of reading, students were assumed to be goal-directed, monitoring coherence of the various levels of representation, and seeking explanations for outcomes and inferences within the text (Zwaan & Singer, 2003). Interestingly, there exists convincing empirical evidence in support of both positions (see van den Broek, Rapp, & Kendou, 2005). Over the last decade, however, the tensions between these two perspectives have given way to cognitive models that integrate the memory-based position with the constructionist position in which some processes take place passively while others require active, conscious processing of the text (Verhoeven & Graesser, 2008). The Landscape Model proposed by van den Broek and colleagues (2005) serves as an example of an empirically supported integrated model. What is important about these cognitive theories of text and discourse comprehension is that they provide a theoretical mapping for researchers to create discussion approaches that will enhance these comprehension processes. As Locke suggested so many years ago, such models would enhance the construction process and the building of meaningful mental models that can aid in comprehension and retention of content.

Social Constructivist and Sociocultural Theory

Social constructivist and sociocultural theory are routinely invoked to explain the role of discussion in promoting students' understandings of discourse and text (Murphy et al., 2009). As perhaps the eminent social constructivist, Vygotsky's theoretical and empirical writings have had a profound effect on models of classroom discussion. Vygotsky (1934/1986) conceived of learning as a culturally embedded and socially mediated process in which discourse plays a primary role in the creation and acquisition of shared meaning making. Moreover, children develop the skills and abilities needed to read through the participation in literacy-rich environments. Within these environments, children are apprenticed into the literate community through authentic, real-world participation with more knowledgeable others including parents, teachers, or more capable peers. Importantly, while the skill development and apprenticeship take place on the social plane, Vygotsky (1978) also conceptualized reading and writing as higher-order psychological processes. Essentially, Vygotsky understood these higher order psychological processes as emerging out of students' participation in literacy communities (Tharp & Gallimore, 1988).

> Vygotsky argues that a child's development cannot be understood by a study of the individual. We must also examine the external social world in which that individual life has developed . . . Through participation in activities that require cognitive and communicative functions, children are drawn into the use of these functions in ways that nurture and "scaffold" them.
>
> (Tharp & Gallimore, 1988, pp. 6–7)

As was advanced in Cooley's (1902/1922) early writings on nature and the social order, students involved in talk about text necessarily bring to the discussion unique cultural and social values, differential levels of prior knowledge, varied background experiences, and potentially disparate assumptions about learning and text. Through interactions in the discussion, learners are exposed to, evaluate, and possibly incorporate ways of thinking about the text that are very different from their individually contrived understandings. When students interact with others in a group in deep and meaningful ways, the outcomes or results that are produced are beyond the abilities and dispositions of the individual students who comprise the group (Wertsch, Del Rio, & Alvarez, 1995). As Dewey (1916) suggested, these new abilities and dispositions are then internalized by learners and can be transferred to other activities that involve independent learning or problem solving (Anderson et al., 2001; Hatano, 1993).

Another key assumption of the social constructivist and sociocultural theory is that reasoning is inherently dialogical and that growth and development are encouraged through dialogic reasoning (Bahktin 1981; Vygotsky, 1978). That is, one's reasoning is necessarily a response to what has been said or experienced as well as an anticipation of what will be said in response. It is not so much that one cannot reason individually but rather that reasoning is mediated by prior experiences and the anticipation of future social experiences. In short, the reasoning process, like the social environment, is dynamic and relational. In the context of text comprehension and classroom discussion, the dialogic process is negotiated and sustained through interpretations of text, high-level reasoning, and standards of interaction that govern group behavior. It is for this reason that approaches like *Collaborative Reasoning* are structured so as to encourage learners to consider their own perspective, as well as the perspectives of their peers (Anderson et al., 2001; Reznitskaya et al., 2001). As Vygotsky suggests, these types of social interactions encourage cognitive growth: "[Growth is] more likely when one is required to explain, elaborate, or defend one's position to others, as well as to oneself; striving for an explanation often make a learner integrate and elaborate in new ways" (Vygotsky, 1978, p. 158).

Summary

Our goal in this section has been to overview the various contemporary theories influencing models of classroom discussion designed to enhance text comprehension. We contend that a deep understanding of the ways in which classroom discourse enhances student learning requires an integration of the cognitive, social constructivist, and sociocultural theoretical perspectives. Simply put, it is not enough to embrace the outward language, tools, and signs that students make use of during discussion without considering how these exchanges are internalized, encoded, and processed by the learner, or the manner in which students justify their views or substantiate their claims. To date, however, the majority of approaches to classroom discussion attend more to the socially-shared and socially-constructed nature of learning than to the cognitive internalization of what is being shared. In the section that follows, we overview trends and issues at play in contemporary research on classroom discussion.

CURRENT TRENDS AND ISSUES

An issue confronting the field is what the different approaches to conducting discussions about text have to offer teachers and their students. As indicated earlier, there is a plethora of approaches to conducting text-based discussions and it is difficult for educators to make informed decisions about when, why, and how to use them. A related issue confronting the field is the strengths and weaknesses of the approaches in terms of their impact on students' learning and comprehension of text. In this section, we identify the major approaches to conducting discussions about text and attempt to make sense of them by describing their similarities and differences. We then examine what is known about their effects on students' learning and comprehension.

Making Sense of the Approaches

Wilkinson, Soter, and Murphy (2007) conducted a synthesis of research on classroom discussions about text and identified nine major approaches. To qualify as a major discussion approach, they stipulated that the approach had to demonstrate consistency of application—it had to *look* the same wherever it was implemented—and have an established place in educational research or practice based on a record of peer-reviewed, empirical research published since 1970. Using these criteria, they identified nine major approaches: *Instructional Conversations* (Goldenberg, 1993), *Junior Great Books Shared Inquiry* (Great Books Foundation, 1987), *Questioning the Author* (Beck & McKeown, 2006), *Collaborative Reasoning* (Anderson, Chinn, Waggoner, & Nguyen, 1998), *Paideia Seminars* (Billings & Fitzgerald, 2002), *Philosophy for Children* (Sharp, 1995), *Book Club* (Raphael & McMahon, 1994), *Grand Conversations* (Eeds & Wells, 1989), and *Literature Circles* (Short & Pierce, 1990).

There are other approaches to conducting classroom discussions about text. These include *Conversational Discussion Groups* (O'Flahavan, 1989), *Dialogical-Reading Thinking Lessons* (Commeyras, 1993), *Idea Circles* (Guthrie & McCann, 1996), and *Point-Counterpoint* (Rogers, 1990). These approaches have some prominence in the field but they did not meet Wilkinson et al.'s criteria because there is relatively little empirical research on them. There are also various instantiations of literature discussion groups based on reader-response theory (see Gambrell & Almasi, 1996), discussion-based envisionments of literature (Langer, 1993, 1995, 2001), and instructional integrations of writing, reading, and talk (Nystrand, Gamoran, & Carbonaro, 2001; Sperling & Woodlief, 1997). These approaches have also received attention in the research literature but they did not meet Wilkinson et al.'s criteria because they do not show consistency of application necessary to consider them as distinct approaches. There is also an approach called *Accountable Talk*, developed by Lauren Resnick and colleagues (Michaels, O'Connor, & Resnick, 2008; Michaels, O'Connor, Hall, & Resnick, 2002). Accountable Talk comprises a set of conditions for productive conversation in academic contexts and forms part of the New Standards Project (Resnick, 1999; Resnick & Hall, 1998). Wilkinson et al. did not include it in their review because it is not specifically designed for conducting text-based discussions (although it has applicability as an approach for promoting reading comprehension; see Wolf, Crosson, & Resnick, 2005).

The similarities and differences in the nine major approaches identified by Wilkinson et al. (2007) can best be described by characterizing them on various dimensions. Table 19.1 describes the nine approaches in terms of several aspects of a discussion: the stance toward the text, who chooses the topic for discussion, who has interpretive authority, who controls turn taking, who chooses the text, the size of the discussion group, and whether the group is peer- or teacher-led. Stance toward the text is largely established by the teacher and classroom context and is usually categorized in terms of an aesthetic, efferent, or critical-analytic stance. An aesthetic or, more appropriately, expressive

Table 19.1 Characterization of approaches by aspect of discussion

Aspect	Approach								
	LC	GC	BC	QtA	IC	JGB	PS	CR	P4C
Expressive stance	High	High	High	Low to Medium	Low	Low	Medium	Medium	High
Efferent stance	Medium	Medium	Medium	High	High	High	Medium	Medium	Medium
Critical-analytic stance	Medium	Medium	Medium	Medium	Medium	Medium	High	High	High
Control of topic	Students	Students	Students	Teacher	Teacher	Teacher	Teacher	Teacher	Teacher
Interpretive authority	Students & Teacher	Students & Teacher	Students	Teacher	Teacher	Teacher	Students & Teacher	Students	Students
Control of turns	Students	Students	Students	Teacher	Students & Teacher	Students & Teacher	Students & Teacher	Students	Teacher
Chooses text	Students	Teacher	Students	Teacher	Teacher	Teacher	Teacher	Teacher	Teacher
Small-group or whole-class	Small group	Small group	Small group	Whole class	Small group / Whole class	Whole class	Whole class	Small group	Whole class
Peer- or teacher-led	Peer	Teacher	Peer	Teacher	Teacher	Teacher	Teacher	Teacher	Teacher

Note: LC = Literature Circles, GC = Grand Conversations, BC = Book Club, QtA = Questioning the Author, IC = Instructional Conversations, JGB = Junior Great Books, PS = Paideia Seminar, CR = Collaborative Reasoning, P4C = Philosophy for Children.

stance (Soter, Wilkinson, Connors, Murphy, & Shen, 2010) privileges a reader's affective response to the text, her spontaneous, emotive connection to all aspects of the textual experience (Rosenblatt, 1978). An efferent stance privileges a more utilitarian response to the text—reading for the purpose of acquiring and retrieving information. The focus is on "the ideas, information, directions, conclusions to be retained, used, or acted on after the reading event" (Rosenblatt, 1978, p. 27). A critical-analytic stance privileges a more objective, critical response in which the reader interrogates or queries the text in search of the underlying arguments, assumptions, worldviews, or beliefs (cf. Wade, Thompson, & Watkins, 1994).

As can be seen from Table 19.1, two important dimensions on which discussions vary are the dominant stance toward the text and the degree of control of the discussion exerted by the teacher versus the students (cf. Chinn et al., 2001). Wilkinson et al. (2007) noticed that these two dimensions of discussions are related. Discussions that give prominence to an aesthetic or expressive stance toward the text tend to be those in which students have the greatest control over topic, interpretive authority, turn taking, and choice of text. These approaches include Literature Circles, Grand Conversations, and Book Club. Conversely, discussions that give prominence to an efferent stance tend to be those in which teachers have the greatest control. These approaches include Questioning the Author, Instructional Conversations, and Junior Great Books Shared Inquiry. Discussions that give prominence to a critical-analytic stance tend to be those in which teachers and students share control. In these approaches, the teacher has considerable control over the choice of text and topic, but students have considerable interpretive authority and control of turns. These approaches include Paideia Seminars, Collaborative Reasoning, and Philosophy for Children.

Another dimension on which discussions vary is the size of the discussion group (small-group versus whole-class). As shown in Table 19.1, Questioning the Author, Junior Great Books Shared Inquiry, Paideia Seminar, and Philosophy for Children tend to use whole-class arrangements or, at least, discussions with large groups of about 10–14 students. The other approaches tend to use smaller groups. The available evidence suggests that smaller groups are better for discussion although they should not be so small as to limit the diversity of ideas needed for productive discussion (see Wiencek & O'Flahavan, 1994). Morrow and Smith (1990), in a study of kindergarten students who engaged in discussions of stories that were read aloud, reported benefits of small-group discussions compared to one-on-one discussions with the teacher or whole-class discussions. Sweigart (1991), in a study of 58 twelfth grade students, found that student-led small-group discussions produced greater effects on students' recall and understanding of essays they had read than did lecture or whole-class discussions. Smaller groups provide more opportunities for students to speak, interact, and exchange points of view in discussion, thus contributing to greater knowledge and understanding of the text and of how to make sense of text.

Yet another dimension on which discussions vary is whether they are peer- or teacher-led. Book Club discussions (those that occur in small groups rather than the whole class 'Community Share') and many Literature Circles are peer-led whereas the other types of discussions are teacher-led. The relative merits of the two formats have been the subject of some debate and available research has not yielded a definitive answer on the issue. Peer-led discussions can enable students collectively to explore topics more fully and to have more control and interpretive authority (Almasi, 1996). However, in teacher-led discussions, the teacher can play an important role in keeping students on topic, fostering norms for productive discourse, and modeling and scaffolding talk to enhance the quality of learning opportunities for students (O'Flahavan, Stein, Wiencek, & Marks, 1992; see also Michaels, O'Connor, & Resnick, 2008; Soter et al., 2008; Wells, 1989). Most likely the key question is not so much whether the teacher or students should lead the group as it is how much structure and focus is provided while giving students the flexibility and responsibility for thinking and reasoning together (cf. Mercer, 1995). Productive discussions need to be structured and focused but flexible enough to foster generative learning—and these can be peer- or teacher-led.

Examining Effects

Research has examined whether discussion improves the learning and comprehension of the texts that were the subject of discussion as well as the learning and comprehension of new texts not discussed in class or performance on new but related tasks. It stands to reason that enabling students to engage in discussions about texts should improve their comprehension of those texts. For example, in an experimental study, Fall, Webb, and Chudowsky (2000) analyzed tenth grade students' performance on language arts tests in which students either discussed or did not discuss a story they were required to read and interpret. Their results showed that allowing students to engage in a 10-minute discussion of the story in three-person groups improved students' factual knowledge of the story as well as their understanding of characters' motives and feelings and the story's theme. Similarly, in a quasi-experimental study, Van den Branden (2000) showed that allowing fifth grade Dutch students, many of whom were non-native speakers, to negotiate the meaning of story by means of discussion improved their comprehension of the main ideas relative to that of students who simply read the story.

The more interesting and important issue for educational research is whether discussion enables students to acquire the habits of mind to transfer their comprehension and learning capabilities to new texts and novel tasks. In this section we examine the role of discussion in enhancing students' comprehension and learning outcomes giving particular attention to the results of studies where researchers have assessed the effects of discussion on measures that are independent of the texts that were discussed. We first consider correlational studies, then quasi-experimental and experimental studies in general, then the subset of quasi-experimental and experimental studies that addressed the issue of transfer.

Correlational Studies

Applebee et al. (2003) conducted a large-scale correlational study of the relationship between discussion and students' literary performance. They observed instructional practices in 64 middle- and high-school English classrooms across the U.S. on four occasions over the school year. They also assessed the students' literary performance in terms of their ability to write essays, scored for levels of abstraction and elaboration, collecting data on 974 students. One of the writing tasks related to a novel, short story, or play that they had studied during the year, but the other task related to writing about a general experience. Their results showed that discussion-based practices, used in the context of academically challenging tasks, were positively related to students' literary performance on the writing tasks.

Similar results have been reported in other correlational studies. Langer (2001) studied the instructional practices associated with student achievement in 25 middle and high schools, involving 44 teachers and 88 classes. The study involved a nested, multiple-case design comparing practices in schools with higher-than-expected achievement in literacy with those in more typically performing schools. She found that whole-class and small-group discussion was one of the characteristics of instruction in the schools that showed higher-than-expected achievement in reading, writing, and English.

In another correlational study, Taylor, Pearson, Clark, and Walpole (2000) observed the instructional practices in first through third grade classrooms in 14 high-poverty schools in Virginia, Minnesota, Colorado, and California, and compared the practices in schools categorized as most, moderately, or least effective in promoting student reading achievement. They showed that asking higher-level, aesthetic-response questions in discussions about text was a feature of instruction of the most accomplished teachers and of teachers in the most effective schools (see also, Taylor, Pearson, Clark, & Walpole, 1999). In subsequent school change work to promote the cognitive engagement of students in grades 1–5 in high-poverty schools, Taylor, Pearson, Peterson, and Rodriguez (2003, 2005) again found that the incidence of teachers' higher-level questions about text predicted students' end-of-year achievement on a number of measures of reading and writing (though not always on measures of reading comprehension).

Quasi-Experimental and Experimental Studies

Murphy et al. (2009) conducted a meta-analysis of 42 quantitative studies of the effects of the nine major approaches to text-based discussions described earlier. They included single-group, pre-test and post-test design studies and multiple-group studies and examined effects on measures of teacher and student talk as well as on measures of individual student comprehension and learning outcomes. Results showed that the approaches were differentially effective in promoting comprehension. Many of the approaches were effective at promoting students' literal and inferential comprehension especially those that had a more efferent stance toward the text, namely Questioning the Author, Instructional Conversations, and Junior Great Books Shared Inquiry. Some of the approaches were particularly effective at promoting students' critical-thinking, reasoning, and argumentation about text, namely Collaborative Reasoning and Junior Great Books Shared Inquiry. Another finding from Murphy et al.'s meta-analysis was that increases in student talk did not necessarily result in concomitant increases in student comprehension. Rather, a particular kind of talk was necessary to promote comprehension. This is consistent with observations from other research that the success of discussion hinges not on increasing the amount of student talk per se, but in enhancing the quality of the talk (Wells, 1989). Results of the meta-analysis also suggested that the approaches exhibited greater effects for students of below-average ability than for students of average or above-average ability. Murphy et al. interpreted this finding to mean that the higher-ability students might be able to read a text and think independently about the nuances of meaning even without participating in discussion.

In the discussion that follows, we expand upon the aforementioned general trends emerging from the meta-analytic study conducted by Murphy et al. In doing so, we offer specific effect sizes emerging from noteworthy studies within each of the given approaches as estimates of the effectiveness of the various approaches to classroom discussion. In Table 19.2, we summarize across the various studies conducted by researchers pertaining to each approach both single group (i.e., within-subjects designs) and multiple groups (i.e., between-subjects designs). In doing so, we hoped to provide a somewhat comprehensive picture of the nature of the effectiveness of the various approaches to classroom discussion.

Quasi-Experimental and Experimental Studies Addressing Transfer

In the balance of this section, we focus on the multiple-group studies that examined the effects of discussion on measures of transfer to new texts or novel tasks. Anderson and colleagues (Dong, Anderson, Kim, & Li, 2008; Kim, 2001; Reznitskaya, Anderson, & Kuo, 2007; Reznitskaya et al., 2001) conducted a number of quasi-experimental studies of Collaborative Reasoning with fourth and fifth-grade students. They compared the

Table 19.2 Effect sizes by construct comparing single and multiple group studies within approach

Stance approach	Construct measured						
Grouping	TT	ST	Comp	TE	TI	SI	CT/R
Critical-analytic							
CR							
Single	−1.924	4.097	—	.490	.082	—	2.465
Multiple	—	—	.262	—	—	.668	—
P4C							
Single	—	—	—	—	—	—	—
Multiple	−.291	—	.333	—	—	—	.236
PS							
Single	−.030	−.006	—	—	—	—	—
Multiple	−.655	.446	—	—	—	.428	—
Efferent							
QtA							
Single	.098	.330	−.205	.949	—	—	2.499
Multiple	—	—	—	.800	—	.627	—
IC							
Single	—	2.735	2.798	2.988	—	1.263	—
Multiple	−.408	1.653	—	.509	.568	.610	—
JGB							
Single	—	—	—	2.345	2.135	—	2.392
Multiple	—	—	.176	−.005	.786	—	.408
Expressive							
LC							
Single	−.439	1.637	.633	—	2.136	—	—
Multiple	—	—	.114	—	—	—	—
GC							
Single	.043	—	—	—	.822	—	—
Multiple	—	—	—	—	—	—	—
BC							
Single	—	.050	—	—	—	—	—
Multiple	—	—	—	—	—	—	—

Note: CR = Collaborative Reasoning, P4C = Philosophy for Children, PS = Paideia Seminar, QtA = Questioning the Author, IC = Instructional Conversation, JGB = Junior Great Books, LC = Literature Circles, GC = Grand Conversation, BC = Book Club, TT = Teacher Talk, ST = Student Talk, Comp = General Comprehension, TE = Text-Explicit Comprehension, TI = Text-Implicit Comprehension, SI = Scriptally-Implicit Comprehension, and CT/R = Critical-Thinking/Reasoning performance of students who participated in anywhere from four to ten Collaborative Reasoning discussions with that of students in control conditions who received regular classroom reading instruction. Students' performance was assessed on a persuasive essay-writing task measured by counting the numbers of arguments, counterarguments, and rebuttals in the essays. Anderson and colleagues' results showed that the essays of students who participated in the Collaborative Reasoning discussions contained a greater number of argument components than the essays of students in the control conditions. The magnitude of the effects on the total number of argument components was moderate to large with effect sizes ranging from $d = 0.45$ to 0.68 (Reznitskaya et al., 2008). One interpretation of these results is that the students internalized an argument schema from the oral group discussions and transferred this capability to written argumentation performed individually and independently.

The most stringent tests of the benefits of discussions come from quasi-experimental and experimental studies that examined the effects of discussion, relative to a control condition, on norm- or criterion-referenced standardized measures (rather than researcher-developed measures). Bird (1984) conducted a quasi-experimental study of the effects of the Junior Great Books program on fifth graders' critical reading and thinking skills. One hundred and eight higher-level readers in four school districts of Monmouth County, New Jersey participated in the study. One group received instruction full-time in the Junior Great Books program, one group received instruction in a basal reading program, and one group received instruction in a combination of Junior Great Books and a basal program. Students from different districts were given different treatments and the duration of treatment varied between groups (three to six months with a mean = 4.1 months). At the end of the treatment, students' performance was assessed on the Worden Test of Critical Thinking and Reading and the Ross Tests of Higher Cognitive Processes. Results showed that students' full or part-time participation in Junior Great Books resulted in significant gains in scores on both measures as compared to participation in the basal program only (median $d = 0.46$). There were no significant differences between the scores of the full-time and combination groups.

Heinl (1988) conducted another quasi-experimental study of the effects of the Junior Great books program on fifth graders' comprehension over a period of six months. Thirty students were allocated to three groups of equal reading ability. One group met every two weeks to discuss stories from Junior Great Books; one group read and wrote summaries of the same stories; and one served as a control group that read materials from the fifth grade basal series. At the end of the program, students' performance was assessed on the Iowa Tests of Basic Skills (ITBS). Results showed that there were no significant differences between the three groups on the ITBS reading comprehension post-test. However, there was a significant difference for the low-ability students. The low-ability students who discussed stories from the Junior Great Books program scored higher than the low-ability students in the other two groups on the ITBS reading comprehension post-test. Heinl concluded that the Junior Great Books benefited low-ability students in reading comprehension but did not benefit the high-ability students. It should be noted that all three groups read the materials from the fifth grade basal series, so the Junior Great Books program was a supplement to students' regular reading instruction.

Lipman (1975) carried out an early pilot study of Philosophy for Children in a New Jersey school during 1970–1971. Forty middle and low-income African American students participated. These students were organized into small groups and the groups were randomly assigned to experimental and control conditions. Lipman and two graduate students taught the students in the experimental group according to the Philosophy for Children framework while the control group was given social science instruction. The classes met twice a week for nine weeks. The results of the initial post-test apparently showed that the experimental group students made significant gains over the control group but the original data were lost, so these results cannot be verified. Two and one-half years later, Lipman administered the reading subtest of the Iowa Test of Basic Skills to the students when they were in seventh grade. Results showed a statistically significant and large difference ($d = 0.56$) between the experimental and control group students in favor of Philosophy for Children. This is the strongest effect found for Philosophy for Children on a standardized test and the result needs to be interpreted cautiously. It is not known what instruction students received in the two and one-half years intervening between the implementation of the program and the follow-up testing and whether it differed for students in the experimental and control conditions.

Yeazell (1982) conducted another quasi-experimental study of Philosophy for Children. One hundred fifth grade students from five classes and three schools participated. Four classes were assigned to the experimental group and one class to the control group. The teacher of the control class also taught one of the experimental classes. Students in the experimental condition participated in the *Harry Stottlemeier's Discovery* component of the Philosophy for Children program once a week over the school year as a supplement to the regular reading program. Students completed the Comprehensive Test of Basic Skills (CTBS) the year before and at the end of the school year. Students in the experimental group made statistically significant gains on the CTBS over the year whereas students in the control group did not. Those students taught by the same teacher showed the same results; the experimental group made a significant gain in test scores while the control group did not. Yeazell concluded that implementing philosophical discussions into reading curriculum enhanced the reading comprehension of students.

The effect of Philosophy for Children on students' reading comprehension was also examined in a quasi-experimental study by Banks (1987). The teachers of three grade 2 classes, four grade 4 classes, and two grade 5 classes volunteered to use the Philosophy for Children program over a school year, while equal numbers of teachers at each grade level, selected by school district administrators, served as the control classrooms. Students completed the California Achievement Test before and after the school year and gain scores were calculated. In reading, results showed no significant differences in gain scores between groups at second grade ($d = -0.18$), a significant difference in favor of Philosophy for Children at fourth grade ($d = 0.46$), and no significant difference at fifth grade ($d = 0.27$). We note that the teachers self-selected into the Philosophy for Children program and it was reported that implementation of the program varied between teachers.

Firmer conclusions about the effects of Philosophy for Children can probably be drawn from an experimental study conducted by Chamberlain (1993). Eighty fourth and fifth grade gifted students in two elementary schools participated in the study with students being randomly assigned to experimental and control group within each class. Students in the experimental condition studied the *Harry Stottlemeier's Discovery* component of the Philosophy for Children program five times a week, for one hour each session, for 12 weeks. The students in control groups studied other literature selections for the same amount of time. Students completed the New Jersey Test of Reasoning

Skills and the Ross Test of Higher Cognitive Processes at the end of the 12 weeks. Results showed statistically significant differences between groups in favor of Philosophy for Children in scores on the New Jersey Test of Reasoning Skills ($d = 0.29$) but not on the Ross Test of Higher Cognitive Processes ($d = 0.29$). The latter non-significant finding might have been due to ceiling effects on the Ross Test.

Summary

The findings from the correlational, quasi-experimental and experimental studies reviewed here indicate that there is, at least, a moderate level of evidence that classroom discussions have positive effects on reading and literacy-related outcomes including those that are independent of the texts discussed. The correlational studies are large in scale but suffer from the problems of interpretation typical of such studies, namely that other factors might have been responsible for the observed "effects" or that the causal direction of the effects is the opposite of that assumed (i.e., students who are better readers engage in more discussion-based practices than do other students). The quasi-experimental studies of Collaborative Reasoning by Anderson and colleagues (Dong, Anderson, Kim, & Li, 2008; Kim, 2001; Reznitskaya, Anderson, & Kuo, 2007; Reznitskaya et al., 2001) are rigorous in design and show moderate to large positive effects on a researcher-developed measure. The quasi-experimental studies of Junior Great Books by Bird (1984) and Heinl (1988) and those of Philosophy for Children by Lipman (1975), Yeazell (1982), and Banks (1987) are less rigorous and show small to moderate positive effects on norm- and criterion-referenced measures. Both sets of quasi-experimental studies are open to the interpretation that the observed effects are due to factors specific to the classes or groups under study rather than to the discussion per se. Chamberlain's (1993) experimental study of Philosophy for Children is probably the most rigorous in design and shows small effects on standardized measures of critical thinking and reading. It might be argued that teacher effects are at work in the quasi-experimental and experimental studies but this argument becomes less tenable as the number of studies showing positive effects of discussion grows. Taken together, the studies reviewed in this section suggest that classroom discussions about text can enable students to acquire the habits of mind to transfer their comprehension capabilities to new texts and novel tasks.

FUTURE DIRECTIONS

Although discussion is an integral part of our lived experiences, discussions in classrooms seem to be relatively rare. Commeyras and DeGroff (1998) surveyed the pedagogical practices of a random sample of 1,519 K-12 literacy teachers and related professionals in the U.S. and reported that only 33% of respondents said they frequently or very frequently had students discuss literature in their classrooms. Similarly, Nystrand (1997) observed the instructional practices of teachers in 58 eighth-grade and 54 ninth-grade language arts and English classes in eight Midwestern communities in the U.S. He found that open-ended, whole-class discussion averaged only 52 seconds per class in eighth grade and only 14 seconds per class in ninth grade. By contrast, anecdotal reports suggest that recitation, where teacher and student exchanges follow a traditional IRE or IRF pattern, is still pervasive in elementary and high school classrooms (Almasi, 1996; Cazden, 2001; Goldenberg, 1993; Tharp & Gallimore, 1988; Worthy & Beck, 1995).

If discussions are to become a staple feature of classroom instruction, there is need for developments in three areas. First, although there is a convergence of theory and data suggesting that high-quality discussions can improve students' comprehension and learning of text, there is a need for more experimental and more rigorous research. As we have indicated, much of the research on classroom discussions has used correlational and single-group pre-test and post-test designs. More quasi-experimental and experimental studies of discussion practices, involving rigorous designs, are needed to assess the effects on the quality of classroom discourse as well as on individual student comprehension and learning outcomes. It is important especially to assess students' comprehension and learning on measures that are independent of the discussion to gauge whether students acquire the habits of mind to transfer their abilities to new texts and novel situations. It is also important for research to examine the conduct and effects of discussions with texts in science, social studies and other content areas. Most studies reviewed in this chapter have focused on discussions of literary texts in the language arts. Discussions of informational texts in the content areas likely involve a different set of instructional and design considerations and research is needed to examine how these discussions are best conducted and their effects on students' comprehension and learning.

Second, beyond examining comprehension and learning outcomes as the product of discussions, there is a need to examine the dynamics by which students construct mental models of discussions about and around text. As we have indicated, the majority of approaches to classroom discussion attend more to the socially-shared and socially-constructed nature of learning than to the cognitive internalization of what is being shared. However, as students process discourse, they construct a mental representation in the form of propositions, semantic networks, scripts, or the like. There is a need for more microgenetic research that examines how students make use of the outward language tools and signs during discussion and internalize, encode, and process the information in conjunction with the text to construct an elaborated mental representation. As Dewey (1916) and Vygotsky (1978) suggested, the language of the text, the discourse of discussion, as well as the rhetorical skills and dispositions of the discourse community are probably all implicated in the mental representation students construct from discussion. As we outlined earlier, understanding the ways in which classroom discourse enhances students' comprehension and learning of text will require an integration of the cognitive, social constructivist, and sociocultural theoretical perspectives on discussion.

Third, there is a need for enhanced professional development to enable teachers to make informed decisions about the use of discussion practices. We have seen in this chapter that there are a plethora of approaches to conducting classroom discussions, that they differ on a number of dimensions relevant to classroom practice, and that the approaches are differentially effective for supporting students' comprehension and learning. It is important that pre-service and in-service teachers have an in-depth understanding of the similarities and differences among the approaches and their strengths and weaknesses. This will enable teachers to select approaches that are suited to their purposes, to their students, to the subject areas they teach, and to the contexts in which they work. Also important in professional development is for teachers to understand talk and the role of talk in classroom discussions. We know from the research that the success of discussion depends not on simply increasing the amount of student talk, but in enhancing the quality of the talk. We also know, with some degree of reliability, those aspects of discourse and attendant classroom norms that help shape student comprehension and learning. Teachers need to be familiar with the discourse tools and signs they can use to promote and to recognize productive talk about text and with the kind of classroom culture that is most beneficial for fostering such talk.

REFERENCES

Almasi, J. (1996). A new view of discussion. In L. Gambrell, & J. Almasi (Eds.), *Lively discussions! Fostering engaged reading* (pp. 7–29). Newark, DE: International Reading Association.

Almasi, J. F., & Garas-York, K. (2009). Comprehension and discussion of text. In S. E. Israel, & G. G. Duffy (Eds.), *Handbook of research on reading comprehension* (pp. 470–493). New York: Routledge,

Anderson, R. C., Chinn, C., Waggoner, M., & Nguyen, K. (1998). Intellectually stimulating story discussions. In J. Osborn, & F. Lehr (Eds.), *Literacy for all: Issues in teaching and learning* (pp. 170–186). New York: Guilford Press.

Anderson, R. C., Nguyen-Jahiel, K., McNurlen, B., Archodidou, A., Kim, S., Reznitskaya, A., et al. (2001). The snowball phenomenon: Spread of ways of talking and ways of thinking across groups of children. *Cognition and Instruction, 19,* 1–46.

Applebee, A.N., Langer, J.A., Nystrand, M., & Gamoran, A. (2003). Discussion-based approaches to developing understanding: Classroom instruction and student performance in middle and high school English. *American Educational Research Journal, 40,* 3, 685–730.

Aquinas, St. T. (1947). *Summa theologica.* (Fathers of the English Dominican Province, Trans.). New York: Benzinger Brothers.

Baddeley, A. (2003). Working memory: looking back and looking forward. *Nature Reviews Neuroscience 4*(10): 829–839.

Bakhtin, M.M. (1981). *The dialogic imagination: Four essays.* (C. Emerson, & M. Holdquist, Trans.). Austin: University of Texas Press.

Banks, J. C. R. (1987). A study of the effects of the critical thinking skills program, Philosophy for Children, on a standardized achievement test. Unpublished doctoral dissertation, Southern Illinois University, Carbondale.

Beck, I. L, & McKeown, M. G. (2006). *Improving comprehension with Questioning the Author: A fresh and expanded view of a powerful approach.* New York: Scholastic.

Billings, L., & Fitzgerald, J. (2002). Dialogic discussion and the Paideia Seminar. *American Educational Research Journal, 39,* 907–941.

Bird, J. B. (1984). Effects of fifth graders' attitudes and critical thinking/reading skills resulting from a Junior Great Books program. Unpublished doctoral dissertation, Rutgers-The State University of New Jersey, New Brunswick.

Bostock, D. (1988). *Plato's Theaetetus.* Oxford: Oxford University Press.

Carpenter, P. A., Miyake, A., & Just, M. A. (1994). Working memory constraints in comprehension: Evidence from individual differences, aphasia, and aging. In M. A. Gernsbacher (Ed.), *Handbook of psycholinguistics* (pp. 1075–1122). San Diego, CA: Academic Press.

Cazden, C. B. (2001). *Classroom discourse: The language of teaching and learning* (2nd ed.). Portsmouth, NH: Heinemann.

Cazden, C. B., & Beck, S. W. (2003). Classroom discourse. In A. C. Graesser, M. A. Gernsbacher, & S. R. Goldman (Eds.), *Handbook of discourse processes* (pp. 165–197). Mahwah, NJ: Lawrence Erlbaum Associates.

Chamberlain, M. A. (1993). Philosophy for Children program and the development of critical thinking of gifted elementary students. Unpublished doctoral dissertation, University of Kentucky, Lexington.

Chinn, C. A., Anderson, R. C., & Waggoner, M. A. (2001). Patterns of discourse in two kinds of literature discussion. *Reading Research Quarterly, 36,* 378–411.

Cole, M. (1996). *Cultural psychology: A once and future discipline.* Cambridge, MA: Belknap Harvard.

Commeyras, M. (1993). Promoting critical thinking through dialogical-thinking reading lessons. *The Reading Teacher, 46*(6), 486–494.

Commeyras, M., & DeGroff, L. (1998). Literacy professionals' perspectives on professional development and pedagogy: A national survey. *Reading Research Quarterly, 33,* 434–472.

Cooley, C. H. (1922). *Human nature and the social order* (Rev. Ed.). New York: Charles Scribner's Sons. (Original published in 1902.)

Cooper, L. (1932). *The rhetoric of Aristotle.* New York: Appleton-Century.

Cornford, F. M. (1935). *Plato's theory of knowledge.* London: Routledge.

Coté, N., Goldman, S. R., & Saul, E. U. (1998). Students making sense of informational text: Relations between processing and representation. *Discourse Processes, 25*(1), 1–53.

Dewey, J. (1916). *Essays in experimental logic.* Chicago: University of Chicago Press.

Dewey, J. (1991). *How we think.* New York: Prometheus Books.

Dong, T., Anderson, R. C., Kim, I., & Li, Y. (2008). Collaborative reasoning in China and Korea. *Reading Research Quarterly, 43*, 400–424.

Eeds, M., & Wells, D. (1989). Grand Conversations: An exploration of meaning construction in literature study groups. *Research in the Teaching of English, 23*, 4–29.

Fall, R., Webb, N., & Chudowsky, N. (2000). Group discussion and large-scale language arts assessment: Effects on students' comprehension. *American Educational Research Journal, 37*(4), 911–942.

Fletcher, C. R., & Bloom, C. P. (1988). Causal reasoning in the comprehension of simple narrative texts. *Journal of Memory and Language, 27*(3), 235–244.

Foltz, P. W. (2003). Quantitative cognitive models of text and discourse processing. In A. C. Graesser, M. A. Gernsbacher & S. R. Goldman (Eds.), *Handbook of discourse processes* (pp. 487–523). Mahwah, NJ: Lawrence Erlbaum Associates.

Gadamer, H. G. (1980). *Dialogue and dialectic: Eight hermeneutical studies in Plato* (P.C. Smith, Trans.). New Haven, CT: Yale University Press.

Gambrell, L. B., & Almasi, J. F. (Eds.). (1996). *Lively discussions! Fostering engaged reading.* Newark, DE: International Reading Association.

Gernsbacher, M. A. (1985). Surface information loss in comprehension. *Cognitive Psychology, 17*(3), 324–363.

Giddens, A. (1979). *Central problems in social theory: Action, structure, and contradiction in social analysis.* Berkley, CA: University of California Press.

Goldenberg, C. (1993). Instructional conversations: Promoting comprehension through discussion. *The Reading Teacher, 46*, 316–326.

Goldman, S. R., Varma, S., & Coté, N. (1996). Extending capacity-constrained construction integration: Toward "smarter" and flexible models of text comprehension. In B. K. Britton, & A. C. Graesser (Eds.), *Models of understanding text* (pp. 73–113). Hillsdale, NJ: Lawrence Erlbaum Associates.

Graesser, A. C., Gernsbacher, M. A., & Goldman, S. R. (Eds.). (2003). *Handbook of discourse processes.* Mahwah, NJ: Lawrence Erlbaum Associates.

Graesser, A. C., Singer, M., & Trabasso, T. (1994). Constructing inferences during narrative text comprehension. *Psychological Review, 101*(3), 371–395.

Graesser, A. C., Swamer, S. S., Baggett, W. B., & Sell, M. A. (1996). New models of deep comprehension. In B. K. Britton, & A. C. Graesser (Eds.), *Models of understanding text* (pp. 1–32). Hillsdale, NJ: Lawrence Erlbaum Associates.

Great Books Foundation (1987). *An introduction to shared inquiry.* Chicago: Author.

Guthrie, J. T., & McCann, A. D. (1996). Idea circles: Peer collaboration for conceptual learning. In L. B. Gambrell, & J. F. Almasi (Eds.), *Lively discussions! Fostering engaged reading* (pp. 87–105). Newark, DE: International Reading Association.

Hatano, G. (1993). Time to merge Vygotskian and constructivist conceptions of knowledge acquisition. In E. A. Forman, N. Minick, & C. A. Stone (Eds.), *Contexts for learning: Sociocultural dynamics in children's development* (pp. 153–166). New York: Oxford University Press.

Heinl, A. M. (1988). The effects of the Junior Great Books program on literal and inferential comprehension. Unpublished master's thesis, University of Toledo.

Jarvella, R. J. (1971). Syntactic processing of connected speech. *Journal of Verbal Learning & Verbal Behavior, 10*(4), 409–416.

Johnson-Laird, P. N. (1996). Space to think. In P. Bloom, M. A. Peterson, L. Nadel, & M. F. Garrett (Eds.), *Language and space* (pp. 437–462). Cambridge, MA: MIT Press.

Just, M. A., & Carpenter, P. A. (1992). A capacity theory of comprehension: Individual differences in working memory. *Psychological Review, 99*(1), 122–149.

Kim, S.-Y. (2001). The effects of group monitoring on transfer of learning in small group discussions. Unpublished doctoral dissertation, University of Illinois at Urbana-Champaign, Urbana-Champaign, IL.

Kintsch, W. (1988). The role of knowledge in discourse comprehension: A construction-integration model. *Psychological Review, 95*(2), 163–182.

Kintsch, W. (1998). *Comprehension: A paradigm for cognition.* New York: Cambridge University Press.

Kintsch, W. (2005). An overview of top-down and bottom-up effects in comprehension: The CI perspective. *Discourse Processes, 39*(2–3), 125–128.

Langer, J. (1993). Discussion as exploration: Literature and the horizon of possibilities. In A. G. E. Newell, & R. K. Durst (Eds.), *Exploring texts: The role of discussion and writing in the teaching and learning of literature* (pp. 23–43). Norwood, MA: Christopher-Gordon.

Langer, J. A. (1995). *Envisioning literature: Literary understanding and literature instruction.* Newark, DE: International Reading Association.

Langer, J. A. (2001). Beating the odds: Teaching middle and high school students to read and write well. *American Educational Research Journal, 38*, 837–880.

Lave, J., & Wenger, E. (1991). *Situated learning: Legitimate peripheral participation.* Cambridge: Cambridge University Press.

Lipman, M. (1975). *Philosophy for children.* (ERIC Document Reproduction Service No. ED103296).

Locke, J. (1917). *Locke's An Essay Concerning Human Understanding* (3rd ed.). (M. W. Calkins, Ed.). Chicago, IL: The Open Court Publishing Co.

Locke, J. (1968). *The Educational Writings of John Locke.* (J. L. Axtell, Ed.). Cambridge, MA: Harvard University Press.

Marx, K. H. (1973). *Grundrisse.* (M. Nicolaus, Trans.). New York: Penguin Books. (Original published in 1939.)

Marx, K., & Engels, F. (2004). *Communist manifesto.* (L. M. Findley, Trans.). Ontario: Broadview Press Ltd.

Mason, L. (2001). Introducing talk and writing for conceptual change: A classroom study. *Learning and Instruction, 11*, 305–329.

McKoon, G., Gerrig, R. J., & Greene, S. B. (1996). Pronoun resolution without pronouns: Some consequences of memory-based text processing. *Journal of Experimental Psychology: Learning, Memory, and Cognition, 22*(4), 919–932.

Mehan, H. (1979) *Learning lessons.* Cambridge, MA: Harvard University Press.

Mercer, N. (1995). *The guided construction of knowledge: Talk amongst teachers and learners.* Clevedon: Multilingual Matters.

Mercer, N. (2002). Developing dialogues. In G. Wells, & G. Claxton (Eds.), *Learning for life in the 21st Century: Sociocultural perspectives on the future of education* (pp. 141–153). London: Blackwell.

Michaels, S., O'Connor, M. C., Hall, M. W., & Resnick, L. B. (2002). *Accountable talk: Classroom conversation that works* (3 CD-ROM set). Pittsburgh, PA: University of Pittsburgh Press.

Michaels, S., O'Connor, C., & Resnick, L. (2008). Reasoned participation: Accountable talk in the classroom and in civic life. *Studies in Philosophy and Education, 27*(4), 283–297.

Morrow, L. M., & Smith, J. K. (1990). The effects of group size on interactive storybook reading. *Reading Research Quarterly, 25*, 213–231.

Murphy, P. K., & Alexander, P. A. (2004). Persuasion as a dynamic, multidimensional process: An investigation of individual and intraindividual differences. *American Educational Research Journal, 41*, 337–364.

Murphy, P. K., Wilkinson, I. A. G., & Soter, A. O. (2004). Making sense of group discussions: A conceptual framework. Paper presented at the annual meeting of the American Educational Research Association, San Diego, April.

Murphy, P. K., Wilkinson, I. A. G., Soter, A. O., Hennessey, M. N., & Alexander, J. F. (2009). Examining the effects of classroom discussion on students' comprehension of text: A meta-analysis. *Journal of Educational Psychology 101*(3), 740–764.

Nystrand, M. (1997). *Opening dialogue: Understanding the dynamics of language and learning in the English classroom.* New York: Teachers College Press.

Nystrand, M. (2006). Research on the role of discussion as it affects reading comprehension. *Research in the Teaching of English, 40*(4), 392–412.

Nystrand, M., Gamoran, A., & Carbonaro, W. (2001). On the ecology of classroom instruction: The case of writing in high school English and social studies. In P. Tynjala, L. Mason, & K. Lonka (Eds.), *Writing as a learning tool: Integrating theory and practice* (pp. 57–81). Dordrecht: Kluwer Academic Publishers.

O'Flahavan, J. F. (1989). Second-graders' social, intellectual, and affective development in varied group discussions about narrative texts: An exploration of participation structures. Unpublished doctoral dissertation. University of Illinois at Urbana-Champaign, Urbana-Champaign, IL.

O'Flahavan, J. F., Stein, S., Wiencek, J., & Marks, T. (1992). *Interpretive development in peer discussion about literature: An exploration of the teacher's role.* Final report to the trustees of the National Council of Teachers of English, Urbana, IL.

Paivio, A. (1986) *Mental representations: A dual coding approach.* Oxford: Oxford University Press.

Piaget, J. (1967). *Biologie et connaissance* [Biology and knowledge]. Paris: Gallimard.

Plato (1962). *Plato's epistles.* (G. R. Morrow, Trans.). New York: Bobbs-Merrill.

Raphael, T. E., & McMahon, S. I. (1994). Book Club: An alternative framework for reading instruction. *The Reading Teacher, 48*, 102–116.

Resnick, L. (1999). Making America smarter. *Education Week, 8*, 38–40.

Resnick, L. B., & Hall, M. W. (1998). Learning organizations for sustainable education reform. *Daedalus, 127*, 89–118.

Reznitskaya, A., Anderson, R. C., Dong, T., Li, Y., Kim, I., & Kim, S. (2008). Learning to think well: Application of argument schema theory to literacy instruction. In C. C. Block, & S. R. Parris (Eds.), *Comprehension instruction: Research-based best practices* (2nd ed., pp. 196–213). New York: Guilford Press.

Reznitskaya, A., Anderson, R. C., & Kuo, L.-J. (2007). Teaching and learning argumentation. *Elementary School Journal, 107*, 449–472.

Reznitskaya, A., Anderson, R. C., McNurlen, B., Nguyen-Jahiel, K., Archodidou, A., & Kim, S. (2001). Influence of oral discussion on written argument. *Discourse Processes, 32*, 155–175.

Robinson, R. (1953). *Plato's earlier dialectic* (2nd ed.). Oxford: Clarendon Press.

Rogers, T. (1990). A point, counterpoint response strategy for complex short stories. *Journal of Reading, 34*(4), 278–282.

Rosenblatt, L. M. (1978). *The reader, the text, and the poem: The transactional theory of the literary work.* Carbondale, IL: Southern Illinois University Press.

Rubin, D. C. (1995). *Memory in oral traditions: The cognitive psychology of epic, ballads, and counting-out rhymes.* New York: Oxford University Press.

Sawyer, R. K. (2002). Unresolved tensions in sociocultural theory: Analogies with contemporary sociological debates. *Culture & Psychology, 8*(3), 283–306.

Sharp, A. M. (1995). Philosophy for children and the development of ethical values. *Early Child Development and Care, 107*, 45–55.

Short, K. G., & Pierce, K. M. (Eds.). (1990). *Talking about books: Creating literate communities.* Portsmouth, NH: Heinemann.

Sinclair, J., & Coulthard, M. (1975). *Toward an analysis of discourse: The English used by teachers and pupils.* London: Oxford University Press.

Soter, A. O., Wilkinson, I. A. G., Connors, S., Murphy, P. K., & Shen, V. (2010). Deconstructing "aesthetic response" in small-group discussions about literature: A possible solution to the "aesthetic response" dilemma. *English Education, 42*, 204–225.

Soter, A. O., Wilkinson, I. A. G., Murphy, P. K., Rudge, L., Reninger, K., & Edwards, M. (2008). What the discourse tells us: Talk and indicators of high-level comprehension. *International Journal of Educational Research, 47*, 372–391.

Sperling, M., & Woodlief, L. (1997). Two classrooms, two writing communities: Urban and suburban tenth graders learning to write. *Research in the Teaching of English, 31*, 205–239.

Sweigart, W. (1991). Classroom talk, knowledge development, and writing. *Research in the Teaching of English, 25*, 497–509.

Taylor, B. M., Pearson, P. D., Clark, K., & Walpole, S. (1999). Effective schools/accomplished teachers. *The Reading Teacher, 53*, 156–159.

Taylor, B. M., Pearson, P. D., Clark, K., & Walpole, S. (2000). Effective schools and accomplished teachers: Lessons about primary grade reading instruction in low-income schools. *Elementary School Journal, 101*, 121–165.

Taylor, B. M., Pearson, P. D., Peterson, D. P., & Rodriguez, M. C. (2003). Reading growth in high-poverty classrooms: The influence of teacher practices that encourage cognitive engagement in literacy learning. *Elementary School Journal, 104*(1), 3–28.

Taylor, B. M., Pearson, P. D., Peterson, D. P., & Rodriguez, M. C. (2005). The CIERA school change framework: An evidenced-based approach to professional development and school reading improvement. *Reading Research Quarterly, 40*(1), 40–69.

Tharp, R. G., & Gallimore, R. (1988). *Rousing minds to life: Teaching, learning, and schooling in social context.* Cambridge: Cambridge University Press.

Van den Branden, K. (2000). Does negotiation of meaning promote reading comprehension? A study of multilingual primary school classes. *Reading Research Quarterly, 35*, 426–443.

Van den Broek, P., Rapp, D. N., & Kendeou, P. (2005). Integrating memory-based and constructionist processes in accounts of reading comprehension. *Discourse Processes, 39*(2–3), 299–316.

van Dijk, T. A., & Kintsch, W. (1983). *Strategies of discourse comprehension.* New York: Academic Press.

Verhoeven, L., & Graesser, A. (2008). Cognitive and linguistic factors in interactive knowledge construction. *Discourse Processes, 45*(4–5), 289–297.

Vygotsky, L. (1978). *Mind in society: The development of higher psychological processes* (M.Cole, V.John-Steiner, S. Scribner, & E.Souberman, Eds.). Cambridge, MA: Harvard University Press.

Vygotsky, L. (1986). *Thought and language.* Cambridge, MA: The MIT Press.

Wade, S., Thompson, A., & Watkins, W. (1994). The role of belief systems in authors' and readers' constructions of texts. In R. Garner, & P. A. Alexander (Eds.), *Beliefs about text and instruction with text* (pp. 265–293). Hillsdale, NJ: Lawrence Erlbaum.

Wells, G. (1989). Language in the classroom: Literacy and collaborative talk. *Language and Education, 3*, 251–273.

Wertsch, J. V., Del Rio, P., & Alvarez, A. (Eds.). (1995). *Sociocultural studies of mind.* Cambridge: Cambridge University Press.

Wiencek, J., & O'Flahavan, J. F. (1994). From teacher-led to peer discussions about literature: Suggestions for making the shift. *Language Arts, 71*, 488–498.

Wilkinson, I. A. G. (2009). Discussion methods. In E. M. Anderman, & L. H. Anderman (Eds.), *Psychology of classroom learning: An encyclopedia* (pp. 330–336). Detroit, MI: Gale/Cengage.

Wilkinson, I. A. G., Soter, A. O., & Murphy, P. K. (2007). *Group discussions as a mechanism for promoting high-level comprehension of text: Final grant performance report* (PR/Award No. R305G020075). Columbus, OH: Ohio State University Research Foundation.

Wilkinson, I. A. G., Soter, A. O., & Murphy, P. K. (2010). Developing a model of Quality Talk about literary text. In M. G. McKeown, & L. Kucan (Eds.), *Bringing reading researchers to life: Essays in honor of Isabel L. Beck.* New York: Guilford Press.

Wolf, M. K., Crosson, A. C., & Resnick, L. B. (2005). Classroom talk for rigorous reading comprehension instruction. *Reading Psychology, 26*(1), 27–53.

Woods, B. S., & Murphy, P. K. (2001). Separated at birth: The shared lineage of research on conceptual change and persuasion. *International Journal of Educational Research, 35,* 633–649.

Worthy, J., & Beck, I. L. (1995). On the road from recitation to discussion in large-group dialogue about literature. In K. Hinchman, & C. Kinz (Eds.), *Perspectives on literacy research and practice: Forty-fourth yearbook of the national reading conference* (pp. 312–324). Chicago: The National Reading Conference.

Yeazell, M. I. (1982). Improving reading comprehension through philosophy for children. *Reading Psychology: An International Quarterly, 3,* 239–246.

Zwaan, R. A. (1996). Toward a model of literary comprehension. In B. K. Britton, & A. C. Graesser (Eds.), *Models of understanding text* (pp. 241–255). Hillsdale, NJ: Lawrence Erlbaum Associates.

Zwaan, R.A., Langston, M.C., & Graesser, A.C. (1995) The construction of situation models in narrative comprehension: an event-indexing model. *Psychological Science, 6,* 292–297.

Zwaan, R. A., & Singer, M. (2003). Text comprehension. In A. C. Graesser, M. A. Gernsbacher, & S. R. Goldman (Eds.), *Handbook of discourse processes* (pp. 83–121). Mahwah, NJ: Lawrence Erlbaum Associates.

20

INSTRUCTION BASED ON TUTORING
Arthur C. Graesser, Sidney D'Mello, and Whitney Cade

This chapter reviews research on human tutoring, a form of one-on-one instruction between a tutor and a tutee. In most cases the tutor is knowledgeable about the subject matter and helps the tutee (i.e., the student) improve mastery of the knowledge base or skill. However, sometimes the tutor is a peer of the tutee who plays the role of a tutor, even though the tutor and tutee are at approximately the same level of subject matter mastery. The hope is that the tutorial session is tailored to the needs of the individual student by building on what the student already knows, filling in gaps in knowledge, and correcting conceptual errors. We distinguish between tutors and mentors, although the distinction is not entirely clear-cut. A tutor typically is an expert on a particular subject matter and has tight control over the tutorial session—turn by turn and moment by moment. In contrast, a mentor has a broader repertoire of knowledge, skills, and wisdom, with only occasional suggestions to the student as the student proceeds with a more self-regulated agenda.

Tutoring is the typical solution that students, parents, teachers, principals and school systems turn to when the students are not achieving expected grades and educational standards. There are serious worries in the community when a school is not meeting the standards of a high stakes test, and teachers are anxious about the prospects of losing their jobs due to the criteria and policies of *No Child Left Behind*. Schools and families worry when a student runs the risk of losing a scholarship or when an athlete may be cut from a team. Tutors step in to help under these conditions. Wealthier families might end up paying $200 per hour for an accomplished tutor to rescue a son or daughter. However, these expectations may be rather high, considering that most tutors are same-age peers of the students, slightly older cross-age tutors, citizens in the community, and paraprofessionals who have had little or no training on tutoring pedagogy (Cohen, Kulik, & Kulik, 1982; Graesser & Person, 1994). Nevertheless, their tutoring can be effective in helping students learn, as we will document in this chapter.

Although most tutors in school systems have little or no tutoring training, there are many examples of excellent tutoring programs that are grounded in the science of learning. One notable example is the *Reciprocal Teaching* method that helps students learn how to read text at deeper levels (Palincsar & Brown, 1984, 1988). The tutoring method engages the tutor and students in a dialogue that jointly constructs the meaning of the text. The dialogue is supported with the use of four strategies: (1) generating questions; (2) summarizing text segments; (3) clarifying unfamiliar words and underlying global ideas; and (4) predicting what will happen next in the text. These strategies are applied in a context-sensitive manner rather than mechanically applied in scripted lessons. Moreover, the tutors systematically change their style of tutoring as the lessons proceed. When students are initially introduced to reciprocal teaching, the tutor models the application of these strategies by actively bringing meaning to the written word (called content strategies) and also monitoring one's own thinking and learning from text (called metacognitive strategies). Over the course of time, the students assume increased responsibility for leading the dialogues. That is, after the modeling phase, the tutor has the students try out the strategies while the tutor gives feedback and scaffolds strategy improvements. Eventually the students take more and more control as the tutor fades from the process and occasionally intervenes much like a coach. This *modeling–scaffolding–fading* instructional process has a long history in the psychology of learning (Collins, Brown, & Newman, 1989; Rogoff & Gardner, 1984; Vygotsky, 1978).

The reciprocal teaching method has been tested in dozens of studies and has been shown to improve students' reading skills. Rosenshine and Meister (1994) conducted a meta-analysis of 16 studies of reciprocal teaching that were conducted with students from age 7 to adulthood. The method was compared with traditional basal reading instruction, explicit instruction in reading comprehension, and reading and answering questions. When experimenter-developed comprehension tests were used, the median effect size was 0.88 sigma. A sigma is a measure in standard deviation units that compares a mean in the experimental treatment to the mean in a comparison condition. According to Cohen (1992), effect sizes of 0.20, 0.50, and 0.80 are considered small, medium, and large, respectively, so the 0.088 effect size would be considered large. When standardized measures were used to assess comprehension, the median effect size favoring Reciprocal Teaching was $d = 0.32$. This effect size is considered small to medium according to Cohen, but it is important to acknowledge that it is much more difficult to obtain large effect sizes on standardized tests, particularly on the skill of reading (as opposed to mathematics and science). According to Hattie (2009), a meta-analysis of meta-analyses revealed that a 0.4 effect size is routinely reported in educational studies for successful interventions. The reciprocal teaching method has also been applied in classroom contexts with trained teachers applying the method in front of a classroom of students or in small groups. Given the promise of this method, it was recently accepted as an effective method to try in What Works Clearinghouse, a mechanism funded by the U.S. Department of Education to test promising methods of instruction in a large number of schools throughout the country.

Despite encouraging examples like reciprocal teaching, there are practical challenges in relying on humans to supply high-quality, one-on-one human tutoring (Conley, Kerner, & Reynolds, 2005; Hock, Schumaker, & Deshler, 1995). For example, it is very costly to train tutors on tutoring strategies. There is a high dropout rate when both skilled and unskilled tutors face the realities of how difficult it is to help students learn. Fortunately, the tutoring enterprise has expanded beyond human tutoring and into the realm of computer tutoring. Computers are available 24/7, do not get fatigued, do not burn out, and can reliably apply pedagogical strategies. There are now intelligent tutoring systems (ITS) and other advanced learning environments that implement sophisticated instructional procedures (VanLehn, 2006; VanLehn et al., 2007; Woolf, 2009). Intelligent tutoring systems are able to induce the characteristics of individual learners at a fine-grained level, to assign problems or tasks that are sensitive to the students' profile, and to generate specific tutoring actions that attempt to optimize learning according to scientific principles. Unlike human tutors, ITS provide precise control over the instructional activities, which of course is a methodological virtue. ITS have the capacity to scale up in delivering learning assistance to many more students than can be provided by human tutors.

The Cognitive Tutors developed by the Pittsburgh Science of Learning Center is one noteworthy ITS family (Anderson, Corbett, Koedinger, & Pelletier, 1995; Koedinger, Anderson, Hadley, & Mark, 1997; Ritter, Anderson, Koedinger, & Corbett, 2007). The Cognitive Tutors help students learn algebra, geometry, and programming languages by applying learning principles inspired by the ACT-R cognitive model (Anderson, 1990). There is a textbook and curriculum to provide the content and the context of learning these mathematically intensive subject matters, but the salient contribution of the Cognitive Tutors is to help students solve problems. The tutor scaffolds the students to take steps in solving the problem by prompting them to actively take the steps, by comparing the students' actions to ideal models of correct solutions, by giving students feedback on their actions, and by providing hints and other forms of help. The Cognitive Tutor mechanism incorporates a combination of declarative knowledge (facts) and procedural knowledge. Students are expected to learn through enough practice in varied contexts on problems that are tied to the curriculum.

The Cognitive Tutors are now used in over 2,000 school systems throughout the country and are among the methods being assessed by What Works Clearinghouse. These tutors have been heavily evaluated over the course of 35 years. The effect sizes on experimenter-developed tests are approximately 1.0 sigma compared to normal classroom teaching (Corbett, 2001). According to Ritter et al. (2007), standardized tests show overall effect sizes of 0.3 sigma, but particularly shine for the subcomponents of problem solving and multiple representations, which show effect sizes of $d = 0.7$ to 1.2. The What Works Clearinghouse investigations show an effect size of 0.4 sigma. The Cognitive Tutors are an excellent example of how scientific principles of learning can be implemented in a technology that not only helps learning but also scales up to widespread use in thousands of school systems.

This chapter reviews the research on human tutoring. We examine the pedagogical theories, conversation patterns, and empirical evidence for the effectiveness of one-on-one human tutoring. Although computer tutors are becoming more prevalent, it is beyond the scope of this chapter to cover intelligent tutoring systems and other advanced computer environments that attempt to adapt to individual students. The final section identifies some future directions for the field to pursue.

DOES HUMAN TUTORING HELP LEARNING?

It could be argued that tutoring was the very first form of instruction. Children were trained one-on-one by parents, other relatives, and members of the village who had particular specialized skills. The apprenticeship model reigned for several millennia before we encountered the industrial revolution and classroom education (Collins & Halverson, 2009). Throughout that part of history, the modelling-scaffolding-fading process was probably the most sophisticated form of early tutoring. The alternative, lecturing, may have been more prevalent: The master simply lectured to the apprentice, the apprentice nodded (knowingly or unknowingly), and the master undoubtedly grew frustrated when very few of the ideas and skills were sinking in. Lecturing is ubiquitous in the repertoire of today's unskilled tutors (Graesser, Person, & Magliano, 1995), but there are some other strategies that come naturally, as will be elaborated in this chapter.

Evaluations of one-on-one tutoring have shown that the method is quite effective, even when the tutors are unskilled tutors. Unskilled tutors are defined in this chapter as tutors who are not experts on subject matter knowledge, are not trained systematically on tutoring skills, and are virtually never evaluated on their impact on student learning. Unskilled tutors are paraprofessionals, parents, community citizens, cross-age tutors, or same-age peers. Meta-analyses show learning gains from typical human tutors, the majority being unskilled, of approximately 0.4 sigma when compared to classroom controls and other suitable controls (Cohen, Kulik, & Kulik, 1982).

There are many possible explanations of these learning gains from tutors who are unskilled. Perhaps the tutor can detect whether or not the student is generally mastering the subject matter on the basis of the student's verbal responses, from their nonverbal reactions, or from the student's attempts to perform a task. The tutor would then re-plan and make adjustments to help the student move forward. Perhaps the one-on-one attention motivates the student or encourages sufficient mastery to prevent embarrassing performance deficits. Perhaps the nature of conversation encourages a meeting of the minds, with sufficient common ground for learning to be built on a solid discourse foundation. The question is still unsettled as to why one-on-one tutoring is so effective when the tutor is unskilled.

Available evidence suggests that the expertise of the tutor does matter, but the evidence is not strong. Collaborative peer tutoring shows an effect size advantage of 0.2 to 0.9 sigma (Johnson & Johnson, 1992; Mathes & Fuchs, 1994; Slavin, 1990; Topping, 1996), which appears to be slightly lower than older unskilled human tutors. Peer tutoring is a low-cost solution because expert tutors are expensive and hard to find. Unfortunately, there have not been many systematic studies on learning gains from expert tutors because they are expensive, they are difficult to recruit in research projects, and tutors tend to stay in the tutoring profession for a short amount of time (Person, Lehman, & Ozbun, 2007). Certified tutors appear to yield the largest gains in tutoring (Slavin, Karweit, & Madden, 1989), so there is some evidence that training facilitates tutoring quality. Available studies report effect sizes of 0.8 to 2.0 (Bloom, 1984; Chi, Roy, & Hausmann, 2008; VanLehn et al., 2007), which is presumably higher than other forms of tutoring. The question is still unsettled on the impact of tutoring expertise on learning gains.

The impact of tutoring expertise on student learning is complicated by the fact that much of the answer lies in what the student does, not what the tutor does. Constructionist theories of learning have routinely emphasized the importance of getting the student to construct the knowledge, as opposed to an instruction delivery system that transfers the knowledge to the student (Bransford, Brown, & Cocking, 2000; Mayer, 2009). Students learn by expressing, doing, explaining, and being responsible for their knowledge construction, as opposed to being passive recipients of exposure to information. There is considerable evidence for the constructivist thesis in general (Bransford et al., 2000), but this chapter considers the evidence for constructivism in tutoring per se.

One form of evidence is that the tutors in these same-age and cross-age collaborations tend to learn more than the tutees (Cohen et al., 1982; Mathes & Fuchs, 1994; Rohrbeck, Ginsburg-Block, Fantuzzo, & Miller, 2003). Playing the role of tutor rather than tutee undoubtedly increases study, effort, initiative, and organization, all of which contribute to learning. In peer tutoring, students often are randomly assigned to tutor versus peer, so any advantages of the tutor role cannot be explained by prior abilities. Another form of evidence lies in who contributes most to the tutoring session. Is it the student or tutor? Correlational evidence reveals that students learn more when they contribute a higher percentage of the words and ideas to the tutoring sessions (Chi, Siler, Jeong, Yamauchi, & Hausmann, 2001; Litman et al., 2006). A good tutor apparently says very little when the student is on a roll and learning. Yet another form of evidence is that it does not help much for the tutor to articulate explanations, solutions, and other critical content in the form of information delivery, without making any attempt to connect with what the learner knows (Chi et al., 2001; VanLehn, Siler, Murray, Yamauchi, & Baggett, 2003). Explanations and other forms of high quality information are of course important when students are maximally receptive, for example, after they try to solve a problem and fail (Schwartz & Bransford, 1998). However, information delivery very often has a limited impact on the student when the content involves complex conceptualizations.

The obvious question that learning scientists have been asking over the years is why tutoring is effective in promoting learning. There are many approaches to answering this question. One approach is to conduct meta-analyses that relate learning gains with characteristics of the subject matter, tutee, tutor, and general structure of the tutoring session. There is evidence, for example, that (a) learning gains tend to be higher for well-structured, precise domains (mathematics, physics) than for ill-structured domains (reading); (b) that learning gains are more pronounced for tutees who start out with comparatively lower amounts of knowledge and skill; (c) that the quality of tutor training is much more important than the quantity of training; and (d) that a tutoring session shows more benefits when there are particular pedagogical activities (Cohen et al., 1982; Fuchs et al., 1994; King, Staffieri, & Adelgais, 1998; Mathes & Fuchs, 1994; Rohrbeck et al., 2003).

A second approach is to perform a very detailed analysis of the tutoring session structure, tasks, curriculum content, discourse, actions, and cognitive activities manifested in the sessions and to speculate how these might account for the advantages of tutoring (Chi, Roy, & Hausmann, 2008; Chi et al., 2001; Graesser & Person, 1994; Graesser, Person, & Magliano, 1995; Hacker & Graesser, 2007; Lepper, Drake, & O'Donnell-Johnson, 1997; McArthur, Stasz, & Zmuidzinas, 1990; Merrill, Reiser, Merrill, & Landes, 1995; Person & Graesser, 1999; Person, Kreuz, Zwaan, & Graesser, 1995; Shah, Evens, Michael, & Rovick, 2002; VanLehn et al., 2003). This chapter addresses these process factors in more detail.

A third approach is to manipulate the tutoring activities through trained human tutors or computer tutors and to observe the impact of the manipulations on learning gains (Chi et al., 2001, 2008; Graesser, Lu et al., 2004; Litman et al., 2006; VanLehn et al., 2003; VanLehn et al., 2007). Manipulation studies allow us to infer what characteristics of the tutoring directly cause increases in learning gains, barring potential confounding variables.

WHAT ARE THE COMMON TUTORING STRATEGIES AND PROCESSES?

As discussed, the typical tutors in school systems are unskilled. These tutors are nonetheless effective in helping students learn, so it is worthwhile to explore which tutoring strategies and processes they frequently implement. Graesser and Person analyzed the discourse patterns of 13 unskilled tutors in great detail (Graesser & Person, 1994; Graesser et al., 1995; Person & Graesser, 1999). They videotaped over 100 hours of naturalistic tutoring in a corpus of unskilled tutors who tutored middle school students in mathematics or college students in research methods. The research team transcribed the tutorial dialogues, classified the speech act utterances into discourse categories, and analyzed the rate of particular discourse patterns. We refer to this as the Graesser–Person *unskilled tutor corpus*. Regarding expert tutors, Person et al. (2007) conducted a literature review of studies with accomplished tutors. Unfortunately, the sample sizes of expert tutors have been extremely small (N < 3) in empirical investigations of expert tutoring and often the same expert tutors are used in different research studies; occasionally the tutors are co-authors of publications. Claims about expert tutoring may therefore be biased by the idiosyncratic characteristics of the small sample of tutors and the tutors' authorship role. Person et al. (2007) recently conducted a study on a sample of 8 tutors who were nominated by school personnel in the Memphis community as truly outstanding. The discourse patterns of these outstanding tutors in Person's *expert tutor corpus* were dissected in great detail.

Unfortunately, neither the unskilled tutor corpus nor the expert tutor corpus had outcome scores. There is a large gap in the literature on detailed analyses of human tutorial dialogue that are related to outcome measures and that have a large sample of tutors. Part of the problem lies in logistical problems in obtaining such data. The subject matters of the tutoring sessions are difficult to predict in advance so it is difficult to proactively identify suitable pre-test and post-test measures from normative testbanks. Nevertheless, these tutoring corpora can be analyzed to identify the tutoring processes.

Sophistication of Tutoring Strategies

As one might expect, unskilled human tutors are not prone to implement sophisticated tutoring strategies that have been proposed in the fields of education, the learning sciences, and developers of ITS (Graesser et al., 1995; Graesser, D'Mello, & Person, 2009; Person et al., 1995). Tutors rarely implement pedagogical techniques such as *bona fide* Socratic tutoring strategies, modeling–scaffolding–fading, reciprocal teaching, frontier learning, building on prerequisites, or diagnosis/remediation of deep misconceptions. In Socratic tutoring, the tutor asks learners illuminating questions that lead the learners to discover and correct their own misconceptions in an active, self-regulated fashion (Collins et al., 1975). Thus, Socratic tutoring is not merely bombarding the student with a large number of questions, as some practitioners and researchers erroneously believe. In modeling–scaffolding–fading, the tutor first models a desired skill, then gets the learners to perform the skill while the tutor provides feedback and explanation, and finally fades from the process until the learners perform the skill all by themselves (Rogoff & Gardner, 1984). As discussed, in reciprocal teaching, the tutor and learner take turns reading and thinking aloud with the goal of lacing in question generation, summarization, clarification, and prediction (Palincsar & Brown, 1984). Tutors who use frontier learning select problems and give guidance in a fashion that slightly extends the boundaries of what the learner already knows or has mastered (Sleeman & Brown, 1982). Tutors who build on prerequisites cover the prerequisite concepts or skills in a session before moving to more complex problems and tasks that require mastery of the prerequisites (Gagné, 1985). Tutors who diagnose and remediate deep misconceptions are on the lookout for errors that are manifestations of more global, problematic mental models (Lesgold, Lajoie, Bunzo, & Eggan, 1992). When a deep misconception is recognized, the tutor attempts to supplant the error-ridden mental model with a correct mental model.

One would expect tutors to be able to help the students correct their idiosyncratic deficits in knowledge and skills. Tutors are no doubt sensitive to some of these deficits, but available data suggest that there are limitations. Two examples speak to such limitations. First, if a tutor is truly adaptive to the student's learning profile, then the tutor should initiate some discussion or activity at the beginning of the session that diagnoses what the student is struggling with. This adaptation is manifested when the tutor: (a) inspects previous test materials and scores of the student; (b) selects problems in the tutoring session that are associated with the student's deficits; and (c) asks the tutee what they are having problems with. A tutor would lack the principle of adaptation if the tutor immediately presents problems to work on in a scripted fashion for all students. Whereas (a) and (c) occur with some frequency, tutors are not prone to do (b) (Chi et al., 2008; Graesser et al., 1995).

The second example of the tutor's limited ability to detect student's knowledge deficits addresses metacognitive knowledge. Tutors frequently ask students comprehension gauging questions, such as Do you understand?, Are you following?, and Does that make sense? If the student's comprehension calibration skills are accurate, then the student should answer YES when the student understands and NO when there is little or no understanding. One counterintuitive finding in the tutoring literature is that there sometimes is a positive correlation between a student's knowledge of the material (based on pre-test scores or post-test scores) and their likelihood of saying NO rather than YES to the tutor's comprehension gauging questions (Chi, Bassock, Lewis, Reimann, & Glaser, 1989; Graesser et al., 1995). Thus, it is the knowledgeable students who tend to say "No, I don't understand." This result suggests that deeper learners have higher standards of comprehension (Baker, 1985; Otero & Graesser, 2001) and that many students have poor comprehension calibration skills. The finding that students have disappointing comprehension calibration is well documented in the metacognitive literature, where meta-analyses have shown only a 0.27 correlation between comprehension scores on expository texts and the students' judgments on how well they understand the texts (Dunlosky & Lipko, 2007; Glenberg, Wilkinson, & Epstein, 1982; Maki, 1998). It is perhaps not surprising that the students' comprehension calibration is poor because they are low in domain knowledge. From the perspective of the tutor, many tutors mistakenly believe the students' answers to the comprehension gauging questions, which reflects insensitivity to the students' knowledge states. A good tutor would periodically ask follow-up questions when students say YES, they understand.

The aforementioned examples suggest that human tutors are insensitive to the students' knowledge states, but such a generalization would be too sweeping. Tutors are often adaptive to the students' knowledge and skills at a micro-level, as opposed to the macro-levels in the above two examples. The distinction is what VanLehn (2006) calls the *inner loop* versus the *outer loop*. The inner loop consists of covering individual steps or expectations within a problem whereas the outer loop involves the selection of problems, the judgment of mastery of a problem, and other more global aspects of the tutorial interaction. Available analyses of human tutoring suggest that human tutors are more sensitive to the students' knowledge at the inner loop than the outer loop.

Dialogue Patterns in Tutoring

Graesser and Person's analyses of tutorial dialogue uncovered a number of frequent dialogue structures (Graesser & Person, 1994; Graesser et al., 1995; Graesser, Hu, & McNamara, 2005). Many of these structures were also prominent in the work of other researchers who have conducted fine-grained analyses of tutoring (Chi et al., 2001; 2004; 2008; Evens & Michael, 2005; Litman et al., 2006; Shah et al., 2002). The following three dialogue structures are prominent: (a) the 5-step tutoring frame; (b) expectation and misconception tailored dialogue; and (c) conversational turn management. All of these structures are in the inner loop: (c) is embedded in (b), which in turn is embedded in (a). It should be noted that it is the tutor who takes the initiative in implementing these structures, not the student. It is rare to have the student take charge of the tutorial session in a self-regulated manner.

5-Step Tutoring Frame

Once a problem or difficult main question is selected to work on, the 5-step tutoring frame is launched, as specified below.

1 TUTOR asks a difficult question or presents a problem.
2 STUDENT gives an initial answer.
3 TUTOR gives short feedback on the quality of the answer.
4 TUTOR and STUDENT have a multi-turn dialogue to improve the answer.
5 TUTOR assesses whether the student understands the correct answer.

This 5-step tutoring frame involves collaborative discussion, joint action, and encouragement for the student to construct knowledge rather than merely receiving knowledge.

The first three steps often occur in a classroom context, but the questions are easier short-answer questions. The Initiate–Respond–Evaluate (IRE) sequence in a classroom consists of the teacher initiating a question, the student giving a short-answer response, and the teacher giving a positive or negative evaluation of the response (Sinclair & Coulthart, 1975). This is illustrated in the exchange below on the subject matter of Newtonian physics.

1 *Teacher:* According to Newton's second law, force equals mass times what?
2 *Student:* Acceleration.
3 *Teacher:* Right, mass times acceleration.

Or

(2) *Student:* Velocity.
(3) *Teacher:* Wrong, it's not velocity, it is acceleration.

Thus, tutoring goes beyond the IRE sequence in the classroom by having more difficult questions and more collaborative interactions during step 4 of the 5-step tutoring frame.

Expectation and Misconception Tailored Dialogue

Human tutors typically have a list of expectations (anticipated good answers, steps in a procedure) and a list of anticipated *misconceptions* associated with each main question. For example, expectations E1 and E2 and misconceptions M1 and M2 are relevant to the example physics problem below:

PHYSICS QUESTION: If a lightweight car and a massive truck have a head-on collision, upon which vehicle is the impact force greater? Which vehicle undergoes the greater change in its motion, and why?

E1. The magnitudes of the forces exerted by A and B on each other are equal.
E2. If A exerts a force on B, then B exerts a force on A in the opposite direction.
M1: A lighter/smaller object exerts no force on a heavier/larger object.
M2: Heavier objects accelerate faster for the same force than lighter objects.

The tutor guides the student in articulating the expectations through a number of dialogue moves: *pumps*, *hints*, and *prompts* for the student to fill in missing words. A pump is a generic expression to get the student to provide more information, such as "What else?" or "Tell me more." Hints and prompts are selected by the tutor to get the student to articulate missing content words, phrases, and propositions. A hint tries to get the student to express a complex idea (e.g., proposition, clause, sentence) whereas a prompt is a question that tries to get the student to express a single word or phrase. For example, a hint to get the student to articulate expectation E1 might be "What about the forces exerted by the vehicles on each other?"; this hint would ideally elicit the answer "The magnitudes of the forces are equal." A prompt to get the student to say "equal" would be "What are the magnitudes of the forces of the two vehicles on each other?" As the learner expresses information over many turns, the list of expectations is eventually covered and the main question is scored as answered.

Human tutors are dynamically adaptive to the learner in ways other than prompting them to articulate expectations. There also is the goal of correcting misconceptions that arise in the student's responses. When the student articulates a misconception, the tutor acknowledges the error and corrects it. There is another conversational goal of giving feedback to the student on their contributions. For example, the tutor gives short *feedback* on the quality of student contributions. The tutor accommodates a mixed-initiative dialogue by attempting to answer the student's questions when the student is sufficiently inquisitive to ask questions. However, it is well documented that students rarely ask questions, even in tutoring environments (Graesser & Person, 1994; Graesser, McNamara, & VanLehn, 2005), because they have limited self-regulated learning strategies (Azevedo & Cromley, 2004). Tutors are considered more adaptive to the student to the extent that they correct student misconceptions, give correct feedback, and answer student questions.

Conversational Turn Management

Human tutors structure their conversational turns systematically. Nearly every turn of the tutor has three informational components after the main problem or question has been introduced and the collaboration is flowing in step 4 of the tutoring frame:

Tutor Turn → Short Feedback + Dialogue Advancer + Floor Shift

The first component of most turns is feedback on the quality of the student's last turn. This feedback is either positive (*very good, yeah*), neutral (*uh huh, I see*), or negative (*not quite, not really*). Sometimes the tutor expresses this short feedback through nonverbal paralinguistic cues, such as intonation, facial expressions, gestures, or body movements. The second dialogue advancer component moves the tutoring agenda forward with either pumps, hints, prompts, assertions with correct information, corrections of misconceptions, or answers to student questions. The third floor shift component is a cue for the conversational floor to shift from the tutor as the speaker to the student. For example, the human ends each turn with a question or a gesture to cue the student to do the talking. Questions strongly invite responses from the conversation partner so the student is expected say something after the tutor asks a question. Alternatively, the tutor can signal a floor shift through a hand gesture, posture display, or facial expression that invites the student to contribute. These floor shift signals need to be dramatic when the student is reluctant to contribute.

The three conversational structures together present challenging problems or questions to the student, adaptively scaffold good answers through collaborative interactions, provide feedback when students express erroneous information, and answers student questions that infrequently are asked. What is absent is sophisticated pedagogical strategies. This is perhaps unsurprising because these strategies are complex and took centuries to discover by scholars. However, it is a very important finding to document because it is conceivable that deep learning could improve tremendously by training human tutors and programming computer tutors to implement the sophisticated strategies.

The pedagogical strategies of expert tutors are very similar to those of unskilled tutors in most ways (Cade, Copeland, Person, & D'Mello, 2008; Person, Lehman, & Ozbun, 2007). However, Cade et al. (2008) did identify a few notable trends in pedagogy in the expert tutor corpus. The expert tutors did occasionally implement elements of modeling–scaffolding–fading, although the relative frequencies of the dialogue moves for this pedagogical strategy were not impressively high. The tutors did a modest amount of modeling, a large amount of scaffolding, and very little fading. These tutors periodically had just-in-time direct instruction or mini-lectures when the student was struggling with a particular conceptualization. These content-sensitive mini-lectures allegedly were sensitive to what the student was having trouble with rather than being routinely delivered to all students.

The expert tutors also appeared to differ from unskilled tutors on some metacognitive dimensions, as addressed below. However, it is important to qualify these claims about expert tutors because there was never a systematic comparison of tutors with different expertise in any given study. Instead, the relative frequencies of tutor strategies and discourse moves were computed in the expert tutor corpus and compared with the relative frequencies of the same theoretical categories in published studies with unskilled tutors. One pressing research need is to systematically compare tutors with varying expertise.

WHAT IS THE ROLE OF METACOGNITION AND META-COMMUNICATION IN TUTORING?

Graesser, D'Mello, and Person (2009) have documented some of the illusions that typical human tutors have about cognition and communication. These illusions may get in the way of optimizing learning. Expert tutors also may be less likely to fall prey to these illusions. The five illusions below were identified:

1 *Illusion of grounding.* The unwarranted assumption that the speaker and listener have shared knowledge about a word, referent, or idea being discussed in the tutoring session. Failure to establish common ground threatens successful communication and the joint construction of knowledge (Clark, 1996). A good tutor is sufficiently skeptical of the student's level of understanding, and so the tutor troubleshoots potential communication breakdowns between the tutor and student.

2 *Illusion of feedback accuracy.* The unwarranted assumption that the feedback that the other person gives to a speaker's contribution is accurate. For example, tutors incorrectly believe the students' answers to their comprehension gauging questions (e.g., "Do you understand?").

3 *Illusion of discourse alignment.* The unwarranted assumption that the listener does understand or is expected to understand the discourse function, intention, and meaning of the speaker's dialogue contributions. For example, tutors sometimes give hints, but the students do not realize they are hints.

4 *Illusion of student mastery.* The unwarranted assumption that the student has mastered much more than the student has really mastered. For example, the fact that a student expresses a word or phrase does not mean that the student understands an underlying complex idea.

4 *Illusion of knowledge transfer.* The speaker's unwarranted assumption that the listener understands whatever the speaker says and thereby knowledge is accurately transferred. For example, the tutor assumes that the student understands whatever the tutor says, when in fact the student absorbs very little.

Both the tutor and student may each have these illusions and thereby compromise the effectiveness of tutoring.

These illusions undermine the tutor's ability to build an accurate and detailed model of the cognitive states of the student, or what is called the *student model.* Indeed, there are reasons for being pessimistic about the quality of the student model that tutors construct. A more realistic picture is that the tutor has only an approximate appraisal of the cognitive states of students and that they formulate responses that do not require fine-tuning of the student model (Chi et al., 2004; Graesser et al., 1995).

There are three sources of evidence for this claim. First, the short feedback to students on the quality of the students' contributions is often incorrect. In particular, the short feedback has a higher likelihood of being positive rather than negative after student contributions that are vague or error-ridden (Graesser et al., 1995). Tutors have the tendency to be polite or to resist discouraging the student by giving a large amount of negative feedback (Person et al., 1995). Second, tutors do not have a high likelihood of detecting misconceptions and error-ridden contributions of students (Chi, Siler, & Jeong, 2004; VanLehn et al., 2007). Third, as mentioned earlier, tutors do not select new cases or problems to work on that are sensitive to the abilities and knowledge deficits of students (Chi et al., 2008). One would expect the selection of problems to be tailored to the student's profile according to the zone of proximal development, i.e., not too easy or not too hard, but just right. However, Chi et al. (2008) reported that there was no relation between problem selection and student's profile. Data such as these lead one to conclude that tutors have a modest ability to conduct student modeling.

A good tutor is sufficiently skeptical of the student's level of understanding. The tutor troubleshoots potential communication breakdowns between the tutor and student. This is illustrated in the simple hypothetical exchange below.

Tutor: We know from Newton's law that net force equals mass times acceleration. This law . . .
Student: Yeah, that is Newton's second law.
Tutor: Do you get this?
Student: Yeah. I know that one.
Tutor: Okay, let's make sure. Force equals mass times what?
Student: Times velocity.
Tutor: No, it's mass times acceleration.

A good tutor assumes that the student understands very little of what the tutor says and that knowledge transfer approaches zero. Person et al. (2007) has reported that expert tutors are more likely to verify that the student understands what the tutor expresses by asking follow-up questions or giving follow-up troubleshooting problems.

What Is the Role of Emotions During Tutoring?

It is important to consider motivation and emotion in tutoring in addition to the cognitive subject matter. Indeed, connections between complex learning and emotions have received increasing attention in the fields of psychology and education (Deci & Ryan, 2002; Dweck, 2002; Gee, 2003; Lepper & Henderlong, 2000; Linnenbrink & Pintrich, 2002; Meyer & Turner, 2006). Studies that have tracked the emotions during tutoring have identified the predominate emotions, namely confusion, frustration, boredom, anxiety, and flow/engagement, with delight and surprise occurring less frequently (Baker, D'Mello, Rodrigo, & Graesser, in press; Craig, Graesser, Sullins, & Gholson, 2004; D'Mello et al., 2008; D'Mello, Picard, & Graesser, 2007; Lehman, Matthews, D'Mello, & Person, 2008). These data are informative, but the important question is how these emotions can be coordinated productively with learning.

The central assumption is that it is important for tutors to adopt pedagogical and motivational strategies that are effectively coordinated with the students' emotions. Lepper, Drake, and O'Donnell (1997) proposed an INSPIRE model to promote this integration. This model encourages the tutor to nurture the student by being empathetic and attentive to the student's needs, to assign tasks that are not too easy or difficult, to give indirect feedback on erroneous student contributions rather than harsh feedback, to encourage the student to work hard and face challenges, to empower the student with useful skills, and to pursue topics they are curious about. One of the interesting tutor strategies is to assign an easy problem to the student, but to claim that the problem is difficult and to encourage the student to give it a try anyway. When the student readily solves the problem, the student builds self-confidence and self-efficacy in conquering difficult material (Zimmerman, 2001).

Several theories linking emotions and learning have been proposed. Meyer and Turner (2006) identified three theories that are particularly relevant to understanding the links between emotions and learning: academic risk taking, flow, and goals (Meyer & Turner, 2006). The academic risk theory contrasts (a) the adventuresome learners who want to be challenged with difficult tasks, take risks of failure, and manage negative emotions when they occur and (b) the cautious learners who tackle easier tasks, take fewer risks, and minimize failure and the resulting negative emotions. According to flow theory (Csikszentmihalyi, 1990), the learner is in a state of flow when the learner is so deeply engaged in learning the material that time and fatigue disappear. When students are in the flow state, they are at an optimal zone of facing challenges and conquering the challenges by applying their knowledge and skills. Goal theory emphasizes the role of goals in predicting and regulating emotions (Dweck, 2002; Stein & Hernandez, 2007). Outcomes that achieve challenging goals result in positive emotions whereas outcomes that jeopardize goal accomplishment result in negative emotions.

A complementary perspective is to focus on learning impasses and obstacles rather than on flow and goals. Obstacles to goals are particularly diagnostic of both learning and emotions. For example, the affective state of confusion correlates with learning gains perhaps because it is a direct reflection of deep thinking (Craig et al., 2004; D'Mello et al., 2008; Graesser, Jackson, & McDaniel, 2007). Confusion is diagnostic of *cognitive disequilibrium*, a state that occurs when learners face obstacles to goals, contradictions, incongruities, anomalies, uncertainty, and salient contrasts (Graesser, Lu, Olde, Cooper-Pye, & Whitten, 2005; Otero & Graesser, 2001). Cognitive equilibrium is ideally restored after thought, reflection, problem solving and other effortful deliberations. It is important to differentiate being productively confused, which leads to learning and ultimately positive emotions, from being hopelessly confused, which has no pedagogical value.

Research is conspicuously absent on how the tutees perceive the causes and consequences of these emotions and what they think they should do to regulate each affect state. The negative emotions are particularly in need of research. When a student is frustrated from being stuck, the student might attribute the frustration either to themselves ("I'm not at all good at physics"), the tutor ("My tutor doesn't understand this either"), or the materials ("This must be a lousy textbook"). Solutions to handle the frustration would presumably depend on these attributions of cause of the frustration. When a student is confused, some students may view this as a positive event to stimulate thinking and test their mettle in conquering the challenge; other students will attribute the confusion to their poor ability, an inadequate tutor, or poorly prepared academic materials. When students are bored, they are likely to blame the tutor or material rather than themselves. Tutors of the future will need to manage the tutorial interaction in a fashion that is sensitive to the students' emotions in addition to their cognitive states.

What Are Tutoring Strategies that Influence Deep Learning?

So far this chapter has provided evidence for the effectiveness of human tutoring and has identified various strategies and processes of naturalistic human tutoring. The obvious next question is, which of the strategies help learning? Surprisingly, there is not an abundance of research on this question because it is difficult to control what human tutors do in controlled experiments, but we review some relevant research on tutoring strategies in this section.

Chi, Roy, and Hausmann (2008) compared five conditions in order to test a hypothesis they were advancing called the *active/constructive/interactive/observing* hypothesis. As the expression indicates, the hypothesis asserts that learning is facilitated from active student learning, knowledge construction, and collaborative interaction, as we have discussed in this chapter. The other aspect of the expression refers to observing a tutoring session vicariously. Their ideal experimental condition involves four people: two student participants watching and discussing a tutorial interaction that occurs between a tutor and another student. According to the hypothesis, the participants would learn a great deal from this interactive vicarious observation condition because it has all four components (action, construction, interaction, observation). To test this hypothesis, students trying to learn physics were randomly assigned to the ideal treatment (condition 1) versus to one-on-one tutoring (condition 2), vicarious observation (all alone) of the tutoring session (condition 3), collaboratively interacting with another student without observing the interaction (condition 4), and studying from a text alone (condition 5). Conditions 1 and 2 were approximately the same in learning gains and significantly higher than conditions 3–5. Thus, it appears that multiple components are needed for learning to be optimal.

As discussed earlier, there is evidence that learning from tutorial interactions improves when the learner constructs explanations and when the student does more of the talking than the tutor (Litman et al., 2006; Siler & VanLehn, 2009). However, Chi et al. (2001) examined the tutor moves in detail for students learning physics. For deep learners, it was the tutor moves that encouraged reflection that helped; for shallow learners, the tutor's responses to scaffolding and explanations were important. Unfortunately, the sample sizes in these studies reported by Chi, Litman, and Siler are modest and very much in need of replication. The door is clearly open for discovering the particular dialogue moves of tutors that predict learning.

Research on reading tutors have also investigated what aspects of tutoring help reading at deeper levels of comprehension (McNamara, 2007). Three notable examples are *Reciprocal Teaching* (Palincsar & Brown, 1984), *Self Explanation Reading Training, SERT* (McNamara, 2004), and *Questioning the Author* (Beck, McKeown, Hamilton, & Kucan, 1997). Reciprocal teaching was mentioned at the beginning of this chapter and we reported that this method has solid learning gains. The key strategies were clarifying, questioning, summarizing, and predicting content as students read text. The SERT method helps students build self-explanations when reading the text, which includes the strategies of paraphrasing, generating inferences, bridging ideas expressed in the text, and connecting the text to what the student knows. Questioning the Author encourages the student to critically evaluate the content of what is writing by asking the author such questions as "What is the evidence for this claim?" and "Why did the author mention this?" The available evidence, including meta-analyses and reviews of research (Roscoe & Chi, 2007; Rosenshine & Meister, 1994; Rosenshine, Meister, & Chapman, 1996), is that the scaffolding of explanations and of deep questions and answers are particularly important components. Explanations involve causal chains and networks, plans of agents, and logical justifications of claims. Deep questions have been defined systematically (Graesser & Person, 1994) and include questions stem such as why, how, what if, what if not, and so what? In contrast, the strategy to predict future content in the text has little or no impact on improving reading at deeper levels, whereas summarization and clarification are somewhere in between.

Part of the challenge of conducting experimental research on human tutoring is that it is difficult to train tutors to adopt particular strategies. They rely on their normal conversational and pedagogical styles. It is nearly impossible to run repeated measures designs where a tutor adopts a normal style on some days and an experimental style on other days. The treatments end up contaminating each other, and it is difficult to force the human tutors to adopt changes in their language and discourse, particularly those levels that are unconscious and involuntary. However, computers can supply such experimental control. Therefore, computer tutors are expected to play a more important role both in future scientific investigations and also in increasing tutoring pedagogy to an increasing number of students.

FUTURE DIRECTIONS

This chapter has made a convincing case that tutoring by humans is a powerful learning environment. It could be argued that tutoring is the most effective learning environment we know of in addition to being the oldest. Tutoring has been around for millennia and has been shown to help learning in several meta-analyses, as we have documented in this chapter. However, there are still a large number of unanswered fundamental questions that need attention in future research.

Rather surprisingly, there needs to be a systematic line of research that investigates the impact of tutoring expertise on learning gains as well as learner emotions and motivation. We had hoped to find a rigorous study that randomly assigns students to human tutors with varying levels of expertise and that collects suitable outcome measures. The fact that we came up empty is remarkable, but it also sets the stage for new research initiatives. To what extent is student learning and motivation facilitated as a function of increased tutor training on pedagogy and/or increased subject matter knowledge? To what extent does tutoring experience matter? How do different schools of tutoring pedagogy compare? Are there interactions between tutor pedagogy, subject matter, and student profiles? How do we best train tutors? Decades of research is needed to answer these questions.

Computer tutors have some promise in providing more control over the tutoring process than human tutors can provide. This opens up the possibility of new programs of research that systematically compare different versions of computer tutors and other advanced learning environments. These systems have multiple modules, such as the knowledge base, the profile of student ability and mastery on particular topics, decision rules that select problems, scaffolding strategies, help systems, feedback, media on the human–computer interface, and so on. Which of these components are responsible for any learning gains of the computer tutors? It is possible to systematically manipulate the quality or presence of each component in "lesion" studies that systematically remove particular components and then assess the impact of the removal on learning? The number of conditions in manipulation studies of course grows with the number of components. If there are six major components, with each level varying in two levels of quality, then there would be $2^6 = 64$ conditions in a factorial design. That would require nearly 2,000 students in a between-subjects design with 30 students randomly assigned to each of the 64 conditions. It indeed might be realistic to perform such a lesion study to the extent that the computer tutor enterprise scales up and delivers training on the web (see Heffernan, Koedinger, & Razzaq, 2008). The alternative would be to selectively focus on one or two modules at a time.

The same comparisons could be made between alternative human tutors. Studies could be conducted to carefully train human tutors to include versus exclude particular tutoring components. For example, should the human tutor respond to the student emotions or ignore their emotions? Should the tutor give negative feedback or stick with positive feedback? Should the human tutor explain the rationale behind answers, or merely give the correct answers? Once again, there are many variables and combinations to test, so this is a research area that could attract the attention of researchers for years.

One of the provocative tests in the future will pit human versus machine as tutors. Most people place their bets on the human tutors under the assumption that they are more sensitive to the student's profile and are more creatively adaptive in guiding the student. However, the detailed analyses of human tutoring challenge such assumptions in light of the many illusions that humans have about communication and the modest pedagogical strategies in their repertoire. Computers may do a better job in cracking the illusions of communication, in inducing student knowledge states, and in implementing complex intelligent tutoring strategies. A plausible case could easily be made for betting on the computer over the human tutor. Perhaps the ideal computer tutor emulates humans in some ways and performs complex non-human computations in other ways. Comparisons between human and computer tutors need to be made in a manner that equilibrates the conditions on content, time on task, and other extraneous variables that are secondary to pedagogy. As data roll in from these needed empirical studies, we need to be open to the prospects of some unpredictable and counterintuitive discoveries.

ACKNOWLEDGMENTS

The research was supported by the National Science Foundation (SBR 9720314, REC 0106965, REC 0126265, ITR 0325428, REESE 0633918, ALT-0834847, DRK-12-0918409), the Institute of Education Sciences (R305H050169, R305B070349, R305A080589, R305A080594), and the Department of Defense Multidisciplinary University Research Initiative (MURI) administered by ONR under grant N00014-00-1-0600. Any opinions, findings, and conclusions or recommendations expressed in this material are those of the authors and do not necessarily reflect the views of NSF, IES, or DoD. The Tutoring Research Group (TRG) is an interdisciplinary research team comprised of researchers from psychology, computer science, physics, and education (visit http://www.autotutor.org, http://emotion.autotutor.org, http://fedex.memphis.edu/iis/). Requests for reprints should be sent to Art Graesser, Department of Psychology, 202 Psychology Building, University of Memphis, Memphis, TN 38152-3230, a-graesser@memphis.edu.

REFERENCES

Anderson, J. R. (1990). *The adaptive character of thought.* Hillsdale, NJ: Erlbaum.

Anderson, J. R., Corbett, A. T., Koedinger, K. R., & Pelletier, R. (1995). Cognitive tutors: Lessons learned. *Journal of the Learning Sciences, 4,* 167–207.

Azevedo, R., & Cromley, J. G. (2004). Does training on self-regulated learning faciliate students' learning with hypermedia? *Journal of Educational Psychology, 96,* 523–535.

Baker, L. (1985). Differences in standards used by college students to evaluate their comprehension of expository prose. *Reading Research Quarterly, 20,* 298–313.

Baker, R. S., D'Mello, S. K., Rodrigo, M. T., Graesser, A. C. (in press). Better to be frustrated than bored: The incidence, persistence, and impact of learners' affect during interactions with three different computer-based learning environments. *International Journal of Human-Computer Studies.*

Beck, I. L., McKeown, M. G., Hamilton, R. L., & Kucan, L. (1997). *Questioning the Author: An approach for enhancing student engagement with text.* Delaware: International Reading Association.

Bloom, B. S. (1984). The 2 sigma problem: The search for methods of group instruction as effective as one-to-one tutoring. *Educational Researcher, 13,* 4–16.

Bransford, J. D., Brown, A. L., & Cocking, R. R. (Eds.). (2000). *How people learn.* Washington, DC: National Academy Press.

Cade, W., Copeland, J. Person, N., and D'Mello, S. K. (2008). Dialogue modes in expert tutoring. In B. Woolf,

E. Aimeur, R. Nkambou, & S. Lajoie (Eds.), *Proceedings of the Ninth International Conference on Intelligent Tutoring Systems* (pp. 470–479). Berlin: Springer-Verlag.

Chi, M. T. H., Bassok, M., Lewis, M., Reimann, P., & Glaser, R. (1989). Self-explanations: How students study and use examples in learning to solve problems. *Cognitive Science, 13*, 145–182.

Chi, M. T. H., Roy, M., & Hausmann, R. G. M. (2008) Observing tutorial dialogues collaboratively: Insights about human tutoring effectiveness from vicarious learning. *Cognitive Science, 32*(2), 301–341.

Chi, M. T. H., Siler, S. A., & Jeong, H. (2004). Can tutors monitor students' understanding accurately? *Cognition and Instruction, 22*(3), 363–387.

Chi, M. T. H., Siler, S., Jeong, H., Yamauchi, T., & Hausmann, R. (2001). Learning from human tutoring. *Cognitive Science, 25*, 471–534.

Clark, H. H. (1996). *Using language.* Cambridge: Cambridge University Press.

Cohen, J. (1992). A power primer. *Psychological Bulletin, 112*, 155–159.

Cohen, P. A., Kulik, J. A., & Kulik, C. C. (1982). Educational outcomes of tutoring: A meta-analysis of findings. *American Educational Research Journal, 19*, 237–248.

Collins, A., Brown, J. S., & Newman, S. E. (1989). Cognitive apprenticeship: Teaching the crafts of reading, writing, and mathematics. In L. B. Resnick (Ed.), *Knowing, learning, and instruction: Essays in honor of Robert Glaser* (pp. 453–494). Hillsdale, NJ: Lawrence Erlbaum Associates.

Collins, A., & Halverson, R. (2009). *Rethinking education in the age of technology: The digital revolution and schooling in America.* New York: Teacher College Press.

Collins, A., Warnock, E. H., Aeillo, N., Miller, M. L. (1975). Reasoning from incomplete knowledge. In D. G. Bobrow, & A. Collins (Eds.), *Representation and understanding* (pp. 453–494). New York: Academic Press.

Conley, M., Kerner, M., & Reynolds, J. (2005). Not a question of should, but a question of how: Literacy knowledge and practice into secondary teacher preparation through tutoring in urban middle schools. *Action in Teacher Education, 27*, 22–32.

Corbett, A.T. (2001). Cognitive computer tutors: Solving the two-sigma problem. *User Modeling: Proceedings of the Eighth International Conference, UM 2001*, 137–147.

Craig, S. D., Graesser, A. C., Sullins, J., & Gholson, B. (2004). Affect and learning: An exploratory look into the role of affect in learning. *Journal of Educational Media, 29*, 241–250.

Csikszentmihalyi, M. (1990). *Flow: The psychology of optimal experience.* New York: Harper-Row.

D'Mello, S. K., Craig, S.D., Witherspoon, A. W., McDaniel, B. T., and Graesser, A. C. (2008). Automatic detection of learner's affect from conversational cues. *User Modeling and User-Adapted Interaction, 18*(1–2), 45–80.

D'Mello, S. K., Picard, R., & Graesser, A.C. (2007). Toward an affect-sensitive AutoTutor. *IEEE Intelligent Systems, 22*, 53–61.

Deci, E. L., & Ryan, R. M. (2002). The paradox of achievement: The harder you push, the worse it gets. In J. Aronson (Ed.), *Improving academic achievement: Impact of psychological factors on education.* Orlando, FL: Academic Press.

Dunlosky, J., & Lipko, A. (2007). Metacomprehension: A brief history and how to improve its accuracy. *Current Directions in Psychological Science, 16*, 228–232.

Dweck, C. S. (2002). Messages that motivate: How praise molds students' beliefs, motivation, and performance (in surprising ways). In J. Aronson (Ed.), *Improving academic achievement: Impact of psychological factors on education.* Orlando, FL: Academic Press.

Evens, M. W., & Michael, J. (2005). *One-on-one tutoring by humans and computers.* New York: Taylor & Francis.

Fuchs, L., Fuchs, D., Bentz, J., Phillips, N., & Hamlett, C. (1994). The nature of students' interactions during peer tutoring with and without prior training and experience. *American Educational Research Journal, 31*, 75–103.

Gagné, R. M. (1985). *The conditions of learning and theory of instruction* (4th ed.). New York: Holt, Rinehart, & Winston.

Gee, J. P. (2003). *What video games have to teach us about language and literacy.* New York: Macmillan.

Glenberg, A. M., Wilkinson, A. C., and Epstein, W. (1982). The illusion of knowing: Failure in the self-assessment of comprehension. *Memory & Cognition, 10*, 597–602.

Graesser, A. C., D'Mello, S. K., & Person, N. (2009). Meta-knowledge in tutoring. In D. J. Hacker, J. Dunlosky, & A. C. Graesser (Eds.), *Metacognition in educational theory and practice.* Mahwah, NJ: Erlbaum.

Graesser, A. C., Hu, X., & McNamara, D. S. (2005). Computerized learning environments that incorporate research in discourse psychology, cognitive science, and computational linguistics. In A. F. Healy (Ed.), *Experimental cognitive psychology and its applications: Festschrift in honor of Lyle Bourne, Walter Kintsch, and Thomas Landauer* (pp. 183–194). Washington, DC: American Psychological Association.

Graesser, A. C., Jackson, G. T., & McDaniel, B. (2007). AutoTutor holds conversations with learners that are responsive to their cognitive and emotional states. *Educational Technology, 47*, 19–22.

Graesser, A. C., Lu, S., Jackson, G. T., Mitchell, H., Ventura, M., Olney, A., & Louwerse, M. M. (2004). AutoTu- tor: A tutor with dialogue in natural language. *Behavioral Research Methods, Instruments, and Computers, 36*, 180–193.

Graesser, A. C., Lu, S., Olde, B.A., Cooper-Pye, E., & Whitten, S. (2005). Question asking and eye tracking during cognitive disequilibrium: Comprehending illustrated texts on devices when the devices break down. *Memory and Cognition, 33*, 1235–1247.

Graesser, A. C., McNamara, D. S., & VanLehn, K. (2005). Scaffolding deep comprehension strategies through Point&Query, AutoTutor, and iSTART. *Educational Psychologist, 40*, 225–234.

Graesser, A. C., & Person, N. K. (1994). Question asking during tutoring. *American Educational Research Journal, 31*, 104–137.

Graesser, A. C., Person, N. K., & Magliano, J. P. (1995). Collaborative dialogue patterns in naturalistic one-to-one tutoring. *Applied Cognitive Psychology, 9*, 1–28.

Hacker, D. J., & Graesser, A. C. (2007). The role of dialogue in reciprocal teaching and naturalistic tutoring. In R. Horowitz (Ed.), *Talk about text: How speech and writing interact in school learning*. Mahwah, NJ: Erlbaum.

Hattie, J. (2009). *Visible learning: A synthesis of over 800 meta-analyses related to achievement*. New York: Taylor & Francis.

Heffernan, N. T., Koedinger, K. R., & Razzaq, L. (2008). Expanding the model-tracing architecture: A 3rd genera- tion intelligent tutor for Algebra symbolization. *The International Journal of Artificial Intelligence in Educa- tion. 18*(2), 153–178.

Hock, M., Schumaker, J., & Deshler, D. (1995). Training strategic tutors to enhance learner independence. *Journal of Developmental Education, 19*, 18–26.

Johnson, D. W., & Johnson, R. T. (1992). Implementing cooperative learning. *Contemporary Education, 63*(3), 173–180.

King, A., Staffieri, A., & Adelgais, A. (1998). Mutual peer tutoring: Effects of structuring tutorial interaction to scaffold peer learning. *Journal of Educational Psychology, 90*, 134–152.

Koedinger, K. R., Anderson, J. R., Hadley, W. H., & Mark, M. (1997). Intelligent tutoring goes to school in the big city. *International Journal of Artificial Intelligence in Education, 8*, 30–43.

Lehman, B. A., Matthews, M., D'Mello, S. K., and Person, N. (2008). Understanding students' affective states during learning. In B. P. Woolf, E. Aimeur, R. Nkambou, & S. Lajoie (Eds.), *Intelligent Tutoring Systems: 9th International Conference*. Heidelberg: Springer.

Lepper, M. R., Drake, M., & O'Donnell-Johnson, T. M. (1997). Scaffolding techniques of expert human tutors. In K. Hogan, & M. Pressley (Eds.), *Scaffolding student learning: Instructional approaches and issues* (pp. 108– 144). New York: Brookline Books.

Lepper, M. R., & Henderlong, J. (2000). Turning "play" into "work" and "work" into "play": 25 years of research on intrinsic versus extrinsic motivation. In C. Sansone, & J. M. Harackiewicz (Eds.), *Intrinsic and extrin- sic motivation: The search for optimal motivation and performance* (pp. 257–307). San Diego, CA: Academic Press.

Lesgold, A., Lajoie, S. P., Bunzo, M., & Eggan, G. (1992). SHER-LOCK: A coached practice environment for an electronics trouble-shooting job. In J. H. Larkin, & R. W. Chabay (Eds.), *Computer assisted instruction and intelligent tutoring systems: Shared goals and complementary approaches* (pp. 201–238). Hillsdale, NJ: Erlbaum.

Linnenbrink, E. A., & Pintrich, P. (2002). The role of motivational beliefs in conceptual change. In M. Limon, & L. Mason (Eds.), *Reconsidering conceptual change: Issues in theory and practice*. Dordrecht: Kluwer Academic Publishers.

Litman, D. J., Rosé, C. P., Forbes-Riley, K., VanLehn, K., Bhembe, D., & Silliman, S. (2006). Spoken versus typed human and computer dialogue tutoring. *International Journal of Artificial Intelligence in Education, 16*, 145–170.

Maki, R. H. (1998). Test predictions over text material. In D. J. Hacker, J. Dunlosky, & A. C. Graesser (Eds.), *Meta- cognition in educational theory and practice* (pp. 117–144). Mahwah, NJ: Erlbaum.

Mathes, P. G., & Fuchs, L. S. (1994). Peer tutoring in reading for students with mild disabilities: A best evidence synthesis. *School Psychology Review, 23*, 59–80.

Mayer, R. E. (2009). *Multimedia learning* (2nd ed.). New York: Cambridge University Press.

McArthur, D., Stasz, C., & Zmuidzinas, M. (1990). Tutoring techniques in algebra. *Cognition and Instruction, 7*, 197–244.

McNamara, D. S. (2004). SERT: Self-explanation reading training. *Discourse Processes, 38*, 1–30.

McNamara, D. S. (Ed.). (2007). *Theories of text comprehension: The importance of reading strategies to theoretical foundations of reading comprehension*. Mahwah, NJ: Erlbaum.

Merrill, D. C., Reiser, B. J., Merrill, S. K., & Landes, S. (1995). Tutoring: Guided learning by doing. *Cognition and Instruction, 13*(3), 315–372.

Meyer, D. K., & Turner, J. C. (2006). Re-conceptualizing emotion and motivation to learn in classroom contexts. *Educational Psychology Review, 18*, 377–390.

Otero, J., & Graesser, A. C. (2001). PREG: Elements of a model of question asking. *Cognition & Instruction, 19*, 143–175.

Palincsar, A. S., & Brown, A. L. (1984). Reciprocal teaching of comprehension- fostering and monitoring activities. *Cognition and Instruction, 1*, 117–175.

Palincsar, A. S., & Brown, A. L. (1988). Teaching and practicing thinking skills to promote comprehension in the context of group problem solving. *Remedial and Special Education (RASE), 9*(1), 53–59.

Person, N. K., & Graesser, A. C. (1999). Evolution of discourse in cross-age tutoring. In A. M. O'Donnell and A. King (Eds.), *Cognitive perspectives on peer learning* (pp. 69–86). Mahwah, NJ: Erlbaum.

Person, N. K., Kreuz, R. J., Zwaan, R., & Graesser, A. C. (1995). Pragmatics and pedagogy: Conversational rules and politeness strategies may inhibit effective tutoring. *Cognition and Instruction, 13*, 161–188.

Person, N., Lehman, B., & Ozbun, R. (2007). Pedagogical and motivational dialogue moves used by expert tutors. Paper presented at the 17th Annual Meeting of the Society for Text and Discourse. Glasgow, Scotland.

Ritter, S., Anderson, J. R., Koedinger, K. R., Corbett, A. (2007) Cognitive Tutor: Applied research in mathematics education. *Psychonomic Bulletin & Review, 14*, 249–255.

Rogoff, B., & Gardner, W. (1984). Adult guidance of cognitive development. In B. Rogoff, & J. Lave (Eds.), *Everyday cognition: Its development in social context* (pp. 95–116). Cambridge, MA: Harvard University Press.

Rohrbeck, C. A., Ginsburg-Block, M., Fantuzzo, J. W., & Miller, T. R. (2003). Peer assisted learning interventions with elementary school students: A meta-analytic review. *Journal of Educational Psychology, 95*(2), 240–257.

Roscoe, R. D., & Chi, M. T. H. (2007). Understanding tutor learning: Knowledge-building and knowledge-telling in peer tutors' explanations and questions. *Review of Educational Research, 77*, 534–574.

Rosenshine, B., & Meister, C. (1994). Reciprocal teaching: A review of the research. *Review of Educational Research, 64*(4), 479–530.

Rosenshine, B., Meister, C., & Chapman, S. (1996). Teaching students to generate questions: A review of the intervention studies. *Review of Educational Research, 66*, 181–221.

Schwartz, D. L., & Bransford, J. D. (1998). A time for telling. *Cognition & Instruction, 16*(4), 475–522.

Shah, F., Evens, M. W., Michael, J., & Rovick, A. (2002). Classifying student initiatives and tutor responses in human keyboard to keyboard tutoring sessions. *Discourse Processes, 33*, 23–52.

Siler, S.A., & VanLehn, K. (2009). Learning, interactional and motivational outcomes in one-to-one synchronous computer-mediated versus face-to-face tutoring. *International Journal of Artificial Intelligence in Education, 19*(1), 73–102.

Sinclair, J. , & Coulthart, M. (1975) *Towards an analysis of discourse: The English used by teachers and pupils.* London: Oxford University Press.

Slavin, R. E. (1990). *Cooperative learning: Theory, research, and practice.* Englewood Cliffs, NJ: Prentice Hall.

Slavin, R. E., Karweit, N., & Madden, N. (1989). *Effective programs for students at risk.* Boston: Allyn and Bacon.

Sleeman D., & Brown, J. S. (Eds.). (1982) *Intelligent tutoring systems.* Orlando, FL: Academic Press, Inc.

Stein, N. L., & Hernandez, M. W. (2007). Assessing understanding and appraisals during emotional experience: The development and use of the Narcoder. In J. A. Coan, & J. J. Allen (Eds.), *Handbook of emotion elicitation and assessment* (pp. 298–317). New York: Oxford University Press.

Topping, K. (1996). The effectiveness of peer tutoring in further and higher education: A typology and review of the literature. *Higher Education, 32*, 321–345.

VanLehn, K. (2006) The behavior of tutoring systems. *International Journal of Artificial Intelligence in Education, 16*(3), 227–265.

VanLehn, K., Graesser, A. C., Jackson, G. T., Jordan, P., Olney, A., & Rosé, C. P. (2007). When are tutorial dialogues more effective than reading? *Cognitive Science, 31*, 3–62.

VanLehn, K., Siler, S., Murray, C., Yamauchi, T., & Baggett, W.B. (2003). Why do only some events cause learning during human tutoring? *Cognition and Instruction, 21*(3), 209–249.

Vygotsky, L.S. (1978). *Mind in society.* Cambridge, MA: Harvard University Press.

Woolf, B.P. (2009). *Building intelligent tutoring systems.* Burlington, MA: Morgan Kaufman.

Zimmerman, B. (2001). Theories of self-regulated learning and academic achievement: An overview and analysis. In B. Zimmerman, & D. Schunk (Eds.), *Self-regulated learning and academic achievement: Theoretical perspectives* (pp. 1–37). Mahwah, NJ: Erlbaum.

21

INSTRUCTION BASED ON VISUALIZATIONS

Richard E. Mayer

INTRODUCTION

People learn better from words and pictures than from words alone. This proposal, which can be called the *multimedia instruction hypothesis*, is examined in this chapter. For thousands of years, the main medium of instruction has involved the use of words—including oral scripts, discussions, lectures, and more recently, textbooks. Recently, advances in computer-based visualization technology have enabled the incorporation of sophisticated graphics in instruction—including animation, video, illustrations, and photos. In this chapter, I explore the question of whether adding visualizations to words in instructional messages can improve student learning.

Multimedia instruction occurs when instructional messages contain both words and pictures (Mayer, 2009). An *instruction message* is a communication intended to promote learning, whereas a *multimedia instruction message* is a communication that contains both words and pictures, and is intended to promote learning (Mayer, 2009). As summarized in Table 21.1, words are verbal representations such as printed text (delivered on a page or screen) or spoken text (delivered face-to-face or via speakers); and pictures are visual-spatial representations such as static graphics (including illustrations, drawings, photos, maps, diagrams, charts, figures, and tables delivered on a page or screen) or dynamic graphics (including animation and video delivered on a screen). In this chapter, I use the terms pictures, graphics, and visualizations interchangeably, although in some venues visualizations refer only to computer-rendered visual-spatial representations.

Table 21.1 The distinction between words and pictures

Mode	Example	Implementation
Words	Printed text	Words (on page or screen)
	Spoken text	Speech that is live, recorded, or synthesized
Pictures	Static graphics	Illustrations, drawings, photos, maps, graphs, charts, figures, tables (on page or screen)
	Dynamic graphics	Animation, video (on screen)

An *instructional visualization* (or instructional picture or instructional graphic) is a visual-spatial representation intended to promote learning. Instructional visualizations can vary along several dimensions:

- *Realism*—pictures can vary from high realism (e.g., a photo or video) to low realism (e.g., a line drawing or an animated line drawing);
- *Dynamism*—pictures can be static (e.g., a drawing or photo) or dynamic (e.g., an animation or video);
- *Interactivity*—pictures can be interactive (e.g., a series of drawings that can be paced by the learner or an animation that can be stopped and started by the learner) or non-interactive (e.g., a drawing or continuous animation);
- *Dimensionality*—pictures can be presented in 2D or 3D form;
- *Visual-spatial character*—pictures can be visual representations (e.g., a drawing or photo of an object) or spatial representations (e.g., a chart or table or map);
- *Delivery medium*—pictures can be presented on a page or screen.

In most of the research presented in this chapter, I focus on pictures that are low in realism, non-interactive, visual, and two-dimensional; that can be either static or dynamic; and that can be delivered on a page or screen.

A BRIEF HISTORY OF INSTRUCTIONAL VISUALIZATIONS

There have been three major phases in the technology supporting instructional visualizations: books, film, and computers.

Books

A major breakthrough in multimedia instruction occurred more than 350 years ago, when the Czech educator, John Amos Comenius ([1658] 1887), published a children's illustrated book entitled, *Orbis Pictus* (*The World in Pictures*). As exemplified in Figure 21.1, each page contained a line drawing of a scene with numbered objects along with accompanying text that named and explicated each object in both the reader's first language and in Latin. Comenius's book was a sort of illustrated encyclopedia containing what he called "nomenclature and pictures of all the chief things that are in the world" (Comenius, 1887, p. xi). *Orbis Pictus* is widely recognized as the first instructional book to combine words and pictures, and stands as "the most popular illustrated textbook ever written for children" (Saettler, 2004, p. 31). Thus, *Orbis Pictus* is the forerunner of modern illustrated textbooks in particular and multimedia instruction in general.

In his Preface, Comenius offered a theoretical rationale for why words and pictures should be learned together: "There is nothing in our understanding that was not before in the sense" (Comenius, 1887, p. xiv). He objected to the words-only approach to instruction on the grounds that when "things which are to be learned are offered to scholars without being understood or being rightly presented to the senses, it cometh to pass, that the work of teaching and learning goeth heavily onward and affordeth little benefit" (Comenius, 1887, p. xiv). In short, the rationale for multimedia instruction is that learners' understanding of text depends on their being able to relate the words to corresponding concrete visual representations and situations.

(200)

XCVIII.

The Study.   Muséum.

The Study 1.	Muséum 1.
is a place	est locus,
where a Student, 2.	ubi *Studiosus*, 2.
a part from men,	secretus ab hominibus,
sitteth alone,	solus sedet,
addicted to his Studies,	*Studiis* deditus,
whilst he readeth	dum lectitat
Books, 3.	*Libros*, 3.
which being within	quos penes se
his reach, he layeth	super *Pluteum* 4.
open upon a Desk 4.	exponit, & ex iliis
and picketh all the	in *Manuale* 5. suum
best things out of	optima quæq; excerpit,
them into his own	
Manual, 5.	

Figure 21.1 A page from Comenius's Orbis Pictus, the world's first illustrated textbook

Motion Pictures and TV

Another milestone in multimedia instruction occurred approximately 100 years ago (1911–1914), when Thomas Edison released the world's first instructional films for classroom showing, with titles in history such as *The Minute Men* and in science such as *Life History of the Silkworm* (Saettler, 2004). Edison predicted that "the motion picture is destined to revolutionize our educational system" (Cuban, 1986, p. 9), and indeed by 1931, 25 states had bureaus dedicated to visual education using motion pictures (Saettler, 2004). In 1954, the first educational television station (KUHT) began broadcasting in Houston, Texas, and in the 1970s the Children's Television Workshop created landmark educational television programming such as *Sesame Street* and *The Electric Company*.

Computers

Beginning in the 1960s, widespread use of computer-based instructional systems became feasible (Cuban, 1986), and within the past decades, we have witnessed important advances in communication technology, including the widespread availability of the Internet, and in graphics technology, including affordable graphics software for producing educational illustrations, animation, and video. Today, it is possible to create compelling computer-based visual simulations on laptop computers, to deliver stunning graphics via hand-held devices, and to offer the experience of immersive virtual reality (Mayer, 2005). An important educational issue concerns how best to use the graphics capabilities in book-, film-, and computer-based technologies to improve student learning.

THEORETICAL FRAMEWORK

Does Multimedia Instruction Work?

It is important to determine whether there is any value added to student learning outcomes by adding graphics to words. In short, a fundamental research question is, Does adding graphics to words help people learn better than presenting words alone? For example, if someone looks up "brakes" in an online encyclopedia, they may come across a section on hydraulic brakes that contains the following explanation of how brakes work:

> When the driver steps on the car's brake pedal, a piston moves forward inside the master cylinder. The piston forces brake fluid out of the master cylinder and through the tubes to the wheel cylinders. In the wheel cylinders, the increase in fluid pressure makes a smaller set of pistons move. When the brake shoes press against the drum both the drum and wheel stop or slow down.
>
> (Mayer, 2009, p. 40)

This explanation provides a step-by-step description of the causal chain in which a change in state in one part (e.g., piston moves forward in master cylinder) causes a change in state in another part (e.g., brake fluid is forced through the tubes) which causes a change in state in another part (e.g., smaller set of pistons move), and so on. The text is intended to help the learner build a *causal model* of the braking system, consisting of each component, the changes in each component, and the relations among the changes in the components.

How well do people learn the explanation from printed words? On an immediate retention test in which they were asked to write all they can remember about how brakes work, people generated less than 25% of the important information (Mayer, 2009). On an immediate transfer test in which they were asked to generate as many answers as possible to open-ended questions (e.g., "Suppose you press the brake pedal in your car but the brakes don't work. What could have gone wrong?"), people averaged less than one acceptable answer per question (Mayer, 2009). In short, people do not appear to learn much from reading a text that explains how something works. Similar results were obtained when people listened to an explanation rather than read it (Mayer, 2009).

What can be done to improve people's understanding of verbal explanations? We can add a series of frames consisting of line drawings that depict the actions described in the verbal explanation. Figure 21.2 shows line drawings depicting the braking system before and after the driver steps on the car's brake pedal along with accompanying printed text. Alternatively, we can add animation (based on line drawings) to a narration. Figure 21.3

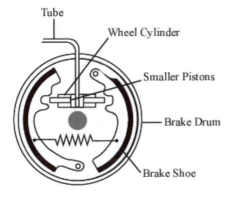

When the driver steps on the car's brake pedal...

A piston moves forward inside the master cylinder (not shown).

The piston forces brake fluid out of the master cylinder and through the tubes to the wheel cylinders.

In the wheel cylinders, the increase in fluid pressure makes a set of smaller pistons move.

When the brake shoes press against the drum both the drum and the wheel stop or slow down.

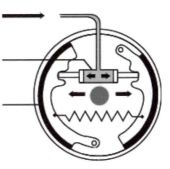

Figure 21.2 A page from a paper-based illustrated text on how a car's braking system works

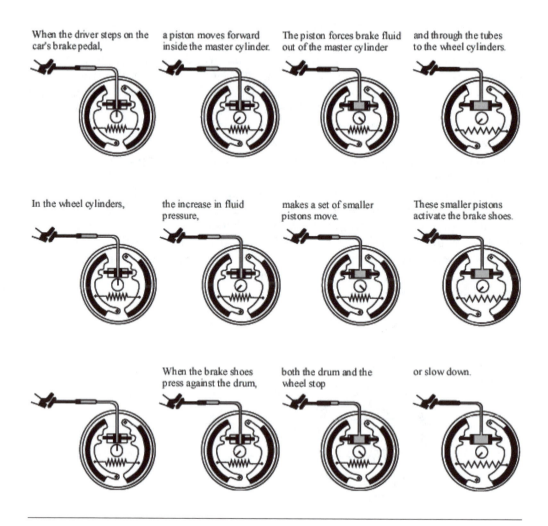

When the driver steps on the car's brake pedal,

a piston moves forward inside the master cylinder.

The piston forces brake fluid out of the master cylinder

and through the tubes to the wheel cylinders.

In the wheel cylinders,

the increase in fluid pressure,

makes a set of smaller pistons move.

These smaller pistons activate the brake shoes.

When the brake shoes press against the drum,

both the drum and the wheel stop

or slow down.

Figure 21.3 Frames from a computer-based narrated animation on how a car's braking system works

shows frames from a computer-based animation along with accompanying narration. As you can see, the added visualizations provide a concrete context for making sense of the words.

Overall, across 13 experimental comparisons involving lessons on topics such as how brakes, pumps, or lighting works, people performed better on transfer tests when they learned from printed text and illustrations than from printed text alone (Mayer, 1989, Experiments 1 and 2; Mayer & Gallini, 1990, Experiments 1, 2, and 3; Mayer, Bove, Bryman, Mars, & Tapangco, 1996, Experiment 2; Moreno & Valdez, 2005, Experiments 1a and 1b) or from narration and animation than from narration alone (Mayer & Anderson, 1991, Experiment 1; Mayer & Anderson, 1992, Experiments 1 and 2; Moreno & Mayer, 1999, Experiment 1; Moreno & Mayer, 2002a, Experiment 1). The median effect size favoring words and pictures over words alone is $d = 1.35$, which is considered a large effect. These results are evidence for the *multimedia principle*: People learn better from words and pictures than from words alone (Mayer, 2009).

An important consideration is whether the multimedia principle applies in more authentic learning situations. For example, a reasonable criticism of the foregoing studies is that they were mainly conducted in lab settings and used very short lessons. In a set of three studies, students who learned about learning principles from a lecture followed by a video showing a case example performed better on a transfer test than did students who learned from a lecture followed an equivalent text booklet describing a case example (Moreno & Ortegano-Layne, 2008, Experiment 1; Moreno & Valdez, 2007, Experiments 1 and 2). In two studies, beginning trade apprentices and trainees in a work-related training program performed better on subsequent transfer tests if their training materials consisted of text and printed diagrams rather than text alone, or audio narration and printed diagrams rather than diagrams alone (Kalyuga, Chandler, & Sweller, 1998, Experiment 1; Kalyuga, Chandler, & Sweller, 2000, Experiment 1). Thus, there is promising evidence that the multimedia principle may extend to more authentic learning environments.

In a recent review, Fletcher and Tobias (2005, p. 117) concluded that the multimedia principle is "supported by research studies" but also noted that the effectiveness of combining words and pictures may depend on individual differences. In particular, the learner's prior knowledge may serve as a boundary condition for the multimedia principle (Mayer, 2009) in which adding pictures to words is particularly helpful for low-knowledge learners but not for high-knowledge learners. For example, Mayer and Gallini (1990) asked students to read a booklet explaining how brakes, pumps, or electrical generators work and then take a transfer test. For students who reported low levels of prior mechanical knowledge, adding line drawings to the printed text greatly improved transfer test performance as compared to presenting text alone. In contrast, for students who reported high levels of prior mechanical knowledge, adding diagrams to printed text did not greatly improve transfer test performance.

In another set of experiments, Kalyuga, Chandler, and Sweller (1998, 2000) taught students how to solve practical engineering problems using diagrams accompanied by printed text or audio narration. Beginning trainees learned better from words and pictures than from words or pictures alone, but as trainees gained more experience, they learned worse from words and pictures than from words or pictures alone. Kalyuga (2005) refers to this pattern as the *expertise reversal effect*: Instructional methods that improve learning for low-knowledge learners may be ineffective or even harmful for high-knowledge learners. It appears that domain-specific prior knowledge may be a useful variable to consider when designing instruction involving visualizations. In particular, adding pictures to words may be particularly helpful for low-knowledge learners, presumably because they are less able to create and link images to words on their own.

Another individual differences dimension that has received much attention in education is cognitive style—such as the distinction between visualizers and verbalizers (Massa & Mayer, 2006). In particular, a common claim is that visualizers would benefit more from adding pictures to words than would verbalizers (Pashler, McDaniel, Rohrer, & Bjork, 2008). However, in a systematic set of studies, Massa and Mayer (2006) gave students a computer-based lesson on electronics that consisted mainly of text along with help frames that combined mainly text or mainly pictorial material. Both visualizers and verbalizers performed better on subsequent transfer tests if they had received pictorial help fames rather than text help frames. Overall, Pashler, McDaniel, Rohrer, and Bjork (2008) conclude that there is not sufficient evidence to provide visual instruction to visualizers and verbal instruction to verbalizers. Thus, it appears that cognitive style is not a major individual differences variable for teaching with visualizations.

How Does Multimedia Instruction Work?

In the previous section, I examined some evidence showing that adding visualizations to a word-based lesson can improve students' understanding of the material. In this section, my goal is to examine how the additional visualizations affect the process of learning. I begin with three principles from cognitive science concerning how learning works—dual channels, limited capacity, and active processing. The dual channels principle is that people have separate channels for processing words and pictures (Baddeley, 1986, 1999; Paivio, 1986, 2001). The limited capacity principle is that people are able to engage in only a limited amount of cognitive processing in each channel at any one time (Baddeley, 1986, 1999; Sweller, 1999). The active processing principle is that meaningful learning occurs when people engage in appropriate cognitive processing during learning, including selecting relevant incoming words and pictures for further processing, organizing the selected words and pictures into coherent mental representations, and integrating the representations with each other and with relevant prior knowledge activated from long-term memory (Mayer, 2009; Wittrock, 1989).

Figure 21.4 summarizes a cognitive model of how multimedia instruction works. There are two channels—a *verbal channel* across the top row for processing words and verbal representations, and a *pictorial channel* across the bottom row for processing pictures and pictorial representations. The three boxes in the columns of the model represent sensory memory, working memory, and long-term memory. *Sensory memory* briefly holds incoming sounds and images in sensory form with unlimited capacity. *Working memory* can be used to temporarily hold and manipulate selected verbal and pictorial representations with limited capacity. *Long-term memory* is the learner's permanent storehouse of knowledge with unlimited capacity.

The arrows in the model represent cognitive processes during learning required for meaningful learning—selecting, organizing, and integrating. *Selecting words* refers to paying attention to some of the incoming spoken words that are fleeting in auditory sensory memory, thereby transferring them to working memory for further processing in the verbal channel. *Selecting images* refers to paying attention to some of the incoming pictures and printed words that are fleeting in visual sensory memory, and transferring them to working memory for further processing in the pictorial channel. Printed words

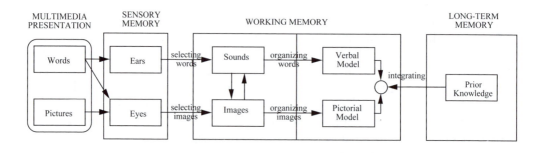

Figure 21.4 A cognitive model of learning with words and pictures

are initially processed in the pictorial channel in working memory and then shifted to the verbal channel in working memory (indicated by the arrow from images to sounds). Organizing words refers to building a coherent verbal representation in the verbal channel of working memory, and organizing images refers to building a coherent pictorial representation in the pictorial channel of working memory. Integrating refers to building connections between the verbal and pictorial representations and with relevant prior knowledge activated from long-term memory.

What happens when a learner is in an instructional situation involving words and pictures (e.g., reading an illustrated text, viewing a narrated animation, or interacting with a multimedia instructional simulation)? If the instruction is well designed and appropriate for the learner, we can expect that all five cognitive processes will be activated, resulting in a meaningful learning outcome, which is then stored in long-term memory. The act of integrating verbal and pictorial representations with each other is an important step in promoting deep understanding.

In contrast, consider what happens when the learner receives only words (e.g., printed or spoken text). In this case, inexperienced learners may not be able to generate relevant pictorial representations on their own, so they do not have the opportunity to build a pictorial representation (i.e., indicated by the organizing images arrow) or to integrate verbal and pictorial representations (i.e., indicated by the integrating arrow within working memory). Thus, the learning outcome for words-only instruction is not as well developed as for multimedia instruction.

In learning with words and pictures, learners may experience three kinds of demands on their limited processing capacity in working memory: extraneous processing, essential processing, and generative processing (Mayer, 2009; Mayer & Moreno, 2003; Sweller, 1999, 2005). *Extraneous processing* refers to cognitive processing that does not support the learning objective and can be caused by poor layout. For example, placing the illustration on one page and the corresponding text on another page causes the learner to have to scan back and forth, wasting precious cognitive processing capacity. It follows that an important instructional goal is to reduce extraneous processing, so that the learner has sufficient remaining capacity to engage in essential and generative processing.

Essential processing refers to cognitive processing that is required to mentally represent the material and is caused by the inherent complexity of the material for the learner. Essential processing requires the process of selecting in Figure 21.4, as well as some initial amount of organizing. Even if we could eliminate extraneous processing, the demands of essential processing might overwhelm the learner's cognitive system. Thus, an important instructional goal is to manage essential processing in a way that prevents cognitive overload.

Generative processing refers to cognitive processing aimed at making sense of the material and is caused by the learner's motivation. Generative processing requires the processes of integrating and organizing in Figure 21.4. Even if we reduce extraneous processing and manage essential processing so processing capacity is available, learners may not use that available capacity to engage in generative processing. Thus, an important instructional goal is to foster generative processing.

In short, based on the model of multimedia instruction presented in Figure 21.4, there are three kinds of threats to appropriate cognitive processing during learning: (1) too much extraneous processing (so a goal is to reduce extraneous processing); (2) too much essential processing (so a goal to manage essential processing); and (3) too little generative processing (so a goal is to foster generative processing).

CURRENT TRENDS AND ISSUES

When Does Multimedia Instruction Work?

Although learning from words and pictures can result in deeper learning than learning from words alone, not all pictorial visualizations are equally effective. In this section, I examine how to design effective visualizations for meaningful learning, based on the three goals described in the previous section. In short, this section briefly examines instructional design principles for reducing extraneous processing, managing essential processing, and fostering generative processing.

As shown in Table 21.2, principles for reducing extraneous processing include the coherence principle, the signaling principle, the redundancy principle, the spatial contiguity principle, and the temporal contiguity principle. The coherence principle is that people learn better from multimedia lessons when extraneous words and pictures are excluded rather than included. For example, a seductive detail is interesting but irrelevant verbal information, such as verbal descriptions of airplanes or people being struck by lightning in a lesson on how lightning storms develop. Similarly, pictorial seductive details are interesting but irrelevant visualizations, such as interspersed pictures or video of lightning storms in a lesson on how lightning storms develop. In six experimental tests, adding seductive details to an illustrated text (Harp & Mayer, 1997, Experiment 1; Harp & Mayer, 1998, Experiments 1, 2, 3, and 4) or a narrated animation (Mayer, Heiser, & Lonn, 2001, Experiment 3) on lightning formation resulted in lower performance on transfer tests, with a median effect size of $d = 1.66$ favoring the more concise lesson.

Similarly, in six experimental comparisons, students performed better on transfer tests if extraneous words had been eliminated from lessons containing printed text and illustrations on ocean waves (Mayer & Jackson, 2005, Experiments 1a and 1b), or lightning (Mayer, Bove, Bryman, Mars, & Tapangco, 1996, Experiments 1, 2, and 3), or lessons containing narration and animation on ocean waves (Mayer & Jackson, 2005, Experiment 2), yielding a median effect size of $d = 0.82$. Finally, students performed better on transfer tests when background music was deleted from computer-based narration and animation on lightning (Moreno & Mayer, 2000a, Experiment 1), or brakes (Moreno & Mayer, 2000a, Experiment 2), with a median effect size of $d = 1.11$. When extraneous material is eliminated, people can focus their cognitive processing on the essential words and pictures in the lesson.

The signaling principle is that people learn better from multimedia lessons when the essential words are highlighted. Signaling can involve adding voice emphasis to essential words, adding an outline, adding headings, or adding a graphic organizer. In this way, the learner may be better able to make connections between the essential verbal

Table 21.2 Five principles for reducing extraneous processing

Principle	Description	n	d
Coherence	Reduce extraneous words and pictures	14	0.97
Signaling	Highlight essential words and pictures	6	0.52
Redundancy	Do not add onscreen text to narrated graphics	12	0.79
Spatial contiguity	Place printed words near corresponding graphics	13	1.08
Temporal contiguity	Present corresponding words and graphics simultaneously	13	0.87

Note: n = number of comparisons; d = median effect size.

material and the corresponding portions of the visualization. Modest preliminary support for the signaling principle can be seen across six experimental comparisons involving a computer-based multimedia lesson on how airplanes achieve lift (Mautone & Mayer, 2001, Experiments 3a and 3b), and paper-based lessons on lightning (Harp & Mayer, 1998, Experiment 3a) and biology (Stull & Mayer, 2007, Experiments 1, 2, and 3), yielding a median effect size of $d = 0.52$. Signaling may be more effective when the display is complex (Jeung, Chandler, & Sweller, 1997) and when it used sparingly (Stull & Mayer, 2007).

The redundancy principle is that people learn better from onscreen visualizations with narration than from onscreen visualizations with narration and onscreen text. In short, the redundancy principle advises against adding onscreen text to a narrated animation or narrated still graphics. The redundancy principle is supported across 12 experimental comparisons involving computer-based lessons on lightning (Craig, Gholson, & Driscoll, 2002, Experiment 2; Mayer, Heiser, & Lonn, 2001, Experiments 1 and 2; Moreno & Mayer, 2002a, Experiment 2), on human memory (Jamet & Bohec, 2007, Experiment 1), on electrical engineering (Kalyuga, Chandler, & Sweller, 1999, Experiment 1; Kalyuga, Chandler, & Sweller, 2000, Experiment 1), on computer-based simulation games in botany (Moreno & Mayer, 2002a, Experiments 2a and 2b), and on paper-based lessons on math problems (Mousavi, Low, & Sweller, 1995, Experiments 1 and 2) and on temperature graphs (Leahy, Chandler, & Sweller, 2003, Experiment 2), yielding a median effect size of $d = 0.79$. When people pay attention to the onscreen text, they are not able to attend to the visualization, and they may waste cognitive capacity by trying to reconcile the two verbal streams. Some important boundary conditions for the redundancy principle are that onscreen text can be helpful when the words are unfamiliar to the learner, the learner is not a native speaker of the language, the learner has hearing difficulties, or the onscreen text is short and placed next to the corresponding part of the graphic (Mayer, 2009; Mayer & Johnson, 2008).

The spatial contiguity principle is that people learn better from multimedia lessons when printed words are placed near rather than far from the corresponding part of the graphic on the screen or page. By placing corresponding words and graphics near each other, the learner is less likely to have to scan around the page or screen trying to figure out where to look. Strong and consistent support for the spatial contiguity principle can be found across 13 experimental comparisons involving paper-based lessons on lighting (Mayer, Steinhoff, Bower, & Mars, 1995, Experiments 1, 2, and 3), on brakes (Mayer, 1989, Experiment 2), on the heart (Chandler & Sweller, 1991, Experiment 6), on engineering (Chandler & Sweller, 1991, Experiment 1; Chandler & Sweller, 1992, Experiment 1; Tindall-Ford, Chandler, & Sweller, 1997, Experiment 1), and on mathematics (Sweller, Chandler, Tierney & Cooper, 1990, Experiment 1); and computer-based lessons on lightning (Moreno & Mayer, 1999, Experiment 1), on pumps (Bodemer, Ploetzner, Feuerlein, & Spada, 2004, Experiment 1), on statistics (Bodemer, Ploetzner, Feuerlein, & Spada, 2004, Experiment 2), and on physics (Kester, Kirschner, & van Merrienboer, 2005, Experiment 1), yielding a median effect size of $d = 1.08$. In recent reviews of the spatial contiguity effect, Ginns (2006) and Ayres and Sweller (2005) have reported strong supporting evidence, but there are some possible boundary conditions (Mayer, 2009): the spatial contiguity principle may apply most strongly for low-knowledge learners (Kalyuga, 2005), when the material is complicated (Ayres & Sweller, 2005), and when the learner places the words next to graphics through interactivity (Bodemer, Ploetzner, Feuerlein, & Spada, 2004).

The temporal contiguity principle is that people learn better when pictures and narration are presented simultaneously rather than successively. Learners are better able to make connections between words and pictures when the spoken words correspond to the visualizations being presented on the screen. Across 13 experimental comparisons, transfer test performance is generally better for simultaneous rather than successive presentation, yielding a median effect size of $d = 1.39$. The evidence comes from computer-based lessons on pumps (Mayer & Anderson, 1991, Experiments 1 and 2a; Mayer & Anderson, 1992, Experiment 1; Mayer & Sims, 1994, Experiment 1), on brakes (Mayer & Anderson, 1992, Experiment 2; Mayer, Moreno, Boire, & Vagge, 1999, Experiment 2), on lungs (Mayer & Sims, 1994, Experiment 2), on lightning (Mayer, Moreno, Boire, & Vagge, 1999, Experiment 1), and on bandaging procedures (Michas & Berry, 2000, Experiment 3); and movies involving carnivorous plants (Baggett & Ehrenfeucht, 1983, Experiments 1a and 1b) and toy construction (Baggett, 1984, Experiments 1a and 1b).

Similarly, Ginns (2006) identified 13 experimental comparisons testing the temporal contiguity principle, yielding a median effect size of $d = 0.87$. Some possible boundary conditions are that the effect is eliminated when learners can control the pace and order of presentation (Michas & Berry, 2000) and when the segments are very short (Mayer, Moreno, Boire, & Vagge, 1999; Moreno & Mayer, 1999).

As shown in Table 21.3, principles for managing essential processing include the segmenting principle, the pretraining principle, and the modality principle. The segmenting principle is that people learn better from a multimedia lesson when the lesson is broken down into learner-paced segments. For example, there is generally consistent support for the pretraining principle across nine experimental comparisons including computer-based multimedia lessons on lightning (Mayer & Chandler, 2001, Experiment 2), on electric motors (Mayer, Dow, & Mayer, 2003, Experiments 2a and 2b), on geography (Mautone & Mayer, 2007, Experiment 2), on chemistry (Lee, Plass, & Homer, 2006, Experiment 1), and on probability problem solving (Gerjets, Scheiter, & Catrambone, 2006, Experiments 1a and 1b); and a paper-based mathematics lesson (Ayres, 2006, Experiments 1a and 2a). Overall, students performed better on transfer tests if they received segmented lessons in which they could control the pacing of segments rather than lessons in which all the material was presented at the same time or continuously, yielding a median effect size of $d = 0.82$. Thus, when the material is presented in bite-size chunks, the learner is able to completely process the words and pictures in one segment before moving on the next.

The pretraining principle is that people learn better from multimedia lessons when they receive pretraining in the names and characteristics of the key concepts. The pretraining principle is generally supported across 10 experimental comparisons involving computer-based presentations on brakes (Mayer, Mathias, & Wetzell, 2002, Experiments 1 and 2), on pumps (Mayer, Mathias, & Wetzell, 2002, Experiment 3), on statistics

Table 21.3 Three principles for managing essential processing

Principle	Description	n	d
Segmenting	Highlight essential words and pictures	9	0.82
Pretraining	Provide pretraining in names and characteristics of each main concept	10	0.88
Modality	Do not add onscreen text to narrated graphics	36	0.88

Note: n = number of comparisons; d = median effect size,

(Kester, Kirschner, & van Merrienboer, 2004, Experiment 1), and on electronics (Kester, Kirschner, & van Merrienboer, 2006, Experiment 1); computer-based simulation games in geology (Mayer, Mautone, & Prothero, 2002, Experiments 2 and 3); and paper-based multimedia lessons on electrical engineering (Pollock, Chandler, & Sweller, 2002, Experiments 1 and 2) and on mathematics (Clarke, Ayres, & Sweller, 2005, Experiment 1a), yielding a median effect size of $d = 0.88$. Thus, when visualizations are presented along with a verbal explanation, people are better able to make connections between the words and visualizations when they know the names and characteristics of the key elements in the verbal explanation and the visualizations.

The modality principle is that people learn better from visualizations with spoken words than from visualizations with printed words. In 36 experimental comparisons involving computer-based multimedia lessons with recorded voice or onscreen text (Atkinson, 2002, Experiments 1a, 1b, and 2; Craig, Gholson, & Driscoll, 2002, Experiment 2; Harskamp, Mayer, Suhre, & Jansma, 2007, Experiments 1 and 2a; Jeung, Chandler, & Sweller, 1997, Experiments 1, 2, and 3; Kalyuga, Chandler, & Sweller, 1999, Experiment 1; Kalyuga, Chandler, & Sweller, 2000, Experiment 1; Mayer, Dow, & Mayer, 2003, Experiment 1; Mayer & Moreno, 1998, Experiments 1 and 2; Moreno & Mayer, 1999, Experiments 1 and 2; Tabbers, Martens, & van Merrienboer, 2004, Experiment 1), paper-based multimedia lessons with tape-recorded voice or printed text (Leahy, Chandler, & Sweller, 2003, Experiment 1; Mousavi, Low, & Sweller, 1995, Experiments 1, 2, 3, 4, and 5; Tindall-Ford, Chandler, & Sweller, 1997, Experiments 1, 2, and 3), and computer-based multimedia simulation games with spoken or onscreen text (Moreno & Mayer, 2002b, Experiments 1a, 1b, 1c, 2a, and 2b; Moreno, Mayer, Spires, & Lester, 2001, Experiments 4a, 4b, 5a, and 5b; O'Neil et al., 2000, Experiment 1), researchers have found generally strong and consistent support for the modality principle, yielding a median effect size of $d = 0.88$. When people pay attention to printed words, they are not paying attention to the visualization, so using spoken text allows the learner to free up capacity in the visual channel. According to recent reviews, the modality principle has received the most research support of any of the principles (Ginns, 2005; Low & Sweller, 2005; Mayer, 2005), but it is important to note that the modality principle is strongest when the material is complex for the learner (Tindall-Ford, Chandler, & Sweller, 1997) and when the pace is fast and not under learner control (Tabbers, Martens, & van Merrienboer, 2004).

As shown in Table 21.4, principles for fostering generative processing include the personalization principle and the voice principle. The personalization principle is that people learn better when words in a multimedia lesson are presented in conversational style rather than formal style. For example, there is strong and consistent support for the personalization principle across 11 experimental tests including learning about lightning in a computer-based multimedia presentation (Moreno & Mayer, 2000b, Experiments 1

Table 21.4 Two principles for fostering generative processing

Principle	Description	n	d
Personalization	Put words in conversational style	11	1.11
Voice	Use friendly human voice for speaking words	3	0.78

Note: n = number of comparisons; d = median effect size.

and 2), about the human respiratory system in a computer-based multimedia presentation (Mayer, Fennell, Farmer, & Campbell, 2004, Experiments 1, 2, and 3), about botany in a multimedia game (Moreno & Mayer, 2000b, Experiments, 3, 4, and 5; Moreno & Mayer, 2004, Experiments 1a and 1b), and about engineering in a multimedia game (Wang et al., 2008, Experiment 1). Overall, students who received multimedia lessons with conversational style performed better on subsequent transfer tests than did students who received lessons with formal style, yielding a median effect size of $d = 1.11$. Thus, the communication style of the words that accompany a visualization can influence how much effort a learner puts into trying to see how the visualization relates to the words.

The voice principle is that people learn better from multimedia lessons when the words are spoken by a friendly human voice than by a machine voice. For example, there is preliminary support for the voice principle across three experimental comparisons involving computer-based lessons on lightning (Mayer, Sobko, & Mautone, 2003, Experiment 2) and on mathematics word problems (Atkinson, Mayer, & Merrill, 2005, Experiments 1 and 2). Overall, students who received multimedia lessons with human voices performed better on transfer tests than did students who learned with machine voices, yielding a median effect size of $d = 0.78$. Thus, the quality of the instructor's voice can influence how much effort a learner puts into trying to see how the verbal explanation meshes with the visualizations.

Where Does Multimedia Instruction Work?

There are many venues in which visualizations can be added to verbal instruction, including book-based lessons (e.g., illustrated textbooks), computer-based multimedia lessons (e.g., narrated animations or interactive simulations and games), face-to-face lessons (e.g., PowerPoint presentations), and lessons with hand-held devices (e.g., illustrated textbooks on Kindle or interactive games and simulations on a cell phone). Additionally, visualizations can be incorporated into many different subject areas including reading (e.g., graphics in phonics instruction), writing (e.g., graphic organizers for planning an essay), mathematics (e.g., concrete manipulatives to help represent word problems or computational procedures), science (e.g., interactive simulations and games for complex systems), history (e.g., figures, graphs, and maps to depict data, or photos and drawings to depict places and people), and second language learning (e.g., as photos, drawings, video, animation to aid in vocabulary learning). Much of the research presented in this chapter focuses on illustrated text, narrated animations, and computer-based interactive games, using content mainly in science and mathematics. However, there are encouraging signs that researchers are beginning to identify how best to incorporate visualizations in a full range of venues and subject areas (Hattie, 2009).

PRACTICAL IMPLICATIONS

The major practical implications of this chapter are the 10 design principles for multimedia lessons listed in Tables 21.2, 21.3, and 21.4, and described in the previous sections. Extraneous processing during learning can be reduced by using the coherence, signaling, redundancy, spatial contiguity, or temporal contiguity principles. Essential processing during learning can be managed by applying the pretraining, segmenting, or modality principles. Generative processing during learning can be fostered by incorporating the personalization or voice principles.

These practical implications are examples of *evidence-based practice*—basing instructional methods on research evidence rather than on conventional wisdom, opinion, speculation, fads, or doctrine. In particular, the 10 design principles summarized in this chapter constitute the fruits of a research strategy that can be called *basic research on applied problems* (Mayer, 2011) or *use-inspired basic research* (Stokes, 1997). In basic research on applied problems (or use-inspired basic research), researchers seek to accomplish two overlapping goals—to contribute to theory (such as a cognitive theory of multimedia learning) and to solve a practical problem (such as how to design effective multimedia instruction). For example, the research reported in this chapter helps develop a cognitive theory of multimedia learning by examining boundary conditions of design principles as predicted by the theory and helps improve design of multimedia instruction by providing evidence-based principles.

Stokes (1997) shows how the theoretical and practical goals of researchers yield four different research scenarios—*pure basic research* occurs when researchers seek to contribute to theory but not to practice; *pure applied research* occurs when researchers seek to contribute to practice but not to theory; *poor research* occurs when researchers seek to contribute neither to theory or practice; and *use-inspired basic research* occurs when researchers seek to contribute to both theory and practice. Stokes refers to this final scenario as *Pasteur's quadrant* and shows how it can lead to many advances in science and practice. Instead of viewing applied and basic research as two ends of a continuum, it makes more sense to view them as complementary research goals. This is the approach taken in this chapter, and more widely within this *Handbook*.

FUTURE DIRECTIONS

The research presented in this chapter points to the potential value of adding visualizations to verbal instruction—an instructional approach that I have called the promise of multimedia learning (Mayer, 2009). Advances in computer and communication technologies have created renewed interest in adding visualizations to verbal instruction in order to help people learn. This renewed interest in the promise of multimedia learning can be seen as the continuation of a 350-year old quest dating back to Comenius's well-reasoned rationale for the world's first illustrated textbook in the mid-1600s. Based on the current state of the research on learning with visualizations, I propose some promising and unpromising directions for future research.

Some promising directions include: (a) the continued discovery of evidence-based principles for multimedia design particularly in authentic learning situations; and (b) research that pinpoints the boundary conditions of multimedia design principles. First, the technology of multimedia instruction (i.e., the development of multimedia instruction) is emerging at a faster rate than the science of multimedia instruction (i.e., evidence-based principles for multimedia design and research-based theory). As textbooks continue to migrate from paper-based to computer-based media, students increasingly are exposed to instructional multimedia games and simulations, and multimedia instruction becomes available on hand-held technologies, there is a need for research on how best to design effective multimedia instruction. Although researchers have made substantial progress in identifying some preliminary design principles, developers need more guidance to help them design effective multimedia instruction. Second, research is needed that pinpoints the boundary conditions under which design principles are most (and least) likely to be effective, including for which kinds of learners, which kinds of content, which kinds of outcome measures, and which kinds of learning contexts. The search for boundary conditions should be guided by learning theory, and can be used to help test and refine current theories of how people learn from words and pictures.

Some unpromising directions include educational research focusing on media comparison studies and unscientific studies of the development of new visualization technologies. First, in media comparison studies, researchers compare learning with one medium (e.g., TV, film, books, computers, virtual reality) versus another medium. Although media comparison studies have a long history in educational research (Saettler, 2004), the consensus among educational researchers is that our field does not need more media comparison research (Clark, 2001). Clark notes that instructional media do not cause learning, but rather instructional methods cause learning. The same medium can be used for different instructional methods; thus, useful research focuses on which instructional methods best foster learning rather than on instructional technology per se. This can explain why media comparison studies generally fail to yield strong effects (Hattie, 2009).

Second, some of the research on multimedia instruction focuses mainly on describing the development of new technologies, describing how people use a new technology, or showing that people like using a new technology. In some cases, researchers seek to show that a new technology fosters learning, but they do not include a control group, do not have appropriate learning measures, or do not have sufficient numbers of learners. Instead, what is needed is high-quality, scientific research that answers the research question at hand (e.g., which instructional methods are most effective for producing learning with multimedia instruction?). Overall, there are encouraging signs for continued advances in our understanding of how to use visualizations to help people learn.

ACKNOWLEDGMENTS

Preparation of this chapter was supported by a grant from the Office of Naval Research. The author's email address is mayer@psych.ucsb.edu.

REFERENCES

Atkinson, R. K. (2002). Optimizing learning from examples using animated pedagogical agents. *Journal of Educational Psychology, 94,* 416–427.

Atkinson, R. K., Mayer, R. E., & Merrill, M. M. (2005). Fostering social agency in multimedia learning: Examining the impact of an animated agent's voice. *Contemporary Educational Psychology, 30,* 117–139.

Ayres, P. (2006). Impact of reducing intrinsic cognitive load on learning in a mathematical domain. *Applied Cognitive Psychology, 20,* 287–298.

Ayres, P., & Sweller, J. (2005). The split attention principle in multimedia learning. In R. E. Mayer (Ed.), *The Cambridge handbook of multimedia learning* (pp. 135–146). New York: Cambridge University Press.

Baddeley, A. D. (1986). *Working memory.* Oxford: Oxford University Press.

Baddeley, A. D. (1999). *Human memory.* Boston: Allyn & Bacon.

Baggett, P. (1984). Role of temporal overlap of visual and auditory material in forming dual media associations. *Journal of Educational Psychology, 76,* 408–417.

Baggett, P., & Ehrenfeucht, A. (1983). Encoding and retaining information in the visuals and verbals of an educational movie. *Educational Communications and Technology Journal, 31,* 23–32.

Bodemer, D., Ploetzner, R., Feuerlein, I., & Spada, H. (2004). The active integration of information during learning with dynamic and interactive visualisations. *Learning and Instruction, 14,* 325–341.

Chandler, P., & Sweller, J. (1991). Cognitive load theory and the format of instruction. *Cognition and Instruction, 8,* 293–332.

Chandler, P., & Sweller, J. (1992). The split-attention effect as a factor in the design of instruction. *British Journal of Educational Psychology, 62*, 233–246.

Clark, R. C. (2001). *Learning from media: Arguments, analysis, and evidence.* Greenwich, CT: Information Age Publishers.

Clarke, T., Ayres, P., & Sweller, J. (2005). The impact of sequencing and prior knowledge on learning mathematics through spreadsheet applications. *Educational Technology Research and Development, 53*, 15–24.

Comenius, J. A. (1887). *Orbis pictus.* [*The world in pictures: Nomenclature and pictures of all of the chief things in the world and men's employments therein.*] Syracuse, NY: C. W. Bardeen, Publisher. [Originally published in 1658.]

Craig, S. D., Gholson, B., & Driscoll, D. M. (2002). Animated pedagogical agents in multimedia educational environments: Effects of agent properties, picture features, and redundancy. *Journal of Educational Psychology, 94*, 428–434.

Cuban, L. (1986). *Teachers and machines.* New York: Teachers College Press.

Fletcher, J. D., & Tobias, S. (2005). The multimedia principle. In R. E. Mayer (Ed.), *The Cambridge handbook of multimedia learning* (pp. 117–134). New York: Cambridge University Press.

Gerjets, P., Scheiter, K., & Catrambone, R. (2006). Can learning from molar and modular worked examples be enhanced by providing instructional explanations and prompting self-explanations? *Learning and Instruction, 16*, 104–121.

Ginns, P. (2005). Meta-analysis of the modality effect. *Learning and Instruction, 15*, 313–332.

Ginns, P. (2006). Integrating information: A meta-analysis of spatial contiguity and temporal contiguity effects. *Learning and Instruction, 16*, 511–525.

Harp, S. F., & Mayer, R. E. (1997). The role of interest in learning from scientific text and illustrations: On the distinction between emotional interest and cognitive interest. *Journal of Educational Psychology, 89*, 92–102.

Harp, S. F., & Mayer, R. E. (1998). How seductive details do their damage: A theory of cognitive interest in science learning. *Journal of Educational Psychology, 90*, 414–434.

Harskamp, E., Mayer, R. E., Suhre, C., & Jansma, J. (2007). Does the modality principle for multimedia learning apply to science classrooms? *Learning and Instruction, 18*, 465–477.

Hattie, J. (2009). *Visible learning.* London: Routledge.

Jamet, E., & Le Bohec, O. (2007). The effect of redundant text in multimedia instruction. *Contemporary Educational Psychology, 32*, 588–598.

Jeung, H., Chandler, P., & Sweller, J. (1997). The role of visual indicators in dual sensory mode instruction. *Educational Psychology, 17*, 329–433.

Kalyuga, S. (2005). Prior knowledge principle in multimedia learning. In R. E. Mayer (Ed.), *The Cambridge handbook of multimedia learning* (pp. 325–338). New York: Cambridge University Press.

Kalyuga, S., Chandler, P., & Sweller, J. (1998). Levels of expertise and instructional design. *Human Factors, 40*, 1–17.

Kalyuga, S., Chandler, P., & Sweller, J. (1999). Managing split-attention and redundancy in multimedia instruction. *Applied Cognitive Psychology, 13*, 351–371.

Kalyuga, S., Chandler, P., & Sweller, J. (2000). Incorporating learner experience into the design of multimedia instruction. *Journal of Educational Psychology, 92*, 126–136.

Kester, L., Kirschner, P. A., & van Merrienboer, J. G. G. (2004). Timing of information presentation in learning statistics. *Instructional Science, 32*, 233–252.

Kester, L., Kirschner, P. A., & van Merrienboer, J. J. G. (2005). The management of cognitive load during complex cognitive skill acquisition by means of computer-simulated problem solving. *British Journal of Educational Psychology, 75*, 71–85.

Kester, L., Kirschner, P. A., van Merrienboer, J. J. G (2006). Just-in-time information presentation: Improving learning a troubleshooting skill. *Contemporary Educational Psychology, 31*, 167–185.

Leahy, W., Chandler, P., & Sweller, J. (2003). When auditory presentations should and should not be a component of multimedia instruction. *Applied Cognitive Psychology, 17*, 401–418.

Lee, H., Plass, J. L., & Homer, B. D. (2006). Optimizing cognitive load for learning from computer-based science simulations. *Journal of Educational Psychology, 98*, 902–913.

Low, R., & Sweller, J. (2005). The modality principle in multimedia learning. In R. E. Mayer (Ed.), *The Cambridge handbook of multimedia learning* (pp. 147–158). New York: Cambridge University Press.

Massa, L. J., & Mayer, R. E. (2006). Testing the ATI hypothesis: Should multimedia instruction accommodate verbalizer-visualizer cognitive style? *Learning and Individual Differences, 16*, 321–336.

Mautone, P. D., & Mayer, R. E. (2001). Signaling as a cognitive guide in multimedia learning. *Journal of Educational Psychology, 93*, 377–389.

Mautone, P. D., & Mayer, R. E. (2007). Cognitive aids for guiding graph comprehension. *Journal of Educational Psychology, 99*, 640–652.

Mayer, R. E. (1989). Systematic thinking fostered by illustrations in scientific text. *Journal of Educational Psychology, 81,* 240–246.

Mayer, R. E. (Ed.). (2005). *The Cambridge handbook of multimedia learning.* New York: Cambridge University Press.

Mayer, R. E. (2009). *Multimedia learning* (2nd ed.). New York: Cambridge University Press.

Mayer, R. E. (2011). *Applying the science of learning.* Upper Saddle River, NJ: Pearson Merrill Prentice Hall.

Mayer, R. E., & Anderson, R. B. (1991). Animations need narrations: An experimental test of a dual-coding hypothesis. *Journal of Educational Psychology, 83,* 484–490.

Mayer, R. E., & Anderson, R. B. (1992). The instructive animation: Helping students build connections between words and pictures in multimedia learning. *Journal of Educational Psychology, 84,* 444–452.

Mayer, R. E., Bove, W., Bryman, A., Mars, R., & Tapangco, L. (1996). When less is more: Meaningful learning from visual and verbal summaries of science textbook lessons. *Journal of Educational Psychology, 88,* 64–73.

Mayer, R. E., & Chandler, P. (2001). When learning is just a click away: Does simple user interaction foster deeper understanding of multimedia messages? *Journal of Educational Psychology, 93,* 390–397.

Mayer, R. E., Dow, G., & Mayer, R. E. (2003). Multimedia learning in an interactive self-explaining environment: What works in the design of agent-based microworlds? *Journal of Educational Psychology, 95,* 806–813.

Mayer, R. E., Fennell, S., Farmer, L., & Campbell, J. (2004). A personalization effect in multimedia learning: Students learn better when words are in conversational style rather than formal style. *Journal of Educational Psychology, 96,* 389–395.

Mayer, R. E., & Gallini, J. K. (1990). When is an illustration worth ten thousand words? *Journal of Educational Psychology, 82,* 715–726.

Mayer, R. E., Heiser, H., & Lonn, S. (2001). Cognitive constraints on multimedia learning: When presenting more material results in less understanding. *Journal of Educational Psychology, 93,* 187–198.

Mayer, R. E., & Jackson, J. (2005). The case for conciseness in scientific explanations: Quantitative details can hurt qualitative understanding. *Journal of Experimental Psychology: Applied, 11,* 13–18.

Mayer, R. E., & Johnson, C. I. (2008). Revising the redundancy principle in multimedia learning. *Journal of Educational Psychology, 100,* 380–386.

Mayer, R. E., Mathias, A., & Wetzell, K. (2002). Fostering understanding of multimedia messages through pretraining: Evidence for a two-stage theory of mental model construction. *Journal of Experimental Psychology: Applied, 8,* 147–154.

Mayer, R. E., Mautone, P., & Prothero, W. (2002). Pictorial aids for learning by doing in a multimedia geology simulation game. *Journal of Educational Psychology, 94,* 171–185.

Mayer, R. E., & Moreno, R. E. (1998). A split-attention effect in multimedia learning: Evidence for dual processing systems in working memory. *Journal of Educational Psychology, 90,* 312–320.

Mayer, R. E., & Moreno, R. E. (2003). Nine ways to reduce cognitive load in multimedia learning. *Educational Psychologist, 38,* 43–52.

Mayer, R. E., Moreno, R., Boire, M., & Vagge, S. (1999). Maximizing constructivist learning from multimedia communications by minimizing cognitive load. *Journal of Educational Psychology, 91,* 638–643.

Mayer, R. E., & Sims, V. K. (1994). For whom is a picture worth a thousand words? Extensions of a dual-coding theory of multimedia learning? *Journal of Educational Psychology, 86,* 389–401.

Mayer, R. E., Sobko, K., & Mautone, P. D. (2003). Social cues in multimedia learning: Role of speaker's voice. *Journal of Educational Psychology, 95,* 419–425.

Mayer, R. E., Steinhoff, K., Bower, G., & Mars, R. (1995). A generative theory of textbook design: Using annotated illustrations to foster meaningful learning of science text. *Educational Technology Research and Development, 43,* 31–43.

Michas, I. C., & Berry, D. (2000). Learning a procedural task: Effectiveness of multimedia presentations. *Applied Cognitive Psychology, 14,* 555–575.

Moreno, R., & Mayer, R. E. (1999). Cognitive principles of multimedia learning: The role of modality and contiguity. *Journal of Educational Psychology, 91,* 358–368.

Moreno, R., & Mayer, R. E. (2000a). A coherence effect in multimedia learning: The case for minimizing irrelevant sounds in the design of multimedia messages. *Journal of Educational Psychology, 92,* 117–125.

Moreno, R., & Mayer, R. E. (2000b). Engaging students in active learning: The case for personalized multimedia messages. *Journal of Educational Psychology, 92,* 724–733.

Moreno, R., & Mayer, R. E. (2002a). Verbal redundancy in multimedia learning: When reading helps listening. *Journal of Educational Psychology, 94,* 156–163.

Moreno, R., & Mayer, R. E. (2002b). Learning science in virtual reality multimedia environments: Role of methods and media. *Journal of Educational Psychology, 94,* 598–610.

Moreno, R., & Mayer, R. E. (2004). Personalized messages that promote science learning in virtual environments. *Journal of Educational Psychology, 96,* 165–173.

Moreno, R., Mayer, R. E., Spires, H. A., & Lester, J. C. (2001). The case for social agency in computer-based teaching: Do students learn more deeply when they interact with animated pedagogical agents? *Cognition and Instruction, 19*, 177–213.

Moreno, R., & Ortegano-Layne, L. (2008). Using cases as thinking tools in teacher education: The role of presentation format. *Educational Technology Research and Development, 56*, 449–465.

Moreno, R., & Valdez, A. (2005). Cognitive load and learning effects of having students organize pictures and words in multimedia environments: The role of student interactivity and feedback. *Educational Technology Research and Development, 53*, 35–45.

Moreno, R., & Valdez, A. (2007). Immediate and delayed effects of using a classroom case exemplar in teacher education: The role of presentation format. *Journal of Educational Psychology, 99*, 194–206.

Mousavi, S. Y., Low, R., & Sweller, J. (1995). Reducing cognitive load by mixing auditory and visual presentation modes. *Journal of Educational Psychology, 87*, 319–334.

O'Neil, H. F., Mayer, R. E., Herl, H. E., Niemi, C., Olin, K., & Thurman, R. A. (2000). Instructional strategies for virtual aviation training environments. In H. F. O'Neil, & D. H. Andrews (Eds.), *Aircrew training and assessment* (pp. 105–130). Mahwah, NJ: Erlbaum.

Paivio, A. (1986). *Mental representations: A dual-coding approach.* Oxford: Oxford University Press.

Paivio, A. (2001). *Mind and its evolution: A dual-coding approach.* Mahwah, NJ: Erlbaum.

Pashler, H., McDaniel, M., Rohrer, D., & Bjork, R. (2008). Learning styles: Concepts and evidence. *Psychological Science in the Public Interest, 9*, 105–119.

Pollock, E., Chandler, P., & Sweller, J. (2002). Assimilating complex information. *Learning and Instruction, 12*, 61–86.

Saettler, P. (2004). *The evolution of American educational technology.* Greenwich, CT: Information Age Publishing.

Stokes, D. E. (1997). *Pasteur's quadrant: Basic science and technological innovation.* Washington, DC: Brookings Institution Press.

Stull, A., & Mayer, R. E. (2007). Learning by doing versus learning by viewing: Three experimental comparisons of learner-generated versus author-provided graphic organizers. *Journal of Educational Psychology, 99*, 808–820.

Sweller, J. (1999). *Instructional design in technical areas.* Camberwell, Australia: ACER Press.

Sweller, J. (2005). Implications of cognitive load theory for multimedia learning. In R. E. Mayer (Ed.), *Cambridge handbook of multimedia learning* (pp. 19–30). New York: Cambridge University Press.

Sweller, J., Chandler, P., Tierney, P., & Cooper, M. (1990). Cognitive load and selective attention as factors in the structuring of technical material. *Journal of Experimental Psychology: General, 119*, 176–192.

Tabbers, H. K., Martens, R. L., & van Merrienboer, J. J. G. (2004). Multimedia instruction and cognitive load theory: Effects of modality and cueing. *British Journal of Educational Psychology, 74*, 71–81.

Tindall-Ford, S., Chandler, P., & Sweller, J. (1997). When two sensory modalities are better than one. *Journal of Experimental Psychology: Applied, 3*, 257–287.

Wang, N., Johnson, W. L., Mayer, R. E., Rizzo, P., Shaw, E., & Collins, H. (2008). The politeness effect: Pedagogical agents and learning outcomes. *International Journal of Human Computer Studies, 66*, 96–112.

Wittrock, M. C. (1989). Generative processes of comprehension. *Educational Psychologist, 24*, 345–376.

22

INSTRUCTION BASED ON COMPUTER SIMULATIONS
Ton de Jong

INTRODUCTION

In the scientific debate on what is the best approach to teaching and learning, a recurring question concerns who should lead the learning process, the teacher or the learner (see e.g., Tobias & Duffy, 2009)? Positions taken vary from a preference for direct, expository, teacher-led instruction (Kirschner, Sweller, & Clark, 2006) to fully open student-centered approaches that can be called pure discovery methods (e.g., Papert, 1980), with intermediate positions represented by more or less guided discovery methods (e.g., Mayer, 2004). This discussion also is a recurring theme in this chapter.

In discussing the issue of the role of guidance in instruction, the specific technology of computer simulations occupies a central place. Computer simulations, through their interactive character, offer a special opportunity for student-centered learning, while at the same time offering options for program or teacher led support and guidance of the learning process. Thus, a major goal of this chapter is to examine whether people learn better when simulations include substantial amounts of scaffolding that guides the learner (i.e., guided discovery method) or when simulations allow people to learn freely without much guidance (i.e., pure discovery method). Another goal of this chapter is to examine whether people learn better with computer simulations than with conventional instructional media.

Computer simulations are computer programs that have as their core a computational model of a system or a process. The system or process that is modeled normally has a natural world origin and the model that is created is usually a simplification (i.e., reduction and abstraction) of the real-world phenomenon (de Jong & van Joolingen, 2007). Simplification is used because: (1) it is hard if not impossible to fully model the real world; (2) a simplification often suffices for the goal for which the model is built and greater realism also has costs in time and effort; and (3) a simplification creates less cognitive load for the learner. In our case, the goal of building a model is to offer students an opportunity to learn with and from the model. When learning with simulations, learners interact with the model through an interface that enables them to change values of input variables and observe the effects of these changes on output variables (see de Jong, 2006a).

Simulation programs can be used as the basis for training of knowledge or skills (or a combination of both). In the case of learning practical skills, transfer to real situations is crucial, so high fidelity is often preferred. High fidelity means that the model in the simulation must be realistic and also that the interface (for both input and output) needs to be close to the real situation (Hays & Singer, 1989). In some cases, high fidelity can be accomplished by using a physical interface rather than a computer screen. Parker and Myrick (2009), for example, describe high-fidelity human patient simulators that are rapidly becoming part of nursing education. These simulators are embedded in a mannequin that is able to show physiological responses; modern devices can even speak, breathe, and perspire. In this way, a realistic training environment is created, which is required because nurses need to recognize symptoms in real persons.

Realism need not be high at the start of the training; its level may be increased during training in order to avoid overloading students in the beginning (Alessi, 2000). In the case of acquiring more theoretical knowledge (be it more conceptual or procedural), the fidelity requirements for the interface are not that high, although real-world interfaces are sometimes recommended for motivational reasons (de Hoog, de Jong, & de Vries, 1991). The level of realism of representations could also affect the knowledge that is acquired. Jaakkola, Nurmi, and Veermans (2009) compared two simulation environments on the physics topic of electricity. In one condition only concrete representations were used (bulbs), while in the other there was a transition from concrete to more abstract representations (resistors). The concrete situation was easier for students to learn, but students who could cope with the complexity of the transition condition acquired knowledge that was better transferable to other domains.

Simulations are used for learning in many domains including psychology (Hulshof, Eysink, & de Jong, 2006), mathematics (Tatar et al., 2008), physics (Wieman, Perkins, & Adams, 2008), chemistry (Winberg & Hedman, 2008), biology (Huppert, Lomask, & Lazarowitz, 2002), and medicine (Wayne et al., 2005). The models involved also vary widely, both in complexity and in content. Law and Kelton (2000) distinguish models according to three dimensions: (1) whether time is one of the variables in the model (i.e., static vs. dynamic models); (2) whether change plays a role in the model (i.e., deterministic vs. stochastic models); and (3) whether the variables in the model can take all values on a scale or vary in only in discrete steps (i.e., continuous vs. discrete models). Although differences in complexity and content may influence the learning process, there are sufficient commonalities across simulations to discuss their affordances for learning in a general way.

In the remainder of this chapter, I provide an historical overview of educational computer simulations, a theoretical framework for learning from computer simulations, and summaries of the current state of research on the effects of incorporating scaffolds that guide learning with computer simulations and on the effects of teaching with computer simulations rather than conventional media. The chapter closes with a discussion of practical and theoretical implications, and an examination of future directions.

HISTORICAL OVERVIEW

Simulations have long been used in training to avoid risks for the operators (e.g., aviation), subjects (e.g., medicine) or both operators and subjects (e.g., military, business).

One of the earliest reports on the use of a simulator for learning dates back to the *Ruggles orientator* (see Jones, 1927)—a device to test pilots on very basic skills. These devices gradually became more sophisticated, with today's flight simulators offering a very high level of functional and physical fidelity. Besides these full-fledged simulators, computer-based simulators have been very popular, beginning from the landmark introduction of Microsoft Flight Simulator in 1979/1980. These relatively inexpensive computer-based simulators have also shown their value for training pilots (see, for an overview, Koonce & Bramble, 1998).

In medicine, the use of simulators and simulations has a century-long history, but simulators started to enter medical education at a reasonable level only during the second half of the 20th century have. Nowadays a rapid increase in the use of simulators in medical education is underway, ranging from high fidelity simulators to desktop computer-based simulations (Bradley, 2006).

Possibly the longest history of simulation use can be found in the military. Wargames were often used, with the earliest known version, the German *Kriegspiel*, dating back to the early 19th century. Even before that, the military used sand tables with iconic representations. Nowadays, digital games are dominant and they exist in many variations for professional and private usage (for an overview, see Smith, 2010).

Business games and simulations have a shorter history that dates back to the 1950s. There are many of these games in existence, now using technologies that enable on-line access. However, there is not much research that examines the outcomes of this type of learning, and the research that does exist is not very definitive on the benefits of business games for the acquisition of knowledge (Anderson & Lawton, 2009; Leemkuil & de Jong, in press). The lack of supporting evidence may have to do with the fact that games have characteristics that are not favorable for learning; for example, learners in a game have less freedom to act than learners in a simulation, due to the goal they must reach (Leemkuil & de Jong, in press).

The traditional application areas for the use of computer simulations for training were focused towards practical skills training (e.g., flying, medical diagnosing, waging war, doing business) and no specific guidance for students was built in. In the late 1970s and early 1980s, new systems were developed, often in the form of intelligent tutoring systems which emphasized training of conceptual knowledge along with skills and included forms of student guidance. These simulations also began to involve domains other than the traditional ones sketched above.

Many of these systems had a focus on diagnosis and troubleshooting. SOPHIE, for example, was an environment for teaching electronic troubleshooting skills, but also aimed at acquisition of conceptual knowledge of electronic laws, circuit causality, and the functional organization of particular devices (Brown, Burton, & de Kleer, 1982). Similarly, QUEST (White & Frederiksen, 1989) focused on electronic circuit troubleshooting, with central attention for knowledge of underlying models from different perspectives. Also SHERLOCK (Lesgold, Lajoie, Bunzo, & Eggan, 1992) aimed at troubleshooting skills for electronic devices and provided trainees with individualized feedback. Another system that combined the learning of operational and conceptual knowledge was STEAMER. This system simulated a complex steam propulsion system for large ships (Hollan, Hutchins, & Weitzman, 1984) and students also had to understand the models underlying this system. Systems such as MACH-III on complex radar devices (Kurland & Tenney, 1988) and IMTS (Towne et al., 1990) also focused on troubleshooting, again with associated conceptual knowledge. A further example of early conceptual simulations for physics education was ARK (Scanlon & Smith, 1988; Smith, 1986). ARK (Alternate Reality Kit) was a set of simulations on different physics topics (e.g., collisions) that provided students with direct manipulation interfaces. In another field, the MYCIN software was an expert system that contained a large rule base for medical diagnosis, which the GUIDON software took up and augmented with teaching knowledge to make this learning software. A student model was created through an overlay approach and students could receive dedicated feedback on their diagnosis process (Clancey, 1986).

Smithtown was one of the first educational computer simulations that targeted an exclusively conceptual domain (i.e., economic laws) and that included a range of support mechanisms for students (Shute & Glaser, 1990). In Smithtown, students could explore simulated markets. They could change such input variables as labor costs and population income and observe the effects on output variables such as prices.

Although scaffolds were already present to some degree in the early computer simulation systems cited here, most specifically Smithtown, recent research has shown that learning with simulations is most effective when the student is sufficiently scaffolded (de Jong & van Joolingen, 1998; Mayer, 2004). Cognitive scaffolds can be integrated with the simulation software or can be provided by the teacher; they can aim at a specific inquiry process (e.g., hypothesis generation) or at the structuring of the entire process. These types of systems are discussed later in this chapter.

THEORETICAL FRAMEWORK

Why would learning with simulations be better than more traditional expository explanation-based or "on-the-job training" approaches? There are several considerations why simulation-based learning would improve performance, all depending on the goal of learning: conceptual knowledge, skills, or a combination.

When simulations are used to help learners acquire conceptual knowledge, the rationale is that they foster deeper cognitive processing during learning, which in turn leads to deeper learning outcomes (in comparison to direct instruction). In particular, computer simulations are intended to encourage learners to activate relevant prior knowledge (e.g., in thinking of hypotheses) and to actively restructure knowledge (e.g., when data are found that are not consistent with a hypothesis). For example, some theoretical frameworks, which can be traced back to Piaget's original ideas (1976), consider learning with simulations as involving an inquiry cycle consisting of processes such as hypothesis generation, experiment design, data interpretation, and reflection (see Friedler, Nachmias, & Linn, 1990; de Jong, 2006a). A related approach describes this scientific inquiry as a specific kind of problem solving with associated moves in a problem space, in this case, hypothesis and experiment space (Klahr & Dunbar, 1988; Klahr & Simon, 2001).

A second approach that highlights advantages of simulations for conceptual learning is the work on multiple representations (e.g., Ainsworth, 2006; Mayer, 2009). The basic idea behind this approach is that if multiple representations (e.g., graphs, tables, animations, etc.) are offered, translations must be made between these representations, leading to deeper and more abstract knowledge. Simulations often offer multiple representations and these are often also dynamically linked (van der Meij & de Jong, 2006). In a series of experiments, Kolloffel and colleagues (Kolloffel, de Jong, & Eysink, 2010; Kolloffel,

Eysink, de Jong, & Wilhelm, 2009) found that different combinations of representations have different effects on learning. Their case involved the learning of combinatorics, in which a combination of formulae and text was the most profitable combination of representations for students.

A third, and somewhat different stance is taken by Lindgren and Schwartz (2009) who emphasize the advantages of simulations from the observation that these environments often offer interactive visualizations. These authors show on the basis of more fundamental work that interactive visual information has the advantages over textual information of being more easily remembered, being suitable for showing variation and differences between cases, conveying structure that is not easily depicted in textual information, and giving a more direct experience via manipulations. The advantages of interactive visualizations are supported by research. Studies that compare simulations in which students can make their own choices with an environment where they cannot show an advantage for the action-based form of learning (Trey & Khan, 2008; Windschitl & Andre, 1998) although sometimes only on a delayed test (Hulshof, Eysink, Loyens, & de Jong, 2005). These advantages, however, do not occur when students are left on their own and do not receive support for the inquiry process (Boucheix & Schneider, 2009). Advantages are also mitigated when the environment is simple and when instructional measures are more dominant than interface characteristics (Swaak, de Jong, & van Joolingen, 2004).

An important principle for training skills (e.g., in aviation, medicine) in simulated instead of real environments is that this allows students to receive a more extended experience with the task to be learned. Compared to the real world, simulations offer the possibility of introducing situations independent of place and time, of presenting critical situations that may not occur frequently in reality, and of creating situations that would be too expensive or dangerous in reality (Alessi & Trollip, 2001). The main principle behind this approach is that an element of practice is necessary in the learning of skills. This practicing of skills requires variation in tasks and confrontation with critical tasks (van Merriënboer, 1997); simulations, not having to rely on the natural and possibly rare occurrence of differing and critical situations, offer the best opportunity to effect this. In addition, computer simulations also offer the possibility of augmenting reality by showing features that cannot be seen in reality (Blackwell, Morgan, & DiGioia, 1998). Further, simulations can help to speed up or slow down tasks so that practice can take place more deliberately and moments of reflection may be built in. Comparisons of simulations to laboratory situations address similar notions (Jaakkola, Nurmi, & Lehtinen, 2010).

Critics assert that learning with simulations is not effective because the required processes are too demanding for students, leading to cognitive overload (Kirschner, et al., 2006). However, this criticism is directed at unsupported pure discovery and does not apply to learning environments that offer students support for their inquiry processes. This learner support is essential for successful inquiry and thus for learning from computer simulations. The next section outlines this issue and discusses the effectiveness of learning with computer simulations.

CURRENT ISSUES: THE EFFECTIVENESS OF SIMULATION-BASED LEARNING

One of the central research questions addressed in this chapter is whether simulation-based instruction fosters an effective form of learning. When considering this question, it is important to realize that it is not the technology per se that causes learning but rather the instructional method (Clark, 1994). The question of effectiveness also depends on what is being measured (e.g., different types of knowledge, inquiry skills, attitudes) as an outcome of the learning process, and may vary with the students' characteristics. A short overview of research is presented in the following sections. The first section presents studies comparing different versions of basically the same simulation learning environment. Here, for example, different types of scaffolds are compared. The second section presents studies in which completely designed simulation environments are compared to alternative didactic approaches (e.g., expository instruction or on-the-job training).

The Effects of Providing Students with Cognitive Scaffolds

Work claiming that direct instruction is superior to inquiry learning generally involves unguided inquiry (e.g., Klahr & Nigam, 2004). What is very clear from the literature is that unguided simulation based learning is not effective (Mayer, 2004). For this reason, contemporary inquiry learning as well as simulation-based learning environments contain all kinds of supports and scaffolds (Hmelo-Silver, Duncan, & Chinn, 2007). Guided simulations lead to better performance than open simulations (de Jong & van Joolingen, 1998) and are also experienced by students as being more effective (Winberg & Hedman, 2008). Several overviews have indicated which types of support are available and how they make learning from simulations effective (Chang, Chen, Lin, & Sung, 2008; de Jong, 2005, 2006a, 2006b, 2010; Fund, 2007; Quintana et al., 2004). In this section, the main conclusions from these overview studies will be summarized, complemented by more recent work. The summary of the different types of support is organized following the main inquiry processes: orientation, hypothesis design, experimentation, and drawing conclusions, along with regulative (planning and monitoring) and reflection processes.

Orientation

When working with computer simulations, students may need to be supported in identifying the main variables in the domain. Belvedere (Toth, Suthers, & Lesgold, 2002), for example, is an inquiry environment in which students work with realistic problems, collect data, set hypotheses, etc. An *inquiry diagram* is available to explore the domain under study. This inquiry diagram is a kind of concept mapping tool dedicated to scientific inquiry. It also functions to relate statements and evidence. Toth et al. (2002) report positive effects on reasoning scores for students using the Belvedere inquiry diagram as compared to students who used simple prose to express their view of the domain. Reid, Zhang, and Chen (2003) studied students who learned with a simulation on buoyancy and provided them with "interpretative support," which consisted of multiple choice questions to activate prior knowledge and to make students think about the variables that played a role in the simulation, together with access to a database of background knowledge. This support had a positive effect on students' intuitive understanding (students' ability to predict effects of changes), which effect was confirmed in a follow-up study (Zhang, Chen, Sun, & Reid, 2004). Holzinger, Kickmeier-Rust, Wassertheurer, and Hessinger (2009) compared three versions of a course on blood flow for medical students—a text version, a computer simulation and a computer simulation preceded by a short video explaining the main parameters. Students who received the video plus simulation treatment outperformed the simulation only and text groups on a short multiple-choice test of conceptual knowledge. The text and the simulation-only groups did not differ in performance.

The use of multiple representations presents a specific case with regard to helping students orient themselves and find the right variables. First of all, students need to be supported in making the right interpretations of visualizations (Ploetzner, Lippitsch, Galmbacher, Heuer, & Scherrer, 2009; Tsui & Treagust, 2003), but they also need support in making the correct relations between representations. Wu, Krajcik, and Soloway (2001), for example, worked with a combined modeling and simulation environment for chemistry, more specifically molecular models. In their learning environment they supported students in making references between the different representations by providing them with referential links. A qualitative analysis of the students' results showed that this kind of support helped students to make the correct relation between representations, which also helped them to make adequate translations. Bodemer, Ploetzner, Feuerlein, and Spada (2004), working with a simulation environment in statistics, showed that supporting students in actively relating representations was beneficial for learning. Studying student learning in a multiple representational simulation environment on the physics topic of moment, van der Meij and de Jong (2006) found that helping students to relate representations by dynamic linking (concurrent changes over time), color coding that related similar variables in different representations, and integration of representations led to greater student gains in domain knowledge compared to students for whom relating representations was not supported.

Hypothesis Design

The creation of hypotheses by students can be supported in different ways. Thinkertools/ Inquiry Island environments, for example, present learners with free text blocks to brainstorm about and to present their hypotheses (White et al., 2002). By using sliders, learners can indicate the degree to which they think their hypothesis is "believable," "related to the question they had," and "testable." Students can also indicate if they have alternative hypotheses. A more specific scaffold for hypothesis generation is the *hypothesis scratchpad* (Shute & Glaser, 1990; van Joolingen & de Jong, 1991). In recent versions of this scratchpad (van Joolingen & de Jong, 2003), learners can compose hypotheses by filling in if–then statements and by selecting variables and relations to fill in the slots. For each hypothesis, they can indicate whether it was tested or not, and whether the data confirmed the hypothesis. However, the authors found that working with such a scratchpad is not very easy for students. Following work by Njoo and de Jong (1993), Gijlers and de Jong (2009) provided students with complete, pre-defined, hypotheses. They created three experimental groups of collaborating dyads of learners. One group (control) did not receive specific scaffolds, one group had a shared hypothesis scratchpad combined with a chat, and the final group received a large set of propositions about the domain. As an overall result, students in the proposition group outperformed students in the other two groups on a measure of intuitive knowledge. A broad conclusion might be that for beginning students, support in the form of complete hypotheses is more beneficial than having them compose hypotheses themselves.

Experimentation

There is a range of heuristics that can be used to design "good experiments" (Baker & Dunbar, 2000) of which the *control of variables strategy* (CVS, Chen & Klahr, 1999) is the best known (Wilhelm & Beishuizen, 2003). This strategy implies that only one variable at the time is varied in experiments and the others are kept constant, so that effects can be attributed to that variable that was varied. Kuhn and Dean (2005) showed that even a simple prompt to focus on one variable at a time may help to increase students' performance level. Keselman (2003) had students work with a simulation-based learning environment on a complex domain with multivariable causality (i.e., risks of earthquakes). One group of students received extensive practice on manipulating variables and making predictions, whereas a second group also observed a teacher modeling the design of good experiments. Both groups improved compared to a control group that received no support, but the modeling group improved most on knowledge gained and on skill in designing good experiments. Lin and Lehman (1999) worked with students who learned in a biology simulation learning environment. They provided students with prompts for designing experiments with an emphasis on the control of variables strategy (e.g., "How did you decide that you have enough data to make conclusions?," Lin & Lehman, 1999, p. 841). These prompts helped students to understand experimental design principles and resulted in better transfer compared to a group of students who received different types of prompts.

Reid et al. (2003) gave students explanations on good experimental procedures and helped students structure their experiments. Overall, they found no effect of this support on a range of measures including intuitive knowledge (on which only a marginal effect was found), transfer, and knowledge integration (how far students had related their new knowledge to existing knowledge and how far they acquired deep principles). A follow-up study (Zhang et al., 2004) added the nuance of taking learner's reasoning abilities into account. Zhang et al. found that support that aimed at the experimentation behavior of students was most effective for low reasoning ability students, indifferent for high ability students and detrimental for the mid-range ability students. Veermans, van Joolingen, and de Jong (2006) compared two simulation-based learning environments (containing implicit or explicit heuristics for designing experiments) on the physics topic of collision. They found no overall difference between the two conditions on knowledge gained and strategies acquired, but found indications that the explicit condition favored weak students.

Regulation

One way to support students in regulating their inquiry process is by providing them with an overall structure (Njoo & de Jong, 1993). In Sci-Wise (Shimoda, White, & Frederiksen, 2002) and the follow-up Thinkertools/Inquiry Island (White, et al., 2002) the inquiry process was divided into *question, hypothesize, investigate, analyze, model,* and *evaluate.* Learners had differently structured tabsheets for each of these tasks and dedicated advisors they could call upon to receive domain independent advice on how to perform a specific inquiry task. Manlove, Lazonder, and de Jong (2009b) report a series of studies on a *process coordinator,* a tool that structures the inquiry process for students and that helps and prompts student to plan, monitor, and evaluate. Their work shows that these tools stimulate students to plan, but that students are not very much inclined to monitor their work. The studies also indicated a negative relation between use of regulative facilities and students' model scores. The authors make clear that this could be caused by the general character of the tool and that a stronger embedding of the tool in the domain would be necessary. In a similar vein, Chang et al. (2008) found that providing students with step-by-step guidance in a simulation environment on optics was less effective than giving them detailed experimentation hints and hypothesis support. Providing students with sets of assignments or exercises that give them ideas for questions to ask and variables to manipulate and that give structure in the inquiry process is a very powerful form of support. This conclusion is substantiated by many studies with both an experimental character (Swaak & de Jong, 2001) and more practice-oriented work (Adams et al., 2008). A specific issue here is that students are not greatly inclined to use facilities that are offered to them, especially in connection with monitoring (Manlove, Lazonder, & de Jong, 2007).

Reflection

A number of studies have systematically examined the effect of reflection scaffolds, as in the work by Lin and Lehman (1999) cited above. Davis (2000) examined the effects of activity and self-monitoring prompts on project progress and knowledge integration, in the context of the KIE (Knowledge Integration Environment) inquiry environment. Activity prompts encouraged students to reflect on the content of their activities. An activity prompt may, for example, "ask students to justify their decision or write a scientific explanation of a decision" (Davis, 2000, p. 822). Self-monitoring prompts activated students to express their own planning and monitoring by giving them sentence openers to complete. A sample prompt would be "Pieces of evidence or claims in the article we didn't understand very well included . . ." (Davis, 2000, p. 824). Three studies were conducted in the domain of heat and temperature. Two studies compared conditions with different types of reflection prompts, while the third study looked deeper into students' reactions to prompts. Overall, self-monitoring prompts helped more with creating a well-connected conceptual understanding (knowledge integration) than activity prompts, although Davis also concluded that similar prompts led to quite different reactions from different learners. Zhang et al. (2004) performed a study in which they gave learners *reflective support*, i.e., support that "increases learners' self-awareness of the learning processes and prompts their reflective abstraction and integration of their discoveries" (p. 270). The learning environment centered around a simulation on floating and sinking of objects. The treatment consisted of: (1) showing the students their inquiry processes (goals of experiments, predictions, and conclusions); (2) reflection notes that students had to fill in asking them to reflect on the experiment; and (3) a fill-in form after the experiment that asked students to think over the process they had gone through and the discoveries they had made. Students who received this type of evaluation support outperformed students who did not receive this support on a number of performance measures.

Wichmann and Leutner (2009) studied the effects of reflective prompts in the context of a simulation on photosynthesis. These prompts were related to stating hypotheses, interpreting results, and thinking of new research questions. The students who received these prompts outperformed students from two control groups who did not receive these prompts or who only received explanation prompts. These results emerged for both a knowledge test and a scientific reasoning test.

Conclusions on the Use of Scaffolds

The overall conclusion from studies that evaluated scaffolding for simulations is that support helps. Even when different kinds of composite support are compared and sometimes subtle differences between support measures are found, it is clear that supported students outperform unsupported students (Fund, 2007). As a coarse summary, it can be stated that students need support in identifying relevant variables, that hypotheses could best be provided in a "readymade" way, that training on experimentation heuristics (especially CVS) is fruitful but only for students of poor reasoning ability, that providing students with a general structure for the inquiry process can be helpful but that it should be made domain-specific, such as in the form of a set of more concrete assignments, and that students need to be prompted for reflection. However, most of the results are based on single studies, and it remains to be seen what support students need when they have a longer term experience with simulation based inquiry learning. Such a situation might lay the basis for fading the scaffolding at some point so that over time a good balance can be reached between taking the inquiry out of students' hands and preserving the inquiry character of the learning process.

Simulation-Based Learning Compared to Other Instructional Approaches

There are many studies showing that learning with scaffolded computer simulations may help students to overcome misconceptions (e.g., Meir, Perry, Stal, Maruca, & Klopfer, 2005; Monaghan & Clement, 1999). A next step then is to compare these results to learning from direct instruction or other didactic approaches. Such work has been limited, but there is an emerging set of studies that present large scale comparative evaluations of simulation-based learning. In these cases the simulation is often embedded in a larger instructional arrangement and it includes a composite of different scaffolds, which means that no specific data on individual scaffolds are available for these large-scale evaluations,. There is also a set of studies that compares simulation-based learning to learning in the real laboratory.

Simulations vs. Traditional Teaching

One of the first examples of such a large-scale evaluations concerns Smithtown, a supportive simulation environment in the area of economics, which underwent a large-scale evaluation with a total of 530 students. Results showed that after 5 hours of working with Smithtown, students reached a degree of micro-economics understanding that would require approximately 11 hours of traditional teaching (Shute & Glaser, 1990).

White and Frederiksen (1998) describe the ThinkerTools Inquiry Curriculum, a simulation-based learning environment on the physics topic of force and motion. In the ThinkerTools software, students are guided through a number of inquiry stages that include experimenting with the simulation, constructing physics laws, critiquing each other's laws, and reflecting on the inquiry process. ThinkerTools was implemented in 12 classes with approximately 30 students each. Students worked daily with ThinkerTools over a period of a little more than 10 weeks. A comparison of the ThinkerTools students with students in a traditional curriculum showed that the ThinkerTools students performed significantly better on a conceptual test (68% vs. 50% correct).

With regard to large-scale comparisons in the domain of science, Hickey, Kindfield, Horwitz, and Christie (2003) assessed the effects of the introduction of a simulation-based inquiry environment on the biology topic of genetics (GenScope). In GenScope, students can manipulate genetic information at different levels: DNA, chromosomes, cells, organisms, pedigrees, and populations. A large-scale evaluation was conducted involving 31 classes (23 experimental, 8 comparison) taught by 13 teachers, and a few hundred students in total. Overall, the evaluation results showed better performance by the GenScope classes compared to the traditional classes on tests measuring genetic reasoning. A follow-up study with two experimental classes and one comparison class also showed significantly higher gains for the two experimental classes on a reasoning test, with a higher gain for students from the experimental group in which more investigation exercises were offered. Linn, Lee, Tinker, Husic, and Chiu (2006) evaluated modules created in the TELS (Technology-Enhanced Learning in Science) center. These modules are inquiry-based and contain simulations (e.g., on the functioning of airbags). Over a sample of 4,328 students and 6 different TELS modules, an overall effect size of 0.32 was observed in favor of the TELS subjects over students following a traditional course for items measuring how well students' knowledge was integrated.

The domain of mathematics has also been an area for large-scale comparisons. Eysink et al. (2009) compared four technology-based learning environments on the same topic of probability theory. These environments were based on hypermedia learning, observational learning, explanation based learning, and simulation based learning. The study involved a total of 624 participants who all received the same knowledge tests with items on situational, intuitive, procedural, and conceptual knowledge. Overall results show that the explanation-based learning environment led to the highest performance, followed by the simulation-based learning environment and then the observational and hypermedia learning environments. However, explanation-based learning was the least efficient (in terms of achievements related to learning time) of the four approaches, hypermedia learning and observational learning the most efficient, and simulation-based learning held an intermediate position.

Tatar et al. (2008) compared performances of a few hundred students and 25 teachers using a SIMCALC-based curriculum vs. a standard curriculum. The SIMCALC curriculum was primarily based on mathematic simulations. Results showed large advantages for the SIMCALC students on mathematical knowledge; the teachers' knowledge in the SIMCALC classes also improved significantly over that of the teachers in the standard curriculum groups. De Jong, Hendrikse, and van der Meij (2010) compared a simulation-based mathematics course to traditional instruction. Over 12 weeks of lessons, students followed either their traditional regular course or an experimental course in which simulation-based exercises were used in conjunction with the book. The data from a total of 418 students from 20 classes could be analyzed. Results indicate that students from both groups score similarly well overall on a post-test, but students from the traditional lectures score especially high on procedural knowledge, while the simulation-based students tend to get better scores on conceptual items. In the related area of statistics (correlations) Liu, Lin, and Kinshuk (2010) found that students using simulation-based training clearly outperformed students who followed a lecture-based approach in repairing misconceptions and on tests measuring understanding.

Simulations Compared to Laboratories

There is now a growing number of studies comparing learning from simulations to learning in real laboratories. These studies can be divided into two groups. The first group compares a simulation with a real laboratory. Here, advantages for the simulation are found in effectiveness and/or efficiency. The second group compares real laboratories and some combination of simulations and laboratories. Overall, students who receive a combination outperform the pure laboratory students. These results all refer to measures of conceptual knowledge.

Chang, Chen, Lin, and Sung (2008) compared learning of the physics topic of optics with three simulation-based environments (that included support in the form of experimentation prompts and hypothesis support) with learning in a laboratory, and concluded that students in all three simulation environments scored better on a test of conceptual knowledge than the laboratory students. Huppert et al. (2002) compared a group of students who followed a combination of traditional lecture and laboratory-based instruction on microbiology with a group who learned with a computer simulation integrated in the laboratory. They found better scores on a conceptual test for the simulation group and some advantages for the simulation group on acquiring science process skills. Bell and Trundle (2008) compared the conceptual knowledge of moon phases for students who gathered data by observing the moon itself and students who worked with a simulation and found large advantages for the simulation group.

A number of other studies found no differences in outcomes between simulated environments and real laboratories, but in these cases simulation-based training was more efficient. Klahr, Triona, and Williams (2007) compared students' performance in a simulated and a real environment in which students had to design a car. They found no difference between the two conditions in resulting knowledge about factors contributing to the car's performance. Triona and Klahr (2003) compared students' mastery of the control of variables strategy in physics domains after learning with a simulation or with physical material and found no differences.

In a somewhat different but comparable setting, Winn et al. (2006) compared the knowledge gained by students who gathered data on oceanographic knowledge (e.g., tides) on a trip on a real boat with students learning from a simulation. Overall both groups scored equally well, with some advantages for the simulation group on two subtests measuring conceptual and structural knowledge. Zacharia and Constantinou (2008) compared two groups of students working in either a physical or a virtual laboratory on heat and temperature; both groups learned equally well. Zacharia and Olympiou (in press) compared a condition where the instruction centered around lectures and textbooks with four experimental conditions in which over 200 students learned about the physics topic of heat and temperature using either a physical laboratory, a simulation, or combinations of a physical laboratory and simulation. All courses were inquiry-based, followed the same instructional principles and lasted 15 weeks. No differences between the four experimental conditions were found on a test measuring conceptual knowledge, but a clear difference in favor of these conditions over the more traditional approach was evident.

A second group of studies found advantages for the combination of simulated and real environments. Akpan and Andre (2000) compared learning the skill of dissecting a frog, and found that students who worked with a simulation alone or with a simulation preceding actual dissection outperformed students performing the hands-on dissection alone or preceding a simulation on a test measuring knowledge of frog anatomy. Zacharia and Anderson (2003) compared learning with a simulation before the real laboratory and with the real laboratory only (and additional textbook material). The domains included were the physics topics of mechanics, optics, and thermal physics. Results showed that adding a simulation to the laboratory helped to increase scores on a conceptual test which required making predictions and giving explanations.

Zacharia (2007) compared two groups of learners where one group learned about electrical circuits in a virtual environment and the other started in a real environment and then moved to a virtual environment. The second group scored better than the first on a conceptual test; this difference could be attributed to the specific parts of the curriculum for which one group learned in the virtual environment and the other in the laboratory environment. Similar results were found by Zacharia, Olympiou, and Papaevripidou (2008). Jaakkola and Nurmi (2008), studying the learning of electrical circuits, found that a succession of a simulated and a real environment led to better performance than either a simulated or a laboratory environment alone. The advantage of combining simulated and real environments was confirmed in another study where video data were analyzed to try to explain why this was the case (Jaakkola et al., 2010). From the video data the authors concluded that students focus on different issues in the simulated and real laboratories and this helps them to create a complete view. In a follow-up study (Jaakkola, Nurmi, & Veermans, in press) the advantages of the combination of real and virtual laboratories against a simulation alone were confirmed.

Conclusions on the Effectiveness of Simulation-Based Learning

In summary, and as a very general conclusion, large-scale evaluations of carefully designed simulation-based learning environments show advantages of simulations over traditional forms of expository learning and over laboratory classes. These results may become slightly more nuanced when we look at the different types of learning outcomes. Most studies focused on conceptual (intuitive) knowledge. For example, Reid et al. (2003) found the largest differences between conditions on a test of intuitive knowledge. Day and Goldstone (2009), studying the transfer abilities of students learning with a simulation on oscillatory movement, concluded that any transfer that occurred was based on implicit knowledge. Making this knowledge more explicit by asking learners to seek for rules even reduced the level of transfer. This work shows that simulation-based learning may be very well suited for gaining intuitive knowledge.

There are, however, other relevant forms of domain knowledge that may be stimulated by learning with simulations such as inquiry skills, nature of science, and attitudes towards science. These areas, although having already received attention in work cited above, need more research, because there are indications that learning with simulations may have impact on such aspects as *systems thinking* (Evagorou, Korfiatis, Nicolaou, & Constantinou, 2009).

A second shortcoming of this body of work is that individual differences are not often taken into account. For example, gender is scarcely considered, although there is work suggesting that simulations are more favorable for boys than for girls (e.g., de Jong, et al., 2010; Holzinger, et al., 2009). Other characteristics such as prior knowledge or spatial ability also seem to influence learning with simulations or the effects of scaffolds. Based on a qualitative analysis of students working with a computer simulation on electrochemistry, for example, Liu, Andre, and Greenbowe (2008) found that students with higher prior knowledge provided more verbal explanations during their work than students with lower prior knowledge.

Liu et al. (2008) speculate that a highly structured environment is more suited for lower prior knowledge students, whereas those with higher prior knowledge profit more from an open environment. There are indications that prior knowledge is especially important when the simulations are highly interactive (i.e., they have many variables to manipulate; (Park, Lee, & Kim, 2009)). An example of the influence of spatial ability is seen in work by Urhahne, Nick, and Schanze (2009), who found that spatial ability had a strong influence on the level of conceptual knowledge that students gained from two- and three-dimensional simulations in chemistry. Finally, students also need sufficient regulative skills to be able to work in simulation-based learning environments (Hsu & Thomas, 2002).

Practical Implications

Overall, results encourage the use of computer simulations in the classroom. At this time, however, we do not see extensive use of simulations in daily school practice. Upscaling and implementing simulations in actual teaching practices are obviously still a challenge. There are several reasons for this, which have mainly to do with technical and didactic issues. First, schools are often not prepared for the technical challenges of introducing software into their curriculum. In addition, software is not always stable enough and well enough tested to survive in the classroom climate. Software developed in a safe laboratory environment needs a few more rounds of testing and debugging before it can be used safely in actual classrooms.

Further, most available software that comes from research projects has no maintenance guarantee, which means that schools are not sure that what runs today will run next year as well. Second, for the didactic issues, most simulations, including the ones described in this chapter, are not developed in alignment with the method and curriculum used in the schools. Simulations as available on the web or off the shelf typically do not have the instructional scaffolding that was seen in this chapter to be required to ensure effectiveness of the simulation software. In addition, working with simulations often takes more time (compared to direct instruction), and teachers do not have that additional time. Teachers also need also to be trained, not only on technical skills but also on didactic techniques such as inquiry learning. This often does not happen. There is a clear need for commercial publishers and teacher training departments to take up these challenges.

CONCLUSION AND FUTURE DIRECTIONS

This chapter gave an overview of advantages and disadvantages of simulation-based learning. The overall conclusion is that simulation-based inquiry learning can be effective if the learners have adequate knowledge and skills to work in such an open and demanding environment and if they are provided with the appropriate scaffolds and tools. In those cases where adequate support is given, simulation-based learning may lead to better results than direct instruction or laboratory based exercises. This conclusion fits within the general conclusion from a meta-analysis of 138 studies that inquiry learning leads to better learning results than direct instruction (Minner, Levy, & Century, 2010).

The discussion on the relative effectiveness of direct instruction vs. simulation-based learning (or inquiry learning in general) will remain a lively one (see e.g., Kirschner et al., 2006; Klahr & Nigam, 2004; Kuhn, 2007; Kuhn & Dean, 2005). This discussion, however, will have no final "winner." There are surely domains and/or learners for which a more direct approach is favorable (Kirschner et al., 2006) and even within domains and learners a variation in instructional methods covering both inquiry approaches and direct instruction might be necessary. The better question is, for what goals and for what learners in what circumstances is what instructional approach the best approach (Schwartz & Bransford, 1998)? The central issue here is what we want students to learn (Kuhn, 2007). In that respect it is noteworthy that the vast majority of the work has concentrated on the effects of simulation-based learning on conceptual (or intuitive) knowledge. There are some examples of work that takes other knowledge aspects (e.g., inquiry skills) into account, but more attention to other types of knowledge than just conceptual knowledge is one of the necessary future directions for the field of learning with computer simulations.

The relative effectiveness of instructional approaches may also depend on the time frame taken into account. Dean and Kuhn (2007), for example, found that when introducing a more extended time frame (10 weeks) and several moments of delayed testing, direct instruction loses its initial advantages and inquiry learning takes over results, which contradicts the results presented by Klahr and Nigam (2004). Students normally lack extensive experience with inquiry learning and some inquiry skills need longer exposure to be developed (Kuhn, Black, Keselman, & Kaplan, 2000). There are indications from more prolonged work (e.g., Fund, 2007, that lasted over six months) that the effects of scaffolds increase over time. Related work on inquiry learning that is not simulation-based (Sadeh & Zion, 2009) shows that effects may only appear after an extended experience with this form of learning. Studies that use a single shot evaluation may therefore not do justice to inquiry environments; more work that looks at students over a longer period of time is necessary.

A promising road for research and development is collaborative learning with simulations. Studies have shown the potential advantages of doing inquiry with simulations in a collaborative way (Gijlers & de Jong, 2009; Kolloffel, Eysink, & de Jong, submitted; Manlove, Lazonder, & de Jong, 2009a) and more research is needed on identifying conditions that optimize confrontations of opinions between students, on how to design shared representations and on tools and scaffolds specifically geared towards collaborative inquiry with simulations.

An interesting technological innovation is the addition of sensory augmentations to a simulation. Minogue and Jones (2009) studied the effects of adding such a haptic device to a simulation in the domain of cell biology which simulated transport through a cell membrane. This haptic device enabled students to *feel* the forces that accompanied transport of substances through the cell membrane. Results showed that learners using the haptic version of the simulation reached higher levels of understanding compared to students who had no access to the haptic device. Tolentino et al. (2009) and Birchfield and Megowan-Romanowicz (2009) describe a similar approach in SMALLlab, a simulation environment in which students engage in haptic and auditory experiences through sensory peripherals.

As discussed in this chapter, scaffolds generally are static, in the sense that they do not adapt to developing characteristics of the students. Ideally, scaffolds would only be launched as they are needed by students and scaffolds would adapt (e.g., fade) to the evolving knowledge and skills of learners. An adequate on-line analysis of student knowledge and characteristics is necessary to create such adaptive systems. New techniques, sometimes based on educational data-mining, that enable this are now being developed (Bravo, van Joolingen, & de Jong, 2006, 2009).

A final development that needs further research is the embedding of simulations in more extensive environments in which students are invited to create things. Objects that can be constructed are, for example, computer models (Hestenes, 1987; Pata & Sarapuu, 2006), physical objects and artefacts (Crismond, 2001), drawings (Hmelo, Holton, & Kolodner, 2000), and concept maps (Novak, 1990). Simulations can then be used to inform the creation of these objects and the object itself can be tested against simulation data (de Jong & van Joolingen, 2007).

Simulations play a specific role in education because they allow student actions (i.e., fast interactions with complicated models) that often are hard or impossible to be realized in another way. This chapter showed that scaffolded simulations may form the basis of effective forms of teaching. New developments including adaptive support and the combination with other affordances such as modelling techniques may further enhance the significance of simulations for learning.

REFERENCES

Adams, W. K., Reid, S., LeMaster, R., McKagan, S. B., Perkins, K. K., Dubson, M., et al. (2008). A study of educational simulations, part I: Engagement and learning. *Journal of Interactive Learning Research, 19*, 397–419.

Ainsworth, S. (2006). Deft: A conceptual framework for considering learning with multiple representations. *Learning and Instruction, 16*, 183–198.

Akpan, J. P., & Andre, T. (2000). Using a computer simulation before dissection to help students learn anatomy. *Journal of Computers in Mathematics and Science Teaching, 19*, 297–313.

Alessi, S. M. (2000). Simulation design for training and assessment. In J. H.F. O'Neil, & D. H. Andrews (Eds.), *Aircrew training and assessment* (pp. 197–222). Mahwah, NJ: Lawrence Erlbaum Associates.

Alessi, S. M., & Trollip, S. R. (2001). *Multimedia for learning; methods and development* (3rd ed.). Boston: Allyn and Bacon.

Anderson, P. H., & Lawton, L. (2009). Business simulations and cognitive learning: Developments, desires, and future directions. *Simulation Gaming, 40*, 193–216.

Baker, L. M., & Dunbar, K. (2000). Experimental design heuristics for scientific discovery: The use of "baseline" and "known standard" controls. *International Journal of Human-Computer Studies, 53*, 335–349.

Bell, R. L., & Trundle, K. C. (2008). The use of a computer simulation to promote scientific conceptions of moon phases. *Journal of Research in Science Teaching, 45*, 346–372.

Birchfield, D., & Megowan-Romanowicz, C. (2009). Earth science learning in SMALLlab: A design experiment for mixed reality. *International Journal of Computer-Supported Collaborative Learning, 4*, 403–421.

Blackwell, M., Morgan, F., & DiGioia, A. M. (1998). Augmented reality and its future in orthopaedics *Clinical Orthopaedics and Related Research, 354*, 111–122.

Bodemer, D., Ploetzner, R., Feuerlein, I., & Spada, H. (2004). The active integration of information during learning with dynamic and interactive visualisations. *Learning and Instruction, 14*, 325–341.

Boucheix, J. M., & Schneider, E. (2009). Static and animated presentations in learning dynamic mechanical systems. *Learning and Instruction, 19*, 112–127.

Bradley, P. (2006). The history of simulation in medical education and possible future directions. *Medical Education, 40*, 254–262.

Bravo, C., van Joolingen, W. R., & de Jong, T. (2006). Modeling and simulation in inquiry learning: Checking solutions and giving intelligent advice. *Simulation: Transactions of the Society for Modeling and Simulation International, 82*, 769–784.

Bravo, C., van Joolingen, W. R., & de Jong, T. (2009). Using co-lab to build system dynamics models: Students' actions and on-line tutorial advice. *Computers & Education, 53*, 243–251.

Brown, J. S., Burton, R. R., & de Kleer, J. (1982). Pedagogical, natural language and knowledge engineering techniques in Sophie I, II, and III. In D. Sleeman, & J. S. Brown (Eds.), *Intelligent tutoring systems* (pp. 227–282). London: Academic Press.

Chang, K. E., Chen, Y. L., Lin, H. Y., & Sung, Y. T. (2008). Effects of learning support in simulation-based physics learning. *Computers & Education, 51*, 1486–1498.

Chen, Z., & Klahr, D. (1999). All other things being equal: Acquisition and transfer of the control of variables strategy. *Child Development, 70*, 1098–1120.

Clancey, W. J. (1986). From guidon to neomycin and heracles in twenty short lessons: Orn final report 19794985. *AI Magazine, 7*, 40–60.

Clark, R. E. (1994). Media will never influence learning. *Educational Technology, Research and Development, 42*, 21–29.

Crismond, D. (2001). Learning and using science ideas when doing investigate-and-redesign tasks: A study of naive, novice, and expert designers doing constrained and scaffolded design work. *Journal of Research in Science Teaching, 38,* 791–820.

Davis, E. A. (2000). Scaffolding students' knowledge integration: Prompts for reflection in KIE. *International Journal of Science Education, 22,* 819–837.

Day, S. B., & Goldstone, R. L. (2009). Analogical transfer from interaction with a simulated physical system. Paper presented at the Thirty-First Annual Conference of the Cognitive Science Society, Amsterdam.

Dean, D., & Kuhn, D. (2007). Direct instruction vs. discovery: The long view. *Science Education, 91,* 384–397.

de Hoog, R., de Jong, T., & de Vries, F. (1991). Interfaces for instructional use of simulations. *Education & Computing, 6,* 359–385.

de Jong, T. (2005). The guided discovery principle in multimedia learning. In R. E. Mayer (Ed.), *Cambridge handbook of multimedia learning* (pp. 215–229). Cambridge: Cambridge University Press.

de Jong, T. (2006a). Computer simulations: Technological advances in inquiry learning. *Science, 312,* 532–533.

de Jong, T. (2006b). Scaffolds for computer simulation based scientific discovery learning. In J. Elen, & R. E. Clark (Eds.), *Dealing with complexity in learning environments* (pp. 107–128). London: Elsevier Science Publishers.

de Jong, T. (2010). Technology supports for acquiring inquiry skills. In B. McGaw, E. Baker, & P. Peterson (Eds.), *International encyclopedia of education* (pp. 167–171). Oxford: Elsevier.

de Jong, T., Hendrikse, H. P., & van der Meij, H. (2010). Learning mathematics through inquiry; a large scale evaluation. In M. Jacobson, & P. Reimann (Eds.), *Designs for learning environments of the future: International perspectives from the learning sciences* (pp. 189–205). Berlin: Springer Verlag.

de Jong, T., & van Joolingen, W. R. (1998). Scientific discovery learning with computer simulations of conceptual domains. *Review of Educational Research, 68,* 179–202.

de Jong, T., & van Joolingen, W. R. (2007). Model-facilitated learning. In J. M. Spector, M. D. Merrill, J. J. G. van Merriënboer, & M. P. Driscoll (Eds.), *Handbook of research on educational communication and technology* (3rd ed., pp. 457–468). Hillsdale, NJ: Lawrence Erlbaum.

Evagorou, M., Korfiatis, K., Nicolaou, C., & Constantinou, C. (2009). An investigation of the potential of interactive simulations for developing system thinking skills in elementary school: A case study with fifth-graders and sixth-graders. *International Journal of Science Education, 31,* 655–674.

Eysink, T. H. S., de Jong, T., Berthold, K., Kollöffel, B., Opfermann, M., & Wouters, P. (2009). Learner performance in multimedia learning arrangements: An analysis across instructional approaches. *American Educational Research Journal, 46,* 1107–1149.

Friedler, Y., Nachmias, R., & Linn, M. C. (1990). Learning scientific reasoning skills in microcomputer-based laboratories. *Journal of Research in Science Teaching, 27,* 173–191.

Fund, Z. (2007). The effects of scaffolded computerized science problem-solving on achievement outcomes: A comparative study of support programs. *Journal of Computer Assisted Learning, 23,* 410–424.

Gijlers, H., & de Jong, T. (2009). Sharing and confronting propositions in collaborative inquiry learning. *Cognition and Instruction, 27,* 239–268.

Hays, R. T., & Singer, M. J. (1989). *Simulation fidelity in training system design.* New York: Springer-Verlag.

Hestenes, D. (1987). Towards a modeling theory of physics instruction. *American Journal of Physics, 55,* 440–454.

Hickey, D. T., Kindfield, A. C. H., Horwitz, P., & Christie, M. A. (2003). Integrating curriculum, instruction, assessment, and evaluation in a technology-supported genetics environment. *American Educational Research Journal, 40,* 495–538.

Hmelo, C. E., Holton, D. L., & Kolodner, J. L. (2000). Designing to learn about complex systems. *Journal of the Learning Sciences, 9,* 247–298.

Hmelo-Silver, C. E., Duncan, R. G., & Chinn, C. A. (2007). Scaffolding and achievement in problem-based and inquiry learning: A response to Kirschner, Sweller, and Clark (2006). *Educational Psychologist, 42,* 99–107.

Hollan, J. D., Hutchins, E. L., & Weitzman, L. (1984). Steamer: An interactive inspectable simulation-based training system. *AI Magazine, 5,* 15–27.

Holzinger, A., Kickmeier-Rust, M. D., Wassertheurer, S., & Hessinger, M. (2009). Learning performance with interactive simulations in medical education: Lessons learned from results of learning complex physiological models with the haemodynamics simulator. *Computers & Education, 52,* 292–301.

Hsu, Y.-S., & Thomas, R. A. (2002). The impacts of a web-aided instructional simulation on science learning. *International Journal of Science Education, 24,* 955–979.

Hulshof, C. D., Eysink, T. H. S., & de Jong, T. (2006). The ZAP project: Designing interactive computer tools for learning psychology. *Innovations in Education & Teaching International, 43,* 337–351.

Hulshof, C. D., Eysink, T. H. S., Loyens, S., & de Jong, T. (2005). ZAPS: Using interactive programs for learning psychology. *Interactive Learning Environments, 13,* 39–53.

Huppert, J., Lomask, S. M., & Lazarowitz, R. (2002). Computer simulations in the high school: Students' cognitive stages, science process skills and academic achievement in microbiology. *International Journal of Science Education, 24,* 803–821.

Jaakkola, T., & Nurmi, S. (2008). Fostering elementary school students' understanding of simple electricity by combining simulation and laboratory activities. *Journal of Computer Assisted Learning, 24,* 271–283.

Jaakkola, T., Nurmi, S., & Lehtinen, E. (2010). Conceptual change in learning electricity: Using virtual and concrete external representations simultaneously. In L. Verschaffel, E. de Corte, T. de Jong, & J. Elen (Eds.), *Use of external representations in reasoning and problem solving* (pp. 133–153): New York: Routledge.

Jaakkola, T., Nurmi, S., & Veermans, K. (2009). Comparing the effectiveness of semi-concrete and concreteness fading computer-simulations to support inquiry learning. Paper presented at the EARLI conference.

Jaakkola, T., Nurmi, S., & Veermans, K. (in press). A comparison of students' conceptual understanding of electric circuits in simulation only and simulation-laboratory contexts. *Journal of Research in Science Teaching.*

Jones, G. M. (1927). Are you fit to drive an airplane? *The Science News-Letter, 12,* 113–120.

Keselman, A. (2003). Supporting inquiry learning by promoting normative understanding of multivariable causality. *Journal of Research in Science Teaching, 40,* 898–921.

Kirschner, P. A., Sweller, J., & Clark, R. E. (2006). Why minimally guided instruction does not work. *Educational Psychologist, 41,* 75–86.

Klahr, D., & Dunbar, K. (1988). Dual space search during scientific reasoning. *Cognitive Science, 12,* 1–48.

Klahr, D., & Nigam, M. (2004). The equivalence of learning paths in early science instruction: Effects of direct instruction and discovery learning. *Psychological Science, 15,* 661–668.

Klahr, D., & Simon, H. A. (2001). What have psychologists (and others) discovered about the process of scientific discovery? *Current Directions in Psychological Science 10,* 75–79.

Klahr, D., Triona, L. M., & Williams, C. (2007). Hands on what? The relative effectiveness of physical versus virtual materials in an engineering design project by middle school children. *Journal of Science Teaching, 44,* 183–203.

Kolloffel, B., de Jong, T., & Eysink, T. H. S. (2010). The influence of learner-generated domain representations on learning combinatorics and probability theory. *Computers in Human Behavior, 26,* 1–11.

Kolloffel, B., Eysink, T., & de Jong, T. (submitted). Do representational tools support understanding in combinatorics instruction? Comparing effects in collaborative and individual learning settings.

Kolloffel, B., Eysink, T. H. S., de Jong, T., & Wilhelm, P. (2009). The effects of representational format on learning combinatorics from an interactive computer-simulation. *Instructional Science, 37,* 503–517.

Koonce, J. M., & Bramble, W. J. (1998). Personal computer-based flight traing devices. *The International Journal of Aviation Psychology, 8,* 277–292.

Kuhn, D. (2007). Is direct instruction an answer to the right question? *Educational Psychologist, 47,* 109–113.

Kuhn, D., Black, J., Keselman, A., & Kaplan, D. (2000). The development of cognitive skills to support inquiry learning. *Cognition and Instruction, 18,* 495–523.

Kuhn, D., & Dean, D. (2005). Is developing scientific thinking all about learning to control variables? *Psychological Science, 16,* 866–870.

Kurland, L., & Tenney, Y. (1988). Issues in developing an intelligent tutor for a real-world domain: Training in radar mechanics. In J. Psotka, L. D. Massey, & S. Mutter (Eds.), *Intelligent tutoring systems: Lessons learned* (pp. 59–85). Hillsdale, NJ: Lawrence Erlbaum Associates.

Law, A. M., & Kelton, W. D. (2000). *Simulation modelling and analysis* (3rd ed.). New York: McGraw-Hill.

Leemkuil, H., & de Jong, T. (in press). Instructional support in games. In S. Tobias, & D. Fletcher (Eds.), *Can computer games be used for instruction?* New York: Routledge.

Lesgold, A., Lajoie, S., Bunzo, M., & Eggan, G. (1992). SHERLOCK: A coached practice environment for an electronics troubleshooting job. In J. H. Larkin, & R. W. Chabay (Eds.), *Computer-assisted instruction and intelligent tutoring systems: Shared goals and complementary approaches* (pp. 201–239). Hillsdale, NJ: Erlbaum.

Lin, X., & Lehman, J. D. (1999). Supporting learning of variable control in a computer-based biology environment: Effects of prompting college students to reflect on their own thinking. *Journal of Research in Science Teaching, 36,* 837–858.

Lindgren, R., & Schwartz, D. (2009). Spatial learning and computer simulations in science. *International Journal of Science Education, 31,* 419–438.

Linn, M. C., Lee, H.-S., Tinker, R., Husic, F., & Chiu, J. L. (2006). Teaching and assessing knowledge integration in science. *Science, 313,* 1049–1050.

Liu, H., Andre, T., & Greenbowe, T. (2008). The impact of learners' prior knowledge on their use of chemistry computer simulations: A case study. *Journal of Science Education and Technology, 17,* 466–482.

Liu, T. C., Lin, Y. C., & Kinshuk. (2010). The application of simulation-assisted learning statistics (SALS) for correcting misconceptions and improving understanding of correlation. *Journal of Computer Assisted Learning, 9999.*

Manlove, S., Lazonder, A. W., & de Jong, T. (2007). Software scaffolds to promote regulation during scientific inquiry learning. *Metacognition & Learning, 2,* 141–155.

Manlove, S., Lazonder, A. W., & de Jong, T. (2009a). Collaborative versus individual use of regulative software scaffolds during scientific inquiry learning. *Interactive Learning Environments, 17,* 105–117.

Manlove, S., Lazonder, A. W., & de Jong, T. (2009b). Trends and issues of regulative support use during inquiry learning: Patterns from three studies. *Computers in Human Behavior, 25,* 795–803.

Mayer, R. E. (2004). Should there be a three-strikes rule against pure discovery learning? *American Psychologist, 59,* 14–19.

Mayer, R. E. (2009). *Multimedia learning* (2nd ed.). New York: Cambridge University Press.

Meir, E., Perry, J., Stal, D., Maruca, S., & Klopfer, E. (2005). How effective are simulated molecular-level experiments for teaching diffusion and osmosis? *Cell Biology Education, 4,* 235–248.

Minner, D. D., Levy, A. J., & Century, J. (2010). Inquiry-based science instruction : What is it and does it matter? Results from a research synthesis years 1984 to 2002. *Journal of Research in Science Teaching, 47,* 474–496.

Minogue, J., & Jones, G. (2009). Measuring the impact of haptic feedback using the solo taxonomy. *International Journal of Science Education, 31,* 1359–1378.

Monaghan, J. M., & Clement, J. (1999). Use of a computer simulation to develop mental simulations for understanding relative motion concepts. *International Journal of Science Education, 21,* 921–944.

Njoo, M., & de Jong, T. (1993). Exploratory learning with a computer simulation for control theory: Learning processes and instructional support. *Journal of Research in Science Teaching, 30,* 821–844.

Novak, J. D. (1990). Concept mapping: A useful tool for science education. *Journal of Research in Science Teaching, 27,* 937–949.

Papert, S. (1980). *Mindstorms: Children, computers, and powerful ideas.* New York: Basic Books.

Park, S. I., Lee, G., & Kim, M. (2009). Do students benefit equally from interactive computer simulations regardless of prior knowledge levels? *Computers & Education, 52,* 649–655.

Parker, B. C., & Myrick, F. (2009). A critical examination of high-fidelity human patient simulation within the context of nursing pedagogy. *Nurse Education Today, 29,* 322–329.

Pata, K., & Sarapuu, T. (2006). A comparison of reasoning processes in a collaborative modelling environment: Learning about genetics problems using virtual chat. *International Journal of Science Education, 28,* 1341–1368.

Piaget, J. (1976). *The grasp of consciousness: Action and concept in the young child.* Cambridge, MA: Harvard University Press.

Ploetzner, R., Lippitsch, S., Galmbacher, M., Heuer, D., & Scherrer, S. (2009). Students' difficulties in learning from dynamic visualisations and how they may be overcome. *Computers in Human Behavior, 25,* 56–65.

Quintana, C., Reiser, B. J., Davis, E. A., Krajcik, J., Fretz, E., Duncan, R. G., et al. (2004). A scaffolding design framework for software to support science inquiry. *The Journal of the Learning Sciences, 13,* 337–387.

Reid, D. J., Zhang, J., & Chen, Q. (2003). Supporting scientific discovery learning in a simulation environment. *Journal of Computer Assisted Learning, 19,* 9–20.

Sadeh, I., & Zion, M. (2009). The development of dynamic inquiry performances within an open inquiry setting: A comparison to guided inquiry setting. *Journal of Research in Science Teaching, 46,* 1137–1160.

Scanlon, E., & Smith, R. B. (1988). A rational reconstruction of a bubble-chamber simulation using the alternate reality kit. *Computers & Education, 12,* 199–207.

Schwartz, D., & Bransford, J. D. (1998). Time for telling. *Cognition and Instruction, 16,* 475–522.

Shimoda, T. A., White, B. Y., & Frederiksen, J. (2002). Student goal orientation in learning inquiry skills with modifiable advisors. *Science Education, 88,* 244–263.

Shute, V. J., & Glaser, R. (1990). A large-scale evaluation of an intelligent discovery world: Smithtown. *Interactive Learning Environments, 1,* 51–77.

Smith, R. B. (1986). The alternate reality kit: An animated environment for creating interactive simulations. Paper presented at the IEEE Computer Society workshop on visual languages.

Smith, R. B. (2010). The long history of gaming in military training. *Simulation & Gaming, 41,* 6–19.

Swaak, J., & de Jong, T. (2001). Discovery simulations and the assessment of intuitive knowledge. *Journal of Computer Assisted Learning, 17,* 284–294.

Swaak, J., de Jong, T., & van Joolingen, W. R. (2004). The effects of discovery learning and expository instruction on the acquisition of definitional and intuitive knowledge. *Journal of Computer Assisted Learning, 20,* 225–234.

Tatar, D., Roschelle, J., Knudsen, J., Shechtman, N., Kaput, J., & Hopkins, B. (2008). Scaling up innovative technology-based mathematics. *Journal of the Learning Sciences, 17,* 248–286.

Tobias, S., & Duffy, T. M. (Eds.). (2009). *Constructivist instruction. Success or failure?* New York: Routledge.

Tolentino, L., Birchfield, D., Megowan-Romanowicz, C., Johnson-Glenberg, M., Kelliher, A., & Martinez, C. (2009). Teaching and learning in the mixed-reality science classroom. *Journal of Science Education and Technology, 18,* 501–517.

Toth, E. E., Suthers, D. D., & Lesgold, A. M. (2002). "Mapping to know": The effects of representational guidance and reflective assessment on scientific inquiry. *Science Education, 86,* 264–286.

Towne, D. M., Munro, A., Pizzini, Q., Surmon, D., Coller, L., & Wogulis, J. (1990). Model-building tools for simulation-based training. *Interactive Learning Environments, 1,* 33–50.

Trey, L., & Khan, S. (2008). How science students can learn about unobservable phenomena using computer-based analogies. *Computers & Education, 51,* 519–529.

Triona, L. M., & Klahr, D. (2003). Point and click or grab and heft: Comparing the influence of physical and virtual instructional materials on elementary school students' ability to design experiments. *Cognition and Instruction, 21,* 149–173.

Tsui, C. Y., & Treagust, D. F. (2003). Genetics reasoning with multiple external representations. *Research in Science Education, 33,* 111–135.

Urhahne, D., Nick, S., & Schanze, S. (2009). The effect of three-dimensional simulations on the understanding of chemical structures and their properties. *Research in Science Education, 39,* 495–513.

van der Meij, J., & de Jong, T. (2006). Supporting students' learning with multiple representations in a dynamic simulation-based learning environment. *Learning and Instruction, 16,* 199–212.

van Joolingen, W. R., & de Jong, T. (1991). Supporting hypothesis generation by learners exploring an interactive computer simulation. *Instructional Science, 20,* 389–404.

van Joolingen, W. R., & de Jong, T. (2003). Simquest: Authoring educational simulations. In T. Murray, S. Blessing, & S. Ainsworth (Eds.), *Authoring tools for advanced technology educational software: Toward cost-effective production of adaptive, interactive, and intelligent educational software* (pp. 1–31). Dordrecht: Kluwer Academic Publishers.

van Merriënboer, J. J. G. (1997). *Training complex cognitive skills: A four-component instructional design model for technical training.* Englewood Cliffs, NJ: Educational Technology Publications.

Veermans, K. H., van Joolingen, W. R., & de Jong, T. (2006). Using heuristics to facilitate scientific discovery learning in a simulation learning environment in a physics domain. *International Journal of Science Education, 28,* 341–361.

Wayne, D. B., Butter, J., Siddall, V. J., Fudala, M. J., Lindquist, L. A., Feinglass, J., et al. (2005). Simulation-based training of internal medicine residents in advanced cardiac life support protocols: A randomized trial. *Teaching and Learning in Medicine, 17,* 210–216.

White, B. Y., & Frederiksen, J. (1998). Inquiry, modelling, and metacognition: Making science accessible to all students. *Cognition and Instruction, 16,* 63–118.

White, B. Y., & Frederiksen, J. R. (1989). Causal models as intelligent learning environments for science and engineering education. *Applied Artificial Intelligence, 3,* 83–106.

White, B. Y., Frederiksen, J., Frederiksen, T., Eslinger, E., Loper, S., & Collins, A. (2002). Inquiry island: Affordances of a multi-agent environment for scientific inquiry and reflective learning. Paper presented at the Fifth International Conference of the Learning Sciences (ICLS).

Wichmann, A., & Leutner, D. (2009). Inquiry learning multilevel support with respect to inquiry, explanations and regulation during an inquiry cycle. *Zeitschrift für pädagogische Psychologie, 23,* 117–127.

Wieman, C. E., Perkins, K. K., & Adams, W. K. (2008). Oersted medal lecture 2007: Interactive simulations for teaching physics: What works, what doesn't, and why. *American Journal of Physics, 76,* 393–399.

Wilhelm, P., & Beishuizen, J. J. (2003). Content effects in self-directed inductive learning. *Learning and Instruction, 13,* 381–402.

Winberg, T., & Hedman, L. (2008). Student attitudes toward learning, level of pre-knowledge and instruction type in a computer-simulation: Effects on flow experiences and perceived learning outcomes. *Instructional Science, 36,* 269–287.

Windschitl, M., & Andre, T. (1998). Using computer simulations to enhance conceptual change: The roles of constructivist instruction and student epistemological beliefs. *Journal of Research in Science Teaching, 35,* 145–160.

Winn, W., Stahr, F., Sarason, C., Fruland, R., Oppenheimer, P., & Lee, Y.-L. (2006). Learning oceanography from a computer simulation compared with direct experience at sea. *Journal of Research in Science Teaching, 43,* 25–42.

Wu, H., Krajcik, J. S., & Soloway, E. (2001). Promoting understanding of chemical representations: Students' use of a visualization tool in the classroom. *Journal of Research in Science Teaching, 38,* 821–842.

Zacharia, Z. C. (2007). Comparing and combining real and virtual experimentation: An effort to enhance students' conceptual understanding of electric circuits. *Journal of Computer Assisted Learning, 23,* 120–132.

Zacharia, Z. C., & Anderson, O. R. (2003). The effects of an interactive computer-based simulation prior to performing a laboratory inquiry-based experiment on students' conceptual understanding of physics. *American Journal of Physics, 71*, 618–629.

Zacharia, Z. C., & Constantinou, C. P. (2008). Comparing the influence of physical and virtual manipulatives in the context of the physics by inquiry curriculum: The case of undergraduate students' conceptual understanding of heat and temperature. *American Journal of Physics, 76*, 425–430.

Zacharia, Z. C., & Olympiou, G. (in press). Physical versus virtual manipulative experimentation in physics learning. *Learning & Instruction.*

Zacharia, Z. C., Olympiou, G., & Papaevripidou, M. (2008). Effects of experimenting with physical and virtual manipulatives on students' conceptual understanding in heat and temperature. *Journal of Research in Science Teaching, 45*, 1021–1035.

Zhang, J., Chen, Q., Sun, Y., & Reid, D. J. (2004). Triple scheme of learning support design for scientific discovery learning based on computer simulation: Experimental research. *Journal of Computer Assisted Learning, 20*, 269–282.

AUTHOR INDEX

SUBJECT INDEX